Sharing the Stage:
Biography and Gender in
Western Civilization

VOLUME I

Sharing the Stage: Biography and Gender in Western Civilization

Jane Slaughter

Melissa K. Bokovoy

University of New Mexico

HOUGHTON MIFFLIN COMPANY   Boston   New York

Senior Sponsoring Editor: Nancy Blaine
Development Editor: Julie Dunn
Associate Project Editor: Reba Libby
Editorial Assistant: Kendra Johnson
Associate Production/Design Coordinator: Bethany Schlegel
Manufacturing Manager: Florence Cadran
Senior Marketing Manager: Sandra McGuire

Cover images: Isabella I., die Katholishe, Königin von Kaitlien und Leon (1474–1504), seit 1469 verehl. mit Ferdinand II. von Aragon; Madrigan de las Altas Torres (Avila) 22.4.1451–Medina del Campo 26.11.1504. Portät.-Gemälde, 19. Jh., von Madrazo.

Ferdinand II., der Katholishe, Königin v. Aragon, v. Sizilien, als Ferd. V. v. Kastilien-Leon, als F. III v. Neapel; Sos 10.3.1452-Madrigalejo 23.1.1516. Portät. Ausschnitt aus "Die Madonna der Katholischen Könige." Gemälde, um 1490, von Miquel Zittoz (um 1469–1525). Madrid, Museo del Prado.

Text and photo credits appear on page 459 which is a continuation of the copyright page.

Printed in the U.S.A.

Library of Congress Catalog Card Number: 2001133348

ISBN: 0-618-01177-3

1 2 3 4 5 6 7 8 9-VHG-07 06 05 04 03

CONTENTS

12   Catholic Monarchs in the Old and New Worlds:
Ferdinand of Aragón (1452–1516) and Isabella of
Castile (1451–1504)   *341*

13   The Protestant Reformation in Germany: Martin
Luther (1483–1546) and Katharina von Bora
(1499–1552)   *376*

PREFACE

The intellectual seeds that produced this volume were gathered in many Western Civilization classes spanning almost four decades. As historians, we, the authors, represent quite distinct generations and different training, but we share ideas and goals that we believe will resonate with other teachers of introductory history courses. The power of historical insight and the thrill of historical discovery have shaped and driven our lives; our purpose is to share the quest and the excitement with students. We have experimented with different approaches and material, and what we found to be most effective has shaped this volume. While many of the current generation of students are, at best, skeptical of participation in political, social, intellectual, or religious movements, we believe that such events are among the most exciting and significant subjects in the history of western societies, and our challenge is to give these life and color. One way to do that is to bring men and women who were key players in those events onto the historical stage. We contend that to understand fully an individual's actions in regard to historical events, we must consider the gender of that individual. Gender discussed in abstract terms often falls on deaf ears; our experience has taught us that individual actions, opportunities, and expectations are far more illustrative. A tested mix of historical movements, biography, and gender, brought from our classrooms, is displayed in the chapters that follow.

Each chapter focuses on one woman and one man whose lives reflect major social, cultural, political, and economic developments of the time. Often these individuals were uniquely positioned to alter the conditions of their lives or to influence the course of history, and these chapters raise important questions about differences in autonomy and power between men and women, but also among women, and among men. By pairing individuals who have intimate familial or social connections, we introduce students to the idea that they must always consider gender as an important criterion of analysis when they assess historical significance. Moving together through time, the lives of each pair illustrate the fact that a man's experience is not the universal experience, and a woman's experience is not the exception.

The examples in this text compare not only experiences, but also sources, encouraging students to ask the questions: Whose stories are recorded? Whose records preserved? Each chapter contains a brief introduction to the sources available for the individuals and the time period. Moving from chapter to chapter, students can begin to see how the nature of the historical record changes, as well as how the records available for men and for women vary widely. As we move forward in time, the diversity and breadth of sources for both men and women increases, and the choice of historical figures thereby expands. In the earliest chapters, the figures discussed will be familiar and might fall into the category of great men or women, like Pericles and Aspasia, or Octavius and Livia. In subsequent chapters, at times one partner will be much better known than the other (for example, the emperor Justinian and his wife Theodora, the early church father Jerome and his spiritual partner, Paula, or Catherine of Siena and Pope Gregory XI.) Even as the range of sources becomes richer, inequities and gaps in the records remain, and confronting the ways that sources shape what becomes the narrative of history remains a key contribution of this volume.

We have organized each of the chapters in *Sharing the Stage* into six sections: Setting the Stage; the Actors; Acts; the Finale; Questions; and Documents. The Setting the Stage section provides historical background on the time period and society in which the individuals lived. The Actors section discusses the lives of the paired individuals, as well as some other figures who influenced their lives or society. The drama of these individual's lives is portrayed in the Acts sections of the chapter. Here we witness how the individuals contributed to their societies and how their societies responded. The Finale section outlines the last years of the individuals' lives and attempts to provide some closure to that period of history. At the conclusion of each chapter, suggested discussion questions ask students to consider conflicting relationships, behaviors, and events and their historical meaning, thus allowing many possibilities for analysis and classroom discussion. Finally, we have included a collection of documents at the end of each chapter. Each document opens with a brief introduction and several focus questions, and all of the documents are referenced in the narrative.

We believe that students can learn to appreciate primary documents and benefit from reading and analysis of such materials. We have selected our documents carefully to include both well-known and less famous pieces. In the chapter on Peter Abelard and Heloise, we include an excerpt from Abelard's treatise, *Sic et Non,* and extracts from Abelard's and Heloise's known letters written many years after their affair, but also extracts from the recently published "lost letters" of the pair which were written at the time of their courtship. In addition to familiar political essays and religious tracts like those of Aristotle, St. Jerome, Henry II of England, and Martin Luther, we include public and personal letters exchanged between partners or parents and children, some of them only now made available. The materials include public and private statements of the central figures in each chapter, but also accounts and ideas of other men and women of the time who express different opinions and recount different experiences. This diverse documentary evidence allows the reader to discuss in detail the possible differences between men's and women's experiences and responses in each of the movements being studied. Several questions address each document; the document is placed in context and referred to in the narrative, making it both relevant and intelligible to the reader. It is our intent that this process will acquaint students with what it is that historians do and to encourage them to grapple with historical problems. Ideally, after reading the text and interpreting the documents, students will learn how to construct one of the most understandable of all historical stories, the biography.

Biographies give human form to textbook narratives that often seem remote and lifeless to many students. *Sharing the Stage: Biography and Gender in Western Civilization* is conceived to accompany the Western Civilization course and the standard textbooks used. Each chapter represents a discrete historical movement or event and is easy to assign for individual reading, classroom discussion, papers, and exams. This reader complements the multifaceted ways that today's instructors teach Western Civilization. It builds on historical events and personalities familiar to instructors of the course, while simultaneously offering themes suitable to teachers of history with widely ranging perspectives and interests.

Acknowledgments

Teaching introductory Western Civilization history survey courses is always challenging. The rewards are also manifold when students connect with events and people in the past and share our enthusiasms. Our thanks and acknowledgments in this volume must, therefore begin with all the wonderful students who began to think historically and have contributed unknowingly. Oddly perhaps, we must thank each other as well. From quite different generations of historians, we found common ground in our passions for history, and our commitment to constant revision and experimentation in our teaching. We also owe a debt to friends and colleagues who validated and encouraged our plan for the volume. Most gratefully, the volume would not exist without the enthusiasm of Jean Woy and Nancy Blaine, the editors at Houghton Mifflin who understood what we were trying to do, and bought an idea others might have found risky.

From the beginning, colleagues at UNM, Larry D. Ball, Beth Bailey, David Farber, and Virginia Scharff were our cheerleaders, intellectual advisors, and editors. The first sketches and the development of bibliography were the work of an amazing undergraduate research assistant, Bernadette Miera, who was assigned to us one summer through the university's "Research Opportunity Program." There is probably no way that we can adequately acknowledge the work that Ellen Cain did on this project. Her remarkable assistance for us in research, and preparation of the manuscript, was done while she wrote her dissertation in U.S. Western History at UNM. Richard Robbins, as department chair, gave us financial support. We also want to acknowledge the important secondary and primary materials available at the Library of Congress, which we relied on, and even more important the work that Carol Armbruster, the French and Italian research librarian at LoC, did. She came to our rescue on many occasions, finding materials and copying and sending them to us. Finally, the number of books, articles, and primary source materials necessary for this project meant ordering almost daily from our interlibrary loan department. The ILL staff worked rapidly and carefully on our requests, and without their help our project would not have been possible.

Julie Dunn's capable hands and creative suggestions shaped the development and design of the volume. Reba Libby carefully oversaw the copyediting and proofing. We wish to thank the following teachers and instructors for their excellent insights, critical analyses, and meticulous reading of the chapters in this volume: Dorothea French, Santa Clara University, Margaret Malamud, New Mexico State University, Andrew Muldoon, Saint Anselm College, Thomas L. Powers, University of South Carolina, Sumter, Carole Putko, San Diego State University, Marylou Ruud, University of West Florida, Judith Lynn Sebesta, University of South Dakota, Timothy M. Thibodeau, Nazareth College of Rochester, Elspeth Whitney, University of Nevada, Las Vegas, Laura H. Yungblut, University of Dayton.

PART

I

Ancient and Classical Worlds

The Challenges of Rule in New Kingdom Egypt: Hatshepsut (1479–1458 B.C.E.) and Tuthmosis III (1479–1425 B.C.E.)

▪ SETTING THE STAGE

The individuals and the built environment of ancient Egypt's ruling family, known as the Eighteenth Dynasty (1550–1295 B.C.E.), have attracted popular and scholarly attention for some time. These monarchs were noted for conquests and empire building, commercial activity and economic growth, and openness to new ideas. Their ex-

tensive building activities, particularly in their home region of Thebes (Luxor), reflected their wealth, power, and administrative skill. Previous rulers, living further north along the Nile, had built massive burial pyramids on the broad river plains. Members of the Eighteenth Dynasty chose to build their tombs in a place known

Chapter 1
The Challenges
of Rule in New
Kingdom Egypt:
Hatshepsut
(1479–1458
B.C.E.) and
Tuthmosis III
(1479–1425 B.C.E.)

as the Valley of the Kings, which was situated under a pyramid-shaped mountain west of the city of Thebes.

They also separated their mortuary or memorial temples from the tombs, and these temples became centers celebrating the actions of the kings or sites where offerings could be made to the rulers and their predecessors. Special housing was created for the skilled work force who built the tombs and temples. One such community, Deir el-Medina, also across from Thebes on the western side of the Nile River, provides insights into daily life in ancient Egypt. The tombs, palaces, monuments, and cities of the Eighteenth and other dynasties of the New Kingdom (1550–1069 B.C.E.) are among the richest sources we have for the study of ancient Egypt.

Even with these resources, tremendous challenges exist in writing the histories of the ancient Egyptians. Three general sorts of evidence remain for Egyptian society: (1) archeological: buildings of all sorts, tombs, and monuments; (2) textual: inscriptions on walls, writings on fragments of stone or clay, and letters on papyrus; and (3) representational: statuary and paintings on various surfaces. All of these pieces of evidence must be translated or interpreted for contemporary meaning. In creating an historical narrative, the purposes for the creation of these sources must be taken into account and their creators must be identified. Most of these materials were intended to depict an ideal rather than an actual situation or person, were propaganda created to glorify their subject, or were prescriptive in the sense of providing wisdom

and advice for "right living." They were not supposed to express individual opinions, desires, or observations. The authors or builders were part of a very small elite—near the top of the social pyramid—who were educated, literate, and overwhelmingly male. Occasionally, remnants of homes and everyday life, not planned to illustrate acceptable standards of behavior or ideals, give us a more intimate picture of this ancient world.

Reconstructing the Egyptian story is also difficult because sources are often fragmentary. Time and weather destroyed some material, but human disruption of remains—grave robbing; capture and seizure of pieces of art; and simply defacing, moving, or covering up older sources—has made scholarly inquiry even more challenging. As one historian notes, "researching into ancient Egypt is like trying to repair a tapestry with gaping holes where much of the design is lost."[1] This need to fill in the gaps has created interesting historical questions and debates, as we shall see.

The rulers of the Eighteenth Dynasty (1550–1295 B.C.E.) reunified the Egyptian state after they expelled the western asiatic Hyksos who had invaded and controlled the delta region of the Nile and other parts of Egypt since approximately 1700. The Hyksos had appropriated some forms of Egyptian culture but had also introduced new and foreign elements into the civilization of the Nile. They brought bronze-making technology, horses

---

1. Gay Robins, *Women in Ancient Egypt* (Cambridge, Mass.: Harvard University Press, 1998), p. 16.

and war chariots, the composite bow, new breeds of cattle, olive trees, and new musical instruments. Even though prior Egyptian dynasties had established trade connections with foreign areas, they had also maintained a large degree of cultural and spiritual isolation that Hyksos rule interrupted.

The new family that came to power after 1550 was thus confronted with significant social, economic, and military changes. The vigor and success with which they faced these innovations, and introduced challenges of their own, made their rule one of the last periods of great power and creativity in Ancient Egypt.[2] As important as their unique contributions were, however, these rulers could not abandon centuries of historical traditions, nor did they want to; the very basis for their power lay in the past.

For centuries, unusual stability and prosperity had marked the ancient Egyptian civilization that stretched along 700 miles of the Nile River. The rulers and the people of the unified state that had developed sometime after 3100 B.C.E. believed that tranquility, continuity, and economic well-being were the will of the gods, who had created order out of chaos. Although this state of harmony and balance was considered the "natural order"—*ma'at* in Egyptian—it always had to be protected and promoted by a

divine presence on earth that resided in the office of the king or pharaoh. Kings were mortal, born to mortal mothers, but the divine office they held had the creative powers and responsibilities of the gods, and thus kings were transformed into gods when they took office. The position they held set them apart from other humans, allowed them to communicate with the gods, and required that they mediate between divine and human worlds.

The king sat alone at the apex of a social, political, and religious hierarchy whose "structure, order and organization . . . was symbolized in the form of the pyramid."[3] In addition to his ritual and magical duties, the king owned all the land and was the chief administrator, law giver, and defender of the state. In practice, the ruler had to delegate some of these duties, and the Egyptian kingdom developed an extensive bureaucracy. Generally, only men held bureaucratic offices, most of which required some ability to read and write. The highest ranking officials usually had financial responsibilities or were first priests of the most powerful gods. Wives of powerful bureaucrats occasionally held office, but usually as priestesses of goddesses like Hathor, who was the patron of women. One's rank in the social hierarchy depended on proximity to the king and on the functions or work one contributed to the orderly management and productivity of the society (Document One). Above all, the legitimacy of a ruler was measured by the ability to maintain prosperity, law,

2. Erik Hornung, *History of Ancient Egypt* (Ithaca, N.Y.: Cornell Univ. Press, 1999), p. 75. See also Barbara Watterson, *The Egyptians* (Cambridge, Mass.: Blackwell, 1999), and Nicolas Grimal, *A History of Ancient Egypt* (Cambridge, Mass.: Blackwell, 1992), for the historical significance of this dynasty.

3. Hornung, p. 24.

Chapter 1
The Challenges
of Rule in New
Kingdom Egypt:
Hatshepsut
(1479–1458
B.C.E.) and
Tuthmosis III
(1479–1425 B.C.E.)

and order—the material dimensions of ma'at—throughout the land. Dramatic changes in social and material conditions, and challenges to custom and tradition could be considered dangerous and as evidence of the displeasure of the gods.

Although orderly maintenance of the status quo was the desired condition for Egyptian society, change could not be avoided. At rare times the Nile flooded too much or too little, with disastrous economic consequences. Administrative failure to provide carefully for grain storage might also result in famine. In other instances, technological innovations, contact with foreign cultures, occupation of the king's office by less able rulers, and even invasions brought disruption and challenges to the Egyptian state.

Examining the reigns of two Eighteenth Dynasty rulers, Hatshepsut (1479–1458 B.C.E.) and Tuthmosis III (1479–1425 B.C.E.) opens a window into this fascinating and contradictory world and, at the same time, allows us to consider many of the challenges scholars face in studying the ancient past.

■ THE ACTORS:

HATSHEPSUT AND TUTHMOSIS

The reigns of Hatshepsut and Tuthmosis III typify dynastic accomplishments in the areas of diplomacy and conquest, economic growth, and extensive public building. They also stand out for several reasons. First, Hatshepsut assumed the titles and authority of king in her own right, thus becoming one of only four women in ancient Egyptian history to act as the supreme ruler. Most women who exercised political power did so as first wives or mothers of rulers, and wielded power only as regents. Thus, Hatshepsut is indeed a notable historical figure. For his part, Tuthmosis became the model of the new warrior king. But the lives of this pair of rulers are instructive for other reasons as well. Their royal pedigrees are complex and the nature of their personal relationship is open to question. Taken together, these factors create an interesting vantage point for a discussion of what constitutes the basis for access to royal power and of the different ways that individual rulers exercised that power.

Hatshepsut was the daughter of the first Tuthmosis, who probably ruled anywhere from 1506 to 1482 (B.C.E.).[4] Through her mother, the queen, she was descended from one of the earliest and most influential queens of the dynasty, Ahmose Nefertari. Hatshepsut married her half-brother, Tuthmosis II (1482–1479 B.C.E.), the son of Tuthmosis I and a royal concubine. The only surviving child of Hatshepsut's marriage was a daughter, Neferure. Like his predecessors, Tuthmosis II had several subordinate wives, and the son of one of these women was Tuthmosis III, who was not yet ten years old when his

---

4. Egyptians marked time by the reigns of their rulers; known birth and death dates are almost nonexistent, and even the dates of reigns are not always clear. In the case of Tuthmosis I, the start and finish dates of his rule vary from scholar to scholar.

father died. Thus Hatshepsut, his step-mother and aunt, served as regent. Familial relationships and situations such as these were not uncommon in Egyptian dynastic history. Coregencies, brother-sister unions, and marriage to multiple wives had occurred before Tuthmosis I took the throne. An especially important fact to be recognized in these historical patterns is that daugh-ters, no matter what their placement in the family lineup, were not considered the legitimate heirs. Hatshepsut's blood connections to earlier pharaohs were stronger than those of either her husband or her stepson. No law explicitly forbade female rule, but since the earliest dynasties, divine rule was equated with masculine principles, and men had occupied the office of pharaoh.

■ ACT I:

THE WORLD OF THE TUTHMOSID QUEENS AND KINGS

In the ancient world, the usual social hierarchy and political structure were ones in which a relatively small number of elite men (often elders) controlled other men and all women. Most scholars agree that no single factor explains these conditions. Instead, development of agriculture, population growth and accompanying expansion and conquest, technological innovations, greater diversity in the nature of work and goods produced, creation of surpluses, market exchanges, and accumulation of goods resulted in wealth, power, and opportunities for some and not for others. Along with the political, social, and gender hierarchies that these developments created, there also emerged increased understanding and mental constructs that explained natural and human events. Usually a priestly class and political leaders formulated and articulated values and opinions regarding what was prized or feared. Qualities, behaviors, or objects that were rare, unique, or exclusive were considered valuable, as were actions or functions assumed to contribute to the public good and to ensure survival of the community (Document Two).

Within this intellectual and spiritual framework, it is understandable that a gender division of labor between men and women, originally based on survival needs, might produce differing attitudes over time toward the roles and attributes of men and women. Although women, like men, engaged in various economic activities, a woman's greatest contribution to society and to her family was her fertility and caregiving. Female sexuality and fertility were valued, but could also be seen as mysterious, even dangerous, and subject to control if inheritance to property and power was involved.[5] Very broadly speaking,

5. Barbara Lesko, "Women of Ancient Egypt and Western Asia," in R. Bridenthal et al. (eds.) *Becoming Visible,* Third Edition (Boston, Mass.: Houghton Mifflin, 1998), p. 17. See also Gerda Lerner, *The Creation of Patriarchy* (New York: Oxford, 1986), which carefully details the historical development of these conditions, although in western Asia rather than Egypt.

Chapter 1
The Challenges
of Rule in New
Kingdom Egypt:
Hatshepsut
(1479–1458
B.C.E.) and
Tuthmosis III
(1479–1425 B.C.E.)

the different roles of men and women were thought to be complementary, but they could easily result in inequality, depending on social values and material conditions (Document Three). When compared to women in other ancient Mediterranean societies, Egyptian women had unusual legal rights and independence. They had influence beyond the household and engaged in a wide range of work and commercial activities, and property was handed down through the female line. Since no women occupied the offices that actually governed the land, their power was limited. Most of our sources reflect the experience of elite women; their status was determined by their husbands or fathers, and even they had limited access to areas of activity like education and politics. While women shared in the same afterlife as men, were often represented in art, and were legally capable, these conditions "should not obscure the fact that women occupied a secondary position in relation to men throughout the history of Egypt."[6]

The relationships of men and women, like the absolute earthly powers of the king, were reflected in and reinforced by religious beliefs and practices. Egyptians worshiped multi-ple gods with various powers and responsibilities. They also accepted the supremacy of one god, while not denying the existence and functions of other deities. Depending on shifting political power, a local god might be elevated to a higher and even supreme status. Gods and goddesses could have overlapping and competing powers, while religious beliefs and practices included rituals and spells, as well as ethical or moral strictures and guidelines. Egyptian beliefs generally began with a creative force or god that included both masculine and feminine principles. Then pairs of gods were created to represent complementary ideas, for example, air and moisture, earth and sky. These pairs, in turn, reproduced other pairs with varying powers and functions. Isis and Osiris were one such brother-sister pair who gradually became the central figures in Egyptian beliefs about cycles of life and death, resurrection and the afterworld. Isis was the ideal wife and mother; Osiris, who had been killed and resurrected by Isis, was the god of the afterlife. While living on earth, divine rulers were the human embodiment of Horus, the son of Isis and Osiris, and at death were identified with Osiris, who ruled the netherworld.

By the time the Eighteenth Dynasty came to rule, the sun god Re dominated the realm of all the gods. But the new dynasty came from Thebes, where the local god Amun was prominent. Under the Theban rulers, massive building projects elevated his status, expanded his power, and eventually created a compound god, Amun-Re, the King of the Gods and Lord of the

6. Gay Robins, *Women in Ancient Egypt* (Cambridge, Mass.: Harvard University Press), p. 191. Other useful works for the history of women in Egypt are: Joyce Tydesley, *Daughters of Isis: Women of Ancient Egypt* (New York: Viking Press, 1994); Barbara Watterson, *Women in Ancient Egypt* (Gloucester, Great Britain: Wren's Park Publishing, 1998); and Zahi Hawass, *Silent Images: Women in Pharaonic Egypt* (New York: Harry Abrams, Inc., 2000).

Thrones of the Two Lands [upper and lower Egypt]. The monarchs of this dynasty also inherited the worship of brother-sister/husband-wife deities, and translated their beliefs into earthly practice. On a practical level, this meant that interfamily marriages could be used to maintain the exclusivity of the royal line, or to guarantee that royal daughters had suitable husbands. If a male successor was from a secondary family branch, he could strengthen his claim to royal power by marrying a half-sister. Many scholars have noted that, although brother-sister marriages were not particularly common in the society as a whole, there would be advantages for earthly rulers in the emulation of their divine counterparts. What was good for the gods was assumed to be advantageous for earthly rulers as well.

The era of the New Kingdom ushered in other transformations in Egyptian life and attitudes. While earlier rule had not relied on a standing army, defensive military actions combined with territorial expansion and conquest led to the establishment of a regular army, which was the source of national pride and often the measure of the success of the pharaohs. Positions in the army now became acceptable professions for aspiring members of the middle and upper classes, and military service joined religious and civil service in importance to the state. Well-organized and trained divisions composed of thousands of infantry, chariot units, and other more specialized troops were commanded by a Great Army Commander, or generalissimo, usually the successor to the throne, although the pharaoh retained absolute power over his forces.[7]

In the New Kingdom, visible and influential queens were the consorts of strong and effective warrior kings. They had a wide range of titles, owned their own estates, had administrators and servants, and wore new symbols of office. Queens had always been considered semidivine, but the new Eighteenth Dynasty strengthened these ties. Like everyone else, the queen's position was defined by her relation to the pharaoh, and among her traditional titles were King's Mother and King's Wife, which reflected the veneration of motherhood common in the society, but also the importance of various male-female relations in structuring the general order of the world. Ahmose Nefertari, wife (and sister or niece) of Ahmose (1550–1526 B.C.E.), the first ruler of the New Kingdom, played a prominent role in state affairs, and assumed the priestly office of God's Wife of Amun, which brought with it land, goods, and an administrative staff. She also served as regent for her young son when her husband died, and after her death was deified and made the object of worship throughout the land until the New Kingdom ended. Her extraordinary status is evident in the numerous inscriptions that refer to her and her activities, while the title of God's Wife was inherited and used by the women in her family line, and by Hatshepsut in particular.[8]

7. See Joyce Tydesley, *Hatchepsut: The Female Pharaoh* (Viking, 1996), pp. 27–29. Hornung uses the title *generalissimo*, p. 82.

8. See Tydesley, *Hatchepsut* pp. 58–62; Robins, pp. 43–45; and Grimal, p. 201.

Chapter 1
The Challenges
of Rule in New
Kingdom Egypt:
Hatshepsut
(1479–1458
B.C.E.) and
Tuthmosis III
(1479–1425 B.C.E.)

◼ ACT II:

THE "HATSHEPSUT PROBLEM": FROM
QUEEN TO KING

Hatshepsut's public career began quite typically with her marriage to her half-brother, Tuthmosis II, when she was about fifteen. Their father (Tuthmosis I) was a successful and venerated military leader and ruler. He had pushed southward into Africa, making Upper Nubia a province of the Egyptian empire, and was the first monarch to stake a claim along the Euphrates River. He had also begun the expansion and embellishment of the Karnak Temple complex near Thebes. He died when he was about fifty—an unusually long life at a time when life expectancy at birth was less than twenty years. Those who survived birth and childhood might live to the age of thirty-five, although the elite lived slightly longer. Death in infancy and childhood was common for all social groups, including the royal family, and this helps to explain both the kings' many wives, as well as the choice of a male successor from a lesser or collateral family line.

From the existing sources, Hatshepsut appears to have been a model wife. She bore the usual titles of King's Daughter, King's Wife, and King's Sister, but like Ahmose Nefertari before her, she preferred God's Wife and the rituals and responsibilities that accompanied the position. Under the rule of Tuthmosis II and Queen Hatshepsut, Egypt prospered. Although Tuthmosis protected their territory from external threats, he was thought to suffer from ill health and was not considered an aggressive and

heroic military leader like his father. In assessing his role, some caution should be exercised. Evidence for battles can easily disappear, and burial evidence of his physical condition is fragmentary because looting and tomb robbing were fairly common after his death. Hatshepsut and Tuthmosis had a daughter, Princess Neferure, but she is typically invisible as a young child.

Tuthmosis II died in 1479 (B.C.E.); by then he had a male heir, also named Tuthmosis, whose mother was a lesser wife. Because the heir was too young to rule, Hatshepsut stepped in as regent, a common practice. An inscription in a rock tomb near Thebes describes these events: "[After the king, Tuthmosis II, died] his son took his place as King of the Two Lands and he was the sovereign on the throne of his father. [Tuthmosis' sister], the God's Wife Hatshepsut, dealt with the affairs of the state: the Two Lands were under her government and taxes were paid to her."[9] Hatshepsut was the de facto ruler of Egypt. In the next several years, she proceeded to consolidate her position and to create her own government, with officials of her choosing who would be loyal to her. By the seventh year of the reign, she proclaimed herself king, was crowned king with full titles and regalia, wore the clothing and even the false beard of the king, and performed the duties and rituals of the divine monarch.

This move on her part, her motives, and the possible reaction of Tuthmosis III have produced heated scholarly

9. Cited in Grimal, *A History of Ancient Egypt,* p. 207.

[10]

debate over the years. In the controversies over historical interpretation, sources again play a major role. Monument evidence that might have provided more clarity has disappeared, been defaced, or was carved over with the names of other rulers and events. In addition to evidentiary problems, some scholars who simply could not understand Hatshepsut's unprecedented action have concluded that she was a greedy, even power-hungry, wicked stepmother who usurped her stepson's birthright. In turn, they assumed that he defaced her statues, monuments, and inscriptions in acts of hatred and vengeance. Some even argued that this animosity led him to have her assassinated. In slightly less personal interpretations, she is assumed to have been peace-loving—a characteristic often attributed to feminine nature—and he a warrior, resulting in a constant power struggle between factions in the palace.

The use of new or different sorts of evidence and the search for other explanations have produced a slightly different picture of the reigns of Hatshepsut and Tuthmosis. In answering the question of why she decided to become king in her own right, it is possible that she enjoyed the exercise of power and was fairly good at it. Perhaps she thought, given high mortality rates, that Tuthmosis might not survive, but as he came of age, it became clear that her powers as queen regent would not continue. Perhaps she also believed that, because of her family line, she had a closer connection to the divine inheritance of the pharaohs. Finally, she was able to take advantage of an old law and practice that allowed older kings to rule with younger successors as coregents. In this regard, she claimed her rule and that of Tuthmosis to have begun in the same year; she never denied his royal status or tried to dispatch him to some obscure post. In fact, she encouraged him to train with the army, and she continued the tradition of the heir as commanding general.

Why did Tuthmosis not challenge his stepmother's rule? When he finally did rule alone, he was one of the most famous of the warrior-kings, so he certainly could have staged a coup. Perhaps he, too, was aware of his less glorious familial background and lacked influential male relatives to give him support. Perhaps he simply accepted the idea of coregency and assumed that he would rule eventually.[10] While there is no doubt that in later years Hatshepsut's name was erased from the legitimate royal line, it is not clear when this effort began, nor that it was the result of personal animosity between the two kings. Given Egyptian desires to avoid change, Hatshepsut's unusual reign might have made some people uncomfortable. Elimination of the record of a female pharaoh would not have been the first time that Egypt's historical narrative was reshaped to conform to tradition rather than left to depict reality.

A prevalent belief over the centuries was that legitimate rulers were gods. Thus, claims to and proof of divinity were critical dimensions of

10. The best discussion of these historiographical questions is in Tydesley, *Hatchepsut*, pp. 77–80, 100–115.

Chapter 1
The Challenges
of Rule in New
Kingdom Egypt:
Hatshepsut
(1479–1458
B.C.E.) and
Tuthmosis III
(1479–1425 B.C.E.)

royal rule. For Hatshepsut, in particular, it was important to show her divine origins and to act in ways befitting her unique status (Document Four). Religious belief described the birth of a king as the miraculous result of the dominant god impregnating a mortal woman. Hatshepsut elaborated on this story, using Amun as her divine father, and had the story carved on the walls of her mortuary temple near Thebes at Deir el-Bahri. According to the story, Amun decided it was time to father a princess who would govern all of Egypt, and thus visited Hatshepsut's mother to tell her she would bear a daughter who would be "the One who is joined with Amun, [she is] the Foremost of women."[11] After her birth, Hatshepsut is presented to Amun, who calls her "daughter of my loins." During her reign, she altered one of the king's titles slightly, claiming to be the "Female Horus of Fine Gold," but both she and Tuthmosis, when he assumed the throne, claimed to be the children of Amun and they promoted his cult. Hatshepsut did not pretend to be a man; she was a woman and that was obvious to all around her. But she *was* a king with full powers and responsibilities. As she said, "none rebels against me in all lands . . . All that the sun encompasses works for me. . . ."

▪ ACT III:

HATSHEPSUT AND TUTHMOSIS AS KINGS

In addition to claiming divine parentage and making such claims public in buildings, monuments, and rituals, the rulers of Egypt also proved their divinity by maintaining order and taking care of their people. From Hatshepsut's standpoint, it was very important that members of the elite classes did not oppose her rule and that Egypt was not disturbed by famines or political unrest (Document Five). Members of the male elite who headed the army, civil service, and priesthood apparently accepted her. Some of the older men of the court had actually served her father and her husband, and they were willing to shift loyalty to her. She also selected several new administrators who proved quite capable though they came from humble origins, and their successes no doubt enhanced her prestige.

One of the most famous of these servants was a man named Senenmut. Neither his mother nor his father had titles, but he was extremely well educated and cultured, and most likely came from an upper-class family in one of the provincial cities. His education placed him in the top 10 percent of the population, and he probably moved up in either the priestly or civilian bureaucracy of his home region. He eventually held ninety-one official titles; the most important among these were titles indicating service to Amun, and perhaps his career really began at the Karnak Temple. Eventually he was known as the Overseer of

---

11. Tydesley, *Hatchepsut*, p. 104.

all the Works of the King at Karnak.[12] As a young man, he had served the queen Hatshepsut as her steward, and then later did the same for princess Neferure. Certainly his fortunes were tied to Hatshepsut, and his able administration proved to be a major asset for her. Hatshepsut had other capable servants and officers, many of whom were also of humble or less illustrious backgrounds, but none was as prominent as Senenmut. The fact that he was in charge of the building of her mortuary temple near Thebes, and the fact that he had one of his own tombs built at that site, are perhaps illustrative of his status (Document Six).

By the time that the Eighteenth Dynasty took the throne, Thebes was a large and extensive city surrounded by numerous burial grounds and temple complexes. By then, it was common to separate the burial tombs from the mortuary temples, where rulers could be served and worshiped. Reflecting the shifting centers of political power, the pharaohs were now buried in the Valley of the Kings, to the west of Thebes, while mortuary temples were built on the west bank of the Nile, directly across from the city. The increased stature of the queens by this point is evident in their burial sites at the nearby Valley of the Queens. Senenmut was in charge of building Hatshepsut's mortuary temple, the quite unusual and beautiful structure, known as the Holiest of Holy Places, at Deir el-Bahri. "The great originality

of Hatsheptut's complex lay in its organization into a succession of terraces in which the changes in plane enabled the monument to harmonize with the natural amphitheatre of the cliffs."[13] Senenmut might not have been an architect, but he certainly had considerable organizational and administrative skills, and a keen aesthetic sense.

Within the temple are many of the narratives about Hatshepsut's rule to which we already referred, but other subjects and events are also described there. One of the most prominent of these depicts the tropical scenery and exotic inhabitants of the land of Punt, which is on the coast of Africa and can be reached by the Red Sea. Like most of her predecessors, Hatshepsut promoted trade with other kingdoms, both far and near. Trips to Punt had occurred during the Middle Kingdom and would be continued by Tuthmosis III and subsequent pharaohs. Generally in these missions, the Egyptians were more interested in obtaining luxuries and exotic goods not available at home than in seeking markets for their own goods. They were especially interested in the resins, from which the Egyptians made incense (myrrh and frankincense). Apparently Hatshepsut's expedition, carried out by her chancellor, also brought back bags of gold, ebony and ivory, panther skins, and even live monkeys. Such crosscultural ventures were publicly displayed as evidence of the wealth

---

12. Descriptions of Senenmut can be found in Tydesley, *Hatchepsut,* Chapter Seven; Grimal, pp. 209–211; Watterson, *The Egyptians,* pp. 128–129.

13. Description in Grimal, p. 211; also see Tydesley, *Hatchepsut,* pp. 165–175.

Chapter 1
The Challenges
of Rule in New
Kingdom Egypt:
Hatshepsut
(1479–1458
B.C.E.) and
Tuthmosis III
(1479–1425 B.C.E.)

and international prestige of King Hatshepsut, but we can also assume that she was commercially successful in less glamorous ways because Egypt remained prosperous.

Although Hatshepsut did not engage in expansionist military campaigns, she did uphold the imperial territories and kept their frontiers secure. She also continued to support the army, and it was in excellent condition, both in terms of men and material, when Tuthmosis III took over. As already mentioned, some have argued that she was a pacifist and refused to extend Egypt's power. The fact that no extant records show her leading troops on aggressive military campaigns does not prove very much. Perhaps, like other dimensions of her life, her feelings about warfare will remain a mystery.

▪ FINALE:

THE KING IS DEAD; LONG LIVE THE KING

After ruling for almost twenty years, Hatshepsut died in 1459 or 1458 B.C.E. Her daughter Neferure died three years earlier, and Senenmut also disappeared from the scene about the same time. Once again, we know little about how Hatshepsut died; whether, indeed, she hoped her daughter would marry her stepson or perhaps rule as a king herself; and what exactly happened to her most trusted adviser. We do know that the transition to the reign of Tuthmosis III was a smooth one, and that he, in fact, kept many of Hatshepsut's advisers and officials in his government.

Like previous family members, the new pharaoh justified and legitimized his rule as Amun's wish. In an inscription in the Karnak Temple to Amun, Tuthmosis explains that the great god appeared to him during a festival and appointed him king, as the living Horus, ruler of the Two Lands. Tuthmosis would continue the building programs of Hatshepsut, although he revived the worship of the war god, Montu, an old Theban deity from the Middle Kingdom, by refurbishing his sanctuary and building a special chapel at the Karnak site. This change was in keeping with the new king's reputation as a great military leader and the creator of an even greater Egyptian empire.

At the time of Hatshepsut's death, various of the asiatic territories began to rebel against Egyptian control. During his reign, Tuthmosis carried out seventeen successful campaigns into western Asia, eventually crossing the Euphrates River north and east of Kadesh. In the process, he subdued rebellions; established provincial control or made local rulers in the area pay tribute to Egypt; and captured vast resources, war booty, and prisoners (Document Seven). In his first campaign, after the battle at Megiddo, near the Mediterranean coast north of Joppa, he took "340 living prisoners . . . 2041 mares, 6 stallions, a chariot wrought with gold; . . . 30 chariots belonging to other chiefs plus 892 chariots belonging to the wretched army; . . . 502 bows, . . . [and numerous cattle and goats]."[14] Tuthmosis also maintained Egyptian control of the area of Nubia and extracted large amounts of gold from the mines in his African territories. Overall, Egyptian prestige was so great under his leadership that envoys came from areas as far away as Minoan Crete to bring gifts to the pharaoh of this mighty empire.

Although Thebes remained the capitol and religious center of the empire, Tuthmosis III spent most of his time at Memphis, which was the center of military command and operations. Under him, the officer corps continued to expand and to gain in political importance. Eventually, under subsequent dynasties, contests between the priestly and military bureaucracies would challenge royal authority. Tuthmosis III also followed in his family's footsteps with his intellectual pursuits and cultural interests. He was well educated, and his tomb inscriptions indicate considerable interest, like Hatshepsut before him, in the flora and fauna of other areas. Finally, Tuthmosis was an excellent equestrian, archer, and athlete, but he was a modest and mild-mannered individual, not given to self-aggrandizement or bragging. This characterization would not seem to fit that of a man driven by hatred and the desire for revenge against his step-mother. But as already noted, the erasure of evidence of Hatshepsut's rule probably occurred late in Tuthmosis' reign or under the guidance of subsequent rulers, and may well have been the result of careful political calculations designed to reshape the historical narrative by streamlining royal lineages and reinforcing connections to earlier dynasties with only male rulers.

Tuthmosis III died in 1425 and was buried in a royal tomb in the Valley of the Kings. He was succeeded by a son of a second wife who proved capable of maintaining many Tuthmosid programs and goals. The Eighteenth Dynasty ended in 1295 when the pharaoh, having no male lineal successor, left the throne to one of his most prominent officials, who thus became the first king of the next dynasty. Other rulers in the Eighteenth Dynasty had made names for themselves as warriors, because of the opulence of their courts, or for religious revolution (in the reign of Amenophis IV, 1352–1336 B.C.E., who took the name Akhenaten—"pleasing to the god Aten"). And queens continued to exercise influence as de facto regents with their husbands or as formal regents for their sons. But no queen or consort equaled Hatshepsut's claim to rule as king in her own right.

---

14. From the temple inscription, cited in Watterson, *The Egyptians,* p. 103.

Chapter 1
The Challenges
of Rule in New
Kingdom Egypt:
Hatshepsut
(1479–1458
B.C.E.) and
Tuthmosis III
(1479–1425 B.C.E.)

■ QUESTIONS

1. What made it possible for Hatshepsut to rule as a king? Why do you think she wanted that title instead of the usual titles given to women? What generally explains the fact that women did not rule in Egypt?

2. On the basis of the rules of Hatshepsut and Tuthmosis, what were the most important qualities of a successful ruler? What did Egyptians expect of their kings?

3. In many ways Egyptian society was quite open and flexible; in other ways, quite rigid and limiting. What sort of moral code did the Egyptians live by? What would make Egyptians follow such a code and accept divine dynastic rule?

4. All of the documents included in this chapter, as well as most of the records we have for ancient Egypt, were intended for something other than historians' examination. Why were the records originally created, and how might their purposes affect the way we view and assess them?

■ DOCUMENTS

DOCUMENT ONE

"Exhortations and Warnings to Schoolboys," New Kingdom

Egyptian schoolboys copied extracts from various compositions on papyri, writing boards, or pieces of soft stone or clay. The purpose was to learn to write and to learn something of ancient literature. After that initial education, a young man could become a scribe to someone in an administrative office (for example, the Treasury) and there he would be trained further. The document that follows is a copying made by a schoolboy during the New Kingdom. Although its purpose was a practical one of teaching him to make his "letters," it also was a piece of advice literature. Why is he encouraged to become a scribe? What criticisms are made of other occupations? Can we assume these are accurate depictions of the various careers described? Why or why not?

. . . [Do not be a soldier, a priest, or a baker.]

Be a scribe, who is freed from forced labour, and protected from all work. He is released from hoeing with the hoe, and thou needest not carry a basket.

It separateth thee from plying the oar, and it is free from vexation. Thou hast not many masters, nor an host of superiors.

No sooner hath a man come forth from his mother's womb, than he is stretched out before his superior. The boy becometh a soldier's henchman, the stripling a recruit, the grown man is made into an husbandman, and the towns-man into a groom. The halt (?) is made into a doorkeeper, and the (short-sighted?) into one that feedeth cattle; the fowler goeth upon the . . . , and the fisherman standeth in the wet.

The superintendent of the stable standeth at the work, while his span is left in the field. Corn is thrown down to his wife, and his daughter is on the em-bankment (?). If his span leaveth him and runneth away, he is carried off to the Iwai-troops.[1]

The soldier, when he goeth up to Syria, hath no staff and no sandals. He knoweth not whether he be dead or alive, by reason of the (fierce?) lions. The foe lieth hidden in the scrub, and the enemy standeth ready for battle. The sol-dier marcheth and crieth out to his god: "Come to me and deliver me!"

The priest standeth there as an husbandman, and the we͗eb-priest worketh in the canal[2] – – – – he is drenched in the river; it maketh no difference to him whether it be winter or summer, whether the sky be windy or rainy.

When the baker standeth and baketh and layeth bread on the fire, his head is inside the oven, and his son holdeth fast his feet. Cometh it to pass that he slip-peth from his son's hand, he falleth into the blaze.

But the scribe, he directeth every work that is in this land.

[Be an official.]
Let not thine heart go afluttering like leaves before the wind – – – –. Set not thine heart on pleasures. Alas, they profit not, they render a man no service – – – –. When he worketh and *it is his lot* to serve the Thirty,[3] he worketh *and* extendeth not his strength,[4] *for* evil toil lieth (yet) in front of him. No servant bringeth him water, and no women will make bread for him, whereas his com-panions[5] *live* according to their desire, and their servants act in their stead. (But) the man of no sense standeth there and toileth, and his eye looketh enviously at them.

Therefore give heed, thou naughty one; thou obstinate one, that will not hear when thou art spoken to. Hasten to it, the calling with the gay. . . . It is the one that directeth all Councils of Thirty and the courtiers of the (Royal) Circle. Prithee, know that.

---

1. Meaning probably: if during these non-military activities his horses get lost, he is put into the infantry.
2. Even the priesthood is not immune from forced labour.
3. The college of high officials.
4. He dares not sleep.
5. His erstwhile schoolfellows who have become scribes.

Chapter 1
The Challenges
of Rule in New
Kingdom Egypt:
Hatshepsut
(1479–1458
B.C.E.) and
Tuthmosis III
(1479–1425 B.C.E.)

DOCUMENT TWO

"The Declaration of Innocence Before the Gods of the Tribunal," The Book of the Dead

Originally, books of wisdom or confession had been intended for the king and his family. By the time of the Eighteenth Dynasty however, anyone who could afford a burial would also use these "coffin texts," or "mortuary literature," the purpose of which was to make sure the deceased emerged victorious in the perilous and unpredictable afterlife. In this document, the individual is attempting to convince the gods that she or he has lived a good life. Based on this document, what behaviors or attitudes did the Egyptians admire? What did they consider evil or sinful?

O Wide-strider who came forth from Heliopolis, I have not done wrong.

O Fire-embracer who came froth from Kheraha, I have not robbed.

O Nosey who came forth from Hermopolis, I have not stolen.

O Swallower of Shades who came forth from Kernet, I have not slain people.

O Terrible of Face who came forth from Rosetjau, I have not destroyed the food offerings.

O Double Lion who came forth from the sky, I have not reduced measures.

O He-whose-Eyes-are-in-Flames who came forth from Asyut, I have not stolen the god's property.

O Burning One who came forth backwards, I have not told lies.

O Breaker of Bones who came forth from Heracleopolis, I have not stolen food.

O Orderer of Flame who came forth from Memphis, I was not sullen.

O He-of-the-Cavern who came forth from the West, I have not fornicated with the fornicator.

O He-whose-Face-is-behind-him who came forth from his hole, I have not caused (anyone) to weep.

O Anointed One who came forth from the chapel, I have not dissembled.

O Hot-Legs who came forth at twilight, I have not transgressed.

O He-who-is-Blood who came forth from the place of slaughter, I have not done grain-profiteering.

O Eater of Entrails who came forth from the Council of Thirty, I have not robbed a parcel of land.

O Lord of Truth who came forth from Hall of Two Truths, I have not discussed (secrets).

O Strayer who came forth from Bubastis, I have brought no lawsuits.

O Planter(?) who came forth from Heliopolis, I have not disputed at all about property.

O Doubly Evil One who came forth from the Brusirite Nome, I have not had intercourse with a married woman.

[18]

O He-who-Sees-what-he-has-brought who came forth from the House of Min, I have not (wrongly) copulated.

O He-who-is-over-the-Great-Ones who came forth from -?-, I have not struck terror.

THE BOOK OF GOING FORTH BY DAY

O Demolisher who came forth from -?-, I have not transgressed.

O Proclaimer of Speech who came forth from Weryt, I have not been hot (-tempered).

O Youth who came forth from the Double Scepter Nome, I have not been neglectful of truthful words.

O Dark One who came forth from darkness, I have not cursed.

O He-who-Brings-his-Offering who comes forth from Asyut, I have not been violent.

O Proclaimer of Voice who came forth from Wenis, I have not confounded (truth).

O Possessor of Faces who came forth from Nedjefet, I have not been impatient.

O Captain who came forth from Weten, I have not discussed.

O Possessor of Two Horns who came forth from Asyut, I have not been garrulous about matters.

O Nefertum who came forth from Memphis, I have not done wrong, I have not done evil.

O He-who-does-not-(allow)-Survivors who came forth from Busiris, I have not disputed the King.

O He-who-Acts-as-he-Wishes who came forth from Antinaiopolis, I have not waded in the water.

O Ihy who came forth from the Primordial Waters, my voice was not loud.

O He-who-Prospers-the-Common-People who came forth from Asyut, I have not cursed a god.

O Uniter of Attributes who came forth from the Cavern, I have not made extollings(?).

O Uniter of Good who came forth from the Cavern, I have not harmed the bread-ration of the Gods.

O Upraised of Head who came forth from the shrine, I have not stolen the Khenef-cakes from the Blessed.

O He-who-Brings-his-Portion who came forth from the Hall of the Two Truths, I have not stolen Hefnu-cakes of a youth, (nor) have I fettered the god of my town.

O He-who-Brightens-the-Land who came forth from Faiyum(?), I have not slain sacred cattle.

Chapter 1
The Challenges
of Rule in New
Kingdom Egypt:
Hatshepsut
(1479–1458
B.C.E.) and
Tuthmosis III
(1479–1425 B.C.E.)

DOCUMENT THREE

"The Wisdom of Anii"
(Circa 1000 B.C.E.)

"Books" of wisdom or advice, usually spoken by a father to a son, were common in Egyptian society. Scribes reproduced these books often imitating much older books of wisdom. The following document is well known. In it, a father is teaching his son and exhorting him to good behavior. What values or attitudes are expressed here? On the basis of this document, what would you describe as the ideal behavior of an Egyptian man? What views of women are expressed?

. . . [Follow my words.]
(I tell thee) that which is excellent, that which thou shalt observe (?) in thine heart. Do it, *and so thou wilt be good,* and all evil is far from thee. – – – – *It will be said of thee:* a good character, *and not:* he is ruined, he is idle. *Accept my words,* and so will all evil be far from thee.

[Be prudent in speech?]
Unintelligible. . . .

[Boast not of thy strength?]
Unintelligible.

[Found a family.]
Take to thyself a wife when thou art a youth, that she may give thee a son. Thou shouldest beget him for thee whilst thou art yet young, *and shouldest live to see* him become a man (?). Happy is the man who hath much people, and he is respected because of his children (?). . . .

[Be discreet on visits.]
Enter not the (house?) of another, – – – –. Gaze not on that which is not right in (his?) house; thine eye may see it, but thou keepest silent. Speak not of it to another outside, that it may not become for thee a great crime worthy of death, when it is heard (?).

[Beware of the harlot.]
Beware of a strange woman, one that is not known in her city. Wink (?) not at her – – – – have no carnal knowledge of her (?). (She is) a deep water whose twisting men know not. A woman that is far from her husband, "I am fair," she saith to thee every day, when she hath no witnesses – – – –. It is a great crime worthy of death, when one heareth of it, and although it is not related outside – – – –. . . .

[20]

[Piety towards parents.]

Offer water to thy father and thy mother, who rest in the desert valley – – – –. Omit not to do it, that thy son may do the like for thee.

[Be not a drunkard.]

Take not upon thyself (?)[1] to drink a jug of beer. Thou speakest, and an unintelligible utterance issueth from thy mouth. If thou fallest down and thy limbs break, there is none to hold out a hand to thee. Thy companions in drink stand up and say: *"Away with this sot!"* . . .

[Be grateful to thy mother.]

Double the bread that thou givest to thy mother, and carry her as she carried (thee). She had a heavy load in thee, and never left it to me. When thou wast born after thy months, she carried thee yet again about her neck, and for three years her breast was in thy mouth. *She was not* disgusted at thy dung, she was not disgusted and said not: "What do I?" She put thee to school, when thou hadst been taught to write, and daily she stood there . . . with bread and beer from her house.

When thou art a young man and takest to thee a wife and art settled in thine house, keep before thee how thy mother gave birth to thee, and how she brought thee up further in all manner of ways. May she not do thee harm nor lift up her hands to God, and may he not hear her cry.

[On wealth and its instability.]

Eat not bread, if another is suffering want, and thou dost not stretch out the hand to him with bread. – – – –. One is rich and another is poor – – – –. He that was rich in past years, is this year a groom. Be not greedy about filling thy belly – – – –. The course of the water of last year, it is this year in another place. Great seas have become dry places, and banks have become abysses. – – – –

[Keep thyself far from tumults.]

Enter not into a crowd, if thou findest *that it standeth ready for* beating – – – – that thou mayest not be blamed in the Court before the magistrates after the tendering of evidence, Keep thee far from hostile people – – – –.

[Treat thy wife well.]

Act not the official over thy wife in her house, if thou knowest that she is excellent. Say not unto her: "Where is it? Bring it us," if (?) she hath put (it) in the right place. Let thine eye observe and be silent, that so (?) thou mayest know her good deeds. (She is) happy when thine hand is with her – – – –. Thereby the man ceaseth to stir up strife in his house – – – –.

1. Possible meaning: Boast not that you can drink, etc.

Chapter 1
The Challenges
of Rule in New
Kingdom Egypt:
Hatshepsut
(1479–1458
B.C.E.) and
Tuthmosis III
(1479–1425 B.C.E.)

[Be careful of women.]
Got not after a woman, in order that she may not steal thine heart away.

[Behaviour towards superiors.]
Answer not a superior who is enraged, *get out of his way.* Say what is sweet, when he saith what is bitter to any one, and make calm his heart. Contentious answers carry rods, and thy strength collapseth. *Rage directeth itself (?)* against thy business, *therefore vex (?) not thine own self.* He turneth about and praiseth thee quickly, after his terrible hour. If thy words are soothing for the heart, the heart inclineth to receive them. Seek out silence for thyself, and submit to what he doeth.

[Stand well with the police.]
Make a friend of the herald of thy quarter, and let him not become enraged with thee. . . .

DOCUMENT FOUR

The Birth of Queen Hatshepsut

The following inscriptions have been taken from inscriptions and scenes at the king's famous temple, Deir el-Bahri. This is really a tale in which the court and higher classes heard the story of the monarch's divine origins. Beginning with her birth, it tells of the god Amun's (spelled Amon here) presentation of Hatshepsut to the gods, and describes her coming of age and then the coronation by her father, Tuthmosis I. (Buto is the goddess of the North; Khnum is the god who created humankind.) Why was it important for Hatshepsut to make these claims? What are the events described that give her credibility?

. . . Words of the Queen

Utterance by the king's-wife and king's-mother Ahmose, in the presence of the majesty of this august god, Amon, Lord of Thebes: "How great is thy fame! It is splendid to see thy front; thou hast united my majesty (fem.) with thy favors, thy dew is in all my limbs." After this, the majesty of this god did all that he desired with her.

Words of Amon

Utterance of Amon, Lord of the Two Lands, before her: "Khnemet-Amon-Hatshepsut shall be the name of this my daughter, whom I have placed in thy

[22]

body, this saying which comes out of thy mouth. She shall exercise the excellent kingship in this whole land . . .

Reply of Khnum

"I will form this [thy] daughter [Makere] (Hatshepsut), for life, prosperity and health; for offerings —————— for love of the beautiful mistress. Her form shall be more exalted than the gods, in her great dignity of King of Upper and Lower Egypt."

V. KHNUM FASHIONS THE CHILD

Scene

Khnum is seated before a potter's wheel, upon which he is fashioning two male (!) children,[1]

Words of Amon

Utterance of [Amon] . . . . —————— to see his daughter, his beloved, the king, Makere (Hatshepsut), living, after she was born, while his heart was exceedingly happy.

Utterance of [Amon to] his bodily daughter [Hatshepsut]: "Glorious part which has come forth from me; king, taking the Two Lands, upon the Horus-throne forever." . . .

Words of the Gods

Utterance of all the gods, [to] Amon-[Re]: "This thy daughter [Hatshepsut], who liveth, we are satisfied with her in life and peace. She is now thy daughter of thy form, whom thou hast begotten, prepared. Thou hast given to her thy soul, thy ⌐—⌐, thy ⌐bounty⌐, the magic powers of the diadem. While she was in the body of her that bare her, the lands were hers, the countries were hers; all that the heavens cover, all that the sea encircles. Thou hast now done this with her, for thou knowest the two æons.[2] Thou hast given to her the share of Horus in life, the years of Set in satisfaction. We have given to her . . . .

---

1. This would indicate that the reliefs were made according to old and traditional sketches in which, of course, a female child had no place. All the pronouns used by Khnum in addressing the child are feminine!

2. An aeon is sixty years.

Chapter 1
The Challenges
of Rule in New
Kingdom Egypt:
Hatshepsut
(1479–1458
B.C.E.) and
Tuthmosis III
(1479–1425 B.C.E.)

The Queen's Growth and Beauty

Her majesty saw all this thing[3] herself, which she told to the people, who heard, falling down for terror among them. Her majesty grew beyond everything; to look upon her was more beautiful than anything; her ⌐—¬ was like a god, her form was like a god, she did everything as a god, her splendor was like a god; her majesty (fem.) was a maiden, beautiful, blooming, Buto in her time. She made her divine form to flourish, ⌐favor of¬ him that fashioned her. . . .

Thutmose I's Address to the Court

Said his majesty before them: "This my daughter, Khnemet-Amon, Hatshepsut, who liveth, I have appointed [her] ——; she is my successor upon my throne, she it assuredly is who shall sit upon my wonderful seat. She shall command the people in every place of the palace; she it is who shall lead you; ye shall proclaim her word, ye shall be united at her command. He who shall do her homage shall live, he who shall speak evil in blasphemy of her majesty shall die. Whosoever proclaims with unanimity the name of her majesty (fem.), shall enter immediately into the royal chamber, just as it was done by the name of this Horus (viz., by my name). For thou art divine, O daughter of a god, for whom even the gods fight; behind whom they exert their protection every day according to the command of her father, the lord of the gods. . . .

DOCUMENT FIVE

HATSHEPSUT

"Speech of the Queen"

The following speech is taken from an inscription on the obelisks at Karnak, which Hatshepsut had built and dedicated to Amun. What is the purpose of the king's speech? Has she been a good king, according to this speech?

. . . III. BASE INSCRIPTION

Titulary and Encomium of the Queen

Live the female Horus . . . . daughter of Amon-Re, his favorite, his only one, who exists by him, the splendid part of the All-Lord, whose beauty the spirits of

---

3. What thing is meant is not clear; possibly it refers to the preceding presentation to the gods, which she narrates now to the people. Then follow her growth into youth and beauty, and the journey.

Heliopolis fashioned; who hath taken the land like Irsu,[1] whom he hath created to wear his diadem, who exists like Khepri[2] *(Ḫpry)*, who shines with crowns like "Him-of-the-Horizon," the pure egg, the excellent seed, whom the two Sorceresses[3] reared, whom Amon himself caused to appear upon his throne in Hermonthis, whom he chose to protect Egypt, to ⌈defend⌉ the people; the female Horus, avengeress of her father, the oldest (daughter) of the "Bull-of-his-Mother," whom Re begat to make for himself excellent seed upon earth for the well-being of the people; his living portrait, King of Upper and Lower Egypt, Makere (Hatshepsut), the electrum of kings. . . .

Speech of the Queen

"I have done this from a loving heart for my father Amon; I have entered upon his ⌈project⌉ of the first occurrence, I was wise by his excellent spirit, I did not forget anything of that which he exacted. My majesty (fem.) knoweth that he is divine. I did (it) under his command, he it was who led me; I conceived not any works without his do⌈ing⌉, he it was who gave the directions. I slept not because of his temple, I erred not from that which he commanded, my heart was wise before my father, I entered upon the affairs of his heart, I did not turn my back upon the city of the All-Lord, but turned to it the face. I know that Karnak is the horizon on earth, the August Ascent of the beginning, the sacred eye of the All-Lord, the place of his heart, which wears his beauty, and encompasses those who follow him."

DOCUMENT SIX

"Inscriptions on a Statue Presented by Hatshepsut to Senenmut"

Hatshepsut and Tuthmosis III presented a statue to Senenmut (spelled Senmut here) as a token of honor; it was to be set up in the temple at Karnak. The inscriptions give an idea of Senenmut's positions as well as the power he exercised. What are some of his functions serving the kingdom? What does he see as his greatest accomplishments?

1. A god's name, lit., *"He who made him."*
2. God of continued existence.
3. A divine name, lit., *"two great in sorcery."*

Chapter 1
The Challenges
of Rule in New
Kingdom Egypt:
Hatshepsut
(1479–1458
B.C.E.) and
Tuthmosis III
(1479–1425 B.C.E.)

. . . 1. INSCRIPTIONS ON THE KARNAK STATUE . . .

Statue Was Presented by Queen

[Given as a fav]or of the king's-presence, the King of Upper and Lower Egypt, Makere (Hatshepsut), who is given [life, to the hereditary prince, count], wearer of the royal seal, sole companion, steward of Amon, Senmut, triumphant; in order to be in the temple of [I]shru; in order to receive the plenty that comes forth from before the presence of this great goddess.

[Given] as a favor of the king's-presence, extending the period of life to eternity, with a goodly memory among the people after the years that shall come; to the prince and count, overseer of the granary of Amon, Senmut, triumphant. . . .

His Praise of Himself; His Offices

He says: "I was the greatest of the great in the whole land; one who heard the hearing alone in the privy council, steward of [Amon], Senmut, triumphant."

"I was the real favorite of the king, acting as one praised of his lord every day, the overseer of the cattle of Amon, Senmut."

"I was — of truth, not showing partiality; with whose injunctions the Lord of the Two Lands was satisfied; attached to Nekhen, prophet of Mat, Senmut."

"I was one who entered in [love], and came forth in favor, making glad the heart of the king every day, the companion, and master of the palace, Senmut."

"I commanded in the storehouse of divine offerings of Amon every tenth day; the overseer of the storehouse of Amon, Senmut."

I conducted ———— of the gods every day, for the sake of the life, prosperity, and health of the king; overseer of the ⌐—¬ of Amon, Senmut."

"I was a foreman of foremen, superior of the great, [overseer] of all [works] of the house of silver, conductor of every handicraft, chief of the prophets of Montu in Hermonthis, Senmut."

DOCUMENT SEVEN

"The Annals: First Campaign" of Tuthmosis III

The records of Tuthmosis' various campaigns come from pillars in temples built for the purposes of celebration. These particular inscriptions describe his Megiddo campaign, which lasted about 175 days. On the basis of the inscriptions, what was the purpose of this campaign? What did the Egyptian empire gain from it? How is the king depicted? [Kode: coastal people who probably shipped the gods.]—Editor

. . . *Surrender of Megiddo*

Behold, the chiefs of this country came to render their portions, to do obeisance to the fame of his majesty, to crave breath for their nostrils, because of the greatness of his power, because of the might of the fame of his majesty — — the country ——— came to his fame, bearing their gifts, consisting of silver, gold, lapis lazuli, malachite; bringing clean grain, wine, large cattle, and small cattle—for the army of his majesty. ⌜Each of the Kode⌝ (*Ḳd-(w)* among them bore the tribute southward. Behold, his majesty appointed the chiefs anew for ———.

Spoil of Megiddo

———340 living prisoners; 83 hands; 2,041 mares; 191 foals; 6 stallions;— young—; a chariot, wrought with gold, (its) ⌜pole⌝ of gold, belonging to that foe; a beautiful chariot, wrought with gold, belonging to the chief of [Megiddo]; ———892 chariot[s] of his wretched army; total, 924 (chariots); a beautiful ⌜suit⌝ of bronze armor, belonging to that foe; a beautiful ⌜suit⌝ of bronze armor, belonging to the chief of Megiddo (*M-k-ty*); ——— , 200 suits of armor, belonging to his wretched army; 502 bows; 7 poles of (*mry*) wood, wrought with silver, belonging to the tent of that foe. Behold, the army of [his majesty]took ———, 297—, 1,929 large cattle, 2,000 small cattle, 20,500 white small cattle.

Plunder of the Lebanon Tripolis, Megiddo, Etc.

List of that which was afterward taken by the king, of the household goods of that foe who was in [⌜the city of⌝] Yenoam (*Y-nw-ᶜᵓ-mw*), in Nuges (*Yn-yw-g-sᵓ*), and in Herenkeru (*Ḥw-r-n-kᵓ-rw*), together with all the goods of those cities which submitted themselves, which were brought to [his majesty: 474]—; 38 lords (*[m-rᵓ-y-]nᵓ*) of theirs, 87 children of that foe and of the chiefs who were with him, 5 lords of theirs, 1,796, male and female slaves with their children, noncombatants who surrendered because of famine with that foe, 103 men; total, 2,503. Besides flat dishes of costly stone and gold, various vessels, ———, a large (two-handled) vase (*ᵓ-kᵓ-nᵓ*) of the work of Kharu (*Ḫᵓ-rw*), (—*b*-) vases, flat dishes, (*ḥntw-*) dishes, various drinking-vessels, 3 large kettles (*rhd't*), [8]7 knives, amounting to 784 deben. Gold in rings found in the hands of the artificers, and silver in many rings, 966 deben and 1 kidet.[1] A silver statue in beaten work ——— the head of gold, the staff with human faces; 6 chairs of that foe, of ivory, ebony and carob wood, wrought with gold; 6 footstools belonging to them; 6 large tables of ivory and carob wood, a staff of carob wood, wrought with gold and all costly stones in the fashion of a scepter, belonging to that foe, all of it wrought with gold; a statue of that foe, of ebony wrought with gold, the head of which [⌜was inlaid⌝] with lapis lazuli ———; vessels of bronze, much clothing of that foe. . . .

[1. Deben and kidet are measures of weight. Ed.]

Politics and Private Life in Classical Athens:
Pericles (?494–429 B.C.E.) and Aspasia (?470–?410 B.C.E)

■ SETTING THE STAGE

By the beginning of the fifth century B.C.E., the population of Greece resided in several independent city-states *(poleis)* of varying size located on mainland Greece, the surrounding islands of the Aegean Sea, and on the coast of Anatolia (eastern Turkey). These urban centers, with surrounding cultivated country, shared a common language and a broad cultural identity, and had also developed ideas of citizenship in which the duties and privileges of membership and structures of government were defined by law. At the same time, the poleis were remarkably different, with diverse economic foundations, varying forms of rule, and distinct religious cults and practices. Although the city-states formed alliances or leagues to defend or promote common interests, any challenge to a city's autonomy could produce resistance and conflict. As a result, in the fifth century, the poleis had to balance between cooperation and independence. Similarly, within each city tensions could develop between desires for order, community, and general welfare on the one hand, and demands for change, individualism, and personal ambitions for gain and glory on the other.

Developments in Athens in the fifth century showcase these tensions and the attempts to resolve them. Few would question the historical importance of Athens' democratic government, wealth, power, built environment, and flourishing culture, and the legacy of these accomplishments to the western tradition. But these accomplishments were created by trial and error, contests and disagreements, personal hardships, and war and loss of life. One can imagine that, although it was exciting to be a resident of Athens at this time, it was not always easy, and certainly the experience varied depending on birth, wealth, and gender. Through the lives of Pericles (?494–429 B.C.E.), and Aspasia (?470–?410 B.C.E.) we can get glimpses of the challenges of making democracy work, the popular attitudes and values in this century, and the relationship between personal lives and politics.

Pericles was a key figure in this age of Athenian achievement—well-known as a political leader, a diplomat, a cultural patron, an intellectual, and a military commander. Aspasia was equally well known as his partner (*pallake,* or concubine), but as a foreigner and a woman, Aspasia exemplifies a very different kind of life in democratic Athens. At times, Pericles and Aspasia were admired and praised, but they were also scrutinized and criticized. Through various social and political dialogues, more general norms of behavior and sets of intellectual and popular values emerged. It is possible to learn quite a bit about a society from what its people say about their leaders. In the cases of Pericles and Aspasia, no personal records from either have survived, and if we hope to learn anything about them, we have no choice but to rely on other voices.

Archeological, representational, and textual sources provide the basis for our knowledge of ancient Greece. The specific records for classical Athens are the built environment of the city, sculpture and vase painting, written laws and court records, poetry, literature, and philosophical essays. Though significant numbers of such sources exist, they are often incomplete fragments or pieces, anecdotal and contradictory. The historian must interpret these sources for meaning and at times fill in the gaps with conjecture. In the absence of personal records from Pericles, our most important sources are laws, the various dramatic works of the time, and the history written by his contemporary, Thucydides (ca. 460–ca.400 B.C.E.). One of the most in-depth accounts of Pericles' life is the account by Plutarch, written much later, in the first century (C.E.). He was able to consult sources

[29]

*Chapter 2
Politics and
Private Life in
Classical Athens:
Pericles
(?494–429 B.C.E.)
and Aspasia
(?470–?410 B.C.E.)*

now lost to us, hence the value of his work. In the final analysis, it is important to recognize that "almost every aspect of the life of Pericles is debatable and has been much debated."[1]

We know even less about Aspasia, but that is true for most Greek women of the period, many of whom are not even referred to by name. "The Greek world rarely accorded women a public voice so we have few occasions when they speak to us directly."[2] In most cases, when women are mentioned, it is through asides, in reference to men, or as general types or symbols. Consequently, we know what men thought of women, but little of what women felt or thought about their lives and their world. As might be expected, this situation was especially true for lower-class, foreign, and slave women. Aspasia was often gossiped about, was mentioned

by comedic writers, and appeared in philosophical commentary or history when the speaker intended either to attack or to praise Pericles. Consequently we are aware of her reputation, what she symbolized or came to represent, but we struggle to find the individual on whom the myths are based.[3]

To create whole persons and personalities out of partial facts, we can first place what we know within broader social and political contexts and compare the individuals to more general information we have about men and women at that time. After establishing a sense of what was usual or possible, we can begin to understand what it took for Aspasia and Pericles to assume their unique positions of prominence in fifth-century (B.C.E.) Athenian history.

▪ THE ACTORS:

PERICLES AND ASPASIA

At the time of Pericles' birth, Athens was one of the largest of the Greek city-states. Situated, in 1,000 square miles of territory known as Attica, by the middle of the fifth century (B.C.E.) its estimated population was between 250,000 and 300,000. Of that population, 80,000 to 100,000 were slaves, about 50,000 were *metics* or foreign residents, and the remaining 100,000 to

150,000 were adult male citizens, their wives, and their children. Individuals in Athenian society were connected to each other in various ways. They lived in households (*oikos*) that usually consisted of the immediate family unit and workers or slaves. Some of these households were closely linked by blood relations and formed noble kin groups (*genos*) that had been influential and powerful for some time. Pericles' mother, Agariste, was from one such family, the Alcmaeonids, who possessed wealth from landed property

1. Donald Kagan, *Pericles of Athens and the Birth of Democracy* (New York,: Free Press, 1991), p. xiii. Also see Anthony Podlecki, *Perikles and His Circle* (New York: Routledge, 1998), which is structured around the debates themselves.

2. Sue Blundell, *Women in Ancient Greece* (London: British Museum Press, 1995), p. 10.

3. Madeleine M. Henry, *Prisoner of History: Aspasia of Miletus and Her Biographical Tradition* (New York: Oxford University Press, 1995), p. 4. See also Paul Cartledge, *The Greeks* (New York: TV Books, 2000).

and were known as political leaders. In fact, Cleisthenes, the famous democratic reformer and lawgiver, was Pericles' maternal great uncle, and several other familial ancestors had played leading roles in Athenian politics. Pericles' father, Xanthippus, also came from an old family, and it was probably from him that Pericles inherited some important property north of Athens. Xanthippus, like all male citizens, served in the military and eventually would gain both notoriety and fame in that capacity. This family background placed Pericles in the highest levels of Athenian society. By the time he was growing up, however, birth and wealth alone did not determine political power.

All Athenian citizens were part of loosely connected and somewhat artificial groups called *phratrys*, or brotherhoods, whose primary functions included determining whether children were the legitimate offspring of Athenian parents. The brotherhoods were gathered into larger units, the tribes, while the territory in which people lived was divided into districts or counties, the *demes*.[4] Individuals were known by their father's name and the *deme* in which they were registered. Thus, one's identity and status as a citizen derived from these groups, and they provided the mechanisms for popular participation in the government of Athens. Finally, other distinctions among citizens would rest on their productive capacities and their military functions. What did each head of household contribute to the city-state in terms of goods and fighting capacity? Obviously, this complex mix of identities makes it hard to distinguish clear social and economic lines among the citizen population. "The problem is not that there are too few possibilities for classification, but too many."[5]

Nevertheless, for all who held it, citizenship was a gift, a major component of identity, and carried with it rights and responsibilities. The identification as a *politai* (translated as "citizen") specified those individuals with full political rights, and they were always male. Women, as the possessors of civil rights, were called *astai*, which also means citizen. But it is clear that the privileges and responsibilities of men and women under the heading of citizenship were significantly different. Especially by the fifth century, women were the "conferrers of citizenship," and consistently played an important role "as channels through which political and economic rights were transmitted to the next generation of citizens."[6]

The blurred boundaries among citizens and the various identities for what constituted the basis and rights of citizenship contributed to ideas of homogeneity and equality. Simultaneously the rights and privileges of male citizens were contrasted, and even made possible, by the legal and political limitations and the secondary social status of women (identified as Athenian),

---

4. For a more detailed discussion of these groups, their origins, and functions, see the following. Robert Garland, *Daily Life of the Ancient Greeks* (Westport, Conn.: Greenwood Press, 1998), pp. 43–47; James N. Davidson, *Courtesans and Fishcakes: The Consuming Passions of Classical Athens* (London: HarperCollins Publishers, 1997), pp. 227–235; P. J. Rhodes, *The Greek City States: A Source Book* (London: Croom Helm, 1986), various descriptive documents by name.

5. Davidson, p. 227.

6. Blundell, p. 129.

*Chapter 2
Politics and
Private Life in
Classical Athens:
Pericles
(?494–429 B.C.E.)
and Aspasia
(?470–?410 B.C.E.)*

metics (foreigners with a right to live permanently in the area), and slaves. These groups had no political rights and could not own land; their legal position was different from that of citizens in various ways, including whom they could marry, whether they paid taxes, and the kind of work they "contributed" to the state. Finally, all three groups were characterized as having natures or qualities that distinguished them from the ideals associated with the male citizen population. Aspasia, as a woman and a foreigner, would have a much different life than Pericles. This is evident if we consider what their lives might have been like as they grew up in fifth-century (B.C.E.) Greece.

Pericles' education probably followed the general patterns of the time. By the fifth century, basic literacy for Athenian male citizens began to replace earlier, more restricted elite education by tutors. By the age of seven, a boy would be sent to a school where his studies continued as long as the family could pay the fees and did not need him to be economically productive. Pericles' family background and economic status would have given him the opportunity for a more extensive period of learning. Education for boys generally consisted of reading, writing, physical training, and music. They had to memorize poetry, learn to play the lyre, and, through the teaching of professional trainers, become physically fit. Learning musical skills was thought to improve self-control and foster harmonious actions. From epic poetry, young men could become acquainted with heroic leaders whom they might emulate. Physical training would prevent bodily weakness and cowardice,

and promote competition. In sum, education taught manliness, which consisted of civic consciousness, self-control, and courage—all qualities suited to an adult male who would participate in government, help subsidize the state through taxes, and passionately defend himself and the state.

Pericles' education was somewhat broader, perhaps because of his intellectual talents and curiosity. As a young man, he appears to have studied individually with some of the best minds of his time. Among them was a philosopher from Ionia, Anaxagoras, who came to Athens about 480 and taught there until 432. Like other Ionian thinkers of the time, Anaxagoras sought to define the "single basic building block" of nature out of which all things develop.[7] He argued that everything that exists is made up of differing combinations of *spermata*, or seeds (what we might call atoms). Even more important for his student Pericles and the world of politics, were Anaxagoras' views of purpose and cause in the universe. He argued that the central principle operating in the world is order and control, and that the instrument of this principle is *nous*, or mind, which "controls all things, both the greater and the smaller, that have life."[8] Plutarch later claimed that Pericles learned from Anaxagoras how to use intellectual argument in the realm of politics and to look for natural rather than supernatural causes to explain events. In fact, Pericles' later career would demonstrate that he was

7. Podlecki, p. 23. Chapter 3 generally covers Pericles' intellectual circle.

8. Quoted in Podlecki, p. 24.

governed by reason rather than superstition, and that his abilities as a persuasive speaker were almost without equal among his peers.

Pericles' younger sister, whose name we do not know, probably received little education outside the home. At home, she would have been taught to manage a productive household and its servants and to carry out some ritual responsibilities. She might have been taught music and dancing by outside tutors, but this instruction would not have been systematic. Although vase painting does show girls and women running and swimming, and healthy mothers were central to a healthy society, physical education would not have been a necessary part of her upbringing. Boys reached maturity through lengthy training to become citizens and warriors; women reached maturity when they were able to bear children. These expectations help to explain why the age at marriage for men was about twice that for women. Marriages were arranged by fathers, often with relatives, and women had no rights in the matter. A woman's relationship to the state was through her husband and family, not directly as a productive and involved

citizen. Women were certainly a necessary part of the *oikos* (household); they produced the sons who insured its perpetuity, and they supervised the day-to-day activities that underlay household survival. But "citizen" women were always the wards of the head of the *oikos*, who could be father, husband, or male child (Document One). Thus, the education and upbringing of girls was designed to ensure that they fulfilled their necessary duties, just as the education of boys prepared them to assume their public rights and responsibilities in the Athenian world.

Aspasia was born in Miletus, a wealthy city on the Ionian coast of Asia Minor. Her father, Axiochus, is assumed to have been a man of some substance. Thus, we might speculate that with such a family background, growing up in a slightly different social and intellectual world, perhaps Aspasia was educated. Later, in Athens, she would be both admired and vilified for her intelligence and learning. Did such unusual attributes for a woman explain why Pericles found her interesting? Or did those attributes serve as a means to see them both as abnormal and even dangerous?

ACT I:

GROWING UP IN A POLITICAL WORLD

Even if we have no firsthand accounts of the childhood and adolescence of our major players, we can be assured that the courses of both their lives in these early decades were shaped by broader political events in Greece.

Pericles was a toddler when the Persians launched two punitive invasions of mainland Greece in the early fifth century. In the first invasion, they were forced to withdraw by the Athenian victory at Marathon in 490. A decade later, while Pericles was still a youngster and not yet ready for military service, he would have lived through a

Chapter 2
Politics and
Private Life in
Classical Athens:
Pericles
(?494–429 B.C.E.)
and Aspasia
(?470–?410 B.C.E.)

second, much more massive Persian invasion, occupation, and eventual defeat of the Persians at Salamis (480) and Platea (479). Following these victories, Athens created a naval league to defend Greek cities against further Persian attacks. Aspasia's home city Miletus was a member of this league of cities, but by 460, when she was a young girl, Athenian attempts to dominate the league had begun to produce turbulence in many of the member cities. These broader events directly affected both of their families, though in different ways.

Pericles' father was one of the heroes at Marathon, but following that contest, competition for political power in Athens eventually brought a charge of treachery against the powerful Alcmaeonid clan. In 484, Xanthippus and his family were forced to leave Athens after a procedure of "ostracism," in which the Assembly voted to expel one of its citizens for a period of ten years. This process had been introduced by Cleisthenes as a means of deterring factions and treason.[9] The family was in exile only until 481, when a renewed Persian threat forced the Athenians to recall all of their ostracized citizens. In the subsequent fighting, Xanthippus was a successful leader on several occasions, and he returned to Athens as a hero and consequently a prominent political figure. In this process, the young Pericles gained firsthand knowledge about political competition and the workings of democracy in his home city-state.

Perhaps he also learned from his family's fortunes that maintaining popular support and fending off attacks by competitors would be a rewarding but difficult enterprise.

Aspasia's fate was also influenced by the turbulence of Athenian politics and the process of ostracism. By the 460s, it appears that several leading Athenian citizens who had been ostracized and expelled were living in Miletus. One of them supposedly married Aspasia's older sister (whose name we do not know). Such alliances between Athenian citizens and leading foreign families were not uncommon at the time. When the ostracism of Aspasia's brother-in-law ended he returned to Athens with his wife, children, and his young sister-in-law. Aspasia thus arrived in Athens as "the dependent relation of an Athenian aristocrat, but also a resident alien."[10]

By the time the family landed in Athens, Pericles was a major political figure and, in fact, had sponsored legislation in 451 that mandated that "a child should only have citizenship if both its parents were citizens."[11] This law meant that the legitimate marriage of Aspasia to an Athenian citizen was less likely because it would limit the capacity of their children to inherit citizenship and land. Aspasia was connected to families of good social standing, but she was still a *metic*; thus

---

9. See Kagan, pp. 17–18, for the discussion of the process and the place of Pericles' family in it.

10. See Henry, pp. 9–11.

11. There is much debate about the actual meaning and import of this legislation. Raphael Sealey, "On Lawful Concubinage in Athens," *Classical Antiquity* 3:1 (1984), p. 130. See also K. R. Walters, "Perikles Citizenship Law," *Classical Antiquity* 2:2 (1983), pp. 314–336; and Podlecki, pp. 159–162.

the only realistic option was for her to "become the *pallake* of a well-born Athenian."[12] Foreign women, like their Athenian citizen-wife counterparts, were subject to guardianship, and Aspasia's *kyrios* (lord) was responsible for her personal fate. Concubinage at the time was institutionalized and involved explicit contractual obligations, thus providing some security for the woman, although she remained without most legal rights or civic and social status. From the perspective of Aspasia and her family, a relationship with Pericles would be realistic and highly desirable. By that time, he was at the center of most Athenian political and cultural activity. But how did he arrive at that lofty position, and why would he enter into a relationship with a foreigner?

▧ ACT II:

PERICLES' PUBLIC DEBUT

In the spring of 472, Pericles was poised to take on the responsibilities of an adult Athenian male and emerge into public view. By then he should have served his required two years of military service and become a citizen with full rights and responsibilities. His first recorded public act was not in the military sphere, however, but in a religious and artistic competition held annually in Athens. Each year, a competition was held among three poets whose plays were judged at a festival; producers, who were really the financial backers of the works, were chosen for each poet, thus creating a sort of team effort in the competition. The richest citizens of Athens underwrote the production of the plays just as they helped outfit the newly emerging navy. In 472, Pericles was assigned to Aeschylus (525–456), whose plays eventually won first prize. *The Persians*, one of the plays that survived, showed the suffering of the Persians, especially the women, after the defeat at Salamis. It also depicted Athenian glory, and from Pericles' perspective was a fitting tribute to his father, who was a hero at that battle. This demonstration of devotion to the state and the memory of his father was an excellent way for a young man to be introduced to public life.

By the 470s, political power for Athenian men rested on several factors: wealth; good family ties and social connections; and personal qualities and talents such as good looks, speaking abilities, generosity, honesty, and incorruptibility. Military successes were also becoming increasingly significant and helped to reinforce desirable masculine qualities of physical prowess and bravery. Cimon (510?–450?), a major political figure after the end of the Persian wars, combined most of these characteristics and qualities. He helped to solidify the Delian League, and apparently favored support for Sparta, which he thought would maintain peaceful relations. He expanded Athenian sea power, and while this tended to increase the influence of the lower-class men who

12. Henry, p. 15.

[35]

*Chapter 2
Politics and
Private Life in
Classical Athens:
Pericles
(?494–429 B.C.E.)
and Aspasia
(?470–?410 B.C.E.)*

rowed the ships, Cimon was able to limit their access to power by making himself an aristocratic "political boss" who catered to their material needs and used their votes when necessary.

As Athens became a naval power with extensive influence over the Delian League, it was also clear to many Athenian citizens who had an eye to a public career that military leadership was an effective avenue to power. In particular, ten generals, who originally represented the ten tribes, were now directly elected, could be re-elected without limit, and came to play a dominant role in the government of Athens. Pericles' military experiences, according to Plutarch, won him the reputation of being "brave and fond of danger." In 463 he reached the age of thirty, the minimum age required for a general, and he was elected to the position, which he held almost consistently for the rest of his life.

By about the time Pericles was elected a general, opponents had emerged who sought to challenge Cimon's leadership and to broaden, not limit, Athenian democracy. In 463 Pericles became associated with a faction of radical democrats led by Ephialtes who hoped to discredit Cimon and to limit the authority of the aristocrats while expanding the decision-making role of the assembly of citizens. Pericles' increased visibility in these efforts rested on his rhetorical eloquence, public presence, lineage, and his demonstrated bravery and loyalty to Athens. In 462 or 461, Ephialtes and his associates successfully ostracized Cimon and passed several political reforms that gave more power to the

Council of 500, chosen by lot from members of the Assembly, while decreasing the functions and responsibilities of the traditional elites. These actions understandably produced heightened political tensions and desires for revenge that resulted in the assassination of Ephialtes that same year—a highly unusual event in the history of Athenian democracy. Though by Athenian standards quite young and inexperienced for such a political role, Pericles took his place as the leader of the democratic reformers (Document Two).

In the decade between 461 and 451 or 450, Pericles had to consolidate his power, but he also began to demonstrate his own views of democracy by supporting legislation that made it "possible for greater numbers of Athenians actually to participate in the running of the state, and, conversely, to benefit from the ever-growing national wealth"[13] (Document Three). It is important to remember that in the government of Athens there was no president, prime minister, cabinet, permanent managers, or administrators. Instead, officials were chosen by lot and included the generals, treasurers, vendors, accountants, superintendent of water supplies, jurors, and members of the Council of 500. In the courts, there were no lawyers or judges; all legal outcomes thus rested in the juries of the people, whose usual size was 501 and whose decisions were rendered by secret ballot. Because the jurors often sat for 150 to 200 days a year, participation, though

13. Podlecki, p. 54.

theoretically open to all, was limited to those who could afford it. One of the earliest and most significant legislative initiatives attributed to Pericles provided payment for jurors, thereby opening opportunities for a much larger group of citizens to sit on the panels. It has also been argued that, regardless of what Pericles' motives might have been for introducing a new, more limiting citizenship law in 451 or 450, the law was enacted by the Assembly, thus giving that body the authority to define the requirements for citizenship in Athens.

By 451, Pericles had also begun to establish a view of Athenian foreign policy that would remain fairly constant for the next twenty years. He came to see Sparta and its alliance of cities, the Peloponnesian League, as a possible threat to Athenian power and prosperity, and thus would attempt to neutralize Sparta. But he also began to realize that Athens should not get bogged down in mainland expansion at the expense of her maritime empire. In effect, "no expansion by land was to become the cornerstone of Pericles' imperial policy."[14] This outlook led him to support building of defensive walls for Athens. Pericles was certainly aware that political power in a democracy like Athens' was not permanent and rested on the ability to persuade and convince the electorate. Later, the historian Thucydides would claim that Pericles viewed the ideal statesman as someone who knows "what must be done and [is] able to explain

it; [who] loves his country and is incorruptible."[15]

As Pericles began to acquire the stature of senior statesman, he also assumed the rights and duties of the citizen head-of-household who contributed money and sons to the state. In this capacity, he did what was expected of him. If we look at his subsequent personal life, we can perhaps speculate that a sense of individual fulfillment and accomplishment was more likely to come from the public realm than from his marriage and family. Sometime in the middle to late 450s, Pericles married a woman whose name we do not know. The average age at marriage for an Athenian male was around thirty; for an Athenian female, it was sometime between fourteen and eighteen. Thus, Pericles was fairly typical in this regard. The purpose of Athenian marriage was fulfilled in their relationship because they had two sons, Xanthippus (named after his grandfather), born in 454 or 453, and Paralus, born in 451. The birth of two sons insured property inheritance and transmission of family cult practices. Within the next several years, Pericles and his wife were apparently divorced. Several historians have argued that Pericles' wife "left him on her own initiative to marry again."[16] Divorce was not difficult to obtain at this time and could be initiated by the husband for his wife's adultery or infertility; the wife could

---

14. Podlecki, p. 76. Also see map in Kagan that illustrates defensive walls, p. 81.

15. From Thucydides, quoted in Kagan, p. 9.

16. Robert D. Cromey, "Perikles' Wife: Chronological Calculations," *Greek, Roman and Byzantine Studies* 23 (1982), pp. 203–212.

Chapter 2
Politics and
Private Life in
Classical Athens:
Pericles
(?494–429 B.C.E.)
and Aspasia
(?470–?410 B.C.E.)

also pursue divorce, but usually with the support of her family of origin. Whether the sons stayed with Pericles is not clear, but we do know that he and his elder son did not get along.

By the time of the divorce, Pericles was dedicated to his career in politics and he spent little time managing his own estate, which he put in the hands of a competent steward. Pericles seemed to be indifferent to money, spent little himself, and carefully doled out resources to his sons, who found him stingy. In fact, money caused a break between Pericles and Xanthippus that was never mended. Xanthippus, and perhaps Paralus, failed to live up to their father's expectations of civic activity and virtue and were referred to publicly as simpletons (Document Four). That may help to explain why Pericles accepted the guardianship of two young boys whose mother was an Alcmaeonid, and whose father was a friend who died in battle in 447 or 446. The elder of the two brothers, Alcibaides (III) was quite talented and eventually entered politics successfully, but after Pericles death was driven from Athens in disgrace and died in exile in 404.[17] Given the difficulties in his family life, Pericles must have taken some comfort in the fact that by the mid-440s his popularity was growing and his political career was on the rise. That satisfaction was no doubt enhanced by the fact that he had met Aspasia and they had established a relationship by about 447. As he prepared to become first citizen, she would be his partner.

■ ACT III:

THE SUCCESSES AND PERILS OF LOVE AND POLITICS, 445–429 B.C.E.

No record reveals how Pericles and Aspasia met, but most accounts acknowledge that she was beautiful, intelligent, and perhaps even politically astute given her own situation and family background. He took her into his house and, though they were not legally married, their commitments to each other in practice created an almost equivalent relationship. Some dimensions of their lives together deviated dramatically from those of a typical citizen marriage. Aspasia was still a foreigner; when she and Pericles had a son about 440, he was not entitled to citizenship because of her status. Also, unlike the usual citizen wife, she appears to have been more of a public figure, and some speculated that she and Pericles even discussed matters of importance to the state. If a contemporary favored Pericles, he might overlook or even grudgingly accept this situation. His opponents felt differently and could insist that Aspasia's involvement in politics, however peripheral, would produce only strife and crisis because women had no natural place in the state.

The fifth-century Greek comedies were, of course, filled with political commentary, and the stage was the place where intellectual discussions and popular opinions about sexuality

17. This discussion of Pericles' relationships with his sons and his wards is from Kagan, pp.177–181.

and power were publicly displayed.[18] Some writers called Aspasia a whore or insisted that she was really a madam who ran a brothel and procured prostitutes for Pericles; others compared her to Helen by insisting both were known for sexual impropriety and starting wars. Later fourth-century philosophical discourses are slightly less libelous or appear less burlesque. Three of Plato's dialogues deal with Aspasia. But even when he suggests that she was learned and actually helped in writing Pericles' speeches, Plato does so satirically, not to praise her but to make fun of both Pericles and his "girlfriend" (Document Five). What was most "real" about Aspasia in the classical world was her reputation, not her actual character and deeds. As Pericles' influence and popularity grew, it became harder to discredit him politically, and thus he was made fun of and attacked for other characteristics, including his relationship with Aspasia (Documents Six and Seven). Here again, it is important to emphasize the precarious position of elected leaders in a democracy like that of Athens where not even semipermanent executive positions existed. In democracies, personal behaviors can have political significance, and "violations of public morality that provoke scandal can be terribly damaging."[19] Given these odds, Pericles might have been smarter to follow a more traditional path in his personal life; in

many respects, Aspasia had much less to lose. Unfortunately for us, even though they were slandered and gossiped about in markets, the theater, and *symposia*, (the ritualized drinking parties that were a central part of Greek male social life), their personal motives and feelings remain hidden.[20]

In the 440s and 430s, as Pericles reached the apex of his political power, Athens entered an era of great fame and glory. The massive building program he initiated in 447 symbolizes many of his goals and ideas, as well as the stature of the city (Document Eight). The plan was originally intended to rebuild temples and buildings throughout Attica that had been destroyed in the Persian wars. Funds for the building projects were to come from tributes paid to the Delian League treasury, now located in Athens. In fact, most of the reconstruction was on the Acropolis in Athens, and the showpiece of all was the Parthenon, which would house a gold and ivory statue of Athena by the sculptor Phidias. In very practical terms, the work on the Parthenon, and an accompanying music hall, or odeion, demonstrates Pericles administrative abilities, financial genius, and honesty because he proved impervious to bribes. The vast building program also served as a major source of employment by hiring between 2,200 and 3,300 people. Pericles thus demonstrated those qualities that had made him a respected and popular leader in Athens. But the Parthenon was more than a public works project or an

18. Henry, p. 19. She continues this discussion of the treatment of Aspasia, pp. 30–36. See Podlecki for the interpretation of Plato's writing, pp. 112–114, and Kagan, pp. 174, 183–184 for attacks on both Pericles and Aspasia.

19. Kagan, p. 183.

20. Description of the symposium is in Davidson, pp. 43–49.

Chapter 2
Politics and
Private Life in
Classical Athens:
Pericles
(?494–429 B.C.E.)
and Aspasia
(?470–?410 B.C.E.)

impressive religious site—it was also a symbol of Athenian greatness, a monument to the people of Athens and the great empire they had fought and sacrificed to create. Like monuments in other times and places, the Parthenon not only created pride but also taught the citizenry what it meant to be an Athenian. There were some Athenians who questioned the expense of the project and the ethics of using the League's funds to build it. But Pericles apparently answered the charges adequately, and his major and really final opponent was ostracized in 443 and sent into exile for a decade.

In addition to exercising greater domination over the traditional cities of the Delian League, Pericles expanded Athenian control to other settlements in the Aegean and in southern Italy, and even took an Athenian fleet into the Black Sea. Occasionally, dissatisfaction on the part of some of the allies grew to resistance, but the Athenian empire survived. In 440, the island of Samos, an original member of the Delian League that possessed its own fleet, became embroiled in a conflict with neighboring Miletus. This conflict eventually led to a Samian rebellion against Athens and sparked resistance in other areas. Pericles himself led the forces that finally put down the revolt in 439.

The action against the Samians was telling. Some Athenians who felt the war had been too costly blamed Aspasia for the conflict because of her Miletian origins. Nevertheless, Pericles came home and was chosen to give the funeral oration for those who fell in the campaign. This speech was one of his most popular and effective

because he convinced his listeners that those who died for their country had, like the gods, achieved immortality. The defeat of the Samians also appeared to signal an end to rebellions and to consolidate Athens' hold on its empire. Sparta and its ally Corinth had not come to the aid of Samos, and overall peace had been maintained in the Peloponnesus. Many thought this augured well for the future.

The confidence and pride in empire was evident in the subsequent celebrations of Athens' most important public holiday—the Panathenaia—held in honor of Athena's birthday in late July. All residents of Attica, even foreigners, were given an opportunity to participate, and women were given "the exceptional honor of a share in the Panathenaic sacrifice."[21] Perhaps Aspasia took part in these events, although foreign women carried water and stools for the aristocratic girls in the procession, and that might not have been an acceptable role for Pericles' partner. Sometime in the 430s, Pericles himself appears to have altered some of the ritual and celebration by introducing musical competitions and theater rehearsals in the odeion. The overall intent was to bring people from all over the empire to the celebration, and to broadcast Athens' standing as a world-class power.

This pride and confidence began to wane at the end of the 430s as signs of conflict between Athens and Sparta became more evident. Historians de-

21. Elaine Fantham, Helene Peet Foley, et al., *Women in the Classical World* (New York: Oxford Press, 1994), p. 86. See also Podlecki for a description of the festival and Pericles' use of it, pp. 77–81.

bate Pericles' role in the outbreak of that war. In his most famous history, Thucydides, himself an admirer of Pericles, seems to change his mind about what Pericles' motives for war might have been. Certainly Pericles had shaped Athenian foreign policy for some time and, given a pragmatic assessment of Athens' position and Sparta's interests, might have concluded that war between them was inevitable. In 431, after Athens had used her power against several of Sparta's allies, Sparta took the offensive, and war began. Pericles, recognizing that Athens was a sea power, had no plan for defeating Sparta in a land battle.

Instead his strategy was a defensive one that he hoped would ultimately convince the Spartans that further aggression was useless. But apparently Pericles did not envision how long the conflict would go on, and Athens' resources were sorely tested. Although he had assumed that the citizens of Athens could leave their land and find protection behind the walls he had built, that was not a popular solution, and instead had devastating results when Athens suffered an outbreak of plague that had a mortality rate of about 25 percent. Pericles' sons died in the plague, as did his sister, and by summer 429 Pericles was also ill.

▨ FINALE

In the last years of his life, Pericles faced political opposition, a loss of popular support, a war that was going badly, and the awful effects of the plague. A new generation of politicians had emerged whose influence came from money they had made in commerce and manufacturing, and who previously had not held the highest offices in the city. They resented Pericles' intellect, his aloofness, and even his austerity, and they hoped to remove him from office. In the midst of the war, facing Spartan invasion and the plague, some individuals advocated meeting to deal with the enemy. Pericles made one of his most famous speeches in which he spoke realistically and bluntly to his comrades, telling them they must endure—that far too much was at stake to give in now. The greatness of their empire demanded that they continue to fight,

and if they withstood this trial nothing could stand in their way. Becoming subservient to another would be "a betrayal of all that their ancestors had sacrificed" to create the empire. Their history demanded they remain free.[22] (Document Nine). For a time, they listened to him, but hardships increased and sometime in the winter of 430–429, his opponents took the opportunity to remove Pericles from the generalship and to charge him with corruption. After a trial, he was fined, but almost immediately the political mood in Athens shifted and he was re-elected general in the spring of 429. This was probably about the time that his sons died, and he appealed to the Assembly to grant citizenship to his bastard son, Pericles II. They did so, but Pericles was very ill by that time and died in the fall of 429. Perhaps by

22. Podlecki, p. 150.

[41]

Chapter 2
Politics and
Private Life in
Classical Athens:
Pericles
(?494–429 B.C.E.)
and Aspasia
(?470–?410 B.C.E.)

then he had an inkling of the disasters that lay ahead, but he hardly could have seen the collapse of Athenian power and glory, and the destruction of many of the political values and practices he had held so dear. Pericles II would go on to hold various government positions, eventually being elected general. But shortly thereafter he was among six commanders tried and put to death for their actions at the battle of Arginousaia in 406 or 405, near the end of the war.

As for Aspasia, the year after Pericles' death she established another union, this time with Lysicles, also a political figure, but a "new" man with wealth from commerce, not estates, who represented the social and political changes taking place in Athens. He died not too long afterward; we don't know where or when she died.

Throughout his life, Pericles had believed in the importance of free, independent, and rational citizens, but he had known that only extraordinary leadership and sacrifice could make the system work. As an intelligent, dedicated individual, he chose the difficult path of political leadership and civic educator, and was both rewarded and punished for it. Aspasia, no matter how beautiful, intelligent, or independent, was not offered similar choices. Even the role of the grieving widow of an Athenian hero was not an option for her. The fact that she entered into another liaison so quickly after Pericles' death was entirely understandable and proper, and is no comment on what we can only imagine was a remarkable relationship with Athens' first citizen, Pericles, during its glory days.

▤ QUESTIONS

1. Although Athens undoubtedly provided one of the widest forums for political participation by men in the classical world, one could also argue that some male citizens were more equal than others. Why would that be true?

2. What conditions or attitudes explain the fact that women had no political role in Athens and, in fact, had few opportunities to act in any public or independent way?

3. Pericles became a major political leader because he understood that government by the people also requires a firm hand. How did he learn this, and how was this demon-

strated in his years of political ascendancy in Athens?

4. As a foreigner, Aspasia might be considered to have experienced both advantages and disadvantages living in Athens. What were some of these advantages and disadvantages?

5. Most of the sources we have for the lives of Pericles and Aspasia have a particular point of view, a purpose behind what they have to say about these two people. What were some of the intents of the various authors who wrote about them? How much of the story do you think they made up? Do you think truth can be told in jokes?

▨ DOCUMENTS

▨▨▨▨▨▨▨▨▨▨▨▨▨ **DOCUMENT ONE** ▨▨▨▨▨▨▨▨▨▨▨▨

ARISTOTLE

The Politics

Although Aristotle (384–322 B.C.E.) wrote his book on Greek society and politics after the era of Pericles and Aspasia, he based his descriptions and conclusions on an examination of historical examples. In this selection, he describes the basic social organization of a society like that of Athens, and he argues strongly for distinct attributes and roles for different members of society. How are societies organized and for what purposes? What are the differences in the natures and functions of men and women? How are women and slaves both similar and different?

. . . It is by examining things in their growth from the very beginning that we shall in this, as in other matters, obtain the clearest view. Now, it is necessary, in the first place, to group in couples those elements that cannot exist without each other, such as the female and male united for the sake of reproduction of species (and this union does not come from the deliberate action of the will, but in them, as in the other animals and plants, the desire to leave behind such another as themselves is implanted by nature), and also that which naturally rules, and that which naturally is ruled, connected for the sake of security. For that which has the capacity, in virtue of its intelligence, of looking forward is by nature the ruling and master element, while that which has the capacity, in virtue of its body, of carrying out this will of the superior is the subject and slave by nature. And for this reason the interests of the master and the slave are identical. Now it is by *nature* that the woman and the slave have been marked as separate, for nature produces nothing in a niggard fashion, as smiths make the 'Delphian'[1] knife, but she makes each individual thing for one end; for it is only thus that each instrument will receive its most perfect development, ...

Now that it is clear what the elements are of which the state is composed, we must speak, in the first place, of the Household; for every state is composed of Households, and the parts of the Household are those elements of which the household in its turn consists. Now the Household, when complete, consists of slaves and free persons. But since each individual thing ought first to be examined in its smallest elements, and since the first and smallest elements of the household are master and slave, husband and wife, father and children, we

1. Probably a knife that could be used for various purposes besides cutting, and called the 'Delphian,' because originally made to serve in different parts of the sacrifice at Delphi.

*Chapter 2
Politics and
Private Life in
Classical Athens:
Pericles
(?494–429 B.C.E.)
and Aspasia
(?470–?410 B.C.E.)*

must first inquire into these three relations, and see what each is, and what its character ought to be. These relations are that of the master, that of marriage (for this relation of husband and wife has no name in Greek), and in the third place that of the generation of children (this also having no proper name). Let us then consider these that we have mentioned to be the three parts of the family. . . .

There have been seen to be three elements of household government, the first being the rule of the master over slaves, of which we have spoken before, the second that of the father over children, and the third that of the husband over the wife; for (it was also seen to be part of the householder's duty) to rule both his wife and his children as beings equally free, but not with the same character of rule. His rule over the wife is like that of a magistrate in a free state, over his children it is like that of a king. For both the male is naturally more qualified to lead than the female, unless where some unnatural case occurs, and also the older and more perfect than the younger and imperfect. Now in the government of free states in most cases the positions of ruler and ruled alternate, for there is a tendency that all should be naturally equal and differ in no respect; but, nevertheless, whenever one party rules and the other is ruled, there is a wish that there should be some difference made in garb, titles, honours. . . .

. . . For in different method does the free element rule the slave, the male the female, the man the child; and while in all of these are there present their separate shares of soul, these are present in each in a different manner. For the slave, speaking generally, has not the deliberative faculty, but the woman has it, though without power to be effective; the child has it, but in an imperfect degree. Similarly, then, must it necessarily be with regard to the moral virtues also. We must suppose that all ought to have some share in them, though not in the same way, but only so far as each requires for the fulfilment of his own function. . . .

DOCUMENT TWO

PLUTARCH

Life of Pericles

Plutarch (ca. C.E. 50–120) wrote about the lives of many people in ancient society in his Parallel Lives. *Pericles was one of his subjects, and to write about him he had a large library of sources he could draw on. In this selection, Plutarch describes the kind of man he felt Pericles was. What does he consider to be important traits and behaviors of the Athenian leader as he came to power?*

. . . However, when Aristides was dead, and Themistocles in banishment, and Cimon was kept by his campaigns for the most part abroad, then at last Pericles decided to devote himself to the people, espousing the cause of the poor and the many instead of the few and the rich, contrary to his own nature, which was anything but popular. But he feared, as it would seem, to encounter a suspicion of aiming at tyranny, and when he saw that Cimon was very aristocratic in his sympathies, and was held in extraordinary affection by the party of the "Good and True," he began to court the favour of the multitude, thereby securing safety for himself, and power to wield against his rival.

Straightway, too, he made a different ordering in his way of life. On one street only in the city was he to be seen walking,—the one which took him to the marketplace and the council-chamber. Invitations to dinner, and all such friendly and familiar intercourse, he declined, so that during the long period that elapsed while he was at the head of the state, there was not a single friend to whose house he went to dine, except that when his kinsman Euryptolemus gave a wedding feast, he attended until the libations were made,[1] . . . .

DOCUMENT THREE

THUCYDIDES

History of the Peloponnesian War

Thucydides (ca. 460 to some time after 400 B.C.E.) was a contemporary of Pericles, lived through the war with Sparta and her allies, and, outliving Pericles, saw Athens' defeat. In this selection, he is giving an account of Pericles' first funeral speech in the early part of the war. Pericles gives an account of what he sees as the most important characteristics of Athenian society and government. What is his view of the people of Athens and their government? What responsibilities do citizen men and women have toward the state during the war?

. . . 37. "Our constitution does not copy the laws of neighbouring states; we are rather a pattern to others than imitators ourselves. Its administration favours the many instead of the few; this is why it is called a democracy. If we look to the laws, they afford equal justice to all in their private differences; if to social standing, advancement in public life falls to reputation for capacity, class considerations not being allowed to interfere with merit; nor again does poverty bar the way—if a man is able to serve the state, he is not hindered by the

---

1. That is, until the wine for the symposium was brought in, and drinking began.

Chapter 2
Politics and
Private Life in
Classical Athens:
Pericles
(?494–429 B.C.E.)
and Aspasia
(?470–?410 B.C.E.)

obscurity of his condition. The freedom which we enjoy in our government extends also to our ordinary life. There, far from exercising a jealous surveillance over each other, we do not feel called upon to be angry with our neighbour for doing what he likes, or even to indulge in those injurious looks which cannot fail to be offensive, although they inflict no positive penalty. But all this ease in our private relations does not make us lawless as citizens. Against this, fear is our chief safeguard, teaching us to obey the magistrates and the laws, particularly such as regard the protection of the injured, whether they are actually on the statute book or belong to that code which, although unwritten, yet cannot be broken without acknowledged disgrace.

38. "Further, we provide plenty of means for the mind to refresh itself from business. We celebrate games and sacrifices all the year round, and the elegance of our private establishments forms a daily source of pleasure and helps to banish the spleen; while the magnitude of our city draws the produce of the world into our harbour, so that to the Athenian the fruits of other countries are as familiar a luxury as those of his own. . . .

40. "Nor are these the only points in which our city is worthy of admiration. We cultivate refinement without stinting and knowledge without effeminacy; wealth we employ more for use than for show, and place the real disgrace of poverty not in owning to the fact but in declining the struggle against it. Our public men have, besides politics, their private affairs to attend to, and our ordinary citizens, though occupied with the pursuits of industry, are still fair judges of public matters; for, unlike any other nation, regarding him who takes no part in these duties not as unambitious but as useless, we are able to judge at all events if we cannot originate, and instead of looking on discussion as a stumbling block in the way of action, we think it an indispensable preliminary to any wise action at all. Again, in our enterprises we present the singular spectacle of daring and deliberation, each carried to its highest point, and both united in the same persons; whereas for others decision is the fruit of ignorance, hesitation of reflection. But the palm of courage will surely be adjudged most justly to those who best know the difference between hardship and pleasure and yet are never tempted to shrink from danger. In goodness we are equally singular, acquiring our friends by conferring not by receiving favours. Yet, of course, the doer of the favour is the firmer friend of the two, in order by continued kindness to keep the recipient in his debt; while the debtor feels less keenly from the very consciousness that the return he makes will be a payment, not a free gift. And it is only the Athenians who, fearless of consequences, confer their benefits not from calculations of expediency, but in the confidence of free men.

41. "In short, I say that as a city we are the school of Hellas; while I doubt if the world can produce a man who, where he has only himself to depend upon, is equal to so many emergencies, and graced by so happy a versatility as the Athenian. . . .

. . . 44. "Comfort, therefore, not condolence, is what I have to offer to the parents of the dead who may be here. . . . Yet you who are still of an age to beget children must bear up in the hope of having others in their stead; not only will they help you to forget those whom you have lost, but will be to the state at once a reinforcement and a security; for never can a fair or just policy be expected of the citizen who does not, like his fellows, bring to the decision the interests and apprehensions of a father. While those of you who have passed your prime must congratulate yourselves with the thought that the best part of your life was fortunate, and that the brief span that remains will be cheered by the fame of the departed. For it is only the love of honour that never grows old; and honour it is, not gain, as some would have it, that rejoices the heart of age and helplessness.

45. "Turning to the sons or brothers of the dead, I see an arduous struggle before you. When a man is gone, all are wont to praise him, and should your merit be ever so transcendent, you will still find it difficult not merely to overtake but even to approach their renown. The living have envy to contend with, while those who are no longer in our path are honoured with a good will into which rivalry does not enter. On the other hand, if I must say anything on the subject of female excellence to those of you who will now be in widowhood, it will be all comprised in this brief exhortation. Great will be your glory in not falling short of your natural character; and greatest will be hers who is least talked of among the men whether for good or for bad. . . .

DOCUMENT FOUR

PLUTARCH

Life of Pericles

In this section, Plutarch describes Pericles' character, his economic activity, and his morality, and he hints at his relationships with his sons. According to Plutarch, what kind of public man was Pericles? Is his private character the same?

. . . [He secured] an imperial sway that was continuous and unbroken, by means of his annual tenure of the office of general. During all these years he kept himself untainted by corruption, although he was not altogether indifferent to money-making; indeed, the wealth which was legally his by inheritance from his father, that it might not from sheer neglect take to itself wings and fly away, nor yet cause him much trouble and loss of time when he was busy with higher things, he set into such orderly dispensation as he thought was easiest and most exact. This was to sell his annual products all together in the lump, and then to buy in the market each article as it was needed, and so provide the

*Chapter 2
Politics and
Private Life in
Classical Athens:
Pericles
(?494–429 B.C.E.)
and Aspasia
(?470–?410 B.C.E.)*

ways and means of daily life. For this reason he was not liked by his sons when they grew up, nor did their wives find in him a liberal purveyor, but they murmured at his expenditure for the day merely and under the most exact restrictions, there being no surplus of supplies at all, as in a great house and under generous circumstances, but every outlay and every intake proceeding by count and measure. His agent in securing all this great exactitude was a single servant, Evangelus, who was either gifted by nature or trained by Pericles so as to surpass everybody else in domestic economy. . . .

DOCUMENT FIVE

PLATO

Dialogues, "Menexenus"

Plato (427–348 B.C.E.) did not live while Pericles dominated Athenian politics. However, he did know some of Pericles' contemporaries, and he lived through the worst of the war and saw Athens' defeat. As a philosopher and writer, Plato grappled with questions of good government, ideal societies, and human behaviors. He often wrote dialogues to recapture the kinds of conversations that his teacher Socrates liked to have, and he picked some topic as the focus of conversation. Here he uses Aspasia to make a statement about certain kinds of political people, and also to make comments on women in the public sphere. If a woman like Aspasia is preparing speeches for political leaders, giving them lessons in rhetoric, what does that say about the politicians themselves? Pericles is not mentioned here, but one could argue that he is present. Why?

. . . MEN: You are always making fun of the rhetoricians, Socrates; this time, however, I am inclined to think that the speaker who is chosen will not have much to say, for he has been called upon to speak at a moment's notice, and he will be compelled almost to improvise.

SOC: But why, my friend, should he not have plenty to say? Every rhetorician has speeches ready made; nor is there any difficulty in improvising that sort of stuff. Had the orator to praise Athenians among Peloponnesians, or Peloponnesians among Athenians, he must be a good rhetorician who could succeed and gain credit. But there is no difficulty in a man's winning applause when he is contending for fame among the persons whom he is praising.

MEN: Do you think not, Socrates?

SOC: Certainly 'not.'

MEN: Do you think that you could speak yourself if there should be a necessity, and if the Council were to choose you?

[48]

SOC: That I should be able to speak is no great wonder, Menexenus, considering that I have an excellent mistress in the art of rhetoric,—she who has made so many good speakers, and one who was the best among all the Hellenes— Pericles, the son of Xanthippus.

MEN: And who is she? I suppose that you mean Aspasia.

SOC: Yes, I do; and besides her I had Connus, the son of Metrobius, as a master, and he was my master in music, as she was in rhetoric. No wonder that a man who has received such an education should be a finished speaker; even the pupil of very inferior masters, say, for example, one who had learned music of Lamprus, and rhetoric of Antiphon the Rhamnusian, might make a figure if he were to praise the Athenians among the Athenians.

MEN: And what would you be able to say if you had to speak?

SOC: Of my own wit, most likely nothing; but yesterday I heard Aspasia composing a funeral oration about these very dead. For she had been told, as you were saying, that the Athenians were going to choose a speaker, and she repeated to me the sort of speech which he should deliver, partly improvising and partly from previous thought, putting together fragments of the funeral oration which Pericles spoke, but which, as I believe, she composed.

MEN: And can you remember what Aspasia said?

SOC: I ought to be able, for she taught me, and she was ready to strike me because I was always forgetting.

MEN: Then why will you not rehearse what she said?

SOC: Because I am afraid that my mistress may be angry with me if I publish her speech.

MEN: Nay, Socrates, let us have the speech, whether Aspasia's or any one else's, no matter. I hope that you will oblige me.

SOC: But I am afraid that you will laugh at me if I continue the games of youth in old age. . . . You have heard, Menexenus, the oration of Aspasia the Milesian.

MEN: Truly, Socrates, I marvel that Aspasia, who is only a woman, should be able to compose such a speech; she must be a rare one.

SOC: Well, if you are incredulous, you may come with me and hear her.

MEN: I have often met Aspasia, Socrates, and know what she is like.

SOC: Well, and do you not admire her, and are you not grateful for her speech?

MEN: Yes, Socrates, I am very grateful to her or to him who told you, and still more to you who have told me.

SOC: Very good. But you must take care not to tell of me, and then at some future time I will repeat to you many other excellent speeches of hers.

MEN: Fear not; only let me hear them, and I will keep the secret.

SOC: Then I will keep my promise.

Chapter 2
Politics and
Private Life in
Classical Athens:
Pericles
(?494–429 B.C.E.)
and Aspasia
(?470–?410 B.C.E.)

DOCUMENT SIX

ATHENAEUS

Comments on Pericles and Aspasia

Athenaeus, a second-century (C.E.) Egyptian Greek of some learning, collected numerous sources, anecdotes, and stories, and compiled them in a sort of banquet of learning. Here he is recounting what some earlier writers had to say about Pericles and Aspasia. According to this account, what explains Pericles' attraction to Aspasia?

Did not Perikles the Olympian, as Clearchus says in the first book of the *Erotica*, throw all of Hellas into confusion for the sake of Aspasia— not the 'younger' but the one who held converse with the learned Sokrates—in spite of his possession of great reputation for intelligence and political ability? This man was extremely prone to sexual pleasure. He even had intercourse with his son's wife, as Stresimbrotus of Thasus relates, a man who lived in his time and set eyes on him. (This) in his work entitled *On Themistokles, Thoukydides, and Perikles.* Antisthenes the Socratic says he (Perikles) was in love with Aspasia and embraced the woman twice a day when he entered (the house) and when he left her. Once when she was a defendant on the charge of impiety, he spoke on her behalf and shed more tears than when his life and his property were in danger.

DOCUMENT SEVEN

PLUTARCH

Life of Pericles

This account of Aspasia's background and her relationship with Pericles confronts some of the other stories that had circulated about the pair. Does Plutarch agree with the stories? If not, what is his interpretation of their relationship

. . . Now, since it is thought that he proceeded thus against the Samians to gratify Aspasia, this may be a fitting place to raise the query what great art of power this woman had, that she managed as she pleased the foremost men of the state, and afforded the philosophers occasion to discuss her in exalted terms and at great length. That she was a Milesian by birth, daughter of one Axiochus, is generally agreed; and they say that it was in emulation of Thargelia, an Ionian woman of ancient times, that she made her onslaughts upon the most influential men. This Thargelia came to be a great beauty and was endowed with grace of manners as well as clever wits. Inasmuch as she lived on terms of intimacy with numberless Greeks, and attached all her consorts to the king of Persia, she stealthily sowed the seeds of Persian sympathy in the cities of Greece by means of these lovers of hers, who were men of the greatest power and influence. And so Aspasia, as some say, was held in high favour by Pericles because of her rare political wisdom. Socrates sometimes came to see her with his disciples, and his intimate friends brought their wives to her to hear her discourse, although she presided over a business that was anything but honest or even reputable, since she kept a house of young courtesans. And Aeschines[1] says that Lysicles the sheep-dealer, a man of low birth and nature, came to be the first man at Athens by living with Aspasia after the death of Pericles. And in the "Menexenus" of Plato, even though the first part of it be written in a sportive vein, there is, at any rate, thus much of the fact, that the woman had the reputation of associating with many Athenians as a teacher of rhetoric. However, the affection which Pericles had for Aspasia seems to have been rather of an amatory sort. For his own wife was near of kin to him, and had been wedded first to Hipponicus, to whom she bore Callias, surnamed the Rich; she bore also, as the wife of Pericles, Xanthippus and Paralus. Afterwards, since their married life was not agreeable, he legally bestowed her upon another man, with her own consent, and himself took Aspasia, and loved her exceedingly. Twice a day, as they say, on going out and on coming in from the market-place, he would salute her with a loving kiss. . . .

DOCUMENT EIGHT

PLUTARCH

Life of Pericles

Here Plutarch describes Pericles as a city leader and sponsor of a major building plan, but he also points out some of the criticisms about the funds for that urban project. What were some of the complaints about Pericles' use of funds? How did Pericles answer those complaints? Would you call him an imperialist?

. . . That which gave most pleasure and ornament to the city of Athens, and the greatest admiration and even astonishment to all strangers, and that which now is Greece's only evidence that the power she boasts of and her ancient wealth are no romance or idle story, was his construction of the public and sacred

---

1. Aeschines the Socratic, in a dialogue entitled "Aspasia," not extant.

Chapter 2
Politics and
Private Life in
Classical Athens:
Pericles
(?494–429 B.C.E.)
and Aspasia
(?470–?410 B.C.E.)

buildings. Yet this was that of all his actions in the government which his enemies most looked askance upon and cavilled at in the popular assemblies, crying out how that the commonwealth of Athens had lost its reputation and was ill-spoken of abroad for removing the common treasure of the Greeks from the isle of Delos into their own custody; and how that their fairest excuse for so doing, namely, that they took it away for fear the barbarians should seize it, and on purpose to secure it in a safe place, this Pericles had made unavailable, and how that "Greece cannot but resent it as an insufferable affront, and consider herself to be tyrannised over openly, when she sees the treasure, which was contributed by her upon a necessity for the war, wantonly lavished out by us upon our city, to gild her all over, and to adorn and set her forth, as it were some vain woman, hung round with precious stones and figures and temples, which cost a world of money."

Pericles, on the other hand, informed the people, that they were in no way obliged to give any account of those moneys to their allies, so long as they maintained their defence, and kept off the barbarians from attacking them; while in the meantime they did not so much as supply one horse or man or ship, but only found money for the service; "which money," said he, "is not theirs that give it, but theirs that receive it, if so be they perform the conditions upon which they receive it." And that it was good reason, that, now the city was sufficiently provided and stored with all things necessary for the war, they should convert the overplus of its wealth to such undertakings as would hereafter, when completed, give them eternal honour, and, for the present, while in process, freely supply all the inhabitants with plenty. With their variety of workmanship and of occasions for service, which summon all arts and trades and require all hands to be employed about them, they do actually put the whole city, in a manner, into state-pay; while at the same time she is both beautiful and maintained by herself. For as those who are of age and strength for war are provided for and maintained in the armaments abroad by their pay out of the public stock, so, it being his desire and design that the undisciplined mechanic multitude that stayed at home should not go without their share of public salaries, and yet should not have them given them for sitting still and doing nothing, to that end he thought fit to bring in among them, with the approbation of the people, these vast projects of buildings and designs of work, that would be of some continuance before they were finished, and would give employment to numerous arts, so that the part of the people that stayed at home might, no less than those that were at sea or in garrisons or on expeditions, have a fair and just occasion of receiving the benefit and having their share of the public moneys.

The materials were stone, brass, ivory, gold, ebony, cypresswood; and the arts or trades that wrought and fashioned them were smiths and carpenters, moulders, founders and braziers, stone-cutters, dyers, goldsmiths, ivory-workers, painters, embroiderers, turners; those again that conveyed them to the town for use, merchants and mariners and ship-masters by sea, and by land cartwrights, cattle-breeders, waggoners, rope-makers, flax-workers, shoe-makers and leather-dressers, road-makers, miners. And every trade in the same nature, as a captain in an army has his particular company of soldiers under him, had its own hired company of journeymen and labourers belonging to it banded together as in array, to be as it were the instrument and body for the performance of the service. Thus, to say all in a word, the occasions and services of these public works distributed plenty through every age and condition. . . .

━━━━━━━ **DOCUMENT NINE** ━━━━━━━

THUCYDIDES

History of the Peloponnesian War, Pericles' Second Funeral Speech

Thucydides again reports on Pericles' leadership during the Peloponnesian War. His first funeral speech (Document Three), at the end of the first year of war, was followed by the epidemic of plague in Athens and a second invasion by the enemy. Pericles then gave this funeral speech in the midst of a very difficult time. What does he tell the citizens of Athens? Why must they continue to fight? How is the tone of this speech different from his tone in the first speech?

. . . 'I was expecting this outburst of indignation; the causes of it are not un-known to me. And I have summoned an assembly that I may remind you of your resolutions and reprove you for your inconsiderate anger against me, and want of fortitude in misfortune. In my judgment it would be better for individuals themselves that the citizens should suffer and the state flourish than that the citizens should flourish and the state suffer. A private man, how-ever successful in his own dealings, if his country perish is involved in her de-struction; but if he be an unprosperous citizen of a prosperous city he is much more likely to recover. Seeing then that states can bear the misfortunes of indi-viduals, but individuals cannot bear the misfortunes of the state, let us all stand by our country and not do what you are doing now, who because you are stunned by your private calamities are letting go the hope of saving the state, and condemning not only me who advised, but yourselves who consented to, the war. . . .

'I allow that for men who are in prosperity and free to choose it is great folly to make war. But when they must either submit and at once surrender inde-pendence, or strike and be free, then he who shuns and not he who meets the danger is deserving of blame. For my own part, I am the same man and stand

[53]

Chapter 2
Politics and
Private Life in
Classical Athens:
Pericles
(?494–429 B.C.E.)
and Aspasia
(?470–?410 B.C.E.)

where I did. But you are changed; for you have been driven by misfortune to re-call the consent which you gave when you were yet unhurt, and to think that my advice was wrong because your own characters are weak. . . .

'As to your sufferings in the war, if you fear that they may be very great and after all fruitless, I have shown you already over and over again that such a fear is groundless. If you are still unsatisfied I will indicate one element of your su-periority which appears to have escaped you, although it nearly touches your imperial greatness. . . . Neither the great King nor any nation on earth can hin-der a navy like yours from penetrating whithersoever you choose to sail. When we reflect on this great power, houses and lands, of which the loss seems so dreadful to you, are as nothing. We ought not to be troubled about them or to think much of them in comparison; they are only the garden of the house, the superfluous ornament of wealth; and you may be sure that if we cling to our freedom and preserve that, we shall soon enough recover all the rest. But, if we are the servants of others, we shall be sure to lose not only freedom, but all that freedom gives. And where your ancestors doubly succeeded, you will doubly fail. For their empire was not inherited by them from others but won by the labour of their hands, and by them preserved and bequeathed to us. And to be robbed of what you have is a greater disgrace than to attempt a conquest and fail. . . .

CHAPTER 3

A Roman Matron and Her Revolutionary Sons: Cornelia (Second century B.C.E.), and Tiberius (163–133 B.C.E.), and Gaius Gracchus (154–121 B.C.E.)

■ **SETTING THE STAGE**

As occasional defensive conflicts turned into protracted wars of expansion, the original city-state of Rome became the center of a Mediterranean empire by the second century B.C.E. Vast wealth for some and increasing impoverishment for others accompanied the territorial expansion. The demands for

Chapter 3
A Roman Matron
and Her
Revolutionary
Sons: Cornelia
(Second Century
B.C.E.), and
Tiberius (163–133
B.C.E.), and Gaius
Gracchus
(154–121 B.C.E.)

larger armies consisting of soldiers serving longer tours of duty had an impact on the land ownership and productivity of small farmers, who formed the bulk of the citizen army. These changes placed pressure on existing Roman Republican institutions, officials, and laws, and produced significant changes in the social order. By 200 B.C.E., the original 130 or so patrician families of the early Republic had been forced to share status and power with other influential and wealthy families, thereby creating a new aristocracy defined by both origins and offices held. But ideological divisions and alternative solutions to existing problems divided this elite population because they had to confront the unsettling influences of foreigners, and the demands and challenges from new commercial and business interests, hard-pressed small farmers, slaves, and ever growing numbers of urban poor. The events and people of Rome's second century form a complex web of economic, political, social, and intellectual tensions that eventually exploded in a revolution spelling the end of the Republic and ushering in a new era in Roman history.

The formation and rupture of family alliances were critical factors in the politics of early Rome. Examining the lives, values, and often conflicting aspirations of some of the key players in the second century B.C.E. illustrates how family politics provided both political stability and conflict as individuals with diverse motives and goals made political decisions and influenced public life. Through their lives, we are witness to the private and pub-lic conflicts and even violence that shook the foundations of the Roman Republic between circa 200 and 100 B.C.E.

Although we do not know Cornelia's exact birth and death dates, her life spanned most of the second century. As a member of the Cornelii clan, she was part of a small and almost princely class of families that had maintained wealth and political power in every century of the Republic. She attracts our attention initially as the daughter, wife, and mother of some of Rome's most famous men. She was the daughter of P. Cornelius Scipio (236–183), who took the descriptive title "Africanus" after his victories over Carthage in the Second Punic War (218–201). She married Tiberius Sempronius Gracchus (ca. 220–ca. 154), a respected military leader, consul, and censor, and was the mother of Tiberius and Gaius Gracchus, the "revolutionary" tribunes of the people. In these relationships she is ideally positioned to shed light on many of the contradictory forces, profound changes, and often tragic events of those years. But she catches our eye for her own talents and actions as well. She was the first highly educated woman we know of in Rome, and she was often controversial because of her interference in politics, yet held up as a model to upper-class women of later generations.[1] Even though they are hardly typical of the broader population of Roman men and women in terms of

1. Emily A. Hemelrijk, *Matrona Docta: Educated Women in the Roman Elite from Cornelia to Julia Domna* (London: Routledge, 1999), p. 64.

work, wealth, and power, Cornelia and her family do represent an important elite circle and, more broadly, many traditional Roman values and virtues. As a result, they are often featured prominently in the writings of those interested in the history of Rome and its citizens.

Numerous sources of different kinds provide a rich mix of evidence for studying the life and times of the Gracchi. Temples and tombs, public buildings, inscriptions, funeral orations, legislation and case law, letters, speeches, essays, poetry and drama, and consciously constructed "histories" (which appeared by the end of the third century) constitute a large body of material for historians of the late Republic. As we have seen in other studies of the ancient world, monuments, buildings, or inscriptions are usually intended to praise and idealize events and individuals and to demonstrate successes rather than failures. Poetry, drama, and topical essays must be examined for what they represent, not necessarily for what they depict.

Letters and speeches are especially valuable sources, but they raise additional issues in their use. For example, both contemporaries and later individuals refer to Cornelia's many letters, and they comment on their erudition and graceful style. But only fragments remain, and these fragments have survived because they were probably reworked and recorded by Cornelius Nepos, an antiquarian and biographer of the first century B.C.E. Gaius Gracchus was known for his oratorical skills, and we have diverse versions of his speeches. Some fragments exist because, fortunately, grammarians and teachers of rhetoric of the time used his language and style as teaching tools. Other versions appear in writings of scholars like Plutarch (ca. 50 to after 120 C.E.) or another Greek, Appian (late first century C.E.), and thus reflect their after-the-fact thoughts about the Gracchan revolution and its results. Finally, some of the richest sources are the writings of prominent men, themselves involved in the events of the last century of the Republic. Marcus Tullius Cicero (106–43 B.C.E.), a great orator, lawyer, and consul of Rome, left over fifty speeches, more than 800 letters, and various treatises on politics and philosophy in which he often defends the interests of the ruling and propertied classes. His slightly younger contemporary, Sallust (86–35 B.C.E.), was also a public figure and devoted his later life to writing history. Although he attacks greed and corruption and moralizes throughout his writings, he does attempt to describe the reality of the politics and people of his time.[2] Recognizing the nature of our sources is important as we turn to look at the lives of Cornelia and her family. When we ask questions about what they thought or when we seek the motives for their actions, we must often fill in the gaps or rely on the words of others.

2. For a good summary of sources available, see Naphtali Lewis and Meyer Reinhold (eds.), *Roman Civilization: Selected Readings*, vol. I (New York: Columbia University Press, 1990), especially "Introduction: The Sources," pp. 1–49. For discussion of the debates about Cornelia's letters, see Hemelrijk, pp. 67–68 and 193–196.

Chapter 3
A Roman Matron
and Her
Revolutionary
Sons: Cornelia
(Second Century
B.C.E.), and
Tiberius (163–133
B.C.E.), and Gaius
Gracchus
(154–121 B.C.E.)

■ THE ACTORS:

*CORNELIA, TIBERIUS GRACCHUS, AND
GAIUS GRACCHUS*

Cornelia was probably born around 190 B.C.E. At the time, Rome was a large, flourishing, and vital city with a population that neared 1 million by the end of the second century. Most of the people lived in multiple-story tenements and struggled to survive in a city subject to fire and flooding, with unlighted streets and no police force. Cornelia's wealthy family would have lived in quite different conditions, safe in an elite neighborhood in a walled house with inner gardens. The household she grew up in would include not only her immediate family but perhaps elderly parents and other dependents, as well as slaves and servants who maintained the house and cared for its inhabitants. The house reflected her father's position and his social and political needs, and it would be an arena for a range of social and business activities.[3] Many of the spaces in the *domus* (house) served multiple functions, and exclusive division between private and public areas was not the rule.

Cornelia might well have grown up in a setting where mornings were filled with numerous visits by clients or acquaintances, and various sources indicate that "Roman women, in contrast to their Greek counterparts [were] comfortably present in the front part of the house . . . where they would come in contact with visitors from outside the household."[4] It is not hard to imagine her mother Aemilia (?–162 B.C.E.) moving about this house and interacting with guests because she eventually had a reputation for somewhat ostentatious displays of her wealth in clothing, jewels, and servants. By this time period, it was common for wealthy Roman families to own both townhouses and villas in the country, so perhaps part of Cornelia's youth was spent in a rural setting.

The lives of all individuals in Roman society were structured by their social status, in other words, the family or house they came from, but also by legal status. It was important to have legal capacity, and it was determined by whether the person were free and a citizen. It was also influenced by age, marital status, gender, and census class. Like all members of a Roman *domus*, from the moment of birth Cornelia was under her father's authority and rule *(patria potestas)*. Her mission in life was to marry, bear and raise children, run a household, and devote herself to her family's fortune, thereby contributing to the social good. Sons would also be expected to marry, establish their own households, and continue their family line. Particularly for young men of the upper classes, however, it was assumed that they would acquit themselves well in military service and then begin to climb a ladder of public offices, where they would gain power and prestige.

3. See Michele George, "Repopulating the Roman House," in Beryl Rawson and Paul Weaver (eds.), *The Roman Family in Italy* (New York: Oxford/Clarendon Press, 1997), pp. 299–320.

4. Ibid., p. 305, fn. 13.

Cornelia's life was shaped by laws on marriage, divorce, and transmission of property common to her class.[5] Laws, of course, determine what one *may* do; social norms and values describe what one *should* do. But laws in Rome were subject to change or contained loopholes for alternative behaviors, and social values also shifted and included spaces where people could act and think in individual ways. Marriage required that a daughter be of age, usually between twelve and fifteen. While marriages were arranged by parents, consent of the partners was mandated by law. In the second century B.C.E., among the free citizen classes, there were few restrictions on whom one could marry. Cousins could marry cousins; a brother could marry his brother's ex-wife or his own ex-wife's sister. Divorce was not difficult to obtain, and adoptions, arranged to ensure the continuity of the lineage, were fairly common. Family property was also protected, and elder males were usually privileged. Daughters were not systematically excluded from inheritance, however, and could inherit property from fathers and husbands, transmit property to their children, and in some cases control dowries.[6]

Roman society inherited a tradition of writing from the Greeks, but it amplified this tradition in its own culture of law, political and personal prescriptions, letter writing, biographies, and history. Thus, by the second century, when the ideal of general education was introduced in Rome by Greek scholars, literacy among the upper classes became common.[7] Initially, individual families, parents in particular, were responsible for educating their children. Education for young men was important both as a mark of status and in their pursuit of careers in law and politics. Families usually hired tutors (often Greek slaves) to train their sons in oratory, philosophy, and Greek and Latin literature, but by the end of the Republic, grammar schools also provided education. Literacy among upper-class Roman women probably was the norm, although their education was not as broad or extensive as that of their male counterparts. For elite families, education of a daughter could signify wealth and status, but it could also be controversial because some Romans saw educated women as dangerous. Cornelia's education was unusual for the time. Her father, P. Cornelius Scipio Africanus, showed a keen interest in Greek civilization and culture, and she might have had access to a library that one of her uncles had shipped from Greece to Rome. Her older brother was a man of considerable learning, while her cousin Scipio

5. See Judith Hallett, *Fathers and Daughters in Roman Society* (Princeton, N.J.: Princeton University Press, 1984).

6. Mireille Corbier, "Family Behavior of the Roman Aristocracy, Second Century B.C.–Third Century A.D.," in Sarah B. Pomeroy (ed.), *Women's History and Ancient History* (Chapel Hill, N.C.: University of North Carolina Press, 1991), pp. 173–196; see also Jane F. Gardner, *Women in Roman Law and Society* (Bloomington, Ind.: Indiana University Press, 1986).

7. Hemelrijk, pp. 17–25. See also Antony Kamm, *The Romans: An Introduction* (London: Routledge, 1995), pp. 116–119.

Chapter 3
A Roman Matron
and Her
Revolutionary
Sons: Cornelia
(Second Century
B.C.E.), and
Tiberius (163–133
B.C.E.), and Gaius
Gracchus
(154–121 B.C.E.)

Aemilianus (185–129 B.C.E.) was famous for his interest in Greek literature and philosophy, and for his support of and friendship with various Greek scholars, including his tutor, the historian Polybius (ca. 200–ca. 118 B.C.E.) Thus, she was raised in a stimulating family environment that stressed learning and culture. While we have no details of Cornelia's educational experience, her later reputation for erudition points to exceptional training at an early age.

Cornelia's princely family background and educational opportunities placed her in an unusual position in Roman elite society, but her life was completely different from that of the majority of women in ancient Italy in many other ways. Consider the contrasting experiences of the wives of peasant soldiers, who were at home only periodically. Peasant women who bore multiple children (losing many of them), had to figure how to plant and harvest the land, and provide for the family on a daily basis. A manual on agriculture describes such women: [they] "should be strong and not ill-looking. In many places they are not inferior to the men at work . . . being able either to tend the herd or carry firewood and cook the food, or to keep things in order in their huts."[8] Although work and economic and living conditions separated the free women of Rome, all were expected to be fertile and virtuous mothers, and to be modest, frugal, and chaste women who were devoted to their families. Similarly, ideologies of masculinity instructed men to be serious, strong, and dedicated to their families, the gods, and the state.

▪ ACT I:

CORNELIA AS DAUGHTER, WIFE, AND MOTHER, 190–154 B.C.E.

Cornelia's childhood coincided with a period of considerable historical change and accompanying fears about the meaning of those changes. The Punic Wars had had devastating effects on the Italian countryside and the people of Rome. High male death rates had an impact not only on the ability of Rome to produce adequate armies of citizens who met appropriate property-holding qualifications, but they also meant that women in all census classes were often left to manage properties. "Marriages became more unstable, while sterner attitudes prevailed in morals and behaviors."[9] In 195 B.C.E., women gathered in the Forum to show their support for the repeal of the *lex Oppia*, which had been passed during the conflict with Carthage to limit the amount of luxury goods a woman could own. Debates among Rome's leaders ensued, not simply on the merits of the repeal but also because some, like Marcus Porcius Cato (234–149 B.C.E.), an up-

8. From Varro, *On Agriculture,* quoted in Elaine Fantham, Helen Foley, et al. (eds.), *Women in the Classical World* (New York: Oxford University Press, 1994), p. 267.

9. Corrado Petrocelli, "Cornelia the Matron," in Augusto Fraschetti (ed.), *Roman Women,* translated by Linda Lappin (Chicago: University of Chicago Press, 2001), p. 44.

holder of tradition, accused the women of "unnatural" public actions, which he felt threatened society (Document One). As Cornelia neared marriage age, some of the constraints on women's behaviors and rights appeared to be loosening, even though formally women were still disciplined by their families.

Because the unfolding of Cornelia's life is almost completely defined by events in the lives of her father, husband, relatives, and sons, we have no concrete evidence of her childhood and adolescence. She appears to us historically just prior to her marriage.[10] Cornelia's father was one of the great heroes of Rome, perhaps the greatest of all time, according to Polybius. His first victories in Spain were followed by his brilliant defeat of the Carthaginians in North Africa at Zama in 202 B.C.E., and eventually he led armies in Asia Minor. Africanus held some of the most important offices in the Roman government. He was elected twice as a consul, first in 205 and then again in 194. In this capacity, he was one of two presidents of the powerful Senate, had judicial powers, was responsible for public order and security, executed the law, and exercised authority as supreme military commander. Later he served as one of two censors, a highly coveted position that, among other functions, filled vacancies in the 300-member Senate every five years.

Given his stature and the importance of marriage for political alliances and advancement, it would not be sur-

prising if the elite of Rome eagerly awaited Africanus's choice of a husband for his daughter, Cornelia. According to both Polybius and Plutarch, however, when Africanus died about 183, Cornelia was neither betrothed nor married, and her marriage was subsequently arranged by a family council. The man chosen for her was Tiberius Gracchus. He was considerably older than she, from the Sempronii Gracchi family, whose origins were plebeian but whose male members had been military commanders and consuls for at least three generations and thus had joined the aristocracy of office. It was the intermarriage of this class with older, princely Senate families that helped to create a new nobility.

They married sometime around 175 B.C.E., and because her father was no longer living, Cornelia probably passed under the authority of her new husband. For the next twenty years we know a great deal about Tiberius's life and career, but almost none of the events in Cornelia's life. Tiberius embodied many of the traditional Roman virtues and became known for his upright moral character, frugality, and sternness.[11] He was a good soldier and won important victories in Sardinia and Spain as Rome continued its expansion. He was a flexible politician, elected first as one of ten tribunes who

10. Petrocelli, pp. 34–65.

11. For information on the Gracchi family, the following are useful: Keith Richardson, *Daggers in the Forum: The Revolutionary Lives and Violent Deaths of the Gracchus Brothers* (London: Cassell and Company, 1976); H. H. Scullard, *From the Gracchi to Nero* (New York: Barnes and Noble, Inc., 1963), and David Stockton, *The Gracchi* (Oxford: Oxford University Press, 1979).

Chapter 3
A Roman Matron
and Her
Revolutionary
Sons: Cornelia
(Second Century
B.C.E.), and
Tiberius (163–133
B.C.E.), and Gaius
Gracchus
(154–121 B.C.E.)

presided over the plebeian assembly, then as consul twice (177 and 163 B.C.E.) and as censor in 169.

While Tiberius was thus occupied, we can assume that Cornelia was fulfilling the obligations of an upper-class Roman woman, which included supervising the work of household slaves, receiving and entertaining guests, and accompanying her husband to social events like birthday parties, weddings, funerals, dinner parties, and religious gatherings. Women also attended the theater and public games, and traveled freely to visit friends and relatives.[12] Although women were denied a formal political role and their lives centered on home and family, they were not confined to the home and could expand their activities and influence beyond the walls of their *domus*. Childbearing was, of course, a primary fe-

male function, and in that regard Cornelia was exemplary; she bore twelve children, only three of whom reached adulthood, a common situation for Rome's ruling families at the time.[13] Sempronia was the eldest of the three surviving children, followed by Tiberius, born in 163 and probably the eldest son, since he carried his father's name. Gaius was born nine years later, in 154, the same year in which his father died. Cornelia was thus left a widow in her mid-thirties, with the responsibility of finding a suitable husband for her daughter and of raising and educating her young sons. She could have remarried, but she chose to remain a widow, which earned her the unusual and admirable status of *univira*, or a woman with only one husband in her lifetime.

◼ ACT II:

THE WIDOW CORNELIA AND HER SONS, 154–134 B.C.E.

Among the stories that circulated and helped to create the legendary Cornelia was that once, when another matron proudly showed Cornelia her jewels, Cornelia countered by stating that her sons were *her* jewels. This declaration fit with the ideal model of a Roman mother who prized her family above all else. Nearer the truth is the fact that, as a widow, Cornelia could control and manage great wealth and exercise considerable influence over her children. Her mother died in 162,

so it was possible Cornelia could have inherited some of the family patrimony. She might have regained the dowry she took to her marriage, and she would have inherited a portion of her husband's estate and administered the remainder until her sons were of age.[14] As a wealthy widow, Cornelia undoubtedly had considerable autonomy. As a mother with sole responsibility for raising her children,

12. Hemelrijk, pp. 9–11.

13. Corbier, p. 179.

14. Her dowry of 50 talents was not huge by elite standards, but it was far more than a solider was paid per year. A talent = 6000 denarius, and a solider's pay was 120 denarius per year. Petrocelli, p. 46; Richardson, p. 22; and Stockton, p. viii.

she had to educate them and help to arrange appropriate marriages for them (Document Two).

Later writers and contemporaries of Tiberius and Gaius agreed on their intellectual abilities, particularly on their excellent oratorical skills. Such prowess was considered to be a natural disposition of the two brothers, but also the result of an exceptionally good education directed by their mother. She hired Greek tutors for her children, who taught them rhetoric and literature as well as acquainting them with Greek political theory and philosophy. One especially influential figure was Blossius of Cumae, a Stoic philosopher whose family had a long association with liberal, democratic ideas and who probably passed these ideas on to the two Gracchi brothers.

Sempronia apparently also received a fairly good education, given her later testimony in an important legal case. Sometime around 150 B.C.E. she married Scipio Aemilianus. He was her mother's cousin by birth but had been adopted by one of Cornelia's brothers, who was childless and wished to keep the Scipio family line alive. This adoption made him the grandson of the great Scipio Africanus. Scipio Aemilianus, as already noted, was famous (and controversial) for his admiration of things Greek. Although by all accounts this was not a particularly happy marriage, perhaps some of his knowledge and Hellenism influenced Sempronia's life. Tiberius and Gaius also married well into prominent and related aristocratic families. Tiberius married Claudia in 143; she was the daughter of Appius Claudius Pulcher (185–130 B.C.E.), a man whose family

had lineage equal to that of the Cornelii. He served as consul (143 B.C.E.), moved to head the Senate, became censor probably in 136, and was a key player in Roman politics in the 140s and 130s. One of his political allies, his brother-in-law P. Licinius Crassus Mucianus (180–130 B.C.E.) of plebeian origins, was a well-known and very wealthy jurist who also was a consul and headed the state religion as *pontifex maximus*. He became connected to the Gracchi when his well-educated daughter Licinia married Gaius in 133, bringing to the marriage a considerable dowry. As already noted, such complex familial relations were the means of building political alliances among members of the elite classes.

By the time Tiberius and Gaius entered the political arena, electoral struggles among Senate families and their allies were increasingly common, and the political circle in which their fathers-in-law operated actually was at odds with the circle around their illustrious kinsman, Scipio Aemilianus, and his relatives. Marriage alliances thus could be advantageous but were not a guarantee of unqualified familial allegiance.

Tiberius and Gaius became adults during a period in which the troubles of Rome deepened. How and by whom these problems should be resolved brought conflict, debate, and contested elections for numerous public offices. Some individuals sought to use the traditional authority of the Senate to control change or reform. Others began to look for their power in the tribal assemblies, which were presided over by tribunes of the people and could pass binding legislation.

In economic terms, wealth increased for members of Rome's upper classes, from the highest senatorial families to rich and intelligent men of a lower class (the knights or *equites*), who were a mix of landowners, military officers, and men engaged in trade, banking, and fulfillment of government contracts and on whom the empire increasingly relied. This economic growth helped to redefine the social order, but it would take time and political contests to change government structures and laws to reflect actual practice. This wealth did not necessarily filter down to the lower orders, nor did it end up in the coffers of the Roman government, so economic and financial pressures grew.

More worrisome and potentially more revolutionary changes occurred in landowning and agricultural production as Rome expanded. The small citizen farmers, who were the bulk of the army, had trouble keeping their farms afloat. Tours of military duty that often lasted six years or more, and competition with much larger farms producing for the market, undermined the older landowning peasantry, many of whom sank into poverty or were forced to abandon their land. Through takeovers of such farms and acquisition of public lands gained through conquest, rich landowners created vast estates (*latifundia*) worked by slaves producing for the market.

Most of the slaves and a great deal of the new wealth came from Rome's expansion to the east into Greece and Asia Minor. Added to those campaigns was the final destruction of Carthage, which became another of Rome's provinces in the Mediterranean. While Rome had taken Spain after the second Punic war, that area remained unstable and was an ongoing problem and a drain on manpower. Heightened resentment over Rome's increasing interference in their affairs caused many of her allies in Italy to demand equal citizenship or to threaten breaking away from Rome. Mutinies and insubordination in the army, combined with slave unrest and a major slave uprising in Sicily in 135 B.C.E., made it clear that something had to be done.

First Tiberius and then Gaius Gracchus became political actors in this setting of economic, political, and social unrest. Although tied together by family and what were seen as their revolutionary politics, the two brothers were certainly not identical. Plutarch describes them both as brave, self-disciplined, and eloquent, but he claims that Tiberius was mild-mannered and somewhat restrained, while Gaius was more passionate and aggressive in his behavior (Document Three). Tiberius gave cool and persuasive speeches, standing in one place; Gaius paced up and down, speaking with "fire and fury [and] hammering every point home with a rich and colorful vocabulary."[15] Both of them married at about the age of twenty. We know little about Claudia and her marriage to Tiberius, although apparently they had three sons who were quite young when their father died in 133, and did not live to play a prominent role in Roman society. Licinia, Gaius's wife, is slightly more visible historically be-

---

15. Richardson, p. 3.

cause of the size of her dowry and the contests over it after Gaius's death in 121. She also had a reputation for education and was thought to have brought Gaius in touch with important intellectuals of the time.

We know much more of the public careers of the two brothers because, on the one hand, they followed a fairly typical pattern of advancement in Roman society. Both entered military service at sixteen or seventeen, when they would be considered adult males, and gave the requisite ten or twelve years. Tiberius began his military service in North Africa under the command of his uncle, Scipio Aemilianius, during the third Punic war (146–147 B.C.E.). According to Plutarch, Tiberius showed both good sense and courage in his military service, and by 137 was chosen *quaestor* by one of the popular assemblies. Quaestorships were often the first step on the ladder of upward mobility for aristocratic young men.

Quaestors usually were assistants to consuls or provincial governors, and they were responsible for financial controls and recordkeeping. Tiberius was assigned as assistant to one of the commanders in Spain, where warfare continued because Rome seemed unable either to govern or subdue the area. About a decade later, Gaius followed in his brother's footsteps, entering military service as he became an adult, and after election as quaestor in 126, serving with a consul in Sardinia.

But the two brothers were not typical in other respects. Like others of their social class, they both became convinced of the needs for economic and political reform. Unlike many of their peers, who felt such reforms could best be accomplished through the traditional authority of the Senate, Tiberius and Gaius would turn to the popular assemblies and exercise their influence as tribunes of the people.

ACT III:

A FAMILY OF REVOLUTIONARIES, 134–121 B.C.E.

In December 134, Tiberius was elected tribune of the people for the following year. The major reform he proposed was legislation for agrarian reform, which was quite controversial. He had been thinking about this issue for some time, feeling that such change could answer both economic and military problems, but he was not the first to propose reforming land ownership. In 140, a consul and one of Scipio Aemiliaus's allies had produced a plan to

deal with public lands, perhaps giving land to army veterans, but heavy opposition from aristocratic landowners and business people led him to withdraw the proposal.

So why did Tiberius take on this thorny problem and risk alienating many people in his social class (Document Four)? Most scholars agree that his travel and experience in Spain as quaestor were significant. By the time he was assigned to the Spanish campaign, opposition to the troop levies was becoming heated and a movement to negotiate a peaceful settlement was under way. On his way to Spain in 137,

Chapter 3
A Roman Matron
and Her
Revolutionary
Sons: Cornelia
(Second Century
B.C.E.), and
Tiberius (163–133
B.C.E.), and Gaius
Gracchus
(154–121 B.C.E.)

Tiberius saw deserted farms and large landholdings being worked by slaves, and he became more conscious of the connections between the unrest in the army and the economic plight of small farmers. In a later speech dealing with the landless veterans, he asked: "Was not a man who could serve in the army more useful than one who could not? Was not a man who had a stake in his country more likely to be devoted to its common interests?"[16]

Handling of the war in Spain, as well as growing discontent at home, had created considerable political tension and division by the time Tiberius returned from Spain and stood for election as tribune in 134. By then a political circle surrounding his father-in-law, Appius Claudius Pulcher, and Licinius Crassus (Gaius's father-in-law), opposed Aemilianus and his followers on issues of both the war in Spain and solutions to their economic problems. Tiberius saw in the Claudio-Crassan circle an alliance of influential, like-minded men who either inspired or supported his own goals of reform.

To what degree might Cornelia also have influenced her son's political decisions? Most historians agree that a Roman matron generally continued to be a moral mentor to her son even after he had left her home, and that her aspirations and goals would more likely be focused on her sons than her husband.[17] Cornelia might well have supported Tiberius's views; after all, she was responsible for selecting the scholars who tutored him and for creating the intellectual environment in which he was raised. She may also have encouraged her sons in their political careers, reminding them of the luster of their family name and, according to Plutarch, reproaching them because "the Romans still called her the mother-in-law of Scipio [Aemilianus], but not yet the mother of the Gracchi."[18]

Whatever the reasons, Tiberius introduced legislation to reform landholding by taking lands the state had acquired in the conquest of Italy and redistributing these among small farmers for a nominal rent. He also proposed to enforce the law that limited the amount of public lands one could own. As expected, major landholders who would be affected by the bill opposed the legislation. Rather than following the usual procedure of submitting the bill to the Senate for preliminary discussion, Tiberius took it immediately to the popular Assembly, where he knew he had support. When a fellow tribune, Octavius, who was backed by the Senate, prepared to veto the bill as it was being read out, Tiberius took the unprecedented step of asking the Assembly to vote his opponent out of office, which it did readily. The bill was passed by acclamation and, to carry out its provisions, Tiberius appointed a land commission

16. Appian quoted in Stockton, p. 32.

17. This perspective can be found in Hallett, p. 248; Richard A. Bauman, *Women and Politics in Ancient Rome* (New York: Routledge, 1992), pp. 175–176; and Suzanne Dixon, *The Roman Mother* (Norman, Okla.: The University of Oklahoma Press, 1988), pp. 176–177, 188.

18. *Plutarch's Lives*, translated by Bernadotte Perrin, 11 volumes; *Tiberius and Gaius Gracchus*, X (Cambridge, Mass.: Harvard University Press, 1949), p. 163. Petrocelli says that she was tired of being referred to as the *daughter* of Scipio, p. 58.

consisting of himself, his father-in-law, and his brother Gaius.

As Cicero later noted, the agrarian law "appealed to the common people. It looked to safeguard the fortunes of the poor. The best people threw their weight against it, because they saw it was a source of discord, and believed that to remove the rich from their longheld possessions would be to rob the state of its defenders."[19] The reform may have created as many as 75,000 small holdings for farming and perhaps affected some of the largest landholders. But the Senate let the bill stand after Tiberius's death, indicating there was broad support for land reform. More critical and controversial were the procedures Tiberius used, which clearly challenged senatorial authority and trod on customary political practices. At odds with the Senate, Tiberius decided to stand for a second term as tribune, an unusual step that was not constitutionally clear. This decision was the last straw for many senators. The result was a rowdy and contested election during which a group of senators, insisting they were upholding order and tradition, marched on a public meeting Tiberius was addressing and clubbed him to death, killed some 300 of his supporters, and threw their bodies in the Tiber River.

The reactions to his death are contradictory and unclear. The senator who had led the attack on Tiberius was sent out of Rome and died a short time later. Scipio Aemilianus was still fighting in Spain and supposedly responded to the news of Tiberius's death with a quote from Homer: "So perish any other man whose crimes be like to his!"[20] And what were the crimes? Again, without personal statements or verbatim records from the time, it is difficult to know exactly what Tiberius's long-term goals were. Most historians agree that while his land reform had revolutionary implications, he probably did not intend to level aristocratic Roman society and place all power in the hands of the lower orders and their assemblies, nor did he question the righteousness of Roman imperial rule. Nevertheless, the judgment that he was revolutionary would be a logical conclusion when seen against the background of his brother's later actions, and with the hindsight of those who witnessed the dramatic changes of the century following Tiberius's death (Document Five).

We have no record of Cornelia's response to the death of her eldest son. Most evidence indicates that by the time he died and perhaps even before, she was spending most of her time at her villa in Misenum on the Bay of Naples. There she engaged in the patronage of Greek scholars by giving them material support, providing them with an audience, sponsoring their recitations, and circulating their books. She also wrote the letters for which she became so famous, sometimes lengthy epistles in ink on papyrus, and in other cases "short notes scratched on wax-tablets and erased for the reply."[21] One might assume

19. Quoted in Stockton, p. 31.

20. Quoted in Stockton, p. 86.

21. Hemlrijik, pp. 97–98, for patronage, and pp. 188–190 for letter writing.

Chapter 3
A Roman Matron
and Her
Revolutionary
Sons: Cornelia
(Second Century
B.C.E.), and
Tiberius (163–133
B.C.E.), and Gaius
Gracchus
(154–121 B.C.E.)

that she communicated in writing with her sons, perhaps commenting on political affairs and financial matters. No evidence remains of how Cornelia responded to Tiberius's brutal finish. Gaius was not in Rome at the time of his brother's death, but given his own career and later political activities, it is clear that he believed in his brother's causes and sought to avenge his death and to enhance his reputation as a hero of the people.

Although Tiberius's death did not solve Rome's problems, it was followed by a period of respite or a temporary truce. One reason for this truce were the deaths of key leaders in the older generation of Roman aristocrats. The Gracchis' fathers-in-law, Crassus Mucianus and Appius Claudius, both died in 131 or 130. A year later, when their adversary, Scipio Aemilianus, died unexpectedly in the midst of opposing certain aspects of the land reform, Gaius, Cornelia, and her daughter Sempronia were suspected. Whether the result of poison, a stroke, or natural death, the demise of Scipio meant the end of an epoch of heroes in the tumultuous second century. Several years passed before new political alliances formed and a new cadre of leaders emerged.

In the meantime, Gaius withdrew from public life in Rome. Writers then and later speculated on his reasons. Both Appian and Plutarch felt he did so because he feared his enemies and a fate similar to his brother's. That reasoning would seem to make sense, but it was also true that he continued to serve on the land commission, which meant traveling a great deal. He mar-ried Licinia and expressed the desire to devote his energies to his family and then, in 126, stood for quaestor, just as his brother had. In that capacity he was assigned to Sardinia, where a rebellion offered the chance to participate in a major military campaign. His previous public appearances had already shown that he had a flair for public speaking, so perhaps he was simply acquiring further credentials and awaiting the appropriate moment "to make a noteworthy entrance on to the public stage"[22] (Document Six).

That moment came in 124, when he stood for election as tribune and took office the following year. By then Gaius's political star had risen because he was well known "for his superb oratory, personal charm and magnetism, indefatigable energy and attention to detail, immense practical ability and drive"[23] (Document Seven). He also had wide popular support among both urban and rural poor, small tradespeople and craftspeople, and financial and business interests. The exact chronology of Gaius's legislation is not entirely clear, but in 123, his first year as a tribune, and 122, when he was re-elected tribune, he proposed several bills that went significantly beyond what his brother Tiberius had attempted. Initially, there was little opposition, but by the end of 122 he faced growing hostility from the aristocracy.

Among the most important laws Gaius sponsored were various bills that attempted to curb abuse of public

22. Richardson, p. 118.
23. Stockton, p. 174.

office and the courts; a *lex frumentaria* (a grain law) that provided for state collection and distribution of grain to Roman citizens at a fixed price; an extension of the land redistribution law, which included allotments of land outside Italy in the form of the creation of colonies; laws for road-building; and judicial reforms, which gave court authority and positions to nonsenators. In his second tribunate, he also proposed that the collection of taxes for the new province of Asia should be auctioned off, thus giving the equites even more opportunities for wealth. His final act, and the rock on which his ship was wrecked, was a proposal to extend the rights of Roman citizenship to the Latins and other allies. This proposal fully aroused Senate anger and had only lukewarm popular support. In late 122, when he stood for the tribunate for an unprecedented third term, he was not re-elected.

In the meantime, Cornelia remained at Misenum but kept in touch with her son in the urban capital. The two fragments of her letters that still exist, assuming they are authentic, were written in 124 when Gaius was planning to run for office (Document Eight). Here she appears opposed to his political aims and warns him of the dangers to himself and to the Republic. After he was elected, apparently she again wrote to him, this time successfully persuading him not to launch punitive measures against Tiberius's foes, thus demonstrating to the world the strong moral fiber and magnanimous character of the Gracchi. Regardless of whether Cornelia agreed with her sons' political choices and views, there seems to be little doubt that there was considerable love and respect between her and her children.

With Gaius out of office, his franchise reform did not become law, and efforts began to repeal other parts of his legislation. Gaius responded by rallying his supporters and forming a bodyguard of friends. In a minor disturbance between that group and the opposition, a servant of the consul Opimius was killed. Opimius was an old enemy of Gaius, and he seized the opportunity to persuade the Senate to pass a resolution that gave a consul the authority to maintain security and save the Republic. Thus empowered, Opimius summoned to arms senators and equites. Gaius and his allies initially attempted negotiations for peace, but these attempts were unsuccessful and they determined that they would have to resist. The Gracchans were defeated and eventually killed. About to be taken by his opponents, Gaius supposedly had a loyal servant cut his throat. The bodies of Gaius and his supporters were flung into the Tiber, and shortly thereafter 3,000 of their surviving supporters were rounded up and executed without a trial. Vengeance was not complete until Gaius's house had been looted, Licinia and the wives of his supporters were forbidden to wear mourning, and Licinia was stripped of her dowry. Her uncle, the pontifex maximum, stepped in to protect her.

Although the consul Opimius was eventually judged to have committed a "just act" to save the state, there were many people who remembered

Chapter 3
A Roman Matron
and Her·
Revolutionary
Sons: Cornelia
(Second Century
B.C.E.), and
Tiberius (163–133
B.C.E.), and Gaius
Gracchus
(154–121 B.C.E.)

the Gracchi as heroes and who set up statues to them and consecrated the places where they were killed. Cornelia was not harmed physically or financially by the brutal assault on her son and his allies. Perhaps she was untouchable because of her age, her family, and her public reputation as a symbol of female republican virtue. Subsequent commentaries noted how nobly she bore her sorrow, that she continued an active social life and spoke to visitors about her family, praising her illustrious father Scipio Africanus and telling all who would listen of the heroic achievements and events of the lives of Tiberius and Gaius (Document Nine). She probably died sometime before 101 B.C.E. In that year, her daughter Sempronia appeared in court to refute a man claiming to be a son of Tiberius. Were Cornelia still alive, as keeper of the family secrets and their documents, that would have been her role.[24]

■ FINALE

Some changes in landowning survived the deaths of the Gracchi brothers, but much of their legislation did not. In the history of the late Roman Republic, demands for change openly and defiantly confronted a wall of entrenched interest during the tribunates of the Gracchi. Tiberius and Gaius desired social and economic reform; they did not set out to destroy the nobility or the Republic nor to grasp tyrannical power. But their occasional poor judgment and even rashness, combined with their appeal to the popular assemblies, antagonized a fearful and uncompromising Senate, resulting in political conflict that ended in violence. The brothers' vision had clarified the links between "problems of poverty, property holding, the army and extension and retention of the empire."[25] Their efforts also revealed weaknesses in the Senate, and the political importance of wealth, patronage, and military power. Their appeals to nonsenatorial social groups showed that the will of the people was not always rational or civic-minded. Whether people realized it or not, Roman politics had changed, as had the old aristocratic families, some of whom were extinct, and others were divided politically.

The nature of Gracchan activities, whether Tiberius's, Gaius's, or Cornelia's, would generate reactions and bias in those who lived after them and told their stories. Cicero praised the brothers as individuals but loathed the destruction they brought to Rome and argued that they "split a united people into two." Livy condemned their madness and sedition, while Sallust was more willing to apportion some blame to the victors who used violence against the Gracchi. Writing much later, Appian and Plutarch were slightly more balanced in their assessments, acknowledging the value of the Gracchi visions along with the vio-

25. Kamm, p. 34.

24. Petrocelli, p. 60.

lence their passions and causes provoked.

The Gracchi brothers became legendary, either as heroes or as villains. Cornelia became the sentimentalized model of the Roman matron. In reality, she had lived as a patroness of literature and learning, as a woman with de facto control over great wealth, and as a widow with autonomy, respect, and authority. But these dimensions of her life would be overshadowed by her elevation as a devoted mother. A century or more later, the emperor Augustus had a statue of Cornelia placed in a portico in Rome, to honor his sister Olivia. The marble base of the statue was rediscovered in 1878, and its inscription read: "the daughter of Scipio Africanus; the mother of the Gracchi." Cornelia survived, not as an individual historical actor, but as the daughter and mother of famous men.

■ QUESTIONS

1. Describe the general economic and political changes that took place in Rome in the second century B.C.E. How were these changes connected to characteristics of social and family life at the time?

2. Tiberius and Gaius Gracchus and their mother Cornelia can be described as typical of their time and social class and at the same time quite unusual for both. Give examples of this apparent contradiction. Why can both conditions exist simultaneously?

3. What makes a revolutionary, or what are revolutionary acts? Do such descriptions apply to Tiberius and Gaius Gracchus? Why or why not?

4. Both Aspasia and Cornelia were educated women with a public presence in their societies, yet their reputations were quite different. What sorts of images applied to each of these women, and why did they symbolize such different female behaviors and values?

Chapter 3
A Roman Matron
and Her
Revolutionary
Sons: Cornelia
(Second Century
B.C.E.), and
Tiberius (163–133
B.C.E.), and Gaius
Gracchus
(154–121 B.C.E.)

■ **DOCUMENTS**

DOCUMENT ONE

LIVY

History of Rome
Account of Marcus Porcius Cato's Speech in the Debate
over Repeal of the Oppian Law
(195 B.C.E.)

The account of this speech comes from Livy, History of Rome, *which appeared in the first century B.C.E. Cato was noted for his dedication to Republican traditions and institutions, and here he is protesting the fact that women had appeared in public to support the repeal of the Oppian Law. But he (or perhaps Livy?) makes other general points about what such behavior might mean. What are the things that most offend Cato? What is his solution to the problem? What does this segment tell you about attitudes toward Roman women in the second and first centuries B.C.E.?*

. . . The law said that no woman might own more than half an ounce of gold nor wear a multicoloured dress nor ride in a carriage in the city or in a town within a mile of it, unless there was a religious festival. The tribunes, Marcus and Publius Junius Brutus, were in favour of the Oppian law and said that they would not allow its repeal. Many noble men came forward hoping to persuade or dissuade them; a crowd of men, both supporters and opponents, filled the Capitoline Hill. The matrons, whom neither counsel nor shame nor their husbands' orders could keep at home, blockaded every street in the city and every entrance to the Forum. As the men came down to the Forum, the matrons besought them to let them, too, have back the luxuries they had enjoyed before, giving as their reason that the republic was thriving and that everyone's private wealth was increasing with every day. This crowd of women was growing daily, for now they were even gathering from the towns and villages. Before long they dared go up and solicit the consuls, praetors, and other magistrates; but one of the consuls could not be moved in the least, Marcus Porcius Cato, who spoke in favour of the law:

'If each man of us, fellow citizens, had established that the right and authority of the husband should be held over the mother of his own family, we should have less difficulty with women in general; now, at home our freedom is conquered by female fury, here in the Forum it is bruised and trampled upon, and, because we have not contained the individuals, we fear the lot . . .

'Indeed, I blushed when, a short while ago, I walked through the midst of a band of women. Had not respect for the dignity and modesty of certain ones (not them all!) restrained me (so they would not be seen being scolded by a consul), I should have said, "What kind of behaviour is this? Running around in public, blocking streets, and speaking to other women's husbands! Could you not have asked your own husbands the same thing at home? Are you more charming in public with others' husbands than at home with your own? And yet, it is not fitting even at home (if modesty were to keep married women within the bounds of their rights) for you to concern yourselves with what laws are passed or repealed here." Our ancestors did not want women to conduct any—not even private—business without a guardian; they wanted them to be under the authority of parents, brothers, or husbands; we (the gods help us!) even now let them snatch at the government and meddle in the Forum and our assemblies. What are they doing now on the streets and crossroads, if they are not persuading the tribunes to vote for repeal? Give the reins to their unbridled nature and this unmastered creature, and hope that they will put limits on their own freedom; unless you do something yourselves, this is the least of the things imposed upon them either by custom or by law which they endure with hurt feelings. They want freedom, nay licence (if we are to speak the truth), in all things.

'If they are victorious now, what will they not attempt? . . . As soon as they begin to be your equals, they will have become your superiors . . .

'What honest excuse is offered, pray, for this womanish rebellion? "That we might shine with gold and purple," says one of them, "that we might ride through the city in coaches on holidays and working-days, as though triumphant over the conquered law and the votes which we captured by tearing them from you; that there should be no limit to our expenses and our luxury." . . .

'The woman who can spend her own money will do so; the one who cannot will ask her husband. Pity that husband—the one who gives in and the one who stands firm! What he refuses, he will see given by another man. Now they publicly solicit other women's husbands, and, what is worse, they ask for a law and votes, and certain men give them what they want. You there, you, are easily moved about things which concern yourself, your estate, and your children; once the law no longer limits your wife's spending, you will never do it by yourself. Fellow citizens, do not imagine that the state which existed before the law was passed will return. A dishonest man is safer never accused than acquitted, and luxury, left alone, would have been more acceptable than it will be now, as when wild animals are first chafed by their chains and then released. I vote that the Oppian law should not, in the smallest measure, be repealed; whatever course you take, may all the gods make you happy with it.'

After this, when the tribunes of the people, who had declared that they would oppose the motion to repeal, had added a few remarks along the same lines, Lucius Valerius spoke on behalf of the motion which he himself had brought:

Chapter 3
A Roman Matron
and Her
Revolutionary
Sons: Cornelia
(Second Century
B.C.E.), and
Tiberius (163–133
B.C.E.), and Gaius
Gracchus
(154–121 B.C.E.)

'[Cato] used up more words castigating the women than he did opposing the motion, and he left in some uncertainty whether the women had done the deeds which he reproached on their own or at our instigation. I shall defend the motion, not ourselves, against whom the consul has hurled this charge, more for the words than for the reality of the accusation. He has called this assemblage "secession" and sometimes "womanish rebellion", because the matrons have publicly asked you, in peacetime when the state is happy and prosperous, to repeal a law passed against them during the straits of war . . .

'What, may I ask, are the women doing that is new, having gathered and come forth publicly in a case which concerns them directly? Have they never appeared in public before this? Allow me to unroll your own *Origines* before you. Listen to how often they have done so—always for the public good. . . .

DOCUMENT TWO

TACITUS

"A Dialogue on Oratory"
(84–85 C.E.)

Writing long after the Gracchan era, Tacitus emphasizes the importance of education and the role of mothers in that process. What changes had taken place since Cornelia raised her children that bothered Tacitus?

. . . But first I must say a word or two about the rigorous system which our forefathers followed in the matter of the upbringing and training of their children.

In the good old days, every man's son, born in wedlock, was brought up not in the chamber of some hireling nurse, but in his mother's lap, and at her knee. And that mother could have no higher praise than that she managed the house and gave herself to her children. Again, some elderly relative would be selected in order that to her, as a person who had been tried and never found wanting, might be entrusted the care of all the youthful scions of the same house; in the presence of such an one no base word could be uttered without grave offence, and no wrong deed done. Religiously and with the utmost delicacy she regulated not only the serious tasks of her youthful charges, but their recreations also and their games. It was in this spirit, we are told, that Cornelia, the mother of the Gracchi, directed their upbringing, Aurelia that of Caesar, Atia of Augustus: thus it was that these mothers trained their princely children. The object of this rigorous system was that the natural disposition of every child, while still sound at the core and untainted, not warped as yet by any vicious tendencies, might at once lay hold with heart and soul on virtuous accomplishments, and whether its bent was towards the army, or the law, or the pursuit of eloquence, might make that its sole aim and its all-absorbing interest.

Nowadays, on the other hand, our children are handed over at their birth to some silly little Greek serving-maid, with a male slave, who may be any one, to help her,—quite frequently the most worthless member of the whole establishment, incompetent for any serious service. It is from the foolish tittle-tattle of such persons that the children receive their earliest impressions, while their minds are still pliant and unformed; and there is not a soul in the whole house who cares a jot what he says or does in the presence of his baby master. Yes, and the parents themselves make no effort to train their little ones in goodness and self-control; they grow up in an atmosphere of laxity and pertness, in which they come gradually to lose all sense of shame, and all respect both for themselves and for other people. Again, there are the peculiar and characteristic vices of this metropolis of ours, ...

DOCUMENT THREE

PLUTARCH

Life of Tiberius Gracchus
(Sometime Between 46 B.C.E. and 126 C.E.)

In this section of his Parallel Lives, *Plutarch describes Cornelia's widowhood and raising of the two boys, as well as the different personalities of the brothers. How does he describe Cornelia? How do the two brothers differ in their character?*

. . . Cornelia took charge of the children and of the estate, and showed herself so discreet, so good a mother, and so magnanimous, that Tiberius was thought to have made no bad decision when he elected to die instead of such a woman. For when Ptolemy[1] the king offered to share his crown with her and sought her hand in marriage, she refused him, and remained a widow. In this state she lost most of her children, but three survived; one daughter, who married Scipio the Younger, and two sons, Tiberius and Caius, whose lives I now write. These sons Cornelia reared with such scrupulous care that although confessedly no other Romans were so well endowed by nature, they were thought to owe their virtues more to education than to nature.

II. Now, just as, in spite of the likeness between Castor and Pollux as they are represented in sculpture and painting, there is a certain difference of shape between the boxer and the runner, so in the case of these young Romans, along with their strong resemblance to one another in bravery and self-command, as

---

1. Probably Ptolemy VI., surnamed Philometor, king of Egypt 181–146 B.C.

[75]

Chapter 3
A Roman Matron
and Her
Revolutionary
Sons: Cornelia
(Second Century
B.C.E.), and
Tiberius (163–133
B.C.E.), and Gaius
Gracchus
(154–121 B.C.E.)

well as in liberality, eloquence, and magnanimity, in their actions and political careers great unlikenesses blossomed out, as it were, and came to light. Therefore I think it not amiss to set these forth before going further.

In the first place, then, as regards cast of features and look and bearing, Tiberius was gentle and sedate, while Caius was high-strung and vehement, so that even when haranguing the people the one stood composedly in one spot, while the other was the first Roman to walk about upon the rostra and pull his toga off his shoulder as he spoke. So Cleon the Athenian is said to have been the first of the popular orators to strip away his mantle and smite his thigh. In the second place, the speech of Caius was awe-inspiring and passionate to exaggeration, while that of Tiberius was more agreeable and more conducive to pity. The style also of Tiberius was pure and elaborated to a nicety, while that of Caius was persuasive and ornate. So also as regards their table and mode of life, Tiberius was simple and plain, while Caius, although temperate and austere as compared with others, in contrast with his brother was ostentatious and fastidious. Hence men like Drusus found fault with him because he bought silver dolphins at twelve hundred and fifty drachmas the pound. Again, their tempers were no less different than their speech. Tiberius was reasonable and gentle, while Caius was harsh and fiery, so that against his better judgment he was often carried away by anger as he spoke, raising his voice to a high pitch and uttering abuse and losing the thread of discourse. Wherefore, to guard against such digressions, he employed an intelligent servant, Licinius, who stood behind him when he was speaking, with a sounding instrument for giving the tones of the voice their pitch. Whenever this servant noticed that the voice of Caius was getting harsh and broken with anger, he would give out a soft keynote, on hearing which Caius would at once remit the vehemence of his passion and of his speech, grow gentle, and show himself easy to recall.

III. The differences between them, then, were of this nature; but as regards bravery in the face of the enemy, just dealings with subject peoples, scrupulous fidelity in public office, and restraint in pleasurable indulgence, they were exactly alike. Tiberius, however, was nine years older than his brother; and this set a different period for the political activity of each, and more than anything else vitiated their undertakings. They did not rise to eminence at the same time, and so did not combine their powers into one. Such an united power would have proved irresistibly great. We must therefore give an account of each by himself, and of the elder first. . . .

DOCUMENT FOUR

PLUTARCH

Life of Tiberius Gracchus

In this portion of his biographies of Tiberius and Gaius, Plutarch describes Tiberius's motives for proposing legislation to reform landholding. According to this account, what explains Tiberius's decision to take on this issue?

. . . But some put part of the blame upon Cornelia the mother of Tiberius, who often reproached her sons because the Romans still called her the mother-in-law of Scipio, but not yet the mother of the Gracchi. Others again say that a certain Spurius Postumius was to blame. He was of the same age as Tiberius, and a rival of his in reputation as an advocate; and when Tiberius came back from his campaign and found that his rival had far outstripped him in reputation and influence and was an object of public admiration, he determined, as it would seem, to outdo him by engaging in a bold political measure which would arouse great expectations among the people. But his brother Caius, in a certain pamphlet [letter], has written that as Tiberius was passing through Tuscany on his way to Numantia, and observed the dearth of inhabitants in the country, and that those who tilled its soil or tended its flocks there were imported barbarian slaves, he then first conceived the public policy which was the cause of countless ills to the two brothers. However, the energy and ambition of Tiberius were most of all kindled by the people themselves, who posted writings on porticoes, housewalls, and monuments, calling upon him to recover for the poor the public land.

IX. He did not, however, draw up his law by himself, but took counsel with the citizens who were foremost in virtue and reputation, among whom were Crassus the pontifex maximus, Mucius Scaevola the jurist, who was then consul, and Appius Claudius, his father-in-law. And it is thought that a law dealing with injustice and rapacity so great was never drawn up in milder and gentler terms. For men who ought to have been punished for their disobedience and to have surrendered with payment of a fine the land which they were illegally enjoying, these men it merely ordered to abandon their injust acquisitions upon being paid their value, and to admit into ownership of them such citizens as needed assistance. But although the rectification of the wrong was so considerate, the people were satisfied to let bygones be bygones if they could be secure from such wrong in the future; the men of wealth and substance, however, were led by their greed to hate the law, and by their wrath and contentiousness to hate the lawgiver, and tried to dissuade the people by alleging that Tiberius was introducing a re-distribution of land for the confusion of the body politic, and was stirring up a general revolution.

Chapter 3
A Roman Matron
and Her
Revolutionary
Sons: Cornelia
(Second Century
B.C.E.), and
Tiberius (163–133
B.C.E.), and Gaius
Gracchus
(154–121 B.C.E.)

But they accomplished nothing; for Tiberius, striving to support a measure which was honourable and just with an eloquence that would have adorned even a meaner cause, was formidable and invincible, whenever, with the people crowding around the rostra, he took his stand there and pleaded for the poor. "The wild beasts that roam over Italy," he would say, "have every one of them a cave or lair to lurk in; but the men who fight and die for Italy enjoy the common air and light, indeed, but nothing else; houseless and homeless they wander about with their wives and children. And it is with lying lips that their imperators exhort the soldiers in their battles to defend sepulchres and shrines from the enemy; for not a man of them has an hereditary altar, not one of all these many Romans an ancestral tomb, but they fight and die to support others in wealth and luxury, and though they are styled masters of the world, they have not a single clod of earth that is their own."

X. Such words as these, the product of a lofty spirit and genuine feeling, and falling upon the ears of a people profoundly moved and fully aroused to the speaker's support, no adversary of Tiberius could successfully withstand. . . .

--- **DOCUMENT FIVE** ---

Accounts Describing Tiberius's Land Reforms and Responses to Them

LIVY
SUMMARIES
9 B.C.E.

In this summary, Livy describes Tiberius's land reforms, probably using as his source Polybius's history written at the time of the Gracchi. What is the tone of this summary? How do you think Livy felt about the Gracchan "revolution"?

. . . LVIII. Tiberius Sempronius Gracchus, a tribune of the commons, carried a land law against the desires of the senate and the order of knights, to the effect that no one should occupy more than a thousand acres of public land; Gracchus then went so insane as to remove from office by special enactment his colleague Marcus Octavius, who was supporting the other side of the controversy; Gracchus also had himself, his brother Gaius Gracchus, and Appius Claudius his father-in-law elected as the board of three in charge of distributing the land. He also proposed a second land law, in order to put more land at his disposal, that the same commissioners should judge which land was public and which private.

APPIAN
CIVIL WARS

Although he was a lawyer by profession, the Greek scholar Appian (ca. 95–165 C.E.) wrote a history of Rome based on secondary sources he had read. In the second part of this reading selection, he also describes Tiberius's ideas and goals in land reform, as well as the violence that eventually led to his death. In what ways does Appian differ from the previous sources that describe Tiberius's character, his motives, and the results of his legislation?

. . . 11. What Gracchus had in his mind in proposing the measure was not money, but men. Inspired greatly by the usefulness of the work, and believing that nothing more advantageous or admirable could ever happen to Italy, he took no account of the difficulties surrounding it. When the time for voting came he advanced many other arguments at considerable length and also asked them whether it was not just to let the commons divide the common property; whether a citizen was not worthy of more consideration at all times than a slave; whether a man who served in the army was not more useful than one who did not; and whether one who had a share in the country was not more likely to be devoted to the public interests. He did not dwell long on this comparison between freemen and slaves, which he considered degrading, but proceeded at once to a review of their hopes and fears for the country, saying that the Romans possessed most of their territory by conquest, and that they had hopes of occupying the rest of the habitable world; but now the question of greatest hazard was, whether they should gain the rest by having plenty of brave men, or whether, through their weakness and mutual jealousy, their enemies should take away what they already possessed. After exaggerating the glory and riches on the one side and the danger and fear on the other, he admonished the rich to take heed, and said that for the realization of these hopes they ought to bestow this very land as a free gift, if necessary, on men who would rear children, and not, by contending about small things, overlook larger ones; especially since for any labour they had spent they were receiving ample compensation in the undisputed title to 500 jugera each of free land, in a high state of cultivation, without cost, and half as much more for each son in the case of those who had sons. After saying much more to the same purport and exciting the poor, as well as others who were moved by reason rather than by the desire for gain, he ordered the clerk to read the proposed law. . . .

. . . As there was much strife over this question, Gracchus, who was getting the worst of it, adjourned the voting to the following day. In utter despair he went about in black, though still in office, and led his son around the forum and introduced him to each man and committed him to their charge, as if he himself felt that death, at the hands of his enemies, were at hand.

Chapter 3
A Roman Matron
and Her
Revolutionary
Sons: Cornelia
(Second Century
B.C.E.), and
Tiberius (163–133
B.C.E.), and Gaius
Gracchus
(154–121 B.C.E.)

15. The poor when they had time to think were moved with deep sorrow, both on their own account (for they believed that they were no longer to live in a free estate under equal laws, but would be reduced to servitude by the rich), and on account of Gracchus himself, who was in such fear and torment in their behalf. So they all accompanied him with tears to his house in the evening, and bade him be of good courage for the morrow. Gracchus cheered up, assembled his partisans before daybreak, and communicated to them a signal to be displayed if there were need for fighting. He then took possession of the temple on the Capitoline hill, where the voting was to take place, and occupied the middle of the assembly. As he was obstructed by the other tribunes and by the rich, who would not allow the votes to be taken on this question, he gave the signal. There was a sudden shout from those who knew of it, and violence followed. Some of the partisans of Gracchus took position around him like body-guards. Others, having girded up their cloaks, seized the fasces and staves in the hands of the lictors and broke them in pieces. They drove the rich out of the assembly with such disorder and wounds that the tribunes fled from their places in terror, and the priests closed the doors of the temple. Many ran away pell-mell and scattered wild rumours. Some said that Gracchus had deposed all the other tribunes, and this was believed because none of them could be seen. Others said that he had declared himself tribune for the ensuing year without an election.

16. In these circumstances the Senate assembled at the temple of Fides. It is astonishing to me that they never thought of appointing a dictator in this emergency, although they had often been protected by the government of a single ruler in such times of peril; but a resource which had been found most useful in former times was never even recollected by the people, either then or later. After reaching such decision as they did reach, they marched up to the Capitol, Cornelius Scipio Nasica, the pontifex maximus, leading the way and calling out with a loud voice, "Let those who would save our country follow me." He wound the border of his toga about his head either to induce a greater number to go with him by the singularity of his appearance, or to make for himself, as it were, a helmet as a sign of battle for those who saw it, or in order to conceal himself from the gods on account of what he was about to do. When he arrived at the temple and advanced against the partisans of Gracchus they yielded out of regard for so excellent a citizen, and because they observed the Senators following with him. The latter wresting their clubs out of the hands of the Gracchans themselves, or breaking up benches and other furniture that had been brought for the use of the assembly, began beating them, and pursued them, and drove them over the precipice. In the tumult many of the Gracchans perished, and Gracchus himself, vainly circling round the temple, was slain at the door close by the statues of the kings. All the bodies were thrown by night into the Tiber.

17. So perished on the Capitol, and while still tribune, Gracchus, the son of that Gracchus who was twice consul, and of Cornelia, daughter of that Scipio

who robbed Carthage of her supremacy. He lost his life in consequence of a most excellent design too violently pursued; and this abominable crime, the first that was perpetrated in the public assembly, was seldom without parallels thereafter from time to time. On the subject of the murder of Gracchus the city was divided between sorrow and joy. Some mourned for themselves and for him, and deplored the present condition of things, believing that the commonwealth no longer existed, but had been supplanted by force and violence. Others considered that their dearest wishes were accomplished. . . .

DOCUMENT SIX

PLUTARCH

The Life of Gaius Gracchus

Plutarch continues his story of the lives of the Gracchi brothers, and in this segment, he describes Gaius's entry into politics and the substance of some of his legislation. What does he say about Gaius's reluctant entry into politics? How does he describe Gaius's reforms and the ways in which people responded to them?

. . . I. Caius Gracchus, at first, either because he feared his enemies, or because he wished to bring odium upon them, withdrew from the forum and lived quietly by himself, like one who was humbled for the present and for the future intended to live the same inactive life, so that some were actually led to denounce him for disliking and repudiating his brother's political measures. And he was also quite a stripling, for he was nine years younger than his brother, and Tiberius was not yet thirty when he died. But as time went on he gradually showed a disposition that was averse to idleness, effeminacy, wine-bibbing, and money-making; and by preparing his oratory to waft him as on swift pinions to public life, he made it clear that he was not going to remain quiet; and in defending Vettius, a friend of his who was under prosecution, he had the people about him inspired and frantic with sympathetic delight, and made the other orators appear to be no better than children. Once more, therefore, the nobles began to be alarmed, and there was much talk among them about not permitting Caius to be made tribune.

By accident, however, it happened that the lot fell on him to go to Sardinia as quaestor for Orestes the consul. This gave pleasure to his enemies, and did not annoy Caius. For he was fond of war, and quite as well trained for military service as for pleading in the courts. Moreover, he still shrank from public life and the rostra, but was unable to resist the calls to this career which came from the

Chapter 3
A Roman Matron
and Her
Revolutionary
Sons: Cornelia
(Second Century
B.C.E.), and
Tiberius (163–133
B.C.E.), and Gaius
Gracchus
(154–121 B.C.E.)

people and his friends. He was therefore altogether satisfied with this opportunity of leaving the city. And yet a strong opinion prevails that he was a demagogue pure and simple, and far more eager than Tiberius to win the favour of the multitude. But this is not the truth; nay, it would appear that he was led by a certain necessity rather than by his own choice to engage in public matters. And Cicero the orator also relates that Caius declined all office and had chosen to live a quiet life, but that his brother appeared to him in a dream and addressed him, saying: "Why, pray, dost thou hesitate, Caius? There is no escape; one life is fated for us both, and one death as champions of the people."

II. After reaching Sardinia, then, Caius gave proof of every excellence, and far surpassed all the other young men in conflicts with the enemy, in just dealings with the subject peoples, and in the good will and respect which he showed towards his commander, while in self-restraint, frugality, and industry, he excelled even his elders. . . .

. . . There are on record also many things which Caius said about her [Cornelia] in the coarse style of forensic speech, when he was attacking one of his enemies: "What," said he, "dost thou abuse Cornelia, who gave birth to Tiberius?" and since the one who had uttered the abuse was charged with effeminate practices, "With what effrontery," said Caius, "canst thou compare thyself with Cornelia? Hast thou borne such children as she did? And verily all Rome knows that she refrained from commerce with men longer than thou hast, though thou art a man." Such was the bitterness of his language, and many similar examples can be taken from his writings.

V. Of the laws which he proposed by way of gratifying the people and overthrowing the senate, one was agrarian, and divided the public land among the poor citizens; another was military, and ordained that clothing should be furnished to the soldiers at the public cost, that nothing should be deducted from their pay to meet this charge, and that no one under seventeen should be enrolled as a soldier; another concerned the allies, and gave the Italians equal suffrage rights with Roman citizens; another related to the supplies of grain, and lowered the market price to the poor; and another dealt with the appointment of judges. This last law most of all curtailed the power of the senators; for they alone could serve as judges in criminal cases, and this privilege made them formidable both to the common people and to the equestrian order. The law of Gracchus, however, added to the membership of the senate, which was three hundred, three hundred men from the equestrian order, and made service as judges a prerogative of the whole six hundred. . . .

VI. The people not only adopted this law, but also entrusted to its author the selection of the judges who were to come from the equestrian order, so that he found himself invested with something like monarchical power, and even the senate consented to follow his counsel. But when he counselled them, it was always in support of measures befitting their body; . . .

He also introduced bills for sending out colonies, for constructing roads, and for establishing public granaries, making himself director and manager of all

[82]

these undertakings, and showing no weariness in the execution of all these different and great enterprises; nay, he actually carried out each one of them with an astonishing speed and power of application, as if it were his sole business, so that even those who greatly hated and feared him were struck with amazement at the powers of achievement and accomplishment which marked all that he did. And as for the multitude, they were astonished at the very sight, when they beheld him closely attended by a throng of contractors, artificers, ambassadors, magistrates, soldiers, and literary men, with all of whom he was on easy terms, preserving his dignity while showing kindliness, and rendering properly to every man the courtesy which was due from him, ...

DOCUMENT SEVEN

Fragments of Speeches of Gaius Gracchus
(123 B.C.E.)

In these fragments of his speeches, Gaius Gracchus is apparently describing his own behavior during his service in the provinces. While he denounces the sins of other aristocrats of the time, he also warns the people of Rome to beware of certain kinds of "politicians." By giving a description of his own admirable behavior, how is he able to show the flaws of others in high public office? What are the things about politicians that he warns the Roman people about?

. . . I so comported myself in my province as I judged to be to your advantage, and not as I thought would best suit my own interest. I kept no extravagant table, no strikingly pretty boys surrounded me, your own children conducted themselves in my company more properly than even at army headquarters;

I so conducted myself in my province that no one could truthfully say that I had accepted a penny more than was my proper due, or that anyone had been put to expense on my account. I spent two years there. If ever a prostitute crossed my threshold, or anybody's serving-boy was solicited on my behalf, then you may reckon me the most worthless man alive. When I held myself back so chastely from their servants, by that token you can reflect how you should think I behaved myself with your own children.

The money-belts which I took out with me full of silver were empty when I brought them home; others took out great jars full of wine, and brought them back home again stuffed with silver. . . .

If, men of Rome, you are prepared to use your intelligence and common sense, you will realize that there is not one of us politicians who comes here without having his price. All of us who address you are looking for something, no one comes before you on any matter except to take something away with

Chapter 3
A Roman Matron
and Her
Revolutionary
Sons: Cornelia
(Second Century
B.C.E.), and
Tiberius (163–133
B.C.E.), and Gaius
Gracchus
(154–121 B.C.E.)

him. As for myself, who advocate that you should increase your revenues in order that you may the more easily meet your own needs and those of our country, I am not here for nothing. But what I seek from you is not money but your good esteem, and honour. Those who come here to persuade you to reject this bill are not after honour from you, but money from Nicomedes. And those who seek to persuade you to accept this bill are not after your good esteem, but a rich reward from Mithridates to put in their pockets. As for those from our same place and our same order who hold their peace, they are the most cunning of all: they take their price from everyone, and cheat everyone. You suppose that they are far above such things, you give them your confidence as being high-minded men. But the agents of King Nicomedes and King Mithridates think that it is in their rulers' interests that they maintain silence, and so they shower them with gifts and money. There is a story that once upon a time in Greece a dramatist was preening himself on being paid a whole talent for one play he had written; but Demades, the finest public speaker in the land, replied: 'So you think it wonderful that your words have earned you a talent? Let me tell you that I have been paid ten talents by a king just to keep my mouth shut.' It is just the same now: these gentlemen are being very highly paid for their silence.

DOCUMENT EIGHT

Fragments of Cornelia's Letters
(Probably Preserved by Cornelius Nepos in the First Century B.C.E.)

These fragments, which are probably portions of the famous letters Cornelia wrote, address Gaius about the time he was planning to stand for tribune in 124. What does she say about his political plans in the first fragment? What is her tone and message in the second piece? Why do you think she might have written to him in this way?

(A)

You will say that it is a beautiful thing to avenge one's enemies. No one thinks this more important or more beautiful than I do, but only if one can pursue such an undertaking and keep the safety of the republic intact. But insofar as this cannot happen, during much of the time and in many places our enemies will not perish; they will continue to exist just as they are now—better than the republic should go to wrack and ruin.

(B)

If I could think of an oath, I would swear that—except for those who killed Tiberius Gracchus—no enemy has given me more trouble and vexation over these matters than you. It was appropriate that you—of all the children I had before—should sustain their duties and take care that I should have as little disturbance as possible in my old age, and that whatever things you do, you should especially want your actions to be pleasing to me, and that you should regard it wrong to do anything against my judgment on important matters, especially since only a small part of my life remains. Can't even this brief space of time aid in preventing you from opposing me and from ruining the republic? When will there be a respite? When will our family cease its madness? When will there be able to be moderation in this affair? When will we stop both having vexations and offering to desist from them? When will we be thoroughly ashamed that the republic is shaken up and thrown into turmoil?

But if this cannot happen at all, then seek the tribuneship—when I am dead. For my sake, do whatever you please when I am no longer alive to feel the effects. When I am dead, you will make the appropriate offerings to me and call upon me as your ancestral deity. Will it not at that time shame you to seek fulfillment of prayers by those deities whom, while they were alive and present, you treated as abandoned and deserted? Let not Jupiter allow you to persevere in these matters, nor such madness enter your mind. But if you do persevere, I fear that throughout your life you will take on so much work—through your own fault—that at no time will you be able to enjoy yourself.

DOCUMENT NINE

PLUTARCH

Life of Gaius Gracchus

In the conclusion to his biography of the Gracchi brothers, Plutarch describes the response to the deaths of the brothers by the people. He then describes Cornelia's remaining days. According to Plutarch, what was the popular reaction to the two brothers? Do you think Plutarch sees them as heroes or villains? What impression does he give you about Cornelia after the death of her sons?

. . . [A] people [the Romans] which was humble and cowed at the time when the Gracchi fell, but soon afterwards showed how much it missed them and longed for them. For it had statues of the brothers made and set up in a conspicuous

[85]

place, consecrated the places where they were slain, and brought thither offerings of all the first-fruits of the seasons, nay, more, many sacrificed and fell down before their statues every day, as though they were visiting the shrines of gods.

XIX. And further, Cornelia is reported to have borne all her misfortunes in a noble and magnanimous spirit, and to have said of the sacred places where her sons had been slain that they were tombs worthy of the dead which occupied them. She resided on the promontory called Misenum, and made no change in her customary way of living. She had many friends, and kept a good table that she might show hospitality, for she always had Greeks and other literary men about her, and all the reigning kings interchanged gifts with her. She was indeed very agreeable to her visitors and associates when she discoursed to them about the life and habits of her father Africanus, but most admirable when she spoke of her sons without grief or tears, and narrated their achievements and their fate to all enquirers as if she were speaking of men of the early days of Rome. Some were therefore led to think that old age or the greatness of her sorrows had impaired her mind and made her insensible to her misfortunes, whereas, really, such persons themselves were insensible how much help in the banishment of grief mankind derives from a noble nature and from honourable birth and rearing, as well as of the fact that while Fortune often prevails over virtue when it endeavours to ward off evils, she cannot rob virtue of the power to endure those evils with calm assurance.

The Imperial Model:
Augustus né Gaius Octavius
(63 B.C.E.–14 C.E.)
and Livia Drusilla (58 B.C.E.–29 C.E.)

■ SETTING THE STAGE

Rome's expansion within Italy and its conquests of the other peoples and states of the Mediterranean world led to profound changes in its political and social institutions, values, and sense of purpose during the first century B.C.E. At the beginning of this century, the power of the Roman state was shifting away from the Senate, which was composed of men from traditionally prominent and wealthy families, to individual senators turned military commanders and their loyal legions. In the early part of the century, these two powerful factions struggled for control of the Roman

[87]

Chapter 4
The Imperial
Model: Augustus
né Gaius
Octavius
(63 B.C.E.–14 C.E.)
and Livia
Drusilla
(58 B.C.E.–29 C.E.)

state and, with their supporters, eventually went to war against each other. Civil war was halted temporarily when Julius Caesar (100–44 B.C.E.), one of the most powerful and popular of the Roman senators and generals, disobeyed the orders of the Senate, crossed the Rubicon River in 49 B.C.E., and took control of Rome and its political institutions.

Caesar's success was short lived. His assumption of the title Perpetual Dictator, his contempt for the Senate as the ruling body for Rome, and his control of the state prompted a group of senators, led by Marcus Junius Brutus (85–42 B.C.E.) and Gaius Cassius, to plan and execute his assassination. The conspirators killed Caesar on March 15, 44 B.C.E., on the steps of the Roman Senate, and with this act civil war resumed. Strife continued for another thirteen years and ended when Caesar's grand nephew and adopted son, Gaius Octavius (63 B.C.E.–14 C.E.), as Augustus was then named, defeated the other heir apparent, the loyal lieutenant to Caesar, Marcus Antonius (83–30 B.C.E.) and the Egyptian queen and his ally, Cleopatra VII (69–30 B.C.E.), at Actium in 31 B.C.E. With this victory against the only other claimant to Caesar's legacy, no person stood in Octavius's way to control the Roman state. There was a bigger obstacle to conquer, however, to assume power: the political traditions of the Roman Republic. Octavius would have to find a way to concentrate power in his person, as dictator, and maintain the fiction that Rome's republican traditions were still in place.

Octavius, later known as Augustus, brought to Rome a flair for reorganiz-ing and refashioning Roman institutions and values. His reforms and tactics resulted in the transformation of the fragmented, disintegrating, and contentious republic into a well-administered, cohesive, and secure imperial state. In this task, he was aided by his second wife, Livia Drusilla, the daughter of an illustrious Roman family with key alliances to leading senators, and a woman of acute political acumen and savvy. The political importance of marriage and family are well exemplified in their lives and relationships. In addition, their biographies provide the backdrop for the process through which Octavius and Livia created, shaped, and stabilized imperial rule in the Roman world.

As a masterful and imaginative promoter of his own greatness, Augustus employed some of Rome's foremost writers, artisans, and craftspeople to sing his praises throughout the Roman world. Writings by two poets, Horace (65–8 B.C.E.) and Virgil (70–19 B.C.E.), and the historian Livy (54 B.C.E.–17 C.E.) present Augustus and Rome, at this point in its development, in laudatory and heroic terms. In addition, Augustus narrated his achievements in *Res gestae* (*Things Accomplished*). These writings, as well as legal texts, public sculpture, and coins, are good sources to see the extent to which Augustus patronized the arts and propagandized to reserve a place in history for himself and his family. However, the historical record was augmented by the writings of two Roman historians, Suetonius (69–130/140? C.E.) and Tacitus (55–117? C.E.), and a Greek historian, Dio Cassius (155–235?), and they not only provided critical assessments of Augustus's rise to imperial greatness, but they also noted the roles that his wife, Livia, and other elite Roman women played in the founding and maintenance of the first Roman dynasty.

The historian Suetonius, writing several generations after Augustus's and Livia's deaths, had much to say about the political intrigues and personal lives of imperial Rome's rulers and their families. Suetonius and Tacitus represented Livia and other imperial women as operating capriciously and malevolently behind the political scenes, abusing their power and influence over their husbands, brothers, or fathers. Both these historians exploited the existing views and prejudices against women to arouse indignation over the usurpation of power from the Senate and its families by the Julio-Claudians. Most of the sources that detail personal conduct and public ideology carry the bias of their creators, privileged Roman males, who see imperial Roman women as disturbances and threats to Roman political order. Nonetheless, by detailing women's intrigues and political machinations, these sources reveal a political and social world where elite Roman women were socially and politically significant and often highly visible individuals.[1] The women of Augustus's family figured prominently in his ambitions and political plans for absolute power.[2]

▨ THE ACTORS:

GAIUS OCTAVIUS AND LIVIA DRUSILLA

Gaius Octavius was born on September 23, 63 B.C.E., to an affluent Roman family that belonged to the equestrian or knightly class, the second highest order in the republic. This class was composed of men who possessed large tracts of land and whose family origins were mostly outside Rome proper. They were originally discouraged and thwarted from entering public service by men of the first order, the senatorial class. By the first century B.C.E., equestrians were becoming senators. Octavius's father, also Gaius Octavius, was elected to the Senate and rose to the office of praetorship, the rank below the consulship. His mother, Atia, was the daughter of Julia, the sister of Julius Caesar. His mother's family belonged to the senatorial order, and young Gaius's great uncle, Julius Caesar, was an influential senator and general. Through his mother's family, Octavius could claim descent by blood from Venus and the Julian clan. Ascending the political ladder in Rome required connections with eminent men, usually through marriage, as well as a sizable fortune and civilian and military office holding.

According to Tacitus, Octavius received a proper education as a young child from his mother Atia. His father was governor of Macedonia from 61 to

1. Judith Hallett, *Fathers and Daughters in Roman Society* (Princeton, N.J.: Princeton University Press, 1984), p. 12.

2. Susan E. Wood, *Imperial Women* (London: Brill, 1999), p. 27.

Chapter 4
The Imperial
Model: Augustus
né Gaius
Octavius
(63 B.C.E.–14 C.E.)
and Livia
Drusilla
(58 B.C.E.–29 C.E.)

59 B.C.E. and then died shortly after his return to Rome. The elder Gaius appeared to have had little influence on his son's upbringing, but the Greek historian, Dio Cassius, claimed that both parents predicted a grand future for their son (Document One). Like other elite Roman boys, Octavius was educated in Latin and Greek, rhetoric, and the art of politics and governance. Despite the various stories about his relationship with his great uncle, Julius Caesar, Octavius probably did not meet him until he was 15 or 16 years of age. His mother's status as Caesar's niece and as a newly widowed woman meant that she would have to remarry, and that marriage should create some type of political advantage for the Julian family. In 57 or 56, Atia married the Roman consul L. Marcius Phillipus. Phillipus managed to steer a middle course between Rome's powerful factions, never became a major political player, and remained neutral during the civil war between Pompeius and Caesar in the 40s.

Octavius, on the other hand, could not remain neutral. Linked to Caesar through his mother, his allegiance was made clear when he delivered the funeral oration for his grandmother and Caesar's sister, Julia. Funerals and their orations were as much political gestures as they were acts of piety, and an individual's and his or her family's noble deeds were remembered. Julia's death, coming at the same time that Caesar was ending his command in Gaul and hoping to return as consul, provided the Julian clan with a platform to remind Caesar's supporters and detractors of his family's powerful

place and connections in the Roman state. Octavius witnessed and took note of the political maneuverings. He accompanied his great uncle in the triumphant military procession through the streets of Rome in 46 B.C.E. after Caesar's defeat of his enemies in Spain and North Africa. At age 18, Octavius was sent to Apollonia, on the Albanian coast, to complete his academic and military training. While not having the cachet of Athens as a learned place, Apollonia was home to five Roman legions whose officers were frequent guests of Octavius. When word of Caesar's assassination reached him there, Octavius returned to Rome to find that he had been adopted by Caesar before his death. Taking the name Gaius Julius Caesar Octavianus, Octavius embraced his connection to the murdered dictator and staked his claim to Caesar's legacy.

Octavius met resistance from one of Caesar's loyal lieutenants, Marcus Antonius, who had expected to be his benefactor's heir. As result of this betrayal, Marcus Antonius refused to hand over Caesar's papers and assets. Octavius had to find the financial means to honor the Roman people on his great uncle's behalf. For this task, he needed money, loyal supporters, and a greater understanding of Rome's political intrigues. As Caesar's heir, he was able to attract to his side wealthy landowners and many soldiers, equestrians, and freedmen who had supported his great uncle. By sponsoring the Games of Victory of Caesar, which were immensely popular public games, Octavius demonstrated to the Senate that he had not only inherited the dead dictator's name, he had also inherited the loyalty of Caesar's allies.

Fearing Antonius's ambitions to dictatorial powers, the Senate believed that the inexperienced young man with the large army could be easily manipulated and they decided to back him. Cicero stated, "We will praise and honor the youngster and then get rid of him." Led by Cicero, the Senate made Octavius a senator and backed him in his first military campaign against Antonius. After driving Antonius and his army across the Alps in 43 B.C.E., Octavius marched on Rome with his army and demanded that he be made consul. He broke with the Roman tradition that required a man to progress gradually through political and military offices before assuming the consulship. Cicero's prediction could not have been further from the truth.

Octavius discarded his Senate allies and made a deal with Antonius and another of Caesar's lieutenants, Lepidus, to form a triumvirate. The Senate sanctioned this power-sharing agreement. Designed to last for five years with complete dictatorial powers, these three used their office to divide the empire among them and to root out and execute their enemies. Over 300 senators, including Cicero, and 2,000 equestrians were put to death.

Killing his enemies was not enough for Octavius. In 42 B.C.E., he pushed through a law in the Senate that proclaimed Caesar a god. By extension, this proclamation made Octavius the son of a divinity and further legitimized his claims to power. He would use the designation "Caesar Son of a God" on the coins he issued. Yet complete power would not be Octavius's until he vanquished all rivals for control of the empire. His ambitions and those of his rivals plunged the empire into another twelve years of civil war.

During this period of civil war, Octavius sought alliances with men who had noble power, influence, and wealth.[3] Marriage, an important political strategy, gained Augustus a temporary truce with the undisputed ruler of Rome's seas, Sextus Pompeius (Pompey the Great's son) and his other rival Antonius. In 40 B.C.E., he married the aunt of Pompeius's wife, Scribonia, and arranged for the marriage of his sister, Octavia (69 B.C.E.–11 B.C.E.), to Antonius. These marriage alliances did not spare the Romans from another ten years of civil war. Beginning in 39 B.C.E., Octavius waged war against Pompeius until his naval fleet defeated Pompeius's fleet off the coast of Sicily in 36 B.C.E. Soon afterward Octavius drove Lepidus, the third triumvir, from the political scene. Only Antonius stood in his way for complete control of the Roman world.

Having married his wife for political reasons, Octavius divorced Scribonia soon after he went to war with her nephew in 39 B.C.E.—on the same day that she gave birth to their daughter, Julia (39 B.C.E.–14 C.E.?). During his marriage to Scribonia, Octavius had fallen in love with Livia Drusilla (58 B.C.E.–29 C.E.), the pregnant wife of Tiberius Claudius Nero and daughter

3. Pat Southern, *Augustus* (New York: Routledge, 1998), p. 74.

Chapter 4
The Imperial
Model: Augustus
né Gaius
Octavius
(63 B.C.E.–14 C.E.)
and Livia
Drusilla
(58 B.C.E.–29 C.E.)

of another distinguished Roman, Marcus Livius Drusus Claudianus. Her mother was Alfidia, the daughter of a rich counselor from the Italian city of Fundi. Livia's father had not been a supporter of Octavius or Antonius and had fought against both. Her first husband traded allegiances from Caesar to his assassins, from Pompeius to Antonius, and finally to Octavius. During her husband's alliance with Octavius around 39 B.C.E., Livia and Octavius met.

How their affair began is unknown but its notoriety is well documented. Soon after the open affair began, they began to live together. Livia was pregnant by her first husband with their second son, Tiberius. Scribonia, Octavius's wife, was pregnant with their first and only child, Julia. Octavius's motivation for such a flagrant disregard for respectability remains unknown. But the fact that his marriage to Scribonia was a political match that no longer benefitted him and his well-known dislike for her, combined with the prospect of marrying a woman from one of Rome's noblest families, have been cited as reasons for his conduct.[4] The circumstances of the open affair and the unorthodox events surrounding the marriage provided Octavius's opponents with ample ammunition (Document Two). However, Antonius's conduct toward his wife, and Octavius's sister, Octavia, was hardly exemplary.

In the early years of Octavia's and Antonius's marriage, Octavia joined her husband in Athens, the administrative center of the eastern provinces. The marriage produced two daughters and a significant truce between Antonius and Octavius. When Octavius vanquished his challengers in the west, he turned his attention to the east and Antonius. During his marriage to his rival's sister, Antonius remained politically and romantically allied with the Queen of Egypt, Cleopatra VII. Octavius used this liaison to turn Roman public opinion against Antonius. During an unsuccessful campaign against one of Rome's eastern enemies, Octavia hurried to Athens to bring reinforcements and money to her husband. Antonius did not meet her and remained in Egypt with his ally and lover.

Calling this behavior mistreatment, Octavius played on the Roman Senate's disdain for Cleopatra. The Senate was suspicious of Antonius's monarchical ambitions and his liaison with a foreign queen. His public rejection of Octavia, a noble, virtuous, and loyal Roman woman, only furthered their growing distrust of Antonius. To contrast his respect for Roman women with his rival's disdain for his sister, Octavius granted to both his wife and his sister the right to be represented in public statuary, the right to control their own financial affairs, and legal protection of their persons.[5] He made sure that public statues of these two women were quickly commissioned and displayed to publicize his respect. Antonius did not help himself when

4. Marleen Flory, "*Abducta Neroni Uxor*: The Historiographical Tradition on the Marriage of Octavian and Livia," *Transactions of the American Philological Association* 118 (1988), 343–359 (specifically pages 345–346).

5. Wood, p. 33.

he divorced Octavia in 32 B.C.E. and had her evicted from his house in Rome. Taking their two daughters with her, Octavia left the house with poise and dignity (Document Three).

Octavius's campaign of slowly sullying Antonius's reputation climaxed when he read Antonius's last will and testament to the Senate. How he obtained it or whether Octavius forged parts of it are not known. At the meeting of the Senate, Octavius accused Antonius of harboring monarchical ambitions and wanting a separate empire in the east. He highlighted the clauses showing that Antonius wished to be buried in Alexandria and that Cleopatra's children were named his heirs, thus confirming the Senate's and the public's worst fears—that part of the Roman empire would come under foreign and female rule. War was immediately declared against Cleopatra, not Antonius, in 32 B.C.E. The following year, Cleopatra and her consort were defeated at Actium. In 30 B.C.E. Octavius conquered Egypt, making him the undisputed leader of the Greco-Roman world.

■ ACT I:

FROM REPUBLIC TO EMPIRE

The world that Octavius occupied was one that had been scarred by almost a century of war waged on behalf of aristocratic rivals for power. His faction, which slowly came together after his marriage to Livia and his successive victories over his rivals, now dominated the Roman Senate, which approved all of Octavius's political reforms. He also helped his cause in the Senate by reducing the number of senators from 1,000 to 800, getting rid of those who opposed him, and distributing land to veterans of his army. Surveying all that he had conquered, Octavius believed that the Roman Empire, with its collection of lands, needed to be integrated and administered by a single, central authority instead of leaving its development to ad hoc and piecemeal decisions and edicts.[6]

During the wars, the Italian peninsula, its cities and its peoples, had suffered dearly. The countryside could not support the hungry city-dwellers and Rome in particular needed a regular and dependable supply of food. Socially, Roman customs, traditions, and religious practices had to be revived and revitalized. Politically, the vast majority of people wished for stability, security of property and person, protection from internal and external threats, and a period of peace so that they could reclaim their everyday lives.[7] To initiate reform that could address these demands, Octavius had to reinvent himself. The image of ruthless military commander vanquishing all who opposed him had to be shed. Accepting indefinite terms of an office or one that explicitly bestowed indefinite rule, like Perpetual Dictator, evoked images of kingship or Caesar's undisguised absolute authority,

6. Southern, p. 102.

7. Ibid., pp. 103–104.

Chapter 4
*The Imperial
Model: Augustus
né Gaius
Octavius
(63 B.C.E.–14 C.E.)
and Livia
Drusilla
(58 B.C.E.–29 C.E.)*

and they were not options for him (Document Four).

With such thoughts in mind, Octavius formally announced in 27 B.C.E. that it was time for the Senate and the Roman people to decide the fate of the Republic. The Senate kept republican traditions and recognized Octavius's undisputed power by electing him consul yet again. In addition, the Senate conferred on him the honorary name of Augustus. Once Augustus felt that his position was secure, he declined the consulship and embraced the title of princeps, a title bestowed upon the most prestigious man in the Senate, the person that other senators looked to for counsel and leadership. The actual power that Augustus held was never clarified and the titles that he wore and then discarded obscured the fact that he had established one-man rule, eviscerated the Republic's institutions, and created the Roman imperial state. In his testimonial to his accomplishments, *Res gestae,* Augustus claimed that he ruled because of his moral authority, dispensing wisdom and advice to beings of lesser experience and knowledge. Not only did he embrace the title of princeps but the title conferred upon him by the Senate in 2 B.C.E., *pater patriae* (father of the country) (Document Five).

Claiming such authority and accepting these titles did not offend or threaten existing political traditions. The founders of the Republic had conceived the state as an extension of the Roman household, the basic unit of society, and the foundation of government. In the Roman home, the adult male possessed authority over wives, children, and servants, or *patria potes-* *tas* (power of a father). The Republic was based on the concept that male heads of household represented their families and sat in the Senate. The senators, as the most privileged males in society, surrounded themselves with men from less powerful families—clients—and the senators held authority over these lesser males, who themselves had the power of the father in their households. The patron, the more privileged male, provided help and assistance when necessary to the client. In return, the client owed him financially and politically. A man could be both a patron and client and, as a result, citizen males were connected through an intricate network of personal relationships. Thus, the Republic that Augustus inherited was a patriarchal society and to designate its most accomplished male "father of the country" was not outside the understanding of most Romans.

Augustus's reforms went beyond changing Rome's administrative and political structures. He wished to revitalize Rome's moral and religious institutions, especially those pertaining to marriage, procreation, and the family. During his long rule, Augustus enacted extensive social legislation that attempted to restore traditional Roman virtues, encourage thrift and stamp out corruption, secure the Roman elite's dominant position in politics, and restore the Roman family.[8] In these endeavors he was greatly aided by Livia, his wife.

8. Ibid., p. 146.

▪ ACT II:

CIVIC MORALITY IN THE EARLY EMPIRE

Like other Romans, Augustus associated private and public morality with the maintenance of a well-ordered state and pleasing the gods. To appease the gods, he began a crusade to revive temperance and morality, especially among the traditional ruling families. To maintain the stability of the state, he believed that the patrician class had to be replenished and revitalized. His laws concerning marriage, procreation, and the family assumed that Rome's elites were deliberately avoiding marriage and parenthood to such an extent that the continuity of the ruling class was at risk.[9] Thus, his social legislation was as much about ensuring that the patrician class replicated itself as it was about restoring Roman values.

Noble men appeared to be shunning legitimate marriage in favor of the single life, taking pleasure when and wherever they wished, and entertaining and cultivating rich relatives and friends while waiting for their inheritances to materialize. In addition, when elite men did marry, they did not always marry women of their class. By law, senators were prohibited from marrying outside their class. In an argument with Augustus as reported by the historian Dio Cassius, senators maintained that Roman women were difficult and not easily controlled. Therefore, they resorted to marrying slaves whom they had freed. These slaves owed everything to them

and thus would be more willing to obey their husbands. Augustus appeared to offer little practical advice in this exchange.[10] Being the adopted son of Julius Caesar and having a wife who also seemed to be playing by the rules relieved Augustus of having to deal with this problem. The only immediate flaw in this highly public marriage and perfect imperial family was the inability of Livia and Augustus to conceive a child.

Another symbol of social disorder and disharmony was the elite Roman woman who had moved outside the control of her father, husband, or brother and who had assumed control over her person and property, abandoned her domestic duties, and preferred childlessness to children and family. During the civil unrest, Roman noblewomen did have greater public visibility and wider roles. Their men were absent from the home front, performing administrative duties in distant provinces, going on military campaigns, or in flight and exile. In their absence, women had to attend to the family business, negotiate with the authorities on behalf of their absent husbands to stay execution or bring them out of exile, or send finances and troops to their husbands. Roman women were also gaining more power over property and their persons as marriage laws and customs underwent dramatic changes during the late Republic.

Prior to the third century B.C.E. women were legally transferred from their father's authority *(patria potestas)* to their husband's when they married.

---

9. Susan Dixon, *The Roman Mother* (Norman: University of Oklahoma Press, 1988), p. 23.

10. Southern, p. 148.

However, "this ancient form of marriage called marriage with *manus* had been largely superceded by the so-called free marriage by the third century B.C.E."[11] Free marriage, or marriage without *manus* resulted from the transformation of Rome from a small republic into a world empire. During the third and second centuries, female wealth increased as a result of a decrease in the male population. Because of the high casualty rates from Rome's wars of expansion, women now inherited land, property, and wealth without competition from brothers. When a Roman woman married without *manus,* she and her property and wealth remained under the authority of her father. Thus, free marriage may be interpreted as a way for women's fathers to retain control over the wealth of their daughters and not transfer this wealth to a son-in-law and his family.[12]

Free marriage gave to women considerable leverage against the authority of their husbands and enhanced their property rights. However, it did not make a woman legally independent. Theoretically, she was still under the authority of her father. In reality, daughters usually outlived their fathers, and the Roman state had to find a substitute for the father because a woman could not live outside male authority and she did not have independent status before the law. If the father was not available, the state appointed a guardian who would perform the function of paterfamilias.

The strict requirement of guardianship for women living outside male *potestas* was evaded by assertive Roman women until it became an empty form. This development meant that some women could inherit great wealth and could therefore wield informal social and political power. But it must be remembered that these elite women of the late Republic and early Roman Empire, like all Roman women, did not have formal political rights and had no legal status.

Bonds between families were often solidified through marriage, and marriage arrangements were often political negotiations. Women married in such a manner, like Augustus's sister Octavia, asserted themselves on behalf of their father's or their husband's family. In other cases, political marriage and the absence of the husband for long periods of time meant that some women looked for liaisons outside marriage. Historians of the first century B.C.E. and C.E. would have their readers believe that women of this time lived to feed their sexual desires and to enjoy pleasures outside their marriages.[13] Augustus had promoted such images during his propaganda campaign against Marcus Antonius. He often depicted Antonius's ally and lover, the Egyptian queen Cleopatra, as a woman of insatiable appetites that extended from the bedroom to world domination.

Augustus's courtship of and marriage to Livia had provided fodder for their opponents during the civil war,

11. Anne Ewing Hickey, *Women of the Roman Aristocracy as Christian Monastics* (Ann Arbor, Mich.: UMI Research Press, 1987), p. 49.

12. Ibid., pp. 49–52.

13. Elaine Fantham, Helene Peet Foley, et al., *Women in the Classical World* (New York: Oxford University Press, 1994), p. 284.

but their indiscreet beginnings were overshadowed by their public show of marital harmony, fidelity, and proper behavior. "Ovid, the poet, justified Livia's earlier divorce by claiming that no husband but Augustus was worthy of her, while Horace describes her . . . as 'a women rejoicing in only one husband'"[14] (Document Six). Adhering to Augustan ideology, Livia represented herself as the ideal standard for upper-class women, borrowing symbols from Roman legend and mythology.

Weaving cloth for husband and children was a powerful symbol of a wife's virtue and devotion. The symbolism had come from the mythical story of Lucretia, a chaste upper-class wife of a Roman. According to the story, as it was retold by the historian Livy in his *History of Rome,* Lucretia's husband and his friends had been bragging about the virtuousness of their wives and to settle the dispute, the husbands called unexpectedly on their wives. Only Lucretia was at home spinning wool and making cloth; the other wives were out at dinner parties.

Livia played the role of "first lady" by setting a similar example of acceptable female behavior. She wove Augustus's garments to set an example for other Roman wives. Augustus appeared in public and bragged that his wife had spun and woven the clothing that he was wearing.[15] Livia also participated in public displays of marital harmony and togetherness. She often accompanied her husband on trips to the provinces and sometimes took her

son, Tiberius, with them. If he traveled without her, Livia made sure that her husband's homecoming was a public display.

Augustus utilized his family to provide both living and symbolic examples of the same messages that he wished to legislate. To celebrate his great successes and Rome's new-found stability and peace, the *Ara Pacis Augustae* (Altar of Augustan Peace) was built. On the south side of the altar, mortal woman and children were represented along with men for the first time in Roman public art. Of course, the people being depicted in the relief were members of the imperial family—Livia, Julia, Julia's children, and other family members. The procession not only symbolized Augustus's bringing of peace but that his family, through reproduction of heirs, would guarantee that transfer of power would be done peacefully through the prolific Julio-Claudian dynasty. Adopted by Augustus, Livia's son would inherit the throne from his stepfather, thus avoiding a struggle for power. In addition to public statuary and propaganda, Augustus sought to shape and regulate marriage, parenthood, and gender roles through legislation.

Augustus's legislative agenda revolved around two bills. The first, Lex Julia or "the Julian law on marriage between the orders," included laws on adultery and was introduced in 18 B.C.E. The second, *lex Papia Poppaea,* was an amended version of the first, passed twenty-five years later. This latter law was named after the two consuls who sponsored the bill in 9 C.E. Augustus brought into the public arena issues of marriage and reproduction,

14. Wood, p. 76.
15. Ibid., p. 77.

Chapter 4
The Imperial
Model: Augustus
né Gaius
Octavius
(63 B.C.E.–14 C.E.)
and Livia
Drusilla
(58 B.C.E.–29 C.E.)

which had been under private control and discretion. These laws penalized men who did not marry before the age of twenty-five and women who did not marry or who remained unmarried after the death of their husbands. Women were rewarded for having more than three children by bestowing upon them "the right of three children." This honor allowed them to be legal persons, without a male guardian. Augustus lectured men who did not have children and spoke of the state's need for married men who had children (Document Seven). Those who did have multiple children stood to gain a better public office. *Lex Julia* prohibited senators and their descendants from marrying outside their class. Writing in the third century, Ulpianus reported the spirit of this clause: "By the lex Julia senators and their descendants are forbidden to marry freedwomen, or women who have themselves followed the profession of the stage . . . ."[16]

Women's and men's behavior within marriage was also a matter of state scrutiny and regulation. Adultery was made a punishable offense, and a special court was created to review cases. It was the duty of the husband to report his adulterous wife or daughter. If he did not, he could be prosecuted. The law defined a noncompliant husband as a pimp and he could be tried as a man who lived off immoral earnings. A husband had sixty days to alert the court and if his wife was found guilty, it was his duty to divorce her or to kill her. An adulterous wife and her lover could be banished to different islands, with the woman obliged to wear the kind of short tunic worn by prostitutes. Wives could not independently accuse their husbands of adultery. These laws were not interested in equality but sought to bring women's sexual behavior in line with the standards of an idealized, traditional social order and to ensure the legitimacy of the offspring.

Underlying Augustan laws on marriage and reproduction was a reminder to the Roman elite that marriages should be contracted between proper social groups and that their property and political power must be transferred through familial lines. The continuous presence of Rome's elite families in government had created a prosperous and formidable imperial state, and Augustus wished to maintain the moral and social structures that had brought about this success. Augustan legislation could be applied to all citizens but the punishments were specifically designed to penalize the Roman elites.[17]

The effect that these laws had on Roman family life is not clear. Suetonius writes that Augustus "was unable to carry it [the lex Julia] out because of an open revolt against its provisions, until he had abolished or mitigated a part of the penalties, besides increasing the rewards [for more children] and allowing a three years exemption from the obligation to marry after the death of a husband or wife."[18] He did relax some of the re-

17. Dixon, p. 86.

16. Ulpianus, *Epitomé* pp. 13–14. Quoted in Fantham, p. 305.

18. Suetonius, *Augustus*, p. 34. Quoted in Fantham, p. 306.

strictions, but Augustus remained convinced that Roman morality had to be restored and he used his family to make this point.

Augustus had his own daughter, Julia, punished for adultery. Julia had been married twice to allies of Augustus. In 12 B.C.E., at the age of 27, her second husband died. Julia, who had given birth to three sons and two daughters in her second marriage, was exempted by law from marrying again. However, Augustus's political needs dictated that he arrange a marriage between his daughter and his heir apparent. Thus, he arranged a marriage between Julia and Tiberius, Livia's son. This arrangement meant that Tiberius had to leave a happy marriage. Complying with Augustus's wishes, Tiberius married Julia and lived with her long enough to produce one son. When the infant died, the couple ceased to live together and remained married in name only. Julia searched for love and sexual gratification outside her marriage. When Augustus heard of her infidelities, he threatened her with death. After a hearing, he banished her to an island from which she was never to return, and when he spoke of her, he portrayed her as a disease of his flesh.

Augustus's daughter was held to strict standards of female behavior, but Livia, while playing the perfect Roman wife, wielded uncontested and uncharacteristic power in the public arena. She represented what many of the senators had alluded to in their discussion about powerful Roman women. Livia had brought substantial wealth with her when she married Augustus and she was permitted by Roman law to control her own property. In addition, Augustus obtained unusual privileges for both his wife and his sister, Octavia, when he granted them the right to control their financial affairs, be represented in public statuary, and have the legal protection of their person, which was normally reserved for elected officials.[19] Luckily for Augustus, Livia and his sister used their financial resources to complement Augustus's policies. Livia also wished to demonstrate her piety and womanly virtue and used Augustus's revitalization of Roman religion as her public platform, a platform where women legitimately played a role. Using her wealth, Livia sponsored the construction of the Porticus Liviae, which celebrated good wives and the virtue of marital harmony. Her private sponsorship of this public building and many others set the example of how private wealth should be used to promote public interests, an issue Augustus believed was crucial to restoring the stability of the Roman state.[20]

Livia ventured into nontraditional arenas, partly because of her independent holdings and partly because of the evolving nature of Roman imperial politics. She invited into her house her extended family and clients from abroad. This included her two sons, Tiberius and Drusus, and Augustus's daughter Julia and her offspring. From this set of children and their children, the Julio-Claudian dynasty would be drawn. Livia's influence was reflected in the active role that she played in

19. Wood, p. 36.
20. Ibid., p. 78.

Chapter 4
The Imperial
Model: Augustus
né Gaius
Octavius
(63 B.C.E.–14 C.E.)
and Livia
Drusilla
(58 B.C.E.–29 C.E.)

Augustus's decisions concerning his heir. Suetonius remarked how this was "a clear case in which her private role as materfamilias intersected with public affairs."[21] Livia also cultivated a circle of women who had similar influence in public and private affairs. Her sister-in-law, Octavia, was one such woman, while others were clients, like the Jewish princess Salome, the sister of King Herod. Livia forged similar relationships as she traveled around the empire with her husband. Tacitus notes that these relationships, some of which resulted in Livia petitioning her husband on behalf of her clients, were appropriations of male authority (Document Eight). Ovid the poet, who had been exiled, accepted such power and asked Livia to petition Augustus to reduce the conditions of his exile.

Whatever the circumstance, Livia worked unceasingly for the interests of the imperial family and in particular for the future of her sons. After Augustus's two grandsons, whom he designated as heirs apparent, died unexpectedly, Tiberius appeared to be the logical heir to the throne. Tacitus argues in the *Annals* that Livia had somehow arranged for the deaths of Augustus's grandsons to clear the way for her son. Tacitus, writing 100 years later, wished to revise Livia's public image. Prior to Tacitus's *Annals,* Livia's public image as the ideal wife and mother was unchallenged. Tacitus was a harsh critic of Augustus's usurpation of power from the Senate and saw Livia's influence as another example of the corruption and distortion of Republican institutions and values under Augustus. Livia certainly did not deserve to be portrayed as a conniving and ruthless woman. Nor does she deserve the reputation as the ideal Roman woman. Livia wielded unprecedented power for a woman, just as her husband wielded unprecedented power for a Roman man. She and her husband seized the opportunities created by Rome's disintegrating social and political order and together they created a new institution that tolerated female authority for the good of the family— the imperial family.

■ FINALE

Livia and Augustus's relationship united family interests and the affairs of state. When Augustus fell sick in 14 C.E., she used her position as wife and mother to hurry to her husband's side and to recall Tiberius from his trip to the provinces. Awaiting the arrival of her son, Livia admitted very few people to her husband's death bed, and it was only after her son's arrival that public notice of her husband's death was announced. It is not known whether Augustus died before or after Tiberius's arrival, but Livia made sure that there would be no question concerning the transfer of imperial power. Tiberius was immediately named Augustus's successor by the Senate.

Augustus ensured his wife's continued influence and wealth in his will by adopting her into the Julian family, designating her as Julia Augusta, and

21. Ibid., p. 80.

[100]

removing any limitations on her rights to inherit a third of his estate. When Augustus was deified after his death, Livia was made the priestess of his cult. The senate tried to recognize her uncontested authority by conferring the title *Mater Patriae* (Mother of Her Country), but Tiberius vetoed this bill. He wished to avoid such nontraditional titles and honors that were too extravagant and too exalted, fearing the appearance of monarchical ambitions. Even when she died in 29 C.E. at the age of 86, Tiberius did not attend her funeral and did not allow her to be deified. Did Tiberius resent his mother's influence? Such emotions are impossible to discern but it was common knowledge that Tiberius owed his position to her and that until her death, her influence and authority were widely respected by members of the Senate, some of whom owed their lives to her because of her intercessions with Augustus and Tiberius on their behalf.

Augustus's initial successes rested on his ability to vanquish all of his enemies and to use his military strength to secure political rule. The Senate recognized this fact in 27 B.C.E. when Senators asked him to safeguard the Republic and awarded him the title of Augustus. But raw power was not his only ambition. Augustus refashioned himself into a defender of the Republic and of Roman traditions and values, and he reinforced this image with his modest behavior and restraint. He practiced patience and tact in his dealings with the Senate, giving the impression that it had important contributions, equal to his own, to make.[22] He unabashedly used his family for state and dynastic purposes, and he had help from Livia in this endeavor.

Augustus and Livia consciously and carefully cultivated the image of the Julio-Claudian clan as guarantors of peace and prosperity for the Roman state in the past, present, and future. They presented themselves as the dignified and protective father and the fertile and virtuous mother who would lead the Roman people and their children to health and happiness. This vision of the family was transmitted all over the Roman Empire through works of art, coins, shrines, ceremonies, buildings and carefully choreographed public appearances by members of the family. Imperial family members were also expected to possess the same modesty, humility, and restraint as their parents. Such displays masked the family's unrestrained authority and power, especially imperial women's influence and autonomy in the public sphere. When later members of the Julio-Claudian dynasty, like Caligula (r. 37–41) and Nero (r. 54–68), failed to follow the path set by Augustus and Livia, they learned that public displays of arrogance, extravagance, and immorality were met with untimely death. Agrippina the Younger, the mother of Nero, attempted more openly than any woman before her to gain political power and was rewarded with execution on her son's order. The goals and ideals of Augustus and Livia continued to haunt their successors in the centuries that followed.

22. Southern, p. 197.

[101]

Chapter 4
The Imperial
Model: Augustus
né Gaius
Octavius
(63 B.C.E.–14 C.E.)
and Livia
Drusilla
(58 B.C.E.–29 C.E.)

▨ QUESTIONS

1. What was the significance of family and marriage in Rome's political arena? How did family affect Augustus's rise to power?

2. What were Octavia's and Livia's duties as daughters and sisters of elite Roman men?

3. Why was it necessary to call attention to private and public behavior and to accentuate the differences among Octavia, Livia, and Cleopatra? To what extent could accusations of sexual impropriety be believed when used against political rivals?

4. Why did Augustus reform private and public behavior? How did these changes further his goals as absolute ruler of the Roman Empire?

5. What were the duties and rights of Roman men and women?

6. How did Augustus's regulation of Julia's behavior contrast with his regulation of Livia's? What significance do you find in the differences?

7. What was the significance of the family for the transfer of power from Augustus to his successor? To what extent was the state simply an extension of family?

8. Dio Cassius, Suetonius, Plutarch, and Tacitus wrote their histories several generations after Augustus and Livia died and are, in fact, secondary sources. How can we assess their historical accuracy?

▨ DOCUMENTS

DOCUMENT ONE

DIO CASSIUS

Roman History, Book 45

Dio Cassius (Cassius Dio Cocceianus, 155–235? C.E.) was a Roman historian and administrator, born in the eastern part of the empire. His rise in civil and military office was steady, and his positions as senator, praetor, and consul (220?) allowed him to study the political developments of the Roman Empire firsthand. His history of the Roman Republic and Empire (in Greek) numbered eighty books, nineteen of which survived. He tried to locate all available sources at the time and critically assess the process by which Rome moved from a republic to an empire. In this selection, Dio Cassius retells a series of fantastic stories about Augustus that predicted his rise to power. Who are Augustus's heavenly and worldly patrons?

. . . [Octavius] on attaining maturity lived with Caesar. For Caesar, being child-less and basing great hopes upon him, loved and cherished him, intending to leave him as successor to his name, authority, and sovereignty. He was influenced largely by Attia's emphatic declaration that the youth had been engendered by Apollo; for while sleeping once in his temple, she said, she thought she had intercourse with a serpent and it was this that caused her at the end of the allotted time to bear a son. Before he came to the light of day she saw in a dream her entrails lifted to the heavens and spreading out over all the earth; and the same night Octavius thought that the sun rose from her womb. Hardly had the child been born when Nigidius Figulus, a senator, straightway prophesied for him absolute power. This man could distinguish most accurately of his contemporaries the order of the firmament and the differences between the stars, what they accomplish when by themselves and when together, by their conjunctions and by their intervals, and for this reason had incurred the charge of practising some forbidden art. He, then, on this occasion met Octavius, who, on account of the birth of the child, was somewhat late in reaching the senate-house (for there happened to be a meeting of the senate that day), and upon asking him why he was late and learning the cause, he cried out, "You have begotten a master over us." At this Octavius was alarmed and wished to destroy the infant, but Nigidius restrained him, saying that it was impossible for it to suffer any such fate. . . . When he was now a lad and was staying in Rome, Cicero dreamed that the boy had been let down from the sky by golden chains to the Capitol and had received a whip from Jupiter. He did not know who the boy was, but meeting him the next day on the Capitol itself, he recognized him and told the vision to the bystanders. Catulus, who had likewise never seen Octavius, thought in his sleep that all the noble boys had marched in a solemn procession to Jupiter on the Capitol, and in the course of the ceremony the god had cast what looked like an image of Rome into that boy's lap. Startled at this, he went up to the Capitol to offer prayers to the god, and finding there Octavius, who had gone up for some reason or other, he compared his appearance with the dream and convinced himself of the truth of the vision. When, later, Octavius had grown up and reached maturity and was putting on man's dress, his tunic was rent on both sides from his shoulders and fell to his feet. Now this event in itself not only foreboded no good as an omen, but it also distressed those who were present because it had happened on the occasion of his first putting on man's garb; it occurred, however, to Octavius to say, "I shall have the whole senatorial dignity beneath my feet," and the outcome proved in accordance with his words. . . .

Chapter 4
The Imperial
Model: Augustus
né Gaius
Octavius
(63 B.C.E.–14 C.E.)
and Livia
Drusilla
(58 B.C.E.–29 C.E.)

DOCUMENT TWO

SUETONIUS

Life of Augustus

Suetonius (Caius Suetonius Tranquillus, 69–140 C.E.) was the private secretary of Emperor Hadrian. In this position, he was able to gather together all sorts of anecdotes and gossip about the early emperors. His biographies are not only lively and scandalous at times, but they also provide insights into the thinking of Romans about the role that imperial women played in making the empire. Suetonius was taken as a model by many later biographers. In this passage, Suetonius describes Augustus's sexual and social improprieties. What acts does Augustus commit and what are their ramifications? Can such sexual and scandalous anecdotes be believed when used for political purposes?

. . . 68. As a young man Augustus was accused of various improprieties. For instance, Sextus Pompey jeered at his effeminacy; Mark Antony alleged that Julius Caesar made him submit to unnatural relations as the price of adoption; Antony's brother Lucius added that after sacrificing his virtue to Caesar, Augustus had sold his favours to Aulus Hirtius, the Governor-General of Spain, for 3,000 gold pieces, and that he used to soften the hair on his legs by singeing them with red-hot walnut shells. One day at the Theatre an actor came on the stage representing a eunuch priest of Cybele, the Mother of the Gods; and, as he played his timbrel, another actor exclaimed:

'Look, how this invert's finger beats the drum!'

Since the Latin phrase could also mean: 'Look how this invert's finger *sways the world*!' the audience mistook the line for a hint at Augustus and broke into enthusiastic applause.

69. Not even his friends could deny that he often committed adultery, though of course they said, in justification, that he did so for reasons of state, not simple passion—he wanted to discover what his enemies were at by getting intimate with their wives or daughters. Mark Antony accused him not only of indecent haste in marrying Livia, but of hauling an ex-consul's wife from her husband's dining-room into the bedroom—before his eyes, too! He brought the woman back, says Antony, blushing to the ears and with her hair in disorder.

Antony also writes that Scribonia was divorced for having said a little too much when 'a rival' got her claws into Augustus; and that his friends used to behave like Toranius, the slave-dealer, in arranging his pleasures for him—they would strip mothers of families, or grown girls, of their clothes and inspect them as though they were up for sale. A racy letter of Antony's survives, written before he and Augustus had quarrelled privately or publicly:

'What has come over you? Do you object to my sleeping with Cleopatra? But we are married; and it is not even as though this were anything new—the affair started nine years ago. And what about you? Are you faithful to Livia Drusilla? My congratulations if, when this letter arrives, you have not been bed with Ter-tuillia, or Terentilla, or Rufilla, or Salvia Titisenia—or all of them. Does it really matter so much where, or with whom, you perform the sexual act?'

70. Then there was Augustus's private banquet, known as 'The Feast of the Divine Twelve', which caused a public scandal. The guests came dressed as gods or goddesses, Augustus himself represented Apollo; and our authority for this is not only a spiteful letter of Antony's, which names all the twelve, but the following well-known anonymous lampoon:

Those rogues engaged the services
    Of a stage manager;
So Mallia found six goddesses
    And six gods facing her!

Apollo's part was lewdly played
    By impious Caesar; he
Made merry at a table laid
    For gross debauchery.

Such scandalous proceedings shocked
    The Olympians. One by one
They quit and Jove, his thunders mocked,
    Vacates the golden throne.

What made the scandal even worse was that the banquet took place at a time of food shortage; and on the next day people were shouting: 'The Gods have gob-bled all the grain!' or 'Caesar is Apollo, true—but he's Apollo of the Tor-ments'—this being the god's aspect in one City district. Some found Augustus a good deal too fond of expensive furniture, Corinthian bronzes, and the gam-ing table. While the proscriptions were in progress someone had scrawled on the base of his statue:

I do not take my father's line;
His trade was silver coin, but mine
    Corinthian vases—

the belief being that he enlarged the proscription lists with names of men who owned vases of this sort.
    During the Sicilian War another rhyme was current:

Chapter 4
The Imperial
Model: Augustus
né Gaius
Octavius
(63 B.C.E.–14 C.E.)
and Livia
Drusilla
(58 B.C.E.–29 C.E.)

He took a beating twice at sea,
    And threw two fleets away.
So now to achieve one victory
    He tosses dice all day.

71. Augustus easily disproved the accusation (or slander, if you like) of prostituting his body to men, by the decent normality of his sex-life, then and later; and that of having over-luxurious tastes by his conduct at the capture of Alexandria, where the only loot he took from the Palace of the Ptolemies was a single agate cup—he melted down all the golden dinner services. However, the charge of being a womanizer stuck, and as an elderly man he is said to have still harboured a passion for deflowering girls—who were collected for him from every quarter, even by his wife! Augustus did not mind being called a gambler; he diced openly, in his old age, too, simply because he enjoyed the game—not only in December when the license of the Saturnalia justified it, but on other holidays, too, and actually on working days. . . .

DOCUMENT THREE

PLUTARCH

Life of Antony

Plutarch (46?–120 C.E.) was a Greek essayist and biographer who traveled extensively throughout the Roman Empire in the first century C.E. His work, The Parallel Lives, is a series of forty-six biographies that compare one Greek life with one comparable Roman life. The purpose of these biographies was to reveal the essential character of each historical figure and to explore the moral implications of their actions. He uses a lot of anecdotal material and his facts are not always accurate. In the selection below, Plutarch describes Octavia's relationship with her husband Marcus Antonius (Marc Antony). What types of judgments does he make about each? What is his assessment of Cleopatra?

. . . But Octavia, in Rome, being desirous to see Antony, asked Cæsar's leave to go to him; which he gave her, not so much, say most authors, to gratify his sister, as to obtain a fair pretence to begin the war upon her dishonorable reception. She no sooner arrived at Athens, but by letters from Antony she was informed of his new expedition, and his will that she should await him there. And, though she were much displeased, not being ignorant of the real reason of this usage, yet she wrote to him to know to what place he would be pleased she should send the things she had brought with her for his use; for she had brought clothes for his soldiers, baggage, cattle, money, and presents for his friends and officers, and two thousand chosen soldiers sumptuously armed, to form prætorian cohorts. This message was brought from Octavia to Antony by Niger, one of his friends, who added to it the praises she deserved so well. Cleopatra, feeling her rival already, as it were, at hand, was seized with fear, lest if to her noble life and her high alliance, she once could add the charm of daily habit and affectionate intercourse, she should become irresistible, and be his absolute mistress for ever. So she feigned to be dying for love of Antony, bringing her body down by slender diet; when he entered the room, she fixed her eyes upon him in a rapture, and when he left, seemed to languish and half faint away. She took great pains that he should see her in tears, and, as soon as he noticed it, hastily dried them up and turned away, as if it were her wish that he should know nothing of it. All this was acting while he prepared for Media; and Cleopatra's creatures were not slow to forward the design, upbraiding Antony with his unfeeling, hard-hearted temper, thus letting a woman perish whose soul depended upon him and him alone. Octavia, it was true, was his wife, and had been married to him because it was found convenient for the affairs of her brother that it should be so, and she had the honor of the title; but Cleopatra, the sovereign queen of many nations, had been contented with the name of his mistress, nor did she shun or despise the character whilst she might see him, might live with him, and enjoy him; if she were bereaved of this, she would not survive the loss. In fine, they so melted and unmanned him, that, fully believing she would die if he forsook her, he put off the war and returned to Alexandria, deferring his Median expedition until next summer.

. . . When Octavia returned from Athens, Cæsar, who considered she had been injuriously treated, commanded her to live in a separate house; but she refused to leave the house of her husband, and entreated him, unless he had already resolved, upon other motives, to make war with Antony, that he would on her account let it alone; it would be intolerable to have it said of the two greatest commanders in the world, that they had involved the Roman people in a civil war, the one out of passion for, the other out of resentment about, a woman. And her behavior proved her words to be sincere. She remained in Antony's house as if he were at home in it, and took the noblest and most generous care, not only of his children by her, but of those by Fulvia also. She received all the friends of Antony that came to Rome to seek office or upon any business, and did her utmost to prefer their requests to Cæsar; yet this her honorable deportment did but, without her meaning it, damage the reputation of Antony; the wrong he did to such a woman made him hated. . . .

[Antony returns to Athens with Cleopatra and sends orders to remove Octavia from his house in Rome.]

. . . [Antony] set sail for Athens, where fresh sports and play-acting employed him. Cleopatra, jealous of the honors Octavia had received at Athens (for Octavia was much beloved by the Athenians), courted the favor of the

Chapter 4
The Imperial
Model: Augustus
né Gaius
Octavius
(63 B.C.E.–14 C.E.)
and Livia
Drusilla
(58 B.C.E.–29 C.E.)

people with all sorts of attentions. The Athenians, in requital, having decreed her public honors, deputed several of the citizens to wait upon her at her house; amongst whom went Antony as one, he being an Athenian citizen, and he it was that made the speech. He sent orders to Rome to have Octavia removed out of his house. She left it, we are told, accompanied by all his children, except the eldest by Fulvia, who was then with his father, weeping and grieving that she must be looked upon as one of the causes of the war. But the Romans pitied, not so much her, as Antony himself, and more particularly those who had seen Cleopatra, whom they could report to have no way the advantage of Octavia either in youth or in beauty. . . .

DOCUMENT FOUR

TACITUS

The Annals, Book 1

Tacitus (Cornelius Tacitus, 55–117 C.E.) was a Roman historian who examined, in
The Annals, *the beginnings of the Roman Empire. His account concentrates on character sketches, the transformation of Roman institutions, and morality. Only twelve of his books (chapters), books I–VI and XI–XVI, survived. The surviving books of the* Annals *tell of the reign of Tiberius, of the last years of Claudius, and of the first years of Nero. In the selection below, Tacitus describes the process by which Augustus consolidated his power and how his stepson, Tiberius, became his heir. How does Tacitus portray Augustus's rule? Who or what affects Tiberius's ascension?*

1. Rome at the beginning was ruled by kings. Freedom and the consulship were established by Lucius Brutus. Dictatorships were held for a temporary crisis. The power of the decemvirs did not last beyond two years, nor was the consular jurisdiction of the military tribunes of long duration. The despotisms of China and Sulla were brief; the rule of Pompeius and of Crassus soon yielded before Cæsar; the arms of Lepidus and Antonius before Augustus; who, when the world was wearied by civil strife, subjected it to empire under the title of "Prince." But the successes and reverses of the old Roman people have been recorded by famous historians; and fine intellects were not wanting to describe the times of Augustus, till growing sycophancy scared them away. The histories of Tiberius, Caius, Claudius, and Nero, while they were in power, were falsified through terror, and after their death were written under the irritation of a recent hatred. Hence my purpose is to relate a few facts about Augustus—more particularly his last acts, then the reign of Tiberius, and all which follows, without either bitterness or partiality, from any motives to which I am far removed.

2. When after the destruction of Brutus and Cassius there was no longer any army of the Commonwealth, when Pompeius was crushed in Sicily, and when, with Lepidus pushed aside and Antonius slain, even the Julian faction had only Cæsar left to lead it, then, dropping the title of triumvir, and giving out that he was a Consul, and was satisfied with a tribune's authority for the protection of the people, Augustus won over the soldiers with gifts, the populace with cheap corn, and all men with the sweets of repose, and so grew greater by degrees, while he concentrated in himself the functions of the Senate, the magistrates, and the laws. He was wholly unopposed, for the boldest spirits had fallen in battle, or in the proscription, while the remaining nobles, the readier they were to be slaves, were raised the higher by wealth and promotion, so that, aggrandised by revolution, they preferred the safety of the present to the dangerous past. Nor did the provinces dislike that condition of affairs, for they distrusted the government of the Senate and the people, because of the rivalries between the leading men and the rapacity of the officials, while the protection of the laws was unavailing, as they were continually deranged by violence, intrigue, and finally by corruption.

3. Augustus meanwhile, as supports to his despotism, raised to the pontificate and curule ædileship Claudius Marcellus, his sister's son, while a mere stripling, and Marcus Agrippa, of humble birth, a good soldier, and one who had shared his victory, to two consecutive consulships, and as Marcellus soon afterwards died, he also accepted him as his son-in-law. Tiberius Nero and Claudius Drusus, his stepsons, he honoured with imperial titles, although his own family was as yet undiminished. For he had admitted the children of Agrippa, Caius and Lucius, into the house of the Cæsars; and before they had yet laid aside the dress of boyhood he had most fervently desired, with an outward show of reluctance, that they should be entitled "princes of the youth," and be consuls-elect. When Agrippa died, and Lucius Cæsar as he was on his way to our armies in Spain, and Caius while returning from Armenia, still suffering from a wound, were prematurely cut off by destiny, or by their stepmother Livia's treachery, Drusus too having long been dead, Nero remained alone of the stepsons, and in him everything tended to centre. He was adopted as a son, as a colleague in empire and a partner in the tribunitian power, and paraded through all the armies, no longer through his mother's secret intrigues, but at her open suggestion. For she had gained such a hold on the aged Augustus that he drove out as an exile into the island of Planasia, his only grandson, Agrippa Postumus, who, though devoid of worthy qualities, and having only the brute courage of physical strength, had not been convicted of any gross offence. . . . At home all was tranquil, and there were magistrates with the same titles; there was a younger generation, sprung up since the victory of Actium, and even many of the older men had been born during the civil wars. How few were left who had seen the republic!

4. Thus the State had been revolutionised, and there was not a vestige left of the old sound morality. Stript of equality, all looked up to the commands of a

*Chapter 4
The Imperial
Model: Augustus
né Gaius
Octavius
(63 B.C.E.–14 C.E.)
and Livia
Drusilla
(58 B.C.E.–29 C.E.)*

sovereign without the least apprehension for the present, while Augustus in the vigour of life, could maintain his own position, that of his house, and the general tranquillity. When in advanced old age, he was worn out by a sickly frame, and the end was near and new prospects opened, a few spoke in vain of the blessings of freedom, but most people dreaded and some longed for war. The popular gossip of the large majority fastened itself variously on their future masters. . . . Tiberius Nero was of mature years, and had established his fame in war, but he had the old arrogance inbred in the Claudian family, and many symptoms of a cruel temper, though they were repressed, now and then broke out. He had also from earliest infancy been reared in an imperial house; consulships and triumphs had been heaped on him in his younger days; even in the years which, on the pretext of seclusion he spent in exile at Rhodes, he had had no thoughts but of wrath, hypocrisy, and secret sensuality. . . .

DOCUMENT FIVE

AUGUSTUS

Res gestae

> *At the end of his reign, Augustus recorded the "things that he had accomplished" during his rule. He presented his rise to power in favorable terms: he saved Rome, reestablished peace and stability, and gave the people prosperity. In this selection, Augustus describes the appreciation of the Roman people. How do they show their appreciation? How does Augustus describe his ascent to complete power? Do later historians agree with his view?*

. . . 34. In my sixth and seventh consulships, when I had extinguished the flames of civil war, after receiving by universal consent the absolute control of affairs, I transferred the republic from my own control to the will of the senate and the Roman people. For this service on my part I was given the title of Augustus by decree of the senate, and the doorposts of my house were covered with laurels by public act, and a civic crown was fixed above my door, and a golden shield was placed in the Curia Julia whose inscription testified that the senate and the Roman people gave me this in recognition of my valour, my clemency, my justice, and my piety. After that time I took precedence of all in rank, but of power I possessed no more than those who were my colleagues in any magistracy.

35. While I was administering my thirteenth consulship the senate and the equestrian order and the entire Roman people gave me the title of Father of my Country, and decreed that this title should be inscribed upon the vestibule of my house and in the senate-house and in the Forum Augustum beneath the

quadriga* erected in my honour by decree of the senate. At the time of writing this I was in my seventy-sixth year.

DOCUMENT SIX

HORACE

Odes, Book 3

Horace (Quintus Horatius Flaccus, 65 B.C.E.–8 B.C.E.) was educated in both Rome and Athens and became a literary figure when he published Book I of the Satires in 35 B.C.E. He was an unrivaled lyric poet. His poems betray the influence of Greek poets, but as his poetry matures he displays a mastery of Latin verse. In the Odes, *he gives a vivid and favorable picture of the Augustan age. In this selection from* Odes, *Horace describes Augustus's return from Spain. What are his views of Augustus?*

Like Hercules, citizens, they said just now
he had sought the laurel at the cost of death:
returning from Spain, seeking his household gods,
   Caesar has conquered.

After sacrifice to the just gods, let his
wife come forth, happy for her matchless husband,
and the sister of our famous leader, and,
   wearing the bands of

Suppliants, mothers of young men and maidens
who now are safe. You boys and girls who are still
inexperienced, be sparing with your words,
   speak nothing evil.

For me this day is truly a festival,
driving dark worry away: I fear neither
civil war nor violent death while earth is
   governed by Caesar.

Go, my boy, look for the perfume and garlands
and a jar that recalls the Marsian War,

*chariot

[111]

Chapter 4
The Imperial
Model: Augustus
né Gaius
Octavius
(63 B.C.E.–14 C.E.)
and Livia
Drusilla
(58 B.C.E.–29 C.E.)

if a single wine pot was overlooked by
   Spartacus' raiders.

And ask witty Neaera to come quickly,
tying her brown hair back in a simple knot;
if her doorman stays out of sight and creates
   delays, come away.

My hair turns gray, and it softens a spirit
fond of argument and bitter quarreling;
I would not have stood this, when youth was hot and
   Plancus was consul.

DOCUMENT SEVEN

Dio Cassius

Roman History, Book 56

*In this selection, Dio Cassius describes Augustus's speech to the young married
men and bachelors of the equestrian class who were complaining about the new
laws regarding the unmarried and childless. How does Augustus justify his laws
governing private conduct? What reasons does he give for maintaining that they
are necessary for national power and survival? What is a Roman citizen's duty?*

[Augustus to Married Men]

. . . Though you are but few altogether, in comparison with the vast throng that
inhabits this city, and are far less numerous than the others, who are unwilling
to perform any of their duties, yet for this very reason I for my part praise you
the more, and am heartily grateful to you because you have shown yourselves
obedient and are helping to replenish the fatherland. For it is by lives so conducted that the Romans of later days will become a mighty multitude. We were
at first a mere handful, you know, but when we had recourse to marriage and
begot us children, we came to surpass all mankind not only in the manliness of
our citizens but in the size of our population as well. Bearing this in mind, we
must console the mortal side of our nature with an endless succession of generations that shall be like the torch-bearers in a race, so that through one another
we may render immortal the one side of our nature in which we fall short of divine bliss. It was for this cause most of all that that first and greatest god, who
fashioned us, divided the race of mortals in twain, making one half of it male

[112]

and the other half female, and implanted in them love and compulsion to mutual intercourse, making their association fruitful, that by the young continually
born he might in a way render even mortality eternal. Indeed, even of the gods
themselves some are accounted male and others female; and the tradition prevails that some have begotten others and some have been begotten of others. So
even among those beings, who need no such device, marriage and the begetting
of children have been approved as a noble thing.

. . . For is there anything better than a wife who is chaste, domestic, a good
house-keeper, a rearer of children; one to gladden you in health, to tend you in
sickness; to be your partner in good fortune, to console you in misfortune; to restrain the mad passion of youth and to temper the unseasonable harshness of
old age? And is it not a delight to acknowledge a child who shows the endowments of both parents, to nurture and educate it, at once the physical and the
spiritual image of yourself, so that in its growth another self lives again? Is it not
blessed, on departing from life, to leave behind as successor and heir to your
blood and substance one that is your own, sprung from your own loins, and to
have only the human part of you waste away, while you live in the child as your
successor, so that you need not fall into the hands of aliens, as in war, nor perish utterly, as in a pestilence? These, now, are the private advantages that accrue
to those who marry and beget children; but for the State, for whose sake we
ought to do many things that are even distasteful to us, how excellent and how
necessary it is, if cities and peoples are to exist, and if you are to rule others and
all the world is to obey you, that there should be a multitude of men, to till the
earth in time of peace, to make voyages, practise arts, and follow handicrafts,
and, in time of war, to protect what we already have with all the greater zeal because of family ties and to replace those that fall by others. Therefore, men,—for
you alone may properly be called men,—and fathers,—for you are as worthy to
hold this title as I myself,—I love you and praise you for this; and I not only bestow the prizes I have already offered but will distinguish you still further by
other honours and offices, so that you may not only reap great benefits yourselves but may also leave them to your children undiminished. . . .

[AUGUSTUS TO BACHELORS]

. . . A strange experience has been mine, O—what shall I call you? Men? But you
are not performing any of the offices of men. Citizens? But for all that you are
doing, the city is perishing. Romans? But you are undertaking to blot out this
name altogether. Well, at any rate, whatever you are and by whatever name you
delight to be called, mine has been an astonishing experience; for though I am
always doing everything to promote an increase of population among you and
am now about to rebuke you, I grieve to see that there are a great many of you.
I could rather have wished that those others to whom I have just spoken were
as numerous as you prove to be, and that preferably you were ranged with
them, or otherwise did not exist at all. For you, heedless alike of the providence

[113]

Chapter 4
The Imperial
Model: Augustus
né Gaius
Octavius
(63 B.C.E.–14 C.E.)
and Livia
Drusilla
(58 B.C.E.–29 C.E.)

of the gods and of the watchful care of your forefathers, are bent upon annihilating our entire race and making it in truth mortal, are bent upon destroying and bringing to an end the entire Roman nation. For what seed of human beings would be left, if all the rest of mankind should do what you are doing? For you have become their leaders, and so would rightly bear the responsibility for the universal destruction. And even if no others emulate you, would you not be justly hated for the very reason that you overlook what no one else would overlook, and neglect what no one else would neglect, introducing customs and practices which, if imitated, would lead to the extermination of all mankind, and, if abhorred, would end in your own punishment? . . . For you are committing murder in not begetting in the first place those who ought to be your descendants; you are committing sacrilege in putting an end to the names and honours of your ancestors; and you are guilty of impiety in that you are abolishing your families which instituted by the gods, and destroying the greatest of offerings to them,—human life,—thus overthrowing their rites and their temples. Moreover, you are destroying the State by disobeying its laws, and you are betraying your country by rendering her barren and childless; nay more, you are laying her even with the dust by making her destitute of future inhabitants. For it is human beings that constitute a city, we are told, not houses or porticos or marketplaces empty of men. . . .

Indeed, it was never permitted to any man, even in olden times, to neglect marriage and the begetting of children; but from the very outset, when the government was first established, strict laws were made regarding these matters, and subsequently many decrees were passed by both the senate and the people, which it would be superfluous to enumerate here. I, now, have increased the penalties for the disobedient, in order that through fear of becoming liable to them you might be brought to your senses; and to the obedient I have offered more numerous and greater prizes than are given for any other display of excellence, in order that for this reason, if for no other, you might be persuaded to marry and beget children. Yet you have not striven for any of the recompenses nor feared any of the penalties, but have shown contempt for all these measures and have trodden them all underfoot, as if you were not living in a civilized community. You talk, forsooth, about this 'free' and 'untrammelled' life that you have adopted, without wives and without children; but you are not a whit better than brigands or the most savage of beasts. For surely it is not your delight in a solitary existence that leads you to live without wives, nor is there one of you who either eats alone or sleeps alone; no, what you want is to have full liberty for wantonness and licentiousness. . . . For you see yourselves how much more numerous you are than the married men, when you ought by this time to have provided us with as many children besides, or rather with several times your number. How otherwise can families continue? How can the State be preserved, if we neither marry nor have children? . . .

DOCUMENT EIGHT

Roman Historians on Livia and Roman Women

In the first three passages of this selection Dio Cassius, Suetonius, and Tacitus discuss Livia's public role. Contrast Livia's passive image promoted by her and Augustus with the real power she enjoyed, as described by these three historians.

In the fourth passage, Tacitus describes a debate in the Senate concerning the issue of whether or not wives should accompany their husbands to the provinces. The debate reveals his attitudes toward women, their nature, and their influence and power. When compared with the passages about Livia, what are Roman attitudes toward imperial women who ventured into the political sphere?

Dio Cassius
Roman History, Book 57

. . . For she occupied a very exalted station, far above all women of former days, so that she could at any time receive the senate and such of the people as wished to greet her in her house; and this fact was entered in the public records. The letters of Tiberius bore for a time her name, also, and communications were addressed to both alike. Except that she never ventured to enter the senate-chamber or the camps or the public assemblies, she undertook to manage everything as if she were sole ruler. For in the time of Augustus she had possessed the greatest influence and she always declared that it was she who had made Tiberius emperor; consequently she was not satisfied to rule on equal terms with him, but wished to take precedence over him. . . .

. . . Among the many excellent utterances of hers that are reported are the following. Once, when some naked men met her and were to be put to death in consequence, she saved their lives by saying that to chaste women such men are no whit different from statues. When someone asked her how and by what course of action she had obtained such a commanding influence over Augustus, she answered that it was by being scrupulously chaste herself, doing gladly whatever pleased him, not meddling with any of his affairs, and, in particular, by pretending neither to hear nor to notice the favorites of his passion.

Suetonius
Life of Tiberius

. . . 50. Tiberius's first hostile action against his own family was when his brother Drusus wrote to him privately suggesting that they should jointly persuade Augustus to restore the Republican constitution; Tiberius placed the letter in Augustus's hands. After coming to power he showed so little pity for his exiled wife Julia that he did not have the decency to confirm Augustus's decree which merely forbade her to set foot outside the town of Reggio; but restricted her to a single house where visitors were forbidden. He even deprived her of

Chapter 4
The Imperial
Model: Augustus
né Gaius
Octavius
(63 B.C.E.–14 C.E.)
and Livia
Drusilla
(58 B.C.E.–29 C.E.)

the annual sums hitherto paid her by Augustus, as both his daughter and his daughter-in-law, on the pretext that no mention of these had appeared in his will and that consequently, under common law, she was no longer entitled to draw them. Tiberius then complained that his mother Livia vexed him by wanting to be co-ruler of the Empire; which was why he avoided frequent meetings or long private talks with her. Although he did occasionally need and follow Livia's advice, he disliked people to think of him as giving it serious consideration. A senatorial decree adding 'Son of Livia' as well as 'Son of Augustus' to his honorifics so deeply offended him that he vetoed proposals to confer 'Mother of the Country' or any similarly high-sounding title on her. What is more, he often warned Livia to remember that she was a woman and must not interfere in affairs of state. He became especially insistent on this point when a fire broke out near the Temple of Vesta and news reached him that Livia was directing the civilian and military fire-fighters in person, as though Augustus were still alive, and urging them to redouble their efforts.

51. Afterwards Tiberius quarrelled openly with his mother. The story goes that she repeatedly urged him to enroll in the jurors' list the name of a man who had been granted a citizenship. Tiberius agreed to do so on one condition—that the entry should be marked 'forced upon the Emperor by his mother'. Livia lost her temper and produced from a strong-box some of Augustus's old letters to her commenting on Tiberius's sour and stubborn character. Annoyance with her for hoarding these documents so long, and then spitefully confronting him with them, is said to have been his main reason for retirement to Capri. At all events he visited her exactly once in the last three years of her life, and only for an hour or two at that; and when she presently fell sick, made no effort to repeat the visit. Livia then died, and he spoke of attending her funeral, but did not come. After several days her corpse grew so corrupt and noisome that he sent it to have it buried; but vetoed her deification on the pretext that she had herself forbidden this. He also annulled her will, and began taking his revenge on all her friends and confidants—even those whom, as she died, she had appointed to take charge of her funeral rites—and went so far as to condemn one of them, a knight, to the treadmill.

Tacitus

The Annals, Book 1

. . . She [Livia] too, was flattered a great deal by the senate. It was variously proposed that she should be called 'parent' and 'mother' of her country; and a large body of opinion held that the words 'son of Julia' ought to form part of the emperor's name. He, however, repeatedly asserted that only reasonable honours must be paid to women—and that, in regard to compliments paid to himself, he would observe a comparable moderation. In reality, however, he was jealous and nervous, and regarded this elevation of a woman as derogatory to his own person. He would not even allow her to be allotted an official attendant, and forbade an Altar of Adoption and other honours of the kind. . . .

Tacitus

The Annals, Book 3

...33. During this debate Severus Cæcina proposed that no magistrate who had obtained a province should be accompanied by his wife. He began by recounting at length how harmoniously he had lived with his wife, who had borne him six children, and how in his own home he had observed what he was proposing for the public, by having kept her in Italy, though he had himself served forty campaigns in various provinces. "With good reason," he said, "had it been formerly decided that women were not to be taken among our allies or into foreign countries. A train of women involves delays through luxury in peace and through panic in war, and converts a Roman army on the march into the likeness of a barbarian progress. Not only is the sex feeble and unequal to hardship, but, when it has liberty, it is spiteful, intriguing and greedy of power. They show themselves off among the soldiers and have the centurions at their beck. Lately a woman has presided at the drill of the cohorts and the evolutions of the legions. You should yourselves bear in mind that, whenever men are accused of extortion, most of the charges are directed against the wives. It is to these that the vilest of the provincials instantly attach themselves; it is they who undertake and settle business; two persons receive homage when they appear; there are two centres of government, and the women's orders are the more despotic and intemperate. Formerly they were restrained by the Oppian and other laws; now, loosed from every bond, they rule our houses, our tribunals, even our armies."

34. A few heard this speech with approval, but the majority clamorously objected that there was no proper motion on the subject, and that Cæcina was no fit censor on so grave an issue. Presently Valerius Messalinus, Messala's son, in whom the father's eloquence was reproduced, replied that much of the sternness of antiquity had been changed into a better and more genial system. "Rome," he said, "is not now, as formerly, beset with wars, nor are the provinces hostile. A few concessions are made to the wants of women, but such as are not even a burden to their husbands' homes, much less to the allies. In all other respects man and wife share alike, and this arrangement involves no trouble in peace. War of course requires that men should be unincumbered, but when they return what worthier solace can they have after their hardships than a wife's society? But some wives have abandoned themselves to scheming and rapacity. Well; even among our magistrates, are not many subject to various passions? Still, that is not a reason for sending no one into a province. Husbands have often been corrupted by the vices of their wives. Are then all unmarried men blameless? The Oppian laws were formerly adopted to meet the political necessities of the time, and subsequently there was some remission and mitigation of them on grounds of expediency. It is idle to shelter our own weakness under other names; for it is the husband's fault if the wife transgresses propriety. Besides, it is wrong that because of the imbecility of one or two men, all husbands should be cut off from their partners in prosperity and adversity. And further, a

[117]

Chapter 4
The Imperial
Model: Augustus
né Gaius
Octavius
(63 B.C.E.–14 C.E.)
and Livia
Drusilla
(58 B.C.E.–29 C.E.)

sex naturally weak will be thus left to itself and be at the mercy of its own voluptuousness and the passions of others. Even with the husband's personal vigilance the marriage tie is scarcely preserved inviolate. What would happen were it for a number of years to be forgotten, just as in a divorce? You must not check vices abroad without remembering the scandals of the capital."

Drusus added a few words on his own experience as a husband. "Princes," he said, "must often visit the extremities of their empire. How often had the Divine Augustus travelled to the West and to the East accompanied by Livia? He had himself gone to Illyricum and, should it be expedient, he would go to other countries, not always however with a contented mind, if he had to tear himself from a much loved wife, the mother of his many children."

35. Cæcina's motion was thus defeated. . . .

PART

II

Christianity and the Heirs to the Roman Empire

CHAPTER

5

Spiritual Partners in Christian Asceticism:
Jerome (?346–420 C.E.) and
Paula (347–404 C.E.)

■ **SETTING THE STAGE**

Over the course of the fourth century, Christianity became legally acceptable, socially respectable, and politically powerful. In the early years of the century, the Roman emperor Constantine (r. 306–337) converted to Christianity and in 313 issued the Edict of Milan, which gave Christians freedom to worship openly. By 383, the law code of the emperor Theodosius (r. 379–395) proclaimed that all peoples in the empire must practice the Christian religion. These dramatic events were part of a dynamic process of transformation as the Roman Empire was Christianized, and as Christianity

Chapter 5
Spiritual
Partners in Chris-
tian Asceticism:
Jerome (?346–420
C.E.) and Paula
(347–404 C.E.)

absorbed and assimilated Roman values, ideas, and administrative structures. Such momentous changes did not happen smoothly or evenly, and all aspects of life in this century were affected by debates over beliefs and creeds, competition for authority, and tensions between civic goals and spiritual power and behaviors.

During this period, the Roman Empire was divided administratively into eastern and western sectors. In the west, Roman law, language, and social order were planted, but this change was accompanied by the growth of provincial authority, increased reliance on an army composed of members of assimilated Germanic tribes, and accompanying financial burdens. Alliances with various Germanic tribes such as the Visigoths maintained peace for a time, but violent confrontations also occurred, as in 410 when Rome was sacked, and continued as Germanic leaders vied to establish kingdoms in western Europe in the fifth and sixth centuries.

As elements of imperial structure disintegrated, Christian bishops, councils, doctrine, and laws moved into the gaps and vacancies, and helped to construct a distinct identity and their own claims to universal or catholic power. Gradually, insistence on conformity in ideas and practices, and even persecution of heretics or those who chose different teachings and behaviors, replaced an older heterodoxy that could tolerate pagans, Jews, and opportunities for different spiritual expressions. Legitimacy, prestige, and orthodoxy were a far cry from an era when to be Christian meant to risk one's life, or when persecution and

marginality served as the marks of holiness and true belief. As a result, it is important to set the institutional, legal, political, and doctrinal changes of the fourth century against their impact on individual lives and the personal responses to those changes.

The lives of Jerome and Paula allow us to consider the complex relationships between the institutional and the personal dimensions of Christianity in a period of rapid transformation. These two people were deeply involved in numerous areas of social, intellectual, and spiritual change in the fourth century, and their experiences help to illustrate why and how such changes took place. First, during this time the Roman senatorial aristocracy converted to Christianity in large numbers or "drifted into respectable Christianity," as historian Peter Brown describes it.[1] Mothers, wives, and daughters of these families, like Paula, often led the way in the conversions and became the exemplary models of Christian devotion and morality. Second, with legalization, church offices and positions became prestigious and desirable, and a new elite of well-known "specialists"—intellectual men like Jerome who were well educated in philosophy and theology—helped to define what it meant to be Chris-

1. Peter Brown, *Religion and Society in the Age of Saint Augustine* (London: Faber and Faber, 1972), p.178. This is a phrase often cited by other historians. Brown's works are among the most important sources for this period. See also *The Body and Society: Men, Women and Sexual Renunciation in Early Christianity* (New York: Columbia University Press, 1988); and *Power and Persuasion in Late Antiquity: Towards a Christian Empire* (Madison: University of Wisconsin Press, 1992).

tian. Finally, in those years, long-existing Roman and Christian traditions of asceticism blossomed and became institutionalized in Christian monasticism. The founding of affiliated holy communities in Bethlehem by Jerome and Paula typifies these developments. Their motives for adopting such a way of life may have been quite similar, but gender differences shaped their places in these movements, the personal meanings of their adoption of holy virginity, and the social responses to these choices. Jerome and Paula lived in similar environments and struggled against all these issues, together and separately, in practice and in spirit.

▨ THE ACTORS:

JEROME AND PAULA

Jerome was born in an economically comfortable family who owned valuable land in Stridon, in the northwest area of the province of Dalmatia. Later in life, Jerome wrote about slave quarters on their estates, and he remembered being raised by nurses and having his own personal attendants. Uncertainty about the actual date of his birth plagues historians, who are forced to try to deduce when he was born from references to other people in his writing, or to what others say about him.[2] His family probably immigrated from Greece but was thoroughly latinized by the fourth century. Jerome says little about his parents, perhaps because they were not as devout as he might like, although they were Christian. Some speculate that his eventual choice to lead a religious life did not meet their aspirations for their eldest son. Over the years, family tensions intensified because Jerome influenced his younger sister, who took religious vows, and his much younger brother, who was ordained a priest.

Like other boys of his social class, Jerome attended an elementary school from the age of six or seven to eleven or twelve. He learned to read and write, elementary mathematics, and probably some basic Greek in addition to his Latin training. Our fragmentary information about his childhood comes from documents he wrote as an adult, and these documents usually concerned issues important in his life at the time. For example, he confessed that he had always liked good food, and that giving it up in his subsequent ascetic life was difficult.[3] When Jerome was twelve he was sent to Rome for his secondary education. This practice was not uncommon at the time because several schools in Rome offered the best possible training, which in turn could lead to lucrative and prestigious government positions. In a school run by a celebrated master, Jerome received general instruction in mathematics, science, and music, but the focus was grammar, the correct

2. J. N. D. Kelly, Jerome's major biographer, uses the earliest date, 331. See *Jerome: His Life, Writings and Controversies* (London: Duckworth Pub., 1975), Appendix. Peter Brown in *The Body and Society*, p. 366, uses the date 346.

3. Kelly, p. 8.

use of language, and classical literature, as it had been at the time of the Gracchi brothers. Two things are important about this education. First, Jerome became familiar with various classical (and pagan) authors, including Virgil, Terence, Cicero, and even the early playwright Plautus and the Stoic moralist Seneca. Later in his life, he would have to decide the value of these pagan texts in a Christian world. Second, the method of instruction, which included memorization and recitation, followed by a systematic, line-by-line analysis, would be boring to some, but it eventually made Jerome an excellent grammarian and rhetorician, and one of "the finest Latin Christian writers."[4]

Jerome's life as a student in Rome was probably not much different from that of his fellow schoolmates. He did begin to buy volumes of the classics, some of which he transcribed himself. He also fully engaged in the social life of the youth of the time, including "sexual adventures" that he later regretted as failings or stumbling on "the slippery path of youth."[5] He also was formally baptized at some point in his Roman sojourn, and he took advantage of Rome's history to visit the catacombs and to pay homage to earlier Christian martyrs.

Simultaneously, Paula was growing up in the conventional environment of a daughter of the Roman lower senatorial aristocracy. Later, when Jerome wrote the epitaph on Paula's tomb, he claimed that she was "born from the Scipios, sprung from Pauline parents, scion of the Gracchi . . . ."[6] There is no evidence to support this lineage, but such claims reflect the ongoing importance of family bloodlines and noble ancestry, even among Christians like Jerome. Paula's parents, Blaesilla and Rogatus, may not have had illustrious pedigrees, and we don't know if they were Christians, but they were at least on the periphery of the elite, which meant they had considerable wealth.[7]

By this period of Roman history, girls of Paula's social rank were well educated in public grammar schools, where they studied Latin literary masters of the past and probably gained some rudimentary knowledge of Greek. By the age of fifteen they were ready to be married and thus would not have had additional education, like Jerome did. Both the laws and actual practices regarding marriage, family, inheritance, and adultery had been in place for some time when

4. Kelly, p. 13.

5. Kelly, p. 21.

6. Quoted in Jo Ann McNamara, "Cornelia's Daughters: Paula and Eustochium," *Women's Studies*, 11 (1984), p. 9. This claim meant that Paula took her name from the father of Scipio Aemilianus, Aemilius Paulus.

7. Among the various authors who provide details on Paula's life, and on the lives of other women who were her social equals and contemporaries, are Anne Ewing Hickey, *Women of the Roman Aristocracy as Christian Monastics* (Ann Arbor, Mich.: UMI Research Press, 1987); Anne Yarbrough, "Christianization in the Fourth Century: The Example of Roman Women," *Journal of Religious History* 15:1 (1988), pp. 319–335; Patricia Ranft, *Women and the Religious Life in Premodern Europe* (New York: St. Martin's Press, 1996); and Elizabeth Clark, "Patrons, Not Priests: Gender and Power in Late Ancient Christianity," *Gender and History* 2 (1990), pp. 253–273.

Paula came of age. Most unions were free marriages. Thus, a wife did not pass under the control of her husband; instead, a daughter remained under her father's authority, and he could control her marriage until she was twenty-five. Women had had rights to inherit and bequeath property since the time of Cornelia (second century B.C.E.); thereafter, guardianship had been much weakened, and a wife gained rights of succession in her husband's family along with her children. Eventually a law of 390 C.E. acknowledged that a widowed woman could be the guardian of her minor children.

The emperor Constantine had altered some of the Augustan marriage and adultery laws—clamping down on some behaviors, loosening others. For example, although a double standard continued to exist concerning divorce and extramarital affairs, divorce laws were tightened, charges of adultery could be made by close kin rather than by only the wounded party, and punishment for adultery was changed from banishment to death. These changes tended to make women more vulnerable to capricious charges of misconduct, and the threat of gossip and slander carried real consequences. Constantine also repealed earlier legislation that had penalized celibacy. Laws providing protection for virgins and holy widows subsequently were expanded in 364 to "call for capital punishment for anyone who even 'solicited' consecrated maidens or widows."[8]

Centuries of Roman imperial expansion, the mixing of peoples and cultures in the Mediterranean, and the gradual assimilation of so-called barbarian populations in the frontier areas had created social diversity and vast differences in wealth and status. Nevertheless, the models of excellence and ideal comportment for men and women remained remarkably unchanged. Women were expected to follow the pattern of the Republican *matrona*, which had guided women in the era of the Gracchi. Marriage and motherhood were the goals; chastity, modesty, and devotion to family and community remained the desired behavior for all women of the free and freed classes. Self-discipline and order, along with civic duty and loyalty, were to guide male behavior. "The upper classes of the Roman empire in its last centuries lived by codes of sexual restraint and public decorum that they liked to think of as continuous with the virile austerity of archaic Rome."[9] Young men in school were warned that they should not bring shame or dishonor on their families by disgraceful public behavior. At the same time, the tradition of a double standard of sexual behavior persisted, and it allowed men, but not women, marital infidelity, particularly with slaves and servants.

At the age of fifteen (ca. 362) Paula married Toxotius, who came from a senatorial family not unlike her own. We know that, as a married woman, Paula was a Christian, but we do not know when her conversion occurred.

8. Hickey, p. 30.

9. Brown, *The Body and Society,* p. 22.

Chapter 5
Spiritual
Partners in Chris-
tian Asceticism:
Jerome (?346–420
C.E.) and Paula
(347–404 C.E.)

Mixed religious marriages were not uncommon at the time, and perhaps Toxotius was a pagan who converted after his marriage. The marriage was apparently happy and successful; they had five children, four girls and a boy, which was an unusually large family at the time. Jerome later claimed that, after Paula had finally given her husband a male heir, sexual relations between them ceased for religious reasons.[10]

Overall, changes in Roman society in women's status by this time are illustrated in the fact that female children could now be named after mothers, grandmothers, and other respected women and were not necessarily given the feminine derivative of their father's name. Paula named her first daughter Blaesilla, after her own mother; the second, Paulina, after herself. Only the last child, the son, was named Toxotius, clearly connecting him to his father's lineage. As a wife and mother, Paula met the feminine ideals of the day. She probably had an active public life, using her own and her family's wealth to engage in charitable works and meet social obligations. Somewhere around 378 Toxotius senior died, leaving Paula a widow with five children. The Romans had always been divided about remarriage, as evident in the ideal of the *univira*, the woman devoted to one husband in her lifetime. Paula chose not to remarry, and instead substituted religious devotion and life in a Christian community in place of conventional marriage and family.

▪ ACT I:

PATHS TO ASCETICISM

While Paula was embarking on a life of marriage and maternity, Jerome was completing his studies. Sometime in 367 or 368, he and a friend left Rome and traveled to Trier in northern Gaul. Why they chose this destination is not clear, but Trier was the capital of the west for much of the fourth century, and it was the center for a host of imperial officials and ministries. Perhaps Jerome hoped to find a lucrative position there. As it turned out, his time in Trier and then a subsequent stay in Aquileia, the military and commercial center located at the north end of the Adriatic Sea, proved to be "of crucial importance for his personal development and for the shaping of his career."[11] During the time from 367 to 372, Jerome decided to abandon a secular career and to dedicate himself to a Christian life of contemplation and retirement from the public world.

Various factors explain Jerome's decision. Among them are the facts that both Trier and Aquileia were cen-

10. See Letter 108 from Jerome to Eustochium, Paula's daughter, in Joan H. Petersen (editor and translator), *Handmaids of the Lord: Contemporary Descriptions of Feminine Asceticism in the First Six Christian Centuries* (Kalamazoo, Mich.: Cistercian Publications, 1996), p.129.

11. Kelly, p. 25.

ters of Christian activity and energy, and both places had impressive Christian leaders, particularly in the persons of residing bishops who were engaged in heated debates over doctrinal matters. As already mentioned, Christianity acquired legal status, religious stature, and a more formal administrative structure, and leaders emerged who hoped to clarify doctrine and practice, thus unifying the Christian communities and, in theory, protecting the spiritual health of all believers. Throughout the fourth century, doctrinal disputes were features of Christian intellectual and spiritual life. Most controversies focused on efforts to describe the relationship between the divine and the created worlds, and between spirit and body, and over how best to give expression to one's beliefs and to God's will. These questions were at the core of debates surrounding the relationship among Father, Son, and Holy Spirit. A church council meeting at Nicaea in 325 had addressed this problem and had resolved that the Father and Son were of the same substance and time of creation. Nevertheless, treatises continued to be written on the subject and contrary views persisted, with the most heated debates continuing to focus on defining the nature of Christ, or "christology." Specifically at issue was whether the created material essence of the Son could ever be equated with the divine essence of the Father. This dilemma raised questions for human existence as well. If Christian life was a process of spiritual transformation and transcendence of material and bodily constraints, did this mean that

differences between the sexes were also transcendable, or that a life of avowed virginity was the ideal means to further holy transformation? Jerome's educational training gave him the tools to examine these issues, and during his visits to Trier and Aquileia he eagerly read books by leading theologians. The ideas captured his intellectual and spiritual imagination, and he began a pattern of vigorous engagement in theological disputes that continued throughout his life.

Another force that would influence both Jerome and Paula in these years was the growth of asceticism, which was practiced in various forms. A long history of ascetic behaviors in the Roman world insisted that conquest of the body and material desires could lead to purity, enlightenment, and higher truth. Stoics had argued that the self-control one exercised in adopting celibacy, or continence, served as a way to perfect the will and thereby to live in harmony with the natural universe, while Neoplatonists believed that such self-control "would mold one's character to be ready to receive the truth."[12] Christianity had established practices of self-sacrifice and self-denial as a way of escaping this world and achieving communion with God, who was the beginning and the end of human existence. Sexual abstinence in particular became a mark of holiness and an "undivided heart." A document from the second or early third century praising the

12. Thomas J. Heffernan, *Sacred Biography: Saints and Their Biographers in the Middle Ages* (New York: Oxford University Press, 1988), p. 236.

Chapter 5
Spiritual
Partners in Chris-
tian Asceticism:
Jerome (?346–420
C.E.) and Paula
(347–404 C.E.)

virtues of ascetic Christian women proclaimed, "blessed are they who have kept the flesh pure, for they shall become a temple of God. . . . Blessed are the continent, for to them God will speak."[13] In the era of persecution of Christians, both male and female celibate martyrs were revered models in the community.

The legalization of Christianity altered the status and meaning of asceticism, virginity, and celibacy in contradictory ways. For many people, legitimacy also meant secularization, and "respectable" Christianity, which seemed to have lost the inspiration and zeal of the earlier movement, offered them little satisfaction. Others who desired a "strict and simpler life" were "sickened by the hypocrisy of new recruits who joined the church only because it was now safe and fashionable to do so."[14] Jerome, for one, frequently attacked the hypocrisy and materialism of the Christian Roman elite. For some, the disappearance of persecution required a new opportu-

nity for the sacrifices of heroic Christianity, and asceticism offered such a life and identity. Asceticism was accessible to all and provided a new sort of social ranking based on moral superiority and suffering. It offered a method for achieving the higher good that could be practiced alone or in household groups, in cities or remote desert areas. For women, in particular those like Paula with social standing, legal autonomy, and economic resources, asceticism was available as a legitimate choice in their lives. Perhaps just as important, in theory, women were men's equals in ascetic practice and belief. In the broadest possible terms, women and men in the fourth century were both pushed and pulled into ascetic behaviors. As the century progressed, men and women more frequently practiced these behaviors in the Christian households of monasticism.

Individuals like Jerome and Paula adapted their lives and created social spaces in which they could express their religious convictions. But these decisions posed challenges to their families, social peers, and church authorities. Upper-class families in Rome were not always enthusiastic about dedication to ascetic ideals because they feared that the individualism and other-worldliness of asceticism would undermine family lineage and destroy civic responsibility and the common good. Church leaders also had to decide how to incorporate this expanding movement into their emerging structures and how to ensure that believers stayed within the boundaries of established doctrines.

13. Quoted in Brown, *The Body and Society*, p. 61. See Ross Kraemer, *Her Share of the Blessings* (New York: Oxford University Press, 1992), pp. 51–55, for a discussion of Thecla.

14. Petersen, *Handmaids of the Lord*, pp. 18–19. The literature of asceticism in the Empire is vast; however, the following discussion relies on the following most useful works: the works of Peter Brown already cited; Kate Cooper, *The Virgin and the Bride* (Cambridge, Mass.: Harvard University Press, 1996); Susanna Elm, *"Virgins of God": The Making of Asceticism in Late Antiquity* (New York: Oxford University Press, 1994); Anne E. Hickey, *Women of the Roman Aristocracy as Christian Monastics* (Ann Arbor, Mich.: UMI Research Press, 1987); Richard Valantasis and Vincent L. Wimbush (eds.), *Asceticism* (New York: Oxford University Press, 1995).

Nevertheless, people like Paula and Jerome, who entered the ascetic movement at this time of flux and challenge, prevailed and helped to establish a regular tradition of religious life that has lasted into the twenty-first century.

Well before Jerome and Paula met in Rome in the 380s, both were drawn into ascetic life. Given their social positions, intellectual standing, and the limitations or advantages of gender, their paths into dedicated, holy lives were different. For example, Jerome left western Europe in 372, heading for Jerusalem, the destination of many devout pilgrims. He visited Athens and stayed for a time with colleagues in Antioch, where he wrote some of his earliest essays. At this point, the conflict he felt between his secular training and intellectual interests, and his spiritual devotion, caused him great concern. Apparently in a nightmare he had at the time, Jesus appeared, rebuked him for his love of the classics, and convinced him never to read pagan works again. Encouraged by this resolution, he eventually set off for the desert near Chalcis, where numerous colonies of hermits were located. For Jerome, adopting the isolated life of the desert ascetics was not easy; he was, after all, an urban man used to some comforts and social life. He continued to write and receive letters, and even in physical isolation he maintained ties to intellectual debates about issues such as the nature of the trinity. Later Jerome remembered that he was plagued by "sinful" thoughts throughout this period (Document One). He never fit in well with the other desert-dwellers, most of whom were not as educated as he. He eventually returned to Antioch in 376 or 377.

During the next five years, he improved his Greek; engaged in extensive, in-depth biblical studies; and was finally ordained a priest (although he always preferred to be referred to as a monk and never performed pastoral duties). He also began to gain more of an intellectual reputation because he was active in the world of Christian intellectual leaders, and some of his writings caught their attention. Jerome was not a creative or daring thinker, but his learning was impressive and he was capable of persuasive exposition of doctrine, caustic critique of those whom he opposed, and often devastating arguments against those judged to be heretical. In 382, Jerome had the opportunity to accompany several church leaders to a major church conference in Rome, and so he returned to that city for the first time since his school days.

In 366, an old friend and mentor of Jerome's, Damasus, had been named pope. When they met at the conference, Pope Damasus was impressed by Jerome's scholarship and personality. He asked Jerome to help in drafting certain statements of belief and letters on church affairs. When the conference ended, Jerome remained in Rome, and the friendship and working relationship with Pope Damasus made this period one of the happiest of his life. By 384, at Damasus' request, Jerome began a monumental project—one that he would not complete for another twenty-two years: the revision and re-creation of a single

Chapter 5
Spiritual
Partners in Chris-
tian Asceticism:
Jerome (?346–420
C.E.) and Paula
(347–404 C.E.)

standard version of the Bible out of the existing Latin translations. Jerome had never been known for his modesty, gentleness, or self-effacement, and his tendencies to exaggerate and boast of his accomplishment increased as he worked on this project. Revising the Bible was bound to displease many, and Jerome showed no tolerance for others' viewpoints. In fact, he was now able to express considerable self-confidence when he advised a group of upper-class Roman Christian women that they should "learn of me a holy arrogance; know that you are better than them all."[15]

▪ ACT II:

THE FOUNDING OF WOMEN'S RELIGIOUS COMMUNITIES

By 382, when the church council met in Rome, women in that city and throughout western Europe had established their own variations of ascetic life. A few adopted an isolated existence akin to that of the desert hermits, but many more created their own communities of women that were modeled on both the practices and the ideals of household and family. At the same time, they significantly altered these models as they took vows of celibacy, often refused marriage, and even placed children with guardians so they could pursue their goals. Among the upper classes in the Roman Empire, there was a long tradition of retreat for intellectual activity and mental rejuvenation, and both women and men, as far back as the Gracchi, were accustomed to urban circles of friends who gathered for reading and discussion. Christian women, including Paula, continued this sort of activity, but with a spiritual or redemptive focus.

In Rome, the earliest and best known of these religious circles was one created by an upper-class woman,

Marcella (325–410 or 411). Raised as a Christian, Marcella was drawn to the stories of austerity and holiness of the ascetic monks in Egypt, and after a brief marriage left her a widow, she decided not to remarry and to create instead her own version of a religious life.[16] She owned a palace on the Aventine Hill and she turned her home into a religious household dedicated to a routine of prayer, fasting, and acts of mercy and charity. At the age of twenty-seven, she publicly pledged herself to monasticism and scriptural study, and she began to gather other women around her. Starting with her mother, her sister, and a handful of other upper-class women, the numbers in her circle grew. Eventually, Marcella moved part of the community to a farm near Rome, where retirement from public life allowed greater opportunity for peaceful study and contemplation, while the remainder stayed in the Aventine villa under the leadership of her sister Asella. As Marcella's prominence grew, other women emulated her community. In Rome and elsewhere in the western

15. Quoted in Brown, *The Body and Society,* p. 367.

16. Ranft, p. 4.

Roman Empire, this form of expression of religious enthusiasm by women increased (Document Two).

Paula became associated with Marcella's circle after she was widowed in 379. It is important to remember that, although these women from the senatorial class were well educated, their formal education had ended when they were teenagers, and opportunities for religious study were few. Thus, one of the great attractions for Paula was the opportunity to study the Scriptures under the capable tutelage of Marcella. Paula's daughter Eustochium actually took a vow of virginity and moved into Marcella's household. Paula herself gained a reputation for both her religious studies and her acts of charity in the community. She was well known among church leaders, and when Pope Damasus called the conference in 382, one of the eastern bishops stayed at her home during the meetings. The household became a center for visiting churchmen and upper-class Roman women interested in asceticism and the path to holiness. In this setting, she met Jerome.

Apparently Marcella, knowing of Jerome's learning, enlisted him as a teacher of the Scriptures for her group. Jerome responded to her request; he did not lead or dominate the group, but instead was a tremendous resource and guide for them in their search for truth. He later wrote how often Marcella would dispute with him, while also influencing him by reigning in some of his impetuosity. In addition to meetings, conversations, and prayer, they also exchanged letters on various points of scriptural interpretation. Jerome's letters were saved, but none of Marcella's writings or those of the other women survived (as we have seen in cases like that of Cornelia, whose almost entire correspondence was lost).

Jerome was not alone in his admiration for these women and their religious communities. Pope Damasus encouraged Jerome's connections with them throughout 383 and 384 because he supported the development of asceticism in the west. It is also important to remember that Jerome was not the only fourth-century Church Fathers to have close connections to women with similar religious commitments. Ambrose of Milan (340–397) had a sister, Marcellina, who was a consecrated virgin, in other words dedicated to a life of virginity from birth. After he became bishop of Milan in 374, Ambrose helped to found a community of virgins in that city. John of Chrysostom (347–407) had a soulmate, Olympias, a young woman from a very wealthy family, who was orphaned, educated, married, and then a widow by age twenty-five. Like many others, Olympias refused a second marriage and insisted on dedicating herself and her resources to her beliefs.[17] It is also important to acknowledge that all of these women were from elite families, and all had considerable resources at their disposal that they were willing and able to spend or distribute for religious purposes. Paula was probably the least socially and economically powerful of the women, but even she had

17. Elm, pp. 179–180, discusses this relationship and Olympia's devotion.

Chapter 5
Spiritual
Partners in Christian Asceticism:
Jerome (?346–420
c.e.) and Paula
(347–404 c.e.)

strong connections to the inner circles of the Roman aristocracy and had inherited considerable wealth.

Jerome and Paula developed an especially close relationship, often writing letters daily. She was perhaps more softhearted than Marcella, more focused on the moral and imaginative dimensions of Christianity, and more expressive emotionally of her faith. Paula also was a model of ascetic renunciation far more than the moderate Marcella, and perhaps Jerome admired her sense of purpose. Jerome generally did not have warm personal relationships, and perhaps he was seeking the sympathy and kindness that Paula could provide. She evidently had a great impact on him because in a later letter he wrote that there was no other Roman matron "who was able to sway me except Paula. . . . [She was] the only woman who could give me delight."[18]

By early 385, Jerome's position in Rome was becoming uncomfortable for him. As already mentioned, he had antagonized numerous people with his biblical translations, and his campaign for asceticism was gaining publicity and causing concern in influential circles. Numerous elite Roman families did not want their daughters devoted to the church. They opposed the refusal of marriage and the idea of adopting a life of virginity, and were alarmed that women

in their families would give away family wealth. Some took active steps to prevent these developments. Marcella's mother had transferred family wealth to her own brother's children so that Marcella would not give it all away. Marcella, Paula, and Melania the Elder (342–409), who like Paula was part of the second cohort of these religious women, were widows without guardians and therefore in a better position to act independently. More unnerving to the upper-class families were situations where daughters were pledged to virginity even before birth, thus clearly closing the doors on marital prospects and future offspring.

No doubt Jerome became a target for those fearful of the social and familial consequences of asceticism. He added fuel to the fire by writing extensively about the decadence and moral failings of the Roman upper classes, and he also denounced the clergy for hypocrisy if they *didn't* adopt asceticism or encourage virginity in their congregations. The death of one of Paula's daughters, Blaesilla, in late 384 was blamed on her adoption of a severe ascetic lifestyle, and whispering increased about Jerome and Paula's relationship and his influence on her. Pope Damasus died shortly after Blaesilla, and Jerome was thus left without a powerful protector. By then Paula had decided that she would embark on a pilgrimage—travel to holy places was becoming increasingly popular by this time—and spend time in Jerusalem and Bethlehem. Word circulated that Paula and Jerome were planning to go to Jerusalem together, and a church court was convened to examine his actions. Although no par-

18. Quoted in E. Glenn Hinson, "When the World Collapsed: The Spirituality of Women During the Barbarian Invasion of Rome," *Perspectives in Religious Studies*, 20 (1993), p. 122, and in Kelly, p. 109. Both are from his famous Letter 45, written to Asella and defending his connections to the Aventine circle of women.

ticular crimes were proven, his behavior was considered scandalous and Jerome was forced to leave Rome, which he did in August 385. In the meantime, Paula made her pilgrimage plans, including giving up her young son Toxotius to other relatives to raise, and she left Rome in late September 385 with her daughter Eustochium. Jerome and Paula met in Antioch and then traveled to the Holy Land. The first phase of their friendship and their spiritual quest was over; the second was about to begin.

■ ACT III:

MONASTICISM IN PRACTICE

Paula and Jerome first traveled to Egypt because Paula was interested in visiting sites of ascetic life, both of individual desert hermits, and groups of "solitaries," as they were called. Apparently, she even considered joining one of the desert communities, but given his previous experience, Jerome probably opposed that idea, and within a month or so they had returned to Palestine, where they eventually settled in Bethlehem.[19] The small town with a population engaged in agriculture and sheep raising was becoming more of an attraction for pilgrims by this time. In the next three years, Paula and Jerome would make Bethlehem their home, and with her money they built a hospice for travelers; a monastery for men; and standing next to it, a larger, more complex convent for women. In some ways, these communities mirrored already existing institutions in Egypt and Asia Minor.

After his Christian baptism, an Egyptian, Pachomius (290–346), was drawn to the ascetic life, but he also realized that "the solitary way neglected the commandment to active charity," something he believed in deeply. He attracted followers and eventually, in 324, founded a community on the Nile River at Tabennesi. His goal was to "nourish the soul" in a community that was organized and based on firm scriptural grounds.[20] About five years after the founding of this monastery, Pachomius's sister joined them, and together they established a community for her that attracted other women. More and more individuals joined them, forming additional centers, but all were attached to the main monastery, where Pachomius acted much like a *paterfamilias* at the center of his household.

A similar but slightly later development in Asia Minor also sustained ascetic ideals within a community and developed written precepts that they followed. Like Jerome, the individuals in this group were all well trained in classical Greek language and culture, although each was "at the same time intensely critical of that tradition."[21] Basil of Caesarea (329–379) and his

---

19. Kelly, pp. 124–128.

20. Elm, p. 288. Chapter 9 is dedicated to Pachomian monasticism. Chapters 2 and 3 focus on Basil, bishop of Caesarea, and his family.

21. Jaroslav Pelikan, *Christianity and Classical Culture* (New Haven, Conn.: Yale University Press, 1993), p. 8. Quote that follows is from p. 177.

elder sister Macrina established both male and female communities in 357 across the river from their family's estate at Annesi. The two "households" had contact with each other and lived by much the same rules, combining the contemplative life with a life of communal work and prayer. Macrina had decided on an ascetic life when she was twelve; she never married but described herself as a widow. Basil referred to her as "sister and teacher," and she demonstrated her level of erudition by insisting that a training in classicism could "be turned to the overthrow of truth," but it could also be a useful tool for "the detection of falsehood." Her life story was written by another of her brothers, Gregory, a theologian and bishop of Nyssa, and became available to the public about 380, when Macrina died (Document Three). Experiences such as these had become well-known models in the west by the time Jerome and Paula started their journey.

Another woman from Marcella's circle, Melanie the Elder, had gone to Palestine in 372 when her husband and two sons died, and by 378 she was in charge of a convent of fifty women on the Mount of Olives in Jerusalem. She was joined there in 381 by Rufinus, an old schoolfriend and colleague of Jerome's, who worked with Melanie and helped to supervise the men's community.[22] Women like Melanie, Paula, and Paula's daughter Eustochium who traveled to well-known shrines; created gathering places for holy women; often ministered to other women; and took vows of worldly renunciation, celibacy, or virginity, were well respected, even held in awe. Melanie was sometimes referred to as a "female man of God," while one of the early histories of ascetics refers to both sexes as "Fathers, male and female."[23]

Monastic communities like Paula's were modeled along the lines of the Roman households in which the women had been raised. They owned their own property, strove to be economically self-sufficient, shared in the labor, followed prescribed ideals of behavior, and had an internal hierarchy.[24] Paula and the women who joined her community saw their actions as following in Jesus' footsteps by adopting celibacy and by fasting and praying together at numerous times during the day, on retiring, and then again at midnight. They had no servants and shared work assignments. They also read and sang Scriptures together, attended church services together, and carried out a regular program of charity. They had little contact with men, though Jerome was the exception (Document Four).

Jerome found this experience with asceticism much more suitable, although even in this setting he did not follow the rule completely because he did no physical labor. For him, this was a period of heightened intellectual activity. He set up a library or visited libraries close to Bethlehem, had a tutor who gave him lessons in He-

22. See Kelly and Hinson for a discussion of Melania the Elder.

23. The first quote is in Brown, *The Body and Society*, p. 280. The second is quoted in Elm, p. 312. Both are from Palladius' *Historia Lausiaca*.

24. Elm, p. 374.

brew, and hired stenographers to copy his work. Not surprisingly, this activity was funded by Paula's wealth, although that resource eventually would run out, given her generosity. But Paula and her community were also engaged in intellectual activities, often requesting specific translations by Jerome, and some of his writings at this time are dedicated to Paula and Eustochium and acknowledge their instigation for the pieces. Jerome continued to discuss theological issues with Paula, and it appears that Paula also learned to read Hebrew at this time. One of Jerome's ongoing efforts was biblical translation, and around 390 he started the translation of a Hebrew version of the Old Testament and finally finished it in 405. He also translated into Latin Pachomius's writings, including his rules for monasticism, thus making these more available in the west, where monasticism grew as well. But Jerome could or did not choose to adopt Paula's brand of sacrifice, and he watched her severe regimen both with awe and with fear for its devastating effects on her health.

By the 380s, when Paula and Jerome were preparing to pursue their joint spiritual lives, questions about asceticism and adoption of a virginal life were also becoming more frequent among church leaders. As already noted, the purity and holiness that accompanied virginity and celibacy were admirable, but there were apparent dangers in this life if it was not somehow regulated and directed more officially by the recognized authorities of the church—bishops, councils, and of course the pope. Heresy was al-

ways a danger for the solitary communities, and the male and female shared communities continued to present the temptation of sexual attractions and illicit behaviors. Finally at issue was the exact place holy women would have in the church hierarchy. By the fourth century, women were not allowed to occupy official positions of authority in the Christian church, but the following question remained—what to do with the de facto authority women like Melanie and Paula gained through their example? Jerome, for one, seemed to take for granted "the profound identity of the minds of men and women, and saw no reason all aspects of intellectual and spiritual life should not be extended to women as to men."[25] Earlier in his career, Jerome had relied on ideas of Origen, who had argued that the body and sexuality had little to do with defining the human spirit, and that in spiritual transformation men and women overcame the physical differences that separated them. Later it was widely believed that Origen (ca. 206) had gone to a doctor to have himself castrated, thus, in a way, practicing what he preached about sexual identity and spiritual growth.[26]

By the early 390s, Jerome stressed the superior life of virginity and questioned the value of marriage. His essay *Against Jovinian*, written in 393, was a polemical statement of this position (Document Five). Within a few years, Jerome found himself in the

25. Brown, *Body and Society*, p. 369.
26. Ibid., pp. 168–169.

Chapter 5
Spiritual
Partners in Chris-
tian Asceticism:
Jerome (?346–420
c.e.) and Paula
(347–404 c.e.)

unwelcome position of being associated with Origen, who was now considered a heretic by many, and was under attack by other church leaders who either stressed the importance of marriage or felt it important to accept a much more skeptical view of the possibility of asexual, virginal relations between men and women. Similarly, a much more materialist approach to the body, including warnings of the dangers of sexual drives, was regaining ascendancy (Document Six).

Jerome backed away from association with Origen's ideas but continued to believe in the path of virginity, especially for young women. In 401 or 402, he wrote what would become a famous guide for parents who chose to dedicate their daughters to a religious life. He addressed the letter to Paula's son Toxotius and his wife Laeta, by then both devoted Christians who apparently had asked him

how to raise a consecrated virgin (Document Seven). In the letter he suggested that their daughter, named Paula after her grandmother, should come to live in their community in Bethlehem. She eventually did so, but not in time to meet her grandmother, who died in January 404. Jerome was devastated by Paula's death; for over twenty years they had followed the same path, working together and sharing visions and goals. He wrote a consolatory letter to Eustochium that is a memorial to Paula and her works. Eustochium was also inconsolable at her mother's death, but she continued the religious life they had shared, running the monasteries and giving Jerome the affection and support he needed. He was now in his seventies, and in addition to the mental strain and anger that the intellectual controversies were causing him, his physical health was failing.

■ FINALE

The opening years of the fifth century were unstable and threatening for all the inhabitants of the Roman Empire. Germanic tribes moved into Italy, and the Visigothic king Alaric laid seige to Rome, eventually sacking the city in 410. Marcella, the grand figure of early female ascetic communities, perished in one of those attacks. Melanie had been in Rome but had returned to Jerusalem at the time of the attacks and died shortly thereafter. She had a granddaughter to succeed her, Melanie the Younger (385–448), who convinced

her husband to live in chastity with her and to continue her grandmother's work. Jerome saw many of these events as the world collapsing around him and interpreted them as God's punishment of a sinful society. Even so, he continued to be involved in the theological controversies of the day, usually by supporting the established orthodox positions of the church. He relied on Eustochium, but outlived her, and after her death in 418 or 419, the young Paula took on the same responsibilities. The last letter he wrote expresses both his physical and mental fatigue and feebleness, and indicates his willingness to have someone else take on the duties of defending the faith and protecting the true doctrine. When he died in 420, no one wrote about him, and he was buried in Bethlehem near Paula and Eustochium.

By the time of his death, the controversial Jerome probably had more enemies than friends. Over the following centuries, views of him would gradually change and he too would become one of the fathers of the church, along with his contemporaries Ambrose and Augustine. The kind of life that he and Paula led did not disappear, and variations of the early Christian ascetic communities formed the basis for Christian monasticism, one of the lasting achievements of the fourth century and a remarkable illustration of the changes and adaptability of the Roman Church as it was legalized.

Many issues remained unresolved after Paula, Jerome, and their contemporaries died. For some, the appeal of asceticism and the growth of monasticism had its problematic side. As asceticism, virginity, and celibacy gained prestige and even became desirable prerequisites for authority in the church, other questions emerged. Because many of the participants in these movements were female, did this mean that women could occupy formal positions of power in the religious hierarchy? The answer to that question was no, but at the same time asceticism and holiness remained alternative means for female identity and expression of belief. The church tried to define norms of female ascetic behavior, but the very attempt to place limits on female holy charisma "could result in an expanded role for such 'holy' women" whose visions, severe fasts, and austere lives seemed to be the embodiment of saintliness. Also, as the ascetic movement strengthened the priesthood, it also created a kind of separatism that excluded those who didn't meet the new "holy" standards. "Men and women who could claim neither clerical status nor ascetic stature [were] second class citizens in the city of God."[27] Church leaders would try to lessen this division through guides for good marriages, but the message never matched the heroism of bodily renunciation, physical suffering, and self-sacrifice. Another possibility was to develop a hagiography for holy wives, perhaps modeled along the lines of Melanie the Younger, whose life was indeed added to the menu of possible behaviors for married women. As the Roman Empire came to a close, newly Christianized populations in the west and their religious leaders confronted similar issues, and the question of the spiritual value of virginity versus the social, political, and moral value of marriage continued to provoke controversy and debate.

27. For these remarks about the legacies of asceticism, see Elm, pp. 165–166, and Cooper, pp. 115, 126.

Chapter 5
Spiritual
Partners in Chris-
tian Asceticism:
Jerome (?346–420
C.E.) and Paula
(347–404 C.E.)

▥ QUESTIONS

1. How did the legalization of Christianity alter the character of the early Christian Church? What was gained? What was lost?

2. How was the legal church influenced by existing Roman political, social, and economic structures, and Roman values and ideals?

3. What factors explain the appeal of asceticism to people in the fourth century? Were these factors the same for men and women?

4. Historians now argue that women played a much greater role in the Christianization of the Roman Empire, and in the growth of monasticism, than previously thought. What evidence can you cite that might support this argument?

5. What were Jerome's contributions to the development of Christianity in this early period?

6. As it gained strength, monasticism seemed to be a mixed blessing for the authorities of the church. Explain this contradiction.

▥ DOCUMENTS

▬▬▬ DOCUMENT ONE ▬▬▬

JEROME

Letter to Eustochium, Letter 22

Most of Jerome's letters were written after he returned to Rome in 382. In this early letter addressed to Eustochium, he recounts his earlier search for intellectual peace and his struggle to overcome bodily temptations. What is the more general message conveyed in this letter?

. . . Oh, how often, when I was living in the desert, in that lonely waste, scorched by the burning sun, which affords to hermits a savage dwelling-place, how often did I fancy myself surrounded by the pleasures of Rome! I used to sit alone; for I was filled with bitterness. My unkempt limbs were covered in shapeless sackcloth; my skin through long neglect had become as rough and black as an Ethiopian's. Tears and groans were every day my portion; and if sleep ever overcame my resistance and fell upon my eyes, I bruised my restless bones against the naked earth. Of food and drink I will not speak. Hermits have nothing but cold water even when they are sick, and for them it is sinful luxury to partake of cooked dishes. But though in my fear of hell I had condemned myself to this prison-house, where my only companions were scorpions and wild beasts, I often found myself surrounded by bands of dancing girls. My face was pale with fasting; but though my limbs were cold as ice my mind was burning with desire, and the fires of lust kept bubbling up before me when my flesh was as good as dead.

. . . [A]nd if my flesh still rebelled I subdued it by weeks of fasting. I do not blush to confess my misery; nay, rather, I lament that I am not now what once I was. I remember that often I joined night to day with my wailings and ceased not from beating my breast till tranquillity returned to me at the Lord's behest. I used to dread my poor cell as though it knew my secret thoughts. Filled with stiff anger against myself, I would make my way alone into the desert; and when I came upon some hollow valley or rough mountain or precipitous cliff, there I would set up my oratory, and make that spot a place of torture for my unhappy flesh. . . .

. . . I will tell you the story of my own unhappy experience.

Many years ago for the sake of the kingdom of heaven I cut myself off from home, parents, sister, relations, and, what was harder, from the dainty food to which I had been used. But even when I was on my way to Jerusalem to fight the good fight there, I could not bring myself to forgo the library which with great care and labour I had got together at Rome. And so, miserable man that I was, I would fast, only to read Cicero afterwards. I would spend many nights in vigil, I would shed bitter tears called from my inmost heart by the remembrance of my past sins; and then I would take up Plautus again. Whenever I returned to my right senses and began to read the prophets, their language seemed harsh and barbarous. With my blind eyes I could not see the light: but I attributed the fault not to my eyes but to the sun. While the old serpent was thus mocking me, about the middle of Lent a fever attacked my weakened body and spread through my inmost veins. It may sound incredible, but the ravages it wrought on my unhappy frame were so persistent that at last my bones scarcely held together.

Meantime preparations were made for my funeral: my whole body grew gradually cold, and life's vital warmth only lingered faintly in my poor throbbing breast. Suddenly I was caught up in the spirit and dragged before the Judge's judgment seat: and here the light was so dazzling, and the brightness shining from those who stood around so radiant, that I flung myself upon the ground and did not dare to look up. I was asked to state my condition and replied that I was a Christian. But He who presided said: 'Thou liest; thou art a Ciceronian, not a Christian. "For where thy treasure is there will thy heart be also."' Straightway I became dumb, and amid the strokes of the whip—for He had ordered me to be scourged—I was even more bitterly tortured by the fire of conscience, considering with myself the verse; 'In the grave who shall give thee thanks?' Yet for all that I began to cry out and to bewail myself, saying: 'Have mercy upon me, O Lord, have mercy upon me': and even amid the noise of the lash my voice made itself heard. At last the bystanders fell at the knees of Him who presided, and prayed Him to pardon my youth and give me opportunity to repent of my error, on the understanding that the extreme of torture should be inflicted on me if ever I read again the works of Gentile authors. . . .

[139]

Chapter 5
Spiritual
Partners in Chris-
tian Asceticism:
Jerome (?346–420
C.E.) and Paula
(347–404 C.E.)

DOCUMENT TWO

JEROME

Letter to Principia, Letter 127

This letter was written as a memorial to Marcella following her death circa 410. In it, Jerome describes this remarkable woman. What traits most impressed him? What do you see as Marcella's impact on the development of Christianity?

. . . [Marcella's] widow's clothing was meant to keep out the cold and not to shew her figure. Of gold she would not wear so much as a seal-ring, choosing to store her money in the stomachs of the poor rather than to keep it at her own disposal. She went nowhere without her mother, and would never see without witnesses such monks and clergy as the needs of a large house required her to interview. Her train was always composed of virgins and widows, and these women serious and staid; for, as she well knew, the levity of the maids speaks ill for the mistress and a woman's character is shewn by her choice of companions.

4. Her delight in the divine scriptures was incredible. She was for ever singing, "Thy words have I hid in mine heart that I might not sin against thee," as well as the words which describe the perfect man, "his delight is in the law of the Lord; and in his law doth he meditate day and night." This meditation in the law she understood not of a review of the written words as among the Jews the Pharisees think, but of action according to that saying of the apostle, "whether, therefore, ye eat or drink or what soever ye do, do all to the glory of God." She remembered also the prophet's words, "through thy precepts I get understanding," and felt sure that only when she had fulfilled these would she be permitted to understand the scriptures. In this sense we read elsewhere that "Jesus began both to do and teach." For teaching is put to the blush when a man's conscience rebukes him; and it is in vain that his tongue preaches poverty or teaches alms-giving if he is rolling in the riches of Croesus and if, in spite of his threadbare cloak, he has silken robes at home to save from the moth.

Marcella practised fasting, but in moderation. She abstained from eating flesh, and she knew rather the scent of wine than its taste; touching it only for her stomach's sake and for her often infirmities. She seldom appeared in public and took care to avoid the houses of great ladies, that she might not be forced to look upon what she had once for all renounced. She frequented the basilicas of apostles and martyrs that she might escape from the throng and give herself to private prayer. So obedient was she to her mother that for her sake she did things of which she herself disapproved. For example, when her mother, careless of her own offspring, was for transferring all her property from her children and grandchildren to her brother's family, Marcella wished the money to be given to the poor instead, and yet could not bring herself to thwart her parent. Therefore she made over her ornaments and other effects to persons already rich, content to throw away her money rather than to sadden her mother's heart.

5. In those days no highborn lady at Rome had made profession of the monastic life, or had ventured—so strange and ignominious and degrading did it then seem—publicly to call herself a nun. It was from some priests of Alexandria, and from pope Athanasius, and subsequently from Peter, who, to escape the persecution of the Arian heretics, had all fled for refuge to Rome as the safest haven in which they could find communion—it was from these that Marcella heard of the life of the blessed Antony, then still alive, and of the monasteries in the Thebaid founded by Pachomius, and of the discipline laid down for virgins and for widows. Nor was she ashamed to profess a life which she had thus learned to be pleasing to Christ. . . . My revered friend Paula was blessed with Marcella's friendship, and it was in Marcella's cell that Eustochium, that paragon of virgins, was gradually trained. Thus it is easy to see of what type the mistress was who found such pupils.

The unbelieving reader may perhaps laugh at me for dwelling so long on the praises of mere women; yet if he will but remember how holy women followed our Lord and Saviour and ministered to Him of their substance, and how the three Marys stood before the cross and especially how Mary Magdalen—called the tower from the earnestness and glow of her faith—was privileged to see the rising Christ first of all before the very apostles, he will convict himself of pride sooner than me of folly. For we judge of people's virtue not by their sex but by their character, and hold those to be worthy of the highest glory who have renounced both rank and wealth. It was for this reason that Jesus loved the evangelist John more than the other disciples. For John was of noble birth and known to the high priest, yet was so little appalled by the plottings of the Jews that he introduced Peter into his court, and was the only one of the apostles bold enough to take his stand before the cross. For it was he who took the Savior's parent to his own home; it was the virgin son who received the virgin mother as a legacy from the Lord.

6. Marcella then lived the ascetic life for many years, and found herself old before she bethought herself that she had once been young. She often quoted with approval Plato's saying that philosophy consists in meditating on death. A truth which our own apostle indorses when he says: "for your salvation I die daily." Indeed according to the old copies our Lord himself says: "whosoever doth not bear His cross daily and come after me cannot be my disciple." Ages before, the Holy Spirit had said by the prophet: "for thy sake are we killed all the day long: we are counted as sheep for the slaughter." Many generations afterwards the words were spoken: "remember the end and thou shalt never do amiss," as well as that precept of the eloquent satirist: "live with death in your mind; time flies; this say of mine is so much taken from it." Well then, as I was saying, she passed her days and lived always in the thought that she must die. Her very clothing was such as to remind her of the tomb, and she presented herself as a living sacrifice, reasonable and acceptable, unto God.

*Chapter 5
Spiritual
Partners in Chris-
tian Asceticism:
Jerome (?346–420
C.E.) and Paula
(347–404 C.E.)*

7. When the needs of the Church at length brought me to Rome in company with the reverend pontiffs, Paulinus and Epiphanius—the first of whom ruled the church of the Syrian Antioch while the second presided over that of Salamis in Cyprus,—I in my modesty was for avoiding the eyes of highborn ladies, yet she pleaded so earnestly, "both in season and out of season" as the apostle says, that at last her perseverance overcame my reluctance. And, as in those days my name was held in some renown as that of a student of the scriptures, she never came to see me that she did not ask me some question concerning them, nor would she at once acquiesce in my explanations but on the contrary would dispute them; not, however, for argument's sake but to learn the answers to those objections which might, as she saw, be made to my statements. How much virtue and ability, how much holiness and purity I found in her I am afraid to say; both lest I may exceed the bounds of men's belief and lest I may increase your sorrow by reminding you of the blessings that you have lost. This much only will I say, that whatever in me was the fruit of long study and as such made by constant meditation a part of my nature, this she tasted, this she learned and made her own. Consequently after my departure from Rome, in case of a dispute arising as to the testimony of scripture on any subject, recourse was had to her to settle it. And so wise was she and so well did she understand what philosophers call *to prepon,* that is, "the becoming," in what she did, that when she answered questions she gave her own opinion not as her own but as from me or some one else, thus admitting that what she taught she had herself learned from others. For she knew that the apostle had said: "I suffer not a woman to teach," and she would not seem to inflict a wrong upon the male sex many of whom (including sometimes priests) questioned her concerning obscure and doubtful points. . . .

DOCUMENT THREE

GREGORY OF NYSSA

Life of Macrina
(ca. 380)

Macrina becomes a model of asceticism for western women through her brother's narrative of her life. In what ways is Macrina a typical ascetic woman? What parts of her life became standards for women wishing to follow a religious life?

THE PROSPECT OF MARRIAGE

Having grown up amid these and similar pursuits, especially in working with her hands at spinning, she reached her twelfth year, in which the flower of youth begins to blossom in particular splendor. Here it is appropriate for us to wonder whether or not the beauty of the young girl, though it had been kept hidden, would escape notice. Indeed there did not seem anything so marvelous throughout the whole of that region that it could be compared with her beauty and charm. The hands of painters could not do justice to her in her bloom.

Although the art of the painter is altogether ingenious and dares to confront the greatest subjects, so as to create by means of imitation images of the sun and planets themselves, it was unable to represent accurately the harmonious beauty of her form. A swarm of suitors besieged her parents on account of her beauty, but her father (a man of prudence and good judgement) chose out from the rest a well-born young man from those of his own kin, who was remarkable for his good character and had only recently completed his education. It was to him that he decided to betroth his daughter, when she had reached the appropriate age. In the meantime, the young man showed promise for the future and brought to Macrina's father, as a joyful wedding gift, a character which equalled his reputation. In the law-courts he displayed his power of speech on behalf of those who had been wronged. Yet envy cut off these promising hopes by snatching him from life at an age to arouse our pity.

MACRINA'S DECISION TO ADOPT A LIFE OF VIRGINITY

The young girl was not unaware of her father's decision, but when the plans that had been made for her were destroyed by the death of the young man, she came to regard the marriage which her father had arranged for her as though it had actually taken place. She made up her mind to live the rest of her life on her own, and her decision was firmer than might have been expected at her age. Her parents often brought up the subject of marriage with her, because there were many men wishing to be her suitors on account of the fame of her beauty. To them she replied that it was absurd and contrary to law and custom for them not to be satisfied with the marriage which had been concluded for her by her father once and for all, but to require her to look to marriage to another; for marriage was by its nature unique, just as birth and death are unique. She strongly maintained that the man to whom she was united in accordance with the decision of her parents had not died; her judgement was that he was 'living in God' through hope of the resurrection and that he had 'gone away' and was not a corpse. It was absurd, in her opinion, not to keep faith with a bridegroom who was on a journey.

Repelling by such arguments those who tried to overrule her, she decided that the only way of safeguarding her noble resolve was never to be separated

Chapter 5
Spiritual
Partners in Chris-
tian Asceticism:
Jerome (?346–420
C.E.) and Paula
(347–404 C.E.)

from her mother, not even for a single moment, so that her mother used to say that she carried her other children for the normal length of time, but that she carried Macrina everywhere within herself, always enclosed, so to speak, within her heart. However, living in common with her daughter was by no means burdensome or lacking in advantage for the mother, for the loving service that her daughter bestowed upon her replaced the work of several maids. There was a fruitful exchange between them: the mother cared for her daughter's soul and the daughter, her mother's body. Macrina fulfilled the service required of her in every other department; she even frequently prepared bread for her mother with her own hands. This, however, was not the principal activity in which she displayed her zeal; after she had used her hands for liturgical purposes, she then provided food for her mother by her own labors in the time that she had left, as she thought this appropriate to her way of life. Not only did she do this, but she also shared with her mother full responsibility in running the household, for her mother had four sons and five daughters and paid taxes to three rulers, because her property was scattered over as many provinces. For this reason, Macrina shared in her mother's varied concerns, for her father was already dead. In all these affairs she was the partner of her mother's labors, sharing her burdens and lightening the weight of her grief. At the same time she both retained her own purity of life through her mother's training—that life which was throughout directed and witnessed by her mother—and provided her mother with a similar ideal—I mean the ideal of philosophy—by means of her own example, drawing her gradually towards a more simple way of life, detached from material things.

MACRINA'S INFLUENCE OVER HER BROTHER BASIL

At the time when her mother was suitably occupied in regulating the affairs of Macrina's sisters, according to what seemed to her right for each of them, the great Basil returned home. He was the brother of the aforesaid Macrina, and during all this long period, he had been receiving training in rhetoric in the schools. Macrina found that he had become excessively exalted by the idea of his own gift of oratory. He despised all those who held public office and was puffed up with pride, regarding himself as a man above the notabilities of the province. She therefore drew him too towards the ideal of philosophy, so rapidly that he renounced worldly fame. He despised the admiration which he had won through his eloquence and became, as it were, a deserter to a hard life of manual labor. Through his complete detachment from material possessions he prepared for himself a way of life in which he would be unhindered in his pursuit of virtue. However, his life and his subsequent practices, through which he became known in every country under the sun and overshadowed all those who were distinguished for their virtue with his reputation, would need a lengthy narrative and plenty of time. Let my story return once more to its point.

[144]

THE CONVERSION OF THE FAMILY HOME INTO A MONASTERY

As the pretext for every kind of materialistic life had already been taken away from them, Macrina persuaded her mother to abandon the conventions of social life and the manners of a woman of the world, to give up the services of her maids, which she had been accustomed to receive up to that time, and to regard herself as being of the same rank as the mass of the people, involving herself in her personal life with all the virgins she had with her, by sharing their pursuits and making sisters and equals out of slave-women and servants. . . .

DOCUMENT FOUR

JEROME

Letter to Eustochium, Letter 108

This letter is Jerome's memorial to Paula and was written after her death. What are the concrete facts of Paula's life that we can glean from this letter? What aspects seem romantic idealizations and reflections of Jerome's affection for Paula?

. . . And who could find there a greater marvel than Paula? As among many jewels the most precious shine most brightly, and as the sun with its beams obscures and puts out the paler fires of the stars, so by her lowliness she surpassed all others in virtue and influence and, while she was least among all, was greater than all. The more she cast herself down, the more she was lifted up by Christ. She was hidden and yet she was not hidden. By shunning glory she earned glory; for glory follows virtue as its shadow; and deserting those who seek it, it seeks those who despise it. But I must not neglect to proceed with my narrative or dwell too long on a single point, forgetful of the rules of writing.

Being then of such parentage, Paula married Toxotius in whose veins ran the noble blood of Aeneas and the Julii. Accordingly his daughter, Christ's virgin Eustochium, is called Julia, as he is Julius, 'A name from great Iulus handed down.'

I speak of these things not as of importance to those who have them, but as worthy of remark in those who despise them. Men of the world look up to persons who are rich in such privileges. We, on the other hand, praise those who for the Saviour's sake despise them; and strangely depreciating all who keep them, we eulogize those who are unwilling to do so. Thus nobly born, Paula through her fruitfulness and her chastity alike won approval from all, from her husband first, then from her relatives, and lastly from the whole city. She bore five children: Blesilla, for whose death I consoled her while at Rome; Paulina,

[145]

Chapter 5
Spiritual
Partners in Chris-
tian Asceticism:
Jerome (?346–420
c.e.) and Paula
(347–404 c.e.)

who has left the reverend and admirable Pammachius to inherit both her vows and property, to whom also I addressed a little book on her death, Eustochium, who is now in the holy places, a precious necklace of virginity and of the Church; Rufina, whose untimely end overcame the affectionate heart of her mother; and Toxotius, after whom she had no more children. You can thus see that it was not her wish to continue to fulfill a wife's duty, but that she only complied with her husband's longing to have male offspring.

When he died, her grief was so great that she nearly died herself; yet so completely did she then give herself to the service of the Lord, that it might have seemed that she had desired his death. In what terms shall I speak of her distinguished and noble and formerly wealthy house, almost all the riches of which she spent on the poor? How can I describe the great consideration she showed to all and her far-reaching kindness even to those whom she had never seen? What poor man, as he lay dying, was not wrapped in blankets given by her? What bedridden person was not supported with money from her purse? She would seek out such with the greatest diligence throughout the city, and would think it her loss were any hungry or sick person to be supported by another's food. She robbed her children; and, when her relatives remonstrated with her for doing so, she declared that she was leaving to them a better inheritance in the mercy of Christ.

Nor was she long able to endure the visits and crowded receptions which her high position in the world and her exalted family entailed upon her. She received the homage paid to her sadly, and made all the speed she could to shun and to escape those who wished to pay her compliments. It so happened that at that time the bishops of the East and West had been summoned to Rome by letter from the emperors to deal with certain dissensions between the churches, and in this way she saw two most admirable men and christian prelates, Paulinus, bishop of Antioch, and Epiphanius, bishop of Salamis (or, as it is now called, Constantia) in Cyprus. Epiphanius, indeed, she received as her guest; and, although Paulinus was staying in another person's house, in the warmth of her heart she treated him as if he too were lodged with her. Inflamed by their virtues, she thought every moment of forsaking her country. Disregarding her home, her children, her servants, her property, and in a word everything connected with the world, she was eager—alone and unaccompanied (if ever it could be said that she was so)—to go to the desert made famous by its Pauls and by its Antony. And at last when the winter was over and the sea was open, and when the bishops were returning to their churches, she also sailed with them in her prayers and desires. Not to prolong the story, she went down to the harbor accompanied by her brother, her kinsfolk and, above all, her own children [eager by their demonstrations of affection to overcome their loving mother]. At last the sails were set and the strokes of the oars carried the vessel into the deep. On the shore the little Toxotius stretched forth his hands in entreaty, while Rufina, now grown up, with silent sobs besought her mother to wait till she should be married. But still Paula's eyes were dry as she turned them heavenwards;

and she overcame her love for her children by her love for God. She knew herself no more as a mother, that she might prove herself a handmaid of Christ. Yet her heart was rent within her, and she wrestled with her grief, as though she were being torn away from part of herself. The greatness of the affection she had to overcome made everyone admire her victory the more. Among the cruel hardships which attend prisoners of war in the hands of their enemies, there is none severer than the separation of parents from their children. Though it is against the laws of nature, she endured this trial with unabated faith; nay more she sought it with a joyful heart; and spurning her love for her children by her greater love for God, she concentrated herself quietly on Eustochium alone, the partner alike of her vows and of her voyage. Meantime the vessel ploughed onwards and all her fellow-passengers looked back to the shore. But she turned her eyes that she might not see what she could not behold without agony. No mother, it must be confessed, ever loved her children so dearly. Before setting out she gave them all that she had, disinheriting herself upon earth that she might find an inheritance in heaven. . . .

. . . [On Cyprus] she visited all the monasteries in the island, and left, so far as her means allowed, substantial relief for the brothers whom love of the holy man had brought thither from all parts of the world. Then crossing the narrow sea she landed at Seleucia, and going up thence to Antioch allowed herself to be detained for a little time by the affection of the reverend confessor Paulinus. Then, such as the ardor of her faith that she, a noble lady who had always previously been carried by eunuchs, went her way—and that in midwinter—riding on an ass. . . .

I shall now describe the order of her monastery and the method by which she turned the continence of saintly souls to her own profit. She sowed carnal things that she might reap spiritual things; she gave earthly things that she might receive heavenly things; she forewent things temporal that she might in their stead obtain things eternal. Besides establishing a monastery for men, the charge of which she left to men, she divided into three companies and monasteries the numerous virgins whom she had gathered out of different provinces, some of whom are of noble birth while others belonged to the middle or lower classes. But, although they worked and had their meals separately from each other, these three companies met together for psalm-singing and prayer. After the chanting of the Alleluia—the signal by which they were summoned to the Collect—no one was permitted to remain behind. But coming either first or among the first, she used to await the arrival of the rest, urging them to diligence rather by her own modest example than by motives of fear. At dawn, at the third, sixth, and ninth hours, at evening, and at midnight they recited the Psalter each in turn. No sister was allowed to be ignorant of the psalms, and all had every day to learn a certain portion of the holy Scriptures. On the Lord's day only, they proceeded to the church beside which they lived, each company following its own mother-superior. Returning home in the same order, they then devoted themselves to their allotted tasks, and made garments either for

[147]

Chapter 5
Spiritual
Partners in Chris-
tian Asceticism:
Jerome (?346–420
c.e.) and Paula
(347–404 c.e.)

themselves or else for others. If any was of noble birth, she was not allowed to have an attendant from home lest her maid, having her mind full of the doings of old days and of the licence of childhood, might by constant converse open old wounds and renew former errors. All the sisters were clothed alike. Linen was not used except for drying the hands. So strictly did she separate them from men that she would not allow even eunuchs to approach them, lest she should give any occasion to slanderous tongues, always ready to cavil at the religious, to console themselves for their own misdeeds. When anyone was backward in coming to the recitation of the psalms or showed herself remiss in her work, she used to approach her in different ways. Was she quick-tempered? Paula coaxed her. Was she phlegmatic? Paula chided her, copying the example of the Apostle who said: *What do you want? Shall I come to you with a rod or in the spirit of gentleness and meekness?* Apart from food and raiment she allowed no one to have anything she could call her own, for Paul had said: *Having food and raiment we are content.* She was afraid lest the custom of having more should breed covetousness in them—an appetite which no wealth can satisfy, for the more it has, the more it requires, and neither opulence or indigence is able to diminish it. When the sisters quarrelled with another, she reconciled them with soothing words. If the young girls were troubled with fleshly desires, she broke their force by imposing frequent and redoubled fasts; for she wished them to be ill in body rather than to suffer in soul. If she chanced to notice any sister too attentive to her dress, she reproved her for her error with knitted brows and severe looks, saying: 'A clean body and a clean dress mean an unclean soul; a virgin's lips should never utter an improper or an impure word, for such indicate a lascivious mind, and by the outward man the faults of the inward are made manifest.' When she saw a sister verbose and talkative or forward and taking pleasure in quarrels, and when she found after frequent admonitions that the offender showed no signs of improvement, she placed her among the lowest of the sisters and outside their society, ordering her to pray at the door of the refectory and take her food by herself, in the hope that where rebuke had failed, shame might bring about a reformation. The sin of theft she loathed as if it were sacrilege; and that which among men of the world is counted little or nothing, she declared to be a crime of the deepest dye in a monastery. How shall I describe her kindness and attention towards the sick or the wonderful care and devotion with which she nursed them? Yet, although when others were sick she freely gave them every indulgence, and even allowed them to eat meat, whenever she fell ill herself, she made no concessions to her own weakness, and seemed unfair in this respect, that in her own case she exchanged for harshness the kindness which she was always ready to show to others.

No young girl of sound and vigorous constitution ever delivered herself up to a regimen so rigid as that imposed upon herself by Paula, whose physical powers age had impaired and enfeebled. I admit that in this she was too determined, refusing to spare herself or to listen to advice. . . .

DOCUMENT FIVE

JEROME

Against Jovinian
(393)

In this essay, Jerome answers those individuals who were arguing that salvation didn't come from works or way of life but was strictly spiritual. Jovinian, another Christian writer, in particular, had argued that virginity had no special place in Christian doctrine. How does Jerome defend virginity? As a result of his views on virginity, what does he say about marriage?

The battle must be fought with the whole army of the enemy, and the disorderly rabble, fighting more like brigands than soldiers, must be repulsed by the skill and method of regular warfare. In the front rank I will set the Apostle Paul, and, since he is the bravest of generals, will arm him with his own weapons, that is to say, his own statements. . . .

[Jerome then repeats Paul's statements from 1 Corinthians 7.] Let us turn back to the chief point of evidence: "It is good," he says, "for a man not to touch a woman." If it is good not to touch a woman, it is bad to touch one: for there is no opposite to goodness but badness. But if it be bad and the evil is pardoned, the reason for the concession is to prevent worse evil. But surely a thing which is only allowed because there may be something worse has only a slight degree of goodness. He would never have added "let each man have his own wife," unless he had previously used the words "but, because of fornications." Do away with fornication, and he will not say "let each man have his own wife." Just as though one were to lay it down: "It is good to feed on wheaten bread, and to eat the finest wheat flour," and yet to prevent a person pressed by hunger from devouring cow-dung, I may allow him to eat barley. "Does it follow that the wheat will not have its peculiar purity, because such an one prefers barley to excrement? That is naturally good which does not admit of comparison with what is bad, and is not eclipsed because something else is preferred. At the same time we must notice the Apostle's prudence. He did not say, it is good not to have a wife: but, it is good not to touch a woman: as though there were danger even in the touch: as though he who touched her, would not escape from her who "hunteth for the precious life," who causeth the young man's understanding to fly away. "Can a man take fire in his bosom, and his clothes not be burned? Or can one walk upon hot coals, and his feet not be scorched?" As then he who touches fire is instantly burned, so by the mere touch the peculiar nature of man and woman is perceived, and the difference of sex is understood. . . .

[Jovian argued that Solomon accomplished a great deal though he was married, and Jerome answers.] . . . [W]hen our opponent adduced Solomon, who,

Chapter 5
Spiritual
Partners in Chris-
tian Asceticism:
Jerome (?346–420
c.e.) and Paula
(347–404 c.e.)

although he had many wives, nevertheless built the temple, I briefly replied that it was my intention to run over the remaining points. Now that he may not cry out that both Solomon and others under the law, prophets and holy men, have been dishonoured by us, let us show what this very man with his many wives and concubines thought of marriage. For no one can know better than he who suffered through them, what a life or woman is. Well then, he says in the Proverbs: "The foolish and bold woman comes to want bread." What bread? Surely that bread which cometh down from heaven: and he immediately adds "The earth-born perish in her house, rush into the depths of hell." Who are the earth-born that perish in her house? They of course who follow the first Adam, who is of the earth, and not the second, who is from heaven. And again in another place: "Like a worm in wood, so a wicked woman destroyeth her husband." But if you assert that this was spoken of bad wives, I shall briefly answer: What necessity rests upon me to run the risk of the wife I marry proving good or bad? "It is better," he says, "to dwell in a desert land, than with a contentious and passionate woman in a wide house." How seldom we find a wife without these faults, he knows who is married.

[Jerome also argued against second marriages, citing the authority of the Greek philosopher Theophrastus, who lived in the fourth century b.c.e. and whose treatise on marriage is unknown except in Jerome's citing of it.]

. . . But what am I to do when the women of our time press me with apostolic authority, and before the first husband is buried, repeat from morning to night the precepts which allow a second marriage? Seeing they despise the fidelity which Christian purity dictates, let them at least learn chastity from the heathen. A book *On Marriage,* worth its weight in gold, passes under the name of Theophrastus. In it the author asks whether a wise man marries. And after laying down the conditions—that the wife must be fair, of good character, and honest parentage, the husband in good health and of ample means, and after saying that under these circumstances a wise man sometimes enters the state of matrimony, he immediately proceeds thus: "But all these conditions are seldom satisfied in marriage. A wise man therefore must not take a wife. For in the first place his study of philosophy will be hindered, and it is impossible for anyone to attend to his books and his wife. Matrons want many things, costly dresses, gold, jewels, great outlay, maid-servants, all kinds of furniture, litters and gilded coaches. Then come curtain-lectures and live-long night: she complains that one lady goes out better dressed than she: that another is looked up to by all: 'I am a poor despised nobody at the ladies' assemblies.' 'Why did you ogle that creature next door?' 'Why were you talking to the maid?' 'What did you bring from the market?' 'I am not allowed to have a single friend, or companion.' She suspects that her husband's love goes the same way as her hate. There may be in some neighbouring city the wisest of teachers; but if we have a wife we can neither leave her behind, nor take the burden with us. To support a poor wife, is hard: to put up with a rich one, is torture. Notice, too, that in the case of a wife you cannot pick and choose: You must take her as you find her. If she has a bad temper, or is a fool, if she has a blemish, or is proud, or has bad breath, whatever her fault may be—all this we learn after marriage. Horses, asses, cattle, even slaves of the smallest worth, clothes, kettles, wooden seats, cups, and earthenware pitchers, are first tried and then bought: a wife is the only thing that is not shown before she is married, for fear she may not give satisfaction. Our gaze must always be directed to her face, and we must always praise her beauty: if you look at another, we must swear by her health and wish that she may survive us, respect must be paid to the nurse, to the nurse-maid, to the father's slave, to the foster-child, to the handsome hanger-on, to the curled darling who manages her affairs, and to the eunuch who ministers to the safe indulgence of her lust: names which are only a cloak for adultery. Upon whomsoever she sets her heart, they must have her love though they want her not. If you give her the management of the whole house, you must yourself be her slave. If you reserve something for yourself, she will not think you are loyal to her; but she will turn to strife and hatred, and unless you quickly take care, she will have the poison ready. If you introduce old women, and soothsayers, and prophets, and vendors of jewels and silken clothing, you imperil her chastity; if you shut the door upon them, she is injured and fancies you suspect her. But what is the good of even a careful guardian, when an unchaste wife cannot be watched, and a chaste one ought not to be? For necessity is but a faithless keeper of chastity, and she alone really deserves to be called pure, who is free to sin if she chooses. If a woman be fair, she soon finds lovers; if she be ugly, it is easy to be wanton. It is difficult to guard what many long for. It is annoying to have what no one thinks worth possessing. But the misery of having an ugly wife is less than that of watching a comely one. Nothing is safe, for which a whole people sighs and longs. One man entices with his figure, another with his brains, another with his wit, another with his open hand. Somehow, or sometime, the fortress is captured which is attacked on all sides. Men marry, indeed, so as to get a manager for the house, to solace weariness, to banish solitude; but a faithful slave is a far better manager, more submissive to the master, more observant of his ways, than a wife who thinks she proves herself mistress if she acts in opposition to her husband, that is, if she does what pleases her, not what she is commanded. But friends, and servants who are under the obligation of benefits received, are better able to wait upon us in sickness than a wife who makes us responsible for her tears (she will sell you enough to make a deluge for the hope of a legacy), boasts of her anxiety, but drives her sick husband to the distraction of despair. But if she herself is poorly, we must fall sick with her and never leave her bedside. Or if she be a good and agreeable wife (how rare a bird she is!), we have to share her groans in childbirth, and suffer torture when she is in danger. A wise man can never be alone. He has with him the good men of all time, and turns his mind freely wherever he chooses. What is inaccessible to him in person he can embrace in thought. And, if men are scarce, he converses with God. He is never less alone than when alone.

[151]

Chapter 5
Spiritual
Partners in Chris-
tian Asceticism:
Jerome (?346–420
C.E.) and Paula
(347–404 C.E.)

DOCUMENT SIX

John Chrysostom

"Instruction and Refutation Directed Against Those Men Cohabiting with Virgins" and "On the Necessity of Guarding Virginity"
(Probably Written After 398)

In these treatises, John Chrysostom, another major church leader and thinker, of-
fers a different view of virginity and spiritual marriage. Does he oppose cohabita-
tion of celibate men and women? What are his arguments, and how might these
arguments be seen as a direct challenge to Jerome's views?

"Instruction and Refutation Directed Against Those Men Cohabiting with Virgins"

1. In our ancestors' era, two justifications were given for men and women living together. The first, marriage, was ancient, licit, and sensible, since God was its legislator. "For this reason," he said, "a man shall leave his father and mother and cleave to his wife, and the two shall be one flesh." And the other, prostitution, of more recent origin than marriage, was unjust and illegitimate, since it was introduced by evil demons. But in our time, a third way of life has been dreamed up, something new and incredible which greatly perplexes those who wish to discover its rationale. There are certain men who apart from marriage and sexual intercourse take girls inexperienced with matrimony, establish them permanently in their homes, and keep them sequestered until ripe old age, not for the purpose of bearing children (for they deny that they have sexual relations with the women), nor out of licentiousness (for they claim that they preserve them inviolate). If anybody asks the reason for their practice, they have plenty and start rehearsing them; however, I myself think that they have not found a single decent, plausible excuse.

. . . What then is the reason? It seems to me that living with a woman entails a certain pleasure, not only in the lawful state of marriage, but also in cases which do not involve marriage and sexual intercourse.

. . . Thus [Job] says, "I mortify my body and keep it in subjection, lest in preaching to others I myself be rejected as counterfeit coin."

He made these remarks to indicate the rebelliousness of the flesh and the madness which stems from desire, to show that the battle was a constant one and his own life a contest. For this reason Christ also made clear the magnitude of the problem. He did not permit a man even to look into the eyes of a woman, but threatened those who did with the penalty laid on adulterers. When Peter commented, "It is better not to marry," Christ did not make a law prohibiting

[152]

marriage but replied, indicating the importance of the subject, "He that is able to receive it, let him receive it."

We also hear in our own time that many who cover their entire bodies with iron chains and are clad in sackcloth, who have climbed the peaks of mountains and live in constant fasting accompanied by vigils and sleeplessness, who demonstrate great hardiness in every way, forbid all women to enter their chambers and cells and in this way discipline themselves—these men, we are told, scarcely prevail over the frenzy of desire.

You say, however, that if you were to see a man living with virgin, a man who is bound to her and delights in her, who would give up his life rather than his roommate and would choose to suffer and do everything than to part from his beloved, you should not believe anything evil nor view the situation as one involving lust, but rather piety. O wondrous man! . . .

Tell me, why do you live with a virgin? This cohabitation is not based on law but on love and lust. For if this reason is taken away, the need for the practice also disappears. What man, if he were free from the compulsion to have a woman, would choose to put up with the delicacy, wantonness, and all the other faults of that sex? Thus even from the beginning God endowed woman with this strength, knowing that she would be totally despicable unless she were provided with this power, that no man would choose to live with her if he were innocent of desire. For if such a necessity also presses upon us now, in addition to her many other uses (indeed we could also mention the bearing of children, taking care of the house, and the rendering of other services even loftier than these), and if even now women performing such chores for men are often easy to despise and are expelled from their homes, how would you love them if it were not for desire, especially since they cast so much reproach upon you? Now either tell us the reason for cohabitation or we will necessarily suspect that there is no other one than wanton desire and the most shameful pleasure. . . .

"ON THE NECESSITY OF GUARDING VIRGINITY"

If meanwhile I ask you the pretext for this joint homesteading, what can you say? The virgin answers, "I am just a weak woman and am not capable of satisfying my own needs by myself." But when we summoned your housemates, we heard them claim the opposite, that *they* kept *you* because of *your* service to *them!* How come, then, if out of your abundant energy you can give relief to the men, you are not able to help yourselves, since you are women, but need others? For just as a man can live together easily and contentedly with a man, so also can a woman with a woman, and if you are fit for the service of men, how much more so for aiding yourselves? Tell me, how could the company of a man be beneficial and necessary? What kind of service will this man render which could be impossible for a woman to provide for one of her own sex? Can he weave at the loom and spin thread and cloth with you more ably than a woman? Just the opposite is so! For even if a man wanted to, he would not

[153]

Chapter 5
Spiritual
Partners in Chris-
tian Asceticism:
Jerome (?346–420
C.E.) and Paula
(347–404 C.E.)

know how to put his hand to any of these tasks, not unless you have just now taught him the skill; this is the work of woman alone.

5. But to launder a cloak, kindle a fire, boil and pot—is not a woman able to manage these things not less proficiently, but even more so, than a man? In what ways, then, is the man an advantage to you, tell me? Perhaps whenever it is necessary to buy or sell something? But the woman is not inferior to the man here, as the marketplace might also testify: all who wish to buy clothes, buy most of them from women. But if it is disgraceful for a virgin to stand in the marketplace for business dealings of such a kind (and it is in truth shameful), certainly it is much more disgraceful for her to live with men. Besides, you can escape this rather minor problem more easily than that one by entrusting every-thing to a serving girl to minister to your needs or to older women who are use-ful for these purposes. . . .

. . . It is not, then, because you [the female virgin] need comfort that you drag the men inside. "Why is it, then?" someone asks. "For the sake of fornication and debauchery?" I for my part would not support that view. God forbid! Rather, I do not cease to reproach those who hold it. If only it were also possible to convince them! "Then what is the reason which makes the practice agreeable to us?" The love of vanity. Just as the men were motivated by a bleak and wretched pleasure, so also for these women this household companionship is inspired by a desire for esteem. For as it is said, the whole human race is vain, but especially the female sex. Since these women are not in need of relaxation, as has been shown, nor are they corrupted by their sexual involvement with the men, it is apparent that this reason alone remains for us to suspect. . . .

Perhaps these women themselves think this very thing, their overpowering men, is laudable. To the contrary, it is completely ridiculous; certainly only courtesans take pride in it. For it is not characteristic of free and virtuous women to be conceited about such snares. This is also another reason for dis-honor: to the degree that they dominate the men and become harsher in their comandeering, to this extent they rather disgrace themselves in addition to the males. It is not the woman who brings men under her rule who is esteemed and considered remarkable by everyone, but the woman who respects them.

DOCUMENT SEVEN

JEROME

Letter to Laeta, Letter 107

What guidelines does Jerome offer Laeta in the raising of her daughter, Paula, who is a dedicated virgin? These words of advice will be followed by many Christian parents thereafter. What does Jerome think are the most important parts of a young virgin's life? Because you have read several of Jerome's letters, consider also the way in which he uses personal letters to expound on themes of much broader importance. Are the letters really personal documents or something else? What might these examples illustrate about the general tradition of letter writing in the Roman world? Why do you think Jerome's letters are preserved, while the letters of his women contemporaries are not?

. . . It was my intention, in answer to your prayers and those of the saintly Marcella, to direct my discourse to a mother, that is, to you, and to show you how to bring up our little Paula, who was consecrated to Christ before she was born, the child of prayers before the hour of conception. . . .

Thus must a soul be trained which is to be a temple of God. It must learn to hear nothing and to say nothing save what pertains to the fear of the Lord. It must have no comprehension of foul words, no knowledge of worldly songs, and its childish tongue must be imbued with the sweet music of the psalms. Let boys with their wanton frolics be kept far from Paula: let even her maids and attendants hold aloof from association with the worldly, lest they render their evil knowledge worse by teaching it to her. Have a set of letters made for her, of boxwood or of ivory, and tell her their names. Let her play with them, making play a road to learning, and let her not only grasp the right order of the letters and remember their names in a simple song, but also frequently upset their order and mix the last letters with the middle ones, the middle with the first. Thus she will know them all by sight as well as by sound. When she begins with uncertain hand to use the pen, either let another hand be put over hers to guide her baby fingers, or else have the letters marked on the tablet so that her writing may follow their outlines and keep to their limits without straying away. Offer her prizes for spelling, tempting her with such trifling gifts as please young children. . . .

Her very dress and outward appearance should remind her of Him to whom she is promised. Do not pierce her ears, or paint with white lead and rouge the cheeks that are consecrated to Christ. Do not load her neck with pearls and gold, do not weigh down her head with jewels, do not dye her hair red and thereby presage for her the fires of hell. Let her have other pearls which she will sell hereafter and buy the pearl that is of great price. . . .

She should not take her food in public, that is, at her parents' guest-table; for she may there see dishes that she will crave for. And though some people think it shows the higher virtue to despise a pleasure ready to your hand, I for my part judge it part of the surer self-restraint to remain in ignorance of what you would like. Once when I was a boy at school I read this line: 'Things that have become a habit you will find it hard to blame.' Let her learn even now not to drink wine 'wherein is excess.' Until they have reached their full strength, however, strict abstinence is dangerous for young children: so till then, if needs

*Chapter 5
Spiritual
Partners in Chris-
tian Asceticism:
Jerome (?346–420
C.E.) and Paula
(347–404 C.E.)*

must, let her visit the baths, and take a little wine for the stomach's sake, and have the support of a meat diet, lest her feet fail before the race begins. . . .

Let her every day repeat to you a portion of the Scriptures as her fixed task. A good number of lines she should learn by heart in the Greek, but knowledge of Latin should follow close after. If the tender lips are not trained from the beginning, the language is spoiled by a foreign accent and our native tongue debased by alien faults. You must be her teacher, to you her childish ignorance must look for a model. Let her never see anything in you or her father which she would do wrong to imitate. Remember that you are a virgin's parents and that you can teach her better by example than by words. Flowers quickly fade; violets, lilies, and saffron are soon withered by a baleful breeze. Let her never appear in public without you, ...

Let her learn also to make wool, to hold the distaff, to put the basket in her lap, to turn the spindle, to shape the thread with her thumb. Let her scorn silk fabrics, Chinese fleeces, and gold brocades. Let her have clothes which keep out the cold, not expose the very limbs they pretend to cover. Let her food be vegetables and wheaten bread and occasionally a little fish. I do not wish here to give long rules for eating, since I have treated that subject more fully in another place; but let her meals always leave her hungry and able at once to begin reading or praying or singing the psalms. I disapprove especially with young people, of long and immoderate fasts, when week is added to week and even oil in food and fruit are banned. I have learned by experience that the ass on the high road makes for an inn when it is weary. . . .

The Franks and the Transformation of the Roman World: Clotild of Burgundy (475–548) and Clovis I, King of the Franks (466?–511)

■ **SETTING THE STAGE**

During the middle of the third century, a "bold, fierce, and courageous" group of Germanic peoples lived just north and to the west of the Roman province of Gaul. Contemporary Roman sources called them Franci, meaning "fierce." The Franks took advantage of the polit- ical and military tumult in the empire and conducted raids across the Roman frontier at the Rhine River. Embold- ened by their early successes, they pen- etrated deeper into Gaul and caused substantial damage to over half of the 115 Roman towns in the province by

Chapter 6
The Franks
and the
Transformation
of the Roman
World:
Clotild of
Burgundy (475–
548) and Clovis I,
King of the
Franks (466?–511)

275 C.E. The devastation and the Frankish threat posed such a challenge to Roman emperors that many of the present-day border fortifications along the Rhine date from this period. Over the next two centuries, Roman emperors dedicated considerable resources and numerous military campaigns to either the suppression or cooption of the Franks and other so-called barbarians in Roman Gaul.

At the beginning of the fifth century, Roman authorities, sometimes even with the help of the Franks, were unable to defend Gaul from the other Germanic tribes and the province fell to the new invaders. These barbarians (a term used by Romans to describe non-Romans) soon came to possess all of Gaul. By the 480s, Gaul had been partitioned into multiple kingdoms. The Visigoths held the southwest, the Burgundians controlled the east, and the Franks ruled in the north. Over the next thirty years, the Franks, under their king, Clovis I, would become the predominant barbarian authority in Gaul.

When the Franks first penetrated the Roman Empire at frontier posts in Gaul, they encountered a world that had been an integral part of the Roman Empire for almost five hundred years, and its cities and elites reflected Roman civilization. Gallo-Roman provincial elites lived in villas on large latifundia; sent their sons to schools in Bordeaux, Lyon, Trier, and other cities to study Latin and rhetoric; expected efficient and just Roman administration; and adhered to Roman civic and familial values. Gaul's cities possessed all the amenities of any Roman city—temples, monuments, theaters, baths, and schools. The countryside

and its inhabitants were brought into Roman systems of agriculture, and the province's borders were protected by Roman legions. Romanization had succeeded in subduing the indigenous population of Gaul and had created a thriving urban culture. This urban culture proved to be fertile ground for the conversion of Gaul's population to Christianity in the fourth century.

Christianity first took root in Gaul after Constantine's Edict of Toleration for Christianity in 313. The emperor's embrace of this religion facilitated the building of churches throughout the Empire and in many of its major cities. These projects were generously funded by the emperor and his family, and Gaul's imperial capital, Trier, began the building of its cathedral in 321. Lyons had its cathedral built in the late fourth century. The Christian church adopted the Empire's administrative unit, the bishopric, for its organization, and the administrative cities of the Roman Empire became ecclesiastical centers and their leaders were called bishops. Cathedrals and their cities were natural sites for Christian preaching, instruction, and conversion of the urban population. Bishops were often prominent members of their communities and played key roles in leading and organizing local communities.[1]

In southern Gaul, another site of Christian culture and spirituality—the monastery—was developing. Established outside the cities, monasteries played a role in converting the inhabitants of the countryside to Christianity.

1. Anthony King, *Roman Gaul and Germany* (Berkeley: University of California, 1990), p. 196.

The most renowned of the Gallic monks, Martin, the bishop of Tours, was a missionary to the *paganus,* or country-dwellers, of central and northern Gaul. In these regions, Romano-Celtic religion still predominated, and Martin of Tours worked hard to convert the pagans to Christianity, to destroy their shrines, and to establish a rudimentary network of parishes. The parishes were Martin's attempt to maintain a Christian presence in the countryside. Despite Martin's proselytizing and missionary efforts, pagan beliefs and practices remained strong in the countryside. When the Franks and the other Germanic peoples settled in Gaul during the fifth century, the main framework of church organization—bishoprics, churches, monasteries, and some parishes—was in place.[2] As Roman secular authority disappeared, this network allowed church authorities to become standard-bearers of Roman values and culture and to strengthen and bolster Christian communities in the towns and cities.

Roman Gaul of the fifth century was a society and culture in transformation because its Gallo-Roman inhabitants encountered, fought, and negotiated with the Germanic kings and peoples who controlled this province. The peoples living in Roman Gaul did not know or understand that their world was in the midst of a fundamental change. Rome still existed, albeit under the control of the Ostrogoths by the end of the century. Romans still owned land, practiced their Christian religion, educated their sons in Greek and Latin, and followed Roman law. Neither the invasions nor the ensuing violence succeeded in immediately crushing or destroying Roman civilization. Instead the invasion facilitated the settling of Germanic peoples among the Gallo-Romans and the gradual blending of Christianized Gallo-Roman society with Germanic society. Similar processes took place elsewhere in the western Roman Empire, but Roman Gaul during the time of the Frankish King, Clovis, and his Burgundian wife, Clotild, best demonstrates the multifaceted dimensions of barbarian rule, cross-cultural contact, and Christian conversion in the early Middle Ages.

Our understanding of this period of transformation and the roles that Clovis and Clotild played in it is unclear. The mainstream portrait of the royal couple comes from Gregory, bishop of Tours (539–594), and his *History of the Franks.* This history was written a half-century after the couple's death and depicted "the first Frankish king of Gaul as a thoroughgoing barbarian."[3] As a member of an old Gallo-Roman senatorial family, Gregory was concerned with moral decline in Frankish Gaul and interpreted barbarian rule as the end of Roman learning and literary life (Document One). As a Catholic bishop, he wanted to tell of "the rewards granted to good men and followers of the true Christian faith, Catholicism, and the punishments

2. Ibid., p. 201.

3. William M. Daly, "Clovis: How Barbaric, How Pagan?" *Speculum* 69 (1994): p. 619.

Chapter 6
The Franks
and the
Transformation
of the Roman
World:
Clotild of
Burgundy (475–
548) and Clovis I,
King of the
Franks (466?–511)

meted out to wicked pagans and heretical Christians."[4] Moral and religious concerns were the focus of his history, and Gregory's account must be read with his perspective in mind.

While much of what Gregory wrote was based on reports, hearsay, and rumor, he did have access to materials written at the time of Clovis and Clotild's ascendency. Many of these sources have been lost in the intervening centuries, and Gregory's use of them is suspect. Given Gregory's biases, historians have had to turn to the few surviving sources that were written at the time of Clovis's reign. "There are several sources that bring us much closer to the historical Clovis."[5] There are three letters from the Bishop of Reims, two of which are addressed to Clovis; a letter addressed to Clovis from another bishop, Avitus of Vienne; several letters from the Visigothic king, Theodoric the Great (r. 493–526); and the *lex Salica,* the legal

code of the Salian Franks, written under Clovis's direction. In addition, there are the letters of Sidonius Apollinaris, a Gallo-Roman, who wrote about the perils of navigating among the various Germanic powers in southern Gaul, including Clotild's people, the Burgundians.

Determining the historical role that Frankish women, and especially Clotild, played in the transformation of Roman Gaul is difficult. Students of history can turn to the *lex Salica* for insights into women's places in Frankish society as well as a new type of literary genre that emerged in the early Middle Ages: hagiography, or biography of saints. This genre taught "a rough and inexperienced ruling class a new set of Christian heroic models"[6] and tells us quite a bit about the moral and religious expectations placed on Frankish women. As a source of factual historical information, however, hagiography must be doubted.

■ **THE ACTORS:**

CLOVIS I, KING OF THE FRANKS, AND CLOTILD OF BURGUNDY

In 481, Clovis succeeded his father, Childeric (r. 463–481), who was the leader of the Salian Franks and ruler of the Belgica Secunda (Second Belgic Province). Childeric was the last Frankish commander to continue the tradition of military service to Rome as an "imperial German," and evidence

shows that he was able to maintain good relations with the Gallo-Romans who lived under Frankish rule.[7] Part of Childeric's success in winning over the Gallo-Romans was his relationship with the Gallo-Roman bishops, who had replaced Roman authorities as leaders in their communities. In return, the Gallo-Romans saw Childeric as a protector of the Roman way of

4. Edward James, *The Franks* (Oxford: Basil Blackwell, 1988), p. 17.

5. Daly, p. 625.

6. Jo Ann McNamara and John E. Halborg, with E. Gordon Whatley, eds., *Sainted Women of the Dark Ages* (Durham, N.C.: Duke University Press, 1992), p. 2.

7. Patrick Geary, *Before France and Germany* (New York: Oxford University Press, 1988), p. 80.

life, which included the defense of orthodox Christian practices against heretical Christian beliefs. When the fifteen-year-old Clovis succeeded his father in 481, the Gallo-Roman bishops expected him to follow in his father's footsteps and to accept advice from the clergy. Remigius wrote, "You should defer to your bishops and always have recourse to their advice." In addition, Remigius addressed Clovis as if he were a Roman provincial governor and not a conqueror: "a strong report has come to us that you have taken over the administration of the Second Belgic Province" (Document Two). In fact, Clovis may have adopted the Roman organization in the Belgic provinces to help him rule.[8]

In his letter, Bishop Remigius recognized what had been true for over a century in this region: Roman accommodation to and coexistence with the German society. A contemporary of Remigius, Sidonius Apollinaris, a Gallo-Roman noble and bishop of Clermont, in the Visigothic kingdom, accepted the reality of Germanic rule as well. In letters to his friends and family, Sidonius both disparaged and praised his new overlords, but ultimately he recognized the necessity of "working with them as the need arose"[9] (Document Three). Remigius and Sidonius represented the part of Gallo-Roman society who sought to make the best of the barbarian predominance. As one of the most influential leaders of northern Gaul,

Remigius felt it was his duty to instruct the young new king. This letter and two more of Remigius's letters are the only sources that offer personal knowledge of Clovis.

When Clovis was born, his parents, Childeric and Basina, gave him a pagan baptism and christened him Chlodweg, or "combat renowned." He was the only male among three girls. The lack of other males in the family meant that Clovis did not have to endure the constant challenges and threat to his succession or subsequent rule that often plagued other Germanic kings and their male heirs. Inheritance among the Franks and other Germanic peoples meant division of property equally among the male children, and so the royal lands, as well as the royal title, which was also considered a personal possession, were divided among the sons of a dead ruler. His father trained Clovis to be a leader of the Frankish army, and Clovis continued his father's fighting and tactical styles, which "integrated both Germanic and Roman tactics and strategy within the context of civil administration."[10] Living in the Roman province of Belgica Secunda and becoming familiar with his father's civil functions, Clovis most likely learned to speak Latin and perhaps learned to read it as well, at least minimally.[11]

Unlike some of the other Germanic peoples, Childeric, Clovis, and the Salian Franks had resisted conversion to any form of Christianity. During the fifth century, the Burgundians,

8. Ralph Whitney Mathisen, *Roman Aristocrats in Barbarian Gaul* (Austin, Tex.: University of Austin Press, 1993), p. 82.

9. Ibid., p. 70.

10. Daly, p. 631.

11. Patrick Perin, *Clovis,* pp. 42–45. Quoted in Daly.

Chapter 6
The Franks
and the
Transformation
of the Roman
World:
Clotild of
Burgundy (475–
548) and Clovis I,
King of the
Franks (466?–511)

Visigoths, Ostrogoths, and Vandals converted to Arianism, a form of Christianity that rejected the principle that God the Father; his son, Jesus Christ; and the Holy Spirit were united and equal in a trinity. This heretical belief began with Arius (ca. 260–336), a priest from Alexandria, who argued that Christ and the Holy Spirit were lesser beings and were mediators between God the Father and the human world. The official doctrine or orthodox position of the Trinity in Unity was officially accepted within the Roman Empire in 381, but Arius's contention that Christ was not divine by nature and coeternal with God the Father resonated with many ordinary people. They found the doctrine of the Trinity in Unity confusing because it gave the appearance of polytheism; they were not only supposed to worship God the Father but the Son and also the Holy Spirit. Arianism spread throughout the eastern Roman Empire first, and soon their missionaries were converting some of the Germanic tribes living within the Western Roman Empire. Some of these missionaries were Visigoths who were armed with a Bible in their own tongue, and they prepared the way for other Visigoths to convert to Arianism. The Visigoth missionaries then began to convert the other Germanic tribes in the Empire to Arianism. Soon many of the Germanic peoples found that they were not only separated from the Gallo-Romans by culture but increasingly by a heretical religion.[12]

Some Germanic kings, like the Burgundians, appeared willing to tolerate both Christian sects in their kingdom.[13] Like the Franks, the Burgundians, won the respect of the Gallo-Roman bishops and elites who lived under their rule. In the 460s, Sidonius noted how Chilperic I, an early Burgundian king, and his queen were known for good works and how they praised the Catholic bishop of Lyons for his feasts and his fasts. Clovis's wife, Clotild was a Catholic Christian and the daughter of Chilperic II, one of the sons of the king of Burgundy, who was an Arian.

Clotild was probably born in Lyons in 474 to Chilperic II and a Gallo-Roman woman, Caretena. The marriage of Clotild's parents may have adhered to a Burgundian pattern of Catholic Gallo-Roman women marrying into elite Burgundian families and might explain the toleration for both religions in the kingdom. Clotild's mother was purported to have given Clotild and her sister, Chroma, their religious training and to have converted her husband, Chilperic II, to Catholicism. With Clotild's mother, a pattern emerged whereby Burgundian women acted as Catholic female missionaries to the courts of the Germanic kings ruling in Roman Gaul.[14] Chilperic may have been converted to Catholicism by his wife, and Gregory of Tours credited Clotild for bringing Catholicism into Clovis's court. Clotild's daughter, sister-in-law, and granddaughter, all Catholics, married Germanic royalty and attempted to

12. J. N. Hillgarth, *Christianity and Paganism, 350–750* (Philadelphia: University of Pennsylvania Press, 1986), p. 73.

13. Ian Wood, *The Merovingian Kingdoms, 450–751* (New York: Longman, 1994), p. 45.

14. McNamara and Halborg, p. 38.

convert their husbands and their husbands' families to their religion.

The marriage alliances between Catholic and Arian or between Catholic and pagan helped to facilitate the creation of a distinct culture, one that was neither German nor Roman, over the next century. Clotild's marriage and subsequent influence on the conversion of her husband and the Catholic Christian baptism of her children illustrate the role that Germanic women played in the transformation of Gallo-Roman society. "By marrying across ethnic lines and converting their husbands to Christianity, then bearing children and transmitting to them a mixed cultural heritage, they were instrumental in bringing about the demographic and cultural amalgamation of the Germanic and Gallo-Roman peoples in Roman Gaul."[15]

Chilperic was one of four sons born to the king of Burgundy, Gundovic. With Gundovic's death, his kingdom was divided among the four sons. Chilperic ruled in Lyons, Gundobad in Vienne, and Godegisil in Geneva (Gundomar's capital is unknown). According to Gregory, Gundobad murdered Chilperic and later killed his other brother Godegisil to bring all of Burgundy under his control. Gregory reported that Gundobad drowned Caretena by tying a stone around her neck and throwing her down a well. As a result of their parent's death, Clotild and her sister, Chroma, were exiled to their uncle Godegisel's court in Geneva. Chroma became religious and established the church of Saint-Victor, and Clotild remained at court, where Clovis's envoys to her uncle observed "that she was an elegant young woman and clever for her years."

Gregory's account of the blood feud among the Burgundians must be questioned. His narrative of these events perhaps reflected his attempt to justify the Frankish invasion of Burgundy in the 530s by depicting the Franks, led by Clotild's sons, as avenging the wrongs done to their queen and their mother. The historical reality of Clotild's family is quite different. According to Avitus of Vienne, bishop of Vienne and a contemporary of Gundobad, Gundobad lamented his brother's death. In addition, Caretena lived until 506; her epitaph claimed that she died "full of days."

15. Suzanne Fonay Wemple, *Women in Frankish Society: Marriage and the Cloister, 500–900* (Philadelphia: University of Pennsylvania, 1981), p. 9.

Chapter 6
The Franks
and the
Transformation
of the Roman
World:
Clotild of
Burgundy (475–
548) and Clovis I,
King of the
Franks (466?–511)

▪ Act I:

Clovis and the Frankish Conquests

In 481, the fifteen-year-old Clovis became leader of the Salian Franks. From the capital of the Belgica Secunda, Tournai, he began a thirty-year journey that brought Roman Gaul under Frankish rule. Clovis's first step in this process was to attack the lands directly south of Tournai. This territory, centered in the city of Soissons, was defended by a Roman general who hoped that the western imperial government would be restored. In 486, Clovis defeated him in a single battle and moved his capital further south, to the more central and strategic location of Paris.

From Paris, Clovis began a gradual course of territorial expansion and integration. In 496 and 506, Clovis led campaigns against the Alamans to stop their penetration into Ostrogoth territory, which was then ruled by Clovis's brother-in-law, Theodoric the Great. Theodoric had married Clovis's sister in 493. In the same year, Clovis forged a marriage alliance with the Burgundian ruler Gundobad by marrying his niece, Clotild. The alliance with the Burgundians brought Clovis into the familial politics of Burgundy. Gregory of Tours reported how Godegisil conspired with Clovis in Geneva to defeat his brother, Gundobad. They waged a successful campaign in 500, and Clovis forced Gundobad to pay annual tribute to the Franks. The internal divisions within the Burgundian royal house weakened the unity of the kingdom, however, and in the 530s, Clovis and Clotild's sons eventually brought Burgundy directly under Frankish rule.

The last of Clovis's campaigns against the other Germanic rulers was the most successful and significant. In the 490s and early 500s, the Franks and the Visigoths competed for control of central and southern Gaul, but neither group gained the upper hand until Clovis and his allies, the Burgundians and another Frankish tribe, the Rhineland (Ripuarian) Franks, successfully invaded Visigoth territory in 506. The Visigoth king, Alaric II, was killed and the Franks annexed most of southern Gaul, doubling Frankish territory in Gaul and adding a rich and highly Romanized region to Clovis's kingdom.[16] The final step in Clovis's political consolidation of Gaul was the submission of the Rhineland Franks to his rule sometime after 507. Gregory of Tours reported that Clovis had masterminded a plot where the son of the king of the Rhineland Franks would kill his father, and then with Clovis's support assume the throne. What the son did not know was that Clovis also planned to have him killed and have the Rhineland Franks proclaim him king. According to Gregory, all parts of the plot were successfully executed. By the time of Clovis's death in 511, his kingdom was the most powerful in Gaul.

Gregory portrayed Clovis as a pagan Frankish warrior leader who brutally subdued the other kingdoms in Gaul, but it must be remembered that the Salian Franks in northern Gaul had been the mainstay of what was left of Roman authority, and that Clo-

16. James, p. 87.

vis's expansion southward bore a similar quality to the military, administrative, and religious practices that he and his father followed in the Second Belgic province. Remigius portrayed Clovis as having legitimately claimed the right to rule in this province; he did not portray him as a conqueror or uncouth barbarian. The portrayal of Clovis as a slaughtering, conquering, and pagan barbarian who won his position within the empire only by conquest emerged with *The History of the Franks*, written a generation after the king's death by Gregory of Tours[17] (Document Four).

Clovis indeed was a successful military commander who used the Belgica province as a launching pad for a series of campaigns against weaker Germanic powers to the south, and who had brought Roman Gaul under the control of the Franks by the time of his death in 511. While Gregory ascribed the Franks' victories to their fierceness and ruthlessness, the Franks under Clovis continued the traditions of the Roman army. They not only recruited their tribesmen but Gallo-Romans for the military as well. These Gallo-Romans saw Clovis as an heir to the barbarian generals who served the Romans loyally for years. Clovis's behavior as a military commander did not dissuade them from this view.

Gregory of Tours related an anecdote from the now lost *Life of St. Remigius*, which illustrated Clovis's Roman military bearing. According to Gregory, the Frankish pagan army attacked the Gallo-Roman city Soissons, and many of the city's churches were plundered during the conquest. By Roman tradition, war booty was gathered together and distributed equally among the soldiers, including the military commander, Clovis, who received the same portion as a foot soldier. During the raid, the soldiers took a valuable religious pitcher, and the bishop appealed to Clovis for its return. Clovis asked his troops that he be granted the pitcher in addition to his fair share. His troops complied. As Clovis went to retrieve the pitcher, one solider, believing that such a request was unreasonable, stepped forward, snatched the pitcher, and split it in two. Clovis retrieved the two halves, gave them to the bishop, and did not punish the man. To have done so would have confirmed that Clovis believed himself to be above his soldiers, a position no Roman military commander would have taken. However, Clovis did not forget this humiliation. Later that year, Clovis was inspecting his troops and their equipment on the parade-ground, and he purposefully singled out the man who had split the pitcher in two. Clovis found this man's equipment to be in bad condition, and he threw the man's ax on the ground in disgust. When the soldier bent to pick up the ax, Clovis split the man's skull. Clovis's actions must not obscure the fact that in this story, he acted as a Roman general, taking his fair share, reviewing troops, inspecting equipment, and meting out punishment.[18] In this story, Clovis also sought to placate church leaders. Clovis's actions demonstrated his willingness to work within the boundaries of

17. Ibid., p. 79.

18. Ibid., p. 82.

Chapter 6
The Franks
and the
Transformation
of the Roman
World:
Clotild of
Burgundy (475–
548) and Clovis I,
King of the
Franks (466?–511)

Gallo-Roman traditions, and in return the Gallo-Romans accepted Frankish rule. "This acceptance is perhaps the main secret to the Frankish conquest of Roman Gaul."[19]

Clovis allowed local Gallo-Roman elites, talented and effective local rulers, the Catholic religious hierarchy, and other Franks to join his ranks. He concluded an agreement with the Catholic bishops of Gaul that Gallo-Romans, Franks, and other barbarians were to be on equal terms. All free men bore the title of Frank, had the same political status, and were eligible for the same positions within the kingdom. In addition, Clovis allowed each individual, Gallo-Roman, Salian Frank, or Rhineland Frank, to follow the law of their own group. The Gallo-Romans lived by Roman law; the Franks lived by Salian or Ripuarian law. Clovis spent the last years of his reign codifying the laws of the Salian Franks (*lex Salica*).

As a result of these policies, Clovis and the Franks were never threatened, as the other barbarian rulers had been, by the great numbers of their Gallo-Roman subjects. As the Franks slowly and carefully advanced further into Roman Gaul, the majority of Gallo-Romans probably either acquiesced to or welcomed Clovis's rule. For Gregory of Tours, these military, legal, and administrative practices were not the key to winning over the Gallo-Romans; the key for him was the conversion of Clovis to Catholic Christianity through the influence of his wife.

■ ACT II:

CONVERSION OF THE FRANKS

With the help of Gregory of Tours, the marriage of Clovis to the Catholic Clotild took on legendary proportions. She was the elegant orphaned daughter of a king murdered by his own brother, whose husband and sons would prosecute her blood feud against her uncle's family. She was also a devout and pious woman who facilitated Clovis's conversion to Christianity. Her story was not told by Gregory only. Medieval hagiographers wrote about Clotild, and the hagiographic account of her life is available in its tenth-century form, *The Life of Saint Clotild.* The retelling of a saint's life helped instruct Christians in the faith and served as examples of how to live a pious and devote life. Clotild's life story and deeds were frequently recited within convent walls for the instruction of nuns or read publicly on the anniversary of the saint's death or some other important event.[20] As a result, her legendary deeds became known outside the small circle of literate Franks, and her role in the divine mission and historical destiny of the Franks was assured.[21] Her life became the cornerstone in the struggle of the Catholic, Gallo-Roman population against the

19. Ibid. p. 84.

20. McNamara and Halborg, p. 2.
21. Ibid.

Arianism and the paganism of the Germanic tribes.[22]

With the birth of their first son, Ingomer, Clotild went to Clovis and asked that he permit the Catholic baptism of their son. Gregory embellishes the moment by making up a little sermon for her to preach to her husband. She argued, "The gods whom you worship are not good. They haven't even been able to help themselves, let alone others. They are carved out of stone or wood or some old piece of metal." In the hagiographic account of Clotild's life, she begs the king on their wedding night to forsake his pagan idols and "believe in almighty God, Father, Son, and Holy Ghost, and that you will destroy the idols you worship and restore the churches you have burned." This latter account firmly established Clotild's divine mission immediately upon marriage. In both accounts, Clovis permitted the Catholic baptism of their son, and then the son promptly died. Clovis reproached the queen for her decision because her god did not save their son. In Gregory's history, Clovis claimed, "[I]f he had been dedicated in the name of my gods, he would have lived without question; but now that he has been baptized in the name of your God he has not been able to live a single day." Despite her grief and pain, Clotild kept her faith and responded that their son "will be nurtured in the sight of God." A second son, Chlodomer, was born and Clotild had him baptized as well. Like their first son, Chlodomer fell ill, but this time Clotild's prayers were answered and he recovered. Clovis remained unimpressed and still persisted in his pagan beliefs. Gregory meant his narrative to be instructive and in his account, Clotild's sentiments and arguments differed very little from those that he might use to persuade pagans or heretics to convert (Documents Five and Six).

Clovis's conversion came on the battlefield and parallels, perhaps conveniently, the conversion of Constantine. Gregory reported that in 496 Clovis prayed to the Christian god for victory during a battle with the Alamans and victory was granted. Upon his return from the war, Clotild called upon the bishop of Reims, Remigius, to instruct and advise her husband in his decision to convert. Remigius found a contrite Clovis who appeared ready to convert but feared that the Franks under his command would not follow him. He need not have feared their disapproval; Clovis, three thousand of Clovis's army, and his two sisters were baptized shortly after the battle. Clotild had accomplished the mission assigned to her by providence: she had converted Clovis and Franks to the Catholic faith. Gregory easily ascribed this role to Clotild, but her actual role in Clovis's conversion is difficult to assess. The only remaining evidence of Clovis's conversion is a letter written by Avitus, bishop of Vienne, and "he sees Clovis's decision to become a Catholic as the personal choice of an intelligent monarch."[23] Avitus saw that Clovis's choice was between Arianism and Catholicism

22. Ibid., p. 39.

23. Wood, p. 44.

Chapter 6
The Franks
and the
Transformation
of the Roman
World:
Clotild of
Burgundy (475–
548) and Clovis I,
King of the
Franks (466?–511)

and complimented the king in seeing through Arianism. (Document Seven). Avitus hints at the idea that Clovis had shown an interest in this heretical religion, meaning that some members of his court were most likely Arians. Gregory admits as much when he points out that Clovis's sister had accepted the Arian religion before confessing to "the triune majesty of the Father, the Son, and the Holy Ghost," along with Clovis. Clovis may very well have flirted with Arianism but given his complex political world, where he had to deal with the Catholic hierarchy and Arian Germanic allies, he proceeded with caution. Like other Germanic kings, the type of Christianity he adopted was not only a personal and spiritual matter but a political and strategic one as well. In the end, his final commitment to Catholicism most likely came in 508, when he was at war with the Visigoths and their Arian king, Alaric II, for control of southwestern Gaul, the most Romanized and Catholic region of Roman Gaul. "He may have thought that there was propaganda value to be

gained by standing as the defender of the Catholic Church."[24]

The idea that Clovis may have decided to convert to Catholicism because of political and strategic reasons does not diminish the role that Clotild played in Clovis's conversion and rule. Her Catholicism and relationship with the church's hierarchy familiarized Clovis and his court with the Catholic religion. In addition, Clotild bore five children, four of whom were sons. Three of the sons, Clodomir, Childebert, and Clotaire, and one daughter, also named Clotild, survived. She had all the children baptized Catholic, and even if Clovis did not convert to Catholic Christianity, Catholicism was assured in the Frankish kingdom and perhaps elsewhere. As Catholic and Frankish royalty, the children would intermarry with other royal houses and bring Catholicism to other royal courts. The daughter, Clotild, was married to a Visigoth king, and she tried in vain to win over her Arian husband. Clovis and Clotild's granddaughter had greater success in her marriage to the king of the Lombards.

■ FINALE

Clovis died in 511 and prior to his death, he had decided to divide his kingdom among his four sons, three of whom had been born to Clotild. The fourth and the eldest had been born to one of Clovis's mistresses, and he alone was old enough to rule. The other three were still minors, and Clovis's decision to divide his kingdom may have rested not only on custom

but on Clotild's wish to see that part of Frankish Gaul would be passed on to her offspring.[25] The royal descendants of Clovis and Clotild would be known as the Merovingian dynasty, named after Clovis's legendary ancestor, Merovech. As a result of the division, Frankish Gaul would be be-

24. Ibid., p. 48.
25. Ibid. p. 50.

sieged by civil wars and shifting familial alliances over the next two hundred years as heirs to Clovis's kingdom competed to gain a greater share of the patrimony.

Despite this competition, Frankish Gaul continued in existence as the other barbarian kingdoms disappeared from the scene. Much of its continued success rested on Clovis's decision to convert to Catholicism and his support for the Gallo-Roman Catholic hierarchy. Choosing Catholicism meant that Clovis provided the Franks with the opportunity to blend and assimilate with the local population, instead of continuing to be separated.[26] After Clovis died, Clotild continued and consolidated Frankish support for Catholicism for the next thirty years. She patronized the Catholic Church through building projects, alms, and a continual presence at the diocese of Tours, where the most popular of all the Gallo-Roman saints, Martin of Tours, was buried. Merovingian hagiographers solidified her role in the struggle between Catholicism and Arianism by portraying her as devote and pious. In their writings, Clotild played a leading role in the divine mission of the Franks. She matched Clovis's military prowess with her prowess for prayer and generosity. The gifts that she, her husband, and their successors bestowed on the Gallo-Roman churches assured the Catholic hierarchy's support for Frankish rule. The Franks were so confident about their ability to win over the Gallo-Romans that they boasted about it in the prologue to the *lex Salica:* "The famous race of Franks, whose founder is God . . . is the race . . . who, after Baptism, have enclosed in gold and precious stones the bodies of the Holy Martyrs whom the Romans had burned by fire, mutilated by sword, or thrown to wild beasts"[27] (Document Eight). The Franks claimed that they were exceptional and superior to all other tribes, and that they had also saved the true Christian faith through their conversion. The heroic figure of Clovis and the saintly figure of Clotild were at the center of these claims to posterity.

■ QUESTIONS

1. How did Gregory of Tours shape the historical story of Clovis and Clotild? Is *The History of the Franks* a secondary source. Why or why not?

2. What methods, means, and principles did Clovis employ to gain control of Roman Gaul? Was one method more successful than the others?

3. How did the Gallo-Romans view Clovis and the other Germanic rulers?

4. What were the roles that Frankish women played in the transformation of their society and that of the Gallo-Romans? Did Gregory and

26. Hillgarth, p. 73.

27. McNamara and Halborg, p. 4.

Chapter 6
The Franks
and the
Transformation
of the Roman
World:
Clotild of
Burgundy (475–
548) and Clovis I,
King of the
Franks (466?–511)

the hagiographers inflate Clotild's importance? Why or why not?

5. Why did Clovis's conversion and Clotild's role in it become legendary?

6. Are there any objective accounts of Clovis and Clotild? How did Gregory of Tours and the medieval hagiographers shape the accounts of their lives?

■ DOCUMENTS

DOCUMENT ONE

GREGORY OF TOURS

"The Preface of Gregory, Bishop of the Church in Tours," *The History of the Franks*

Gregory of Tours (538–594) was the bishop of that city from 573 until his death in 594. He was a Gallo-Roman from a distinguished senatorial family who spoke and wrote Latin as his native language. During his lifetime, Gregory wrote ten books of histories, seven of miracles, and one each on the Lives of the Fathers, Commentaries on the Psalms *and* Offices of the Church. *His histories are known to us as* The History of the Franks, *and they are largely a parade of Germanic kings and queens from the early fifth century until 591, three years before Gregory's death. What themes does Gregory intend to explore in his history?*

A great many things keep happening, some of them good, some of them bad. The inhabitants of different countries keep quarrelling fiercely with each other and kings go on losing their temper in the most furious way. Our churches are attacked by the heretics and then protected by the Catholics; the faith of Christ burns bright in many men, but it remains lukewarm in others; no sooner are the church-buildings endowed by the faithful than they are stripped bare again by those who have no faith. However, no writer has come to the fore who has been sufficiently skilled in setting things down in an orderly fashion to be able to describe these events in prose or in verse. In fact in the towns of Gaul the writing of literature has declined to the point where it has virtually disappeared altogether. Many people have complained about this, not once but time and time again. 'What a poor period this is!' they have been heard to say. 'If among all our people there is not one man to be found who can write a book about what is happening today, the pursuit of letters really is dead in us!'

I have often thought about these complaints and others like them. I have written this work to keep alive the memory of those dead and gone, and to bring them to the notice of future generations. My style is not very polished, and I have had to devote much of my space to the quarrels between the wicked and the righteous. All the same I have been greatly encouraged by certain kind remarks which, to my no small surprise, I have often heard made by our folk, to the effect that few people understand a rhetorical speechifier, whereas many can follow a blunt speaker.

So that the sequence of time may be properly understood, I have decided to begin my first book with the foundation of the world. I have set out the chapter-headings in proper order.

DOCUMENT TWO

BISHOP REMIGIUS OF REIMS

Instructions to Clovis
(481)

When Clovis succeeded his father in 481, Remigius had been bishop at Reims for over two decades. He was well educated, and socially and politically respected. According to Sidonius and others, he was one of the most influential leaders of northern Gaul. What is the tone of the bishop's letter to the young king? What role does Remigius see the church playing in Clovis's reign?

To the celebrated and rightly magnificent Lord, King Clovis, [from] Bishop Remigius.

A strong report has come to us that you have taken over the administration of the Second Belgic Province. There is nothing new in that you now begin to be what your parents always were. First of all, you should act so that God's Judgement may not abandon you and that your merits should maintain you at the height where you have arrived by your humility. For, as the proverb says, man's acts are judged. You ought to associate with yourself counselors who are able to do honor to your reputation. Your deeds should be chaste and honest. You should defer to your bishops and always have recourse to their advice. If you are on good terms with them your province will be better able to stand firm. Encourage your people, relieve the afflicted, protect widows, nourish orphans, so shine forth that all may love and fear you. May justice proceed from your mouth. Ask nothing of the poor or of strangers, do not allow yourself to receive gifts from them. Let your tribunal be open to all men, so that no man may leave it with the sorrow [of not having been heard]. You possess the riches your father left you. Use them to ransom captives and free them from servitude. If someone is admitted to your presence let him not feel he is a stranger. Amuse yourself

*Chapter 6
The Franks
and the
Transformation
of the Roman
World:
Clotild of
Burgundy (475–
548) and Clovis I,
King of the
Franks (466?–511)*

with young men, deliberate with the old. If you wish to reign, show yourself worthy to do so.

DOCUMENT THREE

SIDONIUS APOLLINARIS

Letters, Letter to Agricola

Sources for the fifth century are scarce and the letters of Sidonius Apollinaris, bishop of Clermont between 469 and 485, provide some insight into the thinking of a Catholic Gallo-Roman aristocrat, man of letters, politician, and churchman who was coming to terms with the rulers of southern Gaul, the Visigoths and Burgundians. Twenty-four panegyrics and nine books of letters survive. In many of his letters, Sidonius tries to explain and justify his cooperation with and respect for the barbarians. How does he describe Theodoric, king of the Visigoths? Why does he describe him in this way? Why does he allow the king to win at backgammon?

Sidonius to His Dear Agricola, Greeting

1. Seeing that report commends to the world the graciousness of Theodoric,[1] King of the Goths, you have often asked me to describe to you in writing the dimensions of his person and the character of his life. I am delighted to do so, subject to the limits of a letter, and I appreciate the honest spirit which prompts so nice a curiosity. Well, he is a man who deserves to be studied even by those who are not in close relations with him. In his build the will of God and Nature's plan have joined together to endow him with a supreme perfection; and his character is such that even the jealousy which hedges a sovereign has no power to rob it of its glories. . . . 4. And now you may want to know all about his everyday life, which is open to the public gaze. Before dawn he goes with a very small retinue to the service conducted by the priests of his faith [Arianism], and he worships with great earnestness, though (between ourselves) one can see that this devotion is a matter of routine rather than of conviction. The administration duties of his sovereignty claim the rest of the morning. Nobles in armour have places near his throne; a crowd of guards in their dress of skins is allowed in so as to be at hand, but excluded from the presence so as not to disturb; and so they keep up a hum of conversation by the door, outside the curtains but within the barriers. Meanwhile deputations from various peoples are intro-

---

1. Theodore II. (reigned A.D. 453–466).

duced, and he listens to a great deal of talk, but replies shortly, postponing business which he intends to consider, speeding that which is to be promptly settled. The second hour comes: he rises from his throne, to pass an interval in inspecting his treasures or his stables. . . . 6. When one joins him at dinner (which on all but festival days is just like that of a private household), there is no unpolished conglomeration of discoloured old silver set by panting attendants on sagging tables; the weightiest thing on these occasions is the conversation, for there are either no stories or only serious ones. The couches, with their spreading draperies, show an array sometimes of scarlet cloth, sometimes of fine linen. The viands attract by their skilful cookery, not by their costliness, the platters by their brightness, not by their weight. Replenishment of the goblets or wine-bowls comes at such long intervals that there is more reason for the thirsty to complain than for the intoxicated to refrain. To sum up: you can find there Greek elegance, Gallic plenty, Italian briskness; the dignity of state, the attentiveness of a private home, the ordered discipline of royalty. But as to the luxury of the days of festival I had better hold my tongue, for even persons of no note cannot fail to note it. 7. To resume the story: after satisfying his appetite he never takes more than a short midday sleep, and often goes without it. In the hours when the gaming-board attracts him he is quick to pick up the dice; he examines them anxiously, spins them with finesse, throws them eagerly; he addresses them jestingly and calmly awaits the result. If the throw is lucky, he says nothing; if unlucky, he smiles; in neither case does he lose his temper, in either case he is a real philosopher. As for a second throw, he is too proud either to fear it or to make it; when a chance of one is presented he disdains it, when it is used against him he ignores it. He sees his opponent's piece escape without stirring, and gets his own free without being played up to. You would actually think he was handling weapons when he handles the pieces on the board; his sole thought is of victory. 8. When it is the time for play he throws off for a while the stern mood of royalty and encourages fun and freedom and good-fellowship. My own opinion is that he dreads being feared. Further, he is delighted at seeing his defeated rival disgruntled, and it is only his opponent's ill-temper which really satisfies him that the game has not been given him. Now comes something to surprise you; the exultation which comes upon him on these trivial occasions often speeds the claims of important transactions. At such times the haven of a prompt decision is thrown open to petitions which have for a long time previously been in distress through the foundering of their advocates. I myself at such times, if I have a favour to ask, find it fortunate to be beaten by him, for I lose my pieces to win my cause. . . .

Chapter 6
The Franks
and the
Transformation
of the Roman
World:
Clotild of
Burgundy (475–
548) and Clovis I,
King of the
Franks (466?–511)

DOCUMENT FOUR

GREGORY OF TOURS

"Clovis, King of the Franks,"
The History of the Franks

In this passage, Gregory describes Clovis's first victory. How does Gregory depict the actions of Clovis and his soldiers? What is the key to Clovis's success?

. . . 27. The next thing which happened was that Childeric died. His son Clovis replaced him on the throne. In the fifth year of his reign Syagrius, the King of the Romans[1] and the son of Aegidius, was living in the city of Soissons, where Aegidius himself used to have his residence. Clovis marched against him with his blood-relation Ragnachar, who also had high authority, and challenged him to come out to fight. Syagrius did not hesitate to do so, for he was not afraid of Clovis. They fought each other and the army of Syagrius was annihilated. He fled and made his way as quickly as he could to King Alaric II in Toulouse. Clovis summoned Alaric to surrender the fugitive, informing him that he would attack him in his turn for having given Syagrius refuge. Alaric was afraid to incur the wrath of the Franks for the sake of Syagrius and handed him over bound to the envoys, for the Goths are a timorouss race. When Clovis had Syagrius in his power he ordered him to be imprisoned. As soon as he had seized the kingdom of Syagrius he had him killed in secret.

At that time many churches were plundered by the troops of Clovis, for he still held fast to his pagan idolatries. The soldiers had stolen an ewer of great size and wondrous workmanship, together with many other precious objects used in the church service. The bishop of the church in question sent messengers to the King to beg that, even if he would not hand back any of the other sacred vessels, this ewer at least might be restored to the church. The King listened to them and replied: 'Follow me to Soissons, where all the objects which we have seized are to be distributed. If this vessel for which your bishop is asking falls to my share, I will meet his wishes.' They came to Soissons and all the booty was placed in a heap before them. King Clovis addressed his men as follows, pointing to the vessel in question: 'I put it to you, my lusty freebooters, that you should agree here and now to grant me that ewer over and above my normal share.' They listened to what he said and the more rational among them answered: 'Everything in front of us is yours, noble King, for our very persons are yours to command. Do exactly as you wish, for there is none among us who has the power to say you nay.' As they spoke one of their number, a feckless fellow, greedy and prompt to anger, raised his battle-axe and struck the ewer. 'You

---

1. Syagrius was not King; he was probably Master of the Soldiers.

shall have none of this booty,' he shouted, 'except your fair share.' All present were astounded at his words. The King hid his chagrin under a pretence of long-suffering patience. He took the vessel and handed it over to the envoy of the church; but in his heart he resented what had happened. At the end of that year he ordered the entire army to assemble on the parade-ground, so that he could examine the state of their equipment. The King went round inspecting them all and came finally to the man who had struck the ewer. 'No other man has equipment in such a bad state as yours,' said he. 'Your javelin is in a shock-ing condition, and so are your sword and your axe!' He seized the man's axe and threw it on the ground. As the soldier bent forward to pick up his weapon, King Clovis raised his own battle-axe in the air and split his skull with it. 'That is what you did to my ewer in Soissons,' he shouted. The man fell dead. Clovis ordered the others to dismiss. They were filled with mighty dread at what he had done. Clovis waged many wars and won many victories. In the tenth year of his reign he invaded the Thuringians and subjected them to his rule. . . .

DOCUMENT FIVE

GREGORY OF TOURS

"Clotild Baptizes Her Sons,"
The History of the Franks

In this chapter, Gregory describes Clotild's role in Clovis's conversion to Catholic Christianity. How does Clotild persuade her husband to convert?

. . . 29. The first child which Clotild bore Clovis was a son. She wanted to have her baby baptized, and she kept on urging her husband to agree to this. 'The gods whom you worship are no good,' she would say. 'They haven't even been able to help themselves, let alone others. They are carved out of stone or wood or some old piece of metal. The very names which you have given them were the names of men, not of gods. Take your Saturn, for examples, who ran away from his own son to avoid being exiled from his kingdom, or so they say; and Jupiter, that obscene perpetrator of all mucky deeds, who couldn't keep his hands off other men, who had his fun with all his female relatives and couldn't even refrain from intercourse with his own sister,

'. . . Jovisque
Et soror et coniunx,'[1]

1. *Aeneid*, 1, 46–7: 'at once sister and wife of Jupiter.'

Chapter 6
The Franks
and the
Transformation
of the Roman
World:
Clotild of
Burgundy (475–
548) and Clovis I,
King of the
Franks (466?–511)

to quote her own words. What have Mars and Mercury ever done for anyone? They may have been endowed with magic arts, but they were certainly not worthy of being called divine. You ought instead to worship Him who created at a word and out of nothing heaven, and earth, the sea and all that therein is, who made the sun to shine, who lit the sky with stars, who peopled the water with fish, the earth with beasts, the sky with flying creatures, at whose nod the fields became fair with fruits, the trees with apples, the vines with grapes, by whose hand the race of man was made, by whose gifts all creation is constrained to serve in deference and devotion the man He made.' However often the Queen said this, the King came no nearer to belief. 'All these things have been created and produced at the command of *our* gods,' he would answer. 'It is obvious that *your* God can do nothing, and, what is more, there is no proof that he is a God at all.'

The Queen, who was true to her faith, brought her son to be baptized. She ordered the church to be decorated with hangings and curtains, in the hope that the King, who remained stubborn in the face of argument, might be brought to the faith by ceremony. The child was baptized; he was given the name Ingomer; but no sooner had he received baptism than he died in his white robes. Clovis was extremely angry. He began immediately to reproach his Queen. 'If he had been dedicated in the name of my gods,' he said, 'he would have lived without question; but now that he has been baptized in the name of your God he has not been able to live a single day!' 'I give thanks to Almighty God,' replied Clotild, 'the Creator of all things, who has not found me completely unworthy, for He has deigned to welcome to His kingdom a child conceived in my womb. I am not at all cast down in my mind because of what has happened, for I know that my child, who was called away from this world in his white baptismal robes, will be nurtured in the sight of God.'

Some time later Clotild bore a second son. He was baptized Chlodomer. He began to ail and Clovis said: 'What else do you expect? It will happen to him as it happened to his brother: no sooner is he baptized in the name of your Christ than he will die!' Clotild prayed to the Lord and at His command the baby recovered.

30. Queen Clotild continued to pray that her husband might recognize the true God and give up his idol-worship. Nothing could persuade him to accept Christianity. Finally war broke out against the Alamanni and in this conflict he was forced by necessity to accept what he had refused of his own free will. It so turned out that when the two armies met on the battlefield there was great slaughter and the troops of Clovis were rapidly being annihilated. He raised his eyes to heaven when he saw this, felt compunction in his heart and was moved to tears. 'Jesus Christ,' he said, 'you who Clotild maintains to be the Son of the living God, you who deign to give help to those in travail and victory to those who trust in you, in faith I beg the glory of your help. If you will give me victory over my enemies, and if I may have evidence of that miraculous power which the people dedicated to your name say that they have experienced, then

I will believe in you and I will be baptized in your name. I have called upon my own gods, but, as I see only too clearly, they have no intention of helping me. I therefore cannot believe that they possess any power, for they do not come to the assistance of those who trust in them. I now call upon you. I want to believe in you, but I must first be saved from my enemies.' Even as he said this the Alamanni turned their backs and began to run away. As soon as they saw that their King was killed, they submitted to Clovis. 'We beg you,' they said, 'to put an end to this slaughter. We are prepared to obey you.' Clovis stopped the war. He made a speech in which he called for peace. Then he went home. He told the Queen how he had won a victory by calling on the name of Christ. This happened in the fifteenth year of his reign. . . .

DOCUMENT SIX

MEDIEVAL HAGIOGRAPHY

The Life of Saint Chrothilda [Clotild]

The retelling of saints' lives served multiple purposes in Merovingian Gaul. In Clotild's case, the hagiographer highlighted her role in the struggle between Catholicism and Arianism. When does she begin to discuss her husband's conversion with him? How does this account differ in tone and fact from Gregory's account in Document Five?

. . . 5. And when the king in his chamber had initiated her into the ways of the flesh, Blessed Chrothilda said to him: "Lord King, hear your handmaid and give me what I ask." And the king said: "Ask what you will and I will give it to you." The queen said: "I ask that you will believe in almighty God, Father, Son, and Holy Ghost, and that you will destroy the idols you worship and restore the churches you have burned." The king answered: "I will not desert my gods and I will not pay honor to your God. If you will ask for something else, you will obtain it easily." And all this was done by the disposition of Him Who saves the unbelieving man through the faithful woman. For after that the queen conceived a son to whom she gave the name of Ingmar. The happy queen decorated the church with altar curtains and precious drapery. She ordered it prepared for a baptism and called the clergy to baptize the boy. But when he had been cleansed by holy baptism, he died in his white garb. At that the king was deeply grieved and exceedingly angry with the queen. He said that the boy would still be alive if he had been dedicated in the name of the gods. The queen answered: "I give thanks to God, for He has received this son who came from my body and yours in His kingdom." Thereafter another son was born and called Chlodomir

[177]

Chapter 6
The Franks
and the
Transformation
of the Roman
World:
Clotild of
Burgundy (475–
548) and Clovis I,
King of the
Franks (466?–511)

in Baptism. And when he was sick, he was restored to health by his mother's prayers.

6. The queen did not cease to tell the king that he should worship God and desert the vain idols he honored. But in no way could she move his mind to belief until he went to war with the Alamans and Suevi. Then he was compelled to believe what he had denied before. For while Franks and Alamans fought, Flodoveus' men began to give way. Seeing this, Aurelian said to the king: "Lord King, believe in the God of Heaven Whom the queen honors and He will free you and yours from imminent peril and give you victory." Raising his eyes to heaven, with flowing tears, the king said: "I believe in You, Jesus Christ, who came to save the world. I adore you, true God, Whom I have refused to honor! Free me from present danger, for I am Your servant." When he said this prayer, the Alamans turned in flight, their king fell dead, and they submitted to Flodoveus. The king brought their land under tribute and, praising God for having gained the victory, he turned back into Francia and told the queen how he had merited victory by invoking the name of Jesus Christ. And this was done in the fifteenth year of his reign.

7. At this time, the great priest and bishop, Remigius strongly ruled over the *cathedra* of the church of Reims. The queen summoned him from there, praying that he might show the king the way to salvation. The bishop came before the king who received him with honors and said: "I hear you willingly, most blessed father, and I will follow your commands obediently." In answer, the Blessed Remigius said to the king: "God in Heaven is King of kings and Lord of lords, for He himself has said: 'By me, kings reign.' If you would believe in Him and be cleansed with holy baptism, you will reign with Him and will have remission of all your sins and you will conquer all your enemies and you will reign with Him forever in the life to come." Hearing these holy words from Bishop Remigius, King Flodoveus said with welling tears: "I believe in God. I want to be baptized. I desire to live through Him and to die in Him." The holy Queen Chrothilda had prayed to God incessantly, supplicatingly beseeching that He might snatch the king and his people from the snares of the Devil so that, by the work of the Holy Spirit within him, he might be purged by holy baptism. Immediately, she decorated the church with drapes and cloaks and other ecclesiastical ornaments. Then the new Constantine came to baptism. Blessed Remigius in the lead and Blessed Chrothilda following. The Holy Spirit ordered these things to show their mystical meaning. For as was fitting in the pagan king's approach to baptism, Saint Remigius took the lead as they entered playing the role of Jesus Christ and the holy Queen Chrothilda followed as the embodiment of God's Church. The holy bishop consecrated the font. The king was stripped of his corporal vestments and baptized by the aforesaid bishop. And since there was not enough chrism, the Holy Spirit descended in the form of a dove, carrying two ampoules full of oil and chrism which Saint Remigius devoutly received. With these he anointed the king according to the custom of the church and called him Ludovic, which means a laudable man. Oh happy

Gaul! Rejoice and exult, praise the Lord, delight in the true God! For through the prayers of Saint Chrothilda, the mystical embodiment of the church, your first king was chosen by the King of Heaven and torn from the cult of demons. He was converted to God by the preaching of Saint Remigius and baptized by him. His flesh was anointed with celestial chrism brought by the Holy Spirit and his heart was anointed spiritally with divine love. Then, with the counsel of Blessed Chrothilda, the king began to destroy the fanes and build churches in his land and endow them with copious gifts. He gave alms generously to the poor and helped widows and orphans and persevered sedulously and devoutly in every good work. Thereafter, Blessed Chrothilda bore a son named Lothar in holy baptism and that is what she called him. . . .

DOCUMENT SEVEN

AVITUS, BISHOP OF VIENNE

Letter to Clovis
(496)

Avitus was the bishop of Vienne from 490 to about 518. He was born in a promi- nent Gallo-Roman family. During his lifetime, he pursued the extinction of the Arian heresy in the kingdom of Burgundy (443–532). He wrote extensively, and close to ninety of his letters survive. Among them is this letter to Clovis on the oc- casion of his baptism. What does Avitus mean when he says, "Your Faith is our victory." How does Avitus portray the division between Catholicism and Arian- ism? What can you conclude about the nature and tone of this religious conflict?

Bishop Avitus to King Clovis.

The followers of [Arian] error have in vain, by a cloud of contradictory and un- true opinions, sought to conceal from your extreme subtlety the glory of the Christian name. While we committed these questions to eternity and trusted that the truth of each man's belief would appear at the Future Judgment, the ray of truth has shone forth even among present shadows. Divine Providence has found the arbiter of our age. Your choice is a general sentence. Your Faith is our victory. Many others, in this matter, when their bishops or friends exhort them to adhere to the True Faith, are accustomed to oppose the traditions of their race and respect for their ancestral cult; thus they culpably prefer a false shame to their salvation. While they observe a futile reverence for their parents [by con- tinuing to share their] unbelief, they confess that they do not know what they should choose to do. After this marvelous deed guilty shame can no longer

[179]

Chapter 6
The Franks
and the
Transformation
of the Roman
World:
Clotild of
Burgundy (475–
548) and Clovis I,
King of the
Franks (466?–511)

shelter behind this excuse. Of all your ancient genealogy you have chosen to keep only your own nobility, and you have willed that your race should derive from you all the glories which adorn high birth. Your ancestors have prepared a great destiny for you; you willed to prepare better things [for those who will follow you]. You follow your ancestors in reigning in this world; you have opened the way to your descendants to a heavenly reign. Let Greece indeed rejoice it has elected an emperor who shares our Faith; it is no longer alone in deserving such a favor. Your sphere also burns with its own brilliance, and, in the person of a king, the light of a rising sun shines over the Western lands. It is right that this light began at the Nativity of Our Redeemer, so that the waters of rebirth have brought you forth to salvation the very day that the world received the birth of its Redemption, the Lord of Heaven. The day celebrated as the Lord's Nativity is also yours, in which you have been born to Christ, as Christ to the world, in which you have consecrated your soul to God, your life to your contemporaries, your glory to posterity.

What should be said of the glorious solemnity of your regeneration? If I could not assist in person among the ministers [of the rite] I shared in its joy. Thanks to God, our land took part in the thanksgiving, for, before your Baptism, a messenger of Your Most Subtle Humility informed us that you were a "competens" [that is, to be baptized within forty days]. Therefore the sacred night [of Christmas] found us sure of what you would do. We saw (with the eyes of the spirit) that great sight, when a crowd of bishops around you, in the ardor of their holy ministry, poured over your royal limbs the waters of life; when that head feared by the peoples bowed down before the servants of God; when your royal locks, hidden under a helmet, were steeped in holy oil; when your breast, relieved of its cuirass, shone with the same whiteness as your baptismal robes. Do not doubt, most flourishing of kings, that this soft clothing will give more force to your arms: whatever Fortune has given up to now, this Sanctity will bestow.

I would wish to add some exhortations to your praises if anything escaped either your knowledge or your attention. Should we preach the Faith to the convert who perceived it without a preacher; or humility, which you have long shown toward us [bishops], although you only owe it to us now, after your profession of Faith; or mercy, attested, in tears and joy to God and men, by a people once captive, now freed by you? One wish remains for me to express. Since God, thanks to you, will make of your people His own possession, offer a part of the treasure of Faith which fills your heart to the peoples living beyond you, who, still living in natural ignorance, have not been corrupted by the seeds of perverse doctrines [that is, Arianism]. Do not fear to send them envoys and to plead with them the cause of God, who has done so much for your cause. So that the other pagan peoples, at first being subject to your empire for the sake of religion, while they still seem to have another ruler, may be distinguished rather by their race than by their prince. [End of letter missing.]

DOCUMENT EIGHT

SALIC LAW

"Prologue"

The prologue to lex Salica narrates the history of the Franks. What is the defining moment for the Franks and Roman Gaul?

The famous race of Franks, whose Founder is God, strong in arms, true to its alliances, deep in counsel, noble in body, untouched in sincerity, beautiful in form, daring, swift, and fierce, now converted to the Catholic Faith, free from heresy; while still held in a barbaric [rite], by God's inspiration, according to the quality of its customs, sought after the key of knowledge, desiring justice, keeping piety. . . .

But when, by God's favor, Clovis, King of the Franks, powerful, glorious, and famous, first received Catholic Baptism, what was held less suitable in the pact was lucidly emended by the blows of Kings Clovis, Childebert, and Lothar.

Long live Christ who loves the Franks! May He guard their kingdom, fill their leaders with the light of His Grace, protect their army, accord them the defense of the Faith! May the Lord of Lords concede them, of His Mercy, the joys of peace and days full of happiness! For this is the race which, brave and valiant, threw off in battle from their necks the most hard Roman yoke, and it is the Franks who, after Baptism, have enclosed in gold and precious stones the bodies of the Holy Martyrs, whom the Romans had burnt by fire, mutilated by the sword, or thrown to wild beasts!

7

The Byzantine Empire: Justinian (483?–565) and Theodora (497–548)

▪ SETTING THE STAGE

When the Germanic ruler, Odoacer, rode into the city of Rome as the self-declared king of Italy in 476, the Western Roman Empire and its long line of Roman emperors came to an end. This was not the end of the Roman Empire, however, because the eastern Greek half of the empire and its capital, Constantinople, continued to thrive, defend itself from the successive waves of con-quering peoples from Central Asia, and claim the indivisibility of the Roman Empire, east and west. Fifty years after the consolidation of Ostrogoth rule in Italy, a young emperor, Justinian (483–565), would make one last effort from the shores of Constantinople to conquer and reintegrate the West into the East and reestablish Roman law and admin-istration throughout the former Empire.

When Justinian became emperor of the Eastern Roman Empire in 527, he lived in an imperial city that held a half million inhabitants and ruled over a state and society that was thoroughly Romanized. Built by the Emperor Constantine in the fourth century on the foundations of the old Greek colony Byzantium, Constantinople was the greatest city in both the East and the West at the beginning of the sixth century. The city possessed all of the amenities of a Roman city—an imperial palace, churches, theaters, amphitheaters, a stadium (the Hippodrome), baths, library, defensive walls, and roads radiating from the city to all parts of the Empire and to Rome itself. The peoples who inhabited this part of the Empire still expected efficient administration, the protection of the army, maintenance of trade routes and commerce, spiritual guidance from the Christian church and its leaders, and to be called Roman.

Blending Roman and Christian conceptions of a universal empire, Justinian strove to free Roman lands from the barbarians, reunite the two halves into a single Roman and orthodox Christian empire, and to restore Roman supremacy in the Mediterranean. The restoration of a universal Christian Roman empire was the constant dream of this emperor. During his thirty-eight-year rule, Justinian redefined the relationship between church and the state, renovated the buildings and fortifications of his capital city, codified Roman law, and rooted out heresy and paganism. In his quest for centralization, orthodoxy, and the assertion of autocratic rule, he depended on the counsel of his common-born actress wife, Theodora. During their lifetimes, the "husband and wife made a remarkable pair."[1] He was the offspring of a peasant family; she was the daughter of an animal trainer. Together they survived military and political challenges from enemies and rivals, urban riots, conflicts in the Christian church, and vicious gossip about Theodora's early life. To tell the story of Justinian and Theodora is to wade into the complex political, social, and religious waters of the early centuries of the Byzantine Empire.

Students of history can learn much about the emperor and empress from several narrative histories written by their contemporaries.[2] Procopius of Caesarea regaled literate Byzantines with three accounts of Justinian's and Theodora's reign. The *History of the Wars of Justinian* narrates Justinian's military campaigns in Africa and Italy; *Buildings* is a flattering and glowing account of Justinian's ambitious building program, and of his and his wife's political skills. *Secret History* is a blistering, tell-all account of Theodora's early life as an actress and her intrigues at court, and of the less-than-noble origins of Justinian and his uncle, the emperor Justin (r. 518–527). Procopius ended his narratives in the early 550s, but Agathias of Myrina in Asia Minor

1. J. A. S. Evans, *The Age of Justinian: The Circumstances of Imperial Power* (New York: Routledge, 1996), p. 2.

2. Robert Browning, *Justinian and Theodora* (New York: Praeger Publishers, 1971), pp. 261–264.

*Chapter 7
The Byzantine
Empire:
Justinian (483?–
565) and
Theodora (497–
548)*

begins where Procopius left off and continued the story of the empire up to 568.

Scholars have often singled out Procopius's *Secret History* as a particularly troubling source because of its scathing indictment of Theodora and her early life. This source must be used with care because of the author's growing disillusionment with the emperor and his policies and because later historians, especially Catholic scholars, seized on Procopius's stories about Theodora and her sexual adventures to discredit her religious beliefs. Theodora was a Monophysite, or follower of a Christian sect that believed Jesus had only one nature, which was divine. This belief contradicted the accepted, or orthodox, Christian position that declared Jesus was of two natures, human and divine.

When Procopius's *Secret History* was rediscovered by Catholic scholars in the seventeenth century, many subsequent histories of the early Byzantine Empire accepted the view that Theodora was immoral, indecent, and wicked. While many of Procopius's stories about Theodora lack evidence, some of the stories appear in the writings of a friend, supporter, and coreligionist of Theodora's, John of Ephesus. In his history of the church from its foundation to 585, written from the Monophysite point of view, he was quick to note that the empress was a pious and devote woman. His history also contains invaluable information about early Byzantine social life and attitudes. Another history of the early church was written by Evagrius of Epiphaneia and covers the period between 431 to 593. Evagrius not only details the conflicts between the different Christian sects but also gives attention to the secular world of the Byzantine Empire.

One can draw upon numerous other sources for a detailed picture of the lives of Justinian and Theodora and their political and social attitudes. During his reign, Justinian ordered the compilation of Roman law, which sorted through all existing statutes, edicts of elected officials, opinions of jurists, and imperial decrees from Rome and beyond. He placed all of them into a single source know as the *Corpus Iuris Civilis (Collected Civil Law)*. Included in this compilation were Justinian's decrees, many of which dealt with the status of women, women's rights in marriage, and family issues and tell us quite a bit about official ideology and propaganda. Justinian's building projects are another invaluable source because they tell us about the political, social, and religious values of the imperial couple. Justinian rebuilt Constantine's Church of Holy Wisdom, or Santa Sophia, and funded the building of hospitals and orphanages to demonstrate his piousness and devotion to the orthodox Christian church. He also funded the refurbishing of a "palace into a monastery for former prostitutes who had been forced into working in brothels 'not of their own free will but under the force of lust' because of extreme poverty."[3]

3. Lynda Garland, *Byzantine Empresses: Women and Power in Byzantium, A.D. 527–1204* (New York: Routledge, 1999), p. 17.

From all of these diverse sources, the student of history not only gains a sense of the political, military, and religious conflicts of the early Byzantine state and its society but also learns that earlier peoples loved gossip, scandal, and intimate scurrilous details about the rich and famous as much as their counterparts in the modern world.

THE ACTORS:

JUSTINIAN AND THEODORA

Justinian's entrance onto the stage of Byzantine politics was sponsored by his uncle, the emperor Justin I. Justin and his family came from a Thracian settlement in the Roman province of Dardania (in present-day southeastern Serbia). In his early twenties, Justin, traveled to Constantinople to find his fortune. At this point in the 470s, the Eastern Roman emperor, Leo I (r. 457–474), was forming a new imperial guard, and he sought residents from all parts of the empire who were fit, brave, and eager to swear loyalty to a powerful patron. Justin and his two traveling companions appeared to be the ideal recruits and soon became part of this elite unit. Recruitment for military service often depended on such young men, and their powerful position within the Roman Empire was noted by the Byzantine general Germanus in 537, another one of Justin's nephews. Addressing his soldiers during the campaign in Africa against the Vandals, Germanus stated, "There is nothing, fellow soldiers, with which you can justly reproach the Emperor . . . for it was he who took you as you came from the fields with your wallets and one short frock apiece and brought you together in Byzantium and has caused you to be so powerful that the Roman state now depends on you."[4] Germanus spoke from experience. His uncle had summoned him and his two brothers to Constantinople to serve the state and also his cousin, Petrus Sabbatius, who would later become Justinian I.

We do not know much about Justinian's early life or when he came to Constantinople because we have little concrete historical evidence about him before 518. Justinian is believed to have been born in 482 or 483 to Justin's sister and the peasant Sabbatius in a small village near the birthplace of his uncle. His first language was probably Thracian, but because of the Romanization of the province, most likely he knew Latin as well. The year when his uncle sent for him is unknown, but it has been argued that Justinian was relatively young because his education, his cultured manner, and his facility with both Greek and Latin probably meant longtime residence in Constantinople.

Once in the imperial city, he lived the life of Constantinople's well-educated elite and enjoyed the privileges bestowed on members of the corps of palace guards. By the time

4. Procopius, *De bello Vandalico* II, 16, 12–13. Quoted in A. A. Vasiliev, *Justin the First: An Introduction to the Epoch of Justinian the Great* (Cambridge, Mass.: Harvard University Press, 1950), p. 65.

Chapter 7
The Byzantine
Empire:
Justinian (483?–
565) and
Theodora (497–
548)

Justin became emperor in 518, Justinian had earned his uncle's confidence and respect, evidenced by the fact that Justin legally adopted his nephew. The young Petrus Sabbatius added Justinianus to his name and then eventually chose to use Justinian as his official name.

Justin's elevation to the imperial throne was unexpected. The previous emperor died in 518 without an heir and designated successor. Justin's powerful position as the commander of the palace guards, his devotion to orthodox Christianity, the respect he enjoyed among the army's military commanders and the rank and file, and the reluctance of the Senate to go against anyone whom the army supported propelled Justin onto the throne. The peasant from the provinces now ruled over the most powerful empire in the world, and he turned to his nephew, Justinian, to help him rule. Justin immediately appointed Justinian to be commander of the troops in the imperial city. This position brought him into the inner cabinet, which gave daily advice to the emperor. From these vantage points, Justinian was able to suppress any plots or conspiracies against his uncle from rival candidates, and he was also able to steer his uncle through the labyrinth of Constantinople's social and political worlds. Now in his thirties, Justinian had had twenty years of experience observing and learning the ways of the imperial city's aristocracy, the army, and the Senate (Document One).

Justin I ruled from 518 until 527. By all accounts, he was a fine soldier, but he depended on his nephew, the imperial bureaucracy, and ministers to keep the empire running smoothly. Historians agree that during this nine-year reign, Justin's nephew was the de facto ruler. The Eastern Roman Empire still functioned efficiently. It had effectively resisted Germanic migrations and invasions; its bureaucracy still collected taxes, dispensed justice, and provided civic and social services; and its military recruited from within the state's borders and did not depend on mercenaries. The Eastern Roman Empire was severed from its western half, however, and this division was not only political, but social and religious as well.

While Latin was the official language of the Eastern Roman Empire, the area was in fact culturally Greek. An additional division occurred during the middle of the fifth century, when the Eastern Roman Empire began a fifty-year schism with the papacy. In the first years of Justin's rule, Justin and Justinian had to address the problem of religious unity. Beginning in the third century, Christian intellectuals and church leaders had been struggling with defining and enforcing the main set of beliefs for Christians. They struggled to define the nature of God, of Jesus, of his mother Mary, and of human beings. Having different definitions meant that the church could fracture and fragment into smaller and smaller pieces or into different sects of Christian believers. Church leaders were not the only ones concerned about this fragmentation. When he declared Christianity a legal religion in the fourth century, the emperor Constantine saw the potential of Christianity as a unifying force for the Roman Empire. Like the Christian church's leaders, he believed it was necessary to define clearly the central tenets of Christianity. In 325, Constantine called together the leaders of the Christian church to settle the dispute over the nature of Jesus. Although the council of Nicaea, in Asia Minor, asserted that Jesus was both human and divine, this assertion did not mean that controversy on this matter ended (Document Two).

By the fifth century, the belief that Jesus was divine only, and not human, emerged as the central tenet of a Christian movement known as Monophysitism, and its adherents were primarily from eastern parts of the empire, Egypt, and Syria. This movement persisted even after 451, when more than five hundred bishops at Chalcedon reiterated that Jesus was both human and divine. At this council, the order of precedence of the great archbishoprics, or patriarchates, was established, and the archbishop or the patriarch of Constantinople came first, immediately after the pope in Rome. Despite the Council of Chalcedon, Monophysitism persisted because it had powerful patrons. Two early Byzantine emperors, Zeno (r. 474–491) and Anastasius (r. 491–518), and several powerful eastern bishops had been followers. In the interest of maintaining stability and unity in the East, Zeno had issued an edict in 482 aimed at reconciling the two positions. The edict caused the papacy in Rome to break off relations with Constantinople. This breach between Roman and Constantinople meant that the empire, which had been divided by conquest, was now divided by religion.

Justinian had dreams of reuniting the two halves of the empire, and he persuaded his uncle to repair the breach with Rome. His uncle, a follower of the orthodox or Chalcedonian position, agreed and forced the patriarch of Constantinople, an appointee of the previous emperor, to reject his pro-Monophysite stance. He demanded that the church root out all Monophysite bishops, priests, and followers in its midst. He left the bastion of Monophysite belief, Egypt, and its powerful bishop of Alexandria, untouched because Egypt was the empire's most important supplier of grain. Rooting out this heretical sect would not be easy, and in 520 Justinian sent a letter to the pope counseling patience "lest, while we wish to win souls, we should lose both the bodies and the souls of many persons."[5] Justinian learned firsthand how hard it was to win souls over to the Chalcedonian position. Not two years after he wrote this letter, he met the woman he was to marry, Theodora, who was an actress and a Monophysite.

Information about Theodora's early life is given by Procopius in his *Secret History,* some of which is confirmed by John of Ephesus. To understand the context of her life and the stories about her is to understand the world surrounding the culture of entertainment and the nature of politics in the early Byzantine state. Like Rome, Constantinople possessed a large oval stadium, the Hippodrome, for chariot races, circus performances, and public

5. Evans, p. 78.

Chapter 7
The Byzantine
Empire:
Justinian (483?–
565) and
Theodora (497–
548)

games. All classes of people gathered here regularly to cheer for their favorite racing teams or performers and to elect or accept a new emperor. Public and popular acclamations were part of the empire's political culture, and Constantinople's mass politics began to revolve around the chariot-racing factions in the Hippodrome: the Greens, the Blues, the Whites, and the Reds. Chariot racing was the primary outlet for the youthful exuberance of Constantinople's young male population, and seating in the Hippodrome was arranged according to team affiliation. Young men quickly developed connections and loyalties to the different factions. Among the factions, the Blues and the Greens emerged as distinct groups and began to play an integral part in the empire's political, social, and religious life. Through their network of supporters, the patrons of these factions could summon a crowd or quickly whip up support for or against an emperor. The Blues were identified with the wealthy upper classes and were predominately Chalcedonian Christians. The Greens drew support from the city's traders, artisans, and people of the lower classes, some of whom were of Syrian origin, where Monophysitism thrived. Theodora's father, Akakios, was a bearkeeper and circus performer employed by the Greens.

Akakios had three daughters. Theodora's mother was most likely an ex-performer, like her husband, and their family occupied one of the lowest rungs of the social ladder. Circus performers, actors, actresses, mimes, and other performers had many legal prohibitions placed on them, espe-

cially the women. According to Roman legal practice, a woman who appeared on stage without the consent of her husband could be divorced immediately, a man who married an actress could not become a bishop, and a senator could not marry an actress.[6] The profession of actress required theatrical talents, but it was also common for an actress to be seen as an available sexual partner. Actors and actresses at the time performed in broad farces, and some of these farces included physical comedy such as suggestive dancing and movements, nakedness, and buffoonery. These performances sometimes caused such disorder that they drew the attention of the authorities. The emperor Anastasius banned certain types of performances in 502, and in 520 Justin banished dancers from the empire's theaters.

Theodora and her two sisters, Comito and Anastasia, were born into this world, and their position in life became even more precarious when their father died. Their mother remarried immediately, and it was assumed that her new husband would take over her late husband's job of bearkeeper for the Green faction. This position had been purchased by another, however, and Theodora's family seemed poised for a descent into poverty. As was the custom of the day, Theodora's mother decided to appeal this decision to the crowds at the Hippodrome, and she placed a wreath of flowers on her daughters' heads and led them into the center of the stadium. Here the family threw itself upon the mercy of the crowd. The

6. Browning, p. 65.

Greens rejected their appeal, but the Blues, who had recently lost their own bearkeeper, accepted it.[7] From this point forward, Theodora preferred the Blues to the Greens.

According to law, the children of actors were required to keep the occupation of their parents. Both Theodora and her older sister, Comito, became successful actresses and courtesans to the powerful and influential in Byzantine society. Theodora's fame grew as word spread about her uninhibited striptease performances and her willingness to serve as a kind of male prostitute by indulging in anal intercourse with interested clients[8] (Document Three). Theodora's choices were few and it is clear from the sources that she was thrown into the courtesan world at an early age, a fact Procopius noted when he wrote, "Theodora was still too underdeveloped to be capable of sharing a man's bed or having intercourse like a woman; but she acted as a sort of male prostitute." She left this life when she accompanied the newly appointed governor to his post in Libya. There she was his concubine and, according to Procopius, "served his unnatural appetites." The reasons why she left his service are not known, but it is clear that she made her way back to Constantinople by way of Alexandria, where it is purported that she converted to Monophysitism. With this conversion, she renounced her profession. Once in Constantinople, sometime in the early 520s, she and Justinian met.

■ ACT I:

PEASANT AND ACTRESS AS EMPEROR AND EMPRESS

How Justinian and Theodora met is unknown, but Justinian believed that he had met his perfect mate and the love of his life. Later in his life, he set forth a legal definition of marriage that probably mirrored his relationship with Theodora. It stated, "Mutual affection creates a marriage, and it does not need the addition of a dowry."[9] Of course, Justinian could make such a statement. He was one of the most powerful men in all of Byzantium and need not have worried about a dowry or the opinion of Constantinople's senatorial class. The only one who stood in their way of marrying was his uncle's wife, Euphemia, herself a former slave. With her death in 524, Justinian had cleared one obstacle to their marriage. The second obstacle, a Roman law that forbade the marriage of a man of his senatorial rank to a woman who had appeared on the stage, was cleared away when Justin issued an edict allowing for a repentant actress who had acquired a high honor to marry a senator. Theodora had already renounced her former life, and Justinian conferred upon her the rank of patrician. With these obstacles conquered, Justinian and Theodora were married

7. Evans, p. 101.

8. Garland, p. 11.

9. Evans, p. 101.

Chapter 7
The Byzantine
Empire:
Justinian (483?–
565) and
Theodora (497–
548)

in 525 in Santa Sophia. Justinian and Theodora also made sure that her sisters married well. If we can use Procopius as the bellwether for senatorial attitudes toward Constantinople's new powerful family, senators were not pleased to have a peasant and an actress at the core of a new dynasty.

Justinian became emperor in 527 when his uncle died. Succession had been assured when Justin made his nephew co-emperor a few months before his death and Justinian and Theodora were proclaimed emperor and empress by the patriarch of Constantinople in a solemn ceremony in Santa Sophia. Even though he had been the designated successor and the patriarch crowned Justinian and Theodora emperor and empress, neither fact meant that their place was secure. Prior to his ascension to the throne, Justinian had spent quite a bit of time and energy cultivating the Blue faction, so much so that the police turned a blind eye to the violence and thievery practiced by the gangs that were part of this faction. Once securely on the throne, Justinian renounced the Blues and embarked on a policy to curb their and the Greens' powers and privileges, which was not any easy task. Their latent power as masters of the crowd still posed a threat to the new emperor.

Justinian set an ambitious agenda for himself as emperor of the Roman Empire. First, he believed that he was the most powerful ruler in the known world, backed by God. In this regard, he conceived of himself as both priest and king, and he felt that he not only could dictate worldly affairs but could intervene at any time in religious disputes and ecclesiastical policy. As a result of these beliefs, Justinian was determined that the imperial government be reformed to make it efficient and just and to be sure that his state was prosperous enough to extract taxes. Finances were particularly important because of Justinian's wish to protect and secure his border with the Persians and to reconquer the western half of the empire. As heaven's "supreme viceroy on earth," he wished to heal the wounds created by the earlier schism with Rome, to root out paganism, and to resolve the problem of the Monophysite dissent.

Beginning in 528, Justinian began a campaign against the Persians that produced mixed results. During this two-year campaign, the young general Belisarius won an impressive victory against the Persians, the first time in many years that a Roman army had defeated the Persians, and led a heroic defense. His skills as a tactician, strategist, and field commander earned him a recall to Constantinople, where he was assigned the task of leading a Roman army against the Vandals in Africa. This successful reconquest of Africa from the Vandals in 533 and 534 was followed with a partial and costly reconquest of Italy from 535 to 555, and an essentially failed campaign in Spain, where the Byzantine army occupied only a few coastal areas. With a second war against the Persians (540–545) that pushed the empire's boundaries beyond Edessa, a Roman emperor once again ruled over most of the Mediterranean world, rivaling the empire of Diocletian and Constantine.

The early years of Justinian's reign were not only spent challenging rivals abroad, but also consolidating his power at home. Justinian was aware of the animosity he inspired in the empire's senatorial class, and he was determined to impress the image of the reign on his subjects. In the second year of his rule, he went through the capital city throwing gold coins from a sack to the cheering crowds who lined the streets. He used imperial funds to rebuild several cities that had fallen on hard times. In these cities, his builders renovated and rebuilt theaters, baths, and porticoes to demonstrate that a new era had begun. When Antioch in Syria suffered a devastating earthquake in late 528, Justinian and Theodora (she is noted for her concern in contemporary accounts) spent lavishly on its reconstruction. Theodora also participated in this early propaganda campaign to legitimize and solidify their rule. During the summer of 529, she made her way to the mineral springs in northwestern Asia Minor with an entourage of over four thousand people. Along the way, this imperial convoy distributed gifts to the churches, villages, and cities. The imperial couple also used ritual, ceremony, and imperial etiquette to elevate the emperor and empress above all others. Justinian and Theodora required all who approached them to prostrate themselves.

In her new role as empress and devout Christian and with Justinian's approval and aid, Theodora built "an extremely fine church of the archangel Michael" and the basilica of Anatolius. She also commissioned a very costly cross set with pearls and sent it to Jerusalem. She possessed a deep sympathy for the empire's destitute and impoverished subjects; an inscription in the church of Saint Sergius and Bacchus in Constantinople proclaims, "[S]he is the 'the God-crowned' Theodora whose mind is adorned with piety, and whose constant toil lies in unsparing efforts to nourish the destitute."[10]

Her concern for the destitute went beyond providing havens for the poor or refuge for former prostitutes. As early as 528, she took action against the pimps and brothel owners who kept young girls under contract and turned them into public prostitutes. Summoning the brothel keepers to the palace, she is purported to have lectured them on the evils of their ways and repaid each of them the five gold coins that they had paid to the girls' parents. She then gave each young girl a set of clothes and a gold coin. This concern for prostitution and its control had been the concern of other emperors. Perhaps because of Theodora, Justinian also made it his concern. Procopius noted, "[S]he [Theodora] was naturally inclined to assist women in misfortune" (Document Four). During the 530s, Justinian outlawed procurers and pimps who exploited girls for prostitution, passed legislation that made pimps subject to corporal punishment for their activities, and condemned those who entrapped girls into thinking that their contracts or promises made with pimps had the force of law.[11] Evagrius, another of the contemporary chroniclers, noted the severity with which men charged with rape were punished under Justinian.

10. Ibid., p. 103.
11. Garland, pp. 6–18.

[191]

Chapter 7
The Byzantine
Empire:
Justinian (483?–
565) and
Theodora (497–
548)

One cannot assume that Theodora had a natural inclination to assist the poor or the destitute because of her background or because she was a woman. She probably had an interest in removing some of the worst abuses of prostitution and helping the disadvantaged; she herself had been quite young when she was drafted into a life of performing sexual acts. However, imperial women traditionally had been expected to help the underprivileged, including prostitutes, and Theodora did bring a greater knowledge to bear on the problems suffered by this class. It is not impossible to draw the conclusion that she provided counsel to her husband on this matter, as she sometimes did on other affairs of state.[12] Procopius reported Justinian's views on his wife's advice: "he [Justinian] has taken counsel with 'the most pious consort given to Us by God.'"[13]

Justinian's respect for his wife and dependence on her counsel is reflected in Procopius's account of the most severe challenge to Justinian's rule: the Nika revolt of 532. In January 532 the Blues and the Greens of the Hippodrome fought a skirmish that blossomed into a larger social and political revolt. Reacting to the street fighting, the prefect of the city ordered the arrests and executions of seven of the ringleaders, both Blue and Green. Five of the seven executions were carried out. Perhaps reacting to the hostility of the crowd that gathered to watch the hanging, the executioners badly bungled the last two hangings,

a Blue and a Green, who fell from the scaffold still alive. They were swept up by the crowd and carried to the sanctuary of the Church of St. Lawrence, where they waited a resolution to their cases. The two warring factions came together in this common cause, and several days later at the races in the Hippodrome, the crowd, acting as one, chanted for the two men's release. Justinian's refusal to release the men incited the crowd, and people surged out of the stadium toward the palace of the city prefect, killed police who offered resistance, released prisoners, and set the palace on fire. The riot escalated into a revolt against Justinian, and the city was quickly engulfed in smoke and flames.

Justinian's refusal to show mercy to the two men reflected popular discontent with his rule. The heavy tax burden imposed on the people because of renovation and fortification projects and the campaigns against the Persians, coupled with Justinian's curtailment of the Blues' and Greens' power, snapped the bond of trust between him and his subjects.[14] They sought to topple him from the throne and presented another choice for emperor: Hypatios, the nephew of Anastasio I. The senatorial class, which had never been satisfied with Justinian's family's usurpation of power, also favored Hypatios. Poor Hypatios had to be dragged against his will, however, to the Hippodrome for the coronation.

As control of the city fell to the crowds, the wealthy fled and Justinian steeled himself and his court for the possibility of flight. According to Pro-

12. Ibid., p. 19.
13. Ibid., p. 15.

14. Evans, p. 121.

copius, Justinian and his kingdom were saved by the intervention of Theodora. In the discussion concerning the merits of leaving the city, she urged defiance. Procopius reports that her courage gave Justinian the resolve to put down the revolt (Document Five).

He ordered his two loyal commanders, Belisarius and Mundus, to lead their troops to the Hippodrome and kill the insurgents. Over thirty thousand were slaughtered. At Theodora's urging, Justinian also put Hypatios and his brother to death.

ACT II:

UNIFYING THE EMPIRE: RELIGION AND LAW

Theodora's influence not only extended into the realm of politics and charitable works but to religion as well. Her husband's conviction that he was both a priest and a king, supreme head on earth in matters ecclesiastical as well as state, permitted Theodora also to enter into religious debates and conflicts. Unlike her husband, she was a committed and pious Monophysite. John of Ephesos had nothing but praise for Theodora and her open support for the Monophysite bishops and monks against Justinian's official championing of the Chalcedonians. He wrote, "The Christ-loving Theodora, who was perhaps appointed queen by God to be a support for the persecuted against the cruelty of the times . . . suppl[ied] them with provisions and liberal allowances."[15] Theodora's open support for and devotion to a heretical movement, which was known to her husband, was remarked on by Evagrius. He reported that the public believed the imperial couple deliberately fostered the appearance of dis-

agreement to keep both sides happy, especially when it became clear in the early 530s that harsh measures against the Monophysites were failing. In his attempts to reconquer the western parts of the empire, Justinian could not have portions of the eastern empire in open revolt or opposition to him.

In 534, Justinian allowed the leading Monophysite, Severos of Antioch, to come to the capital and stay there for over a year. During this time, Severos was able to convince the patriarch Anthimos of the correctness of the Monophysite position and Anthimos changed allegiances. When Pope Agapetus I left Rome to visit Constantinople, he was not happy, to say the least, to find a converted Monsophysite in the patriarchate and he deposed Anthimos. Disunity and instability within the church was not the result Justinian was searching for as he embarked on his reconquest of Italy. Justinian was slowly understanding that to secure his position in Italy, the imperial position toward theology had to be acceptable to the pope. It appeared that the only way to satisfy the pope was by rigorous suppression of all heresies and the

---

15. Garland p. 23.

Chapter 7
The Byzantine
Empire:
Justinian (483?–
565) and
Theodora (497–
548)

heretics who maintained them.[16] On August 6, 536, Justinian made his position clear. He ordered Anthimos, Severos, and their supporters from the capital and all major cities in the east and the burning of Monophysite writings. Despite continued suppression, Monophysitism continued to thrive in the east, and the empress was clearly seen as its most powerful defender and patron.

Theodora's influence on church affairs has been greatly debated. The Chalcedonians argued that she contributed to Christendom's disunity by supporting a heretical movement. She encouraged the spread of Monophysitism in the east by supporting the consecration of two patriarchs in the east and the proselytization of large areas of Asia Minor, Syria, Nubia, and Arabia. Others argue that it delayed the split between eastern and western Christendom for centuries and that it was not the toleration of the heretics that created the disunity, but Rome's insistence on the righteousness of its position. Until the last years of his rule, Justinian tried to reconcile the two positions without success. His last attempt at reconciliation, at the Fifth Ecumenical Council in 553, resulted in the emergence of three different orthodoxies: the western orthodoxy of Rome, a militant Monophysite orthodoxy, and the compromise orthodoxy of Constantinople and Justinian. This third orthodoxy defined the Byzantine Church of the future.

16. P. N. Ure, *Justinian and His Age* (Harmondsworth, England: Penguin Books, 1951), p. 127.

Justinian not only wrestled with the Roman Empire's Christian legacy and its multiple manifestations, but he also inherited its legal traditions and experiences. The emperor believed that collecting and ordering Roman law, like religion, could provide another foundation for reconstituting the empire (Document Six). Within a few months of his uncle's death, Justinian created a commission to begin sorting through the laws and decrees of the senate, the writings of jurists and their pronouncements, and previous codes. The codification of Roman law eventually spread over two commissions, six years, and thirty-nine legal scholars reading over two thousand books. At the end of this process, Justinian produced a new compilation of Roman law, the *Corpus Iuris Civilis* (*Collected Civil Law*). Published in Latin, this compilation was broken into four parts: the *Code*, a revised collection of all imperial edicts; the *Digest*, a compilation of legal opinions and commentaries from jurists; the *Institutes*, a textbook for Roman legal studies; and the *Novels*, a code of imperial edicts and legislation passed after 533, the year the *Code* was completed.

Justinian's codification of Roman law served to erase some of the confusion and chaos that resulted from a thousand years of interpreting Roman law and lay claim to the past for reasons of the present. His own edicts often remade Roman tradition and law, particularly those pertaining to slavery and serfdom, the status of women and their rights in marriage, and civil administration. His attitudes toward these subjects and others are found in the *Novels*. Some of his early edicts demonstrated his concern that existing Roman law protecting slaves be followed and that certain rights be granted to women. He believed that if slaves were granted their freedom, then there should be no restrictions placed upon them by their former masters. He changed the laws so that masters could free as many slaves as they wished, well-born people would be prevented from becoming slaves as a form of punishment, and owners would be prevented from abandoning a sick slave without manumitting him on the slim chance that the slave might survive. In addition, he allowed a child born of a free mother and a father who was a peasant tied to a large estate (in other words, a serf) to be legally free.

Justinian's edicts do not depart from Roman ideals, but he was the first emperor in a long time to return to the principles of protecting slaves from abuse by their masters and preventing Roman citizens from becoming enslaved, going so far as to try to enforce the Roman law of slavery, which ruled that a child of a "free womb" was free. This particular law panicked many landowners in the empire who had been ignoring the fact that some of their slaves had been born of free women. Labor was scarce and they pressured Justinian to reduce the impact of the law.

Justinian departed from Roman tradition with his protection of women and his advocacy of new rights for them. In several places, he stressed the equality of the sexes. He states in the *Novels*, "[I]n the service of God there is no male or female, nor freeman nor slave."[17] As a result of his thinking, he prohibited separate penalties for men and women in divorce; allowed women to reclaim their dowries; increased the penalties for men who were found guilty of rape, abduction, or seduction of women; and affirmed the right of women to own property. Justinian also issued edicts that removed some of the disadvantages endured by freedwomen (ex-slaves), actresses, or other women who, through the "weakness of their sex," fell into an unworthy lifestyle but wished to return to an honest way of life.[18] He allowed a citizen who had married an ex-slave to remain married if he was made senator. Women could not be forced onto the stage. If actresses wished to renounce their profession, they could do so without fear of punishment from their employers (Document Seven).

Justinian struck at corruption in imperial administration and ecclesiastical practices. He placed prohibitions on the buying and selling of civil and ecclesiastical offices. He decreed that when a high official left office, he was to remain in the province for at least fifty days and show himself in public to demonstrate that he had governed justly, honestly, and efficiently. He prohibited high officials from appointing their subordinates, from traveling in their districts without permission from the emperor, and from extracting expenses for this travel from the

---

17. *Novels J.* 21 pr. (A.D. 536). Quoted in Garland, p. 15.

18. Garland, p. 14.

Chapter 7
The Byzantine
Empire:
Justinian (483?–
565) and
Theodora (497–
548)

people of the province. Justinian prevented clergy from holding multiple offices, forbade the buying and selling of ecclesiastical posts, regulated the behavior of the clergy, and prohibited the clergy from transferring property that had come into their possession as a result of their religious duties to their relatives. Justinian's laws and edicts illuminate the many problems and challenges that faced him as he tried to reconstitute the Roman Empire.

The *Novels* show how local and provincial officials benefitted from their offices, extracting favors, monies, and wealth from the people in their districts; how the Eastern Roman Empire's social hierarchies were shifting, as evidenced by the emperor and his wife, who came from the lower orders of society; and how the Christian church suffered from corruption and greed as much as the empire's secular institutions.

■ FINALE

Justinian and Theodora produced no heirs, and when Justinian died on November 14, 565, his nephew, Justin II (r. 565–578), ascended the throne. Justin II inherited from his uncle an expanded empire, but one that was still divided by religious belief, was financially and economically exhausted, and remained politically fragmented. Justinian had not succeeded in unifying the empire through religion, nor did his conquests withstand new invaders from the east, the north, and the south after his death. As emperor, he declared that it was his right to intervene in theological disputes and ecclesiastical practices, thus fusing the church and state together. During his reign, he had worked hard at bringing Rome under his control. The emperor believed that it was in the interest of his subjects to enforce religious uniformity, and he ordered laws against pagans and heretics to be strictly enforced. Theodora's support for and belief in the Monophysite position on the nature of Christ, however, hin-

dered Justinian's ability to crush throughly the Monophysites and other heretical Christian sects in the East. This inability, coupled with his embrace of the Monophysite position after Theodora's death in 548, furthered the conditions for religious schism.

Justinian had tried to strike at the power of the provincial governors, and his attempt to centralize imperial administration and circumvent Constantinople's senatorial class earned him the reputation as an autocrat. He aided this view by forcing his subjects, including the senators, to prostrate themselves in front of the emperor and empress and by spending lavishly on buildings, games, and ceremonies that celebrated his achievements and accomplishments. He and Theodora also adopted a style of dress and ceremony that departed from more modest Roman traditions and practices.

Theodora was Justinian's adviser and trusted confidante, and these roles were often commented on by their contemporaries. Procopius noted that "neither did anything apart from the other to the end of their joint lives."

John the Lydian opined that she was co-sharer of the empire and "superior in intelligence to any man."[19] Other accounts suggest that she had exceptional influence on her husband. Her position as royalty carried tremendous influence and power, but it was her husband's trust in her and her abilities that allowed Theodora to occupy such a powerful place in Byzantine society. Past empresses had not wielded her power, and her position as a royal woman bore little resemblance to lives of most Byzantine women.

Their relationship and Theodora's presence were constant targets for Procopius, who was most likely responding to the sentiments of the empire's powerful political and bureaucrat elites. To them Theodora represented a center of power that did not fit the traditional models. In fact, she was an empress to fear. Her success at discrediting her husband's trusted and able financial adviser, John the Cappadocian, and others whom she saw as a threat to her influence with her husband, was documented by other contemporaries. Procopius frequently noted how Theodora acted in cooperation with her husband and gives an impression of mutual cooperation and respect. The fact that the *Secret History* and other works documented Theodora's actions demonstrates the power and authority that Theodora enjoyed within the Byzantine state.[20]

QUESTIONS

1. What were the religious, political, and social conditions of the Eastern Roman Empire in the sixth century? How did they contribute to the emergence of Justin, Justinian, and Theodora?

2. What were the disintegrative and integrative forces at work during the sixth century in the Byzantine Empire?

3. What was at stake in theological disputes? Why did emperors intervene? What were Justinian's interests in settling the Monophysite dispute?

4. What was Procopius's evaluation of the imperial couple? What were their positive and negative attributes? Why did he focus on Theodora's sexual exploits?

5. What types of reforms and programs did Justinian initiate? What role did Theodora play in the running of the empire?

6. Were Justinian's actions and motivations Roman? Why or why not?

7. Why did ancient historians target women as symbols of disorder and disharmony?

19. Ibid., p. 30, and John Lydus, *Ioannes Lydus: On Powers or the Magistracies of the Roman State*, ed. and trans. A. C. Bandy, (Philadelphia, Pa.: American Philosophical Society, 1983).

20. Garland, p. 30.

Chapter 7
The Byzantine
Empire:
Justinian (483?–
565) and
Theodora (497–
548)

■ **DOCUMENTS**

DOCUMENT ONE

PROCOPIUS

"Ignorance of the Emperor Justin"
Secret History

Procopius (500?–565?) was a native of Caesarea in Palestine. He accompanied Justinian's general Belisarius on his campaigns as his secretary, and later he commanded the imperial navy and served as prefect of Constantinople in 562. His education, high connections, and public offices gave him the ability to write critical, sometimes scathing, and always intimate accounts about Justinian's rule. His chief works are History of the Wars of Justinian, *dealing primarily with the wars against the Goths, Vandals, and Persians, and* Secret History, *a scandalous and often scurrilous court chronicle. He also wrote* Buildings, *a work in six books describing buildings erected throughout the empire by Justinian and glorifying the emperor's accomplishments. Procopius had violent personal prejudices and he made them known in* Secret History. *In this document, he turns his invective to Justinian's uncle, Justin. Why does he say that Justinian and Theodora brought "confusion on the Roman state"? What are Justin's and Justinian's shortcomings?*

I come now to the tale of what sort of beings Justinian and Theodora were, and how they brought confusion on the Roman state.

During the rule of Emperor Leo in Constantinople, three young farmers of Illyrian birth, named Zimarchus, Ditybistus, and Justin of Bederiana, after a desperate struggle with poverty, left their homes to try their fortune in the army. They made their way to Constantinople on foot, carrying on their shoulders their blankets in which were wrapped no other equipment except biscuits they had baked at home. When they arrived and were admitted into military service, the Emperor chose them for the palace guard; for they were all three fine-looking men. . . .

As time went on, this Justin came to great power. For the Emperor Anastasius appointed him Count of the palace guard; and when the Emperor departed from this world, by the force of his military power Justin seized the throne. By this time he was an old man on the verge of the grave, and so illiterate that he could neither read nor write: which never before could have been said of a Roman ruler. It was the custom for an Emperor to sign his edicts with his own hand, but he neither made decrees nor was able to understand the business of state at all.

The man on whom it befell to assist him as Quaestor was named Proclus; and he managed everything to suit himself. But so that he might have some evidence of the Emperor's hand, he invented the following device for his clerks to construct. Cutting out of a block of wood the shapes of the four letters required to make the Latin word, they dipped a pen into the ink used by emperors for their signatures, and put it in the Emperor's fingers. Laying the block of wood I have described on the paper to be signed, they guided the Emperor's hand so that his pen outlined the four letters, following all the curves of the stencil: and thus they withdrew with the FIAT of the Emperor. This is how the Romans were ruled under Justin.

His wife was named Lupicina: a slave and a barbarian, she was bought to be his concubine. With Justin, as the sun of his life was about to set, she ascended the throne.

Now Justin was able to do his subjects neither harm nor good. For he was simple, unable to carry on a conversation or make a speech, and utterly bucolic. His nephew Justinian, while still a youth, was the virtual ruler, and the cause of more and worse calamities to the Romans than any one man in all their previous history that has come down to us. For he had no scruples against murder or the seizing of other persons' property; and it was nothing to him to make away with myriads of men, even when they gave him no cause. He had no care for preserving established customs, but was always eager for new experiments, and, in short, was the greatest corrupter of all noble traditions.

Though the plague, described in my former books, attacked the whole world, no fewer men escaped than perished of it; for some never were taken by the disease, and others recovered after it had smitten them. But this man, not one of all the Romans could escape; but as if he were a second pestilence sent from heaven, he fell on the nation and left no man quite untouched. For some he slew without reason, and some he released to struggle with penury, and their fate was worse than that of those who had perished, so that they prayed for death to free them from their misery; and others he robbed of their property and their lives together. . . .

DOCUMENT TWO

Definition of Faith

The early church leaders had to call bishops together to settle disagreements over Christian teachings and beliefs. Disagreement about the relation of the son to the father and the definition of the Trinity proved divisive in the early church. In this document are two theological statements on these relationships. The first is the Nicene Creed, *which was adopted by the Church Council in Nicaea in 325. The second selection is* Definition of the Faith, *which was adopted in 451 by the Council of Chalcedon. This council was convened to determine the nature of*

[199]

Chapter 7
The Byzantine
Empire:
Justinian (483?–
565) and
Theodora (497–
548)

Christ. The bishops assembled there asserted that Christ had two authentic na-
tures: he was true God and true man. Why is recitation of a definition of faith
necessary? How do these two statements differ? What events and theological
disputes influenced the statement by the Council of Chalcedon?

Council of Nicaea
The Nicene Creed
(325)

We believe in one God, Father, all-sovereign, maker of all things seen and unseen; and in one Lord Jesus Christ, the Son of God, begotten from the Father as
only-begotten, that is, from the substance of the Father, God from God, light
from light, true God from true God, begotten, not made, *homoousios* with the Father, through whom all things came into existence, the things in heaven and the
things on the earth, who because of us men and our salvation came down and
was incarnated, made man, suffered, and arose on the third day, ascended into
heaven, comes to judge the living and the dead; and in one Holy Spirit. And
those who say "there was once when he was not" or "he was not before he was
begotten" or "he came into existence from nothing" or who affirm that the Son
of God is of another *hypostasis* or substance, or a creature, or mutable or subject
to change, such ones the catholic and apostolic church pronounces accursed
and separated from the church.

Council of Chalcedon
Definition of the Faith
(451)

We believe in one God, Father, Ruler of all, the maker of heaven and earth and
of all things seen and unseen.

And in one Lord Jesus Christ, the only-begotten Son of God, begotten from
the Father before all ages, true God from true God, begotten not made, of one
essence with the Father, through whom all things were made; who for us human beings and for our salvation came down and was incarnate and became
human; and suffered, and rose on the third day and went up into the heavens
and is seated at the right hand of the Father, and is coming to judge the living
and the dead.

And in the Holy Spirit.

But those who say, "There was a 'when' when he was not" and "Before he
was begotten he did not exist" and "He came into existence out of nothing," or
who say that the Son of God is "from another hypostasis or essence," or "mutable" or "alterable"—them the catholic and apostolic church anathematizes . . .

DOCUMENT THREE

PROCOPIUS

"How Theodora, Most Depraved of All Courtesans, Won His Love"
Secret History

Procopius reveled in the details of Theodora's life as an actress and courtesan because of his hatred and fear of her. He and others in his class resented her ultimate social and political successes. He intended Secret History *to be read by those already familiar with the empress's early life and her subsequent role as the repentant sinner. In this passage, Procopius not only details her "wantonness" but the choices she did or did not have. What is attributable to her class position? What is attributed to Theodora? In what ways might Procopius have expected his lascivious detailing of Theodora's sexual history to weaken public support for her and those who followed her? What does this selection tell us about the theater and theatrical life in the sixth-century Eastern Roman Empire?*

. . . When these children [Comito, Theodora, and Anastasia] reached the age of girlhood, their mother put them on the local stage, for they were fair to look upon; she sent them forth, however, not all at the same time, but as each one seemed to her to have reached a suitable age. Comito, indeed, had already become one of the leading hetaerae* of the day.

Theodora, the second sister, dressed in a little tunic with sleeves, like a slave girl, waited on Comito and used to follow her about carrying on her shoulders the bench on which her favored sister was wont to sit at public gatherings. Now Theodora was still too young to know the normal relation of man with maid, but consented to the unnatural violence of villainous slaves who, following their masters to the theater, employed their leisure in this infamous manner. And for some time in a brothel she suffered such misuse.

But as soon as she arrived at the age of youth, and was now ready for the world, her mother put her on the stage. Forthwith, she became a courtesan, and such as the ancient Greeks used to call a common one, at that: for she was not a flute or harp player, nor was she even trained to dance, but only gave her youth to anyone she met, in utter abandonment. Her general favors included, of course, the actors in the theater; and in their productions she took part in the low comedy scenes. For she was very funny and a good mimic, and immediately became popular in this art. There was no shame in the girl, and no one ever saw her dismayed: no role was too scandalous for her to accept without a blush.

*concubines

Chapter 7
The Byzantine
Empire:
Justinian (483?–
565) and
Theodora (497–
548)

She was the kind of comedienne who delights the audience by letting herself be cuffed and slapped on the cheeks, and makes them guffaw by raising her skirts to reveal to the spectators those feminine secrets here and there which custom veils from the eyes of the opposite sex. With pretended laziness she mocked her lovers, and coquettishly adopting ever new ways of embracing, was able to keep in a constant turmoil the hearts of the sophisticated. And she did not wait to be asked by anyone she met, but on the contrary, with inviting jests and a comic flaunting of her skirts herself tempted all men who passed by, especially those who were adolescent.

On the field of pleasure she was never defeated. Often she would go picnicking with ten young men or more, in the flower of their strength and virility, and dallied with them all, the whole night through. When they wearied of the sport, she would approach their servants, perhaps thirty in number, and fight a duel with each of these; and even thus found no allayment of her craving. Once, visiting the house of an illustrious gentleman, they say she mounted the projecting corner of her dining couch, pulled up the front of her dress, without a blush, and thus carelessly showed her wantonness. And though she flung wide three gates to the ambassadors of Cupid, she lamented that nature had not similarly unlocked the straits of her bosom, that she might there have contrived a further welcome to his emissaries.

Frequently, she conceived, but as she employed every artifice immediately, a miscarriage was straightway effected. Often, even in the theater, in the sight of all the people, she removed her costume and stood nude in their midst, except for a girdle about the groin: not that she was abashed at revealing that, too, to the audience, but because there was a law against appearing altogether naked on the stage, without at least this much of a fig-leaf. Covered thus with a ribbon, she would sink down to the stage floor and recline on her back. Slaves to whom the duty was entrusted would then scatter grains of barley from above into the calyx of this passion flower, whence geese, trained for the purpose, would next pick the grains one by one with their bills and eat. When she rose, it was not with a blush, but she seemed rather to glory in the performance. For she was not only impudent herself, but endeavored to make everybody else as audacious. Often when she was alone with other actors, she would undress in their midst and arch her back provocatively, advertising like a peacock both to those who had experience of her and to those who had not yet had that privilege her trained suppleness.

So perverse was her wantonness that she should have hid not only the customary part of her person, as other women do, but her face as well. Thus those who were intimate with her were straightway recognized from that very fact to be perverts, and any more respectable man who chanced upon her in the Forum avoided her and withdrew in haste, lest the hem of his mantle, touching such a creature, might be thought to share in her pollution. For to those who saw her, especially at dawn, she was a bird of ill omen. And toward her fellow-actresses she was as savage as a scorpion: for she was very malicious. . . .

DOCUMENT FOUR

PROCOPIUS

Buildings

Later in his life, Procopius turned to documenting the building projects of Justin-ian and Theodora. How does Procopius view the imperial pair in the selection? Is it different in tone from previous accounts? Why?

. . . ix. On this shore there chanced to have been from ancient times a remark-able palace. This the Emperor Justinian has dedicated wholly to God, exchang-ing immediate enjoyment for the reward of piety thereby obtained, in the following manner. There was a throng of women in Byzantium who had carried on in brothels a business of lechery, not of their own free will, but under force of lust. For it was because of their extreme poverty that they were maintained by brothel-keepers, and inmates of such houses were obliged at any and all times to practise lewdness, and pairing off at a moment's notice with strange men as they chanced to come along, they submitted to their embraces. For there had been a numerous body of procurers in the city from ancient times, conducting their traffic in licentiousness in brothels and selling others' youth in the public market-place and forcing virtuous persons into slavery. But the Emperor Justin-ian and the Empress Theodora, who always shared a common piety in all that they did, devised the following plan. They cleansed the state of the pollution of the brothels, banishing the very name of brothel-keepers, and they set free from a licentiousness fit only for slaves the women who were struggling with ex-treme poverty, providing them with independent maintenance, and setting virtue free. This they accomplished as follows. Near that shore of the strait which is on the right as one sails toward the Sea called Euxine, they made what had formerly been a palace into an imposing convent designed to serve as a refuge for women who repented of their past lives, so that there through the oc-cupation which their minds would have with the worship of God and with re-ligion they might be able to cleanse away the sins of their lives in the brothel. Therefore they call this domicile of such women "Repentance," in keeping with its purpose. And these Sovereigns have endowed this convent with an ample income of money, and have added many buildings most remarkable for their beauty and costliness, to serve as a consolation for the women, so that they should never be compelled to depart from the practice of virtue in any manner whatsoever. So much, then, for this. . . .

=== DOCUMENT FIVE ===

Procopius

History of the Wars of Justinian

History of the Wars of Justinian is Procopius's principal narrative account of Justinian's reign. In this selection, Procopius describes Theodora's actions during the Nika revolt. What are Theodora's arguments for remaining in Constantinople?

. . . By this time the members of the senate were assembling,—as many of them as had not been left in the emperor's residence,—and many expressed the opinion that they should go to the palace to fight. But Origenes, a man of the senate, came forward and spoke as follows: "Fellow Romans, it is impossible that the situation which is upon us be solved in any way except by war. Now war and royal power are agreed to be the greatest of all things in the world. But when action involves great issues, it refuses to be brought to a successful conclusion by the brief crisis of a moment, but this is accomplished only by wisdom of thought and energy of action, which men display for a length of time. Therefore if we should go out against the enemy, our cause will hang in the balance, and we shall be taking a risk which will decide everything in a brief space of time; and, as regards the consequences of such action, we shall either fall down and worship Fortune or reproach her altogether. For those things whose issue is most quickly decided, fall, as a rule, under the sway of fortune. But if we handle the present situation more deliberately, not even if we wish shall we be able to take Justinian in the palace, but he will very speedily be thankful if he is allowed to flee; for authority which is ignored always loses its power, since its strength ebbs away with each day. . . . So spoke Origenes. But the rest, as a crowd is accustomed to do, insisted more excitedly and thought that the present moment was opportune, and not least of all Hypatius (for it was fated that evil should befall him) bade them lead the way to the hippodrome. But some say that he came there purposely, being well-disposed toward the emperor.

Now the emperor and his court were deliberating as to whether it would be better for them if they remained or if they took to flight in the ships. And many opinions were expressed favouring either course. And the Empress Theodora also spoke to the following effect: "As to the belief that a woman ought not to be daring among men or to assert herself boldly among those who are holding back from fear, I consider that the present crisis most certainly does not permit us to discuss whether the matter should be regarded in this or in some other way. For in the case of those whose interests have come into the greatest danger nothing else seems best except to settle the issue immediately before them in the best possible way. My opinion then is that the present time, above all others, is inopportune for flight, even though it bring safety. For while it is impossible for a man who has seen the light not also to die, for one who has been an emperor it is unendurable to be a fugitive. May I never be separated from this purple, and may I not live that day on which those who meet me shall not address me as mistress. If, now, it is your wish to save yourself, O Emperor, there is no difficulty. For we have much money, and there is the sea, here the boats. However consider whether it will not come about after you have been saved that you would gladly exchange that safety for death. For as for myself, I approve a certain ancient saying that royalty is a good burial-shroud." When the queen had spoken thus, all were filled with boldness, and, turning their thoughts towards resistance, they began to consider how they might be able to defend themselves if any hostile force should come against them. Now the soldiers as a body, including those who were stationed about the emperor's court, were neither well disposed to the emperor nor willing openly to take an active part in fighting, but were waiting for what the future would bring forth. All the hopes of the emperor were centred upon Belisarius and Mundus, of whom the former, Belisarius, had recently returned from the Persian war bringing with him a following which was both powerful and imposing, and in particular he had a great number of spearmen and guards who had received their training in battles and the perils of warfare. Mundus had been appointed general of the Illyrians, and by mere chance had happened to come under summons to Byzantium on some necessary errand, bringing with him Erulian barbarians. . . .

Chapter 7
The Byzantine
Empire:
Justinian (483?–
565) and
Theodora (497–
548)

JUSTINIAN

Institutes

The Institutes *is the textbook created under Justinian's legal reforms. What are the reasons for good law and codification? What advice does Justinian give to students of Roman law? What does the document reveal about late Roman laws and values?*

In the Name of Our Lord Jesus Christ

The Emperor Caesar Flavius Justinian

Conqueror of the Alamanni Goths
Franks Germans
Antes Alani Vandals Africans

Devout Fortunate Renowned
Victorious and Triumphant
Forever Augustus

to

Young Enthusiasts for Law

Imperial Majesty should not only be graced with arms but also armed with laws, so that good government may prevail in time of war and peace alike. The head of the Roman state can then stand victorious not only over enemies in war but also over trouble-makers, driving out their wickedness through the paths of the law, and can triumph as much for his devotion of the law as for his conquests in battle. 1. Long hours of work and careful planning have, with God's help, given us success in both these fields. Barbarian nations brought beneath our yoke know the scale of our exertions in war. Africa and countless other provinces, restored to Roman jurisdiction and brought back within our empire after so long an interval, bear witness to the victories granted to us by the will of heaven. However, it is by the laws which we have already managed to enact and collect that all our peoples are ruled. 2. The solemn pronouncements of the emperors were in disarray. We collected them into a clear, systematic series. Then we turned our attention to the rolls of the classical law, that boundless ocean of learning, and, passing by heaven's favour as it were through the midst of the deep, we soon completed a task which seemed overwhelming. 3. When with God's help we reached the end of that, we called together Tribonian, of eminent rank, minister and former chancellor of our sacred palace, and also Theophilus and Dorotheus, professors of illustrious rank. From all three we had already received proofs of their brilliance, their learning in the law, and their loyalty in carrying out our wishes. We gave them this specific instruction: to compose with our authority and at our instigation an edition of Institutes. Our intention was to give you an elementary framework, a cradle of the law, not based on obscure old stories but illuminated by the light of our imperial splendour; and to ensure that you hear and adopt nothing useless or out of place but only the true principles at the heart of the subject. Until now even the best students have barely begun to read imperial pronouncements after four years of study; but you have been found worthy of the great honour and good fortune of doing so from the beginning and of following a course of legal education which from start to finish proceeds from the Emperor's lips. 4. It was for these reasons that after the completion of the fifty books of the Digest or Pandects, in which all the classical law has been brought together and which we achieved through this same excellent Tribonian and other learned men of illustrious rank, we gave the order for the Institutes to be composed in these four books, to form the first principles of all learning in the law. 5. They now give a brief account both of how matters used to stand and of the imperial measures which brought light to areas darkened by disuse. 6. They have been compiled from all the books of Institutes written by the classical lawyers, and especially from the works of our own Gaius, both his Institutes and his Everyday Law, though also from many other treaties. When the work was finished, the three learned commissioners presented the books to us. We have read and examined them and have endowed them with the full force of our own pronouncements. 7. Study our law. Do your best and apply yourselves keenly to it. Show that you have mastered it. You can then cherish a noble ambition; when your course in law is finished you will be able to perform whatever duty is entrusted to you in the government of our state. Given at Constantinople on 21st November 533, the year of the third consulate of our lord Justinian, Perpetual Augustus.

Chapter 7
The Byzantine
Empire:
Justinian (483?–
565) and
Theodora (497–
548)

THE INSTITUTES OR ELEMENTS OF OUR LORD
JUSTINIAN PERPETUAL AUGUSTUS,
COMPOSED BY TRIBONIAN, MINISTER AND FORMER CHANCELLOR OF
THE SACRED PALACE, EMINENT IN RANK, UNMATCHED IN LEGAL
KNOWLEDGE; AND THE NOBLE THEOPHILUS, JURIST, AND PROFESSOR
OF LAW IN THIS CAPTIAL CITY; AND THE NOBLE DOROTHEUS,
MINISTER, JURIST, AND PROFESSOR OF LAW IN THE SPLENDID

Book One

1.1 JUSTICE AND LAW

Justice is an unswerving and perpetual determination to acknowledge all men's
rights. 1. Learning in the law entails knowledge of God and man, and mastery
of the difference between justice and injustice. 2. As we embark on the exposition of Roman law after these general statements the best plan will be to give
brief, straightforward accounts of each topic. The denser detail must be kept till
later. Any other approach would mean making students take in a huge number
of distinctions right at the start while their minds were still untrained and short
of stamina. Half of them would give up. Or else they would lose their self-
confidence—a frequent source of discouragement for the young—and at the
cost of toil and tears would in the end reach the very standard they could have
attained earlier and without overwork or self-doubt if they had been taken
along an easier road. 3. The commandments of the law are these: live hon-
ourably; harm nobody; give everyone his due. 4. There are two aspects of the
subject: public and private. Public law is concerned with the organization of the
Roman state, while private law is about the well-being of individuals. Our business is private law. It has three parts, in that it is derived from the law of nature,
of all peoples, or of the state.

DOCUMENT SEVEN

JUSTINIAN

Novels, 22.3–22.7

The Novels *are the decrees and edicts issued by Justinian after the codification of
Roman law. How does Justinian's definition of marriage differ from earlier definitions? Why is marriage and divorce a concern for Roman legislators?*

22.3—In What Way Marriage Is Effected and Dissolved

Reciprocal affection constitutes marriage, without it being necessary to enter into a dotal contract; for when the parties are once agreed and have been influenced by pure affection, it is not requisite to stipulate for a dowry, or a donation on account of marriage. We shall treat of this relation as regards both its origin and end, whether the latter is accompanied by the penalty or not, since every tie effected by men is capable of being dissolved.

A penalty is also prescribed where marriages contracted without a dowry are dissolved; and these We shall consider first.

22.4—Concerning Dissolutions of Marriage and Divorces Which Take Place by Common Consent and in Other Ways

Marriages occasionally are dissolved by common consent during the lives of the contracting parties, but it is not necessary to examine this kind of separation, because the parties interested settle their affairs by agreement among themselves; at other times, they are dissolved for some good reason, and this kind of separation is called divorce by common consent; in other instances, separations take place without any cause whatever, and in others still, for one which is reasonable.

22.5—Concerning Monasticism

Divorce takes place without blame whenever either the husband or the wife enters monastic life, and desires to live in chastity; for another law of Ours specially provides that either a man or his wife, who devotes himself or herself to a monastic life, is authorized to dissolve the marriage, and separate from his or her consort by serving a notice by way of consolation. And whatever the parties may have agreed upon in case of the death of either, as set forth in their marriage contract, shall enure to the benefit of the abandoned wife or husband. The reason for this provision is, that wherever anyone embraces a different mode of life from that of his or her companion, he or she is considered to have died, so far as the marriage is concerned.

22.6—Concerning Impotence

Marriage is dissolved for a necessary and not unreasonable cause, when the husband is incapable of copulation with his wife, and cannot do what nature created him for; and, in conformity with the law which We have already promulgated, if two years should have elapsed after the marriage, and the husband still not be able to show that he is a man, either his wife or her parents shall be permitted to dissolve the marriage, and give notice of repudiation to her

Chapter 7
The Byzantine
Empire:
Justinian (483?–
565) and
Theodora (497–
548)

husband, even if the latter should be unwilling to consent; the wife shall be entitled to the dowry, if one was given, and the husband shall return it if he received it; and the latter, on the other hand, shall be entitled to the ante-nuptial donation, and shall suffer no loss of his property.

We amend this law by making a certain addition thereto; for We decree that not two years, but three, shall elapse from the date of the marriage; as We have ascertained that some persons who were impotent for the term of two years have afterwards showed that they are capable of the procreation of children.

22.7—CONCERNING CAPTIVITY

The effect of captivity is to dissolve marriage by mutual consent, where one of two married persons is in the hands of the enemy; for where the husband suffers a misfortune of this kind, and his wife remains at home; or, on the other hand, the wife is reduced to captivity, and her husband remains in his country, the marriage is dissolved for a reason derived from the condition of slavery; as, where a person is once reduced to servitude, the inequality of condition does not permit the equality derived from the marriage state to continue to exist. Therefore, considering cases of this kind from an humane point of view, We desire that the marriage shall remain undissolved as long as it is clear that either the husband or the wife is still living . . .

8

Public Power in Private Hands: Eleanor of Aquitaine (ca. 1122–1204) and Henry II (1133–1189)

■ SETTING THE STAGE

As the twelfth century began, the geographic area called Europe was well on its way to developing a distinct civilization. Over several centuries, Judeo-Christian, Greco-Roman, and Germanic traditions had merged. By the end of the eleventh century, population growth—accompanied by urban development, increased agricultural output, trade, and markets—provided the basis for an emerging profit-based economy. Schools and education grew steadily, and new social classes appeared, often defined by education, profession, and wealth. These new classes had to find a place on an existing ladder of social hierarchy that had been built by the traditional orders of warriors, worshippers, and workers. Reforming popes like Gregory VII (1073–1085) strengthened the papacy and, in confrontations with secular rulers, insisted on the supremacy of their spiritual authority. Those secular

*Chapter 8
Public Power in
Private Hands:
Eleanor of
Aquitaine
(ca. 1122–1204)
and Henry II
(1133–1189)*

rulers hoped to enhance and consolidate their own power by hiring new officials, claiming new responsibilities, and expanding government institutions in their own contests with powerful nobles in their realms. Side by side with emerging institutional structures (like laws, taxation, and education) were older patterns of personal and familial power and authority. Thus, by the start of the twelfth century, a spirit of reform and intellectual rebirth seemed to hold out possibilities for change and growth, but the following questions remained. Who would benefit from these opportunities? Would men and women be affected similarly by these developments? How much change would be tolerated by those who held the military and financial reins of the society? What would happen to those whose challenges went too far?

Henry II of England and Eleanor of Aquitaine are two individuals who represent both the spirit of change and the desire to maintain traditions. While hardly typical of the population at large, their struggles, desires, and goals reflect the controversies and dynamism of the twelfth century. Feudal structures in England contrasted with those of France, and the monarchy of England was one of the most powerful in Europe. In France and elsewhere, feudalism had developed as an outgrowth of chaotic and violent conditions in the eighth and ninth centuries and the disintegration of central authority. Monarchs encouraged the development of feudalism by granting land (fief), which was held by the king, to a lesser noble (vassal) in return for service. The fief in theory was

still the king's land to distribute, but over the centuries the vassal held de facto control over the land and the vassal's position was strengthened at the expense of the overlord, even a king. In some cases, vassals became more powerful and wealthier than their overlords; the feudal relationship between the dukes of Aquitaine and Normandy and the kings of France illustrates this phenomenon.

In the English case, William the Conqueror (r. 1066–1087) concentrated land in his hands, and he and his successors retained greater control over the distribution of fiefs. Time and circumstance had not yet diminished the English king's power. As a result, William and his successors stood at the top of the political hierarchy and not alongside the great nobles. William and his heirs, including William's great grandson, Henry II (r. 1154–1189) represent the efforts of monarchs in England and on the Continent to subvert the autonomous power of the feudal aristocracy and to create a centralized monarchy. Such efforts were not always successful, and for the next several hundred years the political history of England was dominated by conflicts between the monarch and the feudal lords. English monarchs attempted to consolidate their power over the feudal lords, who in turn resisted monarchical encroachment on their traditional rights and privileges.

The story of Henry II, however, is more than that of a centralizing monarch wrestling with obstreperous nobles, trying to build royal institutions, and unifying a kingdom. Henry II, his marriage to Eleanor of Aquitaine (1122–1204), his ascension to the English throne through familial claims, and his relationship with his sons and wife illuminate the ways in which "rulership and power were thought of in terms of personal inheritance. The king's 'family' and household were the government, ill-defined succession customs allowed many royal family members to hope for the throne, and the queen became a pivotal figure and a player in the politics of royal succession."[1] As a woman, Eleanor exploited the means at her disposal—her position as heir to one of Europe's richest duchies and her roles as a wife and mother—to pursue political power. Queens and noblewomen lived exceptional and extraordinary lives compared to the overwhelming majority of women who lived during the Middle Ages, but queens were the closest of all women to the center of power. A study of Eleanor helps us understand the extent of and the limitations on noblewomen's political roles during the Middle Ages.

Eleanor was more than queen; she was heir to Aquitaine, one of Europe's richest and most cultured lands, and she used its wealth and influence not only to assert political power but to create and maintain an opulent, learned, and luxurious court, and to patronize twelfth-century artists, writers, poets, musicians, and troubadours. During the twelfth century, French and English elites and others witnessed a flurry of artistic and intellectual activity such as the systematization of theological thought; advances in logic

and grammar; and new trends in music, poetry, art, and architecture. Much of this activity was centered at the cathedral schools of Paris (see Chapter 9) and the ducal and royal courts in France and England. New literary trends emerged from the Poitou-Aquitaine region of southern France in the early twelfth century, moving northward to Paris and then across the channel to England around midcentury. Eleanor's life, and that of her husband's, was connected to many of these trends, and their courts became centers of this renaissance in artistic and intellectual life. In addition, both Eleanor's and Henry's proximity to these learned men and their political prominence as royalty exposed them to the scrutiny of their literate contemporaries.

The twelfth century was the zenith of historical writing in medieval England and France. Not only do we have several chronicles (year-by-year records of the events that the chronicler deemed noteworthy), but several biographies and biographical entries in these chronicles recorded the words and deeds of medieval kings, nobles, and religious leaders. The works of these chroniclers and early biographers must be approached cautiously. These men were of the elite, usually monastic or ecclesiastical, and often came from noble and wealthy backgrounds. They were not above altering facts and information to reflect their own and their community's sensibilities, values, and political and social leanings. When writing about an event, the chroniclers may have witnessed it personally or received information from an eyewitness. In either

---

1. John Carmi Parsons, "Family, Sex, and Power: The Rhythms of Medieval Queenship," in John Carmi Parsons, ed., *Medieval Queenship* (New York: St Martin's Press, 1993), p. 3.

*Chapter 8
Public Power in
Private Hands:
Eleanor of
Aquitaine
(ca. 1122–1204)
and Henry II
(1133–1189)*

case, however, accounts could be embellished and events could be distorted or fictionalized.

Women appear in the chronicles as wives, widows, or queens who may have influenced their male counterparts. In Eleanor's case, she attracted some attention because of her multiple roles: heir of Aquitaine, queen of France and England, and mother of future queens and kings. Despite her very public and prominent position in twelfth-century society, she did not have a dedicated biographer or chronicler interested in her rulership, activities, and deeds; therefore, no chronicles or contemporary biographies exist for her life.[2] The narratives that do exist often present a contradictory picture. As a powerful and well-known patron of the arts, she inspired writers, minstrels, and poets to write about her, albeit in fictionalized form. Even these writings, like the chronicles, suspect Eleanor of misdeeds simply because she was a woman and so, by twelfth-century definition, she was unreliable, fickle, deceitful, and sinful. Her political prominence and power further contributed to this view. Eleanor did have admirers who saw her not only as a woman of virtue but as a compassionate, sympathetic, and fair ruler in her own right. Such panegyrics may have been the result of the need to curry favor with her or her sons or simply the result of admiration.

Chronicles and literary accounts are but two types of sources that we have for the lives and events surrounding the rule of Henry II and Eleanor of Aquitaine. Official acts of government such as legislation from the king (assizes), legal treatises, charters granting land and possessions, letters, wills, court documents, and land surveys made by the Crown shed light on the complex feudal, familial, and personal interactions and relationships found in twelfth-century England and France. Such documents depict a small subset of English and French society, primarily the landholding classes, and the activities of their menfolk. Few women were sufficiently educated to contribute to the documentary and historical record, so the stories of Eleanor and other women of comparable rank are not based on their own words directly but the words of intermediaries who had specific reasons for noting their presence.

▨ THE ACTORS:

ELEANOR OF AQUITAINE AND HENRY II OF ENGLAND

Eleanor of Aquitaine was born in Bordeaux in 1122 to William X (1099–1137), duke of Aquitaine, and Aénor

of Chatellerault (11??–1130). According to the late twelfth-century chronicler, Gervase of Canterbury, Eleanor "sprang from a noble race." Her family claimed that they could trace their ancestors back to the time of Charlemagne, and their duchy of Aquitaine, covering most of central and southwest France, was the largest, richest, and most populous region of France in

2. D. D. R. Owens, *Eleanor of Aquitaine: Queen and Legend* (Oxford: Blackwell, 1993), p. 108.

the twelfth and thirteenth centuries. Chroniclers extolled its virtues. "Opulent Aquitaine, sweet as nectar thanks to its vineyards dotted about with forests, overflowing with fruit of every kind, and endowed with a superabundance of pasture land," wrote Heriger of Lobbes.[3] Its abundance and prosperity, built on its trade in wine and salt, meant that Aquitainian dukes enjoyed a luxurious standard of living unknown to their counterparts in northern France or England. The courts of the Aquitainian dukes and their vassals, powerful lords in their own right, were renowned for their elegance and sophistication. Not only did their wealth support and patronize numerous religious orders but also musicians, poets, writers, and troubadours.

As a young girl, Eleanor was exposed to all that Aquitaine had to offer. Her mother and her brother, the only male heir, died when Eleanor was a young girl. Her father, William X, took Eleanor and her younger sister, Aelith de Poitiers (ca. 1123–?) with him when he toured his lands. Much of Eleanor's childhood was spent riding throughout the duchy, watching her father interact with his vassals and peasants, and participating in sporting activities that made her accomplished at riding, hunting, and falconry. When not on the road, Eleanor learned the traditional womanly arts: household management and domestic skills such as sewing and embroidery. Embroidery played an important role in the transmission of familial and historical memories, and women often embroidered historical figures and scenes onto linen at the bequest of a patron or a family member. Through this medium, women transmitted ancestral and historical memories, and Eleanor undoubtedly heard tales about her adventurous, learned, and spirited ancestors while she learned this craft.[4] Eleanor's education extended beyond domestic and sporting skills. She was given an education, not unheard of for her class, but exceptional nonetheless. She learned to read and write Latin and her native language, the Provençal dialect. Evidence for her literacy is found in the comments from her contemporaries who remarked that she could read.

Eleanor inherited from the Aquitainian line the tradition of an active role for women. This position derived from the legal and social place of women in Aquitaine, which differed from other parts of Europe. In Aquitaine, women could inherit property and administer and rule over the lands that they inherited. Even when women married, their land remained in their possession; it did not pass to their husbands or to their husbands' families. These landowning rights differed from the tradition in England, where women could hold land, but they relinquished control of it to their husbands during marriage. When an English woman died, her lands passed to her husband and his family. In Aquitaine, the right to inherit property, to retain legal possession of it after marriage, and to

---

3. Allison Weir, *Eleanor of Aquitaine: A Life* (New York: Ballantine Books, 2000), p. 5.

4. Elisabeth van Houts, *Memory and Gender in Medieval Europe, 900–1200* (Toronto: Toronto University Press, 1999), pp. 147–148.

Chapter 8
Public Power in
Private Hands:
Eleanor of
Aquitaine
(ca. 1122–1204)
and Henry II
(1133–1189)

determine the inheritance of their lands as they saw fit gave extensive power to women. Eleanor had this type of power because her father, William X, did not have a male heir. When he died at the age of thirty-eight, Eleanor, at the age of fifteen, inherited the duchy of Aquitaine and all of its lands and with them some political power.[5] This situation made Eleanor the most desirable and sought-after young woman in France.

Eleanor's father fully understood the position his eldest daughter would be in when he died, and he made arrangements with the French king, Louis VI, to be Eleanor's guardian. The French king was the only man alive who could protect Eleanor's inheritance and interests if her father died before she married. The intended consequence of this agreement was that Eleanor would marry Louis VI's son, Louis VII. Four months after William's death in April 1137, the fifteen-year-old duchess of Aquitaine and Gascony and countess of Poitou married the heir to the French throne. The bride's father-in-law intended that the marriage and subsequent children would bring Eleanor's lands under the control of the French monarchy. The riches of Eleanor's lands were such that the question of the close blood relation-ship (consanguinity) between Eleanor and Louis was not raised by anyone at the time of their marriage. They were

5. Jo Ann McNamara and Suzanne Wemple, "The Power of Women Through the Family in Medieval Europe, 500–1100," in Mary Erler and Maryanne Kowaleski, eds., *Women and Power in the Middle Ages* (Athens, Ga: The University of Georgia Press, 1988), pp. 92–94.

fourth cousins. One month after her marriage to the young heir, her father-in-law died and Eleanor and Louis VII became the queen and king of France.

When Eleanor married Louis VII in 1137, Henry was four years old and living with his mother Matilda, the only surviving child of Henry I of England and duke of Normandy, and his father, Geoffrey Plantagenet, count of Anjou. With this lineage, Henry, as the firstborn son, stood to inherit the crown of England; the duchy of Normandy; and the fiefs of Anjou, Maine, and Touraine, considerable lands in northwestern France. However, his claim to the throne of England rested on Henry I's and Matilda's ability to defend his inheritance. In 1127, Henry took the first step by designating Matilda his successor and forced his vassals to swear fealty to her. Needing allies on the Continent to protect his patrimony in Normandy against the aggressive designs of the French king, he also arranged Matilda's marriage to the fifteen-year-old Geoffrey of Anjou. Six years later, on March 4, 1133, she gave birth to Henry, the first of her three sons.

When Henry I died in 1135, Matilda stood ready to rule England. Norman tradition did not have a precedent for the rule of a woman. In addition, Norman family and property law dictated that all of a wife's property and rights be at the disposal of her husband, and the great nobles feared Geoffrey would use them for French interests. Despite the fact that Henry I, in the summer after his grandson's birth, made his nobles once again swear fealty to Matilda and her infant son, the great landowners decided to swear allegiance to

Henry I's nephew, Stephen of Blois, and to offer him the crown. Angry at this betrayal, Matilda used her resources on the Continent and the discontent among Stephen's enemies to mount an attack on England in 1141.

Over the next decade, King Stephen, and Matilda and her young son, Henry of Anjou, fought for the English throne. In 1142, nine-year-old Henry left France and braved the perilous crossing of the English Channel to rally his family's supporters, who were disheartened by the imperious and haughty bearing of his mother. He remained in England until 1144, providing a focal point for those opposed to Stephen's rule. During Henry's stay in England, his father, Geoffrey, fought for the family's claim to the duchy of Normandy. Occupied by the civil war in England, Stephen could not sufficiently defend Normandy and by 1145, Geoffrey of Anjou won the duchy. The bigger prize had yet to be secured, however, and now that Normandy had been won, Matilda asked her husband to send troops to force the issue with Stephen. Uninterested in English affairs, Geoffrey sent the fourteen-year-old Henry and a small force to England in 1147. This adventure failed abysmally and both Henry and his mother had to leave England. With this retreat, Matilda withdrew from political life and left it to her son to press his claims to the throne, which he did once again in 1149 but without success.

While being introduced to the ways of English politics and military campaigns, Henry also managed to receive an excellent education. His father and his maternal uncle instructed him in the military arts but equally important was both men's attention to Henry's schooling. At his father's and uncle's courts, Henry was tutored in French, Latin, philosophy, history, and law by some of the most learned men in France and England. He retained a passion for learning and scholarship his entire life.

Despite his early failures to unseat Stephen, Henry, his parents, and supporters of the young man's claim to the throne all believed that he was up to the task. In 1149, Geoffrey relinquished the title of duke of Normandy to his son. With this resource in hand and determined to press his claim to the English throne, Henry began to raise an army of Normans and Angevins. As duke of Normandy, Henry was a vassal to the king of France, Louis VII, who was not happy with the prospect of the reunion of the kingdom of England and the duchy of Normandy under one ruler. Louis tried unsuccessfully to dislodge Henry. Eventually Louis accepted Henry, and Henry rode to Paris in 1151 to swear fealty to his king, as was customary. Despite assertions by chroniclers working with hindsight, Eleanor and Henry did not meet in Paris and fall in love. Any union between the two would have to wait until the annulment of Eleanor's and Louis's marriage.

Chapter 8
Public Power in
Private Hands:
Eleanor of
Aquitaine
(ca. 1122–1204)
and Henry II
(1133–1189)

■ ACT I:

ELEANOR, QUEEN OF FRANCE

Eleanor and Louis were married for fifteen years. Eleanor's years as queen of France were marked by her move to Paris, the capital city; learning Parisian French and becoming familiar with the intellectual ferment of midcentury Paris; and an inability to produce a male heir. Eleanor and Louis had two girls, Marie, born in 1145, and Alix in 1150. Louis spent the early part of his rule trying to rein in unruly and insubordinate lords, who chafed at his attempts to impose royal authority. He met fierce resistance and failure in Eleanor's lands when he attempted to assert his rights by marriage. Other attempts in different parts of his dominion resulted in the violent suppression of the local feudal lords and their vassals and peasants.

Eleanor's involvement in Louis's campaigns and his political designs is largely a matter of speculation, but as the inheritor of Aquitaine, she probably supported any efforts to force unruly and independent lords to accept royal submission. Soon after they married, Louis launched a punitive campaign against the count of Champagne for insubordination and treachery. He sent his troops into Champagne, where they ravaged the countryside, burning, pillaging, and killing or expelling its inhabitants.[6] During this rampage, Louis's troops burned a church that was reported to have had thirteen hundred people inside who had taken refuge and who were burned alive.

Bernard, abbé of Clairvaux and one of the leading intellectuals and moral commentators of the twelfth century, wrote several letters condemning young Louis's violent and ruthless campaign. In one, he queried the king: "[F]rom whom but the Devil did this advice come under which you are acting?"[7] Bernard found the answer to this question upon meeting Eleanor. At their meeting, Bernard "recognized the evil genius of the king, the 'counsel of the devil' that had plunged Louis into the abysses of sin and remorse."[8] He then admonished the queen to "put an end to your interference with affairs of state"[9] (Document One). While Eleanor appeared unrepentant to the abbé, Bernard believed that Louis had demonstrated genuine contrition. Some of Louis's contemporaries attribute his decision to embark on a crusade as a kind of self-imposed penance. Louis might indeed have been motivated by guilt, but he also saw an opportunity to become the first Western king to lead a crusade, thus establishing his authority as the leading Christian monarch. Perhaps for different reasons, Eleanor also decided to take the cross in the spring of 1146 and join the second wave of crusaders to Jerusalem.

Preparations for this expedition took more than eighteen months, and Eleanor was instrumental in the recruitment of human and material resources. She encouraged her vassals to

6. Owens, p. 18.

7. Weir, p. 40.

8. Amy Kelly, *Eleanor of Aquitaine and the Four Kings* (Cambridge, Mass.: Harvard University Press, 1950), p. 27.

9. Ibid.

participate, imposed new taxes on her lands, sponsored tournaments, organized supplies, and bestowed or renewed privileges for religious houses in exchange for financial and spiritual support.[10] The majority of the crusaders were from her lands, and there were a considerable number of women who accompanied the crusaders. Three hundred women were said to be Eleanor's attendants. Women participated in the first two crusades as nurses, cooks, prostitutes, washerwomen, and warriors. Eleanor's attendants were dressed in armor and carried lances, but they never fought. The Greek chronicler, Nicetas, noted their presence and bearing during the expedition. He wrote, "[T]here were in the army women dressed as men, mounted on horses and armed with lance and battle axe. They kept a martial mien, bold as Amazons. At the head of these was one in particular, richly dressed, that went by the name of 'lady of the golden boot.' The elegance of her bearing and the freedom of her movements recalled the celebrated leader of the Amazons."[11] While Nicetas was impressed by this vision, other commentators criticized the presence of Eleanor, her attendants, and the wagons of female servants as well as the presence of the other women. Their participation in the crusade posed such a problem that the pope issued a papal bull that expressly forbade women of all sorts, except washerwomen, from joining the Third Crusade.

10. Weir, p. 51.

11. Nicetas Choniate, *Histoire de* (Mich III, 402ff), p. 404, quoted in Kelly, p. 39.

Once again speculations swirled around Eleanor's motivation for participating in the crusade and her subsequent part during the campaigns. Some chroniclers attribute her presence to Louis's jealousy and fear that the beautiful Eleanor would commit adultery during his absence, and it was on his initiative that she accompanied him. Others argued that Eleanor yearned for adventure and wished to renew her friendship with Raymond, her uncle, an educated, cultured, and handsome man, who had been appointed prince of Antioch, one of the four crusader states. The prospect of adventure, seeing the magnificence and antiquity of the Near East, and following a tradition set by her grandfather each might well have played a part in her motivation.

Whatever the reasons, Eleanor's activities and behavior during the two-year expedition (1147–1149), especially her relationship with her uncle, elicited much commentary and gossip. John of Salisbury's account is probably the most reliable. He does tell of the closeness of Raymond and Eleanor and their opposition to Louis's plans to continue to Jerusalem instead of trying to recapture Edessa, a crusader state that had been captured by the Turks in 1144 and put Antioch at risk. Raymond had asked for the crusade and now wanted the crusaders' help. Eleanor saw the logic of her uncle's military reasoning and sided with him. Louis, however, was determined to leave Antioch, which had not lived up to his expectations as a holy and reverent city, and make the pilgrimage to Jerusalem. Eleanor's vocal and stubborn refusal to follow him

Chapter 8
Public Power in
Private Hands:
Eleanor of
Aquitaine
(ca. 1122–1204)
and Henry II
(1133–1189)

caused Louis to spirit his wife away from Antioch under the cover of darkness (Document Two). Furious, Eleanor questioned the validity of their marriage, basing her argument on the question of consanguinity. She now had found a way to end her unhappy marriage and simply had to wait for the most opportune moment.

Little is known about Eleanor during the three months that the crusaders spent in Jerusalem, but Louis, advised by his counselors there, decided that the best way to safeguard the remaining crusader states was to take Damascus, depriving the two main Islamic states in the region, Baghdad and Egypt, of an easy route between them. Internal rivalries, conflicting agendas, and the brave defense by the inhabitants of Damascus caused the Second Crusade to fail. De-

feated, Eleanor and Louis returned to France in separate ships in 1149. Shortly after their return, Eleanor gave birth to their second daughter. After the birth, Louis and his advisers began to wonder if Eleanor could produce a male heir. Females could not inherit the French crown and the replacement of unsatisfactory wives, i.e., those who did not produce sons, was not unknown to the French royal family. Louis decided that the loss of Eleanor's lands was a risk he was willing to take to try to have a son with another, perhaps less headstrong and tempestuous queen. On March 21, 1152, a council of leading French prelates annulled the marriage. Eleanor retained her lands but her two daughters remained with Louis. Not yet thirty, Eleanor was once again the most desirable heiress in Europe.

■ ACT II:

THE KING AND QUEEN OF ENGLAND

Eleanor could have had her pick of suitors and there were some, like Henry's brother and the count of Blois who tried to capture the heiress as she made her way home to Poitiers so they could force her to marry them. Outwitting her suitors, Eleanor reached the safety of her lands but knew that she and her inheritance would not be safe until she found a powerful husband. Of eligible lords, one stood out among all others: Henry, count of Anjou, duke of Normandy, and disputed heir to the English throne. His lands bordered hers and as her only serious rival in the re-

gion, Henry was the obvious choice for the older Eleanor. For Henry, the choice was not as clear. Undisturbed by the eleven-year age difference, Henry realized he was taking a chance because the stigma of possible sterility hung over the ex-queen. In addition, if he were to wed Eleanor, he would be marrying the ex-wife of his lord, which might cause friction between Henry and Louis. Two chroniclers, Walter Map and Gerald of Wales, reported that Henry's father, Geoffrey, who died in 1151, had warned his son that "She [Eleanor] is the wife of your lord [Louis VII], and your father [Geoffrey] has already known her." Geoffrey most likely did not utter these words because he had been dead a year, but they sensationalized and called attention to the protocols and prohibitions broken by the possibility of this union. Henry did not observe the feudal custom of asking his lord for permission to marry, nor did he ask Louis for Eleanor's hand in marriage. Legally, Eleanor was still Louis's ward. The salacious and unsubstantiated gossip about an affair between Geoffrey and Eleanor served to insult both Louis, who was portrayed in this rumor as impotent and powerless, and Eleanor, who appeared wanton and sinful. Sharing the sexual partner of one's lord was considered indecent and disrespectful; to share the sexual partner of your father was incest.[12]

Whether Henry contacted her or she contacted him is a matter of dispute. Gervase of Canterbury suggested that Eleanor sent a secret messenger northward to Henry to suggest their marriage alliance and that Henry accepted because [he was] "tempted by the quality of this woman's blood but even more by her lands." Other commentators attribute their marriage to more romantic impulses. Map claimed that when Henry came to Paris in 1151, they met and felt an immediate attraction; he cast a lustful eye and she "caste her unchaste eyes" at him. In the context of twelfth-century politics, the marriage between Eleanor and Henry on May 18, 1152, in Poitiers cemented a strategic and political alliance that enhanced Henry's status and secured Eleanor's inheritance. Their union also created an assem-

blage of lands in the British Isles and western France held by Henry and Eleanor and their heirs for the next fifty years (1154–1204) (Document Three).

The creation of such a powerful polity, known by the nineteenth century as the Angevin Empire, and the defiance of his two subordinates angered Louis VII. Almost immediately after the wedding, Louis mounted a campaign against Henry in Normandy. Henry quickly and efficiently outmaneuvered the French king and then turned his attention to England. Leaving his pregnant wife behind in Aquitaine, Henry gathered a small force and set sail for England in January 1153. Met by his supporters, Henry waged occasional and strategic battles against King Stephen during the spring, summer, and fall of 1153. Exhausted by eighteen years of sporadic but devastating warfare and weakened politically by the death of his eldest son and heir, King Stephen negotiated a settlement with Henry in November 1153. Henry was made Stephen's successor and Henry's heirs were recognized as next in line for the throne after him. Henry's first heir, William, had been born in August. Henry did not have to wait long to take the throne; Stephen died a year later in October 1154. In December 1154, Henry and Eleanor were crowned king and queen of England at Westminster. Despite his youth, the English nobles recognized Henry as their king and saw in him the prospect of a man who would bring peace and stability to England. In baby William, the nobles had proof that Eleanor could provide England with male heirs. She did not disappoint them.

12. Georges Duby, *Women of the Twelfth Century,* trans. Jean Birrell (Chicago, Ill.: University of Chicago Press, 1997), p. 13.

Chapter 8
Public Power in
Private Hands:
Eleanor of
Aquitaine
(ca. 1122–1204)
and Henry II
(1133–1189)

Over the next ten years, Eleanor gave birth to seven more children, Henry (1155), Matilda (1156), Richard (1157), Geoffrey (1158), Eleanor (1161), Joanna (1165), and John (1166). All except William lived to adulthood.

Eleanor was more than queen mother; she was a ruling queen who served as regent of England when Henry was abroad attending to his duties on the Continent. While no Norman tradition existed for a woman to rule outright, queens were "sharers in the imperial kingship "[13] and Eleanor made sure that her husband's interests were protected while he was away. Despite her consecutive pregnancies, Eleanor was involved in the kingdom's daily business during the first decade of Henry's rule, issuing orders received from the king, overseeing the king's ministers, settling disputes, and reviewing the accounts for her and her husband's lands.[14] Evidence for her involvement survives in the form of official documents or writs stamped with her own seal and in rulings that she issued when she presided over her husband's courts in England and on the Continent. Some of her rulings and letters, drawn up by her own clerks, survive and they show a queen confident in her power and ability to pursue her family's interests and implement her husband's policies (Document Four). She remained active in the politics of Aquitaine, and in 1159, she pressed Henry to move against one of Aquitaine's rivals, the count of Toulouse, but he had little

success.[15] By the mid-1160s, Henry took more of an interest in the formal ruling of England, and Eleanor's active participation in English rule fell off. Needing to control Aquitaine's rebellious nobles and at Henry's request in 1168, Eleanor took over the rule of Aquitaine and moved her court there. Some historians have speculated that she and Henry calculated that if she was in residence with the heir to the duchy, her favorite son Richard, then he would be familiar to the aristocracy and would not be seen as a foreign overlord. From this time, Eleanor's political ambitions focused on her children, especially Richard.

Once in residence, Eleanor also took the opportunity to rejuvenate court life in Aquitaine. Eleanor's family had been patrons of scholars, writers, and troubadours. Eleanor's grandfather, Duke William IX (1071–1127), embodied the qualities associated with the duchy and its leading family. He was educated in the manner of the day, studying liberal arts, theology, Roman law, and the military arts. In 1101, he decided to raise an army, join the First Crusade (1096–1099), and help defend Jerusalem after it had been captured by the crusaders. William's journey introduced him, his court, and his successors to the cultural richness of the East and to dreams of future crusades. Eleanor had followed in her grandfather's footsteps during the Second Crusade (1147–1149) and her son,

13. Parsons, p. 4.
14. Weir, p. 126.

15. Elizabeth A. R. Brown, "Eleanor as Parent, Queen, and Duchess," in William W. Kibler, ed., *Eleanor of Aquitaine: Patron and Politician* (Austin, Tex.: University of Texas Press, 1976), pp. 16–17.

Richard I of England, figured prominently in the Third Crusade (1189–1192).

When William IX returned home, he brought with him an appreciation of the literary forms of the East, not only from Arab writers, but from writers and philosophers of classical antiquity. He found inspiration in the erotic works of the Roman poet, Ovid (43 B.C.–A.D. 17), and he began writing poetry. The duke was not alone in his fascination with literary traditions that broke away from religious themes. He and other writers and poets of southern Europe, especially in Aquitaine and Provençe, observed and absorbed the changes taking place in twelfth century Europe and created new cultural forms, like the *chansons de geste* (songs of heroic deeds), love poetry, and troubadour music.

European society had been beset by numerous invaders over the previous three centuries, and fierce and merciless warriors had been necessary to defend it. By the twelfth century, European settlements had stabilized and began to prosper as the invasions ceased. The warrior ethos no longer held the same value and in fact threatened communities at peace. Society had to tame these men, channel their energies and penchant for violence, and redefine their roles. One of the outlets were the holy crusades of the twelfth century; another was creating a new code of values and behaviors, the code of chivalry. Nobles and knights bred for war, conquest, and acquisition were now expected to be gentle or act with what the French call *courtoisie*. This code meant aristocratic men were to be courteous and to defer

to each other and to less powerful persons in peaceful settings; be generous in thought and deed; be honest and forthright with peers; defend weaker persons, such as women, children, clerics, and noncombatants, defend places of worship; and exhibit courage, loyalty, and honor when at war.

Women were not excluded from this redefinition and reassessment of behaviors and norms. Prior to the twelfth century, Church Fathers had made it clear that women deserved contempt and loathing because Eve was the cause of Adam's expulsion from paradise. By their very nature, women were treacherous, evil, morally inferior, and sexually insatiable. The early Christian theologian, Tertullian (160–230), summarized women's natural inclination when he wrote, "And do you not know that you are Eve? God's sentence hangs still over all your sex and His punishment weighs down on you. You are the devil's gateway; you are who first violated the forbidden tree and broke the law of God."[16] There was, however, another example for women: the Virgin Mary, mother of God, who could inspire men to great deeds and lead them to salvation. Despite the alternative model for women, ecclesiastical writing on women from Tertullian to twelfth-century clerics often took the more negative view of them.

Pragmatism dictated aristocratic views about women. Women were betrothed because of the political advantage it might bring to her family and to her husband and his family, and be-

16. David F. Noble, *A World Without Women* (Oxford: Oxford University Press, 1992), p. 50.

Chapter 8
Public Power in
Private Hands:
Eleanor of
Aquitaine
(ca. 1122–1204)
and Henry II
(1133–1189)

cause of the promise of male offspring. Love or reverence for women played no part in the decision to marry. As the twelfth century began, new sensibilities toward women, love, and courtship emerged for various reasons: to regulate lustful aristocratic behavior, because of Church efforts to give women some of the honor due to the Virgin Mother, and as a result of the emergence of secular romantic literature that often portrayed women as objects of reverence. Eleanor embraced these new sensibilities, and her personal court, separate from her husband's, spread these values and the new cultural forms they spawned throughout England, France, and beyond.

Wherever she established her court, in Poitiers, Normandy, Maine, Anjou, England, and back to Poitiers and Aquitaine, she promoted and diffused the new literary forms and the values depicted by them. The chansons de geste celebrated chivalric ideals such as courage in battle, loyalty, and honor by relating the historical and mythical adventures of Charlemagne, Roland, King Arthur, and others. Romantic poetry extolled the virtues of courtly love, the longing of a young knight for a beautiful, chaste, and often married noblewoman. Many of the early songs and poems hailed from Aquitaine and were written and performed by wandering poets or troubadours in the vernacular language of southern France.

Some noblemen and -women, like William IX, also tried their hand at such verse, and historians regard William as the first troubadour who introduced the figure of the *domna*, the unattainable noblewoman who is an object of reverence as well as desire for a young lover. Female troubadours also existed and used the same conventions as their male counterparts. Some of the songs of the female troubadours allowed their female characters to have emotions and feelings, in contrast to the male convention of women being depicted as projections of men's images and desires.[17] Wherever she settled her court, Eleanor and later her daughter, Marie de Champagne, embraced and promoted different forkloric and narrative traditions from all of their lands. Eleanor was a cultural intermediary and passionate patron of the arts.[18] As a result of her familiarity with these cultural circles, Eleanor had numerous works dedicated to her and she was also the subject of many poems and songs (Document Five).

■ ACT III:

THE KING OF ENGLAND

During the first year of his reign, Henry punished Stephen's allies and solidified his own support with grants of land and office. Knowing that his responsibilities on the Continent would take him away from England, Henry

17. Marty Williams and Anne Echols, *Between Pit and Pedestal: Women in the Middle Ages* (Princeton, N.J.: Markus Wieners Publishers, 1994), p. 9.

18. Moshe Lazar, "Cupid, the Lady, and the Poet: Modes of Love at Eleanor of Aquitaine's Court," in William W. Kibler, ed., *Eleanor of Aquitaine: Patron and Politician* (Austin, Tex.: University of Texas Press, 1976), pp. 38–41.

asked Thomas Becket, the archdeacon of Canterbury and protégé of the archbishop of Canterbury, to be his chancellor. Confident that he had excellent men to look after his interests and leaving much of their oversight to Eleanor, Henry left in 1158 to defend Normandy from royal encroachment. Henry would spend twenty-one years of his thirty-four-year reign defending and at times expanding his family's French possessions.

When he returned to England in 1163, Henry was determined to redefine the king's relationship with his nobles and with the Church and to reestablish royal law and order in the countryside. In the 1160s and 1170s, Henry initiated a series of reforms meant to reassert royal jurisdiction over major crimes; take power away from baronial and ecclesiastical courts; and improve dealings with accused criminals. Henry's major reform of criminal prosecution came in 1166 with the issuing of the Assize of Clarendon, which defined the rights and duties of courts and people in criminal cases and established judicial procedures regarding how criminals would be arrested, charged, and arraigned.

Henry's intention was not to protect citizens from false prosecution or to create a single unified system of royal justice. Instead, Henry II wished to increase his control over the countryside, repress lawlessness, and wrestle power away from baronial and ecclesiastical authorities. To achieve these goals, he revived Henry I's policy of sending itinerant royal justices to the shires who would then determine the nature of the crimes against the crown and the local people. When the justice appeared in a community, he heard cases offered to him by "juries of presentment." Established by the Assize of Clarendon, these juries were the gathering together of twelve "good and lawful" men from the community who acted as the investigative agent of the monarchy. However, the group of jurors did not "investigate" in the contemporary sense of the word. Rather, most evidence originated from the jurors themselves in the form of hearsay, rumor, and personal knowledge.

Henry sought to bring order to civil procedures too, especially cases dealing with land and property disputes. Such disputes had traditionally been in the hands of the local nobles and their courts, but complaints of procedural procrastination, denial of justice, and arbitrary wrong reached Henry.[19] In the 1160s, Henry issued an assize that created new and swifter means for settling civil disputes. The plaintiff purchased from the king a writ that asked the sheriff to summon a jury, under the supervision of a royal justice, to decide the land or property dispute. Whatever decision the jury reached, the Crown enforced it. Because of the swiftness and apparent fairness of these civil proceedings, the king's courts experienced an increase in the volume of civil cases, which had once been heard by local lords. These new procedures and their successful implementation slowly eroded feudal justice and expanded royal authority.

19. Frank Barlow, *The Feudal Kingdom of England, 1042–1216* (New York: Longman, 1999), p. 261.

Chapter 8
Public Power in
Private Hands:
Eleanor of
Aquitaine
(ca. 1122–1204)
and Henry II
(1133–1189)

Henry was displeased with the corrupt practices of the sheriffs, the principal representatives of the monarch at the local level. He wanted to ensure that his royal representatives—sheriffs, bailiffs, and foresters as well as ecclesiastical and baronial officials—were devoted to his interests. During his time on the Continent in the 1160s, he received complaints that the sheriffs, who were responsible for collecting royal revenue and services, took some of the royal revenues for themselves and did not attend properly to the royal manors or to the king's subjects. By 1170, the level of corruption had become unacceptable to Henry and he issued the Inquest of Sheriffs. He sent out itinerant justices to investigate the actions of all sheriffs over the previous four years. These inquiries resulted in the removal of most of the sheriffs and in the appointment of Henry's loyal supporters in their places. Henry also ordered sheriffs to do more. After 1170 in addition to collecting royal revenue, Henry made the sheriffs responsible for the mundane duties of dispensing royal justice. Sheriffs now handled writs, summoned the various juries, guarded prisoners, and prepared for the visits of the king's traveling justices.[20]

Although Henry's reforms eroded local authority and autonomy, he experienced few successful rebellions against his policies. Why? Because Henry was a skilled negotiator, consummate politician, and energetic ruler. He often gained "local acquiescence by identifying mutual self inter-

est or coercion."[21] When Henry issued the assizes and created new offices or duties, he did so based on knowledge about his kingdom and his subjects. Henry was constantly on the move, visiting his royal residences, inspecting his lands, evaluating the work of his subjects and his officials, and learning about the political and military weaknesses of his enemies. His contemporaries remarked on Henry's travels and boundless curiosity.[22] Louis VII, king of France, asked if Henry flew instead of traveling by horse or ship. Walter Map, one of Henry's household clerks, remarked on how Henry covered distances like a courier. Peter Blois described Henry as "hunting through the provinces inquiring into everyone's doing, and especially those whom he made judge of others."[23] On the move and always inquiring, Henry imposed his will and wishes on his subjects (Document Six).

While Henry was successful in bringing the nobility to heel in the 1160s, he faced a more formidable opponent in the Catholic Church and its new archbishop of Canterbury, his friend and former chancellor, Thomas Becket. The issue at stake was the dispensation of justice. Over the centuries, the Church claimed jurisdiction over all spiritual persons and in all spiritual cases. When a member of the clergy committed a crime, that indi-

20. Ibid., p. 258.

21. "Henry II," *Who's Who in British History*, vol. 1, ed., Geoffrey Treasure (Chicago, Ill.: Fitzroy Dearborn Publishers, 1998), p. 616.

22. Richard Barber, *Henry Plantagenet* (Woodbridge, UK: The Boydell Press, 1964), p. 56.

23. W. L. Warren, *Henry II* (London: Eyre Methuen, 1973), p. 617.

vidual fell under the jurisdiction of the Church rather than the king. The accused would be tried in an ecclesiastical court using canon law, not in a manorial or royal court using the king's laws. Henry was not opposed to such claims, but during Stephen's reign, the Church had taken over the right to judge the offenses of clerks, no matter the crime, and to prosecute all breaches of the moral code, whether committed by clerk or layperson.[24] In addition, the ecclesiastical courts were highly corrupt. Even the most heinous crimes committed by clergy, such as murder, resulted in minor penalties imposed by the Church court.

By the early 1160s, Henry wished to reclaim from the Church jurisdiction over clerical offenders who committed offenses against the Crown and over cases concerning land and property disputes, and to prevent the Church from overzealously prosecuting laypeople accused of moral offenses.[25] None of these issues was necessarily explosive and Henry calculated that the time was ripe for the Church to relinquish some of its authority. In 1162, Henry campaigned successfully to have his friend and chancellor, Thomas Becket, appointed archbishop of Canterbury, and he believed that they could negotiate a compromise. The compromise Henry proposed was a return to the privileges and rights that the Church had enjoyed under his grandfather. Henry was determined to establish a written

definition of the king's authority and rights in relation to the Church. In 1164, at Clarendon, one of his courts of inquest convened and recorded sixteen articles detailing royal prerogatives in ecclesiastical affairs. These articles are known as the Constitutions of Clarendon (Document Seven). Henry expected that Becket and the English bishops would swear an oath to observe these prerogatives. Becket, however, vigorously defended the Church's authority and refused to submit to these restrictions on ecclesiastical authority, especially clauses 4 and 8, which hindered clerical travel abroad and recourse to the pope. Feeling betrayed by his friend and angered by his defiance, Henry used the royal and ecclesiastical courts to harass Becket and drive him out of office. Becket went into exile on the Continent but refused to resign as archbishop of Canterbury. During his exile, Becket depended on the diplomatic and financial backing of Henry's old enemy, the king of France, Louis VII.

Eventually, Henry was moved to reconcile with his old friend. He simply could not rule effectively while warring with Becket. In 1169, he was seriously considering going on a crusade and was anxious to have his young son, Henry, crowned king. Traditionally, the prerogative of crowning kings of England belonged to the archbishop of Canterbury, and Henry needed Becket. In June 1170, after years of endless negotiations with Becket, Henry had his son crowned by the archbishop of York, a rival of Becket's. By this time, Henry regarded

---

24. Barlow, p. 100.
25. Ibid., p. 242.

Chapter 8
Public Power in
Private Hands:
Eleanor of
Aquitaine
(ca. 1122–1204)
and Henry II
(1133–1189)

the whole affair a tiresome distraction and finally settled it, allowing Becket to return to England.

On November 29, 1170, Becket returned to England with the firm intention of seeking out and punishing those who had wronged him, especially those who had defied him and participated in the coronation ceremony in June. For a month, Becket traveled the countryside, meting out punishment to those bishops and clerics who had betrayed him and enforcing his rights and claims. By doing so, Becket alienated several powerful nobles and clerics, and these men informed Henry that the archbishop was "roving round with an army in order to enforce his rights and claims."[26] Henry, who was on the Continent at the time, sent a delegation to Becket to order him to stop his activities and retreat to Canterbury. If he did not, Henry authorized his knights to arrest him. When the delegation met with Becket in Canterbury Cathedral, the archbishop defiantly and forcefully refused to retreat, a scuffle broke out when the delegation tried to arrest him, and Becket was struck dead by Henry's knights.

Whether or not Henry ordered the murder did not matter. His enemies on the Continent, Louis VII and the French bishops, immediately implicated Henry, and one of the French bishops ordered an interdict, a general ban on all church services, on Henry's French fiefs. In addition, the pope excommunicated all who had been involved in the murder. Henry was not excommunicated but the pope subjected him to a personal interdict. The king retreated publically and eventually he and the pope negotiated a settlement. With the exception of a few clauses, the Constitutions of Clarendon remained the statement for royal prerogatives in ecclesiastical affairs. In return, Henry granted the pope the right to insist that any change in ecclesiastical affairs be scrutinized by the Church. Henry had never intended to go to war with the Church; he had only been interested in establishing a clear line between the duties and rights of the royal and ecclesiastical courts. Henry understood that the unity of the kingdom of England depended on the peaceful coexistence of the king and the Church. After the Becket affair, Henry treated the church most generously.[27]

During his first two decades of rule, both in England and on the Continent, Henry had made enemies of Louis VII, the Church, and his French vassals, who resented his dominance and his authority. In 1173–1174, Louis VII conspired with the young king, Henry, to unseat Henry II from his French lands. Since his coronation, the young king (as he is referred to by his contemporaries) had grown impatient waiting for his father to give him some responsibility in ruling England. At the very least, the young king wanted his father to relinquish some lands to his control so that he could support himself and his young queen, Margaret, Louis's eldest daughter from his second marriage. Henry's and Eleanor's other lands had been divided among their other sons: Aquitaine to

26. Ibid., p. 250.

27. Ibid, p. 255.

Richard, Brittany to Geoffrey, and Ireland to John.

Bestowing lands on heirs so young was customary. Not only did it diminish questions of inheritance after a father's death, but it also gave the heirs some experience in ruling. In Henry's case, the division also made sense because he had his sons looking after the family's interest. And that is what Henry's lands were, "a partible family estate,"[28] not a unified state. The fact that young Henry felt he had not been given his rightful portion triggered rebellion against his father. Eleanor supported the revolt, and she convinced Richard and Geoffrey to join their brother and Louis.

Chroniclers mention and condemn Eleanor's role in persuading Richard and Geoffrey to join the revolt. Rebellions of sons against fathers were not unusual for this time, but it was rare for a queen to conspire openly against her husband and king. Eleanor's actions were scandalous to her contemporaries and all condemned her

for her treachery. The archbishop of Rouen conveyed this attitude in a letter that pleaded with her to recall her sons:

> The wife is guilty when she parts from her husband, when she does not faithfully respect the marriage contract . . . we all deplore that fact that you separate from your husband in this way. This is the body becoming estranged from the body, the limb no longer serving the head, and, what goes beyond the bounds, you allow the offspring of the lord king and your own to rise up against the father . . . return to your husband, if not, in accordance with canon law, we will make you return to him."[29]

Eleanor refused, and as she traveled to Paris to meet her sons and former husband, wearing men's clothing, she was captured and held for the duration of the year-long rebellion. After the revolt, Henry pardoned his sons but kept his wife in close confinement until his death in 1189.

■ FINALE

Henry lived for another fifteen years after the rebellion, and during that time his sons continued to challenge his power and authority. Henry often manipulated his sons by threatening to disinherit one of them in favor of another to keep their loyalty. Young Henry began to mount an army against his father in 1183, but his untimely

death that same year averted a major rebellion. In 1188–1189, Richard allied with the new French king, Philip II (r. 1180–1223) and forced his father to hand over all of the Angevin possessions. Tired, sick, and disheartened, Henry II died in July 1189. His death brought Eleanor's release.

Eleanor emerged from years of imprisonment to play an active role in both Richard's and John's reigns.

28. John Gillingham, *The Angevin Empire* (London: Arnold Publishers, 2001), p. 32.

29. Duby, p. 15.

Chapter 8
Public Power in
Private Hands:
Eleanor of
Aquitaine
(ca. 1122–1204)
and Henry II
(1133–1189)

During Richard's ten-year rule, the majority of which he spent on crusade, Eleanor was the de facto regent for her son; and she made up for her many years of confinement. Now in her sixties, Eleanor traveled throughout England transacting the business of state for her son, protected his patrimony from his younger brother John, who had designs on Richard's continental land; and successfully negotiated Richard's marriage to the daughter of the king of Navarre, a rival of the king of France. When Richard was captured on his way back from the crusades by the duke of Austria, who demanded an exorbitant ransom, Eleanor rallied Richard's English subjects to pay the ransom. Eleanor delivered the ransom herself, and she and Richard returned triumphantly to England in early 1194. In May, she left with Richard to settle the dispute with John over the continental possession. With Richard and John reconciled, Eleanor retired to Fontévrault Abbey, which had been endowed by her grandfather and was generously patronized by Eleanor. It was a refuge first for women of all classes and then later a refuge for aristocratic women. Six years earlier, Henry II had been buried there.

Eleanor intended to close out her life within the abbey's walls, but the death of Richard in 1199 and the need to secure the succession of her remaining son, John, to the English throne and the Angevin inheritance interrupted her retirement. She successfully secured the support for his coronation and then, wishing to safeguard the Angevin inheritance for her family, she arranged the marriage of her granddaughter to the heir of the French throne. Finally, she fended off a challenge to John's patrimony in Aquitaine. When Eleanor died in 1204, her children could be grateful that she had done what a good aristocratic matron was supposed to do—protect the patrimony at all costs.

As a powerful male ruler with considerable political skills, Henry had various tools at his disposal for achieving his goals. Military force, personal loyalties, economic resources, and the development of institutional powers like laws, courts, police, and bureacratic patronage could be used to protect and extend the authority of his family. His biggest problems, perhaps, were the traditional feudal claims to inheritance and rights that his very family members could launch against him. How exactly could he fight his wife and his sons? Eleanor, on the other hand, began with traditional feudal rights stemming from family interests that had accrued to many noblewomen for some time. She could also utilize maternal obligations to her children to support and defend familial interests. When she stepped into the arena of institutional political power in a visible way, she aroused suspicion and even opposition. She had no claim to bureacratic support, legal authority, or any of the material dimensions of the expanding realm of government. Her impressive cultural contributions and the personal power she exercised in her family inspired sometimes grudging admiration, but in successive generations, women's informal political power would not withstand a growing centralized state.

■ QUESTIONS

1. What was the significance of family and marriage in the political arena of medieval England and France? How did family and marriage influence Henry's and Eleanor's political ascents?

2. Why was it necessary to call attention to Eleanor's and Henry's private and public behavior? To what extent could accusations of immorality and sexual impropriety be believed? Who made these accusations and why?

3. What motivated Henry to undertake his governmental, judicial, and religious reforms? From what did he derive his legitimacy?

4. How and in what form did women enter the political arena? From what did women derive the right to be public persons?

5. Often the most positive images of medieval queens were extensions of their maternal role. Why was this the case? From what did medieval kings derive their positive images?

6. Much of what we know about Eleanor and Henry comes from medieval chronicles. How can we assess the historical accuracy of these chronicles? How do chroniclers' accounts of Eleanor and Henry compare with the Greek and Roman historians' accounts of Augustus and Livia (chapter 4), Clovis and Clotild (chapter 6), and Justinian and Theodora (chapter 7)?

■ DOCUMENTS

DOCUMENT ONE

BERNARD OF CLAIRVAUX

Letter to the Virgin Sophia

Bernard of Clairvaux (1090–1153) was one of the leaders of a new order of monks, the Cistercians, and became abbé of the Cistercian monastery at Clairvaux. He argued passionately for the values of his order: discipline, austerity, and simplicity in all human activity. He was intimately involved in the theological controversies and ecclesiastical politics of his age and was called "the conscience of all Europe." He was also a prodigious letter writer. In the letter below, he describes to young Sophia a scene he witnessed in 1140 when he happened on a group of royal women, most likely Eleanor, queen of France, and her entourage. What are the practices of these noble ladies? What will come from their behavior? What is the proper role for women?

Chapter 8
*Public Power in
Private Hands:
Eleanor of
Aquitaine
(ca. 1122–1204)
and Henry II
(1133–1189)*

'Vain are the winning ways, beauty is a snare: it is the woman who fears the Lord that will achieve renown.' I rejoice with you, my daughter, in the glory of your virtue whereby, you tell me, you have cast away the false glory of the world. It is well to be rid of it, and you deserve praise for not having been deceived in a matter concerning which many people, wise enough in other respects, are exceedingly foolish. . . .

2. Let other women who know no better contend amongst themselves for the tawdry and fleeting glory of short-lived and deceitful things, but do you strive to set your heart upon what can never fail. Do you, I say, strive for that 'eternal weight of glory which our present momentary and light tribulation worketh for us above measure exceedingly.' And if those daughters of Belial who 'put on airs, walk with heads high, and with mincing steps' got up and adorned like a temple, abuse you, answer them: 'My kingdom is not of this world'; answer them: 'My time has not yet come, but your time is always ready'; answer them: 'My life is hid with Christ in God. When Christ shall appear, who is my life, then I also shall appear with him in glory'. . . .

3. So I will pass over what is promised to you in the future and concern myself solely with the present, with what you have already, with the 'firstfruits of the spirit,' the gifts of the Bridegroom, the pledges of betrothal, the 'abundant blessings with which he has met you on the way,' he whom you await to follow you and complete what is lacking. May he come out into the open to be seen by his bride in all his beauty and admired by the angels in all his glory. If the daughters of Babylon have anything like this, let them bring it forth, 'whose only glory is their shame.' They are clothed in purple and fine linen, but their souls are in rags. Their bodies glitter with jewels, but their lives are foul with vanity. You, on the contrary, whilst your body is clothed in rags, shine gloriously within, but in the sight of heaven, not of the world. . . .

. . . Silk, purple, and paint have their beauty, but they do not impart it. They show their own beauty when applied to the body, but they do not make the body beautiful. When the body is taken away, they take their beauty with them. The comeliness which goes on with clothes, comes off with clothes, it belongs to the clothes and not the clothed.

5. Therefore do not emulate evil-doers and those who borrow their beauty elsewhere when they have lost their own. They prove themselves destitute of any proper or natural beauty who go to such pains and such expense to make up after the fashion of the world that passes away so as to be admired by the foolish people who see them. Consider it wholly beneath you to borrow your appearance from the furs of animals and the work of worms, let what you have be suffcient for you. The true and proper beauty of anything needs no help from other sources. The ornaments of a queen have no beauty like to the blushes of natural modesty which colour the cheeks of a virgin. Nor is the mark of self-discipline a whit less becoming. Self-discipline composes the whole bearing of a maid's body and the temper of her mind. It bows her head, smoothes her

brow, composes her face, binds her eyes, controls her laughter, bridles her tongue, calms her anger, and governs her steps. Such are the pearls which adorn the vesture of a virgin. What glory can be preferred to virginity thus adorned? The glory of angels? An angel has virginity, but he has no body. Without doubt he is more happy if less strong in this respect. Excellent and most desirable is the adornment which even angels might envy!

6. There remains another thing concerning the same subject. Without any doubt the more your adornment is your own the safer it is. You see women burdened rather than adorned with ornaments of gold, silver and precious stones, and all the raiment of a court. You see them dragging long trains of most precious material behind them, stirring up clouds of dust as they go. Do not let this trouble you. They leave it all behind them when they die, but you will take your holiness with you. What they carry about does not belong to them. When they die they will not be able to take a thing with them, none of all their worldly glory will go down with them to the grave. These things of theirs belong to the world and the world will send the wearers naked away and keep all their vanities to seduce others equally vain. But your adornments are not like this. They remain securely yours, secure because yours. You cannot be deprived of them by violence nor lose them to guile. Against them the cunning of the thief and the cruelty of the madman are of no avail. They are not corrupted by moth and they do not wear out with age, nor are they spent with use. They survive death, for they belong to the soul and not the body. They do not die with the body, but leave the body in company with the soul. Even those who kill the body are powerless against the soul.

DOCUMENT TWO

ELEANOR AT ANTIOCH

At the end of the Second Crusade, John of Salisbury was a clerk in the papal chancery. He recorded much of what he heard and saw during the years 1148–1153 in his Historia Pontificalis. *In the passage below, John tells of Louis's and Eleanor's arrival and stay at Antioch. What motives does John ascribe to Raymond's, Eleanor's, and Louis's actions?*

The second passage, a tale written almost one hundred years after Eleanor's stay in Antioch, weaves together many of the historical anecdotes about Eleanor. Compare this story with John of Salisbury's account. What explains Eleanor's progressive vilification? Why is Saladin, the Muslim leader during the Third Crusade, substituted for Raymond?

Chapter 8
Public Power in
Private Hands:
Eleanor of
Aquitaine
(ca. 1122–1204)
and Henry II
(1133–1189)

John of Salisbury
Historia Pontificalis

He [Raymond] was as it happened the queen's uncle, and owed the king loyalty, affection and respect for many reasons. But whilst they remained there to console, heal and revive the survivors from the wreck of the army, the attentions paid by the prince to the queen, and his constant, indeed almost continuous, conversation with her, aroused the king's suspicious. These were greatly strengthened when the queen wished to remain behind, although the king was preparing to leave, and the prince made every effort to keep her, if the king would give his consent. And when the king made haste to tear her away, she mentioned their kinship, saying it was not lawful for them to remain together as man and wife, since they were related in the fourth and fifth degrees.* Even before their departure a rumour to that effect had been heard in France, where the late Bartholomew bishop of Laon had calculated the degree of kinship; but it was not certain whether the reckoning was true or false. At this the king was deeply moved; and although he loved the queen almost beyond reason he consented to divorce her if his counsellors and the French nobility would allow it. There was one knight among the king's secretaries, called Terricus Gualerancius [Thierry Galeran], a eunuch whom the queen had always hated and mocked, but who was faithful and had the king's ear like his father's before him. He boldly persuaded the king not to suffer her to dally longer at Antioch, both because 'guilt under friendship's guise could lie concealed' [Ovid, *Heroides,* iv,138], and because it would be a lasting shame to the kingdom of the Franks if in addition to all the other disasters it was reported that the king had been deserted by his wife, or robbed of her. So he argued, either because he hated the queen or because he really believed it, moved perchance by widespread rumour. In consequence, she was torn away and forced to leave for Jerusalem with the king; and, their mutual anger growing greater, the wound remained, hide it as best they might.

Anonymous Minstrel from Reims
Tale About Eleanor

Seeing his weakness and ignorance, Saladin challenged him to battle several times, but without the king being willing to engage. When Queen Eleanor observed how negative the king was and heard of the goodness, prowess, intelligence and generosity of Saladin, she fell madly in love with him. Then, through an interpreter of hers, she sent him greetings and the assurance that, if he could manage to abduct her, she would take him as her husband and renounce her

---

*Fourth cousins

[234]

faith. When Saladin learned this from the letter passed to him by the interpreter, he was delighted, for he was well aware that this was the noblest lady in Christendom. So he had a galley equipped and set out from Ascalon, where he was, to go to Tyre with the interpreter; and they arrived at Tyre shortly before midnight.

Then the interpreter went up by a small concealed entrance into the room of the queen, who was expecting him. 'What news?' she asked when she saw him. 'My lady,' he said, 'the galley is here all ready and waiting for you. Hurry now so we're not spotted!'—'Well done, by my faith!' said the queen. Then she fetched two maidens and two chests crammed with gold and silver, which she wanted to have taken into the galley. One of the girls then realized what was happening. Leaving the room as quietly as she could, she came to the bed of the sleeping king and wakened him with the words: 'There's trouble brewing, sire! My lady's wanting to go to Saladin in Ascalon, and the galley's waiting for her in the harbour. Make haste, sire, in God's name!' On hearing her, the king jumped up, dressed and got ready, then had his household arm and went to the harbour. There he found the queen with one foot already in the galley. Seizing her by the hand, he led her back to her room. And the king's company captured the galley and those in it; for they were so taken by surprise that they were unable to defend themselves.

The king asked the queen why she wanted to do that. 'On account of your cowardice, in God's name,' replied the queen, 'for you're not worth a rotten apple! And I've heard such good reports of Saladin that I love him better than you; so you can be quite sure that you'll never get any satisfaction from holding on to me.' At that the king left her and had her well guarded. Then he decided to return to France, as he was running short of money and achieving nothing but shame where he was.

So he put to sea again with the queen and returned to France. Then he took all his barons' advice on what he should do with the queen, telling them how she had behaved. 'Truly,' said the barons, 'the best advice we could give you is to let her go; for she's a devil, and if you keep her much longer we're afraid she'll have you murdered. Above all, you've had no child by her.' The king acted like a fool and took this advice: he would have done better to have her walled up, so he would have had her great land all his life, and the disasters of which you are about to hear would not have happened.

So the king sent Queen Eleanor back to her country. Then she immediately sent for King Henry of England (the man who had Saint Thomas of Canterbury killed). And he gladly came and married her, paying the king homage for the land he was acquiring, which was vast and rich. He then took the queen off to England and kept her until he had had three sons by her. The first of them was Henry Curtmantle, a worthy man and fine knight; and the second was called Richard, who was valiant, bold, generous and chivalrous; and the third was named John, who was wicked, disloyal, and did not believe in God.

Chapter 8
Public Power in
Private Hands:
Eleanor of
Aquitaine
(ca. 1122–1204)
and Henry II
(1133–1189)

════════ **DOCUMENT THREE** ════════

GERALD OF WALES

"Concerning the Instruction of a Prince"
(ca. 1190)

Gerald of Wales came to Henry II's court in 1184 as a royal chaplain and was well positioned to witness the last five years of Henry's reign. Displeased that the king had not supported him in his election to the see of St. David's, he took his revenge by penning "Concerning the Instruction of a Prince" and revealing the follies and vices of Henry II and his sons. What are Henry's follies and vices?

To judge from the fortunate issues of chance, Henry II, king of the English, seemed to have obtained divine favour in almost everything, not only from the beginning of his reign, but even from his first year and his very birth, and this more by grace than as a reward for his merits. In the first place, William, the only son and heir of King Henry I, was drowned, and to our Henry, as the king's grandson by his eldest daughter, both the duchy of Normandy and the kingdom of England descended by hereditary right. But when King Henry I departed from this world and the young Henry was left the heir as a lad of fifteen years, Stephen of Blois, the king's nephew on his sister's side, took the crown of the kingdom unlawfully. After a reign of nineteen years, and a little after the death of that noble knight, Eustace, his son, King Stephen died. All obstacles having thus been removed from Henry's path, everything that had been unjustly withheld from him, now that he was a grown man, was wholly restored to him . . .

Furthermore he vigorously extended his dominions overseas in Gaul and Aquitaine; to Anjou, Maine and Touraine, which he had inherited from his father, and Poitou and the whole of Gascony as far as the Pyrenees, which had fallen to his lot by marriage, he added Auvergne, Berri and Gisors, together with the Vexin, which had formerly been taken from Normandy.

Moreover he aspired to extend his rule, not only to France, making full use of the good nature of the simple and saintly King Louis, but even also to the Roman empire, through the occasion of the long war and inexorable discord between the Emperor Frederick and his subjects. Having often been invited by the whole of Italy and the city of Rome, an opening for this was afforded him by way of the Alps and the valley of Maurienne, but he could not obtain effective control there. Indeed, he was sometimes wont, since "his mouth spoke from a full heart," to let fall spirited and ambitious words among his intimates to the effect that the whole world was too small a prize for a single courageous and powerful ruler. Thus throughout the world the fame of his honoured name was so spread abroad that it abounded in glory above the kings, princes and liegemen of the whole earth and to the terror of the nations. Moreover the princes of all lands, both Christians and heathen, such as the German king, Frederick, the Greek emperor, Manuel, Noureddin in his time and afterwards Saladin, and the princes of Asia and Europe, even of Spain, both Christian and infidel, were accustomed to visit him and honour him with presents and to send frequient embassies. . . .

. . . His three daughters, whom he had by the noble Queen Eleanor, he gave in marriage in three widely separated regions of Europe. The eldest he bestowed in Saxony to Henry, duke of Saxony; the second, in Spain to Alfonso, king of Toledo and Castile; the third and youngest, in Sicily to be the wife of William, king of the Two Sicilies.

By the same Eleanor he had in addition six illustrious sons, of whom two died prematurely and at a tender age. The other four who grew to manhood, rejoiced their father's heart more in time of flowering than in time of fruiting, more in the stalk than in the ear of harvest, more in childhood than in maturity. . . . Doubtless it came to pass by the just and admirable vengeance of God that he deserved to be punished for his grave excesses and irregularities through his own offspring, whom he had begotten less lawlessly than was fitting, and that his lands and even his last breath should be disturbed with anxiety, as saith the prophet Naaman [*sic*], "The sword shall not depart from the house of the impious man," and again, "God shall raise up thy seed against thee."

In the first place, as is sufficiently well known, he basely stole Queen Eleanor from his liege lord, Louis, king of the French, and then married her. In course of time and by an evil fortune he had by her the offspring mentioned above. By them also, as we have said, on account of this and other grave offences, some of which we shall recount hereafter, and because adversity engenders understanding, God willed he should be humbled and called to repentance, or if he proved obdurate, the father should be punished by his own brood and the torturer tormented by his own victims. From the beginning even unto the end he was an oppressor of the nobility, weighing justice and injustice, right and wrong by his own convenience, a vendor and procrastinator of justice, shifty and cunning in speech, a ready breaker not merely of his word but also of his plighted troth, an open adulterer, ungrateful and impious towards God, the hammer of the Church and a son of perdition. . . .

. . . From the time of this odious crime, this wicked infamy and sacrilege, the revolving wheel of fortune began to run swiftly down to its lowest point and was only slowly raised again to its normal height. The royal state began to weaken a little and the strength of the ruler to decline from day to day. For although after grave and desperate afflictions, by divine permission and also by way of proof, he seemed at times to rise again and mount up courageously to greater heights of glory, yet his sons, now grown men, frequently rose in revolt against him and day by day enticed the hearts of his nobles away from him until he could find no abiding state of happiness or enjoyment of security. . . .

Chapter 8
Public Power in
Private Hands:
Eleanor of
Aquitaine
(ca. 1122–1204)
and Henry II
(1133–1189)

═══ **DOCUMENT FOUR** ═══

ELEANOR OF AQUITAINE

"Charter of Queen Eleanor, Wife of Henry II, Respecting the Knight Service Owed to the Abbey of Abingdon" (1156–1164)

A charter is a deed in the form of a letter that tells of a grant of land or privilege. Charters may be long or short. On whose authority is Eleanor ordering the knights to honor their service to the abbey of Abingdon? How can the historian use the charter as a source?

Eleanor, queen of England, duchess of Normandy and Aquitaine, and countess of Anjou, to the knights and men who hold lands and tenures of the abbey of Abingdon, greeting. I order that justly and without delay you do full service to Walkelin, abbot of Abingdon, as your predecessors did to his predecessors in the time of King Henry, the grandfather of the lord king. And if you do not do this, the justice of the king and my own justice will cause it to be done.
Witness: Jocelyn "de Balliol". At Winchester.
By writ of the king from over the sea.

═══ **DOCUMENT FIVE** ═══

ANDREAS CAPELLANUS

The Art of Courtly Love

Eleanor's role in the promotion of new literary forms has been much debated, and most historians conclude that she was in fact a patron, if not a practitioner, of the arts. Her patronage was such that Andreas Capellanus, in The Art of Courtly Love, *has Eleanor presiding over "courts of love." There is no evidence that Eleanor ever presided over such courts. In the passage below, Andreas Capellanus has Eleanor passing judgment on two cases. Why would he chose Eleanor as one of his subjects? Can a literary text be helpful to historians? Why or why not?*

A worthless young man and an older knight of excellent character sought the love of the same woman. The young man argued that she ought to prefer him to the older man because if he got the love he was after he might by means of it acquire an excellent character, and it would be no small credit to the woman if through her a worthless man was made into a man of good character.

To this Queen Eleanor replied as follows: 'Although the young man may show that by receiving love he might rise to be a worthy man, a woman does not do very wisely if she chooses to love an unworthy man, especially when a good and eminently worthy one seeks her love. It might happen that because of the faults of the unworthy man his character would not be improved even if he did receive the good things he was hoping for, since the seeds which we sow do not always produce a crop.'

This other love affair was submitted to the decision of the same queen. A certain man who had in ignorance joined in love with a woman who was related to him, sought to leave her when he discovered his fault. But the woman was bound by the chain of love and tried to keep him in love's observances, saying that the crime was fully excused by the fact that when they began to enjoy the love it was without any sin.

In this affair the Queen answered as follows: 'A woman who under the excuse of a mistake of any kind seeks to preserve an incestuous love is clearly going contrary to what is right and proper. We are always bound to oppose any of those incestuous and damnable actions which we know even human laws punish by very heavy penalties.'

DOCUMENT SIX

GERALD OF WALES

"Character of Henry II"
(ca. 1190)

In this passage, Gerald describes the physical traits and multiple facets of his king. Why does he admire some traits and criticize others? What features of his situation color his views?

Henry II, king of England, was a man of reddish, freckled complexion with a large round head, grey eyes which glowed fiercely and grew bloodshot in anger, a fiery countenance and a harsh, cracked voice. His neck was somewhat thrust forward from his shoulders, his chest was broad and square, his arms strong and powerful. His frame was stocky with a pronounced tendency to corpulence, due rather to nature than to indulgence, which he tempered by exercise. For in eating and drinking he was moderate and sparing, and in all things frugal in the degree permissible to a prince. To restrain and moderate by exercise the injustice done him by nature and to mitigate his physical defects by

Chapter 8
Public Power in
Private Hands:
Eleanor of
Aquitaine
(ca. 1122–1204)
and Henry II
(1133–1189)

virtue of the mind, he taxed his body with excessive hardship, thus, as it were, fomenting civil war in his own person.

In times of war, which frequently threatened, he gave himself scarcely a modicum of quiet to deal with those matters of business which were left over, and in times of peace he allowed himself neither tranquillity nor repose. He was addicted to the chase beyond measure; at crack of dawn he was off on horseback, traversing waste lands, penetrating forests and climbing the mountain-tops, and so he passed restless days. At evening on his return home he was rarely seen to sit down either before or after supper. After such great and wearisome exertions he would wear out the whole court by continual standing. But since "above everything moderation is beneficial in life" and no remedy is good by itself alone, the swelling of his feet and legs, aggravated by injuries sustained in spurring on his refractory horses, brought on other bodily ailments, and without doubt, old age, the mother and handmaid of many evils.

In stature he was of middle height, and in this he was matched by none of his sons, for the two eldest were a little above the average, while the two youngest stopped short of it. Except when troubled in mind or moved to anger, he was a prince of great eloquence and, what is remarkable in these days, polished in letters.

He was a man easy of access and condescending, pliant and witty, second to none in politeness, whatever thoughts he might conceal within himself; a prince so remarkable for charity that whenever he overcame by force of arms, he was himself vanquished through showing too great compassion. Strenuous in warfare, he was very prudent in civil life. But always he dreaded the doubtful arbitrament of war, and with supreme wisdom, in accordance with the ancient comic poet, he essayed every method before resorting to arms. For those lost in battle he grieved more than any prince, and was more humane to the dead warrior than to him who survived; the dead indeed he mourned with a grief far greater than the love he bore the living. When difficulties pressed hard upon him, none was more amicable, but none sterner once safety was regained. He was fierce towards those who remained untamed, but merciful to the vanquished, harsh to his servants, expansive towards strangers, prodigal in public, thrifty in private. Whom he had once hated he scarcely ever loved, but whom he had once loved he scarcely ever called to mind with hatred. He delighted beyond measure in birds of prey, especially when in flight, and in hounds pursuing wild beasts by their keen scent, both for their resonant and harmonious voices and for their swift running. Would he had given himself as much to his devotions as he did to the chase!

After the grievous injuries inflicted upon him by his sons, at the instigation it is said of their mother, he became an open violator of the marriage bond. Through a certain inconstancy of nature he was always prompt to break his word. For as often as his affairs became difficult he would repent in word rather than in deed, and so the more easily accounted his oath null and void than his deed. In all his affairs he showed cautious anticipation and restraint, so much so

[240]

that the remedy to some extent exceeded the need, and he appeared dilatory in maintaining law and justice. Only by the grievous importunity of his counsellors would he give proper attention to all matters of business. Finally, while the justice which God bestows freely and without price was sold for money, he pre-eminently turned everything to his own profit and left many heirs to Gehazi both in Church and state.

He was most diligent in guarding and maintaining peace, liberal beyond comparison in almsgiving and the peculiar defender of the Holy Land; a lover of humility, an oppressor of the nobility and a contemner of the proud, "filling the hungry with good things and sending the rich empty away, exalting the humble and putting down the mighty from their seat". By his detestable usurpations in the things pertaining to God he was highly presumptuous; out of zeal for justice, but not informed by knowledge, he joined together, or rather confounded the laws of Church and state, making them both one. As a son of the Church, from whom he acquired the sceptre of royalty, he was either forgetful of his sacramental unction or ignored the fact that he had received it, devoting scarcely an hour to the divine mysteries of the sacred Host, and that very time, perchance through pressure of affairs of state, he passed more in taking counsel and in discussion than in his devotions. The revenues of vacant benefices he paid into the public treasury and as the whole lump may be spoilt by a little leaven, while he confiscated the revenues which Christ claims for himself, new difficulties continually arose and he was forced to pour forth his whole treasure, bestowing on the impious soldiery the moneys which should have been given to the priesthood. Through his consummate prudence he devised many changes and ordered them with foresight, but the issue of events was not always favourable and often seemed to work in a contrary end. Never did a great misfortune arise which was not brought about by familiar causes.

On his legitimate children he lavished in their childhood more than a father's affection, but in their more advanced years he looked askance at them after the manner of a stepfather; and although his sons were so renowned and illustrious he pursued his successors with a hatred which perhaps they deserved, but which none the less impaired his own happiness. And because man's prosperity is neither enduring nor perfect, through the outrageous malice of fortune he incurred a sword when he ought to have obtained joy. He found strife instead of safety, ruin instead of repose, ingratitude instead of constancy, and the utmost confusion instead of peace and tranquillity. Whether by some breach of the marriage tie or as a punishment for some crime of the parent, it befell that there was never true affection felt by the father towards his sons, nor by the sons towards their father, nor harmony among the brothers themselves.

Once he had subdued those who had oppressed the realm and disturbed its peace, among whom were his brothers and sons as well as others, including both his own servants and strangers, he for long afterwards governed in all things according to his will. Would that from beginning to end he had recognised this to be a mark of divine favour to himself by deeds appropriate to its

Chapter 8
Public Power in
Private Hands:
Eleanor of
Aquitaine
(ca. 1122–1204)
and Henry II
(1133–1189)

worth, or at least had done so at the very end! Although he was daily set amidst a host of faces, he never again forgot anyone whom he had once closely scanned. Anything he had once heard worthy of remembrance he could never obliterate from his mind. So he had at his fingers' ends both a ready knowledge of nearly the whole of history and also practical experience of almost everything in daily affairs. To compress much in a few words, if he had to the very end remained a chosen vessel to the Lord and had turned himself to his obedience, he would have been beyond comparison among the princes of this world for his many natural gifts.

DOCUMENT SEVEN

HENRY II

Constitutions of Clarendon
(1164)

After Thomas Becket, archbishop of Canterbury, refused to submit the Catholic Church to the king's authority, Henry summoned an inquest to Clarendon. The council investigated and then wrote out the traditions and customs dictating the historical relationship between the Crown and the Church as they existed at the time of Henry I. What clauses challenged the autonomy of the Church to govern its own affairs? What clauses reasserted royal authority?

. . . Now of the acknowledged customs and privileges of the realm a certain part is contained in the present document, of which part these are the heads:

1. If a dispute shall arise between laymen, or between clerks and laymen, or between clerks, concerning advowson and presentation to churches, let it be treated and concluded in the court of the lord king.

2. Churches within the fief of the lord king cannot be granted in perpetuity without his consent and concession.

3. Clerks cited and accused of any matter shall, when summoned by the king's justice, come before the king's court to answer there concerning matters which shall seem to the king's court to be answerable there, and before the ecclesiastical court for what shall seem to be answerable there, but in such a way that the justice of the king shall send to the court of holy Church to see how the case is there tried. And if the clerk shall be convicted or shall confess, the Church ought no longer to protect him.

4. It is not lawful for archbishops, bishops, and beneficed clergy of the realm to depart from the kingdom without the lord king's leave. And if they do so depart, they shall, if the king so please, give security that neither in going, nor in

tarrying, nor in returning will they contrive evil or injury against the king or the kingdom.

5. Excommunicates ought not to give pledges of security for future good behaviour nor take oaths, but only to give sufficient pledge of security to abide by the judgment of the Church in order to obtain absolution.

6. Laymen ought not to be accused save by accredited and lawful accusers and witnesses in the presence of the bishop, in such wise, however, that the archdeacon may not lose his right nor anything due to him thereby. And if the accused persons be such that no one either wishes or dares to prefer a charge against them, the sheriff, when requested by the bishop, shall cause twelve lawful men of the neighborhood or township to swear before the bishop that they will manifest the truth of the matter to the best of their knowledge.

7. No one who holds of the king in chief nor any of the officials of his demesne shall be excommunicated, nor the lands of any of them placed under interdict, unless application shall first be made to the lord king, if he be in the realm, or to his chief justice, if he be abroad, that right may be done him; in such wise that matters pertaining to the royal court shall be concluded there, and matters pertaining to the ecclesiastical court shall be sent thither to be deal with.

8. With regard to appeals, if they should arise, they should proceed from the archdeacon to the bishop, and from the bishop to the archbishop. And if the archbishop should fail to do justice, the case must finally be brought to the lord king, in order that by his command the dispute may be determined in the archbishop's court, in such wise that it proceed no further without the assent of the lord king.

9. If a dispute shall arise between a clerk and a layman, or between a layman and a clerk, in respect of any holding which the clerk desires to treat as free alms, but the layman as lay fee, it shall be determined by the recognition of twelve lawful men through the deliberation, and in the presence of the king's chief justice, *whether* the holding pertains to free alms or to lay fee. And if it be judged to pertain to free alms, the plea shall be heard in the ecclesiastical court; but if to lay fee, it shall be heard in the king's court, unless both of them shall claim from the same bishop or baron. But if each of them appeal concerning this fief to the same bishop or baron, the plea shall be heard in the latter's court, in such wise that he who was originally in possession shall not lose possession by reason of the recognition that has been made, until the matter has been settled by the plea.

10. If any one of a city or castle or borough or demesne manor of the lord king be cited by archdeacon or bishop for any offence for which he is obliged to make answer to them, and he refuse to give satisfaction at their citations, it is highly proper to place him under interdict; but he ought not to be excommunicated until application has been made to the chief officer of the lord king in that town, in order that it may be adjudged meet for him to make satisfaction. But if the king's officer fails to act in this, he himself shall be at the mercy of the lord king,

Chapter 8
Public Power in
Private Hands:
Eleanor of
Aquitaine
(ca. 1122–1204)
and Henry II
(1133–1189)

and thereafter the bishop shall be allowed to coerce the accused by ecclesiastical justice.

11. Archbishops, bishops and all beneficed clergy of the realm, who hold of the king in chief, have their possessions from the lord king by barony and are answerable for them to the king's justices and officers; they observe and perform all royal rights and customs and, like other barons, ought to be present at the judgments of the king's court together with the barons, until a case shall arise involving a judgment concerning mutilation or death.

12. When an archbishopric or bishopric is vacant, or any abbey or priory of the king's demesne, it ought to be in the king's hand, and he shall receive from it all revenues and profits as part of his demesne. And when the time shall come to provide for the church, the lord king ought to summon the more important of the beneficed clergy of the church, and the election ought to take place in the lord king's chapel with the assent of the lord king and the advice of the clergy of the realm whom he shall summon for this purpose. And the clerk elected shall there do homage and fealty to the lord king as his liege lord for his life and limbs and his earthly honour, saving his order, before he is consecrated.

13. If any of the magnates of the realm should forcibly prevent an archbishop or bishop or archdeacon from doing justice to himself or to his people, the lord king ought to bring him to justice. And if perchance anyone should forcibly dispossess the lord king of his right, the archbishops, bishops and archdeacons ought to bring him to justice, so that he may make satisfaction to the lord king.

14. The chattels of those who are under forfeiture to the king may not be retained by any church or cemetery against the king's justice, because they belong to the king, whether they be found within the churches or without.

15. Pleas of debt due under pledge of faith, or even without pledge of faith, are to lie in the justice of the king.

16. Sons of villeins ought not to be ordained without the consent of the lord on whose land they are known to have been born.

This record of the aforesaid customs and privileges of the crown was drawn up by the archbishops, bishops, earls, barons, nobles and elders of the realm at Clarendon on the fourth day previous to the Purification of the Blessed Virgin Mary in the presence of the lord Henry, and of his father, the lord king. There are, moreover, many other great customs and privileges pertaining to holy mother-church and to the lord king and the barons of the realm which are not contained in this document. Let them be safe for holy Church and for our lord, the king and his heirs and the barons of the realm. And let them be inviolably observed for ever and ever.

An Emerging Civilization in the West

The New Culture of Learning: Peter Abelard (1079–1142) and Héloïse (1100/1101–1163/1164)

■ SETTING THE STAGE

The twelfth century in Latin Christendom has long been acknowledged as a time of urban, political, and commercial renewal and spiritual and intellectual vitality. At the dawn of the twelfth century, the peoples of Western Europe enjoyed improved material conditions due to increases in agricultural production, decreases in mortality rates, improved trade, expanding commercial activities, political stability, and the renewal of urban life. With the exception of the Italian peninsula, urban life had all but disappeared during the Early Middle Ages. But now, with increased trade and abundant agricultural goods, towns and cities re-emerged, populated by new types of people—merchants, artisans, innkeepers, and professionals. These people

Chapter 9
The New Culture
of Learning:
Peter Abelard
(1079–1142) and
Héloïse (1100/
1101–1163/1164)

formed a new strata within medieval society, the middle class, which introduced new ways of knowing the spiritual and temporal worlds.

The twelfth century not only experienced the renewal of city life but also a reforming and reinvigorated Roman Catholic Church. Under the direction of Pope Gregory VII (r. 1073–1085), the Catholic Church reiterated and enforced moral and ethical standards for the clergy. Building on earlier papal decrees, Gregory banned clerical marriage, required clerical celibacy, prohibited the selling of church offices (simony), and banned lay investiture. In addition, substandard education for priests, coupled with simony, had created an ill-educated clergy ignorant of the liturgical practices of their Church. In 1079, Gregory issued a papal decree ordering all cathedrals and major monasteries to establish schools for the training of clergy.

Three hundred years earlier, Emperor Charlemagne had issued a similar decree with the hope of creating a body of educated people to administer and govern his empire. Building on the church's tradition of educating priests, Charlemagne believed that the church was the appropriate institution for educating boys and creating a pool of educated men, i.e., clerics and priests. Charlemagne's plan was never carried out, but some schools had been established, albeit in isolation to the larger secular world. As a result, the curriculum of the early cathedral schools was designed to train male priests and little more; the formal education of girls was largely ignored. With the renewal of urban life and Gregory's papal reform, cathedral and monastic schools greatly expanded and modified their curriculum to reflect the educational needs and demands of the urban classes and the secular world.

The expansion of education, the reinvigoration of spiritual life, and the practical educational concerns of the new urban elites stimulated interest in Latin texts and new methods of inquiry, scholarship, and learning. In twelfth-century Europe, cathedral schools flourished in many urban centers, and students flocked to the cities to find teachers who could instruct them in law, logic, and the liberal arts. As a result, cities like Paris, Bologna, Reims, Cambridge, and Oxford became centers of education. Gradually secular and ecclesiastical authorities had to address the logistical, organizational, and intellectual challenges that arose from students and teachers gathering in their towns and dioceses and engaging in intellectual inquiry. The bringing together of students and teachers around a monastery or cathedral and then creating formal rules and regulations governing qualifications for instruction, subjects to be taught, standards for instruction and graduation, the relationship between student and teacher, and the makeup of the student body gave rise to the university at the beginning of the thirteenth century.

The rise of the university corresponded with the papal reform movement of the eleventh and twelfth centuries and the papacy's enforcement of clerical celibacy. Emerging from the confluence of these trends at the end of the twelfth century was the creation of scholarly and ecclesiastical cultures that promoted "a spiritual revival that matched in intensity and reach that of early Christianity,"[1] demanded asceticism and celibacy of all clerics and scholars, and banished women from the church hierarchy and the university. When the twelfth century began, it was not clear that this new age and its people would create such cultures. As one scholar has stated, [it was] a "germinal time, pregnant with a thousand possibilities."[2] The fluidity of Europe's social, religious, and cultural institutions meant that a canon of Notre Dame, Fulbert, could ask one of the cathedral school's masters, Peter Abelard, to tutor his brilliant niece, Héloïse, and "advance her education in letters."[3] The intellectual and deeply passionate relationship that resulted between Héloïse and Abelard has been extensively discussed and written about, not only for its tragic romance and brutal consequences but because their lives demonstrate the promise and limits of the new culture of the Catholic Church and learning.

Héloïse was more than a schoolgirl who fell deeply and passionately in love with her tutor. In letters to Abelard after she became an abbess at a convent outside Paris, Héloïse demonstrated an extensive knowledge of classical authors, the works of the early Church Fathers, and issues of faith and moral-

ity and of logic and reasoning. Abelard was more than a brilliant and arrogant scholar who intellectually dismantled all those in his wake and applied the use of logic and reason to questions of faith. His love letters written to Héloïse during their secret affair revealed "his gift for combining his skill in philosophy with a gift for composing and singing songs of love."[4] In her letters to Abelard, Héloïse used Jerome's writings (see Chapter 5) on love and marriage to opine about "the earlier Christian ideal of spiritual and intellectual companionship between men and women"[5] and how she aspired to this ideal.

The story of Abelard and Héloïse relies on a remarkably rich set of sources, some of which are still in dispute. The love letters mentioned above have been subject to a long-running dispute about their authenticity because they come to us unsigned and are copies of the original transcribed sometime in the late fifteenth century. Scholars discovered these copies in the 1970s, but the letters were dismissed as problematic. One scholar concluded that the letters indeed were an exchange between a man and a woman and that they were written during the first half of the twelfth century. Despite obvious clues to the identity of the two authors, the scholar determined only that the two anonymous lovers were "like Abelard

1. David Noble, *A World Without Women: The Christian Clerical Culture of Western Science* (Oxford: Oxford University Press, 1992), p. 136.

2. Ibid., p. 139.

3. Peter Abelard, *Historia calamitatum*, in *The Letters of Abelard and Héloïse*, trans. Betty Radice (London: Penguin Books, 1974), p. 66. All quotations from *Historia calamitatum* are taken from this edition unless otherwise noted.

4. Constant J. Mews, *The Lost Love Letters of Héloïse and Abelard: Perceptions of Dialogue in Twelfth-Century France* (New York: Palgrave, 2001), p. 82.

5. Noble, p. 144.

Chapter 9
The New Culture
of Learning:
Peter Abelard
(1079–1142) and
Héloïse (1100/
1101–1163/1164)

and Héloïse."[6] The most recent and authoritative biography on Abelard published in 1997 concurred with this opinion, and the biographer ignored the existence of the love letters. Some scholars asserted that a woman could not have written love letters since writing about love was essentially a male invention.[7] In addition, other scholars raised doubts about women's participation in the literary culture of twelfth-century France and dismissed the possibility that any woman could have written them. Recent scholarship, however, has argued that female literacy at this time existed, that Héloïse composed and wrote her own letters, and that the lost love letters in dispute are indeed those of Héloïse and Abelard.

Given the dispute over the lost love letters of Héloïse and Abelard, the most important sources for information about their relationship to date are still the letters that they wrote in the 1130s. Sometime after 1132, Abelard wrote an autobiographical letter to a male friend, titled, *Historia calamitatum* or *The Story of His Misfortunes*. In this lengthy letter, Abelard detailed the love affair and its aftermath and presented his life as a moral example. Upon reading a copy of the letter, Héloïse rekindled their correspondence and wrote three lengthy letters to Abelard. In addition, four more of Héloïse's letters from this period survive. Like the love letters of Héloïse and Abelard, their authenticity has been questioned. Some scholars asserted that Abelard or maybe one of his students wrote the letters; others believed the correspondence to be genuine but subject to editing by church officials. Scholars now accept that Héloïse wrote her letters and that the entire correspondence between them was subject to her editing.

Many other sources exist to round out some of Abelard's personal and scholarly dimensions. Abelard's own writings reveal him to be an intellectual combatant willing to question rigorously conflicting opinions found in the Scriptures and the writings of the early Church Fathers and to examine the ethics of intentionality and love. The treatises, *Sic et Non* (*Yes and No*) and *Theologia Christiana* are but two examples of Abelard's intellectually rigorous and controversial approach to questions of faith and doctrine. Other writings by Abelard include treatises, commentaries on the Scriptures, letters, poems, hymns, and sermons. The writings of Abelard's contemporaries, like Bernard of Clairvaux, Peter the Venerable, Fulk of Deuil, and Otto of Freising, reveal Abelard's complexity, his brilliance, ambition, arrogance, stupidity, and piety. Héloïse, on the other hand, has no detractors or admirers to help us uncover her layers of complexity. Instead, we must depend on Héloïse's letter writing to introduce herself to the outside world as an active agent in her society and as a writer and philosopher familiar with classical texts, rhetoric, and logic, capable of sparring with one of the best minds of the twelfth century, Peter Abelard.

6. Mews, pp. 7–8.
7. Ibid.

▨ THE ACTORS:

PETER ABELARD AND HÉLOÏSE

Much of what we know about Abelard's early life and family is from *Historia calamitatum*. He was born in 1079 in La Pallet, Brittany, a town twelve miles to the southeast of Nantes. He was the eldest of five children, four boys and a girl. His father, Berengar, was a minor Breton noble and his mother, Lucie, was also from Brittany. According to Abelard, his father had "some knowledge of letters before he was a soldier" and believed that his sons should have an education before training as knight. Little is known of Abelard's early education, but like other boys of his class and region, he probably received his early schooling, beginning at the age of seven, from a tutor specializing in Latin grammar.

Grammar was one of the first three subjects of the liberal arts, or the trivium. The other two subjects of the trivium were logic and rhetoric. Grammar trained the student to read, write, and speak Latin, the universal language of the European educated classes. Grammar also acquainted students with the Latin writings of or commentaries on classical authors known at the time: Ovid, Virgil, Cicero, Boëthius, Plato, Aristotle, and others. Rhetoric taught the art of public speaking; it served as an introduction to literature and logic and provided a method of demonstrating the truth. Abelard's education probably included "instruction in the elements of faith: the Lord's Prayer, the Apostles' Creed, the 'Athanasian' Creed, selections from Scriptures, and some instruction in the lives of the saint."[8] (Document One). Once the trivium was mastered, able students graduated to study of the four subjects of the *quadrivium*—arithmetic, geometry, astronomy, and music.

Abelard appeared to have easily mastered the trivium and to fall in love with learning and with a method of discovering and defending philosophical or theological truth by means of Aristotelian logic or dialectic (the art of debate). Abelard came of age at a time when renewed interest in Latin commentaries on Aristotle's writings on logic stimulated the application of logic to many different subjects. This method of inquiry took the form of a debate, or "dispute," and involved three basic steps: the posing of a question, arguments for and against answers proposed by earlier classical or religious authorities, and a conclusion that attempted to resolve the conflict. To pursue his new-found passion, Abelard renounced his privileges and inheritance as the firstborn son in favor of one of his younger brothers and began to travel seeking teachers and scholars interested in dialectic.

During the eleventh century, a new class of professional teacher appeared, the peripatetic or wandering master, who moved from place to place and attracted students by his personal magnetism or dialectical acumen. As a young student, Abelard traveled to the best philosophers and dialecticians of the day: Jean Roscelin, a practiced dialectician, and William of Champeaux,

8. D. W. Robertson, Jr., *Abelard and Héloïse* (New York: The Dial Press, 1972), p. 6.

[251]

Chapter 9
The New Culture
of Learning:
Peter Abelard
(1079–1142) and
Héloïse (1100/
1101–1163/1164)

a formidable master and philosopher whose keen intellect attracted many students to Paris. He and later his pupil, Abelard would be largely responsible for the influx of students to the city. Wherever Abelard went, he found himself in conflict with his teachers and often defeated their arguments. In 1102, confident in his abilities, Abelard joined the ranks of the wandering scholars, set up his own school south of Paris, and began teaching the trivium. His fame as a teacher of logic grew, so he moved his school closer to Paris, but his quick success and furious pace caught up with him. Abelard wrote in his history, "I fell ill through overwork and was obliged to return home." He remained in Brittany for about six years.

Once he recovered, Abelard resumed his studies and soon found himself battling his old teacher, William of Champeaux, over the nature of the universal. At stake in this debate already taking place between two philosophical camps, the Realists and Nominalists, was the "true" nature of the individual. William, a Realist, said that the universal was a real thing, an essential aspect within all humans, independent of human will and reason. The universal could be detected in all individuals or things, regardless of their observable differences. The Nominalist position, less popular and argued by Abelard's first teacher, Roscelin, asserted that the universal was merely a name, or *nomen,* that people gave to a category of experience and that each individual or thing was separate and unique. Application of this method of reasoning to questions of theology could lead to heretical po-

sitions. Roscelin was purported to have applied Nominalism to the doctrine of the Trinity. Instead of upholding the belief that the Father, Son, and Holy Ghost are one, "he was thought to have postulated three individual Gods and not one God."[9] The Church banished him briefly for daring to apply logic to questions of theology. Roscelin's inquiries foreshadowed the emergence of scholasticism, the philosophical and intellectual movement of the twelfth and thirteenth centuries that sought to explain and clarify theological doctrines by subjecting them to logical analysis. Abelard became one of this movement's finest practitioners.

Abelard proved his abilities as a logician in his dispute with William. Abelard bragged about dismantling his teacher's arguments. He wrote, ". . . [I]n the course of our philosophic disputes I produced a sequence of clear logical arguments to make him amend, or rather abandon, his previous attitude to universals." As a result of this humiliation, "his [William's] lectures fell into such contempt that he was scarcely accepted on any other points of dialectic. . . ." Abelard's superior display of rhetoric and logic earned him the contempt of William, but it also spurred Abelard to strike out once again on his own. Sometime after 1108, he opened another school. William's former students and others flocked to Abelard's school. His teaching occupied him for some time until his mother summoned him home to Brittany. Like her husband before her, she was preparing to enter religious life.

9. Radice, p. 12.

After attending to familial duties in Brittany, Abelard returned to Paris and decided to become a student of theology. He enrolled in the theology school of Anselm of Laon, who had taught many of France's leading churchmen over the course of thirty years. According to contemporaries, students crowded into the small cathedral town of Laon to study with the most famous master of scriptural studies and "the most brilliant of Gallic luminaries."[10] Abelard did not share this commonly held opinion. He found Anselm's teaching tedious and rudimentary, relying on the traditional technique of picking a selection from the Scriptures, reading it sentence by sentence aloud, and explaining its meaning using glosses or notes to explain a text. In *Historia*, Abelard heaped scorn on Anselm's powers of reasoning and comprehending a text. "[Anselm] owed his reputation more to long practice than to intelligence or memory. . . . He had a remarkable command of words but their meaning was worthless and devoid of all sense [reason]." Trained as he was in debate and dispute, Abelard was disappointed that this great master would revert to quoting a passage or two from one of the earlier church scholars when asked a question and not engage in what Abelard thought was the more disciplined technique of logical argumentation. Abelard's fellow students challenged him to demonstrate this technique and he rose to the challenge, delivering several lectures on

an obscure passage from the Bible using only a gloss and his powers of reason. According to Abelard, these lectures were a great success, and as result Anselm "was wildly jealous" and attacked Abelard for commenting on the Scriptures.

While Abelard interpreted Anselm's response as envy, Abelard's bold and unconventional exegesis (study of Scripture) caused Anselm to worry that Abelard's opinions might be interpreted as his own. After all, Abelard was technically Anselm's student, and church authorities might believe these commentaries to belong to the teacher. Anselm forbade his student from teaching and with this prohibition, Abelard went to Paris to take up a post teaching philosophy and religion at the cathedral school at Notre Dame. He was appointed *magister scholarum* at Notre Dame and brought into the chapter as a canon. Abelard represented this episode as an entitlement for his brilliance and as a triumph against his rivals, especially his former teacher, William of Champeaux. "A few days after this [prohibition from teaching at Laon] I returned to Paris, to the school which had long ago been intended for and offered to me, and from which I had been expelled at the start." For several years, most likely between 1114 and 1117, Abelard's life at the school was very successful. He increased "enormously" the number of students in the school who were "gathered there eager for instruction in both subjects." His success translated not only into fame but into fortune.

Abelard occupied a privileged position in late medieval society. Men

10. John of Salisbury, quoted in Regine Pernoud, *Héloïse and Abelard* (New York: Stein and Day, 1973), p. 34.

[253]

Chapter 9
The New Culture
of Learning:
Peter Abelard
(1079–1142) and
Héloïse (1100/
1101–1163/1164)

who were literate and dedicated to scholarly pursuits were referred to as clerics and were not necessarily members of the clergy or church hierarchy. Because education took place within the confines of monastic or cathedral schools, masters, students, and scholars were expected to live like monks, practicing celibacy and isolating themselves from ordinary pursuits. Their status was symbolized by appearance. Masters and students alike were tonsured (the tops of their heads were shaved) and wore clothing similar to that of monks. While there was an expectation of celibacy for both scholars and clergy, clerical celibacy was not yet strictly enforced at the beginning of the twelfth century. As a result, women, wives, mistresses, or children of clerical officials were often found living in the church or cathedral cloisters.[11] For this reason, a young woman, Héloïse, the niece of Fulbert, one of the canons of the cathedral of Notre Dame, could live with her uncle within the cathedral close of Notre Dame.

We first meet Héloïse through Abelard's description of her in his *Historia*. "There was in Paris at the time a young girl named Héloïse, the niece of Fulbert, one of the canons, and so much loved by him that he had done everything in his power to advance her education." Little is known about her parents, her birth, or her childhood. It is believed that she was born in Paris into a family with a privileged background. Her mother was identified as Hersende; her father's identity was unknown. Fulbert appeared to be

her maternal uncle. Speculation persisted that Fulbert was her father or that her father was one of the other canons at Notre Dame. Direct evidence does not exist for either position. She appears to have been placed under the guardianship of her uncle at an early age, and in turn, he placed Héloïse under the care of the sisters at the Benedictine convent at Argenteuil, a richly endowed convent with manor houses, lands, vineyards, and fishponds. It possessed a reputation for learning, and Héloïse received her early education at the convent.

Well-endowed convents like Argenteuil offered women opportunities that did not exist for them outside the cloister. Convents offered protection for women and their property, and also intellectual development and sometimes political power. Affluent convents sometimes housed great libraries and, like their counterparts for males, contributed to the production of illuminated manuscripts. The Benedictine abbess, Hildegard of Bingen (1098–1179), was an author, composer, physician, and consultant to popes and kings. However, Hildegard's education showed the limitations of the education offered at the convent schools. She had had rather rudimentary schooling, her command of Latin remained "uncertain," and she had no specialist training in philosophy or theology.[12] This was often the case for most male clerics who completed only the trivium. By the twelfth century, however, male clerics in the higher

---

11. M. T. Clanchy, *Abelard* (Oxford: Blackwell, 1999), p. 45.

12. Peter Dronke, *Women Writers of the Middle Ages* (Cambridge: Cambridge University Press, 1984), pp. 148–149.

orders of the church had had the opportunity to study philosophy and theology at the cathedral schools. This opportunity was not available for women.

Education for girls from elite families usually consisted of learning to read the Psalms, the Scriptures, and secular authorities appropriate for learning grammar. At the beginning of the twelfth century, some elite women were not only reading their prayer books but were beginning to read romances in their private chambers, and "great ladies were patrons of literature."[13] Writing was not a skill often emphasized in a young girl's education, and earlier speculation on Héloïse's writing denied that she had had the necessary training to write lengthy, erudite, and learned letters. Peter the Venerable, abbot of the Cluny monastery, however, testified to Héloïse's abilities in 1142 when he wrote to her detailing the last years of Abelard's life: "At a time when nearly the whole world is indifferent and deplorably apathetic towards such occupations [the study of the liberal arts], and wisdom can scarcely find a foothold not only, I may say, among the women who have banished her completely, but even in the minds of men, you have surpassed all women in carrying out your purpose, and have gone further than almost every man."[14] Most women who attained privileged positions within the clerical orders, like Hildegard of Bingen, had attained them because of reputa-

tions as mystics or as prophetesses sanctioned by the pope and not because of their scholarly abilities.[15]

Héloïse showed her abilities at an early age, excelling at the trivium, quoting with ease from the Church Fathers and Latin authors, and wishing to pursue the study of theology. Typically, such interests led a young woman to enter a religious order, but a few laywomen were now taking advantage of that brief moment during the twelfth century when the social, intellectual, and cultural norms were in flux to pursue philosophical and theological studies. Héloïse was one such woman, and when her intellectual needs surpassed the abilities of her teachers at Argenteuil, her uncle decided that she should be tutored by the scholars at the cathedral school of Notre Dame. In 1116 or 1117, Héloïse came to live with her uncle.

The cathedral of Notre Dame dominated the landscape of Paris in the twelfth century. Its school was becoming the center of intellectual life in Paris because of the reputation of its masters, especially Abelard. Built on the Ile de la Cité, the island in the Seine that was the original site of Paris, the cathedral symbolized the role that ecclesiastical authority played in the lives of the medieval French. Presiding over the educational activities of the students and scholars in residence at the cathedral school was the archbishop's executive secretary, the chancellor. On the island were several small houses for members of the cathedral hierarchy, including the house of Canon Fulbert, as well as churches and

13. Ibid., p. 44.

14. Peter the Venerable, "Letter to Héloïse," in Radice, pp. 277–278.

15. Noble, p. 141.

Chapter 9
The New Culture
of Learning:
Peter Abelard
(1079–1142) and
Héloïse (1100/
1101–1163/1164)

chapels, cloisters and schoolhouses, gardens and private residences. This area enjoyed a considerable amount of autonomy; no crown officials were allowed. Héloïse's presence in this intellectual world was highly unusual but appeared to be accepted given her reputation as the most learned woman in France, even before her lessons with Abelard started.

■ ACT I:

THE LOVERS

Fulbert's motives for educating his niece, the reasons for asking Abelard to tutor her, and the circumstances under which Abelard accepted and chose to live in Fulbert's house are known to us only through Abelard's words. He claimed that Fulbert was consumed by vanity concerning his niece's talent. Having the most distinguished philosopher of the day teach his niece reflected positively on him. Abelard also claimed that when he offered to live in Fulbert's house and pay rent, Fulbert readily accepted because of greed. Why Abelard chose to involve himself with the talented and brilliant young woman had less to do with her abilities and more with his ego. He claimed that he set out from the beginning to seduce her and that she was powerless to resist such advances (Document Two).

No sources exist beyond Abelard's autobiography, but scholarly speculation asserts that Abelard accepted the position as a way of ingratiating himself with Fulbert and his fellow canons. While being appointed a master of the school, Abelard had not yet gained the other privileges awarded to a cleric of his standing. Perhaps Abelard believed that it was simply a matter of time before he was appointed chancellor or archdeacon and that tutoring Fulbert's niece was mutually advantageous for both of them. Having observed Abelard's coolness, dedication to scholarship, and success, Fulbert had no reason to believe that Abelard would seduce his niece. "If these were the circumstances, seducing Héloïse was the most imprudent thing he could have done."[16] What Héloïse thought of this arrangement is unknown, and Abelard did not comment in *Historia* on Héloïse's opinions about it.

Abelard began tutoring Héloïse in 1116 or 1117, and he describes their sessions as follows: "more words of love than of our reading passed between us, and more kissing than teaching." He then detailed how they abandoned their books for sexual pleasure, how he lost interest in his lectures and was inspired only to compose love songs to her. In a letter written to him after she read *Historia calamitatum*, she mentioned how he had inundated her with letters during their affair. His letters and her letters in response, numbering 113, provide a fuller view of their year-long affair—their love, friendship, and intellectual respect for each other. In her love letters, Héloïse demonstrated her facility with biblical allusions and her knowledge of the works

16. Clanchy, pp. 74 and 151.

of Ovid, Virgil, Horace, Cicero, Jerome, and Boethius, along with lesser known and contemporary authors (Document Three). Abelard's love letters revise the perception of him as a cold-blooded seducer, who years later recalled his behavior and his infatuation with Héloïse as shameful aberrations from his formerly chaste life as a philosopher. In the letters during their affair, Abelard is revealed to be a committed and sincere lover (Document Four). In some of his letters, however, Abelard still struggled over the sinful nature of their relationship. The letters stopped just after their affair was discovered by Héloïse's uncle.

Fulbert appeared to be the last one in the community to realize what had happened between Abelard and Héloïse. Fulbert expelled Abelard from his house and forbade him to see Héloïse. Abelard wrote that they met clandestinely and exchanged letters when possible. He reported that he learned Héloïse was pregnant when she wrote a letter to him "rejoicing" about her pregnancy and "to ask what I thought she should do." Abelard responded by arranging for her to travel to his sister's in Brittany disguised as a nun. Soon after her arrival, she gave birth to a boy and baptized him Peter Astralabe, an odd choice for a surname since an astrolabe was a astronomical instrument used to observe the stars. Young Peter was raised by his aunt and years later pursued an ecclesiastical career.

When Fulbert discovered that his niece was missing, he was furious and insisted that Abelard marry her. Abelard agreed, but only on the condition that the marriage remain secret to protect his standing as a scholar. When he went to Brittany to inform Héloïse of his decision, she rejected his proposal, arguing that Fulbert would not be satisfied with a secret marriage and that Peter was too great a scholar and his societal position too dignified to be sullied by the "constant muddle and squalor which small children bring into the home." Héloïse's objections were supported by the climate of the times and the writings of classical and Christian authorities. As master in the cathedral school of Notre Dame, Abelard was expected to set an example for students and clerics alike by remaining celibate and "exclusively dedicated to his clerical vocation." Secular clerics like Abelard were frequently suspected of sexual impropriety and immorality. His marriage to Héloïse all but admitted that Abelard had lapsed and had been consumed by lust and temporal concerns. Such lapses threatened his current position and future prospects within the church hierarchy.

As the niece of a canon, Héloïse understood the sacrifice Abelard would make by marrying her. She objected to his proposal of marriage on the grounds that it would damage his scholarship, and she framed her arguments using examples and ideas from Socrates, Seneca, Saint Paul, and Saint Jerome, all of whom in similar conclusions argued that "the would-be philosopher or cleric must hold himself aloof from all else—whether honors, engagements, or marriage."[17] According to Abelard and then ex-

17. Elizabeth Hamilton, *Héloïse* (New York: Doubleday and Company, Inc., 1967), p. 46.

Chapter 9
The New Culture
of Learning:
Peter Abelard
(1079–1142) and
Héloïse (1100/
1101–1163/1164)

plained more fully in Héloïse's first letter to Abelard in the 1130s, Héloïse argued that she loved him too much and would not be responsible for burdening him with worldly obligations (Document Five). In her writings, she articulated a love between a man and a woman that was based on friendship, "one which combines both *amor,* passionate love, and *dilectio,* a love that actively esteems another person."[18] Héloïse desired a relationship not based on a social convention like marriage, but "a true love that is known to God."[19] Such views emanated from Saint Jerome, who argued for spiritual marriages. Despite her protestations, they secretly married in 1117 or 1118 in a ceremony witnessed by her uncle and a few of his friends and immediately separated.

Héloïse predicted correctly that her uncle would not be content with a secret marriage and word soon leaked out about the marriage of Abelard and Héloïse. Héloïse refused to acknowledge their union and her uncle "heaped abuse on her on several occasions."

Reacting to the situation, Abelard removed Héloïse from her uncle's house; found refuge for her at the convent of her childhood, Argenteuil; and persuaded her to wear the order's religious habit. Fulbert assumed that Abelard wished to dissolve the marriage. Coming on the heels of Héloïse's assertions that she was not Abelard's wife, Fulbert became furious with Abelard and plotted to castrate the man who had brought shame and embarrassment to his family. Abelard described the act of revenge: ". . . [O]ne night as I slept peacefully in the inner room in my lodgings, they bribed one of my servants to admit them and there took cruel vengeance on me of such appalling barbarity as to shock the whole world; they cut off the parts of my body whereby I had committed the wrong of which they complained." His castration was a public humiliation and he insisted that both he and Héloïse enter religious life, she at Argenteuil, he at the monastery at Saint Denis to become a Benedectine monk.

■ ACT II:

THE MONK AND THE NUN

While Abelard's castration and subsequent retreat to Saint Denis ended one phase of his career, it provided him with new opportunities to reshape his intellectual and spiritual life. In the years after his castration, Abelard published all of his major treatises on

theology and philosophy, and after a short while, he resumed teaching. Abelard's loss of his first position as a teacher and his subsequent choice of monastery (which was close to Paris, supported by the inner circle of the royal court, and in possession of an excellent library) enabled him to study the sources of the Christian tradition, both classical authors and early Church Fathers, and to work out a method of discussing Christian faith through philosophical argument. His

18. Mews, p. 84.
19. Ibid.

first treatise was a discussion of the Trinity using dialectical analysis. Abelard claimed that he wrote *On the Unity and Trinity of God* "for the use of my students who were asking for human and logical reasons on this subject. . . . After the treatise had been seen and read by many people it began to please everyone, as it seemed to answer all questions alike on this subject." Not everyone embraced this treatise. A provincial church council in 1121, the Council of Soissons (according to Abelard, convened by his rivals), condemned the book and burned it because of its lack of reference to the Church Fathers.

Abelard was temporarily confined and then allowed to return to Saint Denis. His return was brief, however. He was not only looked on suspiciously by his fellow monks, but he had earned their enmity during his four years with them. Abelard did not refrain from telling them and their abbot, "frequently and vehemently," how morally lax and materially corrupt they were. Such criticisms, which he duly recorded in *Historia*, were intended to bring attention to Abelard's desire to hold to an ideal of the monk as one engaged in a solitary, intellectual, and spiritual search for God. "He entered into monastic life with the same competitive and critical spirit he had shown in the schools. . . . Just as he thought himself 'the only philosopher in the world' when he headed the Paris schools, so now he was the only true monk."[20] Unfortunately for Abelard, even as a monk, he continued

to offend. In an episode shortly after his return, Abelard insulted the memory of Saint Denis, and the monks asked their abbot to punish him. Fearing for his life, Abelard fled and found refuge at another monastery whose abbot "had long been my close friend and loved me dearly." Eventually, Abelard was released from his obligations to the monastery of Saint Denis and promised that he would withdraw to a place of solitude and not join any other abbey.[21]

In 1122, Abelard retired to a small piece of land in the territory of Troyes, given to him by the local bishop. There he built a modest place of prayer and contemplation and dedicated it in the name of the Holy Trinity. Even the choice of a name for his chapel drew the ire of church authorities, who found it unsuitable, and Abelard renamed it the Paraclete (the Comforter, i.e, the Holy Spirit). Once his whereabouts were discovered, "students began to gather there from all parts, hurrying from cities and towns to inhabit the wilderness. . . ."

His three years at the Paraclete (1122–1125) were productive years for Abelard because he refined his arguments concerning the Trinity and drafted his second major treatise, *Theologia Christiana* (*Christian Theology*). In addition, Abelard wrote a response to those who criticized him for not being concerned with the writings of the Church Fathers. He also wished to prove that some logical analysis of the contradictions among them was needed. This work, *Sic et Non* (*Yes and*

20. Clanchy, p. 201.

21. Ibid., p. 237.

Chapter 9
The New Culture
of Learning:
Peter Abelard
(1079–1142) and
Héloïse (1100/
1101–1163/1164)

No) not only demonstrated Abelard's almost encyclopedic knowledge of patristic writing but his daring as well (Document Six). In this book, Abelard listed several topics for discussion and then listed authorities for each one. What was daring about this method was that the authorities he listed did not agree on the topics. He did not want to cast aspersions on the authorities but intended to stir up discussion among his students and force them to use dialectical analysis to reconcile the contradictions.

By the middle of the 1120s, Abelard's reputation as a scholar and teacher had been restored, even if his writings and teachings were troublesome to the church. In 1125, Abelard accepted the position as abbot of Saint Gildas, a monastery in his native country. In medieval society, abbots were among the most admired and influential. They spent much of their time outside their monasteries, spreading God's word to the rich and powerful, who were their patrons and protectors.[22] As abbot of Saint Gildas, Abelard kept the company of such men and traveled to manor houses, the count of Nantes' court, and gatherings of the church's elite. However, his tenure as abbot of Saint Gildas was short-lived. Abelard described a monastery short on funds, beset by moral corruption and material concerns, and unwilling to submit to his discipline. He wrote, "The monks beset me with demands for their daily needs, though there was no common allowance for me to

distribute, but each one of them provided for himself, his concubine and his sons and daughters from his own purse. . . . they also stole and carried off what they could, so that when I reached the end of my resources I should be forced to abandon my attempt at enforcing discipline or leave them altogether." By the early 1130s, Abelard had been released from his duties at Saint Gildas by his bishop, after accusations by Abelard that the monks there had tried to poison him. He was allowed to retain his rank of abbot and return to France to resume his teaching.

While Abelard spent the decade after his separation from Héloïse pursuing personal ambitions, participating in the intellectual and spiritual ferment of the time, and experiencing "misfortune" wherever he went, Héloïse remained at the convent of Argenteuil, living quietly and becoming prioress of her community. She had not entered the convent voluntarily. In her first letter to Abelard in the 1130s, she reminded him that it was his decision alone that they should both enter religious orders. She wrote, "[I]t was not any sense of vocation which brought me as a young girl to accept the austerities of the cloister, but your bidding alone."[23]

Little is known about her life at Argenteuil. Abelard makes a passing reference that she was an excellent prioress, but he concerns himself with

22. Ibid., p. 247.

23. Radice, *The Letters of Abelard and Héloïse*, p. 116. All quotations from the letters of Abelard and Héloïse are taken from this edition unless otherwise noted.

her story only when she and her nuns were expelled from Argenteuil by the abbot of Saint Denis, Suger, in 1129. Abbot Suger claimed that Argenteuil had been granted to the monastery of Saint Denis by an ancient charter and that the nuns there were immoral. The papal legate sent to investigate concluded that the nuns were "polluting all the neighborhood of the place by their foul and debauched way of life."[24] Similar reports were being filed about other convents that were coveted by monasteries. In fact, Suger most likely wanted Argenteuil because it gave him a valuable port on the Seine.

The expulsion of Héloïse and her nuns from Argenteuil presented Abelard with an opportunity to leave his miserable situation at Saint Gildas and help himself, his wife, and her nuns. He offered them the Paraclete, believing that "this was an opportunity sent me by the Lord for providing for my oratory, and so I returned and invited her [Héloïse], along with some other nuns from the same convent who would not leave her, to come to the Paraclete; and once they had gathered there, I handed it over to them as a gift." This meeting was the first between husband and wife in ten years, and with his help, Héloïse and her nuns established their religious community, despite early difficulties and setbacks. Based on his account, Abelard, as founder of the Paraclete and its patron, returned to the convent on different occasions. He claimed that his visits provoked a reaction

from his critics. "This provoked malicious insinuations, . . . [saying] I was still a slave to the pleasures of carnal desire and could rarely or never bear the absence of the woman I had once loved." Despite this criticism, Abelard continued to be involved in shaping the community. But it was Héloïse who won support from bishops, abbots, and lay people for the Order's founding and continuation.

Héloïse's attitudes about her religious vocation and her concerns and activities as abbess of the Paraclete are known to us through the correspondence that she and Abelard exchanged periodically during the 1130s. Her first letter to Abelard, in response to *Historia calamitatum,* reproached him for offering comfort and consolation to a male friend and not to her (Document Seven). She reminded him that her love for him was pure and not concerned with any personal gain or pleasure and that all she wanted from him was recognition of this pure love and comfort for her suffering.[25] Abelard responded rather coolly that she had proven herself so pious and devote that he did not think it was necessary to comfort her. The respectful but distant tone of his letter demonstrated his discomfort with remembrances of his past, especially the nature of their love. In response to his apology and rebuke, Héloïse wrote even more forcefully about her unhappiness and discontent with their circumstances and her religious life. "Of all the wretched women I am the most wretched and amongst the unhappy I

24. Mews, p. 155.

25. Ibid., p. 34.

Chapter 9
The New Culture
of Learning:
Peter Abelard
(1079–1142) and
Héloïse (1100/
1101–1163/1164)

am the unhappiest. The higher I was exalted when you preferred me to all other women, the greater my suffering over my own fall and yours, when I was flung down; for the higher the ascent, the heavier the fall." She claimed that her piety reflected nothing of the inner anguish because she could not forget the pleasures that they had enjoyed in the past and how she had lived her life in devotion to him and not to God.

The harshness of Héloïse's words in her second letter to him provoked a stronger response from Abelard, who condemned Héloïse for drudging up the "old perpetual complaint against God concerning the manner of our entry into religious life and the cruelty of the act of treachery performed on me." In addition, he argued that their previous relationship had been based on debauchery and deceit and that their physical desire was something that should be left in the past. Their love had been nothing except a self-indulgence.[26] This view of their relationship was contrary to that of Héloïse's. She had argued that their relationship was pure and a mutual profession of love, and not an illicit sexual encounter. She lamented the fact that their relationship and love could not be more like Paula's and Jerome's.

Héloïse's last known letter to Abelard respected her husband's wishes to stop bringing up the past. She wrote, "I would not want to give you cause for finding me disobedient in anything, so I have set the bridle of your injunction on the words which

issue from my unbounded grief." In this letter, she moved away from matters of the heart and asked Abelard, as their founder and patron, to explain "how the order of nuns began and what authority there is for our profession" and to "prescribe some Rule for us and write it down." This request reflected Héloïse's belief that the Benedictine rule, under which she and her nuns lived, did not address women's needs. She wanted Abelard to create a monastic rule adapted for women. In two long letters to his wife (in which obviously he felt more comfortable writing to her on a spiritual level), he supplied a treatise on women's religious life based on examples from both Scripture and classical antiquity and a rule for the Paraclete.[27] In addition to these replies, Abelard responded to another request by Héloïse to resolve forty-two questions on problematic scriptural texts and to write sermons, prayers, and hymns for the nuns. Héloïse's reply to these writings are not known; her responses, which would have been in the possession of Abelard, were probably lost.

Héloïse and the Paraclete not only attracted the attention of Abelard. She forged close ties with Bernard, abbot of the Cistercian monastery at Clairvaux; Matilda, countess of Blois and Champagne; and Peter the Venerable, abbot of the Cluny monastery. Like abbots, abbesses had to win the favor and patronage of the powerful and wealthy, and Héloïse proved particularly adept at this task. The Order of the Paraclete thrived under Héloïse's

26. Ibid., pp. 36—37.

27. Ibid.

direction and its ideals of study, simplicity, and the primacy of intention in distinguishing between right and wrong behavior. Abelard advocated that the order should imitate the example of the holy women around Jerome: "you can at least in your love and study of sacred Scriptures model yourselves on those blessed disciples of St. Jerome, Paula, and Eustochium. . . ." Did this assertion mean that he and Héloïse should live in spiritual marriage, as Jerome and Paula did? In a salutation to her, his thoughts were revealed when he greeted her thus, "once dear to me in the world, now dearest in Christ, once in flesh my wife; now in the spirit my sister and in profession of sacred purpose my consort."[28] Perhaps Abelard finally found a "relationship that was acceptable to him." Whether or not this relationship was acceptable to Héloïse will never be known.

▧ FINALE

Abelard's writings for Héloïse and the Order of the Paraclete were only part of his work during the 1130s. Released from his duties at Saint Gildas, Abelard returned to Paris and resumed his teaching and writing, much of which advocated the primacy of dialectics for understanding theology. Some in the church, like the Cistercian abbot, Bernard of Clairvaux, were horrified at Abelard's methods. His critics argued that when faith was the guiding principle, one did not look for or find inconsistency. Bernard represented those in the church who embraced faith above reason. When Abelard was accused of and then condemned for heresy at the Council of Sens in 1140, it was Bernard who had denounced Abelard and his teachings to the pope (Document Eight). After his condemnation, Abelard was given refuge by Bernard's rival, Peter the Venerable, at the monastery at Cluny, where he died in 1142. His confession of faith, was addressed to Héloïse and not to God. He was buried at the Paraclete.

Héloïse died about twenty years later in 1163 or 1164. In the years before her death, she built the Paraclete into one of the most affluent and successful religious institutions of its time. She was much admired for her piety and religiosity by her contemporaries. Peter the Venerable, in the letter of consolation to her after Abelard's death, was "delighted by your [Héloïse's] renowned learning, and far more because I am drawn to you by what many have told me about your religion." He lamented the fact that she was not of the Cluniac order.

Despite her renown and her brilliance, Héloïse would belong to one of the last generations of educated women who maintained close literary contact with male colleagues. In France and elsewhere, the time was approaching when growing reserve toward interaction between men and women in religious life, mounting pressure on the clergy to give up their ecclesiastical positions or their female households, and increasing suspicion toward

28. Clanchy, p. 259.

Chapter 9
The New Culture
of Learning:
Peter Abelard
(1079–1142) and
Héloïse (1100/
1101–1163/1164)

religious communities that embraced both men and women converged with the new culture of learning that had developed within the cathedral and monastic enclosures. By midcentury, all clerics had to accept monastic discipline. With the exception of maids or prostitutes, women were banned from ecclesiastical enclosures. A world without women within the community of scholars had now been created because "students, masters, and other clerics were gradually prohibited from engaging in intellectual intercourse with women of their own class."[29]

The story of Abelard and Héloïse "dramatically delineated the boundaries of this new ecclesiastical culture of learning" and sent a message to those wayward clerics who dared to associate with women.[30] Abelard was punished and he suffered for his transgressions, but it was Héloïse who bore most of the burden. As a now spiritually and physically chaste monk, Abelard resumed his intellectual life and even returned to Paris. By all accounts Héloïse was as brilliant as Abelard, but she was silenced and denied access to this new world of scholarship. According to Abelard's biographer, the real impact of their relationship on European culture was that "the silencing of Héloïse was a prelude to the silencing of academic women as a class for the next eight centuries."[31]

▣ QUESTIONS

1. Why did Abelard title his autobiographical letter, *The Story of His Misfortunes?* Why did he write this letter? What are the potential problems of using an autobiographical letter as a historical source?

2. Why were scholars reluctant to use the "lost love letters" of Abelard and Héloïse? How would the use of these letters influence the story about them?

3. What were Abelard's and Héloïse's attitudes toward marriage. Why did Héloïse argue against marriage? On whose authority did she base her arguments? What were Abelard's views on their marriage after his castration and humiliation?

4. What were the subjects and method of inquiry taught at the cathedral schools? Why was this curriculum controversial? What was Abelard's role in the debate about scholarly inquiry and theology?

5. What were the positions of men and women in the new culture of learning at the beginning of the twelfth century? Who had the final say about what was taught and who was taught in the universities? Why were women excluded from universities by the thirteenth century?

30. Noble, p. 144.

29. Ibid., p. 46.

31. Clanchy, p. 196.

■ **DOCUMENTS**

DOCUMENT ONE

JOHN OF SALISBURY

On the Taught Classical Authors, *Metalogicon*
(1159)

John of Salisbury (1115–1180) was a secretary at the papal court during the middle of the twelfth century. During the 1130s, he had been a student of Peter Abelard's, and his Metalogicon *included a memoir of his student days. In the passage below, John described elementary instruction in the trivium by an early master of the twelfth century, Bernard of Chartres. What are the necessary steps to becoming a learned individual?*

. . . Grammatical figures, rhetorical embellishments, the cavils of sophistry, and the bearings of the passage assigned for reading upon other disciplines he set forth as he went along, not however trying to teach everything at once but dispensing gradually a measured amount of learning according to the capacity of his hearers. . . . And because memory is strengthened and talent is sharpened by exercise, he urged some by admonitions to imitate what they heard and others by blows and penalties. Each was obliged to review on the following day something of what he had heard on the preceding day, some more, others less; for the day after was with them the disciple of the day before. The evening exercise, which was called *declinatio,* was so stuffed with grammar that if anyone took it for a full year, unless he was duller than the average, he would have in hand the principles of speaking and writing and could not remain ignorant of the meaning of words that are in common use.

But since neither school nor any day should be without religion, such material was set before them as would edify faith and morals, and by which those who had assembled, as if for some collation, should be stimulated to good deeds. So the last part of this *declinatio,* or rather philosophical collation, preferred the paths of piety and commended the souls of the dead to their Redeemer by devout repetition of the sixth Psalm in the Penitentials and the Lord's Prayer. As for the boys' preceding exercises, he assigned poets or orators whom they should imitate in prose or poems, bidding them follow in their footsteps, and he showed how to join statements together and how to end them elegantly. If anyone to improve his own work sewed on foreign cloth, he would call attention to the theft but usually would inflict no punishment. Rather if the inept composition merited this, he would with gracious indulgence order and make the person who had been thus detected set to work imitating authors, so that he who imitated the men of the past might come to deserve the imitation of

Chapter 9
The New Culture
of Learning:
Peter Abelard
(1079–1142) and
Héloïse (1100/
1101–1163/1164)

posterity. This, too, he taught among the first rudiments and fixed in their minds, what virtue there is in economy, what in the adornment of things, what words are praiseworthy; when speech should be bare and, as it were, lean; when abundant, when fulsome, when moderate in all respects. He advised them to read over histories and poems carefully, not as if impelled by spurs to flight; and he was always demanding that from each reading one should daily commit something to memory. Yet he said to avoid what was superfluous and that the writings of illustrious authors were sufficient, since "to busy oneself with what any worthless man has ever written is either too wretched a task or a matter of empty boasting, and detains and wastes ability that might better be occupied otherwise. . . .

DOCUMENT TWO

PETER ABELARD

Description of His Love Affair with Héloïse
Historia calamitatum:
The Story of His Misfortunes

The excerpts below describe Abelard's seduction of and affair with Héloïse. Why does Abelard represent their meeting as a seduction? How does he portray Héloïse's actions?

. . . There was in Paris at the time a young girl named Heloise, the niece of Fulbert, one of the canons, and so much loved by him that he had done everything in his power to advance her education in letters. In looks she did not rank lowest, while in the extent of her learning she stood supreme. A gift for letters is so rare in women that it added greatly to her charm and had won her renown throughout the realm. I considered all the usual attractions for a lover and decided she was the one to bring to my bed, confident that I should have an easy success; for at that time I had youth and exceptional good looks as well as my great reputation to recommend me, and feared no rebuff from any woman I might choose to honour with my love. Knowing the girl's knowledge and love of letters I thought she would be all the more ready to consent, and that even when separated we could enjoy each other's presence by exchange of written messages in which we could speak more openly than in person, and so need never lack the pleasures of conversation.

All on fire with desire for this girl I sought an opportunity of getting to know her through private daily meetings and so more easily winning her over; and with this end in view I came to an arrangement with her uncle, with the help of some of his friends, whereby he should take me into his house, which was very near my school, for whatever sum he liked to ask. . . .

. . . We were united, first under one roof, then in heart; and so with our lessons as a pretext we abandoned ourselves entirely to love. Her studies allowed us to withdraw in private, as love desired, and then with our books open before us, more words of love than of our reading passed between us, and more kissing than teaching. My hands strayed oftener to her bosom than to the pages; love drew our eyes to look on each other more than reading kept them on our texts. To avert suspicion I sometimes struck her, but these blows were prompted by love and tender feeling rather than anger and irritation, and were sweeter than any balm could be.* In short, our desires left no stage of love-making untried, and if love could devise something new, we welcomed it. We entered on each joy the more eagerly for our previous inexperience, and were the less easily sated. . . .

[Abelard described their separation following Fulbert's discovery of the affair.] Separation drew our hearts still closer while frustration inflamed our passion even more; then we became more abandoned as we lost all sense of shame and, indeed, shame diminished as we found more opportunities for love-making. And so we were caught in the act as the poet says happened to Mars and Venus. Soon afterwards the girl found that she was pregnant, and immediately wrote me a letter full of rejoicing to ask what I thought she should do. One night then, when her uncle was away from home, I removed her secretly from his house, as we had planned, and sent her straight to my own country. There she stayed with my sister until she gave birth to a boy, whom she called Astralabe. . . .

DOCUMENT THREE

Héloïse

Lost Love Letters, Letter 49

In her response to Abelard's portrayal of their lustful relationship in the Historia calamitatum, *Héloïse accused him of leaving out her arguments about how she preferred "love to marriage, freedom to chains." She had articulated her notion of selfless love to Abelard in a letter during their affair. (The designation given to the speaker, man or woman, was added by the monk who transcribed the letters in the fifteenth century. Constant Mews concluded that these letters were written by Héloïse and Abelard.) What is the basis of this love, lust or true friendship? What*

---

*Striking a student for inattentiveness to his/her lessons was not unusual at this time.

Chapter 9
The New Culture
of Learning:
Peter Abelard
(1079–1142) and
Héloïse (1100/
1101–1163/1164)

is the basis of this true friendship? What type of love does she hold in greater esteem?

. . . WOMAN   To the rose that does not wither, blooming with the flower of blessedness, she who loves you above all men: may you grow as you flourish and flourish as you grow.

You know, greatest part of my soul, that many people love each other for many reasons, but no friendship of theirs will be as constant as that which stems from integrity and virtue, and from deep love. For I do not consider the friendship of those who seem to love each other for riches and pleasures to be durable at all, since the very things on which they base their love seem to have no durability. Consequently, when their riches or pleasure runs out, so too at the same time love may fail, since they loved these things not because of each other but each other because of these things.

But my love is united with you by a completely different pact. And the useless burdens of wealth, more conducive to wrongdoing than anything when the thirst for possession begins to glow, did not compel me to love you—only the highest virtue, in which lies the root of all honors and every success. Indeed, it is this virtue which is self-sufficient and in need of nothing else, which restrains passion, keeps desires in check, moderates joys and eradicates sorrows; which provides everything proper, everything pleasing, everything delightful; and than which nothing better can be found. Surely I have discovered in you—and thus I love you—undoubtedly the greatest and most outstanding good of all. Since it is established that this is eternal, it is for me the proof beyond doubt that you will remain in my love for eternity. Therefore believe me, desirable one, that neither wealth, distinctions, nor all the things that devotees of this world lust after, will be able to sever me from love for you. Truly there will never be a day in which I would be able to think of myself and let it pass without thinking of you. Know that I am not concerned by any doubt that I may hope the same thing from you. . . .

DOCUMENT FOUR

PETER ABELARD

Lost Love Letters, Letter 50

In her writings, Héloïse described a love between a man and a woman that was based on friendship, "one which combines both amor, *passionate love, and* dilectio, *a love that actively esteems another person." Abelard struggled, however, over the meaning of their passion and love. What of his love does he reveal in this*

*letter? Compare this letter with his description, in Document Two, of his seduc-
tion of and affair with Héloïse. How might historians reconcile these two views on
the affair?*

. . . MAN To the only disciple of philosophy among all the young women of
our age, the only one on whom fortune has completely bestowed all the gifts of
the manifold virtues, the only attractive one, the only gracious one, he who
through your gift is nourished by the upper air, he who lives only when he is
sure of your favor: may you advance even further—if she who has reached the
summit can advance any further.

. . . I admire your talent, you who discuss the rules of friendship so subtly
that you seem not to have read Tully but to have given those precepts to Tully
himself! Therefore, so that I may come to the reply, if it can rightly be called a
reply when nothing equal is given back, I shall reply in my own manner. What
you say is true, sweetest of all women, that truly such a love does not bind us as
often binds those who seek only their own interests, who make friendship a
source of profit, whose loyalty stands firm or collapses with their fortunes, who
do not consider virtue to be of value for its own sake, who call friendship to account, those who with busy fingers keep count of what they ought to get back,
for whom indeed nothing is sweet without profit.

Truly we have been joined—I would not say by fortune but rather by God—
under a different agreement. I chose you among many thousands because of
your countless virtues: truthfully for no other benefit than that I might rest in
you, or that you might lighten all my troubles, or that of all the good things in
the world only your charm might restore me and make me forget all sorrows.
You are my fill when hungry, my refreshment when thirsty, my rest when
weary, my warmth when cold, my shade when hot, indeed in every storm you
are my most wholesome and true calm.

Perhaps because of some good report you heard about me, you also thought
fit to invite me to make your acquaintance. I am inferior to you in many ways,
or to speak more truthfully, I am inferior in every way, because you surpass me
even where I seemed to surpass you. Your talent, your command of language,
beyond your years and sex, is now beginning to extend itself into manly
strength. What humility, what affability you accord to everyone! What admirable moderation with such dignity! Do not people esteem you more than
everybody else, do they not set you up on high, so that from there you can shine
forth like a lamp and be observed by all?

I believe and confidently assert that there is no mortal, no relative, no friend
whom you would prefer to me, or to speak more boldly, whom you would compare with me. For I am not leaden, I am not a blockhead, I am not so hard-nosed
that I cannot scent acutely where true love exists and who loves me from the
heart. Farewell, you who make me fare well, and in whatever way I stand in
your favor, make me certain, for your favor is my only enjoyment.

[269]

Chapter 9
The New Culture
of Learning:
Peter Abelard
(1079–1142) and
Héloïse (1100/
1101–1163/1164)

━━━━━━━━━━━━ **DOCUMENT FIVE** ━━━━━━━━━━━━

PETER ABELARD

Héloïse argues against marriage
Historia calamitatum: Abelard to a Friend:
The Story of His Misfortunes

In the excerpt below, Abelard presented Héloïse's arguments against marriage. According to Héloïse, why shouldn't a philosopher marry? Why does she prefer the designation of mistress to that of wife?

. . . But if I would accept neither the advice of the Apostle nor the exhortations of the Fathers on the heavy yoke of marriage, at least, she [Héloïse] argued, I could listen to the philosophers, and pay regard to what had been written by them or concerning them on this subject—as for the most part the Fathers too have carefully done when they wish to rebuke us. For example, St Jerome in the first book of his *Against Jovinian* recalls how Theophrastus sets out in considerable detail the unbearable annoyances of marriage and its endless anxieties, in order to prove by the clearest possible arguments that a man should not take a wife; and he brings his reasoning from the exhortations of the philosophers to this conclusion: 'Can any Christian hear Theophrastus argue in this way without a blush?' In the same book Jerome goes on to say that 'After Cicero had divorced Terentia and was asked by Hirtius to marry his sister he firmly refused to do so, on the grounds that he could not devote his attention to a wife and philosophy alike. He does not simply say "devote attention", but adds "alike", not wishing to do anything which would be a rival to his study of philosophy.'

But apart from the hindrances to such philosophic study, consider, she said, the true conditions for a dignified way of life. What harmony can there be between pupils and nursemaids, desks and cradles, books or tablets and distaffs, pen or stylus and spindles? Who can concentrate on thoughts of Scripture or philosophy and be able to endure babies crying, nurses soothing them with lullabies, and all the noisy coming and going of men and women about the house? Will he put up with the constant muddle and squalor which small children bring into the home? The wealthy can do so, you will say, for their mansions and large houses can provide privacy and, being rich, they do not have to count the cost nor be tormented by daily cares. But philosophers lead a very different life from rich men, and those who are concerned with wealth or are involved in mundane matters will not have time for the claims of Scripture or philosophy. Consequently, the great philosophers of the past have despised the world, not renouncing it so much as escaping from it, and have denied themselves every pleasure so as to find peace in the arms of philosophy alone. The greatest of them, Seneca, gives this advice to Lucilius: 'Philosophy is not a subject for idle moments. We must neglect everything else and concentrate on this, for no time is long enough for it. Put it aside for a moment and you might as well give it up, for once interrupted it will not remain. We must resist all other occupations, not merely dispose of them, but reject them.' . . .

Heloise then went on to the risks I should run in bringing her back, and argued that the name of mistress instead of wife would be dearer to her and more honourable for me—only love freely given should keep me for her, not the constriction of a marriage tie, and if we had to be parted for a time, we should find the joy of being together all the sweeter the rarer our meetings were. But at last she saw that her attempts to persuade or dissuade me were making no impression on my foolish obstinacy, and she could not bear to offend me; so amidst deep sighs and tears she ended in these words: 'We shall both be destroyed. All that is left us is suffering as great as our love has been.' In this, as the whole world knows, she showed herself a true prophet. . . .

DOCUMENT SIX

Peter Abelard

Sic et Non
(ca. 1122)

The excerpt below is the introduction to Abelard's treatise on logic applied to Christian theology. What approach must students use when reading the Church Fathers? Does Abelard advocate dismissing patristic authority and substituting other authorities? Why or why not?

There are many seeming contradictions and even obscurities in the innumerable writings of the church fathers. Our respect for their authority should not stand in the way of an effort on our part to come at the truth. The obscurity and contradictions in ancient writings may be explained upon many grounds, and may be discussed without impugning the good faith and insight of the fathers. A writer may use different terms to mean the same thing, in order to avoid a monotonous repetition of the same word. Common, vague words may be employed in order that the common people may understand; and sometimes a writer sacrifices perfect accuracy in the interest of a clear general statement. Poetical, figurative language is often obscure and vague.

Not infrequently apocryphal works are attributed to the saints. Then, even the best authors often introduce the erroneous views of others and leave the reader

Chapter 9
The New Culture
of Learning:
Peter Abelard
(1079–1142) and
Héloïse (1100/
1101–1163/1164)

to distinguish between the true and the false. Sometime, as Augustine confesses in his own case, the fathers ventured to rely upon the opinions of others.

Doubtless the fathers might err; even Peter, the prince of the apostles, fell into error; what wonder that the saints do not always show themselves inspired? The fathers did not themselves believe that they, or their companions, were always right. Augustine found himself mistaken in some cases and did not hesitate to retract his errors. He warns his admirers not to look upon his letters as they would upon the Scriptures, but to accept only those things which, upon examination, they find to be true.

All writings belonging to this class are to be read with full freedom to criticise, and with no obligation to accept unquestioningly; otherwise the way would be blocked to all discussion, and posterity be deprived of the excellent intellectual exercise of debating difficult questions of language and presentation. But an explicit exception must be made in the case of the Old and New Testaments. In the Scriptures, when anything strikes us as absurd, we may not say that the writer erred, but that the scribe made a blunder in copying the manuscripts, or that there is an error in interpretation, or that the passage is not understood. The fathers make a very careful distinction between the Scriptures and later works. They advocate a discriminating, not to say suspicious, use of the writings of their own contemporaries.

In view of these considerations, I have ventured to bring together various dicta of the holy fathers, as they came to mind, and to formulate certain questions which suggested by the seeming contradictions in the statements. These questions ought to serve to excite tender readers to a zealous inquiry into truth and so sharpen their wits. The master key of knowledge is, indeed, a persistent and frequent questioning. Aristotle, the most clearsighted of all the philosophers, was desirous above all things else to arouse this questioning spirit, for in his *Categories* he exhorts a student as follows: "It may well be difficult to reach a positive conclusion in these matters unless they be frequently discussed. It is by no means fruitless to be doubtful on particular points." By doubting we come to examine, and by examining we reach the truth.

[*Abelard provides arguments for and against 158 different philosophical or theological propositions. The following are a few of the questions he discusses.*]

Should human faith be based upon reason, or no?

Is God one, or no?

Is God a substance, or no?

Does the first Psalm refer to Christ, or no?

Is sin pleasing to God, or no?

Is God the author of evil, or no?

Is God all-powerful, or no?

Can God be resisted, or no?

Has God free will, or no?

Was the first man persuaded to sin by the devil, or no?

Was Adam saved, or no?

Did all the apostles have wives except John, or no?

Are the flesh and blood of Christ in very truth and essence present in the sacrament of the altar, or no?

Do we sometimes sin unwillingly, or no?

Does God punish the same sin both here and in the future, or no?

Is it worse to sin openly than secretly, or no?

DOCUMENT SEVEN

HÉLOÏSE

Letter I. Héloïse to Abelard
(ca. 1132 or 1133)

Héloïse, in her first letter to Abelard after reading Historia calamitatum, *described her interpretation of their affair and her subsequent misfortunes. What are her misfortunes?*

. . . You know, beloved, as the whole world knows, how much I have lost in you, how at one wretched stroke of fortune that supreme act of flagrant treachery robbed me of my very self in robbing me of you; and how my sorrow for my loss is nothing compared with what I feel for the manner in which I lost you. Surely the greater the cause for grief the greater the need for the help of consolation, and this no one can bring but you; you are the sole cause of my sorrow, and you alone can grant me the grace of consolation. You alone have the power to make me sad, to bring me happiness or comfort; you alone have so great a debt to repay me, particularly now when I have carried out all your orders so implicitly that when I was powerless to oppose you in anything, I found strength at your command to destroy myself. I did more, strange to say—my love rose to such heights of madness that it robbed itself of what it most desired beyond hope of recovery, when immediately at your bidding I changed my clothing along with my mind, in order to prove you the sole possessor of my body and my will alike. God knows I never sought anything in you except yourself; I wanted simply you, nothing of yours. I looked for no marriage-bond, no marriage portion, and it was not my own pleasures and wishes I sought to gratify, as you well know, but yours. The name of wife may seem more sacred or more binding, but sweeter for me will always be the word mistress, or, if you

[273]

Chapter 9
The New Culture
of Learning:
Peter Abelard
(1079–1142) and
Héloïse (1100/
1101–1163/1164)

will permit me, that of concubine or whore. I believed that the more I humbled myself on your account, the more gratitude I should win from you, and also the less damage I should do to the brightness of your reputation.

You yourself on your own account did not altogether forget this in the letter of consolation I have spoken of which you wrote to a friend; there you thought fit to set out some of the reasons I gave in trying to dissuade you from binding us together in an ill-starred marriage. But you kept silent about most of my arguments for preferring love to wedlock and freedom to chains. God is my witness that if Augustus, Emperor of the whole world, thought fit to honour me with marriage and conferred all the earth on me to possess for ever, it would be dearer and more honourable to me to be called not his Empress but your whore.

For a man's worth does not rest on his wealth or power; these depend on fortune, but worth on his merits. And a woman should realize that if she marries a rich man more readily than a poor one, and desires her husband more for his possessions than for himself, she is offering herself for sale. Certainly any woman who comes to marry through desires of this kind deserves wages, not gratitude, for clearly her mind is on the man's property, not himself, and she would be ready to prostitute herself to a richer man, if she could. This is evident from the argument put forward in the dialogue of Aeschines Socraticus by the learned Aspasia to Xenophon and his wife. When she had expounded it in an effort to bring about a reconciliation between them, she ended with these words: 'Unless you come to believe that there is no better man nor worthier woman on earth you will always still be looking for what you judge the best thing of all—to be the husband of the best of wives and the wife of the best of husbands.'

These are saintly words which are more than philosophic; indeed, they deserve the name of wisdom, not philosophy. It is a holy error and a blessed delusion between man and wife, when perfect love can keep the ties of marriage unbroken not so much through bodily continence as chastity of spirit. But what error permitted other women, plain truth permitted me, and what they thought of their husbands, the world in general believed, or rather, knew to be true of yourself; so that my love for you was the more genuine for being further removed from error. What king or philosopher could match your fame? What district, town or village did not long to see you? When you appeared in public, who did not hurry to catch a glimpse of you, or crane his neck and strain his eyes to follow your departure? Every wife, every young girl desired you in absence and was on fire in your presence; queens and great ladies envied me my joys and my bed. . . .

Tell me one thing, if you can. Why, after our entry into religion, which was your decision alone, have I been so neglected and forgotten by you that I have neither a word from you when you are here to give me strength nor the consolation of a letter in absence? Tell me, I say, if you can—or I will tell you what I think and indeed the world suspects. It was desire, not affection which bound you to me, the flame of lust rather than love. So when the end came to what you desired, any show of feeling you sued to make went with it. This is not merely my own opinion, beloved, it is everyone's. There is nothing personal or private about it; it is the general view which is widely held. I only wish that it *were* mine alone, and that the love you professed could find someone to defend it and so comfort me in my grief for a while. I wish I could think of some explanation which would excuse you and somehow cover up the way you hold me cheap.

I beg you then to listen to what I ask—you will see that it is a small favour which you can easily grant. While I am denied your presence, give me at least through your words—of which you have enough and to spare—some sweet semblance of yourself. It is no use my hoping for generosity in deeds if you are grudging in words. Up to now I had thought I deserved much of you, seeing that I carried out everything for your sake and continue up to the present moment in complete obedience to you. It was not any sense of vocation which brought me as a young girl to accept the austerities of the cloister, but your bidding alone, and if I deserve no gratitude from you, you may judge for yourself how my labours are in vain. I can expect no reward for this from God, for it is certain that I have done nothing as yet for love of him. When you hurried towards God I followed you, indeed, I went first to take the veil—perhaps you were thinking how Lot's wife turned back when you made me put on the religious habit and take my vows before you gave yourself to God. Your lack of trust in me over this one thing, I confess, overwhelmed me with grief and shame. I would have had no hesitation, God knows, in following you or going ahead at your bidding to the flames of Hell. My heart was not in me but with you, and now, even more, if it is not with you it is nowhere; truly, without you it cannot exist. See that it fares well with you, I beg, as it will if it finds you kind, if you give grace in return for grace, small for great, words for deeds. If only your love had less confidence in me, my dear, so that you would be more concerned on my behalf! But as it is, the more I have made you feel secure in me, the more I have to bear with your neglect.

Remember, I implore you, what I have done, and think how much you owe me. While I enjoyed with you the pleasures of the flesh, many were uncertain whether I was prompted by love or lust; but now the end is proof of the beginning. I have finally denied myself every pleasure in obedience to your will, kept nothing for myself except to prove that now, even more, I am yours. . . .

Chapter 9
The New Culture
of Learning:
Peter Abelard
(1079–1142) and
Héloïse (1100/
1101–1163/1164)

███████████████████ **DOCUMENT EIGHT** ███████████████████

Bernard of Clairvaux

Letters 241 and 249
(1140)

> *Bernard of Clairvaux was Abelard's prosecutor at the council of Sens in 1140. To prosecute his case successfully, he had to elict support from other church leaders, and he wrote a series of letters to them condemning Abelard and his teachings. Extracts from these letters, one addressed to Cardinal Ivo of Saint Victor and the other to Cardinal Haimeric of Castres, are below. Why are Abelard's ideas dangerous? What is Bernard's objection to the teaching of logic for knowing theology?*

Letter 241

To Cardinal Ivo, on the same subject

To his dearest Ivo, by the grace of God Cardinal Priest of the Holy Roman Church, that he may love justice and hate iniquity, from Bernard, styled Abbot of Clairvaux.

Master Peter Abelard is a monk without a rule, a prelate without responsibility. He is neither in order nor of an Order. A man at variance with himself: a Herod within, a John without; a most doubtful character, having nothing of the monk about him except the name and the habit. But this is not my concern. Let each one bear his own burdens. There is another thing which I cannot overlook, a thing which concerns everyone who loves the name of Christ. He speaks iniquity openly. He oversteps the landmarks placed by our Fathers in discussing and writing about faith, the sacraments, and the Holy Trinity; he changes each thing according to his pleasure, adding to it or taking from it. In his books and in his works he shows himself to be a fabricator of falsehood, a coiner of perverse dogmas, proving himself a heretic not so much by his error as by his obstinate defence of error. He is a man who does not know his limitations, making void the virtue of the cross by the cleverness of his words. Nothing in heaven or on earth is hidden from him, except himself

Letter 249

To Cardinal Haimeric

To his most intimate friend, the illustrious Haimeric, Cardinal and Chancellor of the Holy Roman Church, that he may show good things before God and man, from Bernard, Abbot of Clairvaux.

'As we have heard so have we found' the books and maxims of Peter Abelard. I have noted his words and marked his enigmas, and I have found them to be 'mysteries of iniquity'. Our theologian assails law in the words of the law. He casts what is holy before dogs, and pearls before swine. He corrupts the faith of simple people and sullies the purity of the Church. . . .

He has defiled the Church; he has infected with his own blight the minds of simple people. He tries to explore with his reason what the devout mind grasps at once with a vigorous faith. Faith believes, it does not dispute. But this man, apparently holding God suspect, will not believe anything until he has first examined it with reason. . . .

Politics and Sanctity in Fourteenth-Century Europe:
Gregory XI (1330–1378) and Catherine of Siena (1347–1380)

■ SETTING THE STAGE

Life for most people in fourteenth-century Europe was difficult, even disastrous and frightening. Famine in the early decades of the century, plague that struck again and again after midcentury, the Hundred Years' War between England and France, and political instability and conflict in most of the regions of Italy had widespread, harmful effects. It was natural that the population would turn to the Roman Catholic Church for comfort and leadership. The church itself was in crisis, however; papal credibility and authority were weakened. It was not clear that the institutional church could provide the answers or meet the needs of its followers.

One hundred years before, church authority and influence seemed at their peak under Innocent III (r. 1198–1216), whose term in office was "the most dramatic expression of monarchical power of the medieval papacy."[1] He had insisted on the supreme authority of the papacy and had managed to dominate a number of secular rulers. He also had made the Roman Catholic Church a territorial state through acquisition of lands in central Italy. Innocent was a reformer as well, as the results of the Fourth Lateran Council in 1215 indicated. He hoped to correct both monastic and episcopal abuses, and expected his clergy to be models for and active shepherds of their flocks. His belief that reform, preaching, and teaching went together led him to allow new religious communities and movements to emerge within the church. The Franciscans and Dominicans as well as various lay fellowships were founded and grew consistently throughout the thirteenth century. Innocent also sought to stamp out heresy through the crusades, which often carried indulgences as rewards.

This picture of an active, aggressive, and confident church was mostly the result of the character of this unusual man, who lived at a time of unusual opportunities. As it turned out, many of Innocent's plans ran into difficulties under subsequent popes, some of his successes carried hidden dangers, and his constant rhetoric of unlimited papal power did not always match reality. For example, acquisition of the papal states meant that the church was more likely to be embroiled in the politics of flourishing Italian towns and city-states, whose governments, though subject to frequent change, were independent-minded and not always devoted to the papacy. The reforms he hoped to impose on bishops and lesser clergy were not always effective, and the acceptance of some new spiritual movements led to the growth of alternative forms of spirituality that church authorities could not always control. Some of the Franciscan chapters refused to be reined in by moderation, an upsurge of women's piety threatened to go beyond the bounds of orthodoxy, and distinctly urban lay confraternities (brotherhoods) developed their own forms of worship and expressions of faith. Efforts to eliminate heresy and to define the boundaries of acceptable belief through preaching and teaching gained a powerful ally with the creation of the Inquisition in 1231. But heresy did not disappear because many individuals continued to be Christian in their own fashion, while popular religious enthusiasm gained even greater purpose in response to the natural disasters of famine and disease.

Several events in the first decades of the fourteenth century made it clear that the church was in trouble and not in touch with the concerns of many of its members. Boniface VIII (r. 1294–1303), whose papal bull, *Unam sanctum*,

1. Colin Morris, *The Papal Monarchy: The Western Church from 1050 to 1250* (New York: Clarendon/Oxford University Press, 1989), p. 422.

Chapter 10
Politics and
Sanctity in
Fourteenth-
Century Europe:
Gregory XI
(1330–1378) and
Catherine
of Siena
(1347–1380)

insisted on papal supremacy, was seized and terrorized by Philip IV (r. 1285–1314), the king of France, in 1303. Although the resistance of his countrymen saved the pope, this unprecedented assertion of secular authority so shocked and weakened him that he died in October 1303. The reputation of the papacy was eroded even more when, a few years later, Philip's candidate, a Frenchman, was elected pope, and in 1309 moved the papacy to Avignon on the Rhone River in southern France. In 1316, a church council at Vienne confronted the problem of fringe religious groups that fell outside regular scrutiny and control. Communities of laywomen known as Beguines were special targets because they lived without a religious rule or clerical leadership. Their pious activity violated the usual boundary between acceptable cloistered devotions and the public world of work and charity, and they were condemned on suspicion of heresy; subsequently their groups almost completely disappeared[2] (Document One). In this instance, the church reaffirmed previous decrees and law, as well as stereotypes about the nature of women. Church leaders misinterpreted the depth of female piety and women's desires to serve, and women continued to find alternative outlets throughout the fourteenth century.

Finally, the church faced challenges from those more obviously within its

jurisdiction. Various intellectuals and members of religious orders began to deny absolute papal authority openly, arguing instead for the authority of church councils that represented the whole body of the church. Others questioned the scholastic enterprise that had joined reason and faith since the days of Peter Abelard. They posited instead a separation between knowledge of the material world and knowledge of the divine. The official response of the church to such affronts usually was to condemn such ideas and excommunicate the individuals, but there was enough spiritual and intellectual ferment throughout Europe that protectors and safe havens could be found, and criticism of the church mounted. As the fourteenth century unfolded, the voices of challenge and demands for reform became louder, particularly as the disasters mentioned at the beginning of the chapter struck across the map and spiritual authorities seemed unable to provide solutions. Catherine Benincasa and Pierre Roger de Beaufort grew up in this world and were convinced that they had a role to play in the course of history—that it was their destiny and their duty to solve the spiritual dilemmas and political unrest of their time.

It is hard to imagine two people more different in background, resources, style, personality, and philosophy than Saint Catherine of Siena (as she was known after her canonization in 1461), and Pope Gregory XI (the name Pierre Roger took after being elected pope in 1370). Two points make a study of their lives historically revealing and unique. First, they demonstrate vividly the incredible

2. Carol Neel, "The Origins of the Beguines," in Judith Bennett et al. (eds.), *Sisters and Workers in the Middle Ages* (Chicago, Ill.: University of Chicago Press, 1989), p. 243. See also Shulamith Shahar, *The Fourth Estate: A History of Women in the Middle Ages* (New York: Methuen, 1983), pp. 52–56.

spiritual diversity and political complexity of fourteenth-century Europe. They also illustrate how particular experiences do not occur in a vacuum but are shaped by and contribute to larger historical patterns. Second, numerous records of *both* Catherine and Gregory have survived. Both wrote letters, although hers were collected vigorously and enthusiastically so that today 382 of her epistles are available.[3] She wrote prayers and also a *Dialogue,* which expressed her beliefs and included commentary on current issues of her time. As we have already seen in previous chapters, it was common for followers or associates to write the life stories of those whose holiness inspired them, and that was the case for Catherine as well. Several of her followers collected the materials that would support her canonization, and those documents are valuable sources for attitudes and beliefs of the time, as are the testimonies of those who opposed the canonization. Greg-

ory's decrees, church law, and records of council meetings or gatherings of cardinals, as well as meetings with notable figures throughout Europe, are quite different as historical sources but they also broaden our understanding. Because of his position, his acqaintances also wrote about him or noted things that he said.

Catherine's and Gregory's lives allow us to consider an issue that we have encountered before: the ways in which religious experience and authority differ for men and for women, and how both can change over time. Women were never officially elected pope, but both men and women were canonized as saints. That calling varied by time, however: in the eleventh century, less than 1 percent of all saints were female; in the fourteenth, they constituted almost 25 percent of the total.[4] Such simple facts point to the gender dimensions of sanctity, which are key elements in the story that follows.

■ THE ACTORS:

GREGORY XI AND CATHERINE OF SIENA

Gregory XI was born in 1330 to the Roger family. Though members of the knightly nobility, they held very little land and were social unknowns. His father, Guillaume Roger II, married

three times and had seven sons and six daughters whose futures might have been precarious if not for the fact that Guillaume's brother, Pierre Roger I, after whom Gregory was named, was able to launch a very successful career in the church. He entered a Benedictine monastery at the age of ten, received a degree in theology in 1323,

3. See Susanne Noffke (ed. and trans.), *The Letters of St. Catherine of Siena,* Vol. I (Binghamton, N.Y.: Center for Medieval and Early Renaissance Studies, SUNY Binghamton, 1988), pp. 3–15, for the genealogy of the letters. Noffke's fine study and biography are essential to any study of Catherine.

4. Donald Weinstein and Rudolph M. Bell, *Saints and Society: The Two Worlds of Western Christendom, 1000–1700* (Chicago, Ill.: University of Chicago Press, 1982), p. 220. Note that over half of the saints who lived in Europe in the thirteenth and fourteenth centuries were Italian.

Chapter 10
Politics and
Sanctity in
Fourteenth-
Century Europe:
Gregory XI
(1330–1378) and
Catherine
of Siena
(1347–1380)

then climbed the ladder of church office. He was named bishop in 1328, archbishop in 1329, and cardinal in 1338; finally, he was elected pope as Clement VI (r. 1342–1352). Each of these offices carried with it considerable wealth and the power of patronage, as well as obvious spiritual authority. In contrast to some of his successors, Clement's credentials for the papal office were quite respectable, and he had a reputation for being an able theologian and eloquent speaker.

Clement helped his family with property and offices according to the common practices of the time. When Clement was named pope, Gregory's father, Guillaume, became viscount of Beaufort, a small town in Anjou that was strategically located close to English holdings, and the two brothers were able to take advantage of the war between England and France to parlay their loyalty and support for the French monarchy into additional titles and increased power. By 1346, Guillaume was made the baron of Alais and then count of Beaufort. In short, within the span of a generation, Gregory XI's family became a "wealthy, influential clan whose dealings extended to royal houses of both France and England." Perhaps most impressive is the fact that in the fourteenth century, the Roger clan "included 24 bishops and archbishops, 24 cardinals, . . . 2 popes and another family member"[5] who refused the office when it was offered to him.

5. Paul R. Thibault, *Pope Gregory XI: The Failure of Tradition* (Lanham, Md.: University Press of America, 1986), p. 1. For other information on the family and Clement VI, see Guillaume Mollat, *The Popes at Avignon, 1305–1378*, trans. Janet Love (London: Thomas Nelson and Sons, Ltd. 1963).

Gregory, several of his brothers, and numerous cousins were slated for clerical careers from childhood. We know little of Gregory's early education, but we can speculate that he was trained in basic Latin and French, perhaps in a monastery, in a church school, or by itinerant teachers. When Clement VI became pope, the family moved to Avignon to serve in the papal court. Clement's court became known as one of the most civilized in Europe, a magnet for nobles, artists, writers, and scientists and the center of frequent feasts, balls, and tournaments.

As a teenager, Gregory was exposed to this environment and undoubtedly learned from the experience. One of the people he met was Francesco Petrarch (1304–1374), a leading Italian humanist and poet who spent his youth in Avignon, where his father was a notary at the court. Ironically, Petrarch would also become a major critic of the papal court during its residence in France, referring to it as "Unholy Babylon, thou Hell on earth, thou sink of iniquity, thou cess-pool of the world!"[6] (Document Two). Petrarch popularized the idea of a "Babylonian captivity" for the church, an idea that fell on fertile ground because many Italian intellectuals and political leaders denounced the papacy's ties to the French monarchy and the wealth and worldliness of the Avignon court, and insisted that the true home of the church was Rome. This message would be repeated throughout the fourteenth century. By

6. Quoted in Mollat, p. 279.

the time Gregory was seventeen, his uncle had made him a notary of the papal court, and the next year, in 1348, to the astonishment of many because of his youth and limited training, Gregory was named a cardinal. Clement explained his choice by saying that the demands of such a position were better suited to youth than to age, and he hinted that the heir to the French throne had insisted on the appointment. More likely, Clement's actions can be explained by the fact that the plague had just hit Avignon in 1348 and he might have feared for his own health, which was not good by that time. Appointing his namesake, a favored family member, seemed to ensure his posterity.

In 1347, a year before Gregory was named a cardinal, Catherine Benincasa was born in the city-state of Siena. That social and political world, her own family, and her early personal experiences bear no resemblance to those of Gregory. Before the plague, Siena encompassed almost 300 communities with a population of about 52,000 people, making it larger than Paris or London.[7] Siena had a fairly broad-based oligarchy as its government, but as the century wore on, factionalism in the city increasingly brought political challenges and instabilities. Banking, commerce, and some artisan manufacturing were the basis of economic life. The plague disrupted and weakened the prosperity of Siena, as it did elsewhere, producing labor

shortages and abandoned farms and businesses. It is estimated that the population of Italy between 1348 and 1380 "must have been reduced by between a third and a half."[8] As one chronicler in Siena lamented, "[I]t is not possible for human tongue to tell of the horror . . . in many places in Siena huge pits were dug and the multitude of the dead were piled within them . . ." (Document Three).

Like other towns in Italy in the early 1300s, Siena was a "theater for innovative piety."[9] The Franciscan and Dominican mendicant orders flourished in Italy, as did other movements dedicated to voluntary poverty; charity; feats of self-denial, such as extreme fasting; and physical self-abuse or flagellation. It was not difficult for many to interpret the threats of starvation and disease and a too worldly and political church, as God's punishment for their sins. People in Siena and elsewhere searched for saints, for men and women who openly demonstrated their sanctity, and the era was characterized by "a hunger for miracles, an extraordinary cult of relics and images," and pilgrimages.[10]

Catherine of Siena was raised in this milieu. Her father, Giacomo Benincasa, was a wool-dyer, while his wife, Lapa, was the daughter of a poet-artisan. The family lived in a multi-story house, with Giacomo's business

---

7. For information on Siena in this period, see Samuel Cohn, Jr., *Death and Property in Siena, 1205–1800* (Baltimore, Md.: Johns Hopkins Press, 1988).

8. John Larner, *Italy in the Age of Dante and Petrarch, 1216–1380* (New York: Longman, 1980), p. 261. The firsthand account that follows is from p. 265.

9. Weinstein and Bell, p. 169. See also Cohn, pp. 78–81.

10. Larner, p. 247.

Chapter 10
Politics and
Sanctity in
Fourteenth-
Century Europe:
Gregory XI
(1330–1378) and
Catherine
of Siena
(1347–1380)

on the first floor.[11] By no means wealthy, the family can be described as lower middle class. Most of the information we have about the family comes from biographies or hagiographies of Catherine; thus, her parents, brothers, sisters, and other relatives appear on the stage only when relevant to key developments in her life. We do know that she was the twenty-third child in the family, the twenty-fourth was her twin Giovanna, who died shortly after birth. There would be a final, twenty-fifth child named Giovanna as well.

Catherine was described as a lively, bright child, but like most girls of her social station and time period, she received no formal schooling. She learned to read as an adult, probably taught by one of her dear friends and followers, Alessa de'Saracini. A young Dominican friar who was related to the family apparently came to live with the Benincasas after he lost his parents in the 1348 plague, and often in the evenings he read aloud stories of the saints or other religious material. The *Life of St. Macrina* as well as Clare of Assisi's story were very popular at the time, and both could have shaped Catherine's desire to live a virginal life as the bride of Christ. According to her biographer, Raymond of Capua, Catherine knew early on that she was destined for a holy, celibate life. She had her first vision of Jesus when she was seven and a year later, in 1354, took a personal vow of virginity. Her family had other plans for her because they felt her marriage prospects were excellent: she was intelligent, healthy, and quite lovely according to contemporaries. Thus, began almost a decade of struggle within the family as Catherine resisted their efforts to change her mind or to force her to follow prescribed female roles of marriage and childbearing.

Meanwhile, Gregory had moved to Italy in 1348 when he decided (with his uncle's blessing) to attend the new university in Perugia to study law and theology. For the next five years, we know little about the life of Cardinal Pierre Roger, although a famous jurist with whom he studied claimed that Gregory had a "profound" knowledge of the law, which would be useful to him once he became head of the church.

11. There is a vast literature on all facets of Catherine's life, based on the sources mentioned earlier. A National Center of Studies of Catherine is located in Rome, and a journal is dedicated entirely to scholarship on her and related topics. The most important biography in English is that of Suzanne Noffke, *Catherine of Siena: Vision Through a Distant Eye* (Collegeville, Minn.: The Liturgical Press, 1996). Recent works in Italian include Sara Cabibbo (ed.), *Io, serva e schiava* (Palermo: Editore Sellerio, 1991), and Gabriella Anodal, *Caterina da Siena: Patrona d'Europa* (Casale Monferrato: Edizioni PIEMME, 2000).

ACT I:

*PATHS TO GREATNESS
(CA. 1350–CA. 1370)*

In these two decades (1350–1370) Catherine and Gregory developed the personalities, beliefs, and reputations for which they became known, and they established the goals and behaviors that they hoped would fulfill their destinies and leave a mark on history.

The events in Gregory's life as a cardinal were not recorded except when he acted in a legal capacity, sometimes for a family member, but more generally as a judge in the papal court. When his uncle died in 1352, he participated in the election of Innocent IV (r. 1352–1362), an undistinguished French clergyman and law professor who had the backing of the king of France but whose term would be marked by violence, warfare, economic problems, famine, and disease. After his death in 1362, the election of the next pope was contested and Gregory apparently played a larger role in this election. Five Roger kinsmen were members of the college of cardinals at the time, and a family member (another of Gregory's uncles) was chosen, but to most everyone's surprise, he turned down the office on the grounds that the election was fraudulent.

The pope who was finally selected, Urban V (r. 1362–1370), was also a well-known canon lawyer from Marseilles. Gregory served Urban V in diplomatic missions trying to mediate between warring rulers and nobles. Urban also returned to Rome briefly in 1367, and Gregory was one of the cardinals who went with him. In Rome, he was the archpriest of the Saint John Lateran Cathedral, which had suffered from fire damage during the popes' absences, and Gregory was responsible for rebuilding it. Participation in ceremonies and rituals at that church also gained him public recognition. By 1370, Urban had decided that he could not stay in Rome; he returned to Avignon and died in December of that year. The next person the cardinals chose as pope was Pierre Roger, or Gregory XI. It was now his turn to try to tackle the multiple problems facing the church.

In these same years, Catherine was fighting against her family's wishes, developing her identity, beginning to interpret her own mystical experiences, and listening to the commands of divine will. By the early 1360s, it is possible that her father and mother had chosen a marriage partner for her, and it appeared Catherine might have wavered briefly in her resolve. In 1362, however, Bonaventura, her older married sister, died in childbirth, and Catherine's response was greater determination to pursue a spiritual life in the service of others. By 1362, she had begun regular periods of severe fasting, and Bonaventura had apparently used fasting as a way to threaten a straying husband. The sum of these experiences seemed to strengthen Catherine's resolve not to marry and to convince her even more of the efficacy of fasting. In addition to imitating Jesus and the early saints and martyrs, Catherine saw her fasting and suffering as a way to feed and save the souls of others. Historian Caroline Walker Bynum has argued that "food asceticism, like charitable food donations and performance of

Chapter 10
Politics and
Sanctity in
Fourteenth-
Century Europe:
Gregory XI
(1330–1378) and
Catherine
of Siena
(1347–1380)

food-related miracles was particularly the role of women in the later Middle Ages."[12]

A year later, in 1363, when the plague again swept through Siena, Catherine's youngest sister Giovanna died. Catherine announced to her family that she would never marry, vowed to eat only bread and raw vegetables in limited amounts and to drink only water, and then cut off her hair as a symbol of her vow. In anger, her father declared as punishment that she should take the place of a servant in the household. She did so with zeal, likening her service in her family to service to Jesus, Mary, and the Apostles. Since clearly nothing could move Catherine off her course, her father relented and allowed her to join a Dominican third order. The Order of Penance that she joined was made up mostly of older women, often widows, who were known as the *mantellate* because they wore a black mantel over a white robe. Third orders, or tertiaries, as they were called, were not cloistered and did not live by a rule, but dedicated themselves to charity, poverty and a spiritual life.

For the next three years, Catherine lived alone in a tiny room in her family's house, devoting herself to prayers, confession, fasting, and flagellation. She ventured out only to attend church services. She gained a reputation for holiness, and then in February 1368, during carnival, she had an experience that changed the course of her life. While revelers were carousing in the streets, she had a vision in which her soul was wed with Christ, according to her, not with a ring of gold or silver, but with a ring of his flesh. (Her biographer, Raymond of Capua, transforms the vision into a more traditional story of a wedding between a saintly bridegroom and a virginal bride.[13]) Sometime after her vision, Catherine also announced that she had received a call to give up her solitude and to serve others. She claimed to have been surprised by this request because she was a nobody, a weakling, and a woman. Jesus had answered by telling her that he was fed up with this age of pride, especially among the learned and powerful, and that he was determined "to confound them, [and thus would] give the world women, unlearned and weak, but endowed by me with virtue to defeat their boldness. . . ."[14]

12. Caroline Walker Bynum, *Holy Feast and Holy Fast: The Religious Significance of Food to Medieval Women* (Berkeley: University of California Press, 1987), p. 87. See pp. 165–180 for her specific discussion of Catherine's case.

13. This distinction is made by E. Ann Matter, "Mystical Marriage," in Lucetta Scaraffia and Gabriella Zarri (eds.), *Women and Faith* (Cambridge, Mass.: Harvard University Press, 1999), p. 38.

14. Quoted in Igino Giordani, *Saint Catherine of Siena*, trans. Thomas J. Tobin (Boston, Mass.: The Daughters of St. Paul, 1959), p. 49.

ACT II:

THE ALLIANCE OF POPE AND SAINT (1370–1380)

Catherine and Gregory shared many concerns and goals. Both sought to solve political problems of the era and to strengthen and rebuild the authority of the papacy. They both recognized that politics and spiritual life were connected, although Catherine saw political conflict and intrigue, violence and warfare as contrary to divine commandments. Gregory knew that the papacy could not return to Rome safely until control was established over the papal states, which meant getting embroiled in city politics in Italy. Victory in that arena depended on his ability to gain the support of secular rulers throughout Europe, in particular the French and the English, and alliances with those two powers in turn required an end to their long-standing conflict. Catherine was more likely to believe that exhortation, admonishment, and even reprimand, when combined with a message of justice and peace, would be successful. Gregory was more pragmatic, relying on reason, timing, and his diplomatic experience and skills. She believed in him and the authority of his office; he was impressed by her convictions and, like many others, could not deny the force of her personality. In the end, they both saw themselves as crusaders, defenders of the church, and mediators among warring Christians. Circumstances made them allies.

Gregory and Catherine had particular skills and resources that they could use to achieve their goals. The personal characteristics for which Gregory was known among his colleagues were "prudence, discretion, modest demeanor, piety, goodness, affability, uprightness of character, steadfastness of purpose in word and deed."[15] He had been brought up in the college of cardinals, and they assumed he would be sympathetic to their opinions and needs. Skeptics have also claimed that they chose him for the papacy because his health was not good, and therefore his pontificate would not be unduly long. Perhaps some supported him because he was a respected scholar with broad intellectual training, which was reflected in his addition to the papal library of rare manuscripts, works of classical authors, and philosophical and theological studies.

Even though the papacy was in trouble, Gregory still had huge resources at his disposal. He had a large bureaucracy and a vast network of clergy and church officials under his command; he could use the mechanism of the crusades to muster considerable military support for his causes; church law and doctrine were also extensive and in theory, had universal applicability. Financially, the papacy had multiple sources of revenue from taxes. By the time that Gregory became pope, however, fiscal problems abounded, in large part due to the spending of his uncle Clement VI. When Clement became pope, his predecessor left him reserves of over a

---

15. Mollat, p. 59. For the views of the cardinals who elected him, see Thibault, p. 31.

Chapter 10
Politics and
Sanctity in
Fourteenth-
Century Europe:
Gregory XI
(1330–1378) and
Catherine
of Siena
(1347–1380)

million florins; when Clement died, the amount in papal coffers had fallen to about 300,000 florins, much of it from loans that the papacy had to repay.[16] The situation was even worse when Gregory took over, so that he had to live from hand to mouth and try to collect more in taxes, a move that was never popular and always difficult. Finally, the pope could still use the threat of excommunication to force recalcitrant subjects into line, but given the spiritual condition of the church, that threat was sometimes ignored.

Catherine was not a theologian or a philosopher, although she had some knowledge of Augustine and Aquinas and did not deny the importance of the intellect in shaping a spiritual life. Her close ties to the Dominican order certainly increased her respect for scholars, but in the end, she developed her own philosophy and truth and was never led by her clerical companions, who were in the "shadow of the authority of the inspired woman [Catherine]."[17] The lay population as a whole venerated her because she performed acts of charity, helped the sick and the needy, served as an effective mediator in family and political disputes, and lived a life of such asceticism that she seemed superhuman. Just as her fasting became more extreme, miracles associated with providing food to those in need were attributed to her. By 1370, she no

longer ate bread, and in 1372 gave up solid food, except for some herbs and the wafers of holy communion. Her colleagues claimed that if she consumed anything, she often used a twig to force herself to vomit even the smallest morsels. Nevertheless, she continued to be energetic, at least until quite near the time of her death. All of these characteristics, in addition to her considerable will and the fact that she claimed to speak the word of God, were her sources of power.

As Catherine's public presence expanded, her followers grew in number. They came from all social classes and were male and female, clergy and lay people, poets, artists, and politicians. For example, Alessa de'Saracini, who may have helped her learn to read and who became the leader of the mantellate after 1382, was a well-to-do noblewoman and widow. Raymond of Capua, her biographer, was chaplain of a Dominican monastery and later general of the Dominican order. He was placed in Catherine's service to be her guide, but instead he was her disciple and she felt free to reprimand him for being too timid or cowardly.[18] Stefano di Corrado Maconi was a young nobleman from Siena who sought out Catherine to end the feud between his and another family. After she successfully mediated their dispute, he was devoted to her, became one of her scribes, and frequently traveled with her.

Sometime in 1372 or 1373, Catherine began to write the letters that provide so much information on her life and character. She wrote to her follow-

16. Mollat, p. 330.

17. Andre Vauchez, *The Laity in the Middle Ages: Religious Beliefs and Devotional Practices,* trans. Margery Schneider (Notre Dame, Ind.: University of Notre Dame Press, 1987), p. 247. Previous discussion is from p. 244.

18. Vauchez, p. 248.

ers, friends, and colleagues, giving advice, comfort, and often criticism. For example, Corrado Maconi remained a layman, and in a letter addressed to him in 1376, she expressed how she felt about his life, admitting that "you are weak and frail so far as your sensuality is concerned, but not so when it comes to reason and spiritual strength. For in Christ's blood we are made strong, even though weakness persists in our sensuality. . . . Remember that it is always harder to dig the foundation, but once the foundation is completed it is easy to work on the building."[19] Another young man, Cristofano di Gano Guidini, a notary from Siena, thought of joining a religious order or a confraternity, but his mother was opposed because she wanted him to marry. Catherine wrote to him in 1375, giving him her views and describing her thoughts on the virtues of a virginal, spiritual life (Document Four). (In this case, Guidini's mother won the battle because he married shortly thereafter.) In these letters and in countless others to her followers, Catherine combined forceful, pragmatic personal advice with spiritual precepts, and this combination proved compelling.

Catherine's followers were her scribes and companions and were important to her physical survival because she insisted on personal poverty, often giving away her own clothing. Her father had died in 1368, and several of her brothers took over the family business, but they lost it all in 1370 in a wool-workers' rebellion. After the loss of their business, they left Siena for Florence. By then, Catherine's mother supported her daughter's mission and had joined the mantellate. For a time, both of them lived with Alessa de'Saracini, and in future years, as Catherine traveled more and more, she often stayed in the castles, villas, and houses of wealthy and influential friends. Thus, no matter what her own choices might be, her created spiritual family was certainly not poor or vowed to poverty.

Catherine herself was aware of this contradiction, and living as she did in a time of economic hardship for many, her ideas on wealth are interesting. How did she feel about money? Was it moral to make a profit? Scholastics had been debating these questions for some time, and Catherine argued that profit was acceptable to make a living but should not be made at the expense of others. She acknowledged a right to subsistence, but not the right to more than was needed to sustain life. Wealth belonged to God, and he intended for those who had it to administer it for him. Some have argued that in matters of economics, Catherine may have listened more to her earthly father's views rather than to those of her spiritual father.[20]

While Catherine was becoming a public figure, Gregory was grappling with problems of warring kingdoms, the need to launch a new crusade to recover the Holy Land and protect Europe from the Turks, the persistence of heresy throughout Europe, and the long-standing political struggles in

19. Noffke, *The Letters of St. Catherine*, pp. 264–266.

20. The discussion of her economic views is from Noffke, *Catherine of Siena*, pp. 87–105.

Chapter 10
Politics and
Sanctity in
Fourteenth-
Century Europe:
Gregory XI
(1330–1378) and
Catherine
of Siena
(1347–1380)

Italy, including rebellion in the papal states. He had little time or perhaps inclination to consider innovative reform of the church and to address the needs of a changing society. Early in his pontificate, he had decided that the seat of the church must be in Rome, and by 1372 had made public his desire to return to the ancient city. To make that move possible, he had to deal with some pressing political conflicts.

He needed the military and financial backing of European leaders to put down rebellion in the papal states, which threatened the security of the pope and his administration. Obtaining such backing meant trying to bring peace to England and France. In Italy, competing territorial aspirations created constantly shifting alliances and wars, some of which also had direct bearing on papal lands. Florence, for example, had traditionally been a supporter of the papacy, but by the 1370s new people in Florentine government were convinced that the alliance cost a great deal and gained them little. They also worried that reestablishing strong papal authority in the central regions of Italy would destroy the balance of power to their disadvantage. Between 1372 and 1376, Gregory tried to navigate these stormy political seas, never with resounding success.

On the issues of the return of the pope to Rome and better relations between secular rulers and the papacy, Catherine and Gregory were in agreement. These issues, in fact, became her major cause by 1375. She traveled to cities near Siena, like Florence, Pisa,

and Lucca, trying to persuade their leaders to work peacefully with the church and to assist the pope in his desires to return to Rome. Of her 382 extant letters, sixty-seven are addressed to kings and queens, civic officials, and military leaders throughout Europe. Catherine recognized that the secular rulers of Europe would be responsible for realizing her vision of a truly Christian world because God loaned them his power. As she noted, "Justice will reign within society in exact proportion as it reigns within the individuals who together constitute society."[21]

Catherine wrote to Gregory himself, perhaps as early as 1375, and the correspondence continued until his death three years later. Her major theme is the return of the papacy to Rome, but she also addresses other issues. The earliest letter that still exists, probably from January 1376, advises the pope on how he should govern, criticizes the corruption of church leaders, and suggests that he should choose virtuous men when he appoints cardinals. Addressing the pope as "my dear *babbo*," (colloquial Italian for father, something like "daddy"), she argues that the people are sinful because their leaders are corrupt, and that papal delay in returning to Rome "already has been the cause of a lot of trouble. . . . Up father, no more irresponsibility!" She concludes with an apology for talking to him like that.[22] All of her letters to Gregory, as well as

21. Noffke, *Catherine of Siena,* pp. 76–77.

22. Noffke, *The Letters of St. Catherine of Siena,* Letter 54, pp. 166–170.

those to other rulers, are equally bold and demanding (Document Five). The remarkable thing is that she was not dismissed nor charged with heresy. Unfortunately, we do not possess written responses from the recipients of the letters, so it is hard to tell exactly what they thought of her.

By the end of March 1376, conflict between the papacy and Florence had escalated, and Gregory had placed the city under interdict. Catherine traveled to Florence and then made her way to Avignon in the summer of that year to argue for a peaceful resolution to the conflict with Florence, and again to plead with Gregory to return to Rome. She met with him in Avignon in August and in early September Gregory boarded a ship to take him back to the Holy City. He had sent troops ahead, thus indicating that his decision was made before his talks with Catherine. Nevertheless, Gregory was still facing opposition to his decision from his French cardinals and various political leaders, so her words may have been the encouragement he needed.[23] Certainly her followers thought she was responsible for his action, and in her canonization proceedings in the early fifteenth century, people testified that her influence was considerable. Perhaps in their view, the fact that a woman could have such political impact was proof indeed of her divine inspiration. It should be noted that Catherine was

23. Mollat, p. 171. See also Thibault, "Appendix C: The Question of Catherine of Siena," pp. 211–213, which is devoted to the question of how much influence she had on Gregory.

not the only saintly figure to play such a role in fourteenth-century politics. Saint Bridget of Sweden, who died in Rome in 1373, had encouraged earlier popes to return to that city.

After a difficult journey, Gregory and his entourage arrived in Rome in January 1377. He had not returned in peace, as Catherine hoped, but rather with an escort of two thousand men under the leadership of his nephew. The papal states were subdued, not by spiritual power but through bloody campaigns and the use of force. Catherine returned to Siena; began to dictate what would become her *Dialogue*, a series of discussions between God and a human soul (hers); and then founded a convent at Belcaro in a castle donated to her by a follower, authorized by the commune of Siena, and approved by the pope.

In the meantime, Gregory was trying to establish control over his Roman office and to negotiate with various Italian cities to bring peace to the region. In 1377, he also took action against heresy and ordered the arrest of John Wycliffe. His concerns about Wycliffe included the fact that secular authorities were protecting the radical leader and thereby challenging papal authority (Document Six). By then Gregory's experiences had shown him that secular leaders could not be counted on to support campaigns against heresy or even the work of inquisitorial courts. These challenges would continue to confront the papacy through the time of the Protestant Reformation. By early 1378, Gregory's health was failing rapidly. His primary desire at that point was to

Chapter 10
Politics and
Sanctity in
Fourteenth-
Century Europe:
Gregory XI
(1330–1378) and
Catherine
of Siena
(1347–1380)

secure a free and smooth election of the next pope and guarantee the permanency of the papacy in Rome. To accomplish those ends he drew up a document that gave the cardinals considerable flexibility in their deliberations and action (Document Seven). He died in March 1378 and was buried in Rome.

The cardinals met and elected as Gregory's successor an Italian, the archbishop of Bari, who became Urban VI (r. 1378–1389). He was not a popular or effective leader, with the result that a number of the cardinals left Rome, held another meeting in September, and elected a second pope, one of their own. Clement VII (r. 1378–1394), as he was known, quickly returned to Avignon with his supporters (Document Eight). Thus, the Great Schism in the western church began, representing perhaps the absolute nadir of papal leadership. Gregory's efforts to re-establish a strengthened papal monarchy in Rome were defeated.

■ FINALE

Catherine was pleased with the election of Urban VI, especially when he made peace with Florence in August 1378. The schism was devastating to her, however, and in November she went to Rome to help Urban in his efforts to end the division and reassert his single authority in the church. Perhaps this series of events was too much for her; by then she was much weakened by her years of fasting. Nevertheless, she set up a household in Rome with her mother and several of her disciples. By February 1380, she was confined to bed, eventually refusing to take even water. She died in Rome on April 29, 1380, and like Gregory was buried in the Holy City. Neither Gregory nor Catherine succeeded in realizing their goals of renewed spiritual authority of the church and peace among all true Christians. Some reforms would come to the church, but not through the office of the papacy or the efforts of the saints. Reform came through a series of church council meetings held at Constance (1414–1418), which finally ended the schism with the election of Martin V in 1417.

Gregory helped to restore the base of a papal monarchy in Italy, but at great financial and spiritual costs. Victory over rebellion in the papal states only meant that the church was capable of effectively playing the games of secular politics. Brought up in a traditional hierarchical family and church, Gregory was not prepared to respond in innovative ways to the crises and transformations of fourteenth-century Europe.

Catherine had indeed made her mark on the people she knew. Through her extreme asceticism, her will, and her intellect, she had gained power and defined her own spirituality. But she did not challenge the formal structures of the church and never gained recognized authority in this world. The church accepted Catherine, even though she was bold, because she did not step outside orthodoxy, and the boundaries between male and female religious roles and forms of spiritual expression remained. Gregory, even on his deathbed, had "supposedly advised his followers to be suspicious of holy women and other visionaries" when they became involved in political matters. Radical religious enthusiasm and organizations that asserted independence and the power of individual faith were contrary to the church and had to be controlled and suppressed. Lives of holiness like Catherine's were offered as "imitable models of sanctity."[24] The fourteenth century had offered no definitive answers to Europeans' search for intellectual and spiritual meaning and identity. Instead, different secular and religious perspectives jostled for a place on the path to moral truth and human understanding.

■ QUESTIONS

1. What were the major challenges facing the western church at the start of the fourteenth century? In what ways did the church become more and more like secular authorities? Why did this change occur and what were the results?

2. In what ways could individuals express their religious beliefs in the fourteenth century? What positions of religious authority were open to them, and how were these positions similar or different for men and for women?

3. In what ways does Catherine of Siena reflect the spiritual crises of the fourteenth century? What explains her remarkable rise to prominence?

4. As the fourteenth century came to a close, what were the most important criticisms being leveled against the church? Who voiced these criticisms?

5. In what ways does the growth of an urban culture and the increase in literacy affect religious life in the late Middle Ages?

24. For Gregory's advice, see Vauchez, p. 252; for models of sanctity, see Giulia Barone, "Society and Women's Religiosity," in Scaraffia and Zarri (eds.), p. 70.

Chapter 10
Politics and
Sanctity in
Fourteenth-
Century Europe:
Gregory XI
(1330–1378) and
Catherine
of Siena
(1347–1380)

■ **DOCUMENTS**

DOCUMENT ONE

BONIFACE VIII

Papal Decree, *Periculoso*
(1298)

*For centuries in the monastic movement, monks and nuns had favored enclosure,
or cloistering, as a way to achieve their spiritual goals because they could shut out
the material world. At the same time, flexibility in this structure had allowed
movement in and out of the monastery for economic, missionary, and charitable
activities. When Boniface issued this decree, there were various forms of religious
life for women that permitted and even encouraged more public life for them. This
papal decree would change that because of the threat of excommunication. How
does Boniface justify his action? What does he fear? What is his goal?*

Wishing to provide for the dangerous and abominable situation of certain nuns,
who, casting off the reins of respectability and impudently abandoning nunnish
modesty and the natural bashfulness of their sex, sometimes rove about outside
of their monasteries to the homes of secular persons and frequently admit suspect persons into these same monasteries, to the injury of that to which by free
choice they vowed their chastity, to the disgrace and dishonor of the religious
life and the temptation of many, we do firmly decree by this present constitution which shall forever remain in force, that nuns collectively and individually,
both at present and in future, of whatsoever community or order, in whatever
part of the world they may be, ought henceforth to remain perpetually cloistered in their monasteries, so that none of them, tacitly or expressly professed,
shall or may for whatever reason or cause (unless by chance any be found to be
manifestly suffering from a disease of such a type and kind that it is not possible to remain with the others without grave danger or scandal), have permission hereafter to leave their monasteries; and that no persons, in any way
disreputable, or even respectable, shall be allowed to enter or leave the same
(unless a reasonable and obvious cause exists, for which the appropriate authority may grant a special license) so that [the nuns] be able to serve God more
freely, wholly separated from the public and worldly gaze and, occasions for
lasciviousness have been removed, may most diligently safeguard their hearts
and bodies in complete chastity.

    & 1. Indeed, so that this salutary statute be more easily observed, we most
strictly decree that no sisters shall from this time forward be received in monasteries other than [those of] mendicant orders unless those same monasteries are

able to support them with goods or revenues and without penury; contrary actions shall be considered void.

& 2. But when an abbess or prioress of any monastery shall need to present herself to do homage or swear fealty for a fief that the same monastery holds from any prince or temporal lord (unless, she can do so by a procurator representing her in his presence) she may leave the monastery. In this instance licitly, with respectable and decent company; having done homage or sworn the oath of fealty, let her return to the monastery as soon as it is conveniently possible, so that nothing whatever be done that impairs residence or enclosure.

& 3. Further, lest nuns have any cause or occasion to go abroad we ask, we beg, and we beseech secular princes and other temporal lords, through the merciful heart of Jesus Christ, exhorting them that for the remission of sins, they allow the same abbesses and prioresses or nuns who carry out the administration of business for their monasteries, by whatever titles they may be designated, to litigate in their tribunals and courts through procurators, who in some places are called attorneys, or others of this kind, lest for lack of procurators the nuns themselves be required to go abroad. If anyone presume otherwise and refuse to comply with this kind of reasonable and holy exhortation, since it is against the law to require women, especially religious women, to litigate for themselves, and departs from the honorable path, and may lead to the peril of souls, let them be compelled to do this by their ecclesiastical ordinaries through ecclesiastical censures. Indeed we enjoin bishops and other prelates, whether inferior or superior, that when the aforesaid nuns have to come before them or into their courts for lawsuits or business or to do homage or swear fealty, or for disputes or anything else, that they be allowed to take their actions and transact their business through procurators.

& 4. And since it would be pointless indeed to make laws unless someone were designated to enforce them, we strictly enjoin patriarchs, . . . , archbishops, and all bishops in virtue of holy obedience, under threat of divine judgement and the prospect of eternal damnation, that they take very diligent care that the nuns of any monasteries within their city or diocese subject to them by law as ordinaries and indeed even those that are immediately subject solely to the authority of the Roman church and apostolic see, also abbots and others, exempt as well as non-exempt prelates of the church, with monasteries of whatsoever order subject to them, diligently enforce enclosure in those monasteries in which it is not observed as soon as they can properly provide for this; they shall meet the expenses incurred therein from the alms that they shall procure from the faithful for this purpose if they wish to evade our wrath and divine indignation; those who refuse and resist ought to be constrained through ecclesiastical censure, with no right of appeal, invoking for this, if necessary, the aid of the secular arm. Ordinaries should be aware, however, that they do not acquire in virtue of this [letter] any jurisdiction or power in any other matter over monasteries that are otherwise exempt [from the ordinary's control].

Chapter 10
Politics and
Sanctity in
Fourteenth-
Century Europe:
Gregory XI
(1330–1378) and
Catherine
of Siena
(1347–1380)

DOCUMENT TWO

FRANCESCO PETRARCH

(Undated Letter)

Francesco Petrarch (1304–1374), Italian humanist and poet, spent considerable time in France where his father, a Florentine notary, resided at Avignon. Thus, he had the opportunity to observe the papal court in action. By the time he wrote this letter, he was a renowned scholar and the poet laureate of the city of Rome. Although a secular scholar, Petrarch uses religious themes in his critique. Why do you think he uses this technique? What does he see as the greatest failings of the church? Why do you think his critique became so widely known in Italy at the time?

. . . Now I am living in France, in the Babylon of the West. The sun in its travels sees nothing more hideous than this place on the shores of the wild Rhone, which suggests the hellish streams of Cocytus and Acheron. Here reign the successors of the poor fishermen of Galilee; they have strangely forgotten their origin. I am astounded, as I recall their predecessors, to see these men loaded with gold and clad in purple, boasting of the spoils of princes and nations; to see luxurious palaces and heights crowned with fortifications, instead of a boat turned downwards for shelter.

We no longer find the simple nets which were once used to gain a frugal sustenance from the lake of Galilee, and with which, having labored all night and caught nothing, they took, at daybreak, a multitude of fishes, in the name of Jesus. One is stupefied nowadays to hear the lying tongues, and to see worthless parchments turned by a leaden seal into nets which are used, in Christ's name, but by the arts of Belial, to catch hordes of unwary Christians. These fish, too, are dressed and laid on the burning coals of anxiety before they fill the insatiable maw of their captors.

Instead of holy solitude we find a criminal host and crowds of the most infamous satellites; instead of soberness, licentious banquets; instead of pious pilgrimages, preternatural and foul sloth; instead of the bare feet of the apostles, the snowy coursers of brigands fly past us, the horses decked in gold and fed on gold, soon to be shod with gold, if the Lord does not check this slavish luxury. In short, we seem to be among the kings of the Persians or Parthians, before whom we must fall down and worship, and who cannot be approached except presents be offered. O ye unkempt and emaciated old men, is it for this you labored? Is it for this that you have sown the field of the Lord and watered it with your holy blood? But let us leave the subject. . . .

DOCUMENT THREE

GIOVANNI BOCCACCIO

The Decameron
(1349–1350)

Giovanni Boccaccio (1313–1375) was a well-educated man from a Florentine merchant family. He became well known for his secular writings in vernacular Italian. After the plague struck Florence, in 1349–1350, he completed the set of 100 short stories known as The Decameron. *The following selection is from the Introduction to the stories. How does he describe the impact of the plague and the experience of living through it? Why did the plague have such physical and spiritual impact on Europeans at the time?*

. . . Either because of the influence of heavenly bodies or because of God's just wrath as a punishment to mortals for our wicked deeds, the pestilence, originating some years earlier in the East, killed an infinite number of people as it spread relentlessly from one place to another until finally it had stretched its miserable length all over the West. And against this pestilence no human wisdom or foresight was of any avail; quantities of filth were removed from the city by officials charged with the task; the entry of any sick person into the city was prohibited; and many directives were issued concerning the maintenance of good health. . . .

This pestilence was so powerful that it was transmitted to the healthy by contact with the sick, the way a fire close to dry or oily things will set them aflame. And the evil of the plague went even further: not only did talking or being around the sick bring infection and a common death, but also touching the clothes of the sick or anything touched or used by them seemed to communicate this very disease to the person involved. What I am about to say is incredible to hear, and if I and others had not witnessed it with our own eyes, I should not dare believe it (let alone write about it), no matter how trustworthy a person I might have heard it from. Let me say, then, that the plague described here was of such virulence in spreading from one person to another that not only did it pass from one man to the next, but, what's more, it was often transmitted from the garments of a sick or dead man to animals that not only became contaminated by the disease but also died within a brief period of time. . . .

There were some people who thought that living moderately and avoiding any excess might help a great deal in resisting this disease, and so they gathered in small groups and lived entirely apart from everyone else. They shut themselves up in those houses where there were no sick people and where one could live well by eating the most delicate of foods and drinking the finest of wines (doing so always in moderation), allowing no one to speak about or listen to

Chapter 10
Politics and
Sanctity in
Fourteenth-
Century Europe:
Gregory XI
(1330–1378) and
Catherine
of Siena
(1347–1380)

anything said about the sick and the dead outside; these people lived, entertaining themselves with music and other pleasures that they could arrange. Others thought the opposite: they believed that drinking excessively, enjoying life, going about singing and celebrating, satisfying in every way the appetites as best one could, laughing, and making light of everything that happened was the best medicine for such a disease; so they practiced to the fullest what they believed by going from one tavern to another all day and night, drinking to excess; and they would often make merry in private homes, doing everything that pleased or amused them the most. This they were able to do easily, for everyone felt he was doomed to die and, as a result, abandoned his property, so that most of the houses had become common property, and any stranger who came upon them used them as if he were their rightful owner. In addition to this bestial behavior, they always managed to avoid the sick as best they could. And in this great affliction and misery of our city the revered authority of the laws, both divine and human, had fallen and almost completely disappeared, for, like other men, the ministers and executors of the laws were either dead or sick or so short of help that it was impossible for them to fulfill their duties; as a result, everybody was free to do as he pleased. . . .

Others were of a crueler opinion (though it was, perhaps, a safer one): they maintained that there was no better medicine against the plague than to flee from it; convinced of this reasoning and caring only about themselves, men and women in great numbers abandoned their city, their houses, their farms, their relatives, and their possessions and sought other places, going at least as far away as the Florentine countryside—as if the wrath of God could not pursue them with this pestilence wherever they went but would only strike those it found within the walls of the city! Or perhaps they thought that Florence's last hour had come and that no one in the city would remain alive. . . .

The plight of the lower class and, perhaps, a large part of the middle class was even more pathetic: most of them stayed in their homes or neighborhoods either because of their poverty or because of their hopes for remaining safe, and every day they fell sick by the thousands; and not having servants or attendants of any kind, they almost always died. Many ended their lives in the public streets, during the day or at night, while many others who died in their homes were discovered dead by their neighbors only by the smell of their decomposing bodies. The city was full of corpses. The dead were usually given the same treatment by their neighbors, who were moved more by the fear that the decomposing corpses would contaminate them than by any charity they might have felt toward the deceased: either by themselves or with the assistance of porters (when they were available), they would drag the corpse out of the home and place it in front of the doorstep, where, usually in the morning, quantities of dead bodies could be seen by any passerby; then they were laid out in biers, or for lack of biers, on a plank. . . .

DOCUMENT FOUR

CATHERINE OF SIENA

Letter to Cristofano di Gano Guidini
(1375)

Catherine was a prolific letter writer and kept in touch with family and friends through letters. The recipient of the following letter was a young notary in Siena and one of Catherine's followers. He had plans to join a religious organization of some sort. He later wrote his own memoirs and indicated that by 1375 he had started to change his mind and was thinking of marrying. He wrote to Catherine for her advice, and this letter is her response. What does this letter tell you about Catherine's views of marriage and religion?

Dearest and very loved brother and son in Christ Jesus,

I Caterina [Catherine], servant and slave of Christ's servants, am writing to you in the precious blood of God's Son. I long to see you among those faithful children, always observing and fulfilling what the true heavenly Father tells you when he says, "Those who do not abandon father and mother, sisters and brothers, as well as themselves, are not worthy of me." So it seems he wants us to abandon them. Yet you seem to have no intention of following this, under the pretext of being conscience-stricken at leaving her. That sort of conscience comes more from the devil than from God, to keep you from the perfect way of life the Holy Spirit has apparently called you to. If you should say to me, "God commands me to be obedient to them," true enough, in so far as they don't pull you away from God's path. But if they get in the way of this, we ought to step over their bodies and follow our true Father, with the standard of the most holy cross, drowning and killing our perverse will.

Ah, dearest brother in Christ Jesus, I am truly sorry you resist without even knowing this noble way of life. It seems to me you should be more conscience-stricken at *not* leaving her than at leaving her. But since that's the way it is, I pray supreme eternal Truth to lay his most holy hand on your head and direct you to whatever way of life is most pleasing to him. I beg you, whatever your condition and in all you do, keep your eyes fixed on God, seeking always his honor and the salvation of his creatures. Never forget the price paid for us with such blazing love, the blood of the Lamb.

Concerning the matter of your bride, my answer is that I get into this reluctantly, because it is more the business of worldly people than mine. Still, I can't refuse you. Given the circumstances of each, any of the three is good. If you don't think it would bother you that the one has had another husband, you can make that choice—since you want to get embroiled in this perverse and wicked

[299]

Chapter 10
Politics and
Sanctity in
Fourteenth-
Century Europe:
Gregory XI
(1330–1378) and
Catherine
of Siena
(1347–1380)

world. Otherwise take the daughter of Francesco Ventura da Camporeggi. I'll say no more.

I pray supreme eternal Charity to give you whatever would be best for his honor and your salvation. May he grant both of you the fullness of grace and his supreme eternal benediction. Keep living in God's holy love.

DOCUMENT FIVE

CATHERINE OF SIENA

Letters
(1376)

Catherine wrote letters to many kings, queens, and nobles and to the pope. The first letter that follows was written just before she left for Avignon, where she hoped to persuade Gregory XI to return to Rome (which he actually had already decided to do). What arguments does she present to him? How would you describe the tone of this letter?

The second letter is addressed to Charles V, king of France, and written while she was in Avignon in July 1376. Her goal here was to make sure the king was loyal to the pope and also to give him advice on the role of a monarch. What criticism does she give against secular rulers? What does she advise him to do? What is the tone of this letter? What do both of these letters say about the personality and will of this young, holy woman?

LETTER TO GREGORY XI, APRIL 1376

In the name of Christ crucified and of gentle Mary.

Revered father in Christ gentle Jesus,

I Caterina, your unworthy daughter, servant and slave of the servants of Jesus Christ, am writing to you in his precious blood. I long to see you a courageous man, free of slavish fear, learning from the good gentle Jesus, whose vicar you are. Such was his boundless love for us that he ran to the shameful death of the cross heedless of torment, shame, insult, and outrage. He suffered them all, totally free of fear, such was his hungry desire for the Father's honor and our salvation. For love had made him completely let go of himself, humanly speaking. Now this is just what I want you to do, father. Let go of yourself wherever selfish love is concerned. Do not love yourself selfishly, nor others selfishly, but love yourself and your neighbors for God's sake and God for his own sake, since he is worthy of love, and since he is supreme eternal good. Take as your example

[300]

this slain Lamb, for the blood of this Lamb will give you courage for every battle. In the blood you will lose all fear, and you will become a good shepherd who will lay down your life for your little sheep.

Up then, father; don't sit still any longer! Fire yourself with tremendous desire, expecting divine help and providence. For it seems to me that divine Goodness is about to turn the great wolves into lambs. This is why I am coming there soon, to lay them in your lap, humbled. I am certain that you, as their father, will receive them in spite of their persecution and injustice against you. You will learn from gentle First Truth, who says that the good shepherd, once he has found the little lost sheep, will put it on his shoulders and take it back to the fold. So do that, father. Once your little lost sheep has been found, take it on love's shoulders and put it in the fold of holy Church. And right after that our gentle Savior wants and commands you to raise the standard of the most holy cross over the unbelievers, and let this whole war be picked up and directed against them. As for the soldiers you have hired to come here, hold them back and don't let them come, for they would ruin everything instead of setting things right.

My dear father, you ask me about your coming. I answer you in the name of Christ crucified: come as soon as you can. If you can, come before September, and if you cannot come earlier, don't delay beyond the end of September. Pay no attention to any opposition, but like a courageous and fearless man, come! And, as you value your life, see that you don't come with an army, but with the cross in your hand, as a meek lamb. If you do, you will fulfill God's will. But if you come in any other way you will be violating that will rather than fulfilling it. Be glad, father! Be jubilant! Come! Come!

I'll say no more. Keep living in God's holy and tender love.

Gentle Jesus! Jesus love!

Pardon me, father. I humbly ask your dear blessing.

LETTER TO CHARLES V, KING OF FRANCE, JULY 1376

In the name of Jesus Christ crucified and of gentle Mary.

Dearest lord and father in Christ Jesus,

I Caterina, servant and slave of the servants of Jesus Christ, am writing to you in his precious blood. . . .

There are three specific things I am asking you, in your position, to do for love of Christ crucified.

The first is to make light of the world and of yourself and of all earthly pleasures. Hold your kingdom as something lent to you, not as if it were your own. For you know well that life, health, wealth, honor, status, dominion—none of these belongs to you. If they did, you could own them in your own way. But just when we want to be healthy we are sick; just when we want to be alive we die;

Chapter 10
Politics and
Sanctity in
Fourteenth-
Century Europe:
Gregory XI
(1330–1378) and
Catherine
of Siena
(1347–1380)

just when we want to be rich we are poor; just when we want to be in power we are made servants. And all this because these things are not ours, and we can keep them only as much and as long as it pleases the One who has lent them to us. So it is really foolish to hold as if it were our own what belongs to another: it is, in fact, a thievery worthy of death. This is why I am asking you to act wisely, as a good steward, holding everything as lent to you who have been made God's steward.

The second thing I am asking is that you uphold true holy justice. Let it not be adulterated by selfish love for yourself or by flattery or by human respect. And don't pretend not to see if your officials are inflicting injustice for money, denying the poor their rights. No, be a father to the poor as a dispenser of what God has given you. And see to it that any wrongs in your kingdom are punished, and virtue honored. For all this is the work of divine justice.

The third thing is to follow the teaching given you by this Master on the cross, which is exactly what my soul most longs to see in you: friendship and love between you and your neighbor[1] with whom you have been so long at war. For you know well that without such love as its root the tree of your soul would not bear fruit. . . .

. . . I am surprised you aren't willing to sacrifice even your life if you could— to say nothing of material things—at the sight of all the physical and spiritual destruction there has been, and all the religious and women and children who have been abused and driven away by this war. No more, for love of Christ crucified! Don't you realize that you are the cause of this evil if you don't do what you can? It is evil for Christians and unbelievers alike, for your squabbling has been and still is standing in the way of the mystery of the holy crusade. Even if this last were the only evil coming from your warring, it seems to me we should be expecting divine judgment.

I beg you to stop being the agent of so much evil and the obstacle to such a good as the recovery of the Holy Land and of all those poor souls who have no share in the blood of God's Son. You and the other Christian lords ought to be ashamed of such a thing. What a scandal, humanly speaking, and what an abomination before God, that you should be making war against your brother and leaving your enemy alone, and that you should be seizing what belongs to another and not get back what is yours! Enough of this stupid blindness! . . .

1. England.—Ed.

DOCUMENT SIX

GREGORY XI

Papal Bull Against John Wycliffe
(May 1377)

Like his predecessors, Gregory XI was concerned about stamping out heresy. In England, John Wycliffe (1329–1384), a priest and theologian at Oxford University, was increasingly critical of the church and the clergy. He insisted on the importance of Scripture and the role of individuals in spiritual matters. He also had the protection of important religious and political leaders in England. Gregory clearly saw his ideas as heretical and ordered his arrest. What is Gregory telling the church leaders at Oxford? What are the most important "errors" of belief of Wycliffe? How do these "errors" reflect broader problems in the church?

WYCLIFFITE CONCLUSIONS

I.—That the material substance of bread and of wine remains, after the consecration, in the sacrament of the altar. . . .

IV.—That if a bishop or priest lives in mortal sin he does not ordain, or consecrate, or baptize.

V.—That if a man has been truly repentant, all external confession is superfluous to him or useless.

VI.—Continually to assert that it is not founded in the gospel that Christ instituted the mass. . . .

VIII.—That if the pope is foreordained to destruction and a wicked man, and therefore a member of the devil, no power has been given to him over the faithful of Christ by any one, unless perhaps by the Emperor.

IX.—That since Urban the Sixth, no one is to be acknowledged as pope; but all are to live, in the way of the Greeks, under their own laws.

X.—To assert that it is against sacred scripture that men of the church should have temporal possessions.

XI.—That no prelate ought to excommunicate any one unless he first knows that the man is excommunicated by God. . .s

XV.—To assert that it is allowed to any one, whether a deacon or a priest, to preach the word of God, without the authority of the apostolic see, or of a Catholic bishop, or of some other which is sufficiently acknowledged. . . .

XVIII.—That tithes are purely charity, and that parishioners may, on account of the sins of their curates, detain these and confer them on others at their will.

XIX.—That special prayers applied to one person by prelates or religious persons, are of no more value to the same person than general prayers for others in a like position are to him. . . .

Chapter 10
Politics and
Sanctity in
Fourteenth-
Century Europe:
Gregory XI
(1330–1378) and
Catherine
of Siena
(1347–1380)

XXIII.—That friars should be required to gain their living by the labor of their hands and not by mendicancy.

XXIV.—That a person giving alms to friars, or to a preaching friar, is excommunicate; also the one receiving.

BULL OF POPE GREGORY XI., AGAINST JOHN WYCLIFFE

Gregory, bishop, servant of the servants of God, to his beloved sons the Chancellor and University of Oxford, in the diocese of Lincoln, grace and apostolic benediction.

We are compelled to wonder and grieve that you, who, in consideration of the favors and privileges conceded to your University of Oxford by the apostolic see, and on account of your familiarity with the Scriptures, in whose sea you navigate, by the gift of God, with auspicious oar, you, who ought to be, as it were, warriors and champions of the orthodox faith, without which there is no salvation of souls,—that you through a certain sloth and neglect allow tares to spring up amidst the pure wheat in the fields of your glorious University aforesaid; and what is still more pernicious, even continue to grow to maturity. And you are quite careless, as has been lately reported to us, as to the extirpation of these tares; with no little clouding of a bright name, danger to your souls, contempt of the Roman church, and injury to the faith above mentioned. And what pains us the more, is that this increase of the tares aforesaid is known in Rome before the remedy of extirpation has been applied in England where they sprang up. By the insinuation of many, if they are indeed worthy of belief, deploring it deeply, it has come to our ears that John deWycliffe, rector of the church of Lutterworth, in the diocese of Lincoln, Professor of the Sacred Scriptures, (would that he were not also Master of Errors,) has fallen into such a detestable madness that he does not hesitate to dogmatize and publicly preach, or rather vomit forth from the recesses of his breast certain propositions and conclusions which are erroneous and false. He has cast himself also into the depravity of preaching heretical dogmas which strive to subvert and weaken the state of the whole church and even secular polity, some of which doctrines, in changed terms, it is true, seem to express the perverse opinions and unlearned learning of Marsilio of Padua of cursed memory, . . . This he has done in the kingdom of England, lately glorious in its power and in the abundance of its resources, but more glorious still in the glistening piety of its faith, and in the distinction of its sacred learning; producing also many men illustrious for their exact knowledge of the Holy Scriptures, mature in the gravity of their character, conspicuous in devotion, defenders of the Catholic church. He has polluted certain of the faithful of Christ by sprinkling them with these doctrines, and led them away from the right paths of the aforesaid faith to the brink of perdition.

Wherefore, since we are not willing, nay, indeed, ought not to be willing, that so deadly a pestilence should continue to exist with our connivance, a pestilence which, if it is not opposed in its beginnings, and torn out by the roots in its entirety, will be reached too late by medicines when it has infected very many with its contagion; we command your University with strict admonition, by the apostolic authority, in virtue of your sacred obedience, and under penalty of the deprivation of all the favors, indulgences, and privileges granted to you and your University by the said see, for the future not to permit to be asserted or proposed to any extent whatever, the opinions, conclusions, and propositions which are in variance with good morals and faith, even when those proposing strive to defend them under a certain fanciful wrestling of words or of terms. Moreover, you are on our authority to arrest the said John, or cause him to be arrested and to send him under a trustworthy guard to our venerable brother, the Archbishop of Canterbury, and the Bishop of London, or to one of them.

Besides, if there should be, which God forbid, in your University, subject to your jurisdiction, opponents stained with these errors, and if they should obstinately persist in them, proceed vigorously and earnestly to a similar arrest and removal of them, and otherwise as shall seem good to you. Be vigilant to repair your negligence which you have hitherto shown in the premises, and so obtain our gratitude and favor, and that of the said see, besides the honor and reward of the divine recompense.

Given at Rome, at Santa Maria Maggiore, on the 31st of May, the sixth year of our pontificate.

DOCUMENT SEVEN

GREGORY XI

Guidance for Election of a Pope
(March 1378)

Gregory XI wrote this document after he had returned to Rome. His health was failing rapidly, and he feared what might happen when he died—there was still instability in the papal states, and he suspected some of his cardinals wanted to return to France. In this document, he gives them guidance for the election of a new pope. What is he most concerned about? What advice does he give? What does this document say about the role of the college of cardinals in church affairs?

. . . For the perpetual memory of the matter. With the future dangers and very serious disadvantages which may befall the Holy Church of God as the result of a long vacancy [of the papal throne] on account of wars breaking out, and on the occasion of these and for several other reasons, we, desirous of preventing this by means of a helpful remedy, have determined and do unalterably ordain by virtue of our apostolic authority expressed in this document that, if we

[305]

Chapter 10
Politics and
Sanctity in
Fourteenth-
Century Europe:
Gregory XI
(1330–1378) and
Catherine
of Siena
(1347–1380)

should die between now and the kalends of next September, the cardinals of the Holy Roman Church then present at the Roman curia—or the greater part [*"maior pars"*] of them—with those absent not being called nor in any way awaited, may legally choose, receive and have any other suitable place they wish, either in or out of the City, notwithstanding even the objection of a minority of those present to the change, so as to effect the election at once of the future supreme pontiff our successor, and they may shorten, prolong or completely eliminate—as they or the greater part of them see fit—the time set by law for cardinals to await absent cardinals before proceeding to the election of the supreme pontiff and entering into conclave for this election; and they may change the abovementioned site once or many times . . . just as it seems opportune to them or the greater part of them, with the lesser part not consenting or even contradicting, giving and granting by means of our apostolic authority and from the plenitude of power, to the abovementioned cardinals present or the greater part of them all power and authority to elect the supreme pontiff of the Roman Catholic Church, our immediate successor, ordaining and determining, by our apostolic authority and out of our plenitude of power, that he who will have been elected supreme pontiff and pastor of the Holy Roman Catholic Church by these cardinals present at the Roman curia, or by the greater part of these, even with a lesser segment dissenting or even opposing, will have the loyalty of these cardinals without exception, insisting as we do that they select a good shepherd, imploring them by the bowels of God's mercy and enjoining them no less very strictly and under pain of the law not to postpone proceeding to these aforementioned matters purely, simply, without any deceit, and as quickly as they can according to God and their consciences, notwithstanding any constitutions whatsoever of our predecessors the Roman pontiffs to the contrary which they encounter with respect to the aforementioned or any part of the aforementioned; we want these abrogated this time, though in the future we want them and all their modifications to retain their force. . . .

DOCUMENT EIGHT

The Declaration of the Cardinals, Rome
(1378)

Gregory had hoped to avoid problems in the election of the next pope, but that was not the case. The cardinals elected Urban VI (the archbishop of Bari) first, then repudiated him. They carried out another election, chose another pope (Clement VII), and then fled back to Avignon. The result was the Great Schism in the church because it now had two heads and two seats of government. How do the cardinals explain and justify their actions?

. . . After the apostolic seat was made vacant by the death of our lord, pope Gregory XI, who died in March, we assembled in conclave for the election of a pope, as is the law and custom, in the papal palace, in which Gregory had died. . . . Officials of the city with a great multitude of the people, for the most part armed and called together for this purpose by the ringing of bells, surrounded the palace in a threatening manner and even entered it and almost filled it. To the terror caused by their presence they added threats that unless we should at once elect a Roman or an Italian they would kill us. They gave us no time to deliberate but compelled us unwillingly, through violence and fear, to elect an Italian without delay. In order to escape the danger which threatened us from such a mob, we elected Bartholomew, archbishop of Bari, thinking that he would have enough conscience not to accept the election, since every one knew that it was made under such wicked threats. But he was unmindful of his own salvation and burning with ambition, and so, to the great scandal of the clergy and of the Christian people, and contrary to the laws of the church, he accepted this election which was offered him, although not all the cardinals were present at the election, and it was extorted from us by the threats and demands of the officials and people of the city. And although such an election is null and void, and the danger from the people still threatened us, he was enthroned and crowned, and called himself pope and apostolic. But according to the holy fathers and to the law of the church, he should be called apostate, anathema, Antichrist, and the mocker and destroyer of Christianity. . . .

Renaissance Possibilities: Leon Battista Alberti (1404–1472) and Isotta Nogarola (1418–1466)

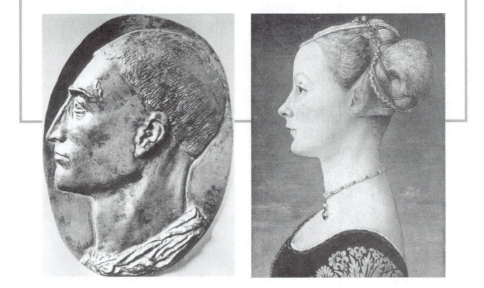

■ SETTING THE STAGE

When Francesco Petrarch died in 1374, the pope had not yet returned to Rome, political contests with secular rulers plagued the church, and questions about the spiritual health of Christianity worried the faithful. Petrarch himself was deeply concerned about the meaning of Christian virtue and morality, and he hoped for church reform. Perhaps fortunately, he did not live to see the Great Schism (1378), which resulted when competing popes were elected and the western Christian community divided. Although the church would be reunited at the start of the next century, its woes did not end because heretical movements continued, and the men elected pope, with some exceptions, were weak, poorly suited to the job, and spiritually uninspiring. Technically, Petrarch was a priest, but he was also a well-educated scholar with considerable secular interests who loved Latin literature and wrote expressive love poems in vernacular Italian. Above all, Petrarch had a sense of history, an awareness of discontinuity between historical epochs, and the importance of understanding discrete or distinct historical eras.[1] He saw the period after the decline of Rome as a "dark age" without culture, an era of "barbarism, and ignorance," and believed that starting with his generation, the study of classical literature could produce a *rinascita*, or "rebirth," of civilization in the West. Petrarch is often associated with the origins of Renaissance humanism, but his disciples and other individuals with resources and learning developed and broadened his perspectives to create the cultural innovations and intellectual revivals that constituted the Italian Renaissance of the fifteenth century.

Before considering some general features of Renaissance life, it is important to remember that new ideas overlapped with the old, and that if Petrarch provided the seeds of this movement, the city-states or communes of Italy were its "midwives."[2]

For a long time, the cities of Italy had demanded civic responsibility and public participation in city life from their leading inhabitants. The welfare of the community depended on action and involvement, not contemplation and retreat, and this idea had been espoused by spiritual leaders like Catherine of Siena (see Chapter 10). By the late fourteenth century, many people in the cities who had survived rounds of the plague, economic depression, and wars with the pope and with other cities felt that they could shape their world and that they were not simply victims of destiny. They began to think of their age as one of opportunity for individuals with energy and talent. The grip of the church had been loosened for some, independent political structures and secular government were more and more common, and lay education was growing, all of which helped to create a receptive environment for intellectual rebirth and renewal. Without a "favorable moral climate, [and] a responsive public," the "cultural program" of a highly literate elite would not have flourished.[3]

It is equally true that the bulk of the population in Italy, which was still rural and lived according to traditional cultures, was probably untouched by the Renaissance. The freedom of opportunity and upward mobility that existed for some would be denied to others. Generally speaking, in the towns of northern Italy, "communal government was increasingly in the

1. Charles Nauert, *Humanism and the Culture of Renaissance Europe* (Cambridge, England: Cambridge University Press, 1995), pp. 19–22.

2. John Larner, *Italy in the Age of Dante and Petrarch, 1216–1380* (New York: Longman, 1980), p. 225. See Lauro Martines, *Power and the Imagination: City-States in Renaissance Italy* (New York: Alfred A. Knopf, 1979), pp. 199, 205, for the ties between communal life and the development of humanism.

3. Martines, p. 205. See also John Larner, *Culture and Society in Italy, 1290–1420* (New York: Charles Scribner's Sons, 1971), pp. 353–354.

Chapter 11
Renaissance
Possibilities:
Leon Battista
Alberti (1404–
1472) and Isotta
Nogarola
(1418–1466)

hands of a minority—[a nobility, or patriciate]—whose ranks were more tightly defined".[4] Thus, Renaissance ideas and practices were the products of a fairly small segment of the fifteenth-century population of Italy. An even "darker side" of the Renaissance is evident in the fact that, regardless of rhetoric, intent, talent, desires, or wealth, women were not men's equals in the project.

A "revolution" in education laid the groundwork for many of the changes associated with the Renaissance. The curriculum and purposes of older communal schools were transformed as a new generation of teachers created independent, urban schools dedicated to humanistic studies (grammar, rhetoric, history, poetry, and ethics). Some Latin texts were rediscovered and others retranslated, while study of Greek literature and philosophy was reintroduced to western scholars. The goal of the new courses of study was to use classical texts and history to confront current social and political problems and to promote self-understanding and expression as well. A range of people who were "restless researchers and experimenters" in multiple disciplines reflected on their

own experiences, observed the world around them, and used the vantage point of their studies for critical analysis.[5] The cities needed men who were capable of practical, political, and economic solutions, not abstract speculation, and communal governments and powerful nobles endorsed the new education. This intellectual tradition did not replace scholasticism, but rather coexisted beside or around it. It was not tied to a single truth and was not centered in the universities, and its revolutionary potential and secular focus could produce condemnation from the church.

Self-consciousness, self-importance, and a sense of history also characterized the literate, urban people of the Renaissance. These traits had quite practical results because individuals described their cities, rulers, and governments, sometimes in glowing terms; provided personal accounts of their own lives; and wrote about family life, often using their experiences as a starting point. Abelard's letters and autobiography (see Chapter 9) attest to the existence of this sort of self-expression in previous centuries, but it had been rare. In the fourteenth century, personal commentary and notes often accompanied tax and financial reports, and more and more people engaged in writing memoirs or had their portraits painted. As the "fashioning of the self" became more wide-

4. Denys Hay and John Law, *Italy in the Age of the Renaissance, 1350–1530* (New York: Longman, 1989), p. 30. For the assessment of women's status, see Samuel J. Cohn, Jr., *Women in the Streets: Essays on Sex and Power in Renaissance Italy* (Baltimore, Md.: Johns Hopkins University Press, 1996); the essays in Judith Brown and Robert C. Davis (eds.), *Gender and Society in Renaissance Italy* (New York: Longman, 1998); and the seminal work of Margaret King, *Women of the Renaissance* (Chicago, Ill.: University of Chicago Press, 1991).

5. Eugenio Garin, "Il filosofo e il mago," in Garin (ed.), *L'uomo del Rinascimento* (Bari: Laterza, 1988), pp. 169, 184; also Paul Grendler, *Schooling in Renaissance Italy* (Baltimore, Md.: Johns Hopkins University Press, 1989), pp. 140–141.

spread, both the "academy and the warehouse were the forges" for an ever increasing number of autobiographical self-revelations.[6] Not only do these works attest to the impact of the ideas and practices of the Renaissance, but they are a gold mine for the historian.

Both Leon Battista Alberti and Isotta Nogarola were well-known figures in intellectual circles and wrote frequent letters to their mentors and peers. Many of these letters were intended for public consumption. They also wrote essays, and Alberti wrote an autobiography. These sources, combined with what others thought of them and with evidence of the social, political, and cultural world in which they lived, provide a fuller sense of the meaning of the Italian Renaissance in the first half of the fifteenth century, of its excitement and diversity, and its possibilities and limitations.

◼ THE ACTORS:

LEON BATTISTA ALBERTI AND ISOTTA NOGAROLA

Circumstances of birth and geography positioned both Leon Battista Alberti and Isotta Nogarola to participate in the intellectual and artistic world of the Renaissance. Both came from wealthy, well-established, upper-class or noble families. The Albertis were a politically prominent, Florentine merchant and banking family; the Nogarolas were nobles from the small city of Verona, which, along with its neighbor Padua, was under Venetian control after 1405. In the arena of Renaissance art, architecture, and writing, Florence was the leader, but Venice was close behind. These cities and their immediate surrounding areas were magnets for talented individuals in a wide range of disciplines. Although neither Florence nor Venice possessed leading universities at this time, they were centers of humanistic studies. Florence could boast about being home to several well-respected and influential teachers. When Venice gained control over Padua, it acquired the benefits of the most important university of this period, as well as access to Padua's independent schools, some of the finest in Italy. A study of six hundred artists and writers of the Italian Renaissance noted that 26 percent of them were from Tuscany (where Florence is located), and 23 percent were from Venice and its territories.[7]

Florence and Venice were independent republics, and although both were governed by oligarchies of elite citizens, they maintained a semblance

---

6. Cohn talks about individualism and the "fashioning of the self," p. 56, while Garin, "L'uomo del Rinascimento," pp. 5, 10, refers to the importance of autobiography in this era. See Giovanni Ciapelli and Patricia Lee Rubin (eds.), *Art, Memory and Family in Renaissance Florence* (New York: Cambridge University Press, 2000), for an in-depth examination of these and other issues of self-commemoration.

7. Peter Burke, *The Italian Renaissance: Culture and Society in Italy,* 2nd ed., (Princeton, N.J.: Princeton University Press, 1999), p. 44.

Chapter 11
Renaissance
Possibilities:
Leon Battista
Alberti (1404–
1472) and Isotta
Nogarola
(1418–1466)

of popular government. The aristocracy of Venice was rigidly set by law. In 1350, there were fifteen hundred nobles; by 1500, there were twenty-five hundred out of a total population of 100,000. Decision-making authority rested in the Greater Council, whose members included all noblemen over the age of 25.[8] The noble class of Florence was more porous, and inclusion in the elite depended on factors such as wealth, prior office holding, family lineage, and marriage alliance. In Florence, an executive committee of 37 members of the leading families, the *Signoria,* had power, although the more democratic *parlamento* still met. Politics in Florence tended to be more unruly than in Venice because additional committees and groups engaged in frequent debate and argument. The head of state in Venice, the *doge,* had a lifetime appointment; the chief administrator in Florence was the chancellor, who was responsible for keeping state papers, composing treaties and laws, and (increasingly by the end of the fourteenth century) writing propaganda and the history of the city. By the time that Battista and Isotta were growing up, it was common in both cities for the individual in charge of either government to be a humanist scholar, and one task was to promote their cities as the heirs to classical republican institutions and as symbols of independence from external domination.

In the first part of the fifteenth century, Leonardo Bruni (1370–1444) was

8. Figures for both Venice and Florence are from Hay and Law, pp. 34, 251–272.

the chancellor of Florence. He inherited many of Petrarch's ideas and studied Greek in Florence. Bruni became most interested in classical republicanism, and was convinced that Florence was the model of freedom from tyranny. In 1406, he wrote *In Praise of the City of Florence,* which clearly illustrated the revival of both the ideas and the form of classical Greek writing and, more specifically relevant to the politics of his time, helped to create the myth of Florentine independence, equality, and liberty (Document One). Men like Bruni, who were humanist scholars, authors, and political leaders, moved easily from government hall to library, to palaces, and to cultural events. They corresponded and met with other well-off, educated people and often traveled to other cities for that purpose. In short, the Italian world of the Renaissance was a small one, and even more extensive connections would be possible with the introduction of printing in the second half of the fifteenth century. Although we have no evidence that Isotta Nogarola and Leon Battista Alberti ever met, their circles overlapped, and we can speculate that as both gained public recognition, they might at least have read each other's works.

Leon Battista was born in 1404 in Genoa because, in the contentious and competitive arena of Florentine politics, the Alberti clan had been defeated and banned from the city—an exile that lasted until 1428. Battista (as he was known until he became an adult and assumed the name Leon) and his older brother Carlo were illegitimate. Some sources say that their mother was a widowed noblewoman from Genoa, but in any case, their father, Lorenzo, recognized the boys as his sons—they were his only children—and gave them his name.[9] (See Galileo's example in Chapter 12.) In 1406, when the plague struck Genoa again, Battista's mother died, and Lorenzo moved to Venice with his two sons. Venice's economic prowess was well known and, as head of the Venetian branch of the family trading company, Lorenzo apparently did quite well. His wedding, which took place when Battista was a young boy, was an opulent and extravagant affair. Lorenzo was also responsible for his son's early education, but at the appropriate time, when Battista was eleven or twelve, he was sent to one of the leading independent boarding schools in Padua run by Gasparino Barzizza (1360–1430).

Barzizza was one of the founders of the new humanistic education. He continued to use some medieval texts and methods, but he introduced his students to classical Latin authors and promoted the use of classical forms and language in modern compositions. Schools like Barzizza's were expensive and thus catered to an elite group who were often drawn from other cities or regions. Battista probably studied with twenty other students (among them his brother Carlo) and remained at the school for three to five years.[10] The training that he received and the intellectual model and morality of his master, Barzizza, shaped Alberti's future character, scholarship, and forms of expression. Attending this school also introduced him to the sons of nobles like the Venetian Francesco Barbaro (1390–1454), like-minded individuals with whom he would maintain ties throughout his life. Barzizza's *gymnasium,* as he called his school, was on the crest of a new wave of schools that earned the endorsement of communal leaders, the patrician class, and the wealthy merchant and banking families, and made possible the establishment of humanistic studies by the mid-fifteenth century.

A contemporary of Barzizza's, the scholar Guarino Guarini (1374–1460), was also from Verona. He had spent five years studying Greek in Constantinople and added that to the curriculum in his famous school. His students were among the future political leaders, princes, and teachers of the fifteenth century. When he eventually moved to Ferrara to tutor Leonello d'Este (1407–1450), the heir

9. This identification of his mother is from Renee Neu Watkins (ed. and trans.), *The Family in Renaissance Florence by Leon Battista Alberti* (Columbia, S.C.: University of South Carolina Press, 1969), p. 4. There are numerous biographies of Alberti and his works; the material in this essay relies on Franco Borsi, *Leon Battista Alberti: The Complete Works* (New York: Electa/ Rizzoli, 1989); Joan Gadol, *Leon Battista Alberti: Universal Man of the Renaissance* (Chicago, Ill.: University of Chicago Press, 1969); and the most recent and quite different study by Anthony Grafton, *Leon Battista Alberti: Master Builder of the Italian Renaissance* (New York: Hill and Wang, 2000).

10. For the development of the most important humanistic schools, see Grendler, *Schooling in Renaissance Italy,* pp. 125–132; Nauert, pp. 45–51. For Alberti's experience at Barzizza's school, see Grafton, pp. 39–46.

Chapter 11
Renaissance
Possibilities:
Leon Battista
Alberti (1404–
1472) and Isotta
Nogarola
(1418–1466)

to the duchy, he also became a star lecturer at the university there and the center of a network of humanist scholars that included both Alberti and Nogarola.

Isotta Nogarola was born in Verona in 1418, at about the same time Alberti was finishing his schooling and preparing to leave that city for university study in Bologna. Her father's family were members of the nobility of Verona. Her mother, Bianca Borromeo, also came from a distinguished lineage and was herself unusually well educated. The Nogarolas had at least six children, including Isotta, a fairly standard family size for the time. In the world in which Isotta and her sisters grew up, women were expected to marry and have children. An alternative might be to enter a convent, and a significant number of women in both Florence and Venice did so, though not necessarily because of personal spiritual goals. Girls were often sent to a female monastery to be raised, at least until their fathers arranged an appropriate marriage. In fact, the Florentines referred to this practice as *serbanza,* which meant being "in reserve or set aside."[11] In the convent, girls learned domestic skills, gained a fundamental vernacular education, and were trained in spiritual matters.

Even if they were educated in a secular environment, girls were usually taught only vernacular reading and writing, a little Latin grammar, and perhaps some arithmetic. A fairly un-usual proposal of the time came from Leonardo Bruni, who wrote an essay sometime in the early 1420s arguing that girls should receive a humanistic education to achieve virtue. Even he, however, said that "public oratory and disputation . . . [were] unbecoming and impractical for women."[12] A few years after that essay appeared, Francesco Barbaro, Alberti's schoolmate, wrote "On Wifely Duties," which was dedicated to Lorenzo de' Medici on his forthcoming marriage. Considering the humanists' admiration for the classical world, it was not surprising that he wanted wives to be like "the leaders of bees, who supervise, receive and preserve whatever comes into their hives [and] unless necessity dictates otherwise, they remain in their honeycombs where they develop and mature beautifully"[13] (Document Two). Most historians agree that in law and property rights, women's options and power were limited during the fifteen century, although loopholes always existed in dowry claims and the provisions of wills. Individual fathers' views and family interests also had a lot to do with the independence and options of their daughters.

We do not know what Leonardo Nogarola expected for his daughters. He died when Isotta was quite young (sometime between 1425 and 1433), and her mother and her aunt Angela, an erudite writer, insisted that she and her sisters be well educated. Like other wealthy noble families, they

11. Grendler, p. 97. See also Margaret L. King, "La donna del Rinascimento," in Garin (ed.), *L'uomo del Rinascimento,* pp. 273–327.

12. Grendler, p. 87.

13. Francesco Barbaro, "On Wifely Duties," in Kohl and Witt, p. 217.

hired tutors, one of whom was Martino Rizzoni, a graduate of Guarino's school in Verona.[14] Isotta thrived in this environment, and she and her sister Ginevra gained reputations fairly quickly for their knowledge and intelligence, not only in Verona, but in the region of Veneto more generally. Like Alberti, they were preparing for their debut into the humanist circles of the Renaissance.

ACT I:

APPEARANCE ON THE PUBLIC STAGE

Alberti's study of canon law at the University of Bologna was interrupted when his father died in 1421. The death of an uncle shortly thereafter created even greater problems because his cousins refused to give Leon Battista or his brother Carlo their inheritance on the grounds that they were illegitimate children. This left Alberti impoverished, and although he continued his legal studies—eventually receiving a degree in 1428—the next years were very difficult for him, not only financially, but also because of exhaustion from overwork and strain. Apparently his humanistic interests sustained him at this time. He managed to write several brief dialogues and also a Latin comedy in which a young man tries to win the hand of a young woman (Glory) with the help of his slave (Intellect). As Alberti explained, "[T]his play has to do with conduct: for it teaches that a man dedicated to study and hard work can attain glory, just as well as a rich and fortunate man."[15] This theme would be consistent in Alberti's life's work. In later reflections he refers to his relatives as "envious and malevolent" and accuses them of conspiring against him "most ungratefully and cruelly." Nevertheless, he continued to insist that "men are themselves the source of their own fortune and misfortune." When he wrote his autobiography much later in life, the picture that he painted of himself in these years as a young scholar emphasized his energy, talents, search for knowledge, enthusiasm and sincerity, not his illnesses and poverty (Document Three).

Although Alberti found legal work boring, his training in canon law provided employment and access to power and status. His first employment

14. The authority on Nogarola's life and ideas is Margaret L. King. In this chapter, I have especially relied on the following works: "Isotta Nogarola: Umanista e devota," in Ottavia Niccoli (ed.), *Rinascimento al femminile* (Bari: Laterza, 1991); "Book-lined Cells: Women and Humanism in the Early Italian Renaissance," in Patricia Labalme (ed.), *Beyond Their Sex: Learned Women of the European Past* (New York: New York University Press, 1980), pp. 66–91; and "Thwarted Ambitions: Six Learned Women of the Italian Renaissance," *Soundings: An Interdisciplinary Journal*, LIX:3 (Fall 1976), pp. 280–304. Also helpful is Lisa Jardine, "Women Humanists: Education for What?" in Lorna Hutson (ed.), *Feminism and Renaissance Studies* (New York: Oxford University Press, 1999), pp. 48–81. Finally, one of the earliest pieces on Nogarola is still a valuable source: see Remigio Sabbadini, "Isotta Nogarola," *Archivio storico italiano* 18 (1886), pp. 435–443.

15. Quoted in Grafton, p. 4. For more of his comments on family and fortune, see his essays in James Bruce Ross and Mary Martin McLaughlin (eds.), *The Portable Renaissance Reader* (New York: The Viking Press, 1953), pp. 329–330, 485.

Chapter 11
Renaissance
Possibilities:
Leon Battista
Alberti (1404–
1472) and Isotta
Nogarola
(1418–1466)

was probably with the bishop of Bologna, who was also a cardinal and a papal legate. From that time, he remained in the service of the church until two years prior to his death. His primary appointment was in the administrative branch of the papal court in Rome. Alberti took holy orders but was not ordained a priest and was never interested in climbing the ladder of church office. He remained a celibate cleric for the rest of his life, and he was a devout Christian who did not challenge doctrine. At the same time, he saw God as the creator, a great architect, who gave humankind "cognition, reason and memory.... Man was born to be useful to himself and others," and devotion was best expressed in work and virtue in this world.[16] His church office provided him with income throughout his life, and when he died, he was well-off and owned several properties that were disposed of in his will.

Working in the papal curia was both advantageous and interesting. Although the church was unified, the conciliar movement remained a crucial voice in church affairs, and the papacy continued to act as a mediator and a major political player in all the regions of Europe. Thus, the popes needed bright young men to draft position papers on all sorts of issues. In addition to the humanist scholars who worked at the court, some of the most powerful families in Italy also had representatives there. Finally, the council meetings of the church were international, and they provided people like Alberti with the opportu-

nity to learn and to acquire new friends. Every bit of news seemed to arrive at the court, and the "discussions of sexual and literary gossip" that went on "spared no one."[17] His employment in the papal court also meant that he traveled with the pope.

Beginning in 1434, when political disturbances in Rome forced the pope to leave the Holy City, Alberti went with him, first to Florence for two years and then to other cities like Bologna and Ferrara. In Florence, the Medici family was rising to power with the backing of the Alberti clan and others. These times were intellectual and cultural glory days for Florence, and also for Alberti because he formed friendships with people like the architect Filippo Brunelleschi and the sculptor Donatello. In the 1430s, he tackled some major topics of interest to Renaissance intellectuals and society. He wrote the first three chapters of *On the Family* while still living in Rome, added a fourth chapter in 1437, and presented the book to the public in 1441.[18] Using fictional dialogues among characters who were supposedly members of his own family, Alberti provided multiple points of view about the family and its functions, dynamics, and internal relationships, and then ultimately about the connection between the family and the community of which it was a part. One of his characters echoed Roman Republican rhetoric when he stated: "Fame is born, not in the midst of private peace, but in public action.... reputation is nourished by the judgement of many

16. Quoted in Gadol, pp. 238–239.

17. Grafton, p. 51.
18. Watkins, p. 2.

people of honor, and in the midst of the people"[19] (Document Four). This was just one of his writings that tackled the problems of the place of the individual in civic life, and the desire for solitude and private reflection versus the need for public action.

Alberti also wrote several treatises that were more technical in nature. *On Painting,* also written in the 1430s, was one such piece. Here Alberti combined his love of artistic expression with his understanding of mathematics and explained how art was a product of geometric rules and the science of optics, but he also insisted that in the largest sense an artistic composition was really painted history. By 1437, he had begun to write his autobiography, and in that same year wrote a satiric eulogy to his dog. The incredible range of his interests and the diversity of the forms of expression he used would mean that some of his essays were more popular than others, or that individual pieces found a particular audience. When he began to add mapmaking, architectural design, and building restorations to his repertoire, many of his contemporaries wondered if there was anything he couldn't do or wouldn't try.

In 1438, he attended a church council meeting at Ferrara and became acquainted with the city's prince, the duke Leonello d'Este, who was Alberti's first well-known patron and eventually a long-time friend. Prior to their meeting, Alberti was certainly familiar with the world of Renaissance patronage and had actually touched

on the subject in earlier writings, in which he questioned whether such a process was indispensable or dangerous in civic life. But now he had the chance to experience this world firsthand, and his public career simultaneously branched out in many different directions. Thus far, his appearance on the public stage seemed to have found a receptive audience.

The same could be said for Isotta Nogarola in her first exposures to public scrutiny, critique, or praise. By 1434, she and her older sister Ginevra were engaged in a standard intellectual activity of the time—the exchange of letters. Their epistles are not concerned with describing daily life, work, household management, or relationships in their family. Instead, they demonstrated their ability to write in Latin, knowledge of a wide variety of classical literature, and awareness of current politics and the issues discussed and debated by Renaissance humanists. Isotta's correspondence, and some of Ginevra's and their aunt Angela's, were collected and preserved by a descendant of the family and all were eventually published in several volumes in the nineteenth century. A few of Isotta's letters and references to her appear in the collections of the individuals with whom she corresponded.[20] The first known letter that Isotta wrote in 1434

19. Quoted in Grafton, p. 179.

20. For discussions of the geneaology of the correspondence, see Sabbadini, p. 435; Margaret L. King, "The Religious Retreat of Isotta Nogarola," 3:4 (Summer 1978), pp. 820–822. The quote that follows from the letter to Barbaro is quoted in Margaret King, "Isotta Nogarola," in Rinaldina Russell (ed.), *Italian Women Writers* (Westport, Conn.: Greenwood Press, 1994), p. 314.

Chapter 11
Renaissance
Possibilities:
Leon Battista
Alberti (1404–
1472) and Isotta
Nogarola
(1418–1466)

was a congratulatory message addressed to Emolao Barbaro in Venice. He was the nephew of Francesco Barbaro and had just received a papal appointment. In true classical form, she "praised his eloquence, important 'for every free people, in every republic,' noted his knowledge of law, and commended his family." Subsequent letters were addressed to other scholars in Venice and also in Padua and Ferrara. The latter city was the location of Guarino's famous school and by the 1430s, under d'Este patronage and leadership, was fast becoming an important center of humanist scholarship. In 1436, Jacopo Foscari, son of the Venetian doge, was sufficiently impressed with Isotta's learning that he forwarded to Guarino a letter he had received from her. Guarino, in turn, praised her "eloquence" to his patron, Leonello d'Este. Shortly thereafter, Isotta received a response from Guarino's *son* expressing his admiration for her intelligence and learning. This epistolary history is significant, first, because Isotta's initial correspondence is with a *second* generation of humanists, the sons of the famous founders of Renaissance thought. Second, the passing around of letters and the reporting on ideas and the works of others were important mechanisms (in a pre–printing press era) by which the "small world" of humanist intellectuals and their reputations—good or bad—were created.

While the number of male humanist scholars was relatively small and the number of female members in those circles even smaller, there were other women humanists. Francesco Barbaro's daughter Costanza was educated by her father in humanist stud-

ies, but in 1440, when she was about twenty years old, she decided to enter a convent. Her father was ambivalent about the decision, probably because he hoped that she would marry, but eventually he supported it and their subsequent correspondence indicates Costanza's ongoing engagement with classical studies.[21] Cecelia Gonzaga (1425–1451) represents a slightly higher social class because her family were the rulers of the city-state of Mantua. She attended a famous humanist school along with her brothers and men who were destined to play intellectual, political, and religious roles in Italian life. By the time she was eight, she had become competent in Greek, and when she was eighteen she decided, like Costanza Barbaro, to enter a convent. Her father refused to allow it and instead arranged a marriage for her. But before the marriage could take place, he died and Costanza and her mother both adopted a religious life. Apparently, she too continued to pursue a serious program of studies within the convent's walls. Subsequent generations of fifteenth-century intellectual women would include the feisty Laura Cereta (1469–1499), who claimed Petrarch as her model, and the more famous Isabella d'Este (1479–1539), who was well educated but best known as one of the major patrons of art in the late fifteenth and early sixteenth centuries. With perhaps the exception of Isabella,

21. Material on Costanza Barbaro and Cecilia Gonzaga is from King, "Thwarted Ambitions," pp. 289–292. One of Francesco's letters to his daughters is in Margaret L. King and Albert Rabli, Jr., , *Her Immaculate Hand,* (Binghamton, N.Y.: Center for Medieval & Early Reniassance Studies, 1983), pp. 106–111.

Isotta's life provides a good comparison with these women and illustrates the opportunities they had and the choices they were forced to make.

After hearing from many other people that her letters were traveling "throughout the world," and that many of the leading scholars, including Guarino, were impressed with her erudition, Isotta decided to write to the great Guarino himself, which she did in early 1437.[22] Several months passed without an answer, and women in Verona began ridiculing her for even thinking that she was worthy of his response. Isotta then wrote Guarino a second, quite desperate letter in which she told him of her humiliation, accused him of unfairly causing her suffering, and exclaimed, "There are already so many women in the world! Why then was I born a woman, to be scorned by men in words and deeds?" Guarino finally sent a reply in which he both scolded and comforted her, insisting that she should be more courageous and stop acting like a weak and foolish woman, and admitted that up until then he had "believed and trusted that your soul was manly." He concluded by telling her to be "noble and firm; [to] create a man within the woman, and face this abuse bravely, ..." We don't know Isotta's reaction to his letter, but undoubtedly she was torn by his words—on the one hand, he seemed to be acknowledging her abilities; on the other, her success would depend on her ability to transcend her gender. How could she become a "manly" woman?

In 1438, Ginevra married a noble *condotierro* from Brescia and left the family *and* her studies. Her married life was not happy. She was often ill and had difficult pregnancies and several miscarriages. Brescia itself was a contested territory and therefore also a battlefield. Shortly after the marriage, Isotta and several other members of her family, including another sister and her brother Antonio, moved to Venice, apparently to avoid the plague in Verona as well as the threat of warfare in that city. In Venice, Isotta resumed her correspondence with a wide circle of educated men, including Damiano dal Borgo, a married friend in Verona. Their letters covered a wide variety of topics, including war, plague, theology, illnesses, family, and love. Isotta's contact with Guarino had probably been unsettling to her, but perhaps even more disturbing was the fact that in all of her other correspondence, admiration and praise for her intellectual ability was usually accompanied by great surprise that a woman was indeed capable of such intelligence, argument, and skillful writing. Isotta became increasingly aware that her "woman's nature" would be hard to overcome, which may explain why, in a letter to dal Borgo in 1438, she included a list of the deeds of great heroines and learned women of the past and asked him, "Did not women exceed men ... in eloquence and virtue?"[23] Isotta was struggling to establish her own identity

22. Guarino exchange is quoted in King, "Thwarted Ambitions," pp. 284–285.

23. Letter to dal Borgo is quoted in King, "Isotta Nogarola," in *Italian Women Writers,* p. 315. The account of the slanderous attack on her in the next paragraph is from King, "Thwarted Ambitions," pp. 285–286.

Chapter 11
Renaissance
Possibilities:
Leon Battista
Alberti (1404–
1472) and Isotta
Nogarola
(1418–1466)

and to mark a path in uncharted territory.

Another blow was struck against Isotta in 1438. An anonymous writer accused her of promiscuity and of incest with her brother, and connected this sort of deviant behavior with her equally deviant intellectual activity, noting that "an eloquent woman is never chaste." Lust and literary studies were connected in this slanderous attack. Although several scholars defended her purity, the struggle to realize her talents and to fulfill her intellectual desires in the public forums, as the men of her time did,

proved too difficult for Nogarola. Shortly after the family returned to Verona in 1441, she declared her retreat from the public world and her dedication to a celibate life. By that time, both she and Alberti had learned a great deal about the sphere of humanist intellectual activity, and both were keenly aware that success in that arena was not always easy. He knew that he had some control, however, over his destiny and could exercise his will; by contrast, the obstacles facing Isotta were old and greater than she alone had the power to change.

▪ ACT II:

FORTUNE AND MISFORTUNE

The 1440s and 1450s found Nogarola in retreat and Alberti on the move. Prior to arriving in Ferrara, Alberti had learned how to approach and gain access to the princely world of patronage, but in that city he first applied the lessons learned.[24] In Ferrara, Alberti had helped Leonello d'Este in the building of a bronze equestrian monument to his father. Throughout the remainder of his life, he would demonstrate his belief in the use of public statues and buildings to "inspire and educate the citizens."[25] He began to study architecture in Ferrara, and when he returned to Rome in 1443, he focused on the ruins in this ancient city and the study of archeology, engineering, and mechanics. In 1447, a new pope, Nicholas V (r. 1447–

1455), was elected. He was an old friend of Alberti's from their university days in Bologna. Nicholas was interested in the restoration of Roman buildings and made Alberti his architectural adviser. This experience and the study of Roman ruins formed the basis for a new treatise, *On the Art of Building*. He presented it to the pope when it was completed in 1452. Although an important technical treatise, the work was also an attempt to combine architecture with politics and social morality. According to Alberti, a town reflected the structure of the society and the character of the people who lived there. Successful towns were run by oligarchies composed of virtuous and fortunate men who were assisted by civil servants. Ultimately, he believed that fine streets and beautiful buildings would increase the prestige of any city and the stature of its citizens.

In the 1450s, Alberti was involved in a wide range of building projects.

24. Grafton, p. 205.
25. Grafton, p. 217.

Sometimes he was the sole planner and overseer of the project; on other occasions, he worked with various artists and craftsmen. As a result, historians have not always been sure exactly which parts of a structure are Alberti's. A church that he built for the Malatesta family in Rimini was one of his earliest and most independent works with a strong classical influence. By the mid-1440s, his circle of patrons had widened to include the Rucellai family, who were wealthy Florentine merchants and backers of the Medici. They hired him to design their palace and a country villa and commissioned him to plan the façade of one of the most famous Florentine churches, the Santa Maria Novella. Alberti took great pleasure in this building, stating that "[it honored] God, the city and my memory."[26] In 1458, another of Alberti's friends was elected pope and took the name Pius II. Although a man of humanist training and ideals, he was also committed to the organization of a vast crusade against the increasingly threatening Turks. For that purpose, a meeting was held in 1460 in Mantua, whose ruling family, the Gonzagas, were also learned and patrons of the arts. Alberti was soon commissioned by the Gonzagas to design a church and then participated in a broader scheme of city renovation and planning. There can be little doubt that his close association and travel with the papacy brought him into contact with important future clients and helped to build his reputation.

As Alberti was expanding his repertoire of Renaissance talents and interests, Nogarola was at home in Verona. She lived with her younger brother Antonio for a while, but then she and her mother lived in the home of her elder brother, Ludovico. Apparently the brothers disputed a family will and the move was the result. The matter was finally settled with Ludovico as the principal heir, but he also had to support his sister, Isotta. She did receive some resources directly, however, and the will stipulated that if Ludovico died, Isotta would be the next in line to inherit. Isotta was not an expensive housemate because she lived in a small room lined with books, did not travel, and was not interested in costly food or clothing. Even though she had proclaimed her retreat from public life, Isotta maintained her correspondence with several people and continued to receive laudatory letters. Another learned noblewoman, Costanza Varano (1428–1447), an accomplished Latinist, wrote to Isotta in the mid-1440s and likened her to Aspasia and Cornelia, claiming that together they all shared a "certain vitality and swiftness of mind."[27] One of her most important correspondents in this period was Lauro Quirini (1420–1479), a Venetian nobleman and another product of Guarino's school, who also appeared to take her intellect quite seriously. In 1442, he wrote to Isotta, setting forth a program of study for her because she was now beyond the "lower studies of literature

26. Quoted in Borsi, p. 48.

27. Letter from Costanza Varano is quoted from King and Rabil (eds.), *Her Immaculate Hand*, pp. 55–56.

Chapter 11
Renaissance
Possibilities:
Leon Battista
Alberti (1404–
1472) and Isotta
Nogarola
(1418–1466)

and languages" and ready to move to a higher plane (Document Five).

In 1451, Isotta initiated a literary correspondence and personal relationship with Ludovico Foscarini that would last until her death fifteen years later. He visited her and her brother, and they had conversations long into the night. Foscarini was a Venetian nobleman, lawyer, and humanist who served as a diplomat and in various civic capacities; at the time she first wrote to him, he was the mayor of Verona, but over the years of their friendship, he would be posted to other cities in Italy. Their correspondence was intense, intimate, and intellectual, but he always idealized her for her sanctity and purity as much as for her intelligence. Perhaps as a result of one of their lengthy conversations, she tackled a fundamental Christian doctrine that had shaped the lives of countless women for centuries: Eve's responsibility for the fall from grace. The treatise that resulted was written as a dialogue between her and Foscarini, and she called it "Of the Equal or Unequal Sin of Adam and Eve " (Document Six). Ironically, Isotta sought to defend Eve and womankind, but she could do so only by admitting female weakness. Contemporaries who read the essay were impressed with her erudition because she cited biblical sources, Aristotle, and Augustine.

A few years later, when Isotta received a sudden proposal of marriage from an admirer in Naples, she wrote to Foscarini asking what she should do. He angrily reminded her that she had forsaken marriage for a virginal life in order to pursue her intellectual interests. She answered him by suggesting that since he too was committed to learning and study, he should renounce his public career and devote himself to a life of purity and religious devotion that matched her own. As historian Margaret King concludes, in his rejection of the idea, he made clear he had no intention of "playing Abelard to her Héloïse."[28] The civic responsibilities he had to fulfill were quite different from any obligations that she might feel.

Isotta continued her scholarship, although with a newly emphasized religious focus. A small essay on Saint Jerome noted his knowledge of Greek and Latin, and pointed to the fact that he had given up his secular studies for spiritual ones. In 1459, she wrote to Pius II, commending him for calling a crusade. Her mother's death in 1461 seemed to weaken her intellectual resolve, and her exchanges with colleagues became fewer and fewer, just as her physical health deteriorated. Fittingly perhaps, in 1464, she received a letter from Ermolao Barbaro, one of the first people she had written to as a very young woman. He was now the bishop of Verona and, along with his letter, sent a book on episcopal administration dedicated to her. The last letter she received before her death in March 1466 was a message from Foscarini expressing concern for her declining health.

Although Alberti continued to pursue his artistic and architectural career in the 1460s, he did not give up his study of the classics or his essay writing on moral, civic, and political

28. King, "Isotta Nogarola," in *Rinascimento al femminile*, p. 22.

themes. No matter where he was working, he always returned to his "native" city, Florence. By the late 1460s, he joined the humanist circle of the young Lorenzo de' Medici (r. 1449–1492). Perhaps membership in that circle helped to inspire one of his last essays, *Icarius*, written in 1468, which dealt with government and advised princes that they must be able to reason abstractly and practically to be virtuous rulers. He also reiterated themes that had characterized much of his previous writings, in particular, the relationship between an individual's religious beliefs and devotion, and public activism and civic responsibility. He repeated his convictions that one was "born to be useful," that individual will and duty could guide one's life, and that work was one of life's sweetest rewards.

◾ FINALE

When Alberti died in 1472, there was little public mention of his death, and he was buried quietly in Rome. Although during his lifetime, many of Alberti's colleagues had praised his skills and the diversity of his pursuits, in later years the impact and importance of his achievements was less clear, perhaps because he worked in too many fields or because his actual contributions to projects were not always evident. Seventy-five years later, the art historian Giorgio Vasari paid Alberti a rather back-handed compliment when he stated that "such has been the influence of his writings on the pens and speech of scholarly men that he is commonly believed to be superior to those who were, in fact, superior to him."[29] By the time Vasari wrote, many of the innovations Alberti had made in the worlds of art and architecture had become almost commonplace and thus were taken for granted. On many levels, Alberti did not fit into neat intellectual or professional categories. He believed in the empirical method, relied on experience, and insisted that practice and action must accompany thought and ideas. Along with profound idealism and optimism, he expressed fears and awareness of human frailties. Nevertheless, his legacy remained and in the mid-nineteenth century, when the Swiss historian Jacob Burckhardt wrote his famous *Civilization of the Renaissance in Italy*, Leon Battista Alberti was the classic "universal man of the Renaissance." During his life, Alberti had hoped to improve his world and inspire his associates, but he had also sought glory and approval from the wealthy and learned circles, and above all knew that "if he lost his audience the lights would be extinguished, the curtain would fall, and he would find himself alone and lost in the dark."[30] That was a lesson Nogarola learned in the hard school of experience. In the face of the gender ideology that underlay the criticisms of her "audience," she chose retreat from the well-lighted public world.

29. Quoted in Borsi, p. 267. See Gadol, pp. 11–12, 233 and Grafton, p. 13 for Alberti's contradictory legacy.

30. Grafton, p. 339.

*Chapter 11
Renaissance
Possibilities:
Leon Battista
Alberti (1404–
1472) and Isotta
Nogarola
(1418–1466)*

Alberti and other humanists of his generation argued that individual will and intellect, a desire to do useful work, and a sense of duty to their communities were natural to men. Realizing these characteristics and talents brought man dignity, the praise of men, and divine approval. These principles did not apply to Isotta Nogarola or her female compatriots and would have been considered "unnatural" for women of the time. As learned and intelligent as Isotto Nogarola was, when she died, a poem had praised her "chaste body, incorruptible heart," but not her intellect and learning. Nogarola had hoped for a different life, but she confronted major obstacles to her will and desire to work, and she in turn felt that she had to defend women by pointing to their "natural" weaknesses. Several decades after her death, Laura Cereta from Brescia confronted the problems of the learned woman more directly, demanding that women's education be equal to men's, and arguing that for *both* men and women, "a mind

free, keen and unyielding in the face of hard work always rises to the good" (Document Seven). Building on what Nogarola and the women of earlier generations had done, Cereta claimed for her gender the Renaissance humanist ideals of men.

The educational and intellectual revolution that the humanists began did not disappear but instead spread into different forums and assumed different focuses. But it had to do so in turbulent times. By 1500, Italy was a battleground for the French and the Habsburg rulers, the Turks were pressing harder on Europe, a whole "new" world was opening up with Spanish and Portuguese expansion, and the spiritual revolution of the Protestant Reformation was about to rock Europe. Nevertheless, some of the intellectual threads of the Renaissance were picked up by individuals like Galileo Galilei, and educated women continued to challenge the closed male club of scholarly pursuits throughout the centuries that followed.

▪ QUESTIONS

1. What forces created a renaissance in the fifteenth century? What kinds of people were involved in this movement?

2. What was the relationship between the church and the cities, and humanist thinkers?

3. What was revoluntionary about education during the Renaissance? What educational traditions remained unchanged?

4. What was the impact of classical studies on Renaissance views of women? Did the Renaissance introduce any "new" ideas about women's nature and abilities? How would you compare Nogarola's life and status with those of her predecessors, Catherine of Siena and Héloïse?

5. What do you think were the most important legacies of the fifteenth-century Italian Renaissance?

DOCUMENT ONE

LEONARDO BRUNI

"In Praise of the City of Florence"
(ca. 1406)

When the Florentine humanist wrote this essay, who was his audience and what was his purpose? What does Bruni see as the outstanding attributes of the citizens of Florence? What makes the city itself unique in Italy, according to him? How realistic a picture do you think he is painting?

. . . So the Florentines were ready to do anything if they felt it would vouchsafe for them the good reputation that had been handed down to them by their ancestors. It was with these things in mind that the Florentine people set out for war in great and high spirits. So this people thought that it would live with great glory or perish fighting valiantly for its principles. Moreover, the Florentines believed that the position inherited from their ancestors had to be protected, so that they could never place concern for their wealth before their own self-esteem. Indeed, they were prepared to lose money and life itself to maintain their freedom, considering their situation both realistically and courageously. . . .

. . . There is nothing here that is ill proportioned, nothing improper, nothing incongruous, nothing vague; everything occupies its proper place, which is not only clearly defined but also in right relation to all the other elements. Here are outstanding officials, outstanding magistrates, an outstanding judiciary, and outstanding social classes. These parts are so distinguished so as to serve the supreme power of Florence, just as the Roman tribunes used to serve the emperor.

Now, first of all, great care is taken so that justice is held most sacred in the city, for without justice there can be no city, nor would Florence even be worthy to be called a city. Next there is provision for freedom, without which this great people would not even consider that life was worth living. These two principles are joined (almost as a stamp or goal) to all the institutions and statutes that the Florentine government has created. . . .

Therefore, what ornament does this city lack? What category of endeavor is not fully worthy of praises and grandeur? What about the quality of the forebears? Why are they not the descendants of the Roman people? What about glory? Florence has done and daily continues to do great deeds of honor and virtue both at home and abroad. What about the splendor of the architecture, the buildings, the cleanliness, the wealth, the great population, the healthfulness and pleasantness of the site? What more can a city desire? Nothing at all.

Chapter 11
Renaissance
Possibilities:
Leon Battista
Alberti (1404–
1472) and Isotta
Nogarola
(1418–1466)

What, therefore, should we say now? What remains to be done? Nothing other than to venerate God on account of His great beneficence and to offer our prayers to God. . . .

Therefore, under these magistracies this city has been governed with such diligence and competence that one could not find better discipline even in a household ruled by a solicitous father. As a result, no one here has ever suffered any harm, and no one has ever had to alienate any property except when he wanted to. The judges, the magistrates are always on duty; the courts, even the highest tribunal is open. All classes of men can be brought to trial; laws are made prudently for the common good, and they are fashioned to help citizens. There is no place on earth where there is greater justice open equally to everyone. Nowhere else does freedom grow so vigorously, and nowhere else are rich and poor alike treated with such equality. In this one also can discern Florence's great wisdom, perhaps greater than that of other cities. Now when very powerful men, relying on their wealth and position, appear to be offending or harming the weak, the government steps in and exacts heavy fines and penalties from the rich. It is consonant with reason that as the status of men is different, so their penalties ought to be different. The city has judged it consistent with its ideals of justice and prudence that those who have the most need should also be helped the most. Therefore, the different classes are treated according to a certain sense of equity; the upper class is protected by its wealth, the lower class by the state, and fear of punishment defends both. From this arises the saying that has been directed very often against the more powerful citizens when they have threatened the lower classes; in such a case the members of the lower class say: "I also am a Florentine citizen." . . .

DOCUMENT TWO

Francesco Barbaro

"On Wifely Duties"
(Sometime After 1414)

Francesco Barbaro was a Venetian humanist. With Guarino Guarini, he traveled to Florence, where he met members of the de' Medici family. This essay was written in honor of the marriage of Lorenzo de' Medici. What does Barbaro see as the most important roles of wives and the most desirable personal characteristics of a wife? What kinds of classical influences do you see in these ideas?

. . . Therefore, there are three things that, if they are diligently observed by a wife, will make a marriage praiseworthy and admirable: love for her husband, modesty of life, and diligent and complete care in domestic matters. We shall discuss the first of these, but before this I want to say something about the faculty of obedience, which is her master and companion, because nothing more important, nothing greater can be demanded of a wife than this. . . .

In the first place, let wives strive so that their husbands will clearly perceive that they are pensive or joyful according to the differing states of their husbands' fortunes. Surely congratulations are proper in times of good fortune, just as consolations are appropriate in times of adversity. Let them openly discuss whatever is bothering them, provided it is worthy of prudent people, and let them feign nothing, dissemble nothing, and conceal nothing. Very often sorrow and trouble of mind are relieved by means of discussion and counsel that ought to be carried out in a friendly fashion with the husband. If a husband shares all the pressures of her anxieties he will lighten them by participating in them and make their burden lighter; but if her troubles are very great or deeply rooted, they will be relieved as long as she is able to sigh in the embrace of her husband. . . .

I therefore would like wives to evidence modesty at all times and in all places. They can do this if they will preserve an evenness and restraint in the movements of the eyes, in their walking, and in the movement of their bodies; for the wandering of the eyes, a hasty gait, and excessive movement of the hands and other parts of the body cannot be done without loss of dignity, and such actions are always joined to vanity and are signs of frivolity. Therefore, wives should take care that their faces, countenances, and gestures (by which we can penetrate by careful observation into the most guarded thoughts) be applied to the observance of decency. If they are observant in these matters, they will merit dignity and honor; but if they are negligent they will not be able to avoid censure and criticism. Still, I am not asking that a wife's face be unpleasant, with a sour expression, but, rather, it should be pleasant. And her demeanor should not be clumsy but gracefully dignified. Moreover, I earnestly beg that wives observe the precept of avoiding immoderate laughter. This is a habit that is indecent in all persons, but it is especially hateful in a woman. On the other hand, women should not be censured if they laugh a little at a good joke and thus lapse somewhat from their serious demeanor. . . .

We who follow a middle way should establish some rather liberal rules for our wives. They should not be shut up in their bedrooms as in a prison but should be permitted to go out, and this privilege should be taken as evidence of their virtue and propriety. Still, wives should not act with their husbands as the moon does with the sun; for when the moon is near the sun it is never visible, but when it is distant it stands resplendent by itself. Therefore, I would have wives be seen in public with their husbands, but when their husbands are away wives should stay at home. . . .

. . . I consider such speechmaking to be, in the main, repugnant to the modesty, constancy, and dignity of a wife. For this reason the author Sophocles, who is certainly no worse than the Venetian I am discussing—and most men

[327]

Chapter 11
Renaissance
Possibilities:
Leon Battista
Alberti (1404–
1472) and Isotta
Nogarola
(1418–1466)

consider him better—has termed silence the most outstanding ornament of women. Therefore, women should believe they have achieved glory of eloquence if they will honor themselves with the outstanding ornament of silence. Neither the applause of a declamatory play nor the glory and adoration of an assembly is required of them, but all that is desired of them is eloquent, well-considered, and dignified silence. But what am I doing? I must be very careful, especially since I am treating silence, that I do not perhaps seem to you too talkative. . . .

We are interested in the care of our property and the diligence proper to our servants and staff because it is necessary to have both property and servants, without whose help family life itself cannot exist. Surely it is in these two things that the management of domestic matters primarily is involved, for unless a wife imposes her own judgment and precepts on these matters, the operation of the household will have no order and will be in great disarray. Men are naturally endowed with strength of mind and body; both for these and other reasons, they provision their homes by their labor, industry, and willingness to undergo hardships. Conversely, I think we may infer that since women are by nature weak they should diligently care for things concerning the household. For weakness can never be separated from cares nor cares from vigilance. What is the use of bringing home great wealth unless the wife will work at preserving, maintaining, and utilizing it? . . .

. . . We beg and exhort the most noble women to follow this example of feeding her infant her own milk, for it is very important that an infant should be nourished by the same mother in whose womb and by whose blood he was conceived. No nourishment seems more proper, none more wholesome than that same nourishment of body that glowed with greatest life and heat in the womb and should thus be given as known and familiar food to newborn infants. The power of the mother's food most effectively lends itself to shaping the properties of body and mind to the character of the seed. That may be discerned quite clearly in many instances; for example, when young goats are suckled with sheep's milk their hair becomes much softer, and when lambs are fed on goats' milk, it is evident that their fleeces become much coarser. In trees it is certain that they are much more dependent on the qualities of both sap and soil than on the quality of the seed; thus, if they are transplanted to other ground when flourishing and well leafed, you will find them changed enormously by the sap from the less fertile ground. . . .

. . . Mothers should often warn their children to abstain from excessive laughter and to avoid words that denote a rash character. That is the mark of stupidity, the evidence of passion. Moreover, children should be warned not ever to speak on those matters that are base in the act. Therefore, mothers should restrain them from vulgar or cutting words. If their children should say anything that is obscene or licentious, mothers should not greet it with a laugh or a kiss, but with a whip.

Moreover, they should teach their children not to criticize anyone because of his poverty or the low birth of his lineage or other misfortunes, for they are sure to make bitter enemies from such actions or develop an attitude of arrogance. . . .

. . . Therefore, my Lorenzo, your compatriots ought to be stirred by your example and follow you with great enthusiasm, for in Ginerva you have taken a wife who is a virgin well endowed with virtue, charm, a noble lineage, and great wealth. What more outstanding, more worthy model could I propose than yours? What more shining, more worthy example than yours, since in this outstanding city of Florence you are most eminently connected through your father, grandfather, and ancestors? You have taken a wife whose great wealth the entire world indeed admires but whose chastity, constancy, and prudence all men of goodwill esteem highly. . . .

DOCUMENT THREE

Leon Battista Alberti

Anonymous Life
(1438)

Although Alberti disguised his authorship, this is his autobiography, written later in his career. In the section that follows, he describes himself as a young man, his values, interests, and social behavior. What does he seem to think are the most important of his character attributes and interests? How do these features relate to what he would see as the ideal adult Renaissance man, as described in the text?

. . . "From early youth he was instructed in all that was most fitting for a noble, liberal education, so that he certainly could not be considered the least among the most prominent young men of his age . . . he practised riding, jousting, and music, and he was passionately fond of literature and the fine arts. There was nothing too mean or too difficult he did not desire to master. His studies and reflections were all praiseworthy. He worked extremely hard at sculpture and painting, not to mention the rest, and neglected nothing in his effort to win the esteem of the best. His talent was of the highest order, and he may be said to have mastered all the arts. He was never idle or lazy, and once he started something he always went through with it. He often said that he found literature free from the cloying quality that is held to be common to all things. He loved literature so much that sometimes it gave him the same pleasure as the buds of sweetly smelling flowers, and then neither hunger nor sleep could make him

Chapter 11
Renaissance
Possibilities:
Leon Battista
Alberti (1404–
1472) and Isotta
Nogarola
(1418–1466)

leave his books. But so late did he stay up sometimes that his books assumed the aspect of piles of scorpions, so that he could see nothing, let alone his books. Whenever he was reduced to this state, he sought relief in music, painting, and physical exercise. He used to play ball-games and darts, and he ran, wrestled, and danced. Above all, he practised mountaineering, but more to strengthen his body than for relaxation or pleasure. He distinguished himself in military exercises when still a boy, and could jump the height of a man from a standing position; no one could beat him at high-jumping. He could throw a javelin with such power that it would pierce the thickest of iron breast-plates. With his left foot touching the cathedral wall, he could throw an apple right over the rooftops. Once he threw a little silver coin up against the roof of a high church with such power that his companions heard it strike the vault. He could ride for hours without showing the slightest trace of fatigue, with one end of a rod touching his foot and the other in his hand, without the slightest movement of the part of the rod. He was such a fine horseman that even the proudest, most mettlesome horses seemed to fear and tremble when he mounted them. He was a self-taught musician and his compositions were highly esteemed by the music-masters. All his life he was given to singing, but he did this when alone or in private, especially at home with his brother and relatives. He loved to play the organ and was reputed one of the best organ-players. Indeed, his advice helped many others to become more proficient in music." . . .

"He used to summon the friends he was accustomed to discussing literary matters with, and while dictating pamphlets to them, he would make sketches or make wax models of them. He suffered pain and the extremes of heat and cold with great patience. Once, when not yet fifteen years old, he was wounded in the foot and did not so much as flinch when the surgeon stitched the wound. On the contrary, he helped the surgeon, and in spite of a high temperature, dressed the wound himself. Another time, when a fierce attack of lumbago caused him to come out in a cold sweat, he summoned some musicians and forced himself to overcome the pain with a couple of hours of singing. His head was by nature sensitive to the slightest breeze, but little by little he overcame this handicap during the summer months, after which he always rode bareheaded through fog and wind. Through some quirk of nature he was allergic to garlic and especially to honey so that the mere sight of either would make him feel sick. But he overcame this repugnance by forcing himself to look at and touch these things, so that they ceased to have any effect on him in the end. Thus he proved the truth of the saying, 'where there's a will there's a way'. He could not have been more scrupulous, sincere, naively enthusiastic, even touchingly faithful . . . .

"When he sought relief by walking out-of-doors, he would spend his time watching the artisans at work in their workshops. But as if rebuked by some stern judge, he would often go straight back home saying, 'But we too are workmen in the exercise of our profession'. Seeing the sown fields flower in springtime and all the trees and plants rich with the promise of fruit, he would be seized by melancholy and rebuke himself thus: 'You too, Battista, must give man the fruit of your studies'. And when he saw the fields ripe for harvesting and the trees laden with fruit in autumn, he would become so downcast that some even saw him weep and heard him exclaim: 'There you are, Leon, everything bears witness to and accuses your sloth. What do you do in a year that is of use to mankind? Tell me, what have you done to show you have fulfilled your purpose?' He took extraordinary delight in looking at things in which there was some beauty or ornament. Once he saw a venerable old man full of health and vigour, and he couldn't take his eyes off him. He used to say he worshipped the beauties of nature, and that quadrupeds, birds, and other resplendent animals should be loved, for all that nature granted in her bounty was beautiful. When his own beautiful dog died he wrote a panegyric for it. He looked upon every skilled or beautiful product of man's invention as divine, and so highly did he esteem anything expressed with a certain grace that he could even find something to praise in a poor writer. When ill, the mere sight of jewels, flowers, or some pleasant natural scene would often cure him." . . .

DOCUMENT FOUR

Leon Battista Alberti

On the Family
(1440–1441)

Like Bruni before him, Alberti was interested in the place of families in society. In this essay he uses a series of conversations that supposedly took place at a gathering of his own family in 1421 when his father was dying. He wrote the essay in the vernacular of Tuscany at the time and portrays the viewpoints of men who represent different ages and practical positions in Florentine society. (No women speak in this essay. Adovardo is supposedly a cousin who represents the humanist view; Lionardo is a young bachelor intellectual, while Giannozzo is a 64-year-old uncle, a man of experience.) Why does Alberti feel families are important to the cities of Italy? Why do you think he included men at different stages of life? What does he see as the responsibilities of a father and husband in the family? Of a wife and mother? How does he describe the relationship between husband and wife? In what ways does he seem to echo what Bruni said? Which of his viewpoints are different from Bruni's?

ADOVARDO: . . . You know I don't see myself as one of those who spend their time collecting for their children that which fortune can snatch away in a moment, not only from the heirs but even from those who acquired it. I do certainly

[331]

Chapter 11
Renaissance
Possibilities:
Leon Battista
Alberti (1404–
1472) and Isotta
Nogarola
(1418–1466)

say that I would rather leave my children rich and fortunate than poor. I heartily desire by working as hard as I can to leave them in such a state of fortune that they need seldom ask for anyone's charity. I am not unaware what misery it is to be forced in one's need to call on the hands of others for help. But don't imagine that a father who need fear neither death nor poverty for his children is free of trouble. Whose is the burden of shaping their character? The father's. The task of having them taught letters and morals? The father's. The immeasurable responsibility of making them learn various sorts of knowledge, art, and science? The father's too, as you well know. To this add the anxious decision which falls upon a father concerning the particular art, science, and career most suited to the temperament of his son, the status of his family, the customs of his country, the circumstances, times, situation, opportunities, and expectations of his fellow citizens. . . .

LIONARDO: A father should make sure that his sons devote themselves seriously to their studies. He should teach his children to read and to write correctly. He should never consider his task as teacher finished until the boys are excellent writers and readers. This is a case, perhaps, where half-knowledge is hardly better than no knowledge. They must learn the abacus, and also, insofar as it may be useful, they should make the acquaintance of geometry. These two sciences are well suited to a boy's intellect, and enjoyable. They are also of no small advantage in my career and at my age. Then the children may go back and savor the poets, orators, and philosophers. Above all be sure they have responsible teachers, from whom good morals may be gained as well as a knowledge of literature. . . .

A father should realize that education never does any harm, but is of great help in any activity whatsoever. Among all the learned men of whom there have been such a number of excellent ones in our family, none has ever been, by his education, made less than perfectly fit for other tasks. There is no need to explain here at length how much the knowledge of letters always helps achieve fame and success in whatever one undertakes. . . .

Young people, however, very often do not cherish the good of the family enough to do this. Marriage, perhaps, seems to them to take away their present liberty and freedom. It may be, as the comic poets like to tell us, that they are held back and dissuaded by some mistress. Sometimes, too, young men find it hard enough to manage one life, and fear as an excessive and undesirable burden the task of supporting a wife and children besides. They may doubt their capacity to maintain in honorable estate a family which grows in needs from day to day. Viewing the conjugal bed as a troublesome responsibility, they then avoid the legitimate and honorable path to the increase of a family.

If a family is not to fall for these reasons into what we have described as the most unfortunate condition of decline, but is to grow, instead, in fame and in the prosperous multitude of its youth, we must persuade our young men to take wives. We must use every argument for this purpose, offer incentive, promise reward, employ all our wit, persistence, and cunning. A most appropriate reason for taking a wife may be found in what we were saying before, about the evil of sensual indulgence, for the condemnation of such things may lead young men to desire honorable satisfactions. As other incentives, we may also speak to them of the delights of this primary and natural companionship of marriage. Children act as pledges and securities of marital love and kindness. At the same time they offer a focus for all a man's hopes and desires. Sad, indeed, is the man who has labored to get wealth and power and lands, and then has no true heir and perpetuator of his memory. No one can be more suited than a man's true and legitimate sons to gain advantages by virtue of his character, position, and authority, and to enjoy the fruits and rewards of his labor. If a man leaves such heirs, furthermore, he need not consider himself wholly dead and gone. His children keep his own position and his true image in the family. . . .

. . . In the race of human life and for general contest for honor and glory, likewise, I think the first step is to choose an appropriate, manageable vessel for your powers and talents, then to strive hard for first place. For spirits which are neither lazy nor mean, it is best to hope and desire and fight wholeheartedly for a place among the first, if not for first place. One must surpass entirely that obscure and forgotten crowd behind. One must struggle with all the force and cunning at his disposal for a certain fame and a measure of glory.

To gain glory a man must have excellence. To gain excellence he need only will to be, and not merely to seem, all that he wishes others might think him. For this reason they say there are few prerequisites to excellence. As you see, only a firm, whole, and unfeigned will, will do. What is false will in a man? Is it to show the desire to pursue something one does not actually care for? We shall not here undertake to prove at length how easy it is to attain excellence. That will be better told in another place. We shall merely state here the fact that a man who strives for first place may with honor sit in the second. No one comes in among the last, however, without incurring obscurity and ignominy. No one takes last place with honor.

We should consider at this point how much reward and profit, how much honor and fame, you can gain from any work or achievement you undertake to perform. The only condition is that you surpass everyone else in the field. In every craft the most skilled master, as you know, gains most riches and has the best position and the greatest stature among his companions. . . .

GIANNOZZO: . . . Let the father of the family follow my example. Since I find it no easy matter to deal with the needs of the household when I must often be engaged outside with other men in arranging matters of wider consequence, I have found it wise to set aside a certain amount for outside use, for investments and purchases. The rest, which takes care of all the smaller household affairs, I leave to my wife's care. I have done it this way, for, to tell the truth, it would hardly win us respect if our wife busied herself among the men in the marketplace, out in the public eye. It also seems somewhat demeaning to me to remain shut up in the house among women when I have manly things to do among men, fellow citizens and worthy and distinguished foreigners. . . .

*Chapter 11
Renaissance
Possibilities:
Leon Battista
Alberti (1404–
1472) and Isotta
Nogarola
(1418–1466)*

LIONARDO: . . . I agree, for you are, indeed, precisely of the opinion of the ancients. They used to say that men are by nature of a more elevated mind than women. They are more situated to struggle with arms and with cunning against the misfortunes which afflict country, religion, and one's own children. The character of men is stronger than that of women and can bear the attacks of enemies better, can stand strain longer, is more constant under stress. Therefore men have the freedom to travel with honor in foreign lands, acquiring and gathering the goods of fortune. Women, on the other hand, are almost all timid by nature, soft, slow, and therefore more useful when they sit still and watch over our things. It is as though nature thus provided for our well-being, arranging for men to bring things home and for women to guard them. The woman, as she remains locked up at home, should watch over things by staying at her post, by diligent care and watchfulness. The man should guard the woman, the house, and his family and country, but not by sitting still. He should exercise his spirit and his hands in brave enterprise, even at the cost of sweat and blood. No doubt of it, therefore, Giannozzo, those idle creatures who stay all day among the little females or who keep their minds occupied with little feminine trifles certainly lack a masculine and glorious spirit. They are contemptible in their apparent inclination to play the part of women rather than that of men. A man demonstrates his love of high achievements by the pride he takes in his own. But if he does not shun trifling occupations, clearly he does not mind being regarded as effeminate. It seems to me, then, that you are entirely right to leave the care of minor matters to your wife and to take upon yourself, as I have always seen you do, all manly and honorable concerns. . . .

GIANNOZZO: "Therefore, dear wife," said I, "we should have order and system in all that we do. It does not befit a woman like you to carry a sword, nor to do other manly things that men do. Nor is it always and in all places fitting for a woman to do everything that is proper to woman, for instance holding a distaff, wearing gold brocade, having one's head tied up in a kerchief. These things are all proper in their place and time. Your duty, dear lady, shall be to stand first in the household, not to be aloof and proud but with great gentleness to keep the whole house in order and in harmony through your conscientious supervision. You shall see that things are done in their proper time. What is needed in autumn is not to be consumed in May. What should be enough for a month is not to be used up in a day."

DOCUMENT FIVE

Lauro Quirini

"Greetings to the most noble and most eloquent virgin Isotta Nogarola"
(1442)

On the basis of this letter, what did Quirini, the Venetian nobleman and scholar, think of Isotta Nogarola's intelligence and learning? What additional studies does he recommend for her? How do his recommendations compare to what both Bruni and Barbaro said about women's roles and education?

. . . This letter asks of you nothing else than that you pursue in the most splendid way, until death, that same course of right living which you have followed since childhood. But if you find this letter dry and uncultivated, forgive me. For at this time we are especially interested in that philosophy which does not value an ornamented style. Therefore, let your delicate ears put up with sometimes dry figures of speech, I beg you. For you who have been trained in the polished and exquisite art of rhetoric and are accustomed to elegant discourses and melodious style, rightly can demand the most ornate eloquence; but we semi-orators and petty philosophers are content for the most part with little eloquence, and that clumsy. Wherefore I rejoice for you and offer congratulations for your virtue. And should we not greatly rejoice that you can be named among those admittedly few but certainly famous women [of the past], when we see that the ancients gloried in the learning of such outstanding women? . . . Rightly, therefore, should you also, famous Isotta, receive the highest praises, since you have indeed, if I may so speak, overcome your own nature. For that true virtue which is proper to men you have pursued with remarkable zeal—not the mediocre virtue which many men seek, but that which would befit a man of the most flawless and perfect wisdom. Thus Cicero rightly said: "You young men have a womanly spirit, but that girl has a man's spirit." Therefore, dissatisfied with the lesser studies, you have applied your noble mind also to the higher disciplines, in which there is need for keenness of intelligence and mind. . . .

. . . But after you have mastered dialectic, which is the method of knowing, you should read diligently and carefully the moral books of Aristotle, which he writes divinely, in which you may unfailingly recognize the essence of true and solid virtue. And if you also, as you should, act upon his excellent teaching in your life, he will lead you as no one else can to the height and extremity of the good. But after you have also digested this part of philosophy, which is concerned with human matters, with a certain nobility of soul you should also set out for that ample and vast other part, which is threefold. [Here] you should

Chapter 11
Renaissance
Possibilities:
Leon Battista
Alberti (1404–
1472) and Isotta
Nogarola
(1418–1466)

begin especially with those disciplines which we call by the Greek name mathematics, which offer knowledge of such certainty (even though it is very difficult) that many philosophers, and these the most serious, think that we can know nothing with certainty unless mathematicians have demonstrated it. Afterwards, strive unceasingly and determinedly to pursue that philosophy which we call natural, in which we are taught about sensible things and those having continuous motion. But finally, you should engage yourself in metaphysics, which our Peripatetics call a divine science, so that you may be able to know God and the three substances. This is the right path and famous order of truth which caused the ancient philosophers who observed it to arrive, as we see, at such a degree of excellence that we do not hesitate to call them divine. . . .

You should also make use of those studies which you have splendidly embraced . . . from your youth, particularly history, for history is as it were the teacher of life, somehow making ours the wisdom of the ancients, inflaming us to imitate great men. For why did our ancestors study history so zealously unless they thought it to be nothing other than the example of a good and holy life? . . .

DOCUMENT SIX

ISOTTA NOGAROLA

"Of the Equal or Unequal Sin of Adam and Eve"
(ca. 1453)

In this most famous of Nogarola's writings, she and her friend Foscarini debate whether the original sin of humankind should be blamed on Adam or Eve. What are the opposing positions presented in this dialogue? If Nogarola was trying to defend women, why do you think she chose the arguments that she did? Who wins the debate and why?

LUDOVICO BEGINS: If it is in any way possible to measure the gravity of human sinfulness, then we should see Eve's sin as more to be condemned than Adam's [for three reasons]. [First], she was assigned by a just judge to a harsher punishment than was Adam. [Second], she believed that she was made more like God, and that is in the category of unforgivable sins against the Holy Spirit. [Third], she suggested and was the cause of Adam's sin—not he of hers; and although it is a poor excuse to sin because of a friend, nevertheless none was more tolerable than the one by which Adam was enticed.

ISOTTA: But I see things—since you move me to reply—from quite another and contrary viewpoint. For where there is less intellect and less constancy, there

[336]

is less sin; and Eve [lacked sense and constancy] and therefore sinned less. Knowing [her weakness] that crafty serpent began by tempting the woman, thinking the man perhaps invulnerable because of his constancy. . . .

[Adam must also be judged more guilty than Eve, secondly] because of his greater contempt for the command. For in Genesis 2 it appears that the Lord commanded Adam, not Eve, where it says: "The Lord God took the man and placed him in the paradise of Eden to till it and to keep it," (and it does not say, "that they might care for and protect it") ". . . and the Lord God commanded the man" (and not "them"): "From every tree of the garden you may eat" (and not "you" [in the plural sense]), and, [referring to the forbidden tree], "for the day you eat of it, you must die," [again, using the singular form of "you"]. [God directed his command to Adam alone] because he esteemed the man more highly than the woman.

Moreover, the woman did not [eat from the forbidden tree] because she believed that she was made more like God, but rather because she was weak and [inclined to indulge in] pleasure. Thus: "Now the woman saw that the tree was good for food, pleasing to the eyes, and desirable for the knowledge it would give. She took of its fruit and ate it, and also gave some to her husband and he ate," and it does not say [that she did so] in order to be like God. And if Adam had not eaten, her sin would have had no consequences. For it does not say: "If Eve had not sinned Christ would not have been made incarnate," but "If Adam had not sinned." Hence the woman, but only because she had been first deceived by the serpent's evil persuasion, did indulge in the delights of paradise; but she would have harmed only herself and in no way endangered human posterity if the consent of the first-born man had not been offered. . . .

I have written this because you wished me to. Yet I have done so fearfully, since this is not a woman's task. But you are kind, and if you find any part of my writing clumsy you will correct it.

LUDOVICO: You defend the cause of Eve most subtly, and indeed defend it so [well] that if I had not been born a man, you would have made me your champion. But sticking fast to the truth, which is attached by very strong roots, I have set out [here] to assault your fortress with your own weapons. I shall begin by attacking its foundations, which can be destroyed by the testimony of Sacred Scripture, so that there will be no lack of material for my refutation.

Eve sinned from ignorance and inconstancy, from which you conclude that she sinned less seriously. [But] ignorance—especially of those things which we are obligated to know—does not excuse us. For it is written: "If anyone ignores this, he shall be ignored." The eyes which guilt makes blind punishment opens. He who has been foolish in guilt will be wise in punishment, especially when the sinner's mistake occurs through negligence. For the woman's ignorance, born of arrogance, does not excuse her, in the same way that Aristotle and the [lawyers], who teach a true philosophy, find the drunk

[337]

*Chapter 11
Renaissance
Possibilities:
Leon Battista
Alberti (1404–
1472) and Isotta
Nogarola
(1418–1466)*

and ignorant deserving of a double punishment. Nor do I understand how in the world you, so many ages distant from Eve, fault her intellect, when her knowledge, divinely created by the highest craftsman of all things, daunted that clever serpent lurking in paradise. For, as you write, he was not bold enough to attempt to persuade her but approached her with a question. . . .

Nor is Adam's companion excused because Adam was appointed to protect her, [contrary to your contention that] thieves who have been trustingly employed by a householder are not punished with the most severe punishment like strangers or those in whom no confidence has been placed. Also, the woman's frailty was not the cause of sin, as you write, but her pride, since the demon promised her knowledge, which leads to arrogance and inflates [with pride], according to the apostle. . . .

ISOTTA: I had decided that I would not enter further into a contest with you because, as you say, you assault my fortress with my own weapons. [The propositions] you have presented me were so perfectly and diligently defended that it would be difficult not merely for me, but for the most learned men, to oppose them. But since I recognize that this contest is useful for me, I have decided to obey your honest wish. Even though I know I struggle in vain, yet I will earn the highest praise if I am defeated by so mighty a man as you.

Eve sinned out of ignorance and inconstancy, and hence you contend that she sinned more gravely, because the ignorance of those things which we are obligated to know does not excuse us, since it is written: "He who does not know will not be known." I would concede your point if that ignorance were crude or affected. But Eve's ignorance was implanted by nature, of which nature God himself is the author and founder. In many people it is seen that he who knows less sins less, like a boy who sins less than an old man or a peasant less than a noble. Such a person does not need to know explicitly what is required for salvation, but implicitly, because [for him] faith alone suffices. . . .

[You argue further that] "the fragility of the woman was not the cause of sin, but rather her inordinate appetite for seeking that which was not suited to her nature," which [appetite] is the product, as you write, of pride. Yet it is clearly less a sin to desire the knowledge of good and evil than to transgress against a divine commandment, since the desire for knowledge is a natural thing, and all men by nature desire to know. . . .

Let these words be enough from me, an unarmed and poor little woman.

LUDOVICO: So divinely have you encompassed the whole of this problem that I could believe your words were drawn not from the fonts of philosophy and theology but from heaven. Hence they are worthy of praise rather than contradiction. Yet, lest you be cheated of the utility [you say you have begun to receive from this debate], attend to these brief arguments which can be posed for the opposite view, that you may sow the honey-sweet seeds of paradise which will delight readers and surround you with glory. . . .

The issues which you have cleverly joined I shall not divide. The inconstancy of Eve which has been condemned was not an inconstancy of nature but of habit. For those qualities which are in us by nature we are neither praised nor blamed, according to the judgment of the wisest philosophers. Actually, the woman's nature was excellent and concordant with reason, genus and time. For just as teeth were given to wild beasts, horns to oxen, feathers to birds for their survival, to the women mental capacity was given sufficient for the preservation and pursuit of the health of her soul.

DOCUMENT SEVEN

LAURA CERETA

"Letter to Bibolo Semproni"
(January 13, 1488)

In this letter—perhaps to a fictional person—Cereta attacks those who criticize women and deny them education. What does she say about women's abilities to study and to learn? According to her, are there innate differences between men's and women's intellects? Why is her defense of women different from Nogarola's? Why is this essay historically important?

Your complaints are hurting my ears, for you say publicly and quite openly that you are not only surprised but pained that I am said to show this extraordinary intellect of the sort one would have thought nature would give to the most learned of men—as if you had reached the conclusion, on the facts of the case, that a similar girl had seldom been seen among the peoples of the world. You are wrong on both counts, Semproni, and now that you've abandoned the truth, you are going to spread information abroad that is clearly false. . . .

. . . My point is that your mouth has grown foul because you keep it sealed so that no arguments can come out of it that might enable you to admit that nature imparts one freedom to all human beings equally—to learn. But the question of my exceptionality remains. And here choice alone, since it is the arbiter of character, is the distinguishing factor. For some women worry about the styling of their hair, the elegance of their clothes, and the pearls and other jewelry they wear on their fingers. Others love to say cute little things, to hide their feelings behind a mask of tranquility, to indulge in dancing, and lead pet dogs around on a leash. For all I care, other women can long for parties with carefully appointed tables, for the peace of mind of sleep, or they can yearn to deface with paint the pretty face they see reflected in their mirrors. But those women for whom the quest for the good represents a higher value restrain their young spirits and ponder better plans. They harden their bodies with sobriety and toil, they control their tongues, they carefully monitor what they hear, they ready their

Chapter 11
Renaissance
Possibilities:
Leon Battista
Alberti (1404–
1472) and Isotta
Nogarola
(1418–1466)

minds for all-night vigils, and they rouse their minds for the contemplation of probity in the case of harmful literature. For knowledge is not given as a gift but by study. For a mind free, keen, and unyielding in the face of hard work always rises to the good, and the desire for learning grows in depth and breadth.

So be it therefore. May we women, then, not be endowed by God the grantor with any giftedness or rare talent through any sanctity of our own. Nature has granted to all enough of her bounty; she opens to all the gates of choice, and through these gates, reason send legates to the will, for it is through reason that these legates can transmit their desires. I shall make a bold summary of the matter. Yours is the authority, ours is the inborn ability. . . .

In addition, I, who have always held virtue in high esteem and considered private things as secondary in importance, shall wear down and exhaust my pen writing against those men who are garrulous and puffed up with false pride. I shall not fail to obstruct tenaciously their treacherous snares. And I shall strive in a war of vengeance against the nortorious abuse of those who fill everything with noise, since armed with such abuse, certain insane and infamous men bark and bare their teeth in vicious wrath at the republic of women, so worthy of veneration. . . .

Catholic Monarchs in the Old and New Worlds: Ferdinand of Aragón (1452–1516) and Isabella of Castile (1451–1504)

▦ SETTING THE STAGE

Many of the historical developments, debates, and contests that have been covered in earlier chapters also characterized Iberian history through the fifteenth century. At the time of the Gracchi, Rome fought to establish control in Iberia, and the peninsula remained a critical part of the Roman Empire thereafter. Like the rest of the West, the inhabitants of Iberia were Christianized by the fourth century and then participated in debates over doctrine, the founding of monasteries, and the expansion of Roman Catholic Church institutions. Invasions by the Visigoths in the fifth century and internal conflicts for power thereafter kept the area in tumult for several

Chapter 12
Catholic
Monarchs in the
Old and New
Worlds:
Ferdinand of
Aragón (1452–
1516) and
Isabella of
Castile
(1451–1504)

centuries. More stable dynastic monarchies eventually began to emerge, but like Eleanor and Henry, the individuals involved had to fight to keep their families in power. Like the rest of Europe, Spain would experience the return of urban and commercial life, and the rise of universities and scholasticism in the Middle Ages. Spain also experienced new expressions of popular piety in lay brotherhoods, in the establishment of the Franciscan and Dominican mendicant orders and their affiliated "tertiaries," and in the emergence of popular female sanctity in the *beatas,* who were much like the Beguines in other parts of Europe. Renaissance ideas also spread to Spain by the mid-fifteenth century.

But some features of Spanish life were also quite distinct from those of most of the rest of Western Europe. Of central importance was the Muslim invasion and occupation of most of Spain and the establishment of a kingdom centered at Cordoba in 711. The tremendous cultural, intellectual, religious, and economic influence of that conquest, as well as the Spanish efforts beginning in 1031 to drive the Moors out of Spain, had a lasting impact on subsequent history. That struggle, known as the *reconquista,* ended with the fall of Granada in 1492. That year signaled the beginning of another singular characteristic of Iberian development—global expansion and conquest. Spain created an empire "on which the sun never set" long before the British. These dramatic events were carried out by the famed Catholic monarchs, Isabella of Castile and Ferdinand of Aragón, and their stories both added to and transformed how Spaniards viewed themselves and how their history would be written. Isabella and Ferdinand came from dynasties that based their legitimacy on commitments to the Catholic faith and to the *reconquista*; the imperial ventures would both enhance and detract from their reputations, depending on who was telling the story.

In the mid-fifteenth century, the marriage of Isabella of Castile and Ferdinand of Aragón forged a political union of the kingdoms of Castile and Aragón. The nascent Spanish state emerged from both these kingdoms. The marriage, the couple's sense of religious purpose, and their subsequent rule moved Spain away from an uneasy but historical religious plurality, political fragmentation, and disparate cultural practices toward a state of political and religious unity and confessional conformity. Isabella and Ferdinand accomplished all this by embarking on the reconquest of Granada, expanding Spanish rule into Italy and Africa and across the Atlantic, reviving the Inquisition, persecuting and expelling the Jews from Spain, and backing the voyage of the Genoese adventurer, Christopher Columbus.

The reign of Isabella and Ferdinand has been the subject of numerous controversies over the centuries. For over five hundred years, chroniclers, historians, intellectuals, politicians, and others have questioned the actions and motivations of these two monarchs, often by reflecting on their own political and intellectual temperaments. Such questioning began with fifteenth-century chroniclers. How these chroniclers depicted the history of Isabella's and Ferdinand's reign has affected all subsequent historical interpretations and political and national remembrances of the pair. The most important contemporary sources available on the two monarchs are from the Spanish chroniclers, and their writings reflected the political and intellectual climate of fifteenth-century Castile and Aragón. When the two kingdoms of Aragón and Castile emerged as the dominant states in Iberia, Spanish intellectuals attempted to legitimize the claims of the dynastic house of Trastámara, which claimed both thrones in 1412.[1] "Loyalists of the new dynasty embarked upon a massive propaganda campaign—in the form of chronicles—to clothe their revolutionary triumph in credible respectability."[2]

What type of historical writing would bring them that respectability? By the fifteenth century, two types of historical writing emerged in Spain: (1) Renaissance humanist historical writing, as practiced by one group at court, the *cabelleros* (military professionals); and (2) the more traditional medieval scholastic approach, as practiced by the other group at court, the *letrados* (bureaucrats trained in canon or civil law). These two groups wrote their histories with the intent of establishing a theory of monarchy where none had existed before and that would create a preeminent position in the political hierarchy for their class.

1. For an extensive discussion of political propaganda and the writing of history in fifteenth-century Castile, see Helen Nader, *The Mendoza Family in the Spanish Renaissance, 1350–1550* (New Brunswick, N.J.: Rutgers University Press, 1979), p. 1.

2. Ibid.

In the cabelleros' histories, the monarch was a man who led armies, dispensed justice, acted chivalrously, and shared power with the cabelleros, who were military and political advisers to the king. However, the monarch's deeds and character could be judged and found wanting. In this type of historical writing, male biography was emphasized, and women's actions and influences were not a consideration. Isabella's authority and rule tended to be overshadowed by Ferdinand's military deeds and chivalrous behavior. When she was portrayed, she was characterized as having the qualities of a king—moral certitude, courage, decisiveness, ambition, curiosity, and prudence.

In the letrados' chronicles, the monarchs and their actions were inspired by God, and Castile and Aragón were divinely ordered states ruled by pious monarchs and administered wisely by clerics and bureaucrats. In these accounts, all events and actions were explained as the fulfillment of a larger divine order and God enabled Isabella and Ferdinand to complete the plans of their divinely inspired predecessors—the reconquest of Granada, the persecution of heretics, the political and religious unity of Iberia, and the conversion of indigenous peoples in the New World to Catholicism. Isabella played a prominent role in such chronicles. While her kingly qualities were stressed, a letrado and the most influential of Isabella's official chroniclers, Fernando Del Pulgar, emphasized her extreme piety and dependence on prayer for the revelation of God's will. As the Catholic monarchs sought to legitimize their rule,

Chapter 12
Catholic
Monarchs in the
Old and New
Worlds:
Ferdinand of
Aragón (1452–
1516) and
Isabella of
Castile
(1451–1504)

they embraced the letrado interpretation of events. Writers in this group portrayed them as divinely ordained and helped to fend off challenges to their rule.

While the chronicles are rich in detail, Spanish historians have had to rely on other accounts and sources to round out the picture of fifteenth-century Spain and to question the chronicles' panegyric interpretations of Isabella and Ferdinand. Both Ferdinand and Isabella left political testaments to explain their motivations and sentiments, and to provide interpretations of their rule. Decrees, letters, and royal charters detail their political, legal, and financial activities, while letters, dispatches, and diaries from both domestic and foreign visitors to their court and from foreign diplomats and papal representatives assess their reigns and their charac-

ters. Texts survive from the Muslims of Granada and from Spanish Jews before and after their expulsion from Spain. Military accounts, legal texts, and records from the Inquisition abound. The majority of these texts detail the public life of Castile and Aragón and often ignore women's activities and actions. Only a small number of women in fifteenth-century Spain were literate and only a small number of literate women kept records. Those who did were primarily nuns and noblewomen. Isabella's own voice is known to us through her few surviving letters, the chronicles, and writings of her contemporaries. Unlike Eleanor of Aquitaine (See Chapter 8), Isabella had official chroniclers of her every official word and deed, and their writings are exceptional sources, despite their bias.

■ THE ACTORS:

FERDINAND OF ARAGÓN AND ISABELLA OF CASTILE

When Isabella was born in 1451 to Juan II of Castile (1405–1454) and his second wife, Isabel of Portugal (1428–1496), no one predicted that the *infanta* (princess) would became queen of Castile. Juan had a male heir, Enrique IV (r. 1454–1474), born during his first marriage. Soon a second male, Alfonso (1453–1468), was born into the family, and Isabella was third in line for the throne of Castile. When Juan died shortly after the birth of his second son, Enrique became king, and the young widowed queen and her

two young children left court and took up residence in a nearby market town. For the next ten years, the dowager queen, Isabella, and Alfonso lived in comfort and security because Alfonso was the heir-apparent and Isabella the second in line.

During their years away from the intrigues of court life and politics, Isabella lived a privileged and protected life. The extent of her education is unknown. She learned the domestic arts and skills necessary for a Castilian princess to make a good political match. She had some basic schooling in reading and writing Castilian and enough Latin to say her prayers, and was most likely exposed to books praising virtuous women and heroic men. Her education was by no means unusual for noblewomen in late medieval Spain. Clerics tutored her brother and other boys like him. These clerics were inculcated with the belief that women did not possess reason and therefore it was not necessary to give girls an extensive education. Later in her life, Isabella regretted her lack of education, but by all accounts she read extensively, strove to learn Latin as an adult, and wrote many letters.[3] Isabella's piety and religiosity was often noted early in her life. She learned these traits from her deeply devout mother, Isabel of Portugal.

When she was ten years old, Isabella's time away from court came to an end. In 1461, the supposedly impotent Enrique fathered an heir, Juana of Castile, and then summoned his half-brother and half-sister to court. He claimed that it was to "have them properly educated," but it was most likely to keep an eye on them, ensure their loyalty, and keep them away from his aristocratic opponents who saw the prince and princess as claimants to the throne. Isabella and her chroniclers made much out of her removal from court after the death of her father and her mandated return, her supposed isolation and "internment" away from court, and her mother's purported madness as a way to present Enrique in the worst possible light and to demonstrate Isabella's moral and spiritual fortitude. The royal chronicler, Pulgar, helped shape the myth of Isabella's childhood by concluding that "her early years were spent 'in extreme lack of necessary things' and that she was without a father and 'we can even say a mother.'"[4]

The politics of succession overshadowed the late childhood and early adulthood of Isabella. Enrique was an unpopular and weak ruler who was dominated by court politics and its different factions. One faction in disfavor spread the rumor that the king was impotent; the queen was unfaithful; and a court favorite, Beltrán de la Cueva, was Juana's father. With the princess Juana's legitimacy in question and counterclaims that Alfonso was the legitimate heir, a succession crisis broke out in the mid-1460s. Nobles opposed to Enrique's rule rallied around Alfonso. When he died in 1468, they transferred their support to Isabella, who declined to join the rebellion against Enrique. Remaining loyal to her half-brother prevented a prolonged civil war at this time. In return for her loyalty and condemnation of the rebels, Enrique acknowledged Isabella in 1468 as his successor and denounced his own daughter's claim.

Isabella's refusal to participate in the uprising against Enrique demonstrated an acute understanding and knowledge of Castilian politics. She understood that if she ascended the throne unmarried and allied with powerful, ambitious, and ruthless nobles, she would perpetuate the destructive factionalism that plagued Castilian politics and she would be

---

3. Nancy Rubin, *Isabella of Castile: The First Renaissance Queen* (New York: St Martin's Press, 1991), p. 30.

4. Peggy K. Liss, *Isabel the Queen: Life and Times* (Oxford, England: Oxford University Press, 1992), p. 13.

Chapter 12
Catholic
Monarchs in the
Old and New
Worlds:
Ferdinand of
Aragón (1452–
1516) and
Isabella of
Castile
(1451–1504)

bound to one faction. Isabella needed to establish her legitimacy through her own efforts. To do so, she had to marry a man who would champion her vision and not the cause of a particular faction. That man was the young heir to Aragón and newly crowned king of Sicily, Ferdinand of Aragón.

Ferdinand was born on March 10, 1452, in the neighboring kingdom of Aragón to Juan II of Aragón and king of Sicily and his second wife, Juana Enríquez, the daughter of a Castilian admiral of Jewish ancestry. Ferdinand was not the firstborn son; his half-brother, Carlos de Viana, had been designated his father's successor. When Carlos died in 1461, Ferdinand was nine years old, and his path to the throne became clear and he was sworn in as heir at a ceremony in Barcelona. Unlike Isabella, Ferdinand had not been sequestered from the rough and tumble life of court and politics. He was groomed for a political and military role in his father's kingdom and already at the age of nine had traveled frequently between his father's courts in Sicily and Aragón.

Ferdinand liked to depict his early life and education as "seen much but read little." This view appealed later to his chroniclers, who presented him as "a warrior prince rich in practical experience"[5] and downplayed his intellectual gifts and abilities. Pulgar wrote, "He rode horseback very

well . . . ; he jousted easily and with such skill, that no one in his Kingdoms did it better. He was a great hunter of birds, and a man of good effort and great commander in war."[6] Such depictions overshadow the fact that Ferdinand was given a "princely" education, in the Renaissance meaning of the word. He was not only schooled in his own vernacular but also in Latin and the liberal arts. Ferdinand's education was a slow but uninterrupted process undertaken at the "Court of the Prince," which functioned from 1462 to 1479. Beginning in 1466, when the prince turned fourteen years old, his father brought several tutors from Catalán, Aragón, Valencia and Sicily and Ferdinand was exposed to the new learning of the Renaissance.[7] We do not know the full influence of these humanists and men of letters on the intellectual development of the future king. Later in his life, however, Ferdinand demonstrated a consistent preoccupation with Renaissance ideas and institutions.

Ferdinand's formal education was matched by his experience in the political arena of Aragón. After his brother's death in 1461, Aragón was plunged into civil war for the next decade (1462–1472). During the war, Ferdinand distinguished himself for

5. Felipe Fernández-Armesto, *Ferdinand and Isabella* (London: Weidenfeld and Nicolson, 1975), p. 35.

6. Fernando Del Pulgar, *Crónica de los señores Reyes Católicos, don Fernando y Doña Isabel de Castilla y de Aragón*, volume LXX (Madrid: Biblioteca de Autores Españoles, 1943), p. 256.

7. Salvador Claramunt, "La Política Universitaria de Fernando II" in *Fernando II de Aragón: El Rey Católico* (Zaragoza, Spain: Institución Fernando el Católico, 1996), pp. 73–74.

his valor on the battlefield, but the war severely weakened the country politically, economically, and socially. Ferdinand, his father, and the Aragonese needed the marriage union with Isabella and Castile. Given the weakness of Ferdinand's kingdom, however, Isabella and her advisers could dictate the terms of any marriage agreement.

■ ACT I:

THE QUEEN OF CASTILE AND THE KING OF ARAGÓN

According to Pulgar, in choosing a husband, Isabella demonstrated remarkable independence of thought and careful consideration of her dynasty's future as the political, social and religious cornerstone. In reality, much politicking and consultation with her advisers occurred before Isabella married the seventeen-year-old heir to the kingdom of Aragón and recently crowned king of Sicily, Ferdinand of Aragón. Ferdinand's father had cultivated marriage plans for his son to marry either Isabella or her niece, Juana. Either match would bring together the two halves of the Trastámaras dynasty, give them an advantage in the civil war, and protect Aragón from an increasingly hostile and expansionist France. In return, the princess who married Ferdinand would also win over many Castilians, who loathed the prospect of one of the princesses marrying into the despised houses of Portugal or France. Isabella and her advisers moved quietly and quickly to secure a match with Ferdinand.

In January 1469, advisers for Isabella and Ferdinand met to arrange the terms of their marriage, which took place in October 1469. Enrique IV was not consulted at all concerning Isabella's marriage, despite the fact that he argued she was his ward. Isabella had rejected this position, maintaining that she was an orphan and without a guardian. According to the terms of the marriage agreement, Isabella, when she became queen of Castile, was the sole authority in Castile. "Her will was to prevail over Ferdinand," who could act only as her consort but received the title of king. The prince promised to reside in Castile, to respect Enrique, and "to do no harm to the nobles . . . members of the Council or of the Royal House, nor to anyone who had any commission by royal will."[8] This matrimonial agreement limited the ability of the Aragonese heir to intervene in Castile and demonstrated Castilian aristocratic concerns that Ferdinand might enter Castilian politics with his own agenda and supporters. Under this agreement, Ferdinand was given a specific role in the marriage, one that the queen herself could not assume, to be

8. Ma. Isabel del Val Valdivieso, "Fernando II de Aragón Rey de Castilla," in *Fernando II de Aragón: El Rey Católico* (Zaragoza, Spain: Institución Fernando el Católico, 1996), pp. 31–36.

Chapter 12
Catholic
Monarchs in the
Old and New
Worlds:
Ferdinand of
Aragón (1452–
1516) and
Isabella of
Castile
(1451–1504)

"the armored arm" and "at the fore-front of four thousand lances, defend-ing the princess's cause."[9] In a feudal kingdom such as Castile, the queen could not assume the most important responsibility of a feudal lord, mili-tary service, and Ferdinand, as her consort, was charged with this duty. This military role gave Ferdinand the ability, sometime in the future, to ar-gue for and gain royal prerogatives and powers in Castile.

Such an occasion presented itself in 1474, when Enrique died and the war for Isabella's succession began. She had to take up arms to defend her claim to the throne. Some at Enrique's court adopted the cause of Isabella's niece, Juana, and civil war broke out between the two princesses and their respective supporters. Thus, Isabella ceded ample powers to Ferdinand on recommendation of her advisers. But the queen made it very clear that it was a cession on her part and these powers could be revoked at any time: "Considering that for the good regi-ment, guard and defense of my king-doms and dominions . . . I therefore give power to the king my hus-band. . . . I transfer to him, all power, high and low, and even supreme, that I have, and that belongs to me as heir and legitimate successor that I am of the said kingdoms and domin-ions. . . ."[10] From this time forward,

decrees were issued in both of their names, but nothing could be done without Isabella's consent. Finally, Ferdinand's rights in Castile expired on his wife's death. Despite these con-cessions, the image of the king that predominated was that of the de-fender of Castile's interests by means of arms.

The war of the Castilian succession lasted four years, and it was decided in Isabella's favor by 1479. As the war came to an end, Ferdinand assumed the Aragonese throne when his father passed away, and his ascendency at last cleared the way for Isabella and Ferdinand to become joint sovereigns of Aragón and Castile. "Spain as Castile-Aragón, not Castile-Portugal, was now an established fact."[11] Since the union of the two kingdoms was at first only a personal one, the question remained throughout their rule whether or not the union would sur-vive Ferdinand and Isabella.

Ferdinand and Isabella laid the foundations for the early modern Spanish state by extending royal au-thority to all parts of their kingdoms at the expense of the feudal aristoc-racy. It must be said, however, that their union did not create a single kingdom. Castile and Aragón re-mained administratively and politi-cally separate; a reform in one kingdom did not necessarily translate into a reform in the other. What each monarch did was restore and build on existing institutions and then modify

9. Ibid., p. 33.

10. Proclamation published by D. J. Dormer, *Discursos varios de historia* (Zaragoza, Spain: 1683), pp. 302–305. See also J. Vicens Vives, *Historia crítica de la vida y reinado de Fernando II de Aragón* (Zaragoza: Institución Fernando el Católico, 1962), pp . 399–400.

11. J. H. Elliott, *Imperial Spain* (Harmonds-worth, England: Penguin Books, 1963), pp. 23–24.

and adapt them to meet new needs. In Castile, the monarchs summoned the *Cortes,* or assembly of nobles, clergy, and municipalities, and with its acquiescence revived the medieval institution of town militias, or brotherhoods. These militias reestablished law and order in the countryside after the lawlessness of the civil-war period and were closely monitored by the crown to prevent them from falling under the influence of local nobles. Isabella and Ferdinand also strengthened their royal authority by acquiring control of the three great military religious orders. These institutions, military in character but bound by religious vows, were founded in the twelfth century to help drive the Moors out of Spain. By the fifteenth century, each possessed enormous resources that had previously been at the disposal of a small number of great nobles. The dispensing of justice, the policing of the kingdom, and the meting out of punishment were now in the crown's hands.

In the past, political decision making in Castile had been controlled by the nobility, and Isabella and Ferdinand wished to break its influence. To do so, they established the Council of Castile, which was to advise and assist them in appointments, charters, the dispensing of justice, and local governance. Staffed largely by the letrados, the council became the principal policymaking body for Castile. To watch over royal interests in the municipalities, Isabella and Ferdinand appointed royal governors to reside in the kingdom's most important cities. They enacted similar reforms in Aragón,

where a royal council was configured much like Castile's. Ferdinand also revitalized the office of viceroy so that royal representatives would be present in each of the three parts of Aragón because he spent the majority of his time in Castile. Finally, Ferdinand and Isabella were able to tax the wealth of their kingdoms by improving the system of royal tax collection.

Despite these political reforms aimed at ensuring the primacy of the crown in Castile and Aragón, Isabella, Ferdinand, and their advisers understood that they would also have to bring the Catholic Church, with its vast resources and wealth and its corrupt but powerful clergy, under their control. One strategy was to demand from the pope the crown's previous privilege of nominating all bishops and prelates so the monarchs could appoint men who would correct some of the church's abuses—pluralism, absenteeism, violation of celibacy, and low educational standards. While the pope maintained that appointments were his right, Isabella and Ferdinand won an important concession: the crown could appoint bishops and clergy to church offices in reconquered and newly acquired territory. Such an arrangement not only suited Isabella politically but also spiritually. Her faith was fervent, mystical, and intense, and she believed that it was the duty of Christian rulers to implement God's will on earth. This duty meant tackling corruption within the church *and* defending the church from the outside threats of heretics and infidels (Document One).

Chapter 12
Catholic
Monarchs in the
Old and New
Worlds:
Ferdinand of
Aragón (1452–
1516) and
Isabella of
Castile
(1451–1504)

■ ACT II:

THE CATHOLIC MONARCHS

Both Isabella and Ferdinand adhered to the cultural and religious mission of previous Iberian monarchs—the reconquest of Iberia from the Moors. Reconquest was not only a secular mission with the possibility of great wealth and acquisition of vast territories; it was also considered a sacred duty. Both Ferdinand and Isabella believed that they had been divinely inspired to complete the mission, and in 1481 they began planning a campaign against Granada, the last remaining Moorish kingdom in Iberia. Pulgar reported that the king and queen, "knowing that no war should be started except for faith or for security, always had in mind the great thought of conquering the kingdom of Granada and of casting out from all the Spains the rule of the Moor and the name of *Mohamat*."[12] Ferdinand declared that his aim was "to expel from all Spain the enemies of the Catholic faith and dedicate Spain to the service of God."[13] Isabella called all of her feudal lords and knights to the cause, and they came motivated by the possibility of completing the mission and receiving the spoils of war.

Precariously balanced between hostile Christian powers to the north and rival Muslim rulers in Morocco to the south, Granada was the last of the Moorish kingdoms in Iberia and had

survived as such for almost two centuries. During the fourteenth and fifteenth centuries, the kingdom fought numerous border skirmishes, gradually ceding territory to its Christian neighbors. As long as the Portuguese, the Castilians, and the Aragonese had fought among themselves, Granada held its ground. With the cessation of hostilities among the three states and the beginning of political stability in Castile, Granadines now faced the determined Catholic monarchs, who were armed with an aggressive and virulent Christian ideology born of three centuries of crusades and wars against Muslims, both Moors and the Ottoman Turks. In addition, Isabella and Ferdinand understood that a successful war against Granada could rally their kingdoms behind them and associate "the Crown and its people in a heroic enterprise which would make the name of Spain ring throughout Christendom."[14]

The ten-year war for Granada began with the battle for Alhama in 1482. This battle foreshadowed the new savagery that would be visited on each Granadine town and city once the Christians captured it. Both Moorish and Christian chroniclers remarked on the ferocity of the Moors' defense of the city, and the brutality and the devastation wrought by the Christians once inside the city's walls. The royal Castilian chronicler, Pulgar, pondered the violence of the siege and sought a moral explanation for the conduct of the Christians. He found it

12. Pulgar, *Crónica de los señores Reyes Católicos,* cap. 126, quoted in Liss, p. 191.

13. Henry Kamen, *Spain, 1469–1714* (New York: Longman, 1991), p. 34.

14. Elliot, p. 46.

in God's will and in the Muslim custom of bathing[15] (Document Two).

As a result of the successful capture of Alhama, Isabella and Ferdinand committed all their collective resources to the reconquest of Granada. The war won the blessing of the pope and some papal financing, attracted volunteers from all over Europe, and increased the prestige of the monarchs. On the Muslim side, civil war and struggles over succession weakened the Granadine state, as did poor harvests, Ferdinand's policy of burning and looting the countryside, and Granadine diplomatic and political isolation. The kingdom held out for ten years, but it eventually succumbed to the continuous onslaught of the Christians. By 1492, Granada had lost nearly half of its population of half a million to death, flight, or enslavement, and surrender was simply a matter of time. In January of that year, the kingdom of Granada surrendered to the Catholic monarchs, who agreed to numerous conditions for a peaceful handover of the city of Granada. "The Capitulations of 1491" reflected the medieval tradition of *convivencia* (the coexistence of the Christians, Jews, and Moors) and guaranteed the Mudejars (Iberian Moors under Christian rule) local autonomy and their customs, property, laws, and religion (Document Three). Despite the generous provisions, many Moors found life in Christian Granada intolerable, especially when

faced with the monarchs' dual policy of pressuring the Moors to emigrate or to convert to Christianity. When forced conversions began in 1499, the Moors fled in droves or submitted to the religion of their conquerors.

The conquest of Granada and subsequent policy of forced conversions had been an important part of Isabella's vision to rid Christian Iberia of infidels and heretics. During the ten years of war, she used her power as queen to require cities, villages, and religious orders to supply knights, foot soldiers, and provisions and to lobby Rome for monies and men. She often visited the front, made sure that the army was provisioned according to her husband's requests, and frequently consulted with her council and her husband about how to pursue the war. She maintained this activity and interest throughout the war, despite the births of three more daughters, twin girls in 1482, one of whom survived and was named Maria, and the youngest, Catherine, in 1485. Ferdinand commanded the Christian forces, which at one point in the war numbered fifty thousand foot soldiers and ten thousand cavalry, formidable numbers for medieval warfare.[16] Ferdinand's actions and duties were never in doubt as he led this force to victory (Document Four).

How Isabella saw her mission and duty at the time is revealed in letters that she wrote to Ferdinand while he was at the front. Writing as both a concerned wife and powerful queen, Isabella prayed to the Lord to continue

---

15. L. P. Harvey, *Islamic Spain, 1250–1500* (Chicago, Ill.: University of Chicago, 1992), p. 271.

16. Fernández-Armesto, p. 99.

Chapter 12
Catholic
Monarchs in the
Old and New
Worlds:
Ferdinand of
Aragón (1452–
1516) and
Isabella of
Castile
(1451–1504)

granting victory "until He gives you the city and all the kingdom. This has been a marvelous thing and the most honorable in the world. . . . The dead weigh heavily on me, but they could not have gone better employed."[17] But her concern was not only for him and the troops but the end result. She had her opinions and views about the Moors and their military prowess. In the same letter, she wondered to her husband about the fickleness and inconsistency of their Muslim counterparts in waging the war; the internal dissension of the kingdom of Granada; and how Moorish leaders, particularly the young Granadine king, Boabdil, would do better in cooperation with the Christians. By both actions and words, Isabella showed herself to be an equal force in the war's persecution, so much so that a Muslim ballad noted her presence:

> With armor well burnished, and lances
>   all flashing,
> And banners all waving, and one
>   golden standard
> In front of the general, the King, Don
>   Fernando. . . .
> She also comes riding, Fernando's
>   great Queen,
> So powerful to hearten the hosts of
>   Castile.[18]

One holy crusade apparently was not enough for the pair. Beginning in 1478, they also sought and secured a papal bull to set up the Inquisition to root out and punish heretics.

Isabella believed that there was no bigger threat to the unity of her kingdom than the *conversos*, or new Christians, who had converted from Judaism. She was influenced in Seville in 1478 by the teachings of a Dominican priest, whose sermon had argued that defiance to her rule there and throughout the region was not because the powerful nobles were jealously guarding their privileges but because of religious dissidence. The priest asserted that converted Jews or their descendants "were false Christians, who had accepted baptism for personal gain but who in their hearts, and often in their religious practice, remained Jews."[19] Their false belief and their presence in Castile threatened Isabella's and Ferdinand's regime and the social, economic, and political fabric of Castilian society. Such sentiments were built on popular perceptions, social and economic reasons, and anti-Semitism.

While official toleration of the Jews dated back to the Moorish conquest of the peninsula in the eighth century and convivencia was accepted by the Christian conquerors, Jews were excluded from public office and feudal privileges, prohibited from owning land, and forced to live in ghettos in towns and cities. Despite such prohibitions, Iberian Jews carved out valuable social space for themselves as tradespeople, doctors, bankers, tax collectors, and scholars. Such professions provided important services to the upper classes and wielded signifi-

17. *Cartas autógrafas de los Reyes Catholics (1475–1502)*, Amalia Prieto, ed. (Simancas, 1971) carta 2. Quoted in Liss, p. 221.

18. Liss, p. 210.

19. John Edwards, *The Spain of the Catholic Monarchs, 1474–1520* (Oxford: Blackwell Publishers, 2000), p. 69.

cant political and economic influence. Yet their position in the kingdom was suspect because of this influence. Andrés Bernáldez, chronicler and parish priest near Seville, explained: "[M]erchants, salesmen, tax-gathers, retailers, stewards of the nobility, officials, tailors, shoemakers, tanners, weavers, grocers, pedlars, silkmercers, smiths, jewellers, and other like trades; none broke the earth, or became a farmer, carpenter or builder, but all sought after comfortable posts and ways of making profits without much labor."[20]

Iberian Jews endured periodic outbreaks of violence directed against them. One of the worst outbreaks was in 1391, which resulted in the forced conversion of many Jews and lingering anti-Semitism. Within a century, the conversos and their descendants were a significant minority in Castile's towns and cities, intermarrying with noble families, gaining important ecclesiastical and secular offices, and retaining some residual Jewish cultural customs.[21] In the popular perception, conversos seemed no different from Jews, and anti-Semitism thus affected them. Pulgar, Isabella's official chronicler and royal secretary, was a converso. He observed that some households held both conversos and Jews, resulting in a situation where conversos "lived neither within one law or the other."[22] To Isabella, conversos represented a threat to religious conformity and political unity, and the Inquisition was created to investigate their religious orthodoxy.

The Inquisition was a papally sanctioned court invested with the powers to investigate, try, and punish heretics. Clergy staffed the court, but they were appointed by the crown, which financed its operation. Given these conditions, the Inquisition became an instrument of secular power and reflected the sensibilities of Isabella and Ferdinand. In Isabella's hands, the campaign against the conversos sought a retributive justice, to be meted out to all who were suspected and found guilty of practicing any form of Judaism.[23] She was not interested in a few exemplary cases but instead wanted to root out each and every case of heresy, with the purpose of purging Catholicism of any elements of Judaism. Her exact intent with this policy is not directly known, but one official of the Inquisition captured her opinion when he observed that the Inquisition might punish some innocent people but

the harm from ignoring sin and withholding punishment is greater than the harm that would follow from administering it, for from that error would ensue the breaking of the faith, the corruption of true doctrine, and the destruction of virtuous life; and even though the punishment [of the innocent] create a scandal, it is the doctrine of Christ to punish; and not to open the door of pardon either to the few or to

20. Andrés Bernáldez, *Memorias del reinado de los Reyes Católicos* (Madrid, 1962), Chapter. CXII, p. 256.

21. Liss, p. 163.

22. Pulgar, p. 337. Quoted in Henry Kamen, *Inquisition and Society in Spain in the Sixteenth and Seventeenth Centuries* (London: Weidenfeld and Nicolson, 1985), p. 27.

23. Liss, p. 169.

Chapter 12
Catholic
Monarchs in the
Old and New
Worlds:
Ferdinand of
Aragón (1452–
1516) and
Isabella of
Castile
(1451–1504)

the many; for it is better to enter Paradise with one eye than to suffer in Hell with two.[24]

With such sentiments at work, the Inquisitors took informants at their word, used confiscation of property and torture to obtain confessions, persecuted the innocent, and condemned many to death by burning at the stake (Document Five). The first year of the Inquisition in Seville revealed so many heretics that Isabella sought and received a papal bull to set up the Inquisition for the rest of Castile. In 1482, Ferdinand revived the Inquisition in Aragón and subjected it to his control, essentially usurping the power of the pope. The pope, Sixtus IV, was displeased with Ferdinand's usurpation of his power to set up the court and with information he received about the brutality of the Aragonese Inquisition's methods and its corruption. Sixtus IV issued a strong reprimand in the form of a papal bull to Ferdinand. In this decree, Sixtus IV accused the Aragonese Inquisition for unjustly imprisoning many people, subjecting them to cruel tortures, declaring them false believers when they were not, and confiscating the property of the executed[25] (Document Six). The strong wording and acceptance of converso claims of corruption caused Ferdinand to portray the bull as false. Clearly, the time was past for the pope to intervene because the Inquisition

had become a "wholly royal and Spanish institution."[26]

Once conversos were found guilty of heresy, their sentences were publicly announced and carried out in a religious ceremony known as *auto de fe*, or act of faith. Over the course of a decade, over fifteen thousand conversos were found guilty and suffered "reconciliation," which meant they were imprisoned, their property was confiscated, or they were reprimanded (Document Seven). Two thousand conversos were burned at the stake. The terror of the Inquisition caused many conversos to flock to the Inquisition and confess voluntarily for their lapses of faith and others to flee. It also focused attention on the "enemy from within," the unconverted Jews.

During the 1480s, conditions for Jews deteriorated because anti-Semitism increased among Spaniards. As a result, urban authorities, with the blessing of the Inquisition and the crown, began to expel unconverted Jews from their towns because they provided a bad example to their converted brethren. Local expulsions were not sufficient for the infamous Inquisitor General, Tomás de Torquemada. In 1492, he convinced the two monarchs that Jews had to be expelled if they wanted to stop heresy among the conversos. Shortly after the conquest of Granada, Isabella and Ferdinand ordered the expulsion of the Jews from Spain (Document Eight). In a letter written on the same day as the expulsion, Ferdinand explained the reasoning behind it. He wrote, "The Holy Office of the Inquisition, seeing

24. Ibid. p. 170.

25. Henry Charles Lea, *A History of the Inquisition of Spain*, Volume 1 (New York: The Macmillan Company, 1906–1908), pp. 587, 590 (appendices X and XI). Quoted in Kamen, *Inquisition and Society in Spain*, p. 34.

26. Ibid.

how some Christians are endangered by contact and communication with the Jews, had provided that the Jews be expelled from all our realms and territories, and has persuaded us to give our support and agreement to this, which we now do, because of our debts and obligations to the said Holy Office; and we do so despite the great harm to ourselves, seeking and preferring the salvation of souls above our own profit and that of individuals."[27] Ferdinand's correspondence on this matter has led many historians to conclude that it was his decision to expel the Jews, but the queen's sense of destiny as ordained by God also played a role in the expulsion order. She believed in the imminence of the second coming and that she, Ferdinand, and the Spanish people had been elected "the spiritual heirs of the initial chosen ones and that, the Messiah having arrived, it was past time for Jews to disappear."[28]

This sense of destiny, reinforced by the successful reconquest of Granada, spurred Isabella and Ferdinand to expand their influence and the Christian cause into Africa, across the Atlantic, and beyond. They were poised for empire, and it was no coincidence that the two monarchs finally decided in 1492 to sponsor the Genoese adventurer, Christopher Columbus, on an expedition westward across the Atlantic, ostensibly to find a shorter route to the Far East. In an earlier meeting with Isabella and Ferdinand

in 1486, Columbus had appealed to their sense of religious obligation and historical destiny and had ingratiated himself by playing upon the royal construction of that destiny[29] (Document Nine). Already in 1478, Isabella and Ferdinand had taken a step toward this divine mission by sponsoring an expedition to the Canary Islands. The cabellero chronicler Diego de Valera noted this sense of destiny when he addressed Ferdinand after a victory against the Moors in 1485. He wrote, "It is clear that our Lord intends to carry out what has been prophesied for centuries . . . , to wit, that you shall not merely put these Spains under your royal scepter, but that you will also subjugate regions beyond the sea."[30] When Columbus sailed with Isabella's and Ferdinand's sponsorship in August 1492, he went with the knowledge that finding a new route to the Far East and acquiring riches were not the only goals of the expedition; his mission was also to bring glory and honor to Spain. On October 12, 1492, Columbus and his men reached the Bahamas and opened the way for Spanish conquest of the New World.

Columbus's voyage to the Caribbean under the sponsorship of the Castilian crown allowed Isabella to lay claim to the new-found lands for Spain and to defend that claim against possible claims made by Portugal. She received papal support for her position, but the Portuguese successfully pressed the Catholic monarchs to concede more territory to them in a treaty

27. P. Leon Tello, *Judios de Toledo*, Volume 1 (Madrid: Instituto B. Arias Montano, 1979, p. 347.

28. Liss, p. 271.

29. Ibid., p. 286.

30. Ibid., p. 283.

Chapter 12
Catholic
Monarchs in the
Old and New
Worlds:
Ferdinand of
Aragón (1452–
1516) and
Isabella of
Castile
(1451–1504)

signed at Tordesillas in 1494. Columbus made a total of four voyages to the New World, all of them sponsored by the Catholic monarchs. With each voyage, the hoped-for riches did not appear; but with each return, Isabella honed her plans for the Indies. Claiming royal power over the lands and peoples of the Indies, she parceled out land to new settlers, collected import taxes, and decreed that the people of the Indies were royal vassals. Believing that the "Indians" were her subjects, Isabella rejected Columbus's and others' attempts to enslave the Indi-

ans. Of course, any subjects of the Catholic monarchs had to be converted to Christianity and submit to Spanish rule. To achieve these results, the conquerors utilized the skills that had been perfected during the reconquest, the Inquisition, and the war against the Jews. Ferdinand and Isabella not only laid the foundations for a world empire, but their methods provided their subjects and enemies with sufficient evidence to assess the impact of their rule either positively or negatively.

◼ FINALE

Much has gone unsaid about Ferdinand's and Isabella's personal relationships because most choose to concentrate on the activities and ventures that earned them the designation "Catholic monarchs." By all accounts, Isabella was a devoted mother and faithful wife. She had witnessed firsthand the consequences of questionable paternity, and she crafted her behavior and her image to ensure that the legitimacy of her five children was never questioned and that the dynasty continued. She prepared the heir to the throne, Juan, for rule by providing the best tutors in the liberal and military arts. For her four daughters, she also provided schooling that prepared them for queenship, not like the inadequate preparation that she received. Her daughters learned to read and write in both the vernacular and Latin and had some instruction in the liberal arts. United by their desire to advance both Aragón's and

Castile's dynastic interests, Isabella and Ferdinand shared a relationship of mutual respect, equal partnership, and great affection. In Juan and their daughters, they had produced heirs who could unite and intertwine the interests of the two kingdoms.

Isabella was always conscious of her and her husband's political image as they attempted to forge political and religious unity in their respective kingdoms. She worked hard to allay her subjects' fear regarding women rulers, and she always made sure Ferdinand was on hand for all political decisions. To craft their image as political partners, she instructed the official chroniclers to portray their authority as equal, despite the fact that she was the monarch of Castile, had dictated the terms of their partnership, and was the only one of the two who wielded ultimate royal authority in Castile. Pulgar took this charge to heart and created the view that their rule and partnership were seamless. He even went so far as to comment that "[t]he King and Queen had been delivered of a daughter."[31] Had their position of authority been switched, Pulgar would most likely not have received such instructions from Ferdinand.

In the consciousness of their contemporaries, Ferdinand and Isabella were the quintessential Christian monarchs who achieved religious and political unity through reconquest, war, and ventures that took on the character of an endless crusade against infidels and heretics, both inside and outside Spain. With the unification of Castile and Aragón under the pair, the nascent Spanish state and their rulers were increasingly identified as Catholic monarchs and defenders of the faith. In December 1496, Pope Alexander VI officially designated Isabella and Ferdinand "Catholic Kings" (*Reyes Católicos*) because of their commitment to and advancement of the Catholic faith in Iberia and in the New World. From this time forward, Catholicism became integral to the creation of Spanish identity, and professions of faith were often used by the state to test one's loyalty to Spain

and its enterprises. In 1513, Niccolò Machiavelli (1469–1527), the Florentine Renaissance political philosopher, wrote *The Prince* to instruct Italy's various rulers on how to pursue political goals and power by whatever means were necessary. In this political treatise, Machiavelli cited Ferdinand as an example of a ruler who embraced the Catholic faith to realize political ambitions but ignored its principles of mercy, humanity, and integrity. Machiavelli pointed to Ferdinand's hypocrisy but believed such a position was acceptable and necessary. He wrote, "One prince [Ferdinand] of the present time, whom it is not well to name, never preaches anything else but peace and good faith, and to both he is most hostile, and either, if he had kept it, would have deprived him of reputation and kingdom many a time." By using Ferdinand as a model that should be emulated, and ignoring his partner, Isabella, Machiavelli defined the successful ruler in male terms and ignored the possibility that a woman could be an equally effective "prince."

▓ QUESTIONS

1. What was the role of the chroniclers in shaping the story and image of Isabella and Ferdinand? What sources corroborate or contradict their narratives?

2. How did Isabella, as a claimant to the throne of Castile, legitimize her

claim? What were the conditions of the marriage contract between Ferdinand and Isabella? Why did Ferdinand gain additional powers?

3. How did Isabella's image as a pious and moral queen affect her ability to rule? What was Ferdinand's image in the public imagination?

4. What was the significance of the Reconquista in medieval Spain?

31. Liss, p. 4.

Chapter 12
Catholic
Monarchs in the
Old and New
Worlds:
Ferdinand of
Aragón (1452–
1516) and
Isabella of
Castile
(1451–1504)

What motivated Isabella and Ferdinand to undertake the reconquest of Granada?

5. Why did Isabella and then Ferdinand call for the Inquisition in their respective kingdoms? What were its consequences? Why did they expel the Jews from Spain?

6. What motivated Isabella and Ferdinand to undertake Atlantic explo-

ration? Why did exploration agree with their sense of mission and destiny?

7. What are the points of controversy surrounding the reign of Ferdinand and Isabella? Does one monarch bear greater or lesser responsibility for their activities? Why or why not?

▪ DOCUMENTS

DOCUMENT ONE

ISABELLA OF CASTILE

The Duties of a Monarch

Before each of Christopher Columbus's voyages during the 1490s, Isabella and Ferdinand entered into a contract with the explorer. The preface to one such contract, or capitulation (shown in the first part of this document), revealed how Isabella and Ferdinand interpreted their roles as monarchs. What gave them their right to rule? What were the duties and responsibilities of a good ruler?

In the early 1500s, Isabella endured a long illness that resulted in her death in 1504. Knowing that her death was imminent, she drafted, as was customary, a will (shown in the second part of this document). What were her concerns at the end of her life? What was her legacy to her children and to her subjects?

Preface to 1493 Confirmation of the Granada Capitulations,
Barcelona
(May, 23 1493)

[1] In the name of the Holy Trinity and Eternal Unity, Father, Son, and Holy Spirit, three persons in one divine essence who lives and reigns forever without end, and of the Most Blessed Virgin, glorious Saint Mary, our lady, His mother, whom we accept as sovereign and advocate in all our affairs; in honor and reverence to her, to the most blessed apostle, lord Saint James, light and mirror to all the lands of Spain, patron and guide to the kings of Castile and León, and to all the other saints of the entire celestial court. Although man cannot completely know what God is, however great his knowledge of the world may be, yet he

can know Him by seeing and contemplating His wonders and the works and acts that He has done and does every day, since all works are done by His power, governed by His wisdom, and maintained by His goodness.

[2] And thus man can understand that God is the beginning, middle, and end of all things, and that in Him they are comprehended; and He maintains each one in that state which He has ordained for them, and all have need of Him and He has no need of them, and He is able to change them whenever He may choose, according to His will; and it is not in His nature to change or alter in any manner.

[3] He is called King over all kings, because from Him they derive their name and by Him they reign, and He governs and maintains them, who are His vicars, each one in his own kingdom, appointed by Him over the nations to maintain them in justice and worldly truth.

[4] This is fulfilled in two ways, one being spiritual, as the prophets and saints revealed, to whom our Lord gave the gift of knowing all things accurately and causing them to be understood. The other way is by nature, as was shown by the philosophers who were knowledgeable about things rationally.

[5] For the saints declared that the king is appointed on the earth in place of God to execute justice and give to each his due, and therefore he was known as the heart and soul of the people; and just as the soul is in man's heart, and by it the body lives and is maintained, so justice is in the king, which is the life and sustenance of the people under his dominion; and just as the heart is one, and all the other parts receive their unity from it in order to be a body, even so all those of the kingdom, no matter how many they may be, are one, because the king must be and is one, and therefore they must all be one with him in order to follow and help him in the things he has to do.

[6] The philosophers reasoned that kings are the head of the kingdom, because, as from the head proceed all the senses by which all parts of the body are commanded, just so by the commandment that proceeds from the king, who is lord and head of everyone in the kingdom, must all be commanded and guided, and obey it.

[7] So great is the authority of the power of kings, that all laws and rights are subject to their power, because they do not hold it from men but from God, whose place they supplant in temporal matters: to which, among other things, chiefly pertains to love, honor, and protect their peoples, and among others he should nobly single out and honor those who deserve it for the services they have rendered; and therefore the king or prince has, among other powers, not only the power but also the duty to confer favors on those who deserve them for the services they have rendered him and for the goodness that he finds in them. . . .

[9] This justice consists of two principal parts: the one being commutative, which is between one man and another, the other distributive, in which are obtained the rewards and remunerations for good and virtuous works and

Chapter 12
Catholic
Monarchs in the
Old and New
Worlds:
Ferdinand of
Aragón (1452–
1516) and
Isabella of
Castile
(1451–1504)

services that men perform for kings and princes or for the public welfare of their kingdoms.

[10] Because, as the laws declare, to give rewards to those who well and loyally serve is something that is very becoming to all men but especially to kings, princes, and great lords who have the power to do it, it is their particular privilege to honor and exalt those who serve them well and loyally, and whose virtues and services deserve it. In rewarding good deeds, kings show that they are discerners of virtue and likewise administrators of justice.

[11] For justice does not exist solely to correct the wicked but also to reward the good. Moreover, another great utility proceeds from it, because it encourages the good to be more virtuous and the wicked to reform themselves. If kings did not [reward the good], the contrary could happen.

[12] Because, among other rewards and remunerations that kings can give to those who well and loyally serve them, is the honor and exaltation of them above others of their lineage, and ennoblement, decoration, and honor of them, as well as the conferral on them of many other benefits, gifts, and favors. . . .

Isabella the Catholic

Testamentaria

(1504)

I would like and order to be buried in the Franciscan monastery that is in the Alhambra of the city of Granada, . . . dressed in the habit of . . . Saint Francis . . . however, if the King my husband [*senor*] chooses a sepulcher in another church or monastery in any other place in our kingdoms, I wish and order that my body be transferred and buried next to his because our bodies on the earth represent the joining together that we had while living, and that our souls, I hope in God's mercy, will return to in heaven. . . .

I order that after said debts and obligations [referred to in previous paragraphs] are paid, in churches and monasteries in my kingdoms and territories, twenty thousand masses be said for my soul. . . .

I order that after the payment of said debts and obligations, that sums of money be distributed for the marriages of needy young women, and another sum so that some poor young women may enter the religious life because in that holy state they wish to serve God. . . .

I ask and order that the Princess, my daughter, and the Prince, her husband, pay great attention to the things that honor God and the Holy Faith, . . . that you be obedient to the orders of the holy mother Church, and protectors and defenders of it, and that you do not cease in the conquest of Africa and in the fight for the Faith against the infidels, and that you always support the many acts of the holy Inquisition against depraved heresy, ...

I pray and urge the Prince and Princess, my children, that just as the king, my husband, and I always were in love, union and agreement, that you have that same love, union and agreement that I expect from you, and that you pay great attention to the preservation of the patrimony of the Royal Crown . . . and that you are benign and humanitarian to your subjects. . . .

DOCUMENT TWO

Fernando del Pulgar

"War of Granada"
Cronica de los Reyes Católicos
(1490s)

Pulgar was one of the official royal chroniclers of the Catholic monarchs. His Chronicles of the Catholic Kings *fall into the letrado tradition of historical writing. In this passage, he described the fall of Alhama. To whom or what did he ascribe the Moorish defeat? Did he see the struggle as a clash of civilizations?*

The caballeros and town mayors of whom we have spoken, with the wish to do a notable deed to strengthen the Christian faith and to serve the King and the Queen, gathered their people for the agreed-upon day and, informed of the state and defense of the city of Alhama and of Malaga, agreed to enter Moorish territory and to take the road to Alhama, because according to the information that they of the small guard for the city, believed they could take it with little word or danger . . . [and armed men] 1500 on horseback, 3000 on foot, followed the road by night and by day . . . until they arrived at the city of Alhama.

The Moors, who had not been diligent in guarding the city, were astonished when they heard that the Christians had been able to advance so far into [the kingdom of Granada]. . . .

[In the battle for the city], the Christians were many and well-armed, so the Moors, having fought all day and not being able to withstand the Christian forces, retreated to the large mosque, near the walls of the city, ... The Christians set fire to the mosque. . . . The Moors, as they felt the fire (like desperate people) came out to fight in various places and most of them died; at the end they were defeated and imprisoned.

About four thousand women and children were taken captive there. More than a thousand Moors died, fighting in the streets. A large quantity of household goods, gold and silver and cattle were taken, because that city was very rich and a great trading center. . . .

[Those who witnessed the destruction of that city] done in so few hours, marveled that no live person remained, the dead were eaten by dogs, . . . the goods seized were taken to many places; and God wanted to show his punishment, even on the dogs of that city, so they did not remain alive. And because we find

Chapter 12
Catholic
Monarchs in the
Old and New
Worlds:
Ferdinand of
Aragón (1452–
1516) and
Isabella of
Castile
(1451–1504)

in Sacred Scripture that when God is angry with a people, he threatens them with total destruction, even the dogs, ... Why did it please God to show his great wrath and cruelty against them? We find that close to the city were baths in a very beautiful building where there was a natural hot spring. Men and women from the city and other places came to these baths to bathe. The baths caused some softening of the body [and] so much pleasure that led to idleness, and from luxurious idleness came sins, wickedness and other deceits and evil deeds inflicted on each other to sustain the idleness to which they were accustomed.

Considering this, we believe that it pleased God's justice to give them such punishment, that even the dogs in that city did not remain alive; . . . .

DOCUMENT THREE

The Capitulations of Granada
(1491)

Castilian and Arabic versions of the terms for the surrender of Granada exist. The text printed below is the Castilian version and is the more complete of the two. Because of the length of the document, the editor of the text has translated some clauses in full (indicated by [F]) and summarized others (indicated by [S]). Did the terms reflect the tradition of convivencia? What were the rights and responsibilities of the Moors? Of the Spanish king and queen?

"*Firstly* that the Moorish king and his *alcaides* [sic] and lawyers, judges, *muftīs*, ministers, learned men, military leaders, good men, and all the common folk of the city of Granada and of its Albaicín and other suburbs will in love, peace, goodwill, and with all truthfulness in their dealings and their actions yield and surrender to their highnesses, or to a person by them appointed, within forty days from this date, the fortress of the Alhambra and Alhizan with all towers, gates to the city and the Albaicín and to suburbs connecting directly with the open country, so that they may occupy them in their name with their own troops, at their own free will, on condition that orders be issued to the justices that they should not permit the Christians to climb onto the wall between the Alcazaba and the Albaicín from where the houses of the Moors may be seen; and if anybody should climb up there, he should be punished immediately and sternly." [F] . . .

3. Isabella, Ferdinand, and Prince Juan (their son) would after the surrender accept all Granadans, from King Abi Abdilehi (Boabdil) down, "great and small, men and women," as their vassals and natural subjects. In return the monarchs guaranteed to let them remain in their "houses, estates and heredita-

ments now and for all time and for ever, nor would they allow any harm to be done to them without due legal process and without cause, nor would they have their estates and property nor any part thereof taken from them, rather would they be honored and respected by all their vassals." [S] . . .

6. "Their highnesses and their successors will ever afterwards [*para siempre jamás*] allow King Abi Abdilehi and his *alcaides*, judges, *muftīs, alguaciles*, military leaders, and good men, and all the common people, great or small, to live in their own religion, and not permit that their mosques be taken from them, nor their minarets nor their muezzins, nor will they interfere with the pious foundations or endowments which they have for such purposes, nor will they disturb the uses and customs which they observe." [F]

7. "The Moors shall be judged in their laws and law suits according to the code of the *sharīʿa* which it is their custom to respect, under the jurisdiction of their judges and *qādīs*." [F]

8. "Neither now nor at any future time will their arms or their horses be taken from them, with the exception of cannons, both large and small, which they will within a short space of time hand over to whomsoever their highnesses appoint for that purpose." [F]

9. "Those Moors, both great and small, men and women, whether from Granada or from the Alpujarra and all other places, who may wish to go to live in Barbary or to such other places as they see fit, may sell their property, whether it be real estate or goods and chattels, in any manner and to whomsoever they like, and their highnesses will at no time take them away, or take them from those who may have bought them." [S]

10. Those who wished to leave with their families and all their possessions of any kind whatsoever, except firearms, might do so. Those wishing to cross immediately might make use of the ten large ships provided for the purpose for the next seventy days from the port of their choice to "those ports of Barbary where Christian merchants normally trade." After this, and for three years, ships would be made available free at fifty days' notice. [S] . . .

13. "Neither their highnesses nor the Prince Juan their son nor those who may follow after them for all time will give instructions that those Moors who are their vassals shall be obliged to wear distinctive marks like those worn by the Jews." [F] . . .

15. All Christian captives were to be handed over at the moment of surrender, with no entitlement for ransom or compensation, although if the Granadan owner of the captive had taken him to North Africa and already sold him before the Capitulations came into force, he would not have to hand him back. [S] . . .

17. No Christians might enter mosques where the Muslims perform their prayer without permission of the *alfaquíes:* anyone entering otherwise was to be punished. [S] . . .

19. King Boabdil and all his dignitaries, and all the common people of Granada, etc., would be well treated by their highnesses and their ministers, "and that what they have to say will be listened to, and their customs and rites

Chapter 12
Catholic
Monarchs in the
Old and New
Worlds:
Ferdinand of
Aragón (1452–
1516) and
Isabella of
Castile
(1451–1504)

will be preserved, and all *alcaides* and *alfaquíes* will be allowed to collect their incomes and enjoy their preeminences and their liberties such as by custom they enjoy, and it is only right that they should continue to enjoy." [S] . . .

21. "Law suits which arise between Moors will be judged by their law *sharīʿa*, which they call of the *sunna*, and by their *qāḍīs* and judges, as they customarily have, but if the suit should arise between a Christian and a Moor, then it will be judged by a Christian judge and a Moorish *qāḍī*, in order that neither side may have any grounds for complaint against the sentence." [F] . . .

25. "That the Moors will not be obliged to give or pay more tribute to their highnesses than they used to give to the Moorish kings." [F] . . .

27. If any Moor were to go to North Africa and then find he did not like the way of life, he could return and have all the benefits of the Capitulations, so long as he returned within three years. [S] . . .

29. Nobody would be permitted to abuse by word or by deed any Christian man or woman who before the date of the Capitulations had turned Moor, and if any Moor had taken a renegade for his wife, she would not be forced to become a Christian against her will, but might be questioned in the presence of Christians and Moors, and be allowed to follow her own will; the same was to be understood of children born of a Christian mother and a Moor. [S]

30. "No Moor will be forced to become Christian against his or her will, and if for reasons of love an unmarried girl or a married woman or a widow should wish to become Christian, she will not be received [into the church] until she has been questioned. And if she has taken away from her parents' house clothing or jewels, these will be restored to the rightful owner, and guilty persons will be dealt with by the law." [F] . . .

32. If any Moor had wounded or insulted any Christian man or woman held in captivity, no legal proceedings could be instituted against him ever. [S] . . .

34. "The judges, *alcaides*, and governors which their highnesses appoint in the city and region of Granada will be persons such as will honor the Moors and treat them kindly [*amorosamente*], and continue to respect these Capitulations. And if anyone should do anything which he ought not to do, their highnesses will have him moved from his post and punished." [F]

35. Neither Boabdil nor anybody else would be called to account for things done before the city surrendered. [S] . . .

41. "The pious endowments [*habices*] and the emoluments of the mosques, and the alms and other things customarily given to colleges [*madrasas*] and schools where children are taught will be the responsibility of the *alfaquíes*, to distribute them as they see fit, and their highnesses and their ministers will not interfere in this nor any aspect of it, nor will they give orders with regard to their confiscation or sequestration at any time ever in the future." [F] . . .

47. Christian slaughterhouses would be separated from Muslim ones. [S]

48. "The Jews native to Granada, Albaicín, and other suburbs, and of the Alpujarras and all other places contained in these Capitulations, will benefit

from them, on condition that those who do not become Christians cross to North Africa within three years counting from December 8 of this year." [F]

"And their highnesses will give orders for the totality of the contents of these Capitualtions to be observed from the day when the fortresses of Granada are surrendered onwards. To which effect they have commanded that their royal charter and deed should be signed with their names and sealed with their seal and witnessed by Hernando de Zafra their secretary, and have so done, dated in the *vega* of Granada on this 28th day of the month of November of the year of our salvation 1491." [F]

DOCUMENT FOUR

Historical Approaches to the Reign of the Catholic Monarchs

ANDRES BERNÁLDEZ

Historia de los reyes católicos
(ca. 1500)

A member of the clergy who witnessed firsthand the Inquisition in Seville, Andres Bernáldez represents the letrado tradition of historical writing. He saw the actions of Isabella and Ferdinand as divinely inspired and was uncritical of those he believed were ordained by God to carry out God's will. In this passage, he retold the story of the siege of Granada and the reasons for its fall. What were the causes of the Moorish defeat and the Christians' victory?

[During the siege of Granada] . . . one day, a Saturday, the Queen said that she wanted to go to see Granada at closer range. . . . The King and the Prince mounted up with her and the Infanta and [they went to a nearby town and lodged in a house from which they had a good view of the ensuing battle.] In the course of the battle, between the dead, the wounded, and the captured were more than 2000 Moors . . . and many Moors escaped and fled to the mountains. All of this the King and Queen, Prince and Infanta saw clearly from the window of the house where they were; the King, the Queen and the Infanta, when they saw the fighting, fell to their knees begging God, our Savior, to guard the Christians, and the Ladies who accompanied them did the same, and the Moors even though there were many of them, could not prevail against the sharp and unexpected blow that the Marquis, Duke of Cadiz and his battalion gave them . . . and the Moors began to flee, to run into each other and to knock each other

Chapter 12
Catholic
Monarchs in the
Old and New
Worlds:
Ferdinand of
Aragón (1452–
1516) and
Isabella of
Castile
(1451–1504)

down; and there was no Christian caballero that day who did not fix his lance on a Moor; and no harm came to the Christians that day except some wounds, and a few dead horses. And the King and Queen took great pleasure in this victory, more so because the Queen was the cause of it. . . .

[The area was finally conquered after ten years of fighting.] And thus the sainted and praiseworthy conquest came to a glorious end, and the [King, the Queen and the court] saw what many Kings and princes wished to see, a kingdom of many cities and towns, and a multitude of villages, situated in such sturdy and fertile terrain, all won in ten years. What else could this mean but God wanted to provision it for them and put it in their hands?

DIEGO DE VALERA

Cronica de los Reyes Católicos

Chapter XLVIII: "How the illustrious kings don Fernando y dona Isabel, being in the city of Cordoba, determined to make war on the kingdom of Granada, and the advice that they received on this."
(ca. 1480s)

Diego de Valera was a member of the courts of Juan II and Enrique IV, a partici-
pant in Juan's military conflicts, and a practitioner of the caballero school of his-
torical writing. As a member of court, a successful military man, and an elder
statesman to Ferdinand and Isabella, he saw in their actions both strengths and
weaknesses and the need to consult men like himself. In Valera's opinion, what
were the monarchs' strengths and weaknesses during the siege of Loja? Is the tone
between this account and Bernáldez's different? Why or why not?

Our serene highnesses, the King and Queen, being in the city of Cordoba, sought advice on the form that the war should take, on which they received a great diversity of opinions. And finally, it was determined that they would put the city of Loja under siege because taking this city would be a great help in order to get into the city of Alhama. . . . The Marquez of Cadiz, because he had greater experience in the war against the Moors than any other caballero who was there, was of a contrary opinion, giving obvious reasons for it. But because the will of the King and Queen was determined to put Loja under siege, it was necessary to proceed, from which great inconveniences followed.

[Valera then describes more of the advice of the Duke of Cadiz, which was to attack another city, not Loja.]

Because the king had already stated his intention, he determined to follow it, the result I will relate shortly. [Loja was a military defeat for the Spanish.] But one of the things which a king should consider in taking advice is that he should receive from each person advice on that which they know best: in matters of conscience, from religious; in matters of justice, from the learned doctors; in matters of war, from the caballeros who have the most experience in it.

<hr>

DOCUMENT FIVE

Inquisitorial Trials of Inés López

Inés López was the daughter of conversos, and she was tried by the Inquisition for observing several Jewish customs. Other members of her family were also tried by the Inquisition, not an uncommon phenomenon in Spain. Brought before the court in October 1495 and then again in January 1496, Inés confessed her digressions. The Inquisition sentenced her to wear a penitential garment (sanbenito) *and to life imprisonment. In this case, it meant house arrest, but such sentences were seldom strictly enforced. In 1511, she was brought before the court for violations of her sentence. The Inquisition imprisoned her and confiscated her property. The passages below are excerpts from her first two confessions. What accusations were made against her? To what did she confess?*

CONFESSION OF 22 OCTOBER 1495

Most reverend Lords:

I, Inés López, a resident of Ciudad Real, wife of the late Alonso de Aguilera, appear before Your Reverences with the greatest contrition and repentance for my sins of which I am capable, and I beg Our Lord Jesus Christ for His pardon and mercy, and I beg of Your Reverences a saving penance for my soul, and for those [sins] that I have committed by which I have offended My Lord Jesus Christ and His Holy Catholic Faith, which are the following in this manner:

I declare, My Lords, that I did not do servile work on some Saturdays, and on Saturdays I put on clean clothes. And sometimes I ate food that was prepared on Friday for Saturday, and I lit candles on Friday evening in accordance with Jewish ritual.

Likewise, I observed some of the Jewish fasts, [fasting] until nightfall. Moreover, I sometimes observed Jewish holidays, when I found out about them from a cousin of mine named Isabel de Lobón, when I was [staying] with her, for she was a widow. And she told me to do so for the benefit of my soul, especially [to observe] Passover, for the aforementioned Isabel de Lobón every so often gave me [unleavened bread], warning me not to tell anyone. The aforementioned Isabel de Lobón has left Villarreal [Ciudad Real]; for where, no one knows.

Likewise, I removed the fat from meat whenever I could.

Likewise, My Lords, I declare that I ate on low tables at funeral banquets. . . .

*Chapter 12
Catholic
Monarchs in the
Old and New
Worlds:
Ferdinand of
Aragón (1452–
1516) and
Isabella of
Castile
(1451–1504)*

ADDITIONAL CONFESSION OF 14 JANUARY 1496

My most reverend Lords:

I, Inés López, daughter of Diego López, a resident of Ciudad Real, appear before Your Reverences to say that, because I had made a confession of the sins I had committed against Our Lord in which I said that if any further sin came to mind I would declare and reveal it, I now declare, My Lords, that what I further remember is the following:

I declare and confess to Your Reverences that on some Friday nights my sister [Violante], the [wife] of [Pedro de] San Román, and I tidied up the house and cooked Saturday's food on those nights. We did this sometimes, and other times we didn't, so that we wouldn't be found out, etc.

Moreover, My Lords, I had little desire to eat pork, and when I could, I didn't eat it, and neither did my aforementioned sister, who told me that I shouldn't eat [it] nor anything cooked with it because I was younger than she.

Moreover, My Lords, sometimes when I went to Mass it was my custom and habit to chatter and not to pray . . .

Moreover, My Lords, on Sundays and holidays I sometimes sewed things I needed and also performed other tasks . . .

Moreover, My Lords, on days of abstinence in Lent and the vigils of other holidays and on ember days, I often prepared and ate food, and I saw that my aforementioned sisters ate meat and other [forbidden] delicacies.

Moreover, My Lords, I declare that when my father died, I saw Diego Díez's wife and Sezilla, the wife of Martín González, put a pot of water in the parlor where [his body] was. I don't know why, except that I heard it said that it was to bathe my aforementioned father, who was dirty. And I placed a basin of water and a cloth in said parlor—I don't remember who told me to do so, except that I believe that it was Mayor Alvarez, my sister, who was there.

Moreover, I often lit candles on Friday nights in San Román's house, because I usually lived with San Román and his wife, my sister, for I was twelve or fifteen years old.

Moreover, my Lords, I saw that my mother did not spin on Saturdays, and I saw this during the whole time that I lived [with her]. . . .

ADDITION OF 19 JANUARY 1496

My most reverend Lords:

I, Inés López, a resident of Ciudad Real, appear before Your Reverences and declare that, in addition to what I have declared and confessed to you, I often porged meat and removed the tendons from legs of lamb.

DOCUMENT SIX

Pope Sixtus IV and Ferdinand

Characterization of the Inquisition in Aragón
(April–May 1482)

In the two passages below, Sixtus IV and Ferdinand disagree over how the Inquisition had been carried out in Aragón. What were the pope's concerns? How did Ferdinand respond? What did he accuse the pope of doing?

Sixtus IV
Papal Bull on the Aragonese Inquisition
(April 18, 1482)

. . . [I]n Aragón, Valencia, Mallorca and Catalonia the Inquisition has been moved not by zeal for faith and the salvation of souls, but by lust for wealth, and that many true and faithful Christians on the testimony of enemies, rivals, slaves and other lower and even less proper persons, have without any legitimate proof been thrust into secular prisons, imprisoned, tortured, and condemned as relapsed heretics, deprived of their goods and property and handed over to the secular arm to be executed, to the perils of souls, setting a pernicious example, and causing disgust to many.

Ferdinand of Aragón
Response to the Papal Bull
(May 13, 1482)

Things have been told me, Holy Father which, if true, would seem to merit the greatest astonishment. It is said that Your Holiness has granted the conversos a general pardon for all the errors and crimes they have committed. . . . To these rumors, however, we have given no credence, because they seem to be things which would in no way have been conceded by Your Holiness, who have a duty to the Inquisition. But if by chance concessions have been made through the persistent and cunning persuasion of the said conversos, I intend never to let them take effect. Take care therefore not to let the matter go further, and to revoke any concessions and entrust us with the care of these questions.

Chapter 12
Catholic
Monarchs in the
Old and New
Worlds:
Ferdinand of
Aragón (1452–
1516) and
Isabella of
Castile
(1451–1504)

DOCUMENT SEVEN

Descriptions of an *Auto de Fe*
(1486)

What was the purpose of an auto de fe? What were some of its features, according to this passage?

Toledo, 12 February 1486

On Sunday, 12 February 1486, all the "reconciled" who lived in these seven parishes—Saint Vincent, Saint Nicholas, Saint John of the Milk, Saint Justa, Saint Michael, Saint Justus, [and] Saint Lawrence—marched in a procession; there were as many as seven hundred fifty people [including] both men and women. And they marched in procession from [the monastery of] Saint Peter the Martyr in this fashion. The men were without cloaks, bareheaded, barefoot, and without hose. And because the weather was so cold they were ordered to wear linen soles under their otherwise bare feet, with unlit candles in their hands. And the women were without cloaks or any outer garment whatsoever, their faces uncovered, barefoot like the men, and holding their candles. Many important and respected personages were among such people, and with the extremely cold temperature and the dishonor and disgrace they suffered on account of the great crowd that was watching them— because many people had come from the surrounding areas to see them—they went along shrieking with pain and weeping, and some tore out their hair (it is believed more because of the disgrace they were suffering than because of the offenses they had committed against God).

And thus they marched in great anguish through the entire city, following the same path as the Corpus Christi procession, until they arrived at the cathedral. At the door of the cathedral were two priests who made the sign of the cross on the forehead of each one of them, saying these words: "Receive the sign of the cross that you denied and lost through being grievously deceived." And they went into the cathedral up to a platform, and on another nearby platform was an altar where mass was said for them and a sermon was preached to them. And afterward a notary public arose and began to call each one by name, speaking in this way: "Is so-and-so there?" And the reconciled raised his candle and said: "Yes." And there in public he [the notary] read off all the things in which he [the reconciled] had Judaized, and likewise was done with the women.

And when this was done, there in public they were given their penance which was to march in a procession on six [consecutive] Fridays, whipping their backs with ropes of knotted hemp and without hose or hats, and [also] that they fast on those six Fridays. And it was ordered that as long as they should live they could hold no public office such as mayor or constable or alderman or magistrate or notary public or gatekeeper, and that those who held such offices should lose them, and that they could not be moneychangers or apothecaries or spice-merchants, nor could they hold any suspicious post whatsoever, nor could they wear silk or fine scarlet wool or colored clothing or gold or silver or pearls or mother-of-pearl or coral or any jewel, nor could they act as witnesses, nor could they rent such things. They were ordered on penalty of being considered backsliders, that is, those who fall again into the same error as before, that if they used any one of the above-mentioned [forbidden] articles, they would be condemned to be burned at the stake. And when all these ceremonies were over, they left the cathedral at two in the afternoon.

DOCUMENT EIGHT

ISABELLA AND FERDINAND

"Charter of Expulsion of the Jews"
(1492)

What justification did Isabella and Ferdinand give for issuing the charter? What were the terms and conditions of the Jews' expulsion?

31 March 1492. Granada

. . . Salutations and grace.

[2] You know well, or ought to know, that whereas we have been informed that in these our kingdoms there were some wicked Christians who Judaized and apostatized from our holy Catholic faith, the great cause of which was interaction between the Jews and these Christians, in the cortes which we held in the city of Toledo in the past year of one thousand, four hundred and eighty, we ordered the separation of the said Jews in all the cities, towns, and villages of our kingdoms and lordships and [commanded] that they be given Jewish quarters and separated places where they should live, hoping that by their separation the situation would remedy itself. Furthermore, we procured and gave orders that inquisition should be made in our aforementioned kingdoms and lordships, which as you know has for twelve years been made and is being made, and by it many guilty persons have been discovered, as is very well known, and accordingly we are informed by the inquisitors and by other devout persons, ecclesiastical and secular, that great injury has resulted and still results, since the Christians have engaged in and continue to engage in social interaction and communication they have had and continue to have with Jews, who, it seems, seek always and by whatever means and ways they can to

Chapter 12
Catholic
Monarchs in the
Old and New
Worlds:
Ferdinand of
Aragón (1452–
1516) and
Isabella of
Castile
(1451–1504)

subvert and to steal faithful Christians from our holy Catholic faith and to separate them from it, and to draw them to themselves and subvert them to their own wicked belief and conviction, instructing them in the ceremonies and observances of their law, holding meetings at which they read and teach that which people must hold and believe according to their law, achieving that the Christians and their children be circumcised, and giving them books from which they may read their prayers and declaring to them the fasts that they must keep, and joining with them to read and teach them the history of their law, indicating to them the festivals before they occur, advising them of what in them they are to hold and observe, carrying to them and giving to them from their houses unleavened bread and meats ritually slaughtered, instructing them about the things from which they must refrain, as much in eating as in other things in order to observe their law, and persuading them as much as they can to hold and observe the law of Moses, convincing them that there is no other law or truth except for that one. This proved by many statements and confessions, both from these same Jews and from those who have been perverted and enticed by them, which has redounded to the great injury, detriment, and opprobrium of our holy Catholic faith.

[3] Notwithstanding that we were informed of the great part of this before now and we knew that the true remedy for all these injuries and inconveniences was to prohibit all interaction between the said Jews and Christians and banish them from all our kingdoms, we desired to content ourselves by commanding them to leave all cities, towns, and villages of Andalusia where it appears that they have done the greatest injury, believing that that would be sufficient so that those of other cities, towns, and villages of our kingdoms and lordships would cease to do and commit the aforesaid acts. And since we are informed that neither that step nor the passing of sentence [of condemnation] against the said Jews who have been most guilty of the said crimes and delicts against our holy Catholic faith have been sufficient as a complete remedy to obviate and correct so great an opprobrium and offense to the faith and the Christian religion, because every day it is found and appears that the said Jews increase in continuing their evil and wicked purpose wherever they live and congregate, and so that there will not be any place where they further offend our holy faith, and corrupt those whom God has until now most desired to preserve, as well as those who had fallen but amended and returned to Holy Mother Church, the which according to the weakness of our humanity and by diabolical astuteness and suggestion that continually wages war against us may easily occur unless the principal cause of it be removed, which is to banish the said Jews from our kingdoms. Because whenever any grave and detestable crime is committed by members of any organization or corporation, it is reasonable that such an organization or corporation should be dissolved and annihilated and that the lesser members as well as the greater and everyone for the others be punished, and that those who perturb the good and honest life of cities and towns and by contagion can injure others should be expelled from those places and even if for

lighter causes that may be injurious to the Republic, how much more for those greater and most dangerous and most contagious crimes such as this.

[4] Therefore, we, with the counsel and advice of prelates, great noblemen of our kingdoms, and other persons of learning and wisdom of our council, having taken deliberation about this matter, resolve to order the said Jews and Jewesses of our kingdoms to depart and never to return or come back to them or to any of them. And concerning this we command this our charter to be given, by which we order all Jews and Jewesses of whatever age they may be, who live, reside, and exist in our said kingdoms and lordships, as much those who are natives as those who are not, who by whatever manner or whatever cause have come to live and reside therein, that by the end of the month of July next of the present year, they depart from all of these our said realms and lordships, along with their sons and daughters, manservants and maidservants, Jewish familiars, those who are great as well as the lesser folk, of whatever age they may be, and they shall not dare to return to those places, nor to reside in them, nor to live in any part of them, neither temporarily on the way to somewhere else nor in any other manner, under pain that if they do not perform and comply with this command and should be found in our said kingdom and lordships and should in any manner live in them, they incur the penalty of death and the confiscation of all their possessions by our Chamber of Finance, incurring these penalties by the act itself, without further trial, sentence, or declaration. And we command and forbid that any person or persons of the said kingdoms, of whatever estate, condition, or dignity that they may be, shall dare to receive, protect, defend, nor hold publicly or secretly any Jew or Jewess beyond the date of the end of July and from henceforth forever, in their lands, houses, or in other parts of any of our said kingdoms and lordships, under pain of losing all their possessions, vassals, fortified places, and other inheritances, and beyond this of losing whatever financial grants they hold from us by our Chamber of Finance. . . .

. . . [W]e command that this our charter be posted in the customary plazas and places of the said city and of the principal cities, towns, and villages of its bishopric as an announcement and as a public document. And no one shall do any damage to it in any manner under penalty of being at our mercy and the deprivation of their offices and the confiscation of their possessions, which will happen to each one who might do this. . . .

[7] Given in our city of Granada, the XXXI day of the month of March, the year of the birth of our lord Jesus Christ one thousand four hundred and ninety-two years. I, the king, I the queen, I, Juan de Coloma, secretary of the king and queen our lords, have caused this to be written at their command. Registered by Cabrera, Almacan chancellor.

*Chapter 12
Catholic
Monarchs in the
Old and New
Worlds:
Ferdinand of
Aragón (1452–
1516) and
Isabella of
Castile
(1451–1504)*

DOCUMENT NINE

CHRISTOPHER COLUMBUS

Prologue to Journal of His First Voyage
(1492)

Columbus appealed to the Catholic monarchs' sense of destiny and religious zealotry in the hope of persuading them to sponsor his trip across the Atlantic. What were his motivations for undertaking the voyage? What inspired him to sail?

IN THE NAME OF OUR LORD JESUS CHRIST

Most Christian and most exalted and most excellent and most powerful Princes, King and Queen of the Spains and of the islands of the sea, Our Sovereigns: Forasmuch as in this present year of 1492, after Your Highnesses had brought to an end the war with the Moors who reigned in Europe and had concluded the war in the great city of Granada where this same year on the second day of January I saw Your Highnesses' royal banners placed by force of arms on the towers of the Alhambra, which is the fortress of the said city, and I saw the Moorish king come out to the city gates and kiss Your Highnesses' royal hands and those of My Lord the Prince; and then in the same month from information which I had given Your Highnesses about the lands of India and a prince called the Great Khan, which means in our language King of Kings, and how he and his ancestors had many times sent to Rome for learned men to instruct him in our holy faith, and how the Holy Father had never provided them, and how so many people were being lost, falling into idolatry and embracing doctrines of perdition; and Your Highnesses, as Catholic Christians and princes devoted to the holy Christian faith and the furtherance of its cause, and enemies of the sect of Mohammed and of all idolatry and heresy, resolved to send me, Christopher Columbus, to the said regions of India to see the said princes and the peoples and lands and determine the nature of them and of all other things, and the measures to be taken to convert them to our holy faith; and you ordered that I should not go by land to the East, which is the customary route, but by way of the West, a route which to this day we cannot be certain has been taken by anyone else: So then, after having expelled all the Jews from all your kingdoms and domains, in the same month of January, Your Highnesses commanded me to take sufficient ships and sail to the said regions of India. And in consideration you granted me great favours and honoured me thenceforth with the title 'Don' and the rank of Admiral of the Ocean Sea and Viceroy and Governor in perpetuity of all the islands and mainland that I should discover and take possession of and which should hereafter be discovered and occupied in the Ocean Sea, and that my eldest son should succeed in turn, and so on from generation to generation for ever. And I left the city of Granada on the twelfth day of May of the same year 1492, a Saturday, and came to the town of Palos, which is a seaport, where I prepared three ships suitable for such an undertaking, and I set out from the said port well stocked with supplies and with many seamen on the third day of August of the same year, a Friday, half an hour before sunrise, and I took the route to the Canary Islands, Your Highnesses' possession in the said Ocean Sea, thence to set my course and navigate until I should reach the Indies, and deliver Your Highnesses' embassy to those princes and comply with what you had ordered. And for this purpose I decided to write down the whole of this voyage in detail, day by day, everything that I should do and see and undergo, as will be seen in due course. Furthermore, My Lords, besides writing down each night whatever the day should bring, and each day the course taken during the night, I propose to make a new navigational chart, on which I shall note all the sea and land in the Ocean Sea in their proper places with their bearings and also keep a book in which, in the same way, I shall record them by latitude from the equator and by longitude to the west; above all, I must give no thought to sleep, and must work diligently at my navigation, because such is my duty; all of which will require great effort.

CHAPTER 13

The Protestant Reformation in Germany: Martin Luther (1483–1546) and Katharina von Bora (1499–1552)

■ **SETTING THE STAGE**

The Protestant Reformation of the sixteenth century profoundly affected the political, social, and religious institutions of Europe. At the outset, the reform movements were disorderly and their goals were unclear. Within these movements, the potential for radical change burned brightly. Religious reformers in early sixteenth-century Europe hoped to cure spiritual ailments and rectify abuses in the Christian church centered in Rome. These at-

tempts quickly became direct challenges, not only to the established authorities of the Christian church, but to its political allies and to European social order, intellectual life, and cultural values. Calls for reform became platforms for revolution as the movements, collectively known as the Protestant Reformation, swept through Europe.

But these movements did not appear overnight. They emerged from a world that, for several centuries, had questioned the power of the church and the actions of its leaders. The fourteenth and fifteenth centuries witnessed multiple efforts from within the church to restore spiritual vitality and confidence, as well as secular expressions of rational truth that could guide individuals in their search for meaning in this world and the next. Other factors added to the instability created by the intellectual tumult and the religious contests of the later Middle Ages. Secular rulers had been extending their authority for some time, often at the expense of papal power, and lesser princes and urban leaders pushed for more autonomy at the local level. Economic fluctuations, cycles of poor harvests, and recurring bouts of the plague continued to make life difficult and even precarious for most Europeans. New dimensions were added to European life as the explorations and conquests of the late fifteenth and early sixteenth centuries helped turn perceptions of the world upside down and produced tales of the mysterious and strange populations to the east and west. A technological revolution in the form of the printing press, invented in the fifteenth century, provided the means whereby foreign discoveries, local controversies, or individual rebellions could be communicated quickly to a wide literate audience. At the opening of the new century, many Europeans faced uncertainty and wondered where in this complex world they could find the comfort and security of God. The Protestant Reformation grew out of these conditions.

The Reformation was never a homogeneous movement. Its unfolding was not a simple narrative and its results were often mixed and contradictory. In the first decades of protest, change was often rapid and disorderly because different leaders and groups expressed competing viewpoints and goals, and vied for supporters and legitimacy. Regional political conditions influenced the course of reform, and personal responses and motives varied, depending on the economic, social, and cultural positioning of the individual. By looking at how reform or rebellion appealed to different men and women and at the forms and meaning of individual and group protest and their impact on the men and women involved, we can begin to grasp the complex course and outcomes of the Protestant Reformation.

Martin Luther was a key figure in the movement in Germany. By considering his experiences and those of his wife, Katharina von Bora, the inconsistencies, controversies, and personal dimensions of this religious revolution become more evident. These two people played highly visible roles in the processes of change, but they also represent populations most directly affected by the challenges to the established church. As the Roman Catholic Church began to split in Germany, and as political leaders took sides in the controversies, most of the population was also forced to choose, to "confess" their religious loyalty or identity. For monks or priests like Martin Luther, and for nuns like von Bora, such spiritual choices were obviously public, while the decision to marry was an overt challenge to the church. Others in their religious orbit faced a similar situation because most

Chapter 13
The Protestant
Reformation in
Germany:
Martin Luther
(1483–1546)
and Katharina
von Bora (1499–
1552)

of the early leaders of the movement were married and they and their partners often had been members of religious communities. In this sense, the Luthers are quite typical and, in fact, they are often described as the ideal pastor and his wife. Nevertheless, they were unusual for other reasons. Thus, by looking at their lives in contrast to others around them, both famous and lesser-known men and women, the diversity and contradictions of the Reformation become more apparent.

▣ THE ACTORS:

MARTIN LUTHER AND KATHARINA VON BORA

Martin Luther was born in Saxony in 1483. His father advanced from copper miner to owner of mines and copper-smelting furnaces, probably with help from his mother's family, which was an older, established family in the region. His mother was also the more educated of his parents and may have helped Martin to learn to read, but both parents supported Martin's education, hoping that he would study law, enter the legal profession, and find a career in public service. Luther's upbringing emphasized personal responsibility and punishment for misbehavior, factors he claimed shaped his later outlook.[1]

In 1501, he entered the University of Erfurt, where he earned a master's degree and planned to study law. By then, however, Luther was feeling some discontent with that career choice, and instead hoped for something higher. In the world in which he lived, the ideal would be dedication to God as a monk or priest. He was a sensitive, often emotional young man, and he was religiously inclined. Though uncertain about his own life, he was capable of decision and action derived from intellectual analysis and judgment. The result was that, instead of the legal profession, he chose in 1502 to enter the Augustinian monastery in Erfurt, a religious community dedicated to internal reform and reaffirmation of older values and rules. He eventually was ordained a priest and then earned a doctorate in theology. These accomplishments did not necessarily increase his personal confidence or satisfy his yearnings for fulfillment.

As a young man, Luther lived in a world where the church's spiritual authority was increasingly under attack, not only because of the endemic corruption and rampant materialism of its clergy and pope, but also because men and women of the faith yearned for greater consolation and comfort from their religion and its practices. Luther frequently expressed his feelings of insecurity, even fear, in the face of a harsh and punishing God. He was often plagued by feelings of unworthiness and uncertainty about his spiritual health. Demands for church reform in both material and spiritual terms had been circulating for some time. The highly ritualistic and formulaic practices of the church, led by cor-

1. Heiko Oberman, *Luther: Man Between God and the Devil* (New Haven, Conn.: Yale University Press, 1982), p. 93.

rupt, indifferent, and sometimes illiterate parish priests and bishops, had encouraged individuals like John Wycliffe (1330–1384) of England and Jan Hus (1372–1415) of Bohemia (who was influenced by Wycliffe's ideas) or groups like the Cathars in thirteenth-century France to challenge the Catholic clergy's monopoly on religious practices and spiritual guidance. Wycliffe sought solace in reading the Bible and having the Holy Spirit lead him through the Scriptures' truth. The Cathars (also known as Albigensians), centered in Albi, France, withdrew into asceticism and rejected the flesh, marriage, and procreation.

Whether individuals sought comfort in biblical truth or ascetic practices, each believed that a new path had to be followed to reunite with God in heaven after death—to achieve salvation. Of course, the Catholic Church could not allow for heresy, and the Cathars, Wycliffe, and Hus suffered the consequences: the church launched a crusade against the Cathars, Wycliffe was threatened into silence, and Hus was burned at the stake. Despite such harsh and cruel punishment for seeking religious truth and salvation, men and women of the fifteenth century continued to look for God outside the ordained Catholic practices of the day. Luther was not the first to seek God's salvation elsewhere, nor would he be the last. Armed with a crisis of faith and an intimate knowledge of theology, Luther entered onto the historical stage at a time when the church and its spiritual and temporal kingdoms were in crisis.

In 1512, Luther accepted the position of professor of the Scriptures at the new University of Wittenberg in Saxony. At least on the surface, there was nothing startling about Martin Luther's life up to this point. Others in this era of uncertainty and doubt had fled to monasteries for refuge, and Luther was a good monk with no record of having violated his vows in any way. As he noted, "I was a good monk, and I kept the rule of my order so strictly that I may say that if ever a monk got to heaven by his monkery it was I."[2] The joking tone of this remark reflects a much darker concern. Luther's problem was that he yearned for salvation and was never confident that he had earned it. The church had set forth numerous ways to acquire merit and salvation, but no amount of confession, contrition, penance, observance of the sacraments, or acts of charity gave Luther the spiritual comfort and security he sought. But Luther was an academic after all, trained in the study of the Scriptures, and there he would find the answers to his personal quest and the spiritual solutions and comfort that appealed to many of his equally troubled and uncertain contemporaries.

Between the years 1512 and 1517, as he prepared sermons and lectures and carried on correspondence with his colleagues, Luther gradually moved

2. Quoted in Roland Bainton, *Here I Stand: A Life of Martin Luther* (New York: New American Library, 1950), p. 34. Additional biographical material on Luther can be found in Richard Marius, *Martin Luther: The Christian Between God and Death* (Cambridge, Mass.: Belknap/Harvard, 1999). His early life is discussed in Chapters 2 and 3.

Chapter 13
The Protestant
Reformation in
Germany:
Martin Luther
(1483–1546)
and Katharina
von Bora (1499–
1552)

toward what would at first be his personal epiphany. He gradually came to the conclusion that individual righteousness and salvation were not the results of merit, penance, good works, or any other acts. Individual worthiness was not something God judged on merit. Instead righteousness came simply with faith, a gift God gave to all. Luther now felt at peace—personal failures or sins did not mean destruction. These ideas would be the core of his later religious revolution—the doctrine of justification by faith.

In addition to his fears and depressions, righteous anger was also part of Luther's personality, and in 1517, secure in his beliefs, "his anger became more combative."[3] Luther became a public figure in the latter months of 1517 largely because of his criticism of the church's sale of indulgences and his public request for debate and clarification of the matter. Since the time of the Crusades, the church had given to specific individuals remission of the usual penalties for sin, or an indulgence, by drawing on a "treasury of merits" stored up by Christ and the saints. Thus, if one died without being able to confess or do the appropriate penance, one could still be reconciled with God and be saved. By the sixteenth century, however, the practice was more widespread; indulgences were now given for gifts to the church to meet special financial needs, thereby benefitting various church leaders and their projects. Many people believed that acquiring an indulgence could guarantee entry into heaven.

When a sales campaign began in the area around Wittenberg in 1517, Luther felt compelled to protest. In his view, indulgences could not be equal to legitimate, doctrinal prescriptions for salvation such as the sacraments or good works, and he also questioned on what authority the church was able to grant them. For others, and perhaps for Luther, an additional issue was the selling of salvation by a wealthy and often corrupt church for fundraising purposes. In October 1517, Luther wrote a position paper on these questions, asking for debate and clarification by church authorities. The *Ninety-five Theses* were published and widely distributed, and by December Martin Luther was famous—as a hero or as a potential heretic, depending on one's position.

Luther's questioning of the sale of indulgences was really only a small piece of a spiritual and intellectual revolution that involved much more fundamental challenges to existing church doctrines and institutions. His doubts that the church and its officials could grant or guarantee salvation at all bordered on heresy and directly attacked papal and clerical authority; thus, church leaders took Luther's challenges quite seriously. When the church responded to Luther, he clarified and solidified his ideas and conclusions in public debates, sermons, and written essays. Moving away from initial calls for reforms within the Church, Luther began to develop beliefs that were truly radical after 1517. By the close of 1520, he "looked very much like a revolutionary,"[4] hav-

3. John Todd, *Luther: A Life* (New York: Crossroads Publishers, 1982), pp. 73–80.

4. Ibid, p. 244.

ing articulated the basic tenets of his beliefs in numerous important essays. In these essays, he insisted that the pope and priests were simply office-holders with no special jurisdiction over secular authorities. He concluded that the only source for church or spiritual authority was Scripture, that all people were potentially masters of Scripture, and that the church was a "priesthood of believers." In the last essay, *On the Freedom of a Christian*, he publicly proclaimed the solution to all his doubts about the avenue to salvation by asserting that individuals are saved by faith and God's grace alone (Document One). His idea of raising Scripture to a level higher than tradition and the papacy precipitated the political, social, and economic events to follow.

In January 1521, Pope Leo X excommunicated Luther and urged the Holy Roman Emperor, Charles V, to ban him outright. Instead, Charles summoned Luther to appear at the Diet of Worms in April, where Luther refused to recant. Charles consequently banned him from the empire. Henceforth, Luther was an outlaw in both the spiritual and political worlds. But by that point, Luther had protectors in high places—in particular, Frederick the Wise, the elector of Saxony, who took him to a castle in Wartburg, where Luther remained for a solitary but very productive year. By then, Luther had attracted a critical group of followers. Among them were several individuals who could spread Luther's words by preaching and writing, who widened the scope of spiritual and religious reform, and who worked with Luther to build commu-

nities of "new" men and women committed to their cause. In the process, Luther and his supporters realized that, in addition to the spiritual revolution they promoted, they would have to create visible religious, political, and social institutions to replace the institutions disrupted by their attacks.

The spiritual and material changes they advocated did not occur peacefully. First, the Roman Catholic Church and various political leaders, including the powerful Habsburg ruler and Holy Roman Emperor, Charles V, did everything they could to prevent the strengthening and spread of the protestors' movement. Other rulers supported the reformers, giving them physical protection and economic help, thus imparting important political dimensions to the religious struggle. All German leaders, from the burghers of city councils to the seven electors of the Holy Roman Empire, had to decide their stance. For Luther and other leaders, this situation was difficult because they were often forced to depend on political authorities for income and physical defense. Even more threatening was the fact that in many areas controlled by the Roman Catholic Church, they were "wanted" by the law and would suffer harsh treatment and even death if they fell into enemy hands.

Conflict was not confined to the Protestants versus the Catholics; it occurred with equal violence among the reformers themselves. Because Protestantism emphasized the importance of individual belief and understanding of the Scripture, it automatically encouraged individual interpretation.

Chapter 13
The Protestant
Reformation in
Germany:
Martin Luther
(1483–1546)
and Katharina
von Bora (1499–
1552)

Almost as soon as Luther proclaimed his principles, others began to disagree with him. Having struggled to find the truth, Luther was not about to compromise, and his considerable intellect, acerbic wit, and anger were aimed at those who disagreed with him. Nevertheless, a wide range of reform groups quickly appeared, and intellectual debates often turned into outright warfare as different religious communities fought over spheres of spiritual and political influence. What all this controversy meant, of course, was that Europe was divided by religion, and few people who lived in the first decades of the Reformation remained untouched by the turmoil. Exactly how the Reformation affected you and what your response might be depended on such factors as where you lived, your social position, whether you were married or not, and whether you were a man or a woman.

Martin Luther's ideas were spread in print and by word of mouth. The printing press made the dissemination of Luther's ideas much easier, and he and his followers used this new technology to their advantage. Luther's views were published in pamphlets using the vernacular, and they were often illustrated with inflammatory cartoons portraying the clergy as gluttonous and greedy so that even the illiterate could be reached. Between 1522 and 1545, portions of his works were printed 2,596 times, with between two hundred and one thousand copies for each printing.[5] Most of these printed documents

were essays or sermons covering specific questions or issues, but letters he wrote and conversations he had with friends, colleagues, and students also appeared on the printed page. (Depending on the edition, his completed published works appear in anywhere between fifty-five and sixty-five volumes.) Few of Luther's voluminous writings were actually printed as pamphlets. Most were written in Latin and were thus available only to those with the appropriate education, with the resources to acquire the printed pages, or with access to libraries. The bulk of the population received simplified oral versions of Luther's word when he took the stand or climbed into the pulpit, or when his fellow teachers and preachers did the same. In many cases, the report actually could be secondhand because someone in the audience often carried the words and their impressions home to friends, neighbors, or coworkers.

In 1519, word of Luther's teachings entered the Cistercian cloister of Marienthron at Nimbschen, where twenty-five-year-old Katharina von Bora was a nun.[6] The von Bora family was of noble descent, although Katharina's immediate family was not wealthy. Her mother died in 1504 and Katie (as Luther would call her) was sent to be

Marshall (eds.), *The Process of Change in Early Modern Europe* (Athens, Ohio: Ohio University Press, 1988), pp. 156, 161.

6. An excellent account of her life is in Jeanette C. Smith, "Katharina von Bora Through Five Centuries: A Historiography," *The Sixteenth-Century Journal: The Journal of Early Modern Studies* 30:3 (Fall 1999), pp. 745–774. See also Roland Bainton, *Women of the Reformation in Germany and Italy* (Boston, Mass.: Beacon Press, 1971), pp. 23–44.

5. Mark Edwards, "Statistics on Sixteenth-Century Printing," in Phillip Bebb and Sherrin

educated at a nearby convent school; by the time she was ten, she had entered the convent at Marienthron, a pattern not unusual for noble families with limited resources. By the later Middle Ages, many young men and women joined monastic communities because of familial decisions and needs. A spiritual quest might have mixed with more practical interests, but in Katharina's case, we know little of what her own wishes and spiritual inclinations might have been as a young woman. For women of some social standing, the convent was one of the few alternatives to marriage.

As a result of her convent experience, von Bora was well educated, and later in life she could actually participate in scholarly discussions in Latin. Apparently, by 1519, several of the nuns at Marienthron were increasingly disenchanted with cloistered life and had written home, asking to rejoin their families. That kind of request, of course, could pose problems because the options for women, particularly slightly older ex-nuns, were limited. Luther somehow learned of their situation and helped to arrange an escape from the monastery (Document Two). The convent was in territory controlled by Duke George of Saxony, who was an opponent of the reform movement; hence, secrecy was important. On the evening of April 4, 1523, von Bora, along with eleven other nuns, was transported from the convent with the help of a merchant from a nearby town—legend later said that they escaped in empty smoked-herring barrels. The women were taken to Torgau, in the territory of Luther's friend and supporter,

Frederick of Saxony, and then nine of them traveled to Wittenberg, where Luther welcomed them. In fact, he openly took responsibility for their escape, as he explained in a letter to a friend.

In one sense, von Bora was like many original supporters of Luther. As an educated member of a religious order, she could certainly read church doctrine and writings of the reformers. She might also have been dissatisfied with cloistered life. Records of other members of religious communities, male and female, attest to increasing discontent with authoritarian clerical management, and even corruption, and express desires for the same spiritual renewal and simplicity that Luther had sought. It is also important to acknowledge that, by 1523, Luther and several other Protestant reformers had denounced clerical celibacy and encouraged monks and nuns to flee their monasteries. The marital relationship became "the showcase of Christian living," and Luther and others began to develop their own perspectives on marriage and relations between the sexes.[7] For Luther, virginity was no longer the ideal state—in fact, he argued that marriage was God's mandate, while celibacy, which required individuals to resist their natural human instincts, was hard to maintain and therefore was indeed the work of Satan (Document Three).

7. Lyndal Roper, *Oedipus and the Devil: Witchcraft, Sexuality and Religion in Early Modern Europe* (New York: Routledge, 1994), p. 80.

[383]

Chapter 13
The Protestant
Reformation in
Germany:
Martin Luther
(1483–1546)
and Katharina
von Bora (1499–
1552)

■ ACT I:

CONVERSION AND CHRISTIAN
MARRIAGE

Von Bora no doubt found much that was appealing in Luther's ideas and was equally impressed by his person, much like several of her contemporaries. The priest Matthew Zell (1478?–1548) arrived in the city of Strasbourg in 1520 and was assigned to the post of cathedral priest in that city. He read Luther's tracts, and his sermons increasingly reflected Luther's ideas. For this action, the church charged him with a long list of heresies. In his public response, Zell argued: "I am accused of having read Luther. To be sure I have. . . . If Luther is guilty of some errors that does not make him a heretic. Which of the church fathers was ever free from all error? . . . [Luther] is being read all over Germany and am I alone to be forbidden to read him?"[8] In 1523, Zell took the ultimate step in his confession of religious commitment and identity by marrying Katherine Schutz, the daughter of a well-known Strasbourg carpenter. Though not a nun, she too claimed that, until she heard Martin Luther's words, her spiritual life was incomplete and she had found no peace. Individuals like von Bora and the Zells were drawn to Luther's ideas and would follow their consciences, whatever the cost. Von Bora and Matthew Zell, along with other priests and nuns, were willing to be excommunicated and condemned as heretics by leaving their

monasteries and by renouncing clerical celibacy.

The results of these decisions, however, were not always the same for men and women. When monks and priests renounced their vows and left their orders, they continued to occupy positions of authority in religious life. They were often employed as preachers in the same churches where they had previously officiated. Luther himself continued as a professor and, while certainly never wealthy, earned a salary in that position and also received a small stipend from the elector of Saxony. Philip Melancthon (1497–1560), who was Luther's right-hand man in Wittenberg, had been reluctant at first to marry because he was wed to his scholarship. Eventually he married Katherine Krapp, the daughter of a city magistrate, and later explained: "I am not cool toward her and she has all the qualities that I could wish in a wife. Some of my friends think that this will mean for me the end of scholarship. Rather than give that up I would renounce the light of life."[9] He obviously was able to combine his life's work with his passion for Katherine because he was Luther's successor and his marriage lasted thirty-seven years.

Protestant reformers like Luther, Melancthon, and Zell sought to redefine their own religious and societal roles. While willing to challenge tradition and authority for themselves, they did not necessarily extend the same reasoning to women and their roles in society. No matter how revolutionary their ideas about religion

8. Bainton, *Women of the Reformation*, p. 59.

9. Ibid., p. 159.

might be, the male leaders were part of a society that defined women by marital and family status. What was not readily apparent at the beginning of the Reformation was the role that women, especially pious and religious women, would play in this movement. Catholicism had allocated to women a cloistered space, the convent, to express their religious convictions. For religious women like Katharina von Bora, the move out of the convent seemed to offer other new opportunities. Once outside the walls of the cloister, however, what would happen to her?

Von Bora was not close to her family (her father had remarried after her mother's death), so returning home was not possible once she left the convent. In Wittenberg, she initially worked as a domestic servant, a standard option for women at the time. But the most realistic solution for her situation was marriage. Having taken responsibility for her and the other nuns who fled the convent, Luther attempted to arrange a marriage for von Bora. In one case, the proposed suitor was another pastor, but von Bora thought him too miserly and begged Luther not to marry her off to him. At that point, she suggested that, if Luther asked for her hand, she would not refuse. Apparently, he had been thinking about marriage himself. He had been loaned and then given the former Augustinian Friary as living quarters, but he found the place lonely, the food unappealing, and the housekeeping terrible. He resisted marriage for a time because of the heavy demands made on him as the leader of the Reformation movement

and because he recognized the constant danger in which he lived. Eventually, in May 1525, he announced his intentions: "If I can manage it before I die, I will still marry my Katie to spite the devil"[10] and they were married in June. His parents attended the public wedding feast, and Luther remarked that he wanted to fulfill his father's hope for children to carry on the family line, but also said, "I neither love nor lust for my wife, but I esteem her."[11] Luther's opponents launched virulent attacks on him and von Bora after their marriage, accusing them of marrying because their lust had resulted in pregnancy, and charging her with being a "fallen woman [who] left the cloister in lay clothes and [went] to Wittenberg like a chorus girl. You are said to have lived with Luther in sin. Then you married him, forsaking Christ your bridegroom."[12] Personal behaviors and morality were often the symbols of religious truths and affiliations, and thus were frequently the focal point of accusations and conflict.

Luther may have married von Bora to live up to his theological convictions, because his friends encouraged him to do so, or because it was practical and convenient. She married him perhaps for these same reasons, but also out of necessity. Whatever the reasons, the marriage turned out well and over the years their mutual respect, affection, and companionship strengthened and deepened. Luther expressed his feelings for von Bora in 1531 when he wrote: "I wouldn't give

10. J. Smith, "Katharina von Bora," p. 749.

11. Marius, *Martin Luther*, p. 438.

12. Bainton, *Women of the Reformation*, p. 27.

Chapter 13
The Protestant
Reformation in
Germany:
Martin Luther
(1483–1546)
and Katharina
von Bora (1499–
1552)

up my Katie for France or for Venice."[13] She in turn was devoted to him, and when he died in February 1546, she was inconsolable. No wonder that they become the models for pastoral and, even more generally, Protestant marriage.

Martin Luther and other Protestant writers saw men and women as interdependent and marriage as an institution based on reciprocity and mutual responsibility. At the same time, they did not see husbands and wives as equals or their status and functions in marriage as similar. Wedding sermons from the time are revealing because they prescribed appropriate behavior for the average bride and groom.[14] Husbands should love and respect their wives, treat them fairly, and not abuse them unreasonably. But they must also take charge in a marriage, using reason if possible because women were still seen as emotional creatures, weaker than men, with a greater inclination to sinfulness. Women were to be obedient and submissive to their husbands, to raise Christian children, and to manage household affairs efficiently. Luther addressed the importance of such an arrangement at one of his famous dinnertable conversations in late 1531 or early 1532. Noting how busy he was with preaching, lecturing, hearing cases, and writing letters and essays, he concluded: "It is a good thing that God came to my aid and gave me a

wife."[15] The purpose of the recommended practices was the creation of orderly Christian households that would be the basis for a godly, reformed community.

The Luthers' marriage seems to have lived up to many of these standards. Luther often called Katie "my rib," and described her as "compliant in every way . . . obedient and obliging to me."[16] Von Bora bore six children, two of whom died in infancy, and Luther delighted in their offspring. He rejoiced because von Bora stayed at home and managed household affairs effectively, and he made it clear that he did not expect her (or other women) to engage in intellectual activities. As he said, "There is no dress that suits a woman as badly as trying to become wise."[17] But von Bora was not a household slave, and in many ways Luther depended on her. He was a generous man, but without von Bora's economic activity and financial skills, his generosity would have been limited (Document Four).

After their marriage it was up to von Bora to manage the Friary household. The place had about forty rooms on the first floor, with small cells on the second. Through most of their marriage, all the rooms were occupied by visitors, religious refugees, other family members, servants, or students whom von Bora insisted had to pay

---

13. J. Smith, "Katharina von Bora," p. 750.

14. Susan Karant-Nunn, "Fragrant Wedding Roses: Lutheran Wedding Sermons in Early Modern Germany," *German History* 17:1 (1991), pp. 25–40.

15. Theodore G. Tappert (ed. and trans.), *Luther's Works*, Vol. 54, *Table Talk*, No. 154 (Philadelphia, Pa.: Fortress Press, 1967), p. 23.

16. J. Smith, "Katharina von Bora," p. 762.

17. Merry Wiesner, "Luther and Women: The death of two Marys," in Jim Obelkevich, Lyndal Roper, and Raphael Samuel (eds.), *Disciplines of Faith* (London: Routledge, 1987), p. 300.

rent. There were gardens, pens, and stables attached to the house and von Bora worked hard to make the household self-sufficient. Like other women of the time, she helped to herd, milk, and slaughter cattle; raise pigs and chickens; and make butter and cheese. She also developed a garden and an orchard and built a brewery, and from all these efforts she fed her family, friends, and boarders. If that were not enough to occupy her time, she acquired a farm at Zulsdorf, two days' travel from Wittenberg, and went there for several weeks at a time to oversee the operations. Luther jokingly called her "the rich lady at Zulsdorf" and in a 1541 letter told her "to sell what you can and come home."[18]

At the same time, Luther's frequent letters to von Bora reveal close companionship and even an exchange of ideas. She was, after all, an educated woman and certainly participated in mealtime conversations, as illustrated by the testimony of those present and which was recorded in *Table Talk*. During one dinner conversation in 1532, Luther was joking with von Bora that "the time will come when a man will take more than one wife . . . [because] a woman can bear a child only once a year while her husband can beget many." Luther apparently went on in jest for some time, and finally von Bora told him, "Before I put up with this, I'd rather go back to the convent and leave you and all your children."[19] After Luther's death in 1546, von Bora struggled to maintain the properties, support her family, and educate her sons (Document Five). Religious warfare destroyed her lands, and she and her family were forced to flee on several occasions. In the fall of 1550, she was injured in a wagon accident from which she did not recover. When she died on December 20, her daughter recorded her last words as "I will stick to Christ as a burr to a top coat."

It would be a mistake to either sentimentalize or marginalize von Bora. Equally erroneous would be a view of Luther as a domestic tyrant, a modern liberated man, or a romantic in his views of women and marriage. Recognizing that husbands and wives sometimes disagreed, he stated: "If I can put up with battles with the devil, sin and a bad conscience, then I can also put up with the irritations of Katie von Bora."[20] The theory and practice of Protestant marriage worked in the lives of these two people in ways that made them exemplary. The fact that the model was not absolutely perfect is borne out in the experiences of other reforming men and women.

18. Quoted in Bainton, *Women of the Reformation*, p. 39.

19. Tappert (ed. and trans.), *Table Talk*, No. 1461, April–May 1532, p. 153.
20. Quoted in Todd, p. 327.

Chapter 13
The Protestant
Reformation in
Germany:
Martin Luther
(1483–1546)
and Katharina
von Bora (1499–
1552)

■ ACT II:

CONTRASTING REFORMATION
EXPERIENCES

Other men and women faced more conflict and personal difficulties in their attempts to combine a spiritual quest and convictions with prescribed marriage roles and gender behaviors. The life and beliefs of Argula von Grumbach (1492–1554) are a good example of such conflicts.[21] Her family of origin and the man she married were members of the free nobility of Bavaria. Her family had supported religious reform and, by 1520, Argula von Grumbach's enthusiasm for spiritual renewal was kindled by a local reforming priest. She began to write to various leaders of the Reformation, including Luther. Argula was literate in German (not in Latin) and thus could read Scripture, confess, and write but, like many others, she had no access to a library. Since she was not a pastor's wife, she would not have had opportunities to engage in intellectual discussion and debates, especially since her husband remained loyal to the old church. She read Luther's translation of the Scriptures and agreed that they were the sole source of faith and grace. She also insisted that "every Christian, whether man or woman, has a duty to confess the faith, however painful or difficult it may be"[22] (Document Six). Based on that belief, she felt compelled to publicize her truth and

argued that in time of crisis the spirit of God overcomes women's "natural sense" that they shouldn't speak or write. Her social position gave her access to the printing press and she published over twenty-five thousand copies of eight pamphlets that she wrote. She spent much energy lobbying her noble peers to support the Protestant cause, even attending meetings of the Imperial Reichstag for that purpose. Other scholars have noted as remarkable this "lone woman, sailing off, leaving an angry husband, and having access to princes while she said her piece."[23]

She was remarkable but not successful. The prince of Bavaria had no intention of threatening his political alliance with the emperor and the papacy, and he banned Lutheran teachings in his realm. In 1523, von Grumbach came to the defense of a young local university student imprisoned for his evangelical beliefs. The result was a reprimand sent to her *husband* and *his* suspension from his administrative job for failing to exercise his paternal authority (Document Seven). Numerous public attacks were launched against Argula von Grumbach throughout 1523 and 1524, calling her a "female desperado," a "wretched and pathetic daughter of Eve," and a "shameless whore."[24] She composed a lyrical poem in her own defense, but that poem was the last of her public writings. She and her husband retired to their estates, where she handled most of their financial

21. Peter Matheson, *Argula von Grumbach: A Woman's Voice in the Reformation* (Edinburgh: T&T Clark, 1995), "Introduction," pp. 1–55.

22. Matheson, *Argula von Grumbach*, pp. 38–39.

23. Ibid., p. 20.

24. Ibid., p. 19.

and business matters. Von Grumbach continued to write to outside reformers, apprizing them of religious persecutions in the area, but none of the major Protestant leaders seemed interested in having religious discussions with her and none defended her right to confess and speak publicly. The authority she might have gained through her social position was trumped by gender constraints when it came to a spiritual vocation.

Matthew and Katharine Zell, who were important members of the reformed community of Strasbourg, offer another version of a spiritual partnership and Protestant marriage. Katharine bore two children, both of whom died in infancy, and thus was able to devote herself completely to spiritual and civic duties, often in partnership with Matthew. They traveled together to visit other Protestant leaders; published small pamphlets designed to educate the public, especially children; and often befriended those persecuted in other areas of the empire for their religious beliefs. Because of its unusual status as a free imperial city, Strasbourg frequently was a refuge for such people. Katharine often rose to the challenge, at one time putting up sixty or more people in the parsonage and feeding them for three weeks.[25]

By the late 1520s, theological differences among leaders in the Strasbourg community became increasingly common, as they did in other Protestant centers. Not only did the Protestants have to contend with opposition from the Catholic Church and its imperial backers, but also with friction and even sectarian splits among themselves. In the debates, the Zells were notable for their liberal approach to all believers. As Matthew stated, "Anyone who acknowledges Christ as the true Son of God and the sole Savior of mankind is welcome at my board."[26] Katharine encouraged such toleration and defended her own right to speak and act publicly. Using Scripture, she argued that in Christ there is no difference between Jew or Greek, slave or free person, man or woman; thus, women had the right to participate in the life of the church.

After Matthew died in 1548, Katharine was able to keep the parsonage for several years and continue her works of charity, visiting hospitals and prisons. She also remained in contact with other Christian communities through letters and travel. In 1555, the Peace of Augsburg allowed political authorities the right to determine the religion of their states or cities. The Strasbourg council committed to Lutheranism, which meant that non-Lutheran Protestants could be targeted. In 1557, Katharine came to their defense. For this action, she was called "a disturber of the peace of the church."[27] Like other pastors' wives, she occasionally took over her husband's official duties. For example, right before her death in 1562, she gave a funeral sermon for a woman of

---

25. For information on the Zells, see Bainton, *Women and the Reformation*, pp. 55–78.

26. Ibid., p. 65.

27. Ibid., p. 72.

Chapter 13
The Protestant
Reformation in
Germany:
Martin Luther
(1483–1546)
and Katharina
von Bora (1499–
1552)

a dissident sect in Strasbourg, but this and other examples of women preaching generally caused alarm. Until she died, Katharine continued to challenge what she considered rigid and narrow Protestant doctrines and the civil authorities and laws that enforced them. In the Zell version of Protestant marriage, Matthew indeed had a helper and companion. At the same time, Katharine created her own religious identity and followed an independent and often controversial public course as she pursued and confessed her beliefs.

■ FINALE

As noted before, in the decades between 1520 and 1555, reformed communities and their leaders grappled with both spiritual and practical issues. They entered the existing world of politics as they sought supporters and security, and in the emerging Protestant cities, towns, and states, they were forced to fill the vacuum left when Catholic authorities, courts, and laws no longer reigned. Just as leaders like Luther had begun with the search for individual faith and grace based on scriptural readings, many of the new believers also read Scripture in their own way. The results were debates and tensions among the believers. The attempts at clarification among the various Protestant leaders eventually led to both doctrinal separation and institutional independence among the Protestant groups. Within the emerging religious denominations, individual men and women were expected to follow common behaviors and attitudes in their communities, not only for their own protection and security, but as witness to their common beliefs and the rule of God here on earth.

Leaders in urban centers were usually responsible for articulating the ideals and practices of the new churches. For some time, city governments had been concerned with the "public good" as they confronted issues such as health, economic stability and growth, defense and business practices, wages, and prices. During the sixteenth century, these issues were still important, but additional ordinances were passed that specifically addressed personal behaviors and targeted the Christian household, which was seen as the cornerstone for order and morality.[28] Marriage courts were given jurisdiction in all matters pertaining to marriage and morality. The norms expressed were not necessarily "new" because pre-Reformation marriage guidance literature was often used as the basis for regulating behaviors. In fact, the Protestant norms of marital partnerships, commitment, and efficiency were already accepted values among urban artisans and burghers, many of whom would be influential in city governments.[29]

28. Merry Wiesner, "Paternalism in Practice: The Control of Servants and Prostitutes in Early Modern German Cities," in Bebb and Marshall (eds.), *The Process of Change*, p. 196.

29. Heide Wunder, *He Is the Sun, She Is the Moon* (Cambridge, Mass.: Harvard University Press, 1998), pp. 47–49.

Perhaps the Protestants preached these ideas with greater intensity because marriage was expected of all; it was now the ideal estate that would shoulder the burden for moral attitudes and behaviors. In practice, city councils expected heads of households, just like heads of businesses, to maintain order in their homes, offices, and workshops. Husbands and masters were responsible for and given authority over wives, children, servants, journeymen, and apprentices. As already noted, the "new" marriages of pastors and their wives, like that of Luther and von Bora, set the tone for the affection, companionship, *and* authority that could guarantee virtue and stability. Ideal men were married household heads with the power to govern and chastise, and women were expected to marry, to be obedient, and to find their honor and express their piety in raising good Christian children and doing charitable works. But the civil and religious authorities also recognized the difference between real and ideal; when faced with sinful and lazy patriarchs, and disobedient or wayward wives, they punished infractions, often with fines and imprisonment for men, with whipping and public humiliation for women.

At the outset, the rejection of celibacy and the ideal of virginity had allowed marital and sexual experimentation, but threats of instability and disorder served to limit people to single standards of behavior. The Catholic Church had accused early leaders like Luther and von Bora of lust and sexual license, and Luther and others turned around and accused dissident groups of lack of sex-

ual discipline and control. Thus, age-old debates about the relationship between body and soul were often expressed in conflicts about marriage and sexual behaviors.[30]

In their debates and practices, Protestant reformers like Luther generally upheld centuries-old doctrines of women's nature and the differences between men and women. At the same time, the protestors insisted on ideals of religious freedom that could be applied to and appeal to both men and women of all social groups. Like men, women could express themselves as individuals in terms of conscience and faith, and the household roles of wives like von Bora were given an added religious significance. Neither women nor men had to submit to a priest or pastor, but women did not have access to institutional offices and spiritual authority. Men could come together as intellectuals, as city council leaders, in economic groups, or as reforming preachers to respond to and shape their social, political, and religious environments. For Protestant women in the sixteenth century, there were few places in which they could organize and act together, and individual resistance and claims to authority were usually seen as dangerous to the community.

The doctrines and practices of the Reformation evolved as individual leaders and their communities faced external opponents and internal disagreements. Although Protestantism became more conservative as it divided into institutionalized churches,

30. Roper, *Oedipus and the Devil*, pp. 79, 97–98.

*Chapter 13
The Protestant
Reformation in
Germany:
Martin Luther
(1483–1546)
and Katharina
von Bora (1499–
1552)*

its original calls for personal freedoms and equality in spiritual life did not disappear and would sound again and again in the early modern world.

▪ QUESTIONS

1. What are indulgences? Why does Luther condemn their use?

2. Why did people commit to the Reformation movements? What ideas and goals were most appealing?

3. In what ways did Reformation ideas challenge prevailing attitudes and values? In what ways did the Reformation simply reinforce prevailing norms and traditions?

4. How did individual lives change as a result of this religious revolution?

5. In what ways was marriage changed as a result of the Protestant Reformation? How important were marital and family ties to the movement?

6. The importance of individual faith and the freedom of personal conscience were fundamental to Protestantism. How free were the members of the new religious groups? What kinds of controls might limit a person's options and abilities to act?

7. What were some of the contradictions between beliefs and ideas, and social and political needs, that showed up in the Reformation movements?

8. How did the Protestant Reformation affect the status of women?

▪ DOCUMENTS

DOCUMENT ONE

MARTIN LUTHER

The Freedom of a Christian
(1520)

The Freedom of a Christian, written in November 1520, accompanied a letter addressed to Pope Leo X. Luther hoped his essay, which summarized his views, would clarify his position, persuade the pope of his good intent, and make peace. This essay was Luther's last attempt at reconciliation with Rome. The essay also makes clear Luther's quite revolutionary views of salvation and the role of priests.

How does this document redefine the relationship between the individual and church authorities, and between the individual and God? What is "revolutionary" about these views?

"Yes, since faith alone suffices for salvation, I need nothing except faith exercising the power and dominion of its own liberty. Lo, this is the inestimable power and liberty of Christians. . . . anyone can clearly see how a Christian is free from all things and over all things so that he needs no works to make him righteous and save him, since faith alone abundantly confers all these things. . . . You will ask, "If all who are in the church are priests, how do these whom we now call priests differ from laymen?" I answer: . . . Holy Scripture . . . gives the name 'ministers,' 'servants,' 'stewards,' to those who are now called popes, bishops, and lords and who should according to the ministry of the Word serve others and teach them the faith of Christ and the freedom of believers. Although we are all equally priests, we cannot all publicly minister and teach."

"It is indeed true that in the sight of men a man is made good or evil by his works, but this being made good or evil only means that the man who is good or evil is pointed out and known as such, ... Whoever, therefore, does not wish to go astray with those blind men must look beyond works, and beyond laws and doctrines about works. . . . [H]e must look upon the person and ask how is he justified. For the person is justified and saved, not by works and laws, but by the Word of God, that is, by the promise of his grace, and by faith, . . ."

DOCUMENT TWO

MARTIN LUTHER

How God Rescued an Honorable Nun
(1524)

A young noblewoman from Upper Weimar who had been forced into a convent at a very young age eventually escaped from the convent. She then wrote her story to explain what had happened and to defend her actions. Luther heard about the document and published it himself, with some notations and a comment. Why do you think Luther was so interested in this woman's story? What does it say about the experiences of young women, like Katharina von Bora, who were forced into convent life?

THE BEGINNING

When I was six, my parents, who at the time viewed the religious vocation as good and blessed and were moved by the urgent pleading of my aunt, the

Chapter 13
The Protestant
Reformation in
Germany:
Martin Luther
(1483–1546)
and Katharina
von Bora (1499–
1552)

abbess, delivered me to an Eisleben nunnery, called Neu-Helfte.[1] Here I was trained until my eleventh year. At that age, during my immature youth, I was consecrated at the instigation of the abbess without being consulted. (Even if I had been consulted, it would not have made any difference because of my lack of understanding at the time.)

But when I was fourteen years old and I began to know and understand my mind and my capabilities, I discovered that all my talents and my nature clashed with the religious vocation. On pain of my soul's starvation I found it impossible to keep the vows, and I told this to one of my aunts in Upper Weimar. She immediately relayed this news to the abbess, my mother's sister—may God be merciful to her through whom my plan came to the ears of the abbess—who had her sister tell me that I should forget about my notion; that I would have to be and remain a nun, with or without good intention, and that she would deal with me in such a way that I would be glad to remain. I was told that I was consecrated now and had vowed, by the offering of the ring, eternal chastity to God; that I could not revoke this; and that no pope and no bishop could absolve me from that. I replied by asking them why they had not waited until I had arrived at an age of reasoning so that I could know what was and was not suited to me. Their only answer was that I had been old enough and that I had to remain a nun. Since I was not versed and instructed in the Holy Scriptures at the time, with which I might have defended myself against their pretexts, nor had any consolation, help, or counsel from friends (all of whom did not dare to act contrary to the wishes of the abbess, and, moreover, lived so far away) I was obliged, although very reluctantly and yet not without the particular sufferance of God, to submit to their power, rule, Babylonian captivity,[2] etc. . . .

Thus I assumed my religious vocation against my will. I let every pious Christian and lover of evangelical truth judge for himself how sorely my conscience was daily tried and oppressed because of this. Nevertheless, I placed my full trust and hope in God during this time of woe, misery, and trouble, [aware that] he has no pleasure in the death of the wicked, etc. [Ezek. 33:11]. I was confident that in his own time God would grant me, an orphan committed solely to his care, the comfort of deliverance, etc. . . .

Since I realized that I could derive no solace from the abbess, a persecutor of evangelical truth, but would invite nothing but punishment (which I dreaded like any other human being) I wrote to the very learned Dr. Martin Luther, opened my heart to him, and asked him for consolation, help, and counsel. Some of my associates who shared my secret with me informed my superior of

1. Florentina's aunt, Katharina von Watzdorf, was abbess of the Neu-Helfte convent from 1493 to 1534. She was a foe of the Reformation. The convent was originally located at Helfte and was later moved to a location just outside of Eisleben, where Luther was born and where he died. During the Middle Ages the convent was the home of several well-known mystics: Mechtildis of Magdeburt, Mechtildis of Hackeborn, and "the great Gertrude."

2. Florentina's use of this expression suggests some familiarity with Luther's treatise, *On the Babylonian Captivity of the Church.*

this in violation of Christian love. As a result I was placed by force into close confinement. . . .

After the expiration of those four weeks I had to announce these confessed transgressions publicly before the assembled chapter. Then the abbess put me under the ban. I had to sit in my locked cell. During the canonical hours, however, I had to kneel before the choir stall and prostrate myself to the floor until the collect, and as often as the assembly passed into the choir stall and when they came from it, they all had to step over me. That happened for three days.

Then the abbess put me under the so-called lesser ban. Now I had to go along into the choir stall; but as often as the congregation went into and from the choir stall I had to prostrate myself (as I described before) and let them step over me. During meals I had to sit on the floor before the abbess with a crown of straw on my head. I did penance in that way for three days.

Meanwhile I had to choose five persons who made themselves responsible for me. I had to vow and swear that in the future I would do nothing in word, deed, or writing to make my way out of the religious order. This I did with the kindest words I could muster, but my heart and my mind were not in it. Then she released me from my penance. However, the abbess delegated a person to watch me day and night, to walk with me, to stand with me, to sit and to sleep with me. The abbess also told me in the presence of the chapter that I should henceforth demean myself humbly and regard myself as a prisoner under the heels of my sister nuns and as a person whom no one could ever again trust or believe. I was to be chastised for seven Wednesdays and seven Fridays by ten persons at one time.

I then felt a strong urge to write my dear cousin Kaspar von Watzdorf, a well-known lover of evangelical truth, to inform him of my distress. This I did through one of the convent servants (I handed him a note with the instruction to transmit it to him). But through some treachery the abbess found out. How shamefully, abusively, scandalously, and derisively the abbess and others thereupon inveighed against me, I cannot say or write before pious people, etc.

I was flogged by her and four others until they had to stop from exhaustion. . . .

But God, with whom all things are possible, in his divine wisdom, beside which the wisdom of this world is foolishness, had it come to pass that one day after a meal, as I was going to my cell, the person who was to lock me in left the cell open. I easily escaped with God's manifest help about an hour before sunset when many of my sisters were in their cells and in the dormitory. . . .

But to make mention of everything, I add that when leaving the convent I took a cheap frock, a mantle, and several veils with which to cover my body; but they, in turn, kept my garments,[3] all of which they had taken from me and which were better than those I took with me.

---

3. Florentina probably means her conventual garb, not the clothing she wore when she entered the convent.

Chapter 13
The Protestant
Reformation in
Germany:
Martin Luther
(1483–1546)
and Katharina
von Bora (1499–
1552)

DOCUMENT THREE

Martin Luther

Essays and Comments on Marriage

Luther's essay, On the Babylonian Captivity of the Church, *is a lengthy document in which he discusses church organization and the legitimate functions of the church. In this passage he challenges the idea that marriage is a sacrament. What are the grounds for this argument and why does he take this stance?*

Once Luther had taken up residence at the Friary and especially after he married von Bora, it was common to have numerous guests for meals. Often these visits were also occasions for discussions of Protestant doctrines and ideas, and particularly for Luther to speak more informally on matters of all sorts. In the following passages, he gives his views about marriage. According to Luther, what is the purpose of marriage? Does he seem to approve of marriage? Why has it existed through the ages? Do the ideas he expresses here seem different from his more formal, doctrinal statement in the previous passage?

On the Babylonian Captivity of the Church, 1520

Marriage

There is no Scriptural warrant whatsoever for regarding marriage as a sacrament; and indeed the Romanists have used the same traditions, both to extol it as a sacrament, and to make it naught but a mockery. Let us look into this matter.

We have maintained that a word of divine promise is associated with every sacrament, and anyone who receives the sacrament must also believe in that word of promise, for it is impossible that the sign should in itself be the sacrament. But nowhere in Scripture do we read that anyone would receive the grace of God by getting married; nor does the rite of matrimony contain any hint that that ceremony is of divine institution. Nowhere do we read that it was instituted by God in order to symbolize something, although we grant that all things done in the sight of men can be understood as metaphors and allegories of things invisible. Yet metaphors and allegories are not sacraments, and it is of sacraments that we are speaking.

There has been such a thing as marriage itself ever since the beginning of the world, and it also exists amongst unbelievers to the present day. Therefore no grounds exist on which the Romanists can validly call it a sacrament of the new law, and a function solely of the church. The marriages of our ancestors were no less sacred than our own, nor less real among unbelievers than believers. . . .

SELECTIONS FROM LUTHER'S *TABLE TALK*

Men Cannot Get Along Without Women

BETWEEN JUNE 12 AND JULY 12, 1532   NO. 1658

"Many good things may be perceived in a wife. First, there is the Lord's blessing, namely, offspring. Then there is a community of property. These are some of the pre-eminently good things that can overwhelm a man.

"Imagine what it would be like without this sex. The home, cities, economic life, and government would virtually disappear. Men can't do without women. Even if it were possible for men to beget and bear children, they still couldn't do without women."

Marriage and Cohabitation Are God's Creation

BETWEEN JUNE 12 AND JULY 12, 1532   NO. 1659

"When one looks back upon it, marriage isn't so bad as when one looks forward to it. We see that our mothers and our fathers were saints and that we have the divine commandment, 'Honor your father and your mother' [Exod. 20:12]. When I look beside myself, I see my brothers and sisters and friends, and I find that there's nothing but godliness in marriage. To be sure, when I consider marriage, only the flesh seems to be there. Yet my father must have slept with my mother and made love to her, and they were nevertheless godly people. All the patriarchs and prophets did likewise. The longing of a man for a woman is God's creation—that is to say, when nature's sound, not when it's corrupted as it is among Italians and Turks."

DOCUMENT FOUR

MARTIN LUTHER

"Letter to Katie"
(1532)

Luther traveled a great deal and wrote to von Bora almost daily. The following letter, written in 1532, explains why his return from visiting the Elector John in Torgau has been delayed, but it also reveals something of his relationship with his wife. What does this document tell you about Luther's view of von Bora and her position in the family?

Chapter 13
The Protestant
Reformation in
Germany:
Martin Luther
(1483–1546)
and Katharina
von Bora (1499–
1552)

To my dearly beloved mistress of the house, Catherine Luther:
Personal

God in Christ be with you! My dearly beloved Katie! As soon as Doctor Brück is granted permission to leave the court—he puts me off with this prospect—I hope to come along with him tomorrow or the next day. Pray God to bring us home chipper and healthy! I am sleeping very well, about six or seven hours without interruption, and then thereafter again for two or three hours. It's the beer's fault, I think. But just as in Wittenberg I am sober.

Doctor Caspar says that the gangrene in our Gracious Lord's foot will spread no further. But neither Dobitzsch nor any prisoner on the stretching-rack in jail suffers such agony from John the jailer as His Electoral Grace suffers from the surgeons. His Sovereign Grace is, in his whole body, as healthy as a little fish, but the devil has bitten and pierced His Grace's foot. Pray, and continue to pray! I trust God will listen to us, as he has begun. For Doctor Caspar, too, thinks that in this case God has to help.

Since John is moving away, it is both necessary and honorable that I let him go honorably from me. For you know that he has served me faithfully and diligently, and conducted himself with humility, and done and endured all [he was required to do], according to the gospel. Remember how often we have given something to bad boys and ungrateful students, in which cases all that we did was lost. Now therefore reach into your wallet and let nothing be lacking for this fine fellow, since you know that it is well used and God-pleasing. I certainly know that little is available; yet if I had them I wouldn't mind giving him ten gulden. But you shouldn't give him less than five gulden, since we didn't give him a new suit of clothes [upon his departure]. Whatever you might be able to do beyond this, do it, I beg you for it. The Common Chest might, of course, make a present to my servant in my honor, in view of the fact that I am forced to maintain my servants at my expense for the service and benefit of the local congregation. But they may do as they please. Yet under no circumstances should you let anything be lacking as long as there is still a fine goblet [in the house]. Figure out from where you will take the money. God certainly will provide more; this I know. With this I commend you to God. Amen.

Tell the pastor of Zwickau he really ought to be pleased and content with the quarters. Upon my return I shall tell you how Mühlpfort and I have been guests of Rietesel, and how Mühlpfort has demonstrated much wisdom to me. But I wasn't eager for his wisdom.

Kiss young Hans for me; keep after Hänschen, Lenchen, and Aunt Lena to pray for the dear Sovereign and for me. I am unable to find anything to buy for the children in this town even though there is now a fair here. If I am unable to bring anything special along, please have something ready for me!

February 27, 1532   Doctor Martin Luther

DOCUMENT FIVE

KATHARINA VON BORA

"Letter to Duke Albrecht von Hohenzollern-Ansbach"
(1549)

Many of Katharina von Bora's letters were not preserved. In this one, she writes to Duke Albrecht von Hohenzollern-Ansbach, one of their benefactors, in 1549, three years after Luther's death. Their son Hans had attended the university in Königsberg, and von Bora is writing to appeal to the duke for his help and to request that he continue to support Hans. (Apparently, by 1551, Hans had not done well enough to continue his studies, so further requests were denied.) What does this letter tell you of the difficulties von Bora faced after Luther's death?

―――. *Letter to Duke Albrecht von Hohenzollern-Ansbach of Prussia. Wittenberg, 29 May 1549.*

May the grace and peace of God, together with my poor prayers, be with your Princely Grace. Most illustrious and highborn Prince and Lord!

Since Your Princely Grace always showed such benevolence to my dear master, Dr. Martin, of blessed memory, I have never doubted that Your Princely Grace would also be especially beneficent to me, just as our dear God taught Your Princely Grace to cherish, protect and hold—also for the sake of my dear blessed master, a true prophet of these recent dangerous and turbulent times—taking me and my dear children as bereaved widow and orphans under your gracious protection and sway.

There is no need to remind Your Princely Grace of the severe plight of my household after the recent wars, and how wretchedly I have hitherto had to nourish and maintain myself and my children from my poor devastated and wasted estates. On the advice of Mr. Philippus and following the report of Dr. Sabini as to how well disposed Your Princely Grace is to my children, I dispatched my eldest son Hans to Your Princely Grace, and after Your Princely Grace had most graciously offered to maintain him for some time at his studies, I should most humbly like to thank Your Princely Grace for this same gracious support and care for my poor bereaved children.

Since, however, this is my son's first period away from home and since I sent him away primarily so that he could, alongside his studies, learn how to deal with others, so it is my humble plea to Your Princely Grace that you might take this my son, for the sake of my dear deceased husband, into your grace and protection, and since he has not shown himself fully worthy, I beg you graciously to put this down to his ignorance and his being away from home for the first time and to be patient with him. I do not doubt that he will show submissive

Chapter 13
The Protestant
Reformation in
Germany:
Martin Luther
(1483–1546)
and Katharina
von Bora (1499–
1552)

obedience to Your Princely Grace and due obedience to his mentors, that he will pursue his studies and other duties diligently and show himself honorable and grateful in all submissiveness.

May our dear Lord richly reward in turn Your Princely Grace's gracious support. I shall always studiously supplicate God on behalf of Your Princely Grace for a long-lasting reign and well-being. Dated Wittenberg, 29 May in the year 49.

Your Princely Grace's

humble and submissive

Katharina, bereaved widow

of the blessed Dr. Martin

Luther

DOCUMENT SIX

MARTIN LUTHER

On the Councils and the Church
(1539)

In this essay, On the Councils and the Church, *written in 1539, Luther addresses the issue of who should preach and teach in the church and, in particular, the place of women in the church. Argula von Grumbach had strong views about women speaking out, teaching in the church, and in general assuming public roles in the Protestant movement (see chapter discussion). How are her views contrary to what Luther writes in this passage?*

. . . St. Paul states in Ephesians 4 [:8], "He received gifts among men . . ."—his gifts were that some should be apostles, some prophets, some evangelists, some teachers and governors, etc. The people as a whole cannot do these things, but must entrust or have them entrusted to one person. Otherwise, what would happen if everyone wanted to speak or administer, and no one wanted to give way to the other? It must be entrusted to one person, and he alone should be allowed to preach, to baptize, to absolve, and to administer the sacraments. The others should be content with this arrangement and agree to it. Wherever you see this done, be assured that God's people, the holy Christian people, are present.

It is, however, true that the Holy Spirit has excepted women, children, and incompetent people from this function, but chooses (except in emergencies) only competent males to fill this office, as one reads here and there in the epistles of St. Paul that a bishop must be pious, able to teach, and the husband of one wife—and in I Corinthians 14 [:34] he says, "The women should keep silence in the churches." In summary, it must be a competent and chosen man. Children, women, and other persons are not qualified for this office, even though they are able to hear God's word, to receive baptism, the sacrament, absolution, and are also true, holy Christians, as St. Peter says [I Pet. 3:7]. Even nature and God's creation makes this distinction, implying that women (much less children or fools) cannot and shall not occupy positions of sovereignty, as experience also suggests and as Moses says in Genesis 3 [:16], "You shall be subject to man." The gospel, however, does not abrogate this natural law, but confirms it as the ordinance and creation of God.

DOCUMENT SEVEN

Argula von Grumbach

Letter to Her Mother's Cousin
(1523)

In late 1523, Argula von Grumbach wrote to her mother's cousin, an influential civil and military leader in Bavaria. Apparently he had been critical of her actions, calling them inappropriate for a woman, after she had tried to defend a young university student for his religious beliefs. In this letter, von Grumbach defends herself against what kinds of accusations? What arguments does she use to justify her actions?

To the noble and honourable lord Adam von Thering,
my gracious lord the Count Palatine's administrator in Neuberg . . . ,
my dear lord and cousin.

The grace and peace of God and the presence of his Holy Spirit be with you, my beloved lord and cousin. I have been told that you were informed of my letter to the University of Ingolstadt, and that this made you more than a little angry with me. Perhaps you thought it unbecoming of me as a foolish woman. Which is, of course, exactly how I see myself. However, the wisdom needed to confess God does not derive from human reason, but is to be seen as a gift of God. From this has come—and more may yet come—much malicious gossip on the part of the worldly wise, tending to my disgrace, shame or ridicule. . . . I am called a follower of Luther, but I am not. I was baptised in the name of Christ; it is him I confess and not Luther. But I confess that Martin, too, as a faithful Christian, confesses him. God help us never to deny this, whether faced by disgrace,

Chapter 13
The Protestant
Reformation in
Germany:
Martin Luther
(1483–1546)
and Katharina
von Bora (1499–
1552)

abuse, imprisonment, breaking on the wheel and even death—God helping and enabling all Christians in this. Amen.

I have heard that you are reported as saying that if my own husband would not do it, some relative should act, and wall me up. But don't believe him. Alas, he is doing far too much to persecute Christ in me. In 2 Corinthians 4 Paul says: 'We endure all things without complaint for the name of the Lord.' So it is no difficulty for me, and I am not liable to obey him in this matter, for God says in Matthew 10 and Mark 8: 'We must forsake father, mother, brother, sister, children, life and limb', and then says: 'What good does it do someone to gain the whole world but ruin one's soul? With what would one repurchase one's soul? . . .

Even if all my friends were there (God forbid) I fear they could not do much to entertain me! It's the fault of the parents for failing to have their children taught. If by chance they have been to school it's Terence and Ovid they are taught; for the reason given above. But what is in these books? How to make love, be lover-boys and whores and so on. That's an option, for sure, and every level of society is full of people like that, whether married or not, who boast about it rather than being ashamed of it. Sadly it has come to the stage where whores and their partners often show more fidelity to each other than occurs in marriage. . . .

I have scant enthusiasm or expectation about this meeting of the Reichstag that has been summoned. May God send his Spirit to teach them to recognize the truth when they see it, so that this Reichstag meeting deserves the name, and we may become rich in soul and body; all be governed in true Christian faith, and the wealth of land and people no longer be dissipated, making us poorer still. If as much attention were given to God's word as to eating, drinking, banqueting, gambling, masques and the like, things would soon improve. What hundreds of thousands of florins I can remember being wasted in such Reichstag meetings. And to what purpose? You know better than I! What deliberation is possible when they are so busy gorging themselves day and night that they can hardly sit upright? . . .

I have been told that they wish to deprive my husband of his office. I cannot help that; I weighed everything up carefully beforehand. It will not stand in the way of my salvation, as was the case with Pilate. I am prepared to lose everything—even life and limb. May God stand by me! Of myself I can do nothing but sin; pray to God earnestly for me, that he may increase my faith. Even if that should mean the end of me, do not regard that as a disgrace but rather praise God. Had I the grace, my soul would be like a precious jewel to the Lord God.

The property they can take from me is almost nothing. You know that my father was ruined under the princes of Bavaria, and his children became beggars—although they have treated me and my children well by giving employment to my husband. May God be their reward. Although the priests of Würzburg have devoured my husband's property, God will surely care for my four children, and send the birds of the air to feed them and clothe them with the flowers of the field. He has said it; he cannot lie.

I had intended to keep my writing private; now I see that God wishes to have it made public. That I am now abused for this is a good indication that it is of God, for if the world were to praise it, it would not be of God. Therefore, my beloved lord and cousin, I commend you now and forever to the grace of God; may it be with you now and for ever. Grunbach [*sic*].

Argula von Grunbach, née von Stauffen.

The Scientific Revolution: Galileo Galilei (1564–1642) and Sister Maria Celeste (née Virginia Galilei, 1600–1634)

◼ SETTING THE STAGE

Knowledge and learning in the centuries leading up to the seventeenth had been dominated by respect for and reliance upon philosophers and religious authorities of earlier centuries. Prevailing attitudes about the creation and acquisition of knowledge argued that instead of going directly to nature for investigation of its laws and processes, it was best to go to earlier authorities, either ancient or Christian, who were supposed to have spoken the last word on the natural world and its many phenomena. During medieval times, the most highly respected philosophers and scientists were men of the cloth. These individuals, often called "natural philosophers," did make advancements in mathematical and physical thinking, not by systematic observations of the natural world but by refined logical analysis.

Nonetheless, their conceptualizations and theories about the workings of the universe still depended upon the works and ideas of the ancient Greeks and Romans. The blending of these distinctive ways of understanding the world led to many erroneous conclusions and theoretical contradictions concerning nature and its laws.

Questioning the medieval world view and its reliance on a few ancient authorities gained momentum as Europeans abandoned religious education and training for education in secular subjects such as astronomy, mechanics, and medicine. This inquiry did not happen in a vacuum. In the sixteenth century, Europeans were challenging the authority of the Catholic Church in religious and political matters, as demonstrated by the Protestant Reformation and the religious wars that followed. It is not surprising then that as Christian unity broke down, European men and women challenged the church's authority in the intellectual realm and questioned many of the earlier interpretations of the universe and humanity's place in it. This challenge to previous knowledge and accepted truths drew the learned world into two centuries of intellectual revolt known as the Scientific Revolution.

The transformation to a new world view was not an easy one. It did not occur immediately or rapidly, nor did it displace religion from the everyday lives of Europeans. In fact, the scientists of the sixteenth and seventeenth centuries often justified their pursuit of knowledge and science in religious terms and remained faithful to the Christian church while they pursued secular interpretations and explanations of the natural world. Such pursuits often brought scientists into conflict with religious authorities who sought to protect their monopoly on knowledge, learning, and the interpretation of the universe. Yet it is not the scientist alone who dueled with the established ecclesiastical and academic institutions of the Catholic Church for control of the minds and imaginations of Europeans. To take on the established order, think new ideas, and pursue new forms of knowledge, scientists needed allies to support their endeavors financially, to foster communication with other scientists, and to obtain social status and respectability. Humanists, protestant reformers, new merchant elites, more confident and self-assured aristocrats, princes and monarchs, and artisans helped create new institutions, social and scientific networks, and creative spaces for the growth of European culture beyond the walls of the Vatican, cathedral schools, monasteries, and convents. Relinquishing the power to control knowledge and learning would not be easy for the Catholic Church nor would it be easy for learned men and women to defy the works of the ancients and their Christian disciples.

Central to the historical understanding of the professional and personal conflicts between science and religion is the story of Galileo Galilei, which includes his scientific activity and his relationship, conflicts, and encounters with the Roman Catholic Church. Galileo's story does not have a simple plot line, with science, light, and reason standing on one side and religion, darkness, and lack of reason standing

Chapter 14
The Scientific
Revolution:
Galileo Galilei
(1564–1642) and
Sister Maria
Celeste (née
Virginia Galilei,
1600–1634)

on the other. Nor did Galileo reject everything that the Catholic Church, its institutions, and its doctrines had to offer. Galileo lived in a world where he encountered the church constantly, whether it was in his personal or professional life. While rejecting the church's authority in his search for scientific truth, he remained a devout Catholic and depended on the Catholic Church for patronage and spiritual leadership and as the authority in his daughters' lives. To understand the religious, intellectual, and social milieu of the Scientific Revolution is to understand the lives of Galileo Galilei and his daughter, Sister Maria Celeste.

✱ THE ACTORS:

GALILEO GALILEI AND
SISTER MARIA CELESTE

Galileo Galilei was born in Pisa, Tuscany, on February 15, 1564, to Julia Ammanati of Pescia and Vincenzio Galilei, a cloth merchant and musician. Galileo was the first of seven children born to Vincenzio and Julia, but only three of his siblings, Virginia (b. 1573), Michelangelo (b. 1575), and Livia (b. 1587) lived to adulthood. Their mother, Julia, was a woman of education and intelligence and their father, Vincenzio, belonged to a distinguished merchant family from Florence whose wealth unfortunately was greatly diminished by the time of Galileo's birth. Vincenzio had been broadly educated in the humanist tradition. He had trained as a musician and became an accomplished lutenist and composer, but he studied and mastered mathematics and classical languages as well.

Several of Vincenzio's works on musical theory survive. In these works, he argued stridently against blind acceptance of previous musical ideas and theory. In *A Dialogue on Ancient and Modern Music*, he stated, "It appears to me that they who in proof of any as-sertion rely simply on the weight of authority without adducing any argument in support of it, act very absurdly. I, on the contrary, wish to be allowed freely to question and freely to answer you without any sort of adulation, as well becomes those who are truly in search of the truth."[1] Vincenzio would bequeath his fervent passion for music and mathematics and his distrust of and contempt for arguments based on blind obedience to intellectual authority to his eldest son.

Vincenzio had great ambitions for Galileo and began educating him, as he had been educated, in the humanist tradition. At one point as a boy, Galileo was enrolled at the monastery of Santa Maria di Vallombrosa where he learned the elements of logic. But his father was not about to allow his eldest son to enter the monastic ranks. In 1581, at great sacrifice to his impoverished family, Galileo entered the University of Pisa as a student of medicine. The choice of medicine appeared a logical one for the Galilei

1. *The Private Life of Galileo: Compiled Principally from His Correspondence and That of His Eldest Daughter, Sister Maria Celeste* (London: MacMillan and Co., 1870), p. 2.

family because medicine was becoming a most lucrative profession.

At the University of Pisa, Galileo encountered the works of two of the great ancient authorities in medicine and philosophy, Claudius Galen and Aristotle. Galileo read these works voraciously and attempted to engage his professors in discussion concerning the contradictions and inconsistencies in these texts. This effort to understand the ancients and then ask questions about them won Galileo the reputation of a rebel. It was soon clear that medicine and its training were not for this inquisitive young man, and he began to seek other intellectual pursuits, especially the study of mathematics.

Renaissance men and women had rediscovered the mathematics of the ancients, and they soon believed that mathematics could help explain the workings of the universe and the nature of things. In the fifteenth century, Leonardo da Vinci argued that God eternally geometrizes, and therefore nature, as God's creation, is inherently mathematical. Da Vinci and Renaissance natural philosophers grew increasingly convinced that mathematical reasoning promoted a degree of certainty about the nature of things that was impossible to deduce using only logic and observation.

Despite the embrace of mathematics during the Renaissance, it still was not a widely taught or accepted field of study in the late sixteenth century. The University of Pisa was not known for the study of mathematics and small universities throughout Europe did not teach it at all. In 1583, while on vacation, Galileo asked a friend of the family, Ostillo Ricci, who was a tutor to the Tuscan ducal court, to instruct him in this discipline. Ricci assessed Galileo's abilities quickly and convinced Vincenzio that his eldest son's future lay in mathematical studies.

Galileo did not immediately forsake his other studies at Pisa. He continued to study both mathematics and natural philosophy and prepared himself for a future university post. In 1584, he dedicated much of his energy to the preparation of lectures on natural philosophy because it was more likely that he would find a teaching post in this discipline than in mathematics. As he prepared, he noted that this discipline rested on the foundations that Aristotle had laid eighteen centuries earlier. On all questions concerning the study of nature, Aristotle was the authority, either having the final say from his grave or having his ideas modified or altered by later authorities. Most natural philosophers, even if they observed something different from Aristotle, accepted only those results that could be reconciled with Aristotle's writings on logic, motion, and the structure of the universe. While initially bowing to the Aristotelian view, Galileo dedicated his scholarly life to criticizing, testing, and refuting Aristotle's doctrines and the commentaries of the Aristotelians, past and present.

Galileo left the University of Pisa in 1584 without obtaining his medical degree and spent the next four years in Florence with his family trying to find a university position in mathematics. During this time, Galileo began to explore bodies in motion. According

Chapter 14
The Scientific
Revolution:
Galileo Galilei
(1564–1642) and
Sister Maria
Celeste (née
Virginia Galilei,
1600–1634)

to one of the romantic and mythical tales about Galileo, he had become interested in why objects move when in the cathedral of Pisa he observed a lamp swinging gently to rest after being filled with oil. Eventually this observation led him to the discovery of the isochronism of the pendulum, which he used fifty years later in the design of an astronomical clock. Whatever the truthfulness of this story, historians do know that by the late 1580s, Galileo was wrestling with several commonly held theories about the principles of motion.

The Aristotelians held that the acceleration of falling bodies depended on their weight; a heavier object fell faster than a lighter one. They also believed that an object remained at rest unless a force was applied against it, or it remained in motion only if some force propelled it. Observable fact disputed the latter theorem. Medieval philosophers had noted that a cannonball continued in the air without a force propelling it, and mathematicians and natural philosophers of the sixteenth century continued wrestling with the problem.

By the time Galileo took his first teaching post at the University of Pisa in 1589, several other scholars had worked on inertia and Galileo possibly used their work in his unpublished treatise, *On Motion*. At the University of Pisa, Galileo puzzled over the problems of falling bodies and bodies in motion, and the ideas germinated here eventually blossomed into new theories on motion. Later in life, Galileo embellished his accomplishments at Pisa by telling his biographer, Vincenzio Vivianni, how

he climbed to the top of the Tower of Pisa and dropped two objects of the same material, but of different weights, at the same time to disprove Aristotle's theory that objects fall at a rate proportional to their weight. The objects reached the ground together, disproving Aristotle. The story is not true; Galileo had reached this conclusion without actually performing the experiment. Instead of presenting his case through complicated mathematical formulas, he had invented a simple and dramatic story to illustrate his point.

In 1592, Galileo accepted the chair of mathematics at the University of Padua in the Republic of Venice. The reasons for Galileo's departure are numerous: his Pisan colleagues' discomfort with Galileo's opposition to Aristotelian principles, a higher salary at Padua, the University of Padua's better reputation, and the Republic of Venice's tradition of being an enlightened and well-ruled state. The University of Padua benefitted greatly from the patronage of Venetian nobles, many of whom appreciated all branches of learning and the arts. Some of them fancied themselves scholars and learned men. In an era when there were no formal scientific meetings, these nobles sponsored gatherings at their estates, financed experiments and equipment for the scientists they supported, and even had laboratories or workshops built in their homes. They also hired the professors at the university to teach their sons. Many professors, including Galileo, used this money to supplement their income. One of Galileo's students, Cosimo II de Medici (1590–1621), would later become his biggest patron. In 1610, Cosimo would become grand duke of Tuscany and would lure Galileo away from Padua to Florence with the guarantee of a lifetime appointment and a generous salary.

Venice offered other opportunities as well. At this time, Venice was a great maritime empire, and its extensive trade and diplomatic networks made it easier for scientific ideas, inventions, and books from other parts of Europe to reach Galileo. Galileo also observed and benefitted from artisan innovation that emerged from the Venetian maritime industry. The intellectual and political climate created by the ruling families of Venice was reflected in the policies of the university, where the Venetians guaranteed to all scholars broad freedom of thought. The University of Padua had been founded in 1222 and by the late sixteenth century had become a European center for the study of medicine and philosophy. While many of its faculty still adhered to the works of the ancient and medieval authorities, the school of medicine and its faculty abandoned these teachings and experimented widely. This new bent toward experimentation and an openness to challenging the ancients suited Galileo's temperament.

Galileo spent eighteen years at the University of Padua, where he continued his work in mechanics, that is, the study of the action of forces on matter. He formally established the laws of falling bodies and the laws of projectiles and pondered the laws of motion, which were finally articulated by Sir Isaac Newton a century later. He also studied stationary bodies (statics) and gave the first satisfactory demonstration of the laws of equilibrium and the principle of virtual velocities. Finally, he applied his ideas to the study of objects in water (hydrostatics) and developed the principle of flotation. Galileo virtually created the systematic study of the relationship between motion and the forces affecting motion, or what we now call the field of dynamics. Yet it is not his work in this field that is the most well known; rather, it is his invention of the telescope and his championing of Copernican astronomy.

During one of his regular visits to Venice in 1609, Galileo heard about the creation of a Dutch optician, Hans Lippershey, an invention that magnified remote objects. Recalling the events years later, he wrote, "News arrived that a Fleming had presented to Count Maurice [of Nassau] a glass by means of which distant objects could be seen as distinctly as if they were nearby. That was all. . . . [I] set myself to thinking about the problem. The first night after my return [to Padua] I solved it, and on the following day I constructed the instrument."[2] He then turned this instrument and his thoughts toward the heavens and found, using the telescope's magnification, that the Ptolemaic system could not explain what he saw. Ptolemy's geocentric cosmology, building on Aristotle's, placed the earth at the center of the universe and had the planets and sun revolving around it. Looking through his telescope, Galileo confirmed the ideas of Nicholas Copernicus (1473–1543), the

2. Stillman Drake, *Galileo at Work* (Chicago, Ill.: University of Chicago, 1978), p. 137.

Chapter 14
The Scientific
Revolution:
Galileo Galilei
(1564–1642) and
Sister Maria
Celeste (née
Virginia Galilei,
1600–1634)

Polish astronomer, who argued that the sun was at the center of universe, and the planets, including the earth, revolved around it. Galileo had privately confessed his belief in the Copernican heliocentric system in a letter to the young astronomer, Johannes Kepler (1571–1630), in 1597 but had kept his belief private lest he suffer the ridicule and humiliation experienced by Copernicus.

While not being the first to create the telescope, Galileo was the first to turn it toward the heavens and he began to see objects in the heavens that no one had even seen before. He reported his observations and discoveries in the study, *The Starry Messenger,* in 1610. Galileo's study of the heavens revealed that the seemingly perfect sphere of the moon had craters and mountains, the planet Jupiter had four small bodies or satellites revolving around it, the sun had "blemishes" on its surface, and the planet Venus moved in and out of light and dark phases. The publication of *The Starry Messenger* stunned the educated world and positioned Galileo as the foremost astronomer and scientist of his age (Document One).

The Venetian Republic rewarded its prized scholar with a lifetime appointment at the University of Padua. Despite this generous gesture, Galileo was still drawn to his home city of Florence and the Duchy of Tuscany. One of Galileo's students, Cosimo II de Medici, would later become his biggest patron. Evidence of this allegiance to Tuscany and its ruling family, the Medicis, is found in the dedication of *The Starry Messenger* to the young grand duke, Cosimo II, and

in the glorification of the Medici family by naming Jupiter's moons the "Medicean stars." In September 1610, Galileo triumphantly returned to the Medicean court at Florence as the first mathematician at the University of Pisa, with no obligation ever to work or live in Pisa. He never did. Galileo now had a powerful patron at his side, Cosimo II, but as he would soon find out, the freedom of intellectual pursuit and thought that he enjoyed in the Venetian Republic was not a freedom enjoyed by scholars in the Duchy of Tuscany (Document Two).

While at the University of Padua, Galileo's familial responsibilities increased because of the death of his father, Vincenzio, in 1591. Almost all of the family's financial burdens fell on his shoulders. His beloved sister, Virginia, married shortly after his father's death and he had to provide her dowry, a particularly onerous burden. Italy at this time was experiencing dowry inflation because of the surplus of women on the marriage market. In the late fifteenth and early sixteenth century, in Florence there were five men for every six women. To make an appropriate match for his sister, Galileo would have to pay an exorbitant price. Ten years later, his other sister, Livia, married and again the burden of the dowry fell on him. In the latter case, he asked the Venetian Republic for a two-year advance on his salary to make half of the payment. His brother, Michelangelo, assumed the other half but defaulted on the obligation. Galileo, while happy at Padua, began to seek a better patron than the Venetian Republic and in 1604 seriously entertained an offer from the duke of

Mantua, but the financial terms were not to Galileo's liking and he turned down the offer. During his years at Padua, he supplemented his income by taking students into his home, tutoring, and selling mechanical instruments from his workshop.

In the late 1590s, Galileo met and took as his mistress, Marina Gamba, a Venetian of the lower class. Why they never married has been a point of some speculation. Most likely, Marina's class position and the fact that she was from Venice discouraged any formal union; after all, Galileo came from a distinguished Tuscan family, and being linked in marriage to the Gamba family did nothing to further the family's fortune or prestige. Coming from a lower class family, Marina could not improve Galileo's financial woes by bringing a dowry to the marriage. Her family probably could offer only clothing, household items, and maybe a little cash. Until the birth of their first child, Virginia, in 1600, Marina lived in Venice and Galileo in Padua. From 1600 until Galileo's departure for Florence in 1610, Marina lived in a small house close to Galileo's residence in Padua.

Galileo and Marina had three children together, Virginia (b. 1600), Livia (b. 1601), and Vincenzio (b. 1606). Galileo's name did not appear on any of the parish documents as the father, and therefore the children were illegitimate in the eyes of the church and the Italian city-states. Galileo did recognize the children as his; took financial responsibility for them; and, in the case of his son, arranged for the grand duke of Tuscany to legitimize Vincenzio in 1619. When he left for Florence in 1610, he took his daughter, Livia, with him. Virginia had returned with her paternal grandmother, Julia, to Florence a year earlier. Bringing his lower-class mistress to his home city would not have helped his status, and he left Marina in Padua to care for their young son. Vincenzio remained with his mother until 1612, when his father brought him to Florence on the eve of his mother's marriage to a man of Marina's own social class.

The fact that Galileo accepted responsibility for his children was not at all unusual. Men of the elite often kept mistresses. Their offspring, while not enjoying the same inheritance privileges of children born within the union of marriage, were often supported by their fathers and the boys especially could aspire to positions of privilege. This attitude toward children of such liaisons was changing, however. The Catholic Reformation of the sixteenth century sought to condemn such relationships and put an end to them. The Council of Trent (1545–1563) drew a sharp distinction between lawful childbearing, a birth following a wedding presided over by a priest, and its sinful counterpart, bastard bearing. The result of this distinction was to portray illegitimate children as products of sinful behavior and threats to the sanctity of the true family. Those accused of cohabiting without the benefit of the sacrament of marriage lived under the threat of excommunication and denunciation.[3] Both Galileo and Marina

3. David I. Kertzer, *Sacrificed for Honor: Italian Infant Abandonment and the Politics of Reproductive Control* (Boston, Mass.: Beacon Press, 1993), p. 18.

[411]

Chapter 14
The Scientific
Revolution:
Galileo Galilei
(1564–1642) and
Sister Maria
Celeste (née
Virginia Galilei,
1600–1634)

escaped such a fate but their daughters' illegitimacy, Marina's lower class status, and their parent's sinful behavior would make it difficult for Virginia and Livia to marry well.

As the mathematician and philosopher to the grand duke's court and as a scholar, Galileo had little time to devote to the care and education of his daughters. He obviously hoped that his mother or his sisters would bear the brunt of responsibility for his daughters, but his mother's ill health and quarrelsome temperament prevented such an arrangement. In 1611, he sought advice from several Catholic cardinals concerning the placement of his daughters in a convent. He was told that several obstacles stood in his way. First, Florence did not allow for two sisters to take the veil in the same Florentine convent. Second, Galileo wanted to place his daughters in the Convent of San Matteo in Arcetri. If there was no space for them and room had to be made, then the dowry for each would double. Finally, the girls were too young to enter holy life. Galileo tried to get around this last obstacle but the age requirement at first was not waived. In response to his request, Cardinal Del Monte wrote in December 1611,

> In answer to your letter concerning your daughters' claustration, I had fully understood that you did not wish them to take the veil immediately, but that you wished them to be received on the understanding that they were to assume the religious habit as soon as they had reached the canonical age [16]. But, as I have written to you before, even

this is not allowed, for many reasons: in particular, that it might give rise to the exercise of undue influence by those who wished the young persons to take the veil for reasons of their own. This rule is never broken, . . . [4]

Contrary to the cardinal's assertion, the rule was broken often if the family had the right connections. Galileo used his connections at the ducal court to gain the admittance of his daughters to the Convent of San Matteo in October 1613. Virginia was thirteen and Livia twelve. One year later, they both took the veil. Virginia took the name Sister Maria Celeste and Livia, Sister Arcangela.

Why did Galileo have his daughters take their vows? In the seventeenth century, it was not unusual for young girls to be boarded and educated by nuns. Galileo's sisters had had this experience, but because of their family name and Galileo's willingness to pay the dowries of both, they left the convent and married. Galileo's daughters were illegitimate, and the dowries necessary to make a marriage arrangement with an appropriate family were probably not within Galileo's means or desires, nor were the statistical odds in his favor of finding suitable matches. Like many parents, he resorted to an acceptable life choice for his daughters and placed them in a convent, paying a modest dowry. The climate in Florence also favored such a choice. In late sixteenth-century Florence, there

4. Ibid., p. 69.

were 441 male friars and 2,786 nuns, out of a population of 59,000.[5]

Galileo had another motive as well. In 1613, he had reached a standing within the scientific community that was unrivaled in seventeenth-century Italy. He wanted to place his daughters in a situation where "they would not burden him with new responsibilities and relieve him of all worry on the subject forever."[6] They would see their father only on the rare occasions when he visited the convent. Their mother died in 1619 with no evidence surviving that she had seen her daughters after their departure from Padua in 1613. Galileo had chosen religious lives for his daughters because it was convenient for him and socially acceptable. He chose differently for his son, Vincenzio, whom Galileo legitimized, educated, married off, and supported. His daughters would not enjoy or thrive in the life that Galileo had chosen for them. Livia would suffer numerous breakdowns and Virginia would be dead at the age of 34.

❋ Act I:

GALILEO, THE COPERNICAN SYSTEM, AND THE INQUISITION

The duchy of Tuscany and its ruling house, the Medicis, were intimately tied to Rome and the Catholic ecclesiastical hierarchy. Members of the Medici family served as cardinals, bishops, and popes, and these connections brought the Roman Catholic Church into the political, intellectual, and religious affairs of the duchy. This relationship between the two provided Galileo the opportunity to go to Rome in 1611 and try to convince the theologians there of the truth of the Copernican thesis. He went to Rome not as a heretic but as a man deeply committed and loyal to the Roman Catholic Church.

5. Merry Wiesner, *Women and Gender in Early Modern Europe* (London: Cambridge University Press, 1993), p. 61.

6. Ludovico Geymonat, *Galileo Galilei* (New York: McGraw-Hill, 1965), p. 55. Quoted in David F. Noble, *A World Without Women: The Christian Clerical Culture of Western Science* (New York: Oxford University Press, 1992), p. 217.

Galileo was a man of his time. During his lifetime, Roman Catholicism, in which he had been reared and educated, was under siege from the Reformation and threatened by the spread of Protestantism. To counter the Reformation, the church in Rome embarked upon its own reforms. In the mid-sixteenth century, the Council of Trent initiated policies to revive the clergy and papacy and instituted a new order, the Jesuits, to fight the Reformation. In addition, the church once again convened the Holy Office (Inquisition), a tribunal of church officials authorized to uncover, investigate, and prosecute heretics. Galileo understood the threat that the Reformation posed to his religion, but he did not want his church to support a view of the heavens from which it would have to retreat. His discoveries, coupled with Copernicus's and Kepler's, convinced him that a revolution in the conception of the universe was at hand and that if the church denied these scientific advances, it risked fur-

Chapter 14
The Scientific
Revolution:
Galileo Galilei
(1564–1642) and
Sister Maria
Celeste (née
Virginia Galilei,
1600–1634)

ther challenge to and erosion of its credibility.[7] Dogmatic and doctrinal principles and attitudes had brought about the Protestant Reformation, and Galileo did not want the church to lose further ground. From the favorable reception that he and his telescope received in Rome in 1611, it appeared that the church was willing to entertain discussion about the Copernican system and its implication.

In a letter to a Tuscan official, Galileo described how the learned Jesuits of the Roman College confirmed his discovery of the Medicean planets. He wrote, "The Fathers, being finally convinced that the Medicean planets are realities, have devoted the past two months to continuous observations of them, and these observations are still in progress. We have compared notes and have found that our experiences tally in every respect."[8] Pope Paul V (1605–1621) received Galileo for a private audience and Galileo met with Cardinal Bellarmine, one of the *consultors* of the Inquisition, who went so far as to look through Galileo's telescope. Galileo's final triumph was his election to the Academy of the Lincei. Founded in 1603, the academy, an exclusive association of scholars, was devoted to the study of natural phenomena and shunned the traditional natural philosophy of the universities, which at this point were bastions of conservatism and rhetorical superficiality.

The first of Galileo's confrontations with the church began when he wrote three letters in response to the ideas of Christopher Scheiner (1573–1650), a Jesuit scholar, about sunspots. Scheiner's theories on sunspots rested on Aristotelian belief in the sun's immutability and purity. Scheiner argued that the sunspots were bodies revolving around the sun and were not found on the sun's surface. In three letters to a mutual acquaintance, Mark Welser (1558–1614), Galileo proved that the sunspots could not be stars circling the sun as Scheiner hypothesized, but that they were close to the sun's surface. He also disproved Scheiner's idea that the sun stood still while these bodies revolved around it. Instead, Galileo argued that the sun turned on its axis just like the earth. These letters were published by the Lincean Academy in 1613 and it was the first time that Galileo, in print, used his own observations and discoveries as proof of the Copernican system. While carefully wording his response to avoid insulting Scheiner, Galileo could not resist a jab at the Aristotelians in general. He wrote, "They never wish to raise their eyes from those pages [Aristotle's]—as if this great book of the universe had been written to be read by nobody but Aristotle, and his eyes destined to see for all posterity."[9] Galileo had been sparring with the Aristotelians his entire academic career and he thought little of this exchange. But antagonizing a member of the most powerful priestly order in Rome, which was

7. Laura Fermi and Gilberto Bernardini, *Galileo and the Scientific Revolution* (New York: Basic Books, 1961), p. 73.

8. James Brodrick, *Galileo: The Man, His Work, His Misfortunes* (New York: Harper and Row, 1964), p. 56.

9. Ibid., p. 68.

charged with education matters, would not win him many friends.

Discussions and debates concerning Galileo's heavenly discoveries were not limited only to academic and religious circles, but learned men and women, mingling with scholars and priests, also contemplated the significance and meaning of Galileo's theories. During a dinner party in December 1613 at Cosimo II's residence, the grand duke's mother, Cristina of Lorraine (157?–1637), queried one of Galileo's detractors, Cosimo Boscaglia (1550?–1621), a professor at the University of Pisa and a staunch Aristotelian and Platonist, about whether or not Galileo's theories about the earth moving contradicted the Scriptures. Benedetto Castelli (1578–1643), a close ally of Galileo and a Benedictine monk, who was at the dinner, reported the incident in a letter to Galileo. Castelli wrote, "Dr. Boscaglia had had the ear of Madame for a while; and, conceding as true all of the things you have discovered in the sky, he said that only the motion of the earth had something incredible in it and could not take place, in particular because the holy scripture was obviously contrary to this view."[10] Upon receiving Castelli's letter detailing the discussion, Galileo wrote a response with the intention of setting forth clearly his views on the impropriety of mixing religion and science. In a letter addressed to Castelli and later in a revised version addressed to the Grand Duchess Cristina, Galileo argued that nature and its laws went side by side with his faith in God (Document

Three). He simply distinguished between knowledge that aimed to understand the universe and how it worked and knowledge that aimed to attain salvation. Or more simply put, according to Galileo, the Bible and religious writing teaches "humans how to go to heaven, not how the heavens go." Galileo's letters, eloquently composed and argued, circulated in both the scholarly and religious communities of Florence. Given the informalities associated with such letters, it was simply a matter of time before two church officials read or heard about the letters and denounced Galileo to the Inquisition in Rome.

In December 1615, the Inquisition launched an investigation examining the two main tenets of Copernican theory: 1) the sun is immobile and at the center of the universe, and 2) the earth rotates around the sun in daily revolutions and is not the center of the universe. Believing that he had done no wrong and wishing to defend scientific inquiry, Galileo set off to Rome "with the heroic blindness of an apostle [of science] and the enthusiastic faith of a boy."[11] In Rome, Galileo was warmly and courteously received by scholars and ecclesiastics, who listened patiently to his arguments in favor of Copernicus. As Galileo's detractors and enemies busied themselves denouncing him to the Inquisition, several influential cardinals advised him to mute his public enthusiasm for the heliocentric system. Galileo did not heed their advice and he continued his campaign. On February 23, 1616,

10. Ibid., p. 75.

11. Ibid., p. 98.

Chapter 14
The Scientific
Revolution:
Galileo Galilei
(1564–1642) and
Sister Maria
Celeste (née
Virginia Galilei,
1600–1634)

the Inquisition completed its investigation and declared the first of the main tenets of the Copernican system to be "false and absurd, formally heretical and contrary to Scripture" and the second to be "equally censured, philosophically false and was at least erroneous in faith."[12] It also condemned and banned any books that dealt with the Copernican theory. Prior to Galileo's championing of Copernicus's theories, they were brushed aside as indulgent intellectual musings and mathematical exercises, and only one hypothesis among many. Galileo had made these theories the subject of dinner conversations, however, and Catholic authorities could not ignore this threat to their authority. According to the church, the heliocentric system contradicted Scripture and altered a centuries old conception of the universe with a Christian god as its center. To the church, which had held a monopoly on interpreting the heavens, Galileo's advocacy meant that God's creation had become an object of direct human observation, which could be interpreted without the help of the Scriptures, a priest, or religion.[13]

The Inquisition chose not to condemn Galileo for heresy but warned him that he should abandon the idea that the heliocentric system was fact. Curious, of course, is the nuance of the Inquisition's decisions. They did not outright forbid Galileo from holding his beliefs or from teaching or defending them. Galileo could present Copernicanism as a mathematical

supposition that was not supported by "real proof." Rumors flew around the learned world that Galileo had been forced to renounce his beliefs and repent. The Republic of Venice even offered him refuge.

Upon his return to Florence in June 1616, Galileo appeared content to pursue his other scientific pursuits. However, the appearance of three comets in the sky during the fall of 1618 brought his restraint to an end. Father Horatio Grassis (1590–1654), a Jesuit astronomer, used the comets' appearance to denounce the Copernican doctrine. This was too much for Galileo, who had no intention of retreating from his belief in the heliocentric system, and he searched for indirect ways to disprove the church's continuing endorsement of earth-centered heavens. Using a student as a proxy, he delivered a series of lectures and published *Discourse on Comets,* which again articulated his views. The stage was now set for Grassis to reply, which he did in *The Astronomical and Philosophical Balance.* Galileo could not bear the ignorance of the Aristotelians and the posturing of the churchmen any longer, and he crafted a brilliant and biting polemic, *The Assayer.* Published in 1623, it reiterated Galileo's belief in science, nature and its laws, and rigorous intellectual inquiry, and his contempt for those who when "philosophizing must support oneself upon the opinion of some celebrated author."[14]

The Linceans published *The Assayer* and dedicated it to the new pope, Urban VIII (1623–1644), who as the Cardinal Barberini, had befriended

12. Fermi and Bernardini, p. 83.

13. Ibid., p. 84.

14. Ibid., p. 86.

Galileo upon his arrival in Florence in 1611. In 1616, the cardinal had opposed the church's warning to the scientist. Galileo was quite excited about Barberini's election to the papacy, and in 1624 he visited Rome, where he was warmly and generously received by the new pope. During their cordial meetings together, Urban VIII spoke of his favorite passages in *The Assayer,* promised his old friend a pension, and listened to Galileo's ideas about the heavens. When Galileo returned to Rome, it appears that he took his old friend's generosity, warmth, and curiosity as an opportunity to write a work that openly disputed the Ptole-maic system. His continuing ill health slowed his thinking and writing and this polemic, *Dialogue on the Two Chief World Systems; Ptolemaic and Coperni-can,* was not published until 1632.

During the years that he was working on *Dialogue* and struggling with his health, his daughters, Sister Maria Celeste and Sister Arcangela, reappear in the historical record. They were now young women of twenty-three and twenty-two years old and had spent the last ten years of their lives coping with the austere, impoverished, and cloistered world of the Convent of San Matteo.

ACT II:

GALILEO'S DAUGHTER

Sister Maria Celeste and her sister lived cloistered lives, but this circumstance did not mean that they were disinterested in the world beyond the convent's walls. Scholars have 124 of Sister Maria Celeste's letters to her father, beginning with the year 1623 and ending with her death in 1634. His letters to her have disappeared. Her letters reveal a women who was intensely interested in the affairs of her family, yearned to provide comfort and support to her father, gave advice to her brother, offered domestic help to both of them, and acted as a secretary and confidant to her father. These are not the letters of a woman who was content or satisfied with her enclosed world. As the letters reveal, Sister Maria Celeste wished to perform all of the expected duties of a dutiful daughter, albeit behind the convent's wall. Her letters also allow us to enter into the cloistered world of the Convent of San Matteo and learn of its routines, habits, rules, quality of life, and politics.

The Convent of San Matteo in Arcetri was part of the Order of the Poor Sisters, which was founded by Saint Clare of Assisi in the thirteenth century. The Poor Clares, as they were called, vowed to live a life of poverty, charity, and humility, and to devote themselves to prayer, nursing the sick, and works of mercy for the poor and neglected. The rules of the order called upon each sister and the collective group to live a life of extreme austerity and of absolute poverty. These rules symbolized the sisters' willingness to share the life of the poor through manual labor and their imitation of the poor's total dependence on others by only accepting alms for their support.

Chapter 14
The Scientific
Revolution:
Galileo Galilei
(1564–1642) and
Sister Maria
Celeste (née
Virginia Galilei,
1600–1634)

This was the most austere and severe of all the female orders.

Life as a Poor Clare had improved over the centuries. Originally the sisters slept on twigs with patched hemp for blankets. They ate little, and no meat at all. Whatever food they had was obtained by begging. By the seventeenth century, the spiritual standards of the order had changed and the abject poverty associated with the Poor Clares had lessened. The sisters now slept in beds in a large dormitory. There were a few private cells available to those sisters whose families paid an additional price beyond the dowry. The adornment of the room depended again on familial support. Some rooms sported heavy bed-curtains and door hangings, important for shutting out the cold air and draft. Early in their residence at the convent, Sister Maria Celeste and Sister Arcangela shared a small cell with another sister. When this sister relinquished the cell, Sister Maria Celeste gave it to her sister, who was suffering from ill health. Sister Maria Celeste would not have a room of her own until the last four years of her life. At times, she sought comfort and peace away from the common sleeping quarters by sleeping on the floor of another sister who kindly shared her frigid cell (Document Four).

The sisters ate together, but if they could afford extra provisions, these were allowed and shared by all members of the order. On numerous occasions over the years, Sister Maria Celeste wrote to her father asking for a supply of wine or fresh meat to make broth for herself and others when they fell ill. In keeping with the rules of the order, she distributed these provisions to the other sisters. The sisters spent long hours struggling to support themselves, growing fruits and vegetables in the convent's walled garden. Here they not only grew their own food but much of the garden was dedicated to growing medicinal herbs and plants, which they then sold for extra income. Sister Maria Celeste became the convent's apothecary, creating pills and tonics from the garden's bounty and caring for the convent's sick.[15] The convent also supplemented its meager income by baking, sewing, and embroidery. Sister Maria Celeste used these skills to attend to the needs of her father and brother, often sewing shirts, collars, and bed and table linens for them and sending them confections. She also worked as a scribe for her father as he aged. Galileo's numerous illnesses caused his handwriting to deteriorate, and Sister Maria Celeste began to copy his letters and manuscripts.

Ill health resulting from malnourishment and the cold was common among the sisters of San Matteo. Both of Galileo's daughters are often described in Sister Maria Celeste's letters as being ill or recovering from a recent bout of sickness. Sister Arcangela eventually succumbed to the privation and suffered some type of permanent breakdown. Beginning with the first of the surviving letters, dated October 1623, Sister Maria Celeste wrote letters that often detailed her sister's physical and mental health, her and the convent's need for basic foodstuffs

15. Dava Sobel, *Galileo's Daughter* (New York: Penguin Books, 2000), pp. 112–113 and 151–152.

and supplies, and her melancholy at being physically separated from her father and brother. Absent from the letters are sentiments expressing joy over or satisfaction with life in the convent. She confided in one letter that her fondest dream was not so much to fathom the heavens but to step foot just once inside her father's house. As her father aged, her longing to help him through his sicknesses, infirmities, bouts of loneliness, and intellectual struggles with the church increased. In his last encounter with the Inquisition, which resulted in his confinement at home in Florence, Galileo found great comfort in the attention and love bestowed upon him by his daughter.

In 1632, the most famous and controversial of Galileo's works, *Dialogue on the Two Chief World Systems; Ptolemaic and Copernican,* was published in Florence. Written in Italian, not Latin, to reach as many learned people as possible, the *Dialogue* challenged the authority of the Inquisition, which in 1616 had openly endorsed the Ptolemaic system and condemned the Copernican. In this treatise, Galileo cleverly composed a dialogue between a Ptolemist and two Copernicans. The Ptolemist was utterly confounded and defeated by the superior reasoning and proofs of the Copernicans. Church authorities perceived this work to be a defense of a theory that they had prohibited from scholarly discourse. The church reacted immediately, ordered the publisher of the book to stop selling it, and summoned Galileo to Rome.

Why Galileo was summoned before the Inquisition is a question that scholars have pondered for many years.

Some argue that Galileo's enemies, especially the Jesuits, were taking their revenge. Others argue that it was Galileo's arrogance, ambition, and naïveté. He was not content to leave his ideas in the scholarly realm but sought the church's approval for the Copernican theory. In effect, he wanted the church to reinforce his ideas and overthrow centuries of knowledge; the church was not prepared to yield to the authority of this one scientist and to the new discipline of science.

Galileo did not go to Rome immediately. He was quite ill and asked several times if he could be questioned in Florence or postpone the investigation into his suspected heresy until he was well. The church, flexing its muscle, refused and pressured him to make the trip to Rome and appear in person before the Inquisition. Galileo could have refused and fled to another state where the church's authority was not so influential. Hearing of the Inquistion's summons, the Venetians invited him to return. Galileo politely turned down the invitation and traveled to Rome in February 1633, believing he could defend his ideas before the inquisitors. He left his daughter to monitor his personal and household affairs while he was in Rome.

After spending several weeks at the residence of the Tuscan ambassador to Rome, Galileo was summoned to the Inquisition's building where he was comfortably accommodated until the beginning of the trial. On April 12, 1633, Galileo argued before the Inquisition that he did not hold nor did he teach and defend the Copernican system as fact but had merely presented the Copernican view as one supposition

Chapter 14
The Scientific
Revolution:
Galileo Galilei
(1564–1642) and
Sister Maria
Celeste (née
Virginia Galilei,
1600–1634)

among many. The Inquisition was not interested in the nuance of whether Galileo accepted this view as fact or hypothesis; they wanted to put an end to Galileo's challenges and accused him of not following the Inquisition's instruction, which prohibited the discussion of the Copernican theory. He denied that he had ever received such an instruction. He argued that in 1616 he had only been warned not to teach Copernican theory as fact. The Inquisition probably manufactured the instructions. After his interrogation, Galileo fell ill. Sister Maria Celeste, knowing of her father's frail condition, the fatigue of travel, and the grueling interrogation, wrote to her father detailing the banalities of everyday life at the convent and on his estate to distract him from his trial (Document Five).

The Inquisition, after three interrogations spread over two months, found Galileo guilty of holding heretical opinions that he must denounce to be absolved (Document Six). On June 22, 1633, Galileo stood before the ten cardinals of the Holy Office and abjured (Document Seven). Galileo was then sentenced to life imprisonment in Rome. His sympathizers had the sentence softened, and he was eventually allowed to return to his home in Florence to serve his sentence. Not only would Galileo be prevented from ever again appearing publically, but the Inquistion banned all of Galileo's works, published and unpublished.

His daughter was surprised when she learned of the outcome of the trial. She wrote on July 2, 1633, "... what I hear from him [Signor Geri] of the resolution they have taken concerning you and your book gives me extreme

pain, not having expected such a result. Dearest lord and father, now is the time for the exercise of that wisdom with which God has endowed you. Thus you will bear these blows with that fortitude of soul which religion, your age, and your profession alike demand."[16] His daughter understood the workings of the Holy Office and when two of her father's loyal supporters appeared at the convent asking her for keys to his villa so that they could get to Galileo's papers before the Inquisition did, she did not hesitate.

By December 1633, Galileo was now living on a farm and in a house next door to his daughters' convent at Arcetri. His imprisonment had begun briefly in Siena, but the pope feared that his presence in Siena would sow heretical ideas and thought it was best to send him home where he was a known quantity. During his confinement in Siena, Sister Maria Celeste encouraged her father to continue his scientific work in mechanics. She wrote, "... tell me what subject you are writing about at present: Provided it is something that I could understand, and you have no fear that I might gossip."[17] Galileo was composing the last of his scientific treatises, *Two New Sciences*, which was published in 1638 by a distinguished Dutch publishing firm. The Inquisition had prohibited the printing or reprinting of any of Galileo's works, and the manuscript had to be smuggled out of Tuscany. When the Holy Office heard that the book was published, however, they turned a blind

16. *The Private Life of Galileo Galilei*, p. 263.
17. Sobel, p. 333.

eye to this violation of the terms of his confinement.

Sister Maria Celeste rejoiced at her father's return to Arcetri and for several months, until her death in April 1634, they shared the same neighborhood. Galileo could not receive visitors who might engage him in scientific discussions and he could leave his property only to visit the convent. She could receive visitors only in a parlor where guests were received. However, Galileo was more than a guest. He kept the convent's clock in repair, gave advice on pruning and grafting fruit trees, and provided small carpentry services. The companionship of his daughter, her intelligence and interest in his physical and intellectual well-being, and his continued thinking and writing appear at first to have lessened the impact of Galileo's imprisonment, but to him it was still a prison. He began each letter with the phrase, "From my prison in Arcetri." His imprisonment was made all the worse when his eldest daughter died a few months after his return. In a letter to a friend shortly after Sister Maria Celeste's death, he wrote, "Here I lived on very quietly, frequently paying visits to the neighboring convent, where I had two daughters, both nuns, whom I loved dearly: but the eldest in particular, who was a woman of exquisite mind, singular goodness and most tenderly attached to me."[18]

✳ FINALE

Sister Maria Celeste's death came at the age of thirty-three after years of malnourishment, inadequate living conditions, hard work as a Poor Clare, and numerous illnesses. Her father would die eight years later at the age of seventy-seven after years of plenty; comfortable and pleasurable domestic arrangements; lively, exhilarating, and challenging scientific work and study; and occasional skirmishes with religious and scholarly authorities. Historically, Galileo and not his daughter has been portrayed as the one hindered and restrained by the religious practices and prescriptions of the day. The Inquisition did in fact condemn Galileo and his work, stifling not only the last work of his life, *Two New Sciences*, but in effect intimidating others in Italy and elsewhere and preventing them from challenging sacred intellectual and philosophical traditions. In the seventeenth century, the Catholic Church wished to regain control over access to knowledge, and it was willing to vanquish one of the great scientific minds of its day in this pursuit.

Galileo's hubris did not include forsaking Catholicism. He often described his own ideas as "divinely inspired" and discredited his opponents as "contrary to Scripture." He had close collaborative scientific relations as well as close friendships with leading clerics and benefitted on occasion from papal patronage. Until his sentence, Galileo believed that an enlightened papacy could be an effective instrument of

18. *The Private Life of Galileo*, p. 271.

Chapter 14
The Scientific
Revolution:
Galileo Galilei
(1564–1642) and
Sister Maria
Celeste (née
Virginia Galilei,
1600–1634)

scientific progress. Galileo benefitted from this religious world and its world view. The Catholic Church and its clerical culture, ascetic and male-centered, created a learned world where intellectual activity and scholarly pursuit were separate from the mundane and burdensome responsibilities of everyday life. Secular institutions such as the Academy of the Lincei and universities embraced this tradition of separatism and encouraged celibacy among its members. Women were something to shed as men became scholars, essentially creating an intellectual and scholarly space that excluded women.[19]

"This world without women" meant that Galileo could justify the claustration of his daughters, not only because of the circumstance of their birth or because of the burden of the dowry, but because his chosen profession excluded the presence of women. There were a few notable women who did venture into the learned professions, like Elena Lucrezia Cornaro Piscopia (1646–1684), who was the first European woman to receive a doctorate at the University of Padua in 1678, but their success depended on familial support and scholarly climate. It is not at all surprising that Piscopia's doctorate in philosophy was obtained at the most liberal of all Italian universities, the University of Padua.

Despite the opportunities that the University of Padua and his family had given him, Galileo did not extend to his daughters the same opportunities that he and Piscopia enjoyed. Using his prerogative as a father, he gave his daughters one choice. They entered the convent on his order, and in Sister Maria Celeste's letters, we see a woman who was not content with her life circumstances. The convent for her was not a safe haven, a place where women thrived as intellectuals and freethinking persons. The Convent of San Matteo was a place of deprivation of food, family, and friends; of petty indignities; and of countless hours spent contemplating the world outside. Both Galileo and his daughter lived lives that were bound by their class position, religion, intellectual abilities, and gender. If all these positions were equal, they would have lived similar lives. The "woman of exquisite mind," as Sister Maria Celeste's father described her, was prevented from participating in the world, not because of the illegitimacy of her birth or because of her class position or intellectual abilities, but because she was a woman.

✦ QUESTIONS

1. What type of education did Galileo receive? Why were the ancient Greeks and their medieval interpreters touted as the intellectual authorities of the day?

19. Noble, p. 215.

2. What were the necessary preconditions for questioning the church's monopoly over learning? Why did Galileo question ancient and medieval learned authorities?

3. Describe Galileo's relationship with his children. What choices did his son and his daughters have

for their own lives? Why did they differ?

4. Why was Galileo's exploration of the stars and heavens threatening to the Roman Catholic Church? Was Galileo anti-Catholic? Why or why not?

5. Were education, scientific inquiry, and learned communities open to all based on merit? Why or why not?

6. Why did the Inquisition put Galileo on trial? What were his sins?

7. What role did women play during the centuries of the Scientific Revolution? What were some of the obstacles to their participation?

⭐ DOCUMENTS

DOCUMENT ONE

GALILEO GALILEI

The Starry Messenger
(1610)

Galileo turned the telescope to the heavens and revealed to Europeans for the first time hundreds of stars and natural phenomena. In the following excerpts, Galileo described his observation of the moon and his discovery of the four moons orbiting Jupiter. What does Galileo use for his scientific inquiries of the heavens?

But forsaking terrestrial observations, I turned to celestial ones, and first I saw the moon from as near at hand as if it were scarcely two terrestrial radii [a measure of distance, obscure today] away. After that I observed often with wondering delight both the planets and the fixed stars, and since I saw these latter to be very crowded, I began to seek (and eventually found) a method by which I might measure their distances apart. . . .

Now let us review the observations made during the past two months, once more inviting the attention of all who are eager for true philosophy to the first steps of such important contemplations. Let us speak first of that surface of the moon which faces us. For greater clarity I distinguish two parts of this surface, a lighter and a darker; the lighter part seems to surround and to pervade the whole hemisphere, while the darker part discolors the moon's surface like a kind of cloud, and makes it appear covered with spots. Now those spots which are fairly dark and rather large are plain to everyone and have been seen throughout the ages; these I shall call the "large" or "ancient" spots, distinguishing them from others that are smaller in size but so numerous as to occur all over the lunar surface, and especially the lighter part. The latter spots had never been seen by anyone before me. From observations of these spots repeated many times I have been led to the opinion and conviction that the surface of the moon is not smooth, uniform, and precisely spherical as a great number of philosophers believe it (and the other heavenly bodies) to be, but is uneven, rough, and full of cavities and prominences, being not unlike the face of the earth, relieved by chains of mountains and deep valleys. . . .

[MOONS ORBITING JUPITER]

On the seventh day of January in this present year 1610, at the first hour of night, when I was viewing the heavenly bodies with a telescope, Jupiter presented itself to me; and because I had prepared a very excellent instrument for myself, I perceived (as I had not before, on account of the weakness of my previous instrument) that beside the planet there were three starlets, small indeed, but very bright. Though I believed them to be among the host of fixed stars, they aroused my curiosity somewhat by appearing to lie in an exact straight line parallel to the ecliptic, and by their being more splendid than others of their size. Their arrangement with respect to Jupiter and each other was the following:

East   ✳   ✳   O   ✳   *West*

that is, there were two stars on the eastern side and one to the west. The most easterly star and the western one appeared larger than the other. I paid no attention to the distances between them and Jupiter, for at the outset I thought them to be fixed stars, as I have said. But returning to the same investigation on January eighth — led by what, I do not know — I found a very different arrangement. The three starlets were now all to the west of Jupiter, closer together, and at equal intervals from one another as shown in the following sketch:

East   O   ✳   ✳   ✳   *West*

On the tenth of January, however, the stars appeared in this position with respect to Jupiter:

East   ✳   ✳   O   *West*

that is, there were but two of them, both easterly, the third (as I supposed) being hidden behind Jupiter. . . . There was no way in which such alterations could be attributed to Jupiter's motion, yet being certain that these were still the same stars I had observed . . . my perplexity was now transformed into amazement. I was sure that the apparent changes belonged not to Jupiter but to the observed stars, and I resolved to pursue this investigation with greater care and attention. . . .

I had now decided beyond all question that there existed in the heavens three stars wandering about Jupiter as do Venus and Mercury about the sun, and this became plainer than daylight from observations on similar occasions which followed. Nor were there just three such stars; four wanderers complete their revolutions about Jupiter. . . .

Here we have a fine and elegant argument for quieting the doubts of those who, while accepting with tranquil mind the revolutions of the planets about the sun in the Copernican system, are mightily disturbed to have the moon alone revolve about the earth and accompany it in an annual rotation about the sun. Some have believed that this structure of the universe should be rejected as impossible. But now we have not just one planet rotating about another while both run through a great orbit around the sun; our own eyes show us four stars which wander around Jupiter as does the moon around the earth, while all together trace out a grand revolution about the sun in the space of twelve years.

DOCUMENT TWO

Giovanni Francesco Sagredo

Letter to Galileo on Intellectual Freedom
(1610)

Sagredo, a young Venetian nobleman and friend of Galileo, tried to convince Galileo to remain in the Venetian Republic where his intellectual pursuits would be protected by the republic's tradition of freedom and its ability to keep the Inquisition at bay. He warns Galileo to be careful at Cosimo II's court. What are the potential trouble spots for Galileo in Florence? Of whom must Galileo be wary?

. . . Where will you find freedom and sovereignty of yourself as in Venice? Especially since you had here support and protection, which became more weighty every day as the age and authority of your friends grew. . . . At present you serve your natural Prince, a great, virtuous man of singular promise; but here you had command over those who command and govern others, and you had to serve only yourself. You were as the ruler of the universe. . . . In the tempestuous sea of a court who can be sure not to be . . . belabored and upset by the furious winds of envy? . . . Who knows what the infinite and incomprehensible events of the world may cause if aided by the impostures of evil and envious men . . . who may even turn the justice and goodness of a prince into the ruin of an honest man? I am very much worried by your being in a place where the authority of the friends of the Jesuits counts heavily.

Chapter 14
The Scientific
Revolution:
Galileo Galilei
(1564–1642) and
Sister Maria
Celeste (née
Virginia Galilei,
1600–1634)

DOCUMENT THREE

GALILEO GALILEI

Letter to the Grand Duchess Christina
(1615)

Galileo wrote a lengthy letter to Cosimo II's mother, Christina, arguing that one needed to avoid using Scripture to understand natural phenomena. Why does Galileo object to Scripture as a source for explaining the heavens? How did Copernicus acquire his knowledge of the heavens?

To the Most Serene Ladyship the Grand Duchess Dowager:

As Your Most Serene Highness knows very well, a few years ago I discovered in the heavens many particulars which had been invisible until our time. Because of their novelty, and because of some consequences deriving from them which contradict certain physical propositions commonly accepted in philosophical schools, they roused against me no small number of such professors, as if I had placed these things in heaven with my hands in order to confound nature and the sciences. These people seemed to forget that a multitude of truths contribute to inquiry and to the growth and strength of disciplines rather than to their diminution or destruction, and at the same time they showed greater affection for their own opinions than for the true ones; thus they proceeded to deny and to try to nullify those novelties, about which the senses themselves could have rendered them certain, if they had wanted to look at those novelties carefully. To this end they produced various matters, and they published some writings full of useless discussions and sprinkled with quotations from the Holy Scripture, taken from passages which they do not properly understand and which they inappropriately adduce. . . .

Then it developed that the passage of time disclosed to everyone the truths I had first pointed out, and, along with the truth of the matter, the difference in attitude between those who sincerely and without envy did not accept these discoveries as true and those who added emotional agitation to disbelief. Thus, just as those who were most competent in astronomical and physical science were convinced by my first announcement, so gradually there has been a calming down of all the others whose denials and doubts were not sustained by anything other than the unexpected novelty and the lack of opportunity to see them and to experience them with the senses. However, there are those who are rendered ill-disposed, not so much toward the things as much as toward the author, by the love of their first error and by some interest which they imagine having but which escapes me. Unable to deny them any longer, these people became silent about them; but, embittered more than before by what has mellowed and quieted the others, they divert their thinking to other fictions and try to harm me in other ways.

... These people are aware that in my astronomical and philosophical studies, on the question of the constitution of the world's parts, I hold that the sun is located at the center of the revolutions of the heavenly orbs and does not change place, and that the earth rotates on itself and moves around it. Moreover, they hear how I confirm this view not only by refuting Ptolemy's and Aristotle's arguments, but also by producing many for the other side, especially some pertaining to physical effects whose causes perhaps cannot be determined in any other way, and other astronomical ones dependent on many features of the new celestial discoveries; these discoveries clearly confute the Ptolemaic system, and they agree admirably with this other position and confirm it. Now, these people are perhaps confounded by the known truth of the other propositions different from the ordinary which I hold, and so they may lack confidence to defend themselves as long as they remain in the philosophical field. Therefore, since they persist in their original self-appointed task of beating down me and my findings by every imaginable means, they have decided to try to shield the fallacies of their arguments with the cloak of simulated religiousness and with the authority of Holy Scripture, unintelligently using the latter for the confutation of arguments they neither understand nor have heard.

At first, they tried on their own to spread among common people the idea that such propositions are against Holy Scripture, and consequently damnable and heretical. Then they realized how by and large human nature is more inclined to join those ventures which result in the oppression of other people (even if unjustly) than those which result in their just improvement, and so it was not difficult for them to find someone who with unusual confidence did preach even from the pulpit that it is damnable and heretical; and this was done with little compassion and with little consideration of the injury not only to this doctrine and its followers, but also to mathematics and all mathematicians. Thus, having acquired more confidence, and with the vain hope that the seed which first took root in their insincere mind would grow into a tree and rise toward the sky, they are spreading among the people the rumor that it will shortly be declared heretical by the supreme authority. . . .

[Addressing the Critics of Copernicus's *The Revolution of Heavenly Bodies* (1543)]

... They always shield themselves with a simulated religious zeal, and they also try to involve Holy Scripture and to make it somehow subservient to their insincere objectives; against the intention of Scripture and the Holy Fathers (if I am not mistaken), they want to extend, not to say abuse, its authority, so that even for purely physical conclusions which are not matters of faith one must totally abandon the senses and demonstrative arguments in favor of any scriptural passage whose apparent words may contain a different indication. Here I hope to demonstrate that I proceed with much more pious and religious zeal than they when I propose not that this book should not be condemned, but

Chapter 14
The Scientific
Revolution:
Galileo Galilei
(1564–1642) and
Sister Maria
Celeste (née
Virginia Galilei,
1600–1634)

that it should not be condemned without understanding, examining, or even seeing it, as they would like. This is especially true since the author never treats of matters pertaining to religion and faith, nor uses arguments dependent in any way on the authority of Holy Scripture, in which case he might have interpreted it incorrectly; instead, he always limits himself to physical conclusions pertaining to celestial motions, and he treats of them with astronomical and geometrical demonstrations based above all on sensory experience and very accurate observations. He proceeded in this manner not because he did not pay any attention to the passages of Holy Scripture, but because he understood very well that if his doctrine was demonstrated it could not contradict the properly interpreted Scripture. . . .

[THE BASIS ON WHICH NATURAL PHENOMENA MUST BE ELEVATED]

Therefore, I think that in disputes about natural phenomena one must begin not with the authority of scriptural passages but with sensory experience and necessary demonstrations. For the Holy Scripture and nature derive equally from the Godhead, the former as the dictation of the Holy Spirit and the latter as the most obedient executrix of God's orders; moreover, to accommodate the understanding of the common people it is appropriate for Scripture to say many things that are different (in appearance and in regard to the literal meaning of the words) from the absolute truth; on the other hand, nature is inexorable and immutable, never violates the terms of the laws imposed upon her, and does not care whether or not her recondite reasons and ways of operating are disclosed to human understanding; but not every scriptural assertion is bound to obligations as severe as every natural phenomenon; finally, God reveals Himself to us no less excellently in the effects of nature than in the sacred words of Scripture, as Tertullian perhaps meant when he said, "We postulate that God ought first to be known by nature, and afterward further known by doctrine—by nature through His works, by doctrine through official teaching" (*Against Marcion*, I.18); and so it seems that a natural phenomenon which is placed before our eyes by sensory experience or proved by necessary demonstrations should not be called into question, let alone condemned, on account of scriptural passages whose words appear to have a different meaning.

DOCUMENT FOUR

SISTER MARIA CELESTE

On Life in the Convent
(1623)

In the following excerpts, Sister Maria Celeste describes the cloistered life and her desire to be of assistance to her father and brother. What types of services did Sister Maria Celeste perform for her family beyond the convent's walls?

[ON DOMESTIC MATTERS, OCTOBER 20, 1623]

Most Illustrious and Beloved Lord Father

I send back the rest of your shirts which we have been working at, also the apron, which I have mended as well as I possibly could. I likewise return the letters you sent me to read; they are so beautiful that my desire to see more of them is greatly increased. I cannot begin working at the dinner napkins till you send the pieces to add on. Please bear in mind that the said pieces must be long, owing to the dinner napkins being a trifle short.

I have just placed Sister Arcangela under the doctor's care, to see whether, with the Lord's help, she may be relieved of her troublesome complaint, which gives me great anxiety.

I hear from Salvadore (the servant) that you are coming to see us before very long. We wish to have you very much indeed; but please remember that when you come you must keep your promise of spending the evening with us. You will be able to sup in the parlour, since the excommunication is for the table-cloth, and not for the meats thereon.

I enclose herewith a little composition, which, aside from expressing to you the extent of our need, will also give you the excuse to have a hearty laugh at the expense of my foolish writing; but because I have seen how good-naturedly you always encourage my meager intelligence, Sire, you have lent me the courage to attempt this essay. Indulge me then, Lord Father, and with your usual loving tenderness please help us. I thank you for the fish, and send you loving greetings along with Suor Arcangela. May our Lord grant you complete happiness.

From San Matteo, the 20th day of October 1623.

Most affectionate daughter,

S. M. C.

Chapter 14
The Scientific
Revolution:
Galileo Galilei
(1564–1642) and
Sister Maria
Celeste (née
Virginia Galilei,
1600–1634)

[On a Package Sent to Her by Galileo, October 23, 1623]

Most Illustrious and Beloved Lord Father

If I should begin thanking you in words for the present you have sent us, besides not knowing how to quench our debt with words, I believe that you would not care for them, preferring, as you do, our gratitude, to demonstrative phrases and ceremonies. It will be better, therefore, that in the best way we know of, that is, by praying for you, we endeavour to show our sense of gratitude, and to repay this and all other great benefits which we for such a length of time have received from you.

When I asked for ten *braccia* of stuff, I meant you to get me a narrow width, not this cloth, so wide and fine, and so expensive. This quantity will be more than sufficient for us.

I leave you to imagine how pleased I am to read the letters you constantly send me. Only to see how your love for me prompts you to let me know fully what favours you receive from this gentlemen is enough to fill me with joy. Nevertheless I feel it a little hard to hear that you intend leaving home so soon, because I shall have to do without you, and for a long time too, if I am not mistaken. And your lordship may believe that I am speaking the truth when I say that except you there is not a creature who gives me any comfort. But I will not grieve at your departure because of this, for that would be to complain when you had cause for rejoicing. Therefore I too will rejoice, and continue to pray God to give you grace and health to make a prosperous journey, so that you may return satisfied, and live long and happily; all which I trust will come to pass by God's help.

Though I know it is not necessary for me to do so, yet I recommend our poor brother to your kindness; and I entreat you to forgive him his fault in consideration of his youth, and which, seeing it is the first, merits pardon. I do beg and entreat you to take him to Rome with you, where opportunities will not be wanting to give him that assistance which paternal duty and your natural kindness will prompt you to seek out.

But fearing that you will find me tiresome, I forebear to write more, though I can never cease to recommend him to your favour. And please to remember that you have been owing us a visit for a very long time.

From San Matteo, the 23rd day of October 1623.

Most affectionate daughter,

S. M. C.

[Sister Marie Celeste Reports to Her Father About a New Set of Dinner Napkins She is Making and About the Health of Her Sister, Sister Arcangela, November 21, 1623]

Most Illustrious and Beloved Lord Father

I cannot rest any longer without news, . . . both for the infinite love I bear you, and also for fear lest this sudden cold, which in general disagrees so much with you, should have caused a return of your usual pains and other complaints. I therefore send the man who takes this letter purposely to hear how you are, and also when you expect to set out on your journey. I have been extremely busy at the dinner-napkins. They are nearly finished, but now I come to putting on the fringe, I find that of the sort I send as a pattern, a piece is wanting for two dinner-napkins: that will be four *braccia*. I should be glad if you could let me have it immediately, so that I may send you the napkins before you go; as it was for this that I have been making such haste to get them finished.

As I have no sleeping-room of my own, Sister Diamanta kindly allows me to share hers, depriving herself of the company of her own sister for my sake. But the room is so bitterly cold, that with my head in the state in which it is at present, I do not know how I shall remain, unless you can help me by lending me a set of those white bed-hangings which you will not want now. I should be glad to know if you could do me this service. Moreover, I beg you to be so kind as to send me that book of yours which has just been published, *Il Saggiatore*, so that I may read it, for I have a great desire to see it.

These few cakes I send are some I made a few days ago, intending to give them to you when you came to bid us adieu. As your departure is not so near as we feared, I send them lest they should get dry. Sister Arcangela is still under medical treatment, and is much tried by the remedies. I am not well myself, but being so accustomed to ill health, I do not make much of it, seeing, too, that it is the Lord's will to send me continually some such little trial as this. I thank Him for everything, and pray that He will give you the highest and best felicity.

P.S. You can send us any collars that want getting up.

From San Matteo, the 21st of November 1623.

Most affectionate daughter,

S. M. C.

Chapter 14
The Scientific
Revolution:
Galileo Galilei
(1564–1642) and
Sister Maria
Celeste (née
Virginia Galilei,
1600–1634)

━━━━━━━ **DOCUMENT FIVE** ━━━━━━━

Sᴉꜱᴛᴇʀ Mᴀʀɪᴀ Cᴇʟᴇꜱᴛᴇ

Taking Care of Business
(1633)

During Galileo's trial, Sister Maria Celeste wrote to her father often. He claimed that her letters were a great comfort to him while the trial dragged on and his health deteriorated. What duties did this most dutiful daughter perform for her father while he was in Rome?

Most Illustrious and Beloved Lord Father

Your letter written on the 10th of February was delivered to me on the 22nd of the same month, and by now I assume you must have received another letter of mine, Sire, along with one from our Father Confessor, and through these you will have learned some of the details you wanted to know; and seeing that still no letters have come giving us definite news of your arrival in Rome (and you can imagine, Sire, with what eagerness I in particular anticipate those letters), I return to write to you again, so that you may know how anxiously I live, while awaiting word from you, and also to send you the enclosed legal notice, which was delivered to your house, 4 or 5 days ago, by a young man, and accepted by Signor Francesco Rondinelli, who, in giving it to me, advised me that it must be paid, without waiting for some more offensive insult from the creditor, telling me that one could not disobey such an order in any manner, and offering to handle the matter himself. This morning I gave him the 6 scudi, which he did not want to pay to Vincenzio but chose to deposit the money with the magistrate until you have told him, Sire, what you want him to do. Signor Francesco is indeed a most pleasant and discreet person, and he never stops declaiming his gratefulness to you, Sire, for allowing him the use of your house. I heard from La Piera that he treats her and Giuseppe with great kindness, even in regard to their food; and I provide for the rest of their needs, Sire, according to your directions. The boy tells me that this Easter he will need shoes and stockings, which I plan to knit for him out of thick, coarse cotton or else from fine wool. La Piera maintains that you have often spoken to her about ordering a bale of linen, on which account I refrained from buying the small amount I would need to begin weaving the thick cloth for your kitchen, as I had meant to do, Sire, and I will not make the purchase unless I hear otherwise from you.

The vines in the garden will take nicely now that the Moon is right, at the hands of Giuseppe's father, who they say is capable enough, and also Signor Rondinelli will lend his help. The lettuce I hear is quite lovely, and I have entrusted Giuseppe to take it to be sold at market before it spoils.

From the sale of 70 bitter oranges came 4 lire, a very respectable price, from what I understand, as that fruit has few uses: Portuguese oranges are selling for 14 crazie per 100 and you had 200 that were sold. As for that barrel of newly-tapped wine you left, Sire, Signor Rondinelli takes a little for himself every evening, and meanwhile he makes improvements to the wine, which he says is coming along extremely well. What little of the old wine that was left I had decanted into flasks, and told LaPiera that she and Giuseppe could drink it when they had finished their small cask, since we of late have had reasonably good wine from the convent, and, being in good health, have hardly taken a drop. I continue to give one giulio every Saturday to La Brigida, and I truly consider this an act of charity well deserved, as she is so exceedingly needy and such a very good girl.

Suor Luisa, God bless her, fares somewhat better, and is still purging, and having understood from your last letter, Sire, how concerned you were over her illness out of your regard for her, she thanks you with all her heart; and while you declare yourself united with me in loving her, Sire, she on the other hand claims to be the paragon of this emotion, nor do I mind granting her that honor, since her affection stems from the same source as yours, and it is myself; wherefore I take pride in and prize this most delicious contest of love, and the more clearly I perceive the greatness of that love you both bear me, the more bountiful it grows for being mutually exchanged between the very two persons I love and revere above everyone and everything in this life.

Tomorrow will be 13 days since the death of our Suor Virginia Canigiani, who was already gravely ill when I last wrote to you, Sire, and since then a malevolent fever has stricken Suor Maria Grazia del Pace, the eldest of the three nuns who play the organ, and teacher of the Squarcialupi codex, a truly tranquil and good nun; and since the doctor has already given her up for dead, we are all beside ourselves, grieving over our loss. This is everything I need to tell you for the moment, and as soon as I receive your letters (which must surely have arrived at Pisa by now where the Bocchineri gentlemen are) I will write again. Meanwhile I send you the greetings of my heart together with our usual friends, and particularly Suor Arcangela, Signor Rondinelli and Doctor Ronconi, who begs me for news of you every time he comes here. May the Lord God bless you and keep you happy always.

*From San Matteo, the 26th day of February 1633.**

Most affectionate daughter,

S. M. Celeste Galilei

Signor Rondinelli, having this very moment returned from Florence, tells me he spoke to the Chancellor of the Advisors and learned that the 6 scudi must be paid to Vincenzio Landucci and not be deposited, and this will be done . . .

*On the Florentine calendar, the new year started on 25 March.

Chapter 14
The Scientific
Revolution:
Galileo Galilei
(1564–1642) and
Sister Maria
Celeste (née
Virginia Galilei,
1600–1634)

━━━━━━━━━━━━━━ **DOCUMENT SIX** ━━━━━━━━━━━━━━

Inquisitors General

The Sentence of Galileo
(1633)

Galileo's trial and sentence was a dramatic moment in intellectual history. What
were the crimes and sins committed in the eyes of the Holy Inquisition? What was
his original sentence? Did Sagredo's predictions come true (Document Two)?

. . . We say, pronounce, sentence, and declare that you, the above-mentioned
Galileo, because of the things deduced in the trial and confessed by you as above,
have rendered yourself according to this Holy Office vehemently suspected of
heresy, namely of having held and believed a doctrine which is false and contrary to the divine and Holy Scripture: that the sun is the center of the world
and does not move from east to west, and the earth moves and is not the center
of the world, and that one may hold and defend as probable an opinion after it
has been declared and defined contrary to Holy Scripture. Consequently you
have incurred all the censures and penalties imposed and promulgated by the
sacred canons and all particular and general laws against such delinquents. We
are willing to absolve you from them provided that first, with a sincere heart and
unfeigned faith, in front of us you abjure, curse, and detest the above-mentioned
errors and heresies, and every other error and heresy contrary to the Catholic
and Apostolic Church, in the manner and form we will prescribe to you.

Furthermore, so that this serious and pernicious error and transgression of
yours does not remain completely unpunished, and so that you will be more
cautious in the future and an example for others to abstain from similar crimes,
we order that the book *Dialogue* by Galileo Galilei be prohibited by public edict.

We condemn you to formal imprisonment in the Holy Office at our pleasure. As
a salutary penance we impose on you to recite the seven penitential Psalms once a
week for the next three years. And we reserve the authority to moderate, change,
or condone wholly or in part the above-mentioned penalties and penances.

This we say, pronounce, sentence, declare, order, and reserve by this of any
other better manner or form that we reasonably can or shall think of.

So we the undersigned Cardinals pronounce:

Felice Cardinal d'Ascoli.
Guido Cardinal Bentivoglio.
Fra Desiderio Cardinal di Cremona.
Fra Antonio Cardinal di Sant'Onofrio.
Berlinghiero Cardinal Gessi.
Fabrizio Cardinal Verospi.
Marzio Cardinal Ginetti.

DOCUMENT SEVEN

GALILEO GALILEI

Recantation
(1633)

What did Galileo confess to believing? Why did he recant?

Galileo's Abjuration (22 June 1633)

I, Galileo, son of the late Vincenzio Galilei of Florence, seventy years of age, arraigned personally for judgment, kneeling before you Most Eminent and Most Reverend Cardinals Inquisitors-General against heretical depravity in all of Christendom, having before my eyes and touching with my hands the Holy Gospels, swear that I have always believed, I believe now, and with God's help I will believe in the future all that the Holy Catholic and Apostolic Church holds, preaches, and teaches. However, whereas, after having been judicially instructed with injunction by the Holy Office to abandon completely the false opinion that the sun is the center of the world and does not move and the earth is not the center of the world and moves, and not to hold, defend, or teach this false doctrine in any way whatever, orally or in writing; and after having been notified that this doctrine is contrary to Holy Scripture; I wrote and published a book in which I treat of this already condemned doctrine and adduce very effective reasons in its favor, without refuting them in any way; therefore, I have been judged vehemently suspected of heresy, namely of having held and believed that the sun is the center of the world and motionless and the earth is not the center and moves.

Therefore, desiring to remove from the minds of Your Eminences and every faithful Christian this vehement suspicion, rightly conceived against me, with a sincere heart and unfeigned faith I abjure, curse, and detest the above-mentioned errors and heresies, and in general each and every other error, heresy, and sect contrary to the Holy Church; and I swear that in the future I will never again say or assert, orally or in writing, anything which might cause a similar suspicion about me; on the contrary, if I should come to know any heretic or anyone suspected of heresy, I will denounce him to this Holy Office, or to the Inquisitor or Ordinary of the place where I happen to be.

Furthermore, I swear and promise to comply with and observe completely all the penances which have been or will be imposed upon me by this Holy Office; and should I fail to keep any of these promises and oaths, which God forbid, I submit myself to all the penalties and punishments imposed and promulgated by the sacred canons and other particular and general laws

Chapter 14
The Scientific
Revolution:
Galileo Galilei
(1564–1642) and
Sister Maria
Celeste (née
Virginia Galilei,
1600–1634)

against similar delinquents. So help me God and these Holy Gospels of His, which I touch with my hands.

I, the above-mentioned Galileo Galilei, have abjured, sworn, promised, and obliged myself as above; and in witness of the truth I have signed with my own hand the present document of abjuration and have recited it word for word in Rome, at the convent of the Minerva, this twenty-second day of June 1633.

I, Galileo Galilei, have abjured as above, by my own hand.

INDEX

New Kingdom (Egypt), 4; social transformations under, 9; "Exhortations and Warnings to Schoolboys" from, 16–17
New World: Columbus in, 356
Nicaea: Council of, 127, 187
Nicene Creed (Council of Nicaea, 325), 199; document, 200
Nicetas (chronicler), 219
Nicholas V (Pope): Alberti and, 320
Nika revolt (Byzantine Empire, 532), 192
Ninety-five Theses (Luther), 380
Nobility: in Rome, 95; in Middle Ages, 223; in Florence, 312. *See also* Aristocrats; Elites
Nogarola, Isotta, 311; background, 314–315; education of, 315; correspondence of, 317–318, 319–320, 321–322; lifestyle of, 321; "Of the Equal or Unequal Sin of Adam and Eve" (ca. 1453), 322, 336–339; women's roles and, 323, 324; "Greetings to the most noble and most eloquent virgin Isotta Nogarola" (Quirini, 1442), 335–336
Nogarola family, 314; Ginevra, 315, 319; Antonio, 319; Ludovico, 321. *See also* Nogarola, Isotta
Nominalists: Abelard and, 252
Normandy, 212; Matilda and, 217; women in, 222; Henry II (England) and, 225. *See also* Henry II (England)
Norms: in Roman Republic, 59
Notre Dame cathedral school, 255; Abelard at, 253
Novels (Justinian), 194, 195, 196; document, 208–210
Nubia: Egypt and, 15

Nuns: von Bora as, 377–378; from Marienthron convent, 382, 383; marriage by, 384. *See also* Convents; Monks and monasticism; "Papal Decree," *Periculoso*, 294–295; *see* specific individuals

Octavia (sister of Augustus), 91, 92, 99, 100
Octavius, Gaius, *see* Augustus (Gaius Octavius)
Odes, Book 3 (Horace): document, 111–112
Odoacer: in Rome, 182
Officials: Justinian laws and, 195–196; Henry II's representatives, 226; of Isabel and Ferdinand, 349
"Of the Equal or Unequal Sin of Adam and Eve" (Nogarola, ca. 1453), 322; document, 336–339
Oikos, *see* Household
Oligarchies: in Florence and Venice, 311–312
Olympias, 131
"On Life in the Convent" (Celeste, Maria, 1623): document, 427–429
On Motion (Galileo), 406
On Painting (Alberti), 317
On the Art of Building (Alberti), 320
"On the Councils and the Church" (Luther, 1539): document, 400–401
"On the Family" (Alberti, 1440–1441), 316–317; document, 331–334
On the Freedom of a Christian (Luther), 381
"On the Taught Classical Authors, *Metalogicon*" (John of Salisbury, 1159): document, 265–266
On the Unity and Trinity of God (Abelard), 259
"On Wifely Duties" (Barbaro, after 1414), 314; document, 326–329
Opimius (Rome), 69

Oppian Law (Rome): "Account of Marcus Porcius Cato's Speech in the Debate over Repeal of the Oppian Law" (*History of Rome*, Livy, 195 B.C.E.), 72–74
Order of the Paraclete: Héloïse and, 261, 262–263
Order of the Poor Sisters, *see* Poor Clares
Origen, 135, 136
Orthodox Christianity: Chalcedonian Christianity as, 187, 188; differences in, 194
Osiris (god), 8
Ostracism: Aspasia and, 34; of Pericles' family, 34; of Ephialtes, 36
Ostrogoths, 159, 182; Arianism of, 162; Theodoric the Great and, 164
Ottoman Turks: Spain and, 350
Ovid, 97; Livia and, 100; William IX of Aquitaine and, 223

Pachomius: religious community of, 133; translation of writings of, 135
Padua, 311; Galileo in, 406, 408; women at university of, 420
Pagans, 159; in Rome, 126
Pallake (partner, concubine): in classical Athens, 29, 35
Panathenaia: in Athens, 40
Papacy, 279; schism with Eastern Roman Empire, 186; Gregory XI and, 287–288, 290; secular rulers and, 290; Florence and, 291; Galileo on, 419–420
Papal authority, 279–280, 292; denial of, 280; challenges to, 380–381
Papal bull: *Unam sanctum* (Boniface VIII), 279–280; on Aragonese Inquisition (April 18, 1482), 369. *See also* Sixtus IV (Pope)

CREDITS

CHAPTER 1   Page 3: *(Left)* Sphinx of Pharoah Hatshepsut, one of a pair from her funerary temple at Deir El Bahari, 18th Dynasty 1473-1458 B.C. Photograph from The Art Archive/Egyptian Museum, Cairo/Dagli Orti (A), Ref. AA326331. *(Right)* Bust of Tuthmosis III, Deir El Bahari. Photograph © John P. Stephens/Ancient Art and Architecture Collection Ltd. **Document 1, page 16:** From Adolf Erman, *The Ancient Egyptians: A Sourcebook of their Writings,* translated by A.M Blackman with an introduction by William Kelly Simpson (New York: Harper Torchbooks, 1966), pp. 196–197. © William Kelly Simpson. **Document 2, page 18:** Excerpt from *The Egyptian Book of the Dead: The Book of Going Forth By Day,* translated by Raymond O. Faulkner, with additional translations and commentary by Dr. Ogden Goelete. Chronicle Books, San Francisco. Copyright © 1998. Reprinted by permission of Specialty Book Marketing, Inc. **Document 3, page 20:** From Adolf Erman, *The Ancient Egyptians: A Sourcebook of their Writings,* translated by A.M Blackman with an introduction by William Kelly Simpson (New York: Harper Torchbooks, 1966), pp. 235, 236, 239, 240. © William Kelly Simpson. **Document 4, page 22:** From James Henry Breasted, *Ancient Records of Egypt: Historical Documents*, Volume II, The Eighteenth Dynasty (The University of Chicago Press, 1906), pp. 80, 81, 84, 89, 91, 97. **Document 5, page 24:** From James Henry Breasted, *Ancient Records of Egypt: Historical Documents*, Volume II, The Eighteenth Dynasty (The University of Chicago Press, 1906), pp. 131–132. **Document 6, page 25:** From James Henry Breasted, *Ancient Records of Egypt: Historical Documents,* Volume II, The Eighteenth Dynasty (The University of Chicago Press, 1906), pp. 146–147. **Document 7, page 26:** From James Henry Breasted, *Ancient Records of Egypt: Historical Documents*, Volume II, The Eighteenth Dynasty (The University of Chicago Press, 1906), pp. 186, 187, 188.

CHAPTER 2   Page 28: *(Left)* Roman marble copy of a Greek work from the 5th Century B.C./photograph from The Granger Collection. *(Right)* Bust, 460 B.C., in the Louvre, Paris; photograph by R. Sheridan/Art and Architecture Collection Ltd. **Document 1, page 43:** From *Aristotle's Politics*, Books I, III, IV, The Text of Bekker, with an English translation by W.E. Bolland (London: Longmans, Green and Co., 1877), pp. 108–109, 115, 147, 150–151. **Document 2, page 44:** Reprinted by permission of the publishers and the Trustees of the Loeb Classical Library Vol. III, LCL #65, translated by Bernadotte Perrin, Cambridge, Mass.: Harvard University Press, 1916. The Loeb Classical Library is a registered trademark of the President and Fellows of Harvard College. **Document 3, page 45:** From *The Greek Historians* by M.I. Finley, copyright © 1959 by The Viking Press, Inc., renewed © 1987 by Charles Richard Whittaker. Used by permission of Viking Penguin, a division of Penguin Putnam Inc. **Document 4, page 47:** Reprinted by permission of the publishers and the Trustees of the Loeb Classical Library Vol. III, LCL #65, translated by Bernadotte Perrin, Cambridge, Mass.: Harvard University Press, 1916. The Loeb Classical Library is a registered trademark of the President and Fellows of Harvard College. **Document 5, page 48:** From *The Dialogues of Plato,* 4th edition translated by B. Jowett, pp. 776–788. Copyright 1953. Reprinted by permission of Oxford University Press, UK. **Document 6, page 50:** Excerpt from *Archaic Times to the End of the Peloponnesian War* edited by Charles W. Fornara, p. 131. Reprinted with the permission of Cambridge University Press. **Document 7, page 50:** Reprinted by permission of the publishers and the Trustees of the Loeb Classical Library Vol. III, LCL #65, translated by Bernadotte Perrin, Cambridge, Mass.: Harvard University Press, 1916. The Loeb Classical Library is a registered trademark of the President and Fellows of Harvard College. **Document 9, page 53:** From *History of the Peloponnesian War* by Thucydides, translated by Benjamin Jowett, pp. 143–145 (Amherst, NY: Prometheus Books), published 1998. Reprinted with permission of the publisher.

CHAPTER 3   Page 55: *Cornelia, Mother of the Gracchi*, 1855–1861 by Pierre-Jules Cavelier (1814-1894), in the Musée d'Orsay, Paris; photograph copyright Scala/Art Resource, NY. **Document 1, page 72:** Lefkowitz, Mary R., and Maureen B. Fant, eds. *Women's Life in Greece and Rome: A Source Book in Translation*, pp. 143–145. Copyright © 1992. Reprinted with permission of The Johns Hopkins University Press. **Document 3, page 75:** Reprinted by permission of the Publishers and the Trustees of the Loeb Classical Library from *Plutarch* Vol. X, LCL #102, translated by Bernadotte Perrin, Cambridge, Mass.: Harvard University Press, 1921. The Loeb Classical Library is a registered trademark of the President and Fellows of Harvard College. **Document 4, page 77:** Reprinted by permission of the Publishers and the Trustees of the Loeb Classical Library from *Plutarch* Vol. X, LCL #102, translated by Bernadotte Perrin, Cambridge, Mass.: Harvard University Press, 1921. The Loeb Classical Library is a registered trademark of the President and Fellows of Harvard College. **Document 5, page 78:** Reprinted by permission of the Publishers and the Trustees of the Loeb Classical Library from *Livy* Vol. XIV, LCL #404, translated by T.E. Page, Cambridge, Mass.: Harvard University Press, 1959. The Loeb Classical Library is a registered trademark of the President and Fellows of Harvard College. **Document 5, page 79:** Reprinted by permission of the publishers and the Trustees of the Loeb Classical Library from *Appian* Volume III, Loeb Classical Library Volume L 4, translated by Horace White, Cambridge, Mass.: Harvard University Press, 1913. The Loeb Classical Library is a registered trademark of the President and Fellows of Harvard College. **Document 6, page 81:** Reprinted by permission of the Publishers and the Trustees of the Loeb Classical Library from *Plutarch* Vol. X, LCL #102, translated by Bernadotte Perrin, Cambridge, Mass.: Harvard University Press, 1921. The Loeb Classical Library is a registered trademark of the President and Fellows of Harvard College. **Document 7, page 83:** Excerpt from *The Gracchi*, translated by David Stockton, pp. 183–184. Copyright © 1979. Reprinted by permission of Oxford University Press, UK. **Document 8, page 84:** From *The Woman and the Lyre: Women Writers of Classical Greece and Rome*, by Jane McIntosh Snyder. Copyright © 1989 by the Board of Trustees, Southern Illinois University. Reprinted by permission of the publisher. **Document 9, page 85:** Reprinted by permission of the Publishers and the Trustees of the Loeb Classical Library from *Plutarch* Vol. X, LCL #102, translated by Bernadotte Perrin, Cambridge, Mass.: Harvard University Press, 1921. The Loeb Classical Library is a registered trademark of the President and Fellows of Harvard College.

CHAPTER 4   Page 87: *(Left)* Antique bust of Roman date/photograph from The Granger Collection. *(Right)* Roman bust, from the Glypotek Museum, Copenhagen; photograph by G.T. Garvey/Ancient Art and Architecture Collection, Ltd. **Document 1, page 102:** From *Dio's Roman History*, translated by Earnest Cary (New York, G.P. Putnam's Sons, 1916), pp. 407, 409, 411. **Document 2, page 104:** Excerpts from Suetonius, *The Twelve* Caesars, translated by Robert Graves. Reprinted by permission of Carcanet Press Limited. **Document 4, page 108:** From *The Complete Works of Tacitus*, by Tacitus. Copyright 1942 and renewed 1970 by Random House, Inc. Used by permission of Random House, Inc. **Document 6, page 111:** Excerpt from Horace, *The Odes and Epodes of Horace*, translated by Joseph P. Clancy, p. 129. Reprinted by permission of The University of Chicago Press. **Document 8, page 115:** From *Dio's Roman History*, translated by Earnest Cary (New York, G. P. Putnam's Sons, 1916). **Document 8, page 115:** Excerpts from Suetonius, *The Twelve* Caesars, translated by Robert Graves. Reprinted by permission of Carcanet Press Limited. **Document 8, page 116:** From *The Annals of Imperial Roman*, by Tacitus, translated by Michael Grant (London: Cassel, 1963), p. 39. **Document 8, page 117:** From *The Complete Works of Tacitus*, by Tacitus, translated by copyright 1942 and renewed 1970 by Random House, Inc. Used with permission of Random House, Inc.

CHAPTER 5   Page 121: *(Left) Saint Jerome*, by Fiorenzo di Lorenzo, 15th century/photograph © Arte and Immagini sri/Corbis. *(Right)* Mosaic pavement from Basilica Aquileia, 4th century A.D. Photograph from The Art Archive/Basilica Aquileia, Italy/Dagli Orti (A), Ref. AA325473. **Docu-**

ment 1, page 138: Reprinted by permission of the publishers and the Trustees of the Loeb Classical Library from *St. Jerome: Select Letters*, Loeb Classical Library, Volume L 262, translated by F.A. Wright, Cambridge, Mass.: Harvard University Press, 1933. The Loeb Classical Library is a registered trademark of the President and Fellows of Harvard College. **Document 3, page 142:** From "A Letter from Gregory, Bishop of Nyssa, on the Life of Saint Macrina," (his sister, c. 380), in Petersen, Joan M., trans. and ed., *Handmaids of the Lord: Contemporary Descriptions of Feminine Asceticism in the First Six Christian Centuries* (Kalamazoo, Michigan: Cistercian Publications, Inc., 1996), pp. 54–57. Copyright Cistercian Publications, Inc., 1996. Reprinted by permission. **Document 4, page 145:** From Petersen, Joan M., trans. and ed., *Handmaids of the Lord: Contemporary Descriptions of Feminine Asceticism in the First Six Christian Centuries* (Kalamazoo, Michigan: Cistecian Publications, Inc., 1996), pp. 128–131, 146–149. Copyright Cesterican Publications, Inc., 1996. Reprinted by permission. **Document 5, page 149:** From *The Principal: Works of St. Jerome*, translated by W.H. Fremantle Select Library of Nicene and Post-Nicene Fathers, 2nd series, Volume 6. Reprinted by permission of Wm. B. Eerdman's Publishing Co. **Document 6, page 152:** Excerpts from *Jerome: Chrysostom, and Friends: Essays and Translations* edited by Elizabeth A. Clark, pp. 164–165, 177–179, 220–223, 228–231. Copyright © 1979. Reprinted by permission of The Edwin Mellen Press. **Document 7, page 154:** Reprinted by permission of the publishers and the Trustees of the Loeb Classical Library from *St. Jerome: Select Letters*, Loeb Classical Library, Volume L 262, translated by F.A. Wright, Cambridge, Mass.: Harvard University Press, 1933. The Loeb Classical Library is a registered trademark of the President and Fellows of Harvard College.

CHAPTER 6   Page 157: Detail from an ivory diptych, 9th century/photograph from The Granger Collection. **Document 1, page 170:** From *History of the Franks* by Gregory of Tours, translated by Lewis Thorpe (Penguin, 1974). Copyright © Lewis Thorpe, 1974. Reprinted by permission of Penguin Books Limited. **Document 2, page 171:** From *Christianity and Paganism, 350–750: The Conversion of Western Europe*, edited by J.N. Hillgarth. Copyright © 1986 University of Pennsylvania Press. Reprinted with permission. **Document 3, page 172:** Reprinted by permission of the publishers and the Trustees of the Loeb Classical Library from *Sidonius*, Loeb Classical Library Vol. 1, LCL #296, translated by W.B. Anderson, Cambridge, Mass.: Harvard University Press, 1936. The Loeb Classical Library is a registered trademark of the President and Fellows of Harvard College. **Document 4, page 174:** From *History of the Franks* by Gregory of Tours, translated by Lewis Thorpe (Penguin, 1974). Copyright © Lewis Thorpe, 1974. Reprinted with permission of Penguin Books Limited. **Document 5, page 175:** From *History of the Franks* by Gregory of Tours, translated by Lewis Thorpe (Penguin, 1974). Copyright © Lewis Thorpe, 1974. Reprinted with permission of Penguin Books Limited. **Document 6, page 177:** From *Sainted Women of the Dark Ages* by Jo Ann McNamara and John E. Halborg, Eds. Copyright © 1992 by Duke University Press. All rights reserved. Used with permission of the publisher. **Document 7, page 179:** From *Christianity and Paganism, 350–370: The Conversion of Western Europe* edited by J.N. Hillgarth. Copyright © 1986 University of Pennsylvania Press. Reprinted with permission. **Document 8, page 181:** From *Christianity and Paganism, 350–750: The Conversion of Western Europe* edited by J.N. Hilgarth. Copyright © 1986 University of Pennsylvania Press. Reprinted with permission.

CHAPTER 7   Page 182: *(Left)* Detail from a mid-6th century mosaic in the presbytery of San Vitale, Ravenna, Italy; photograph © Christel Gestenberg/Corbis. *(Right)* Detail from a mid-6th century mosaic in the presbytery of San Vitale, Italy; photograph from The Granger Collection. **Document 1, page 198:** From Procopius, *Secret History*, translated by Richard Atwater. Copyright © 1961. Reprinted by permission of The University of Michigan Press. **Document 2, page 200:** From *The Trinitarian Controversy*, translated and edited by William G. Rusch (Philadelphia: Fortress Press, 1980), p. 49. **Document 2, page 200:** From *The Christological Controversy*, translated and edited by Richard A. Norris (Philadelphia: Fortress Press, 1980): pp. 156–157. **Document 3, page 201:** From Procopius, *Secret History*, translated by Richard Atwater. Copyright © 1961. Reprinted by permission of The University of Michigan Press. **Document 4, page 203:** Reprinted by permission of the publishers and the Trustees of the Loeb Classical Library from *Procopius*, Loeb Classical Library Vol. VII-*On Buildings*, LCL #343, translated by H.B. Dewing, Cambridge, Mass.: Harvard University Press, 1940. The Loeb Classical Library is a registered trademark of the President and Fellows of Harvard College. **Document 5, page 204:** Reprinted by permission of the publishers and the Trustees of the Loeb Classical Library from *Procopius*, Loeb Classical Library Vol. VII—*On Buildings*, LCL #217, translated by H.B. Dewing, Cambringe, Mass.: Harvard University Press, 1928. The Loeb Classical Library is a registered trademark of the President and Fellows of Harvard College. **Document 6, page 206:** Reprinted from Peter Birks and Grant McLeod, *Justinian's Institutes*. Introduction and translation copyright © 1987 by Peter Birks and Grant McLeod. Used by permission of the publisher, Cornell University Press. **Document 7, page 208:** From *The Civil Law*, translated by S.P. Scott, Cincinnati, 1932, Vol. 16, p. 112 from *Readings in Late Antiquity: A Sourcebook* edited by Michael Maas, pp. 231–233. Reprinted by permission of Taylor & Francis.

CHAPTER 8   Page 211: *(Left)* Colored stone tomb effigy, 13th century, Abbey Fontevrault, France; photograph copyright Erich Lessing/Art Resource, NY. *(Right)* Colored stone tomb effigy, 13th century, Abbey Fontevrault, France; photograph copyright Erich Lessing/Art Resource, NY. **Document 1, page 232:** From *The Letters of St. Bernard of Clairvaux*, translated by Bruno Scott James (Chicago: Henry Regnery Company, 1953), pp. 174–177. **Document 2, page 234:** "Eleanor of Antioch, John of Salisbury" from *Historical Pontificalis of John of Salisbury*, edited and translated by Marjorie Chibnall, pp. 52–53. Copyright © Oxford University Press 1956. Reprinted by permission of Oxford University Press. **Document 2, page 234:** Anonymous minstrel from *Recits d'un Menestrel de Reims*, edited by Natalis de Wailly, translated by D.D.R. Owens in *Eleanor of Aquitaine: Queen and Legend*, pp. 105–107. Reprinted by permission of Blackwell Publishing Ltd. **Document 3, page 236:** From Gerald of Wales, "Concerning the Instruction of a Prince" from *English Historical Documents, 1042–1189*, edited by David C. Douglas and George W. Greenaway, pp. 409–412. Reprinted by permission of Routledge, Taylor & Francis Books Ltd. **Document 4, page 238:** From Eleanor of Aquitaine, "Charter of Queen Elizabeth" from *English Historical Documents, 1042–1189*, edited by David C. Douglas and George W. Greenaway, p. 1003. Reprinted by permission of Routledge, Taylor & Francis Books Ltd. **Document 5, page 238:** From *The Art of Courtly Love* by Andreas Cappelanus, translated by John Jay, pp. 168–170. Copyright © 1990 Columbia University Press. Reprinted with the permission of the publisher. **Document 6, page 239:** From Gerald of Wales, "Character of Henry II" from *English Historical Documents, 1042–1189*, edited by David C. Douglas and George W. Greenaway, pp. 415–418. Reprinted by permission of Routledge, Taylor & Francis Books Ltd. **Document 7, page 242:** From Henry II, "Constitutions of Clarendon" from *English Historical Documents, 1042–1189*, edited by David C. Douglas and George W. Greenaway, pp. 415–418. Reprinted by permission of Routledge, Taylor & Francis Books Ltd.

CHAPTER 9   Page 247: From *Roman de la Rose*, an illuminated manuscript, 14th century, in the Musée Conde, Chantilly, France; photograph copyright Giraudon/Art Resource, NY. **Document 1, page 265:** *Ioannis Saresberiensis Episcopi Carnotensis Metalogicon*, ed. C.C.I. Webb, Oxford, 1929, lib. I, cap. 24 (in part); Minge, *Patrologia Latina*, Vol. 199, cols. 854–855 from *University Records and Life in the Middle Ages*, edited by Lynn Thornedike, pp. 7–9. Copyright 1944 by Columbia University Press. Reprinted with the permission of the publisher. **Document 2, page 266:** From *The Letters of Abelard and Heloise*, translated by Betty Radice (Penguin, 1974), pp. 66–69. Copyright © Betty Radice, 1974. Reproduced by permission of Penguin Books Ltd. **Document 3, page 267:** From *The Lost Love Letters of Heloise and Abelard* by Constant J. Mews. Copyright © Mews, Constant J. Reprinted with permission of Palgrave Macmillan. **Document 4, page 268:** From *The Lost Love Letters of Heloise and Abelard* by Constant J. Mews. Copyright © Mews, Constant J. Reprinted with permission of Palgrave Macmillan. **Document 5, page 270:** From *The Letters of Abelard and Heloise*, translated by Betty Radice (Penguin, 1974), pp. 71–74. Copyright © Betty Radice, 1974. Reproduced by permission of Penguin Books Ltd. **Document 7, page 273:** From *The Letters of Abelard and Heloise*, translated by Betty Radice (Penguin, 1974), pp. 113–114, 116–117. Copyright © Betty Radice, 1974. Reproduced by permission of Penguin Books Ltd. **Document 8, page 276:** From *The Letters of St. Bernard of Clairvaux*, translated by Bruno Scott James (Chicago: Henry Regnery Company, 1953), pp. 321, 328.

CHAPTER 10   Page 278: Oil on wood, 1447–1449, by Paolo di Giovanni (1403–1482), in the Fundacion Coleccion Thyssen-Bornemisza, Madrid; photograph copyright Erich Lessing/Art Resource, NY. **Document 1, page 294:** From *Canon Law and Cloistered Women* by Elizabeth Makowski, pp. 135–135. Reprinted by permission of The Catholic University of America Press. **Document 3, page 297:** "Introduction to 'The Decameron'" by Julia Conaway Bondanella & Mark Musa from *The Italian Renaissance Reader*, edited by Julia Conaway Bondanella & Mark Musa, copyright © 1987 by Julie Conaway Bondanella and Mark Musa. Used by permission of Dutton Signet, a division of Penguin Putnam, Inc. **Document 4, page 299:** Letter 4, pp. 140–141 from *The Letters of St. Catherine of Siena*, Vol. 1 edited by Suzanne Noffke. Copyright © 1988. Reprinted by permission of the Center for Medieval & Early Renaissance Studies, SUNY Binghamton. **Document 5, page 300:** Letter 78, pp. 237–240 from *The Letters of St. Catherine of Siena*, Vol. 1 edited by Suzanne Noffke. Copyright © 1988. Reprinted by permission of the Center for Medieval & Early Renaissance Studies, SUNY Binghamton. **Document 7, page 305:** From Paul R. Thibualt, *Pope Gregory XI: The Failure of Tradition*, pp. 181–182. Reprinted by permission of The Rowman & Littlefield Publishing Group.

CHAPTER 11   Page 308: *(Left)* Self-portrait, 1440/photograph: The Granger Collection. *(Right)* Portrait of a Young Woman, c. 1460–1470, by Antonio Pollajulo (1433–1498), Museo Poldi Pezzoli, Milan, Italy; photograph copyright Scala/Art Resource, NY. **Document 1, page 325:** From *The Earthly Republic*, edited by Benjamin G. Kohl and Ronald Witt. Copyright © 1978 University of Pennsylvania Press. Reprinted with permission. **Document 2, page 326:** From *The Earthly Republic*, edited by Benjamin G. Kohl and Ronald Witt. Copyright © 1978 University of Pennsylvania Press. Reprinted with permission. **Document 3, page 329:** From Franco Borsi, *Leon Battista Alberti: The Complete Works* (New York: Electa/Rizzoli, 1989), p. 258. © Franco Borsi. **Document 4, page 331:** Excerpts from *The Family Renaissance Florence, A Translation of I Libri Della Famiglia* by Leon Battista Alberti, pp. 56, 82–83, 112–113, 140, 207, 208, 226, translated by Renee Neu Watkins. Reprinted by permission of Renee Neu Watkins. **Document 5, page 335:** Excerpts from *Her Immaculate Hand*, edited by Margaret King and Albert Rabil, Jr., pp. 113, 115–116, 59–60, 63, 64, 67. Copyright © 1983. Reprinted by permission of the Center for Medieval & Early Renaissance Studies, SUNY Binghamton. **Document 6, page 336:** Excerpts from *Her Immaculate Hand*, edited by Margaret King and Albert Rabil, Jr., pp. 113, 115–116, 59–60, 63, 64, 67. Copyright © 1983. Reprinted by permission of the Center for Medieval & Early Renaissance Studies, SUNY Binghamton. **Document 7, page 339:** From *Laura Cereta: Collected Letters of a Renaissance Feminist*, edited and translated by Diana Robin, pp. 74–75, 78–79, 80. Copyright © 1997. Reprinted by permission of The University of Chicago Press and Diana Robin.

CHAPTER 12   Page 341: *(Left)* Detail from The Virgin of the Catholic Kings, c. 1490, painting by Miguel Zittoz, Museo del Prado, Madrid; photo AKG London. *(Right)* 19th century painting by Madrazo, photo AKG London. **Document 1, page 358:** Excerpts from *The Book of Privileges Issued to Christopher Columbus by King Fernando and Queen Isabale, 1492–1502*, edited and translated by Helen Nader (Berkeley: University of California Press, 1996), pp. 70–72. Reprinted by permission of UCLA Center for Medieval and Renaissance Studies. **Document 3, page 362:** From *Islamic Spain, 1250–1500* by L.P. Harvey, pp. 315–321. Copyright © 1990. Reprinted by permission of The University of Chicago Press. **Document 5, page 367:** From *Medieval Iberia: Readings from Christian, Muslim, and Jewish Sources*, edited by Olivia Remie Constable. Copyright © 1997 University of Pennsylvania Press. Reprinted with permission. **Document 7, page 370:** From *Medieval Iberia: Readings from Christian, Muslim, and Jewish Sources*, edited by Olivia Remie Constable. Copyright © 1997 University of Pennsylvania Press. Reprinted with permission. **Document 8, page 371:** *Medieval Iberia: Readings from Christian, Muslim, and Jewish Sources*, ed. Olivia Remie Constable (Philadelphia: University of Pennsylvania Press, 1997), pp. 353–356. Translated by Edward Peters. **Document 9, page 374:** Excerpts from the *Journal of the First Voyage* by Christopher Columbus, edited and translated by B.W. Ife, pp. 3–4. Copyright © 1990. Reprinted by permission of Aris and Phillips, Ltd.

CHAPTER 13   Page 376: *(Left)* Portrait of Martin Luther, 1533, by Lucas Cranach, The Elder (1472–1533); photograph © Bettmann/Corbis. *(Right)* Portrait of Katharina von Bora, 1529, by Lucas Cranach, The Elder; photograph © Archivio Iconografico, S.A./Corbis. **Document 1, page 392:** Reprinted from *Luther's Works*, Vol. 31. edited by Harold J. Grimm, © 1957 Fortress Press. Used by permission of Augsburg Fortress. **Document 2, page 393:** Reprinted from *Luther's Works*, Vol. 43 edited by Gustav W. Wiencke, general editor Helmut T. Lehman, © 1966 Fortress Press. Used by permission of Augsburg Fortress. **Document 3, page 396:** From Martin Luther, *On the Babylonian Captivity of the Church, also in 1520.* From J. Dillenberger (ed.) *Martin Luther: Selections from his Writings* (Doubleday/Anchor, 1961, © Dillenberger, 1961, p. 326). He reprinted from Bertram Lee Woolf, *The Reformation Writings of Martin Luther*, Vol. 1, London, Lutterworth Press, 1953, pp. 208–329. **Document 3, page 397:** Reprinted from *Luther's Works*, Vol. 54 edited and translated by Theodore G. Tappert, general editor Helmut T. Lehman, © 1968 Fortress Press. Used by permission of Augsburg Fortress. **Document 4, page 398:** Reprinted from *Luther's Works*, Vol. 50 edited by Helmut T. Lehman, © 1975 Fortress Press. Used by permission of Augsburg Fortress. **Document 5, page 399:** From "Katharina von Bora Through Five Centuries" by Jeanette C. Smith from *Sixteenth Century Journal*, 30:3 (Fall, 1999): 771–772. Reproduced by permission. **Document 6, page 400:** Reprinted from *Luther's Works*, Vol. 41 edited by Helmut T. Lehman, © 1967 Fortress Press. Used by permission of Augsburg Fortress. **Document 7, page 401:** From Peter Matheson (ed.), *Argula von Grumbach: A Woman's Voice in the Reformation*, T&T Clark, Edinburgh, 1995 ©, pp. 141, 144–145, 146–147, 149.

CHAPTER 14   Page 404: *(Left)* Chalk drawing by Ottavio Leoni (c. 1578-1630), in the Biblioteca Marucelliana, Florence, Italy; photograph copyright Scala/Art Resource, NY. *(Right)* Painting by an anonymous artist, 16th century, Torre del Gallo, Villa Galletti, Arcetri, Florence, Italy; photograph copyright Alinari/Art Resource, NY. **Document 1, page 423:** From *Discoveries and Opinions of Galileo* by Galileo Galilei, translated by Stillman Drake, copyright © 1957 by Stillman Drake. Used by permission of Doubleday, a division of Random House, Inc. **Document 2, page 425:** Laura Fermi and Gilberto Bernardini, *Galileo and the Scientific Revolution* (New York: Basic Books, Inc., 1961), p. 72. **Document 3, page 426:** Galileo, *The Galileo Affair: A Documentary History*, Maurice A. Finocchiaro, 1989, p. 87–93. **Document 4, page 429:** Mary Allan-Olney, *The Private Life of Galileo, Compiled Principally from His Correspondence and That of His Eldest Daughter, Sister Maria Celeste* (London: Macmillan, 1870), pp. 115–118, 120–121. **Document 5, page 432:** Letter by Sister Maria Celeste, trans. Dava Sobel (1999) from "The Galileo Project," Rice University, <http://es.rice.edu/ES/humsoc/Galileo/MariaCeleste/Letters/077-2_26_33.html>. **Document 6, page 434:** Galileo, *The Galileo Affair: A Documentary History*, Maurice A. Finocchiaro, 1989, pp. 87–93. **Document 7, page 435:** Galileo, *The Galileo Affair: A Documentary History*, Maurice A. Finocchiaro, 1989, pp. 87–93.